The Russian State and Russian Energy Companies, 1992–2018

The Russian State and Russian Energy Companies analyses the development of relations between the state and five major energy companies, and how this shaped Russia's foreign policy in the post-Soviet region. The book argues that the development of Russia's political economy mattered for foreign policy over the quarter of a century from 1992 to 2018. Energy companies' roles in institutional development enabled them to influence foreign policy formation, and they became available as tools to implement foreign policy. The extent to which it happened for each company varied with their accessibility to the Russian state. Institutional development increased state capacity, in a way that strengthened Russia's political regime. The book shows how the combined power of several companies in the gas, oil, electricity, and nuclear energy industry was a key feature of Russian foreign policy, both in bilateral relationships and in support of Russia's regional position. In this way, Russia's energy resources were converted to regional influence. The book contributes to our understanding of Russia's political economy and its influence on foreign policy, and of the formation of policy towards post-Soviet states.

Ingerid M. Opdahl is associate professor at the Norwegian Institute for Defence Studies (IFS) at the Norwegian Defence University College, and heads the IFS's Russian Security and Defence Programme. She obtained a PhD in Russian, European and Eurasian Studies from the University of Birmingham in 2016. Opdahl has earlier published on Russia's relations with Georgia and with Central Asian states. Her current research is part of the international research project Russia's Politicized Economy, Elite Dynamics and the Domestic-Foreign Policy Nexus (RUSECOPOL), funded by the Norwegian Research Council and led by the IFS.

BASEES/Routledge Series on Russian and East European Studies

Series editors:

sociology and anthropology: Judith Pallot (President of BASEES and Chair), University of Oxford economics and business: Richard Connolly, University of Birmingham media and cultural studies: Birgit Beumers, University of Aberystwyth politics and international relations: Andrew Wilson, School of Slavonic and East European Studies, University College London history: Matt Rendle, University of Exeter

This series is published on behalf of BASEES (the British Association for Slavonic and East European Studies). The series comprises original, high-quality, research-level work by both new and established scholars on all aspects of Russian, Soviet, post-Soviet and East European Studies in humanities and social science subjects

128. Security, Society and the State in the Caucasus
Edited by Kevork Oskanian and Derek Averre

129. Memory, the City and the Legacy of World War II in East Central Europe
The Ghosts of Others
Uilleam Blacker

130. US Foreign Policy Towards Russia in the Post-Cold War Era
Ideational Legacies and Institutionalised Conflict and Co-operation
David Parker

131. Tolstoy's Political Thought
Christian Anarcho-Pacifist Iconoclasm Then and Now
Alexandre Christoyannopoulos

132. Azerbaijan and the European Union
Eske Van Gils

133. Freedom of Expression in Russia's New Mediasphere
Edited by Mariëlle Wijermars and Katja Lehtisaaris

134. The Russian State and Russian Energy Companies, 1992–2018
Ingerid M. Opdahl

For a full list of available titles please visit: https://www.routledge.com/BASEES-Routledge-Serieson-Russian-and-East-European-Studies/book-series/BASEES

The Russian State and Russian Energy Companies, 1992–2018

Ingerid M. Opdahl

LONDON AND NEW YORK

First published 2020 by Routledge

2 Park Square, Milton Park, Abingdon, Oxon OX14 4RN
605 Third Avenue, New York, NY 10017

Routledge is an imprint of the Taylor & Francis Group, an informa business

First issued in paperback 2022

Copyright © 2020 Taylor & Francis

The right of Ingerid M. Opdahl to be identified as author of this work has been asserted by him in accordance with sections 77 and 78 of the Copyright, Designs and Patents Act 1988.

All rights reserved. No part of this book may be reprinted or reproduced or utilised in any form or by any electronic, mechanical, or other means, now known or hereafter invented, including photocopying and recording, or in any information storage or retrieval system, without permission in writing from the publishers.

Notice:
Product or corporate names may be trademarks or registered trademarks, and are used only for identification and explanation without intent to infringe.

Publisher's Note

The publisher has gone to great lengths to ensure the quality of this reprint but points out that some imperfections in the original copies may be apparent.

British Library Cataloguing-in-Publication Data
A catalogue record for this book is available from the British Library

Library of Congress Cataloging-in-Publication Data
A catalog record has been requested for this book

ISBN: 978-0-815-35405-5 (hbk)
ISBN: 978-1-03-233610-7 (pbk)
DOI: 10.4324/9781351134071

Typeset in Times New Roman
by Taylor & Francis Books

Contents

	List of illustrations	vi
	Preface and acknowledgements	vii
	Note on translation and transliteration	xiii
	Abbreviations and acronyms	xiv
1	Introduction: Energy and the institutional development of the Russian state	1
2	Energy and Russia's foreign policy towards post-Soviet states	22
3	The electricity industry: RAO UES and Inter RAO	42
4	The nuclear energy industry: Minatom/Rosatom	90
5	The oil industry: Lukoil	143
6	The oil industry: Transneft and pipeline transport	196
7	The gas industry: Gazprom	257
8	Conclusion: Political economy and foreign policy	315
	Index	325

Illustrations

Figures

6.1	Map of oil pipelines of Transneft	198
7.1	Map of selected gas trunk pipelines in Russia and eastern Europe	259

Tables

3.1	Accumulated electricity debts to Russia, 1998–2000	47
3.2	Non-payment and barter in Russia's electricity trade, 1998–2001	48
3.3	Inter RAO's investments in CIS member states	59
6.1	Selected Transneft proposed and completed pipeline projects in Russia and abroad	208
6.2	Transneft share of Russian crude oil export, 2004–2017	214
6.3	Dividends and taxes paid by Transneft, 2001–2018	220
6.4	Transneft's charity donations and sponsorships, 2005–2017	224
7.1	Gazprom's sales to post-Soviet states, 2002–2018	273

Preface and acknowledgements

The young company president was barricaded in his Moscow office, the building surrounded by special police. When they went in early the next morning, to force him to give up his position in favour of a politically desirable replacement, media reported that the office door was opened using an angle grinder.[1] The stand-off ended with the entry of the new company president. While the outgoing had been known for his audacity, his successor was an experienced and adept industry executive. Over the next eight years, he skilfully expanded the business while giving the occasional memorable media statement. Both are now long gone from Transneft, the Russian oil pipeline monopoly. It has since been headed by a loyal, and far less colourful, manager with a similar background to President Vladimir Putin. Conflicts over company management in Transneft and other energy companies are now more low-key, even when dramatic. They involve documents, delaying tactics and the occasional charge of fraud or embezzlement, rather than office sieges broken by police wielding power tools. What has not changed is that the outcome of such conflicts impacts Russian politics and influences institutional change in the economy. After all, they involve control over resource streams – money flows – and relations between the state and energy companies remain crucial in the Russian political economy. This book shows how state–business relations in Russia have developed and made energy companies so important, to the extent that they even became foreign policy tools of the state.

State–company relations are crucial in any political economy, not just Russia's. This is especially the case when the rules of the game change. When every new rule has the potential to upset all short-term plans and long-term strategies, elites make their best effort to control decisive positions, as they did in post-Soviet Russia from 1992 to 2018. Even so, and even in periods of rapid change, the institutions, the rules of the game, evolve more slowly. The scope of this book is a consequence of the theoretical perspective on institutional development. Empirical realities also mattered for the design. The end of the Soviet Union was the beginning of the contemporary post-Soviet states. The centrifugal changes that followed have gradually turned the states into different political entities. It is meaningless to analyse them applying a one-size-fits-all approach. Nevertheless, Russia's energy relations with them exhibit many continuities. Some ties have lost their relevance, whereas others have enhanced their significance. Covering a long time period makes it possible to show how and to arrive at a more complete picture.

Overall social order development here is understood as providing a frame for institutional transformation. Institutions, the rules, regulations and customs that structure relations between actors like companies and ministries, and individuals, are fundamental bricks in any political economy. The concept of the limited access order, where political and economic power are united, and rules are enforced according to principles of privilege and not of impersonal rights, is the starting point. This is highly relevant in Russia today, where privileges are decisive, and political and economic power go hand in hand. Institutional development emphasises the general traits of the Russian political economy, even as three of the five cases of state–business relations belong to the petroleum industry, and all five to the energy industries more generally. I also argue that Russia's institutional development impacted foreign policy towards other post-Soviet states. Domestic institutions enabled Russian policymakers to use company operations as foreign policy tools.

The Russian political economy and its influence on foreign policy come under scrutiny here. The book embeds five cases of state–company relations in the energy industries. Perhaps unsurprisingly, Gazprom is included. Few energy companies have mattered as much in foreign policy. But it is not the only company of importance. In the electricity industry, the vertically integrated monopoly RAO UES (to 2008) and its former subsidiary for foreign operations, Inter RAO, played a similar role to Gazprom's in gas. The nuclear energy industry, organised first under the umbrella of the Nuclear Industry Ministry Minatom, later restructured into the state corporation Rosatom, was central in relations with Ukraine and Kazakhstan. At home, its trajectory epitomises many of the challenges of monopolies and their relations with the state. Lukoil is one of Russia's largest oil companies, a pioneer of the industry and central to the state's relations with the industry. It has long had substantial operations in the post-Soviet region. Transneft represents another side of the oil industry, pipeline transport, which has been singularly important for state power, also in relation to Russia's post-Soviet neighbours. The energy industries' integrated infrastructure extended across the post-Soviet region: gas, oil, electricity and nuclear energy, and the companies here were all at first closely related to the state. The changes that followed in the institutional framework for each industry to some extent propelled them away from the state, at very different speeds. One company, Lukoil, is now privately owned. Transneft, Gazprom and Inter RAO have minority shareholders, while a majority is held by the state, although ownership is exercised in very different ways. Rosatom is organised as a state corporation, and holds a more autonomous position in relation to the state. But regardless of the differences to the formal institutional set-up, their institutional trajectories display considerable similarities. Moreover, as this book will show, they all depended on their relations with the Russian state to conduct business operations in the post-Soviet region.

Preface and acknowledgements ix

This book was written with a diverse audience in mind. It comprises eight chapters, five of which contain case studies. They can be read on their own, if the aim is to gain some insight into only one company and its relations with the state. Nevertheless, I encourage scholars, practitioners and students alike to read much of the book. The five case chapters complement each other. The similarities between gas and the nuclear energy industry and their relations with the state, or the complementarity of gas relations, electricity relations and nuclear energy relations in Russian foreign policy, can best be appreciated by reading more than one case chapter. Together, they illuminate a greater range of state–company relations than an exclusive focus on gas, or gas and oil, would have permitted. This breadth of approach has yielded the book's original contribution, that it looks at the variety of Russia's foreign policy tools and explains how the domestic political economy made them accessible to the state.

The case chapters are preceded by two introductory chapters. Chapter 1 takes as a starting point the central role of state–company relations in bringing about institutional change, on the background of Russia's state of development in the early 1990s. Concepts used in the book, such as informality and formality, rents, and state capacity, are defined and discussed, as are the most relevant characteristics of the Russian elite with regard to the analysis here. The break-up of the Soviet Union led to institutional weakness and a state of flux. The energy companies filled central functions in the political economy, making them important also with regard to other post-Soviet states.

Chapter 2 places Russia's energy policy towards post-Soviet states in the context of overall Russian foreign policy in the years 1992–2018. Russian foreign policy from the mid-1990s gradually saw regional integration processes in terms of the possibilities for Russia to dominate. In the beginning, the approach coexisted with a reality of weakening Russian influence in the region. After the turn of the century, continued asymmetric energy dependence, access to more resources, and a greater demand for Russian involvement increased Russia's overall leverage. But as the 2000s progressed, contradictions emerged between Russia's coercive use of foreign economic relations and the pursuit of more cooperative regional integration. This process came to a head with the annexation of Crimea: the repercussions limit Russia's regional power to this day.

The case chapters, Chapter 3 through 7, contain analyses of one company's relations with the state, both at home and with regard to operations in the post-Soviet Union, from 1992 to 2018. The company is introduced, and industry characteristics outlined. The company's overall, predominantly domestic, relations with the state are analysed first for each time period. This is followed by discussion of the relationship over foreign operations and foreign policy.

The non-hydrocarbon companies, RAO UES/Inter RAO and Minatom/Rosatom, are discussed before the companies of the oil and gas industries, Lukoil, Transneft and Gazprom. Many readers will be familiar with Russia's oil and gas companies, as the petroleum industries have been the topic of much scholarly and media attention. The progression from less to more familiar ground is intended to draw attention to the general characteristics of state–company relations in the energy industries. Institutional development and its impact on foreign policy is a broader phenomenon connected to the political economy. Readers interested in the use of gas relations as a foreign policy tool, or in natural monopolies, will find it useful to read the chapters on electricity and nuclear energy, and vice versa. The analysis of Transneft is particularly revealing when it comes to natural monopolies. The chapter on Lukoil provides insight on the differences between state and private companies, but the impact of these differences on foreign policy and on company development come to life in the Gazprom and RAO UES/Inter RAO chapters.

In the Conclusion, I sum up the importance of mutual advantage for the state and business in the development of foreign operations and foreign policy. Towards the end of the period under study, four of the five companies became tools of national economic interest. This held some advantage for the companies. In the latter years discussed here, Russia's foreign economic policy in the post-Soviet region reached certain limits. I propose that this marks the end of the post-Soviet period. I also argue that resource abundance led to slowed development, pinning this down to the combined effects of institutional informality and privilege and the vested interests generated by vast resources. Last but not least, the Conclusion points out that limited access orders have fewer institutional obstacles to the use of companies as foreign policy tools. Particularly when property rights are weakened, states like Russia may have access to foreign economic tools that there are more barriers against using in other political systems. For state-owned companies, the book presents evidence that considerations of company development and efficiency may act as barriers against becoming tools of the state, at home and abroad.

This book is based on a variety of sources, including news media, trade journals and industry reports, both international and Russian. Company websites and reports provide much information and have been used throughout. This wealth of information is unevenly distributed across the cases. Gazprom is by far best covered in existing research, and it has the most comprehensive company website. Lukoil is also quite well covered, both in the Russian media and in international trade journals and financial media. Rosatom and the nuclear energy industry's development in the 1990s and 2000s were for long far less discussed. This improved in the 2010s, but the smaller size and fewer competitors of the global nuclear energy industry contribute to less abundant international media coverage, and fewer trade journals. Analysis of the Russian electricity industry was detailed during the reform period (1998–2008), but relatively little remains from before 1998. After 2008, much company information from RAO UES was available on a preserved website until 2018. The electricity industry in Russia is still rather well covered by Russian media, but Inter RAO is now a less open and transparent company than in 2008. Transneft is overall the least researched and least accessible company. A dearth of sources was somewhat remedied by Russian oil and gas trade journals. For all cases, the quality and quantity of Russian news media and trade journal sources are best between the late 1990s and the early 2010s, and distinctly poorer after 2014.

The written sources were complemented by two rounds of interviews in Moscow in February 2009 and September 2012, with follow-up contact in November 2017 and April 2018. All in all, 23 interviews with 20 people, evenly split between company/industry representatives on the one hand, and scholars and analysts on the other. Interviews were semi-structured, and lasted from one to two hours. One follow-up interview was conducted by phone. The industry representatives came from every industry discussed in the book.

Writing this book would not have been possible without the generosity and patience of many people. I extend a heartfelt thanks to all my interviewees in Russia for taking time away from busy work schedules to share your insights and long experience with me. Your generosity and curiosity in the project brought a wealth of perspectives into the process, for which I am very grateful.

The book is the result of research that began in Vladimir Putin's second period, and was completed early in his fourth period. I thank my employer, the Norwegian Institute of Defence Studies (IFS) at the Norwegian Defence University College, for the possibility to undertake the project and see it through to this book. IFS colleagues deserve a special thanks for their interest and support; none more than Professor Kåre Dahl Martinsen. Your comments on the book manuscript were always critical, generous and often humorous, and our discussions were really enjoyable. I also thank colleagues in the Russian Security and Defence Programme for our interesting discussions, and in particular, Håvard Bækken, Jardar Østbø and Katarzyna Zysk for criticism and comments on parts of the book.

The map in Chapter 6 is reproduced with the kind permission of Transneft. Anna Therese Klingstedt prepared it for this book; your help was greatly appreciated. And in Chapter 7, there would have been no map without your expertise. I am deeply thankful to you for the time and effort that went into our collaboration, and to the Norwegian Defence University College for providing us with the necessary time and not least software. I am also grateful to Research Professor Arild Moe of the Fridtjof Nansen Institute for helpful advice on maps in particular.

The Norwegian Defence University College library has supported the work throughout, its librarians always seeking even better ways to help. Nina Eskild Riege and Einar Tokvam Jamne were Head Librarian and Special Librarian during particularly challenging periods. It is a pleasure to acknowledge your help.

The project came to life as a PhD thesis at the University of Birmingham, where the Centre for Russian, European and Eurasian Studies (CREES), now housed at the Department for Politics and International Studies, was my intellectual home and a stimulating research environment. Thanks to everyone at CREES and in particular my two supervisors, Julian Cooper and Richard Connolly. You never wavered in your enthusiasm and support, and indispensable advice, for which I will always be grateful.

In 2017–2018, I was fortunate to have the possibility of visiting the Institute for Industrial and Market Studies at the Higher School of Economics National Research University, through the International Center for the Study of Institutions and Development and its visiting research programme, twice during the academic year. Thank you to everyone, and especially to Professor Andrei Yakovlev for your generous welcome and to Olga Masyutina for great administrative support.

The transition from thesis to book, and then progress of the book project, was made much easier by the steady hand and helpful advice of Peter Sowden, my editor at Routledge. Your work was highly appreciated. The last leg of the process took place in the unusual spring of 2020. I could not have had a better guide to the copyediting process than Kristina Wischenkamper. Thanks to your efficient work and kind emails, exceptional times turned into good working days.

Many others have been generous with their time, comments, support and discussion of the project at different points in the process, including Pami Aalto, Margarita Balmaceda, Tatyana Dolgopyatova, Jakub Godzimirski, Jonas Grätz, Caroline Kuzemko, Boris Kuznetsov, Julia P. Loe, Arild Moe, Indra Øverland, Alexandra Prodromidou, Elena Shadrina, Hanna Smith, Aglaya Snetkov, and Veli-Pekka Tynkkynen. I also thank the anonymous reviewer, whose detailed suggestions and advice were really welcome.

With so many people to be grateful to, the book remains subject to the usual disclaimers. For the final result, including all the book's inevitable errors and omissions, I take full responsibility.

Without the support from my family and friends, this book would not have happened. Thank you Inger and Nils for much support over many years, and especially for spending so much time with your grandchildren, to everyone's enjoyment. And Magnar, Knut and Synneva for endless love and joyful distraction, and more encouragement than anyone could reasonably expect when the book often took time away from you. I'm sorry that it still doesn't fit the requirements for the school reading competition. You are the best.

Note

1 According to some reports, the police used a circular saw. Most reports claim that the door was opened forcefully with a power tool, and they form the basis of my account here. However, at least one report claims that such force was not used.

Note on translation and transliteration

All translations from Russian language sources that appear in the text are my own. Names in Russian, Ukrainian and Belarusian are transliterated according to simplified versions of the Library of Congress's romanisation tables, using ya/yu instead of ia/iu. All soft and hard signs (for Ukrainian and Belarusian, diacritic signs (ï, ī)) have been omitted in the text, but retained in the references. There are a few exceptions to the general system of transliteration. Well-known names such as Yeltsin (not Eltsin), are spelled according to English language conventions. The same applies to geographical names, like Moscow, and company names where companies have established English-language versions. For references to English language publications, authors' names are displayed as in the English original.

For sources and names in other languages, the spelling of names conforms as closely as possible to the prevalent forms in the country in question at the time of writing, except where conventions apply in English. Where two alphabets are in use, such as in Uzbekistan, a simplified version of the language's Latin script is used.

Abbreviations and acronyms

ACG	Azeri–Chirag–Gunesli (oil field)
AIOC	Azerbaijan International Operating Company
ARMZ	*Atomredmetzoloto* (company name until 2008) (nuclear energy industry)
ASE	*Atomstroieksport* (name of parts of reorganised company before 2016) (nuclear energy industry)
bcm	billion cubic metres (of gas)
BPS	Baltic Pipeline System (oil), in Russian: *Baltiiskaya truboprovodnaya sistema*—BTS
BTC	Baku–Tbilisi–Ceyhan (oil) pipeline
BTE	Baku–Tbilisi–Erzurum (gas) pipeline
CAATSA	Countering America's Adversaries through Sanctions Act
CEO	chief executive officer
CIR	Caspian Investment Resources
CIS	Commonwealth of Independent States
CNPC	China National Petroleum Corporation
CPC	Caspian Pipeline Consortium (oil), in Russian: *Kaspiiskii truboprovodnyi konsortsium*—KTK
CSR	Corporate social responsibility
EBRD	European Bank for Reconstruction and Development
EEU	Eurasian Economic Union, in Russian: *Evraziiskii ekonomicheskii soyuz*—EAES
ESPO	East Siberia–Pacific Ocean (oil) pipeline, in Russian: *(nefteprovod) Vostochnaya Sibir'–Tikhii Okean*—VSTO
EU	European Union
FAS	*Federal'naya antimonopol'naya sluzhba*, in English: Federal Anti-Monopoly Service
FSK	*Federal'naya setevaya kompaniya*, in English: Federal Grid Company (electricity)
FST	*Federal'naya sluzhba po tarifam*, in English: Federal Tariff Service
G8	Group of Eight
HEU	highly enriched uranium

HPP	hydropower plant
IAEA	International Atomic Energy Agency
IFRS	International Financial Reporting Standards
IOC	international oil company
IPO	initial public offering
IUEC	International Uranium Enrichment Centre, in Russian: *Mezhdunarodnyi tsentr po obogashcheniyu urana*—MTsOU
JV	joint venture
KGB	*Komitet po gosudarstvennoi bezopasnosti*, in English: Committee for state security (obsolete)
KPO	Karachaganak Petroleum Operating Consortium
LEU	low-enriched uranium
LNG	liquefied natural gas
mcm	thousand cubic metres (of gas)
MFA	Ministry of Foreign Affairs, in Russian: *Ministerstvo inostrannykh del*—MID
Minatom	*Ministerstvo po atomnoi energii*, in English: Ministry for atomic energy
Minsredmash	*Ministerstvo srednego mashinostroeniya*, in English: Ministry for Medium Machine-Building
NATO	North Atlantic Treaty Organization
NDPI	*nalog na dobychu poleznykh iskopaemykh*, in English: consolidated production tax
NMMC	Navoi Mining and Metallurgy Combinat
NOC	national oil company
NPP	nuclear power plant
NPT	Treaty on the Non-Proliferation of Nuclear Weapons
OVR	*Otechestvo – Vsya Rossiya*, in English: Fatherland – All Russia (political party)
PSA	production sharing agreement
RAO UES	*Rossiiskoe aktsionernoe obshchestvo "Edinaya Energeticheskaya Sistema"*, in English: Russian shareholding company United Energy System (literally: single energy system)
Rosimushchestvo	*Federal'noe agenstvo po upravleniyu gosudarstvennym imushchestvom*, in English: Federal Agency for State Property Management
RSBU	*Rossiiskie standarty bukhgalterskogo ucheta*, in English: Russian Financial Reporting Standards
RSPP	*Rossiiskii soyuz promyshlennikov i predprinimatelei*, in English: Russian Union of Industrialists and Entrepreneurs, RUIE
SNF	spent nuclear fuel
SOCAR	State Oil Company of Azerbaijan
SVOP	*Sovet po vneshnei i oboronnoi politike*, in English: Council for Foreign and Defence Policy

tpa	tonnes per annum (oil)
TPP	thermal power plant
UES	united energy system (electricity), in Russian: *edinaya energeticheskaya sistema*—EES
UGSS	united gas supply system, in Russian: *edinaya sistema gazosnabzheniya*—ESG
VVER	*vodo-vodyanoi energeticheskii reaktor*, in English: pressurised water reactor (nuclear energy industry)
WTO	World Trade Organization

1 Introduction
Energy and the institutional development of the Russian state

Russia's international position today is built on energy. Energy resources, especially international oil and gas supplies, make up the fundaments for Russia's position as a great power in international relations and provide revenue for power projection, military and otherwise. Russia's return to great power politics during Vladimir Putin's presidency initially surprised the West, which had in the 1990s become accustomed to a more compliant Russia with little capacity to spare for global affairs. For the post-Soviet states, however, Russia never really went away. While much weakened, it remained a great power in the region, especially in economic terms. Energy power was a central pillar of its position, and underpinned its return to global power status after 2000. Russian energy power has therefore played multiple roles in Russian foreign policy since the end of the Soviet Union. In the 2000s, Russian policymakers came to see it as a source of global and regional power. By virtue of Russia's role in global energy supply, energy relations became a backbone of foreign policy towards a wide variety of states, from Germany to Iraq and China. Due to the legacies of the Soviet economy, energy relations in the post-Soviet region were also potential tools of influence on other states. This turned Russian energy companies into a staple of Russian foreign policy in the post-Soviet region.

At home, Russian energy companies were central to the ability of the state to formulate policy, implement, compel and coerce. Just as Russia in 1992 found itself far feebler in relation to the then newly independent states (quickly conceptualised as the "near abroad"), the state was also considerably weakened with regard to its most basic tasks, including the extraction and redistribution of resources. But the weak Russian state of the 1990s managed to keep afloat, relying to a considerable extent on large companies. Gazprom stepped in when there was a hole in the state budget. The power holding United Energy System (hereafter RAO UES) supplied electricity without payment across regions and industries. Oil companies produced as much oil as they could possibly sell, and paid some taxes. Oil and gas pipelines brought crude oil and natural gas to international markets, even when there were no funds for repairs. The gigantic nuclear energy industry did not disintegrate and turn into a source of illicit nuclear materials, but kept it going, somehow.

In this way, the large companies that had been formed from production units and ministries in 1991 were indispensable to the state at home. This relationship influenced Russia's political development for years to come. It placed the companies in positions where they could influence foreign policy and act as foreign policy tools in the post-Soviet region. The development of Russia's political economy mattered for its foreign policy.

To analyse how state–company relations influenced foreign policy, the book applies a theoretical framework that builds on social order development, drawing heavily on new institutional economics (North et al., 2009). Development, both political and economic, is understood as institutional development. Companies' role in institutional development made it possible for them to influence foreign policy formation, and domestic institutions made them available as tools to implement foreign policy. The combined power of several industries was a key feature of Russian foreign policy, both in bilateral relationships and as a support for Russia's regional position.

That institutions matter, also when they are in flux, is a recurrent topic in studies of Russian foreign policy. Institutional weakness and resourceful actors characterised Russian foreign policy formation in the 1990s (Malcolm, 1996; Sharlet, 2001, p.199). It remained a feature into the 2000s, impacting relations with Europe, the post-Soviet region and the Middle East (Wenger et al., 2006; Torbakov, 2013; Gvosdev and Marsh, 2014; Marten, 2015) as well as the accession process to the World Trade Organization (Guriev and Rachinsky, 2005, p.146; Connolly and Hanson, 2012, p.489). In the comparative literature on post-Communist transitions, institutional development provides an important explanation for states' integration into the global economy (Guriev and Rachinsky, 2005; Brada, 2013; Drabek and Benacek, 2013). In analyses of Russian foreign policy formation, the salient institutional feature has been a weakly developed institutional framework, supplemented by extensive informal relations between state actors and businesses (Bukkvoll, 2003; Aalto et al., 2012; Balmaceda, 2012; Kivinen, 2012; Poussenkova, 2012; Marten, 2015). Business interests, also in the energy industries, have exerted significant informal influence on foreign policy. The background is found in Russia's political economy, which has been profoundly shaped both by resource abundance, and by energy companies as actors (cf. Fish, 2005; Sutela, 2012; Cooper, 2013; Malle, 2013; Mau, 2016; 2017; Miller, 2018). How business influence on foreign policy has changed over time is however less studied.

One common premise of the institutional explanation for Russian foreign policy is that informal institutions subvert formal institutions, thereby contributing to state weakness. This explanation originated in a scholarly debate over whether business or state actors were more powerful amid weak institutions (for the former view, see Hellman, J., 1998, and Hellman, J.S. et al., 2000, for the latter view, see e.g. Yakovlev, 2006, and Sakwa, 2008). A related discussion centred on whether state–business relations were less conflictual, with wider elite integration amid a fluid, informal institutional environment (Åslund, 1999; Peregudov et al., 1999, p.290; Rutland, 2001; Frye, 2002; Ledeneva, 2006; 2013). Building on the studies of elite integration, recent works have analysed how networks of economic and political patronage weaken both state and society (e.g. in Easter, G.M., 2012, pp.20–21; Gel'man, 2015; Hale, 2015, p.10). But even when the state is weak, weakness and informality are only part of the overall framework for state–business interaction. It is the combination of formal rules of the game and their informal interpretation in elite networks that shapes Russia's development.

Integration among political and business elites has important implications when discussing state–company relations over foreign policy (cf. Balmaceda, 2012, p.153; Kaczmarski, 2014). For example, in the case of Gazprom, the political use of energy in foreign policy is frequently seen as external to (Stern, 2005, pp.102–104; Pirani, 2009, pp.5–8) or in subversion of companies' genuine, business-related goals (Baev, 2013; Busygina and Filippov, 2013; Closson, 2014). However, when understood in terms of personalised interaction and mutual support, or mutual favours, it can make considerable sense for a company to make itself useful to the state, also from a business perspective. Margarita Balmaceda (Balmaceda, 2012; 2013) has proposed that Gazprom and other companies accumulate "convertible points" with the Russian state in both the foreign and domestic realm. These "points" can later be translated ("converted") into advantages for the company (Balmaceda, 2012, p.143). The advantages may be significant outside the domestic political economy too. Boris Barkanov finds that Gazprom became a vehicle of Russian statecraft in relations with Europe, but this co-optation enabled Gazprom to influence the terms of Russia's integration into international markets (Barkanov, 2018). Likewise, Adam Stulberg shows how Gazprom and the Russian state coordinated their positions when adjusting to changing constraints in the European gas market in 2013–2015, resulting in a compromise that preserved Ukraine as a gas market for Gazprom (Stulberg, 2015). Gazprom influenced its business environment to a greater degree than what could have been achieved without state support.

The relations suggested in these studies are far from a situation where energy companies see their international business strategies subverted by the state. A more complex understanding of state–business relations over foreign policy is inevitably more complete, particularly when analysing it from the point of view of how these relations connect to those of the domestic political economy. To conduct such an analysis, it is necessary to study state–business relations over time, and include companies in other industries than gas. Adding to the relatively few studies to date that look at several companies over more than a few years (Wenger et al., 2006; Stulberg, 2007; Meister, 2013), this book shows how five energy actors, RAO UES/Inter RAO, Minatom/Rosatom, Lukoil, Transneft and Gazprom, interact with the state and shape Russia's political economy. The findings are then used to show how political economy development influences foreign policy.

The development of the state and state–company relations

The reality of the Russian state in the early 1990s was far from the stable, predictable and transparent implementation of an ideal state in the Weberian sense. The Soviet economy by 1990 had a "systemic vacuum" at its heart: "The old planning system has broken down but has not been dismantled; meanwhile, the structures vital to the functioning of a market have yet to be put in place" (IMF et al., 1990, p.1). The systemic vacuum left the state only a nominal force in segments of the economy at the break-up of the Soviet Union at the end of 1991. The reforms introduced by the new Russian government in early 1992 were meant to create private ownership in a market economy. However, as old Soviet institutions were still not dismantled, two sets of institutions existed side by side in two overlapping but incomplete systems until the new Constitution was put in place in late 1993. The chaos of reforms in 1992–1993 further weakened the capacity of the state to regulate the economy, which was in the midst of a transformational recession (Popov, 2013, p.102). The rules of the game were contradictory and in flux, with only a weak rule of law. Private interests and informal networks were prominent in political decision making. When faced with impending financial crisis in 1998, elite disunity and government policies exacerbated Russia's problems. The result was debt default. Ten years later, government policies, once established in 2009, quite successfully met the next international financial crisis. But this response did not use the crisis to embark on structural reform, facilitate new growth, and ease dependence on hydrocarbon production. Instead, it contained sources of stagnation. A few years later, there was a tendency towards state-led development and isolationism in Russia's reaction to the oil crisis in 2014–2016. These four crises, 1991–1993, 1998, 2009–2010 and 2015–2017 (the years of Russia's own economic crises) are milestones in the development of the Russian state.

The trajectory of post-Soviet Russia illustrates how the institutional framework of the state is essential to a functioning modern economy, and that change in the state goes hand in hand with economic change. The Russian state went through a transformation from a fragile state, with little capacity to uphold stable institutions and predictable practices, to an increasingly cohesive organisation with more clearly delineated institutions and interests. The moribund late-Soviet state, incapable of responding forcefully to, let alone shaping, developments in the economy, degraded further into a transitional chaos. Gradually but slowly, the post-Soviet Russian state became more active and flexible, responding with differentiated institutional frameworks for different sectors. Energy companies were integral to this development. They emerged out of state structures in the early 1990s, and by the 2000s they were distinguishable as companies. They had changed from Soviet enterprises wielding control only over the processes of production, to vertically integrated companies with command over input, production, marketing and profits. In return for state and regime support, they shared their rents, which included more than just profits, with the state and wider Russian society, through taxation and other channels. This increased the resources available to the state, and ipso facto state capacity.

Change in the state, and specifically, the state's ability to formulate policy and implement it, also pertains to foreign policy. Foreign policy is a specific policy area, often somewhat removed from everyday domestic politics, but it is still affected by the state's capacity to formulate coherent policies and implement them effectively. In the 1990s, many choices of Russia's economic and political transition were linked to foreign policy, and specifically to relations with other post-Soviet states. This applied to choices concerning the organisation of multilateral relations among the post-Soviet states, the pursuit of integration into the global economy, and how bilateral affairs with other states could be exploited for Russia's benefit. Many issues remained unresolved until the mid-1990s. The institutional framework, moreover, was unclear and in flux, leaving considerable room for actors to influence events and policy.

In the energy industries, Russia was left in control of an overwhelming share of infrastructure. State attempts to introduce institutional change for these industries had consequences for the post-Soviet region. Energy companies' operations in the region represented, to the Russian state, a powerful tool of foreign policy in a situation when the elites in Moscow found themselves with a markedly reduced toolbox of influence in its immediate neighbourhood.

The institutional legacies of the Soviet planned economy

The Soviet economy was a single structure, giant but centralised. Soviet enterprises were not firms in the Western sense, but production units in USSR Inc. (Hanson, 2003, pp.9–13). Institutional transformation was a slow and uneven process. Economic transition, which aimed to change the Soviet economic system into its opposite, was an immense task. In practice, Soviet institutions were in many cases carried over into each post-Soviet state, leading to further degradation (Ericson, 2013, pp.60–61). These institutional remnants continued to function in new circumstances and made it possible to rely on Soviet-type rules and procedures also after 1991. Institutional legacies are here seen to have passed from the Soviet Union to post-Soviet Russia, sometimes in modified form, to become the basis for further institutional and organisational development. This view, that legacies are modified and changed by institutional continuity, sets the definition used here apart from other contributions that define legacies as durable relationships over a longer period of time (Huskey, 2014, p.111; Kotkin and Beissinger, 2014, p.12).

The legacies of USSR Inc. matter in three ways. The first is systemic and concerns the overall structure of the economy. The Soviet economy was characterised by a lack of distinction between economic organisations, at the same level and within and between different hierarchies. Gradually, from the late Soviet years (1987–1990) to the mid-1990s, organisations from the giant Soviet superstructure became tangibly distinct units within a Russian economy undergoing reform. Other parts of the superstructure were torn away in the break-up and became the property of other post-Soviet states. The speed of change was shockingly rapid in terms of economic history and in everyday life. Nevertheless, the process of mutual adaptation was a gradual one. The boundaries between the state and company levels remained somewhat indistinct during the 1990s. Where state organisations were targeted for insider privatisation, as happened in the power industry (with RAO EEK), nuclear energy industry (with TVEL Concern) and in Transneft, the resulting entities were ambiguously affiliated with the state. Also at times in the 2000s, the dividing line between core state organisations, state companies, and partially state-owned companies remained blurred and their responsibilities diffuse in some industries. Even so, there was a centrifugal movement away from the state as an economic superstructure, and towards institutionalisation of eventually more distant, and more clearly delineated, ties between the state and the companies. Likewise, the basic institutions that structured the economy, relations of property and organisational autonomy, continued to bear a Soviet imprint that only gradually changed.

The second legacy of USSR, Inc. was the institutional framework at the industry level. Gazprom, RAO UES, Transneft and Rosatom survived relatively intact and unreformed until the mid-1990s, and even the outlier in this regard, Lukoil, started as a legacy company in the privatised Russian oil industry. The four others survived because they were infrastructural monopolies in their respective sectors. In 1992, the Russian state embarked on a transformation that would eventually turn the economy into a partial market economy. However, the institutions that regulated these companies changed at a more leisurely pace. The organisations took on traits that turned them more (Gazprom) or less (Transneft) into companies, but their relations with the state were based on their status as monopolies and on informal rent sharing. The energy sector's institutional framework remained a legacy of the late Soviet period for at least a decade, with gradually introduced modifications. The companies were therefore capable of influencing state policies to an extent not seen in many other sectors, with the defence industry as a possible exception.

The institutions that structured ties with the other post-Soviet states was the third legacy. USSR Inc. extended throughout the entire Union, and linked enterprises by sector across internal boundaries (Bradshaw, 2008, p.194). Over the 25 years that followed the break-up of the Soviet Union, the post-Soviet states have moved away from what was once the centre of USSR Inc. Post-Soviet states today are now distinctly different to an extent that was difficult to foresee in 1992. This pertains even as subgroups among the post-Soviet states continue to display political and economic similarities. There is an infrastructural side to this legacy. The pipelines and power grids criss-crossing internal borders were a physical, infrastructural expression of the Soviet

Union. As Soviet transport grids were concentrated on Russian territory, Russian energy companies were left with more of the Soviet production and transportation chains under their own control than other companies. The companies studied here were large and forceful entities in the post-Soviet context. Due to widespread Soviet rent addiction (Gaddy and Ickes, 2010, p.293), discussed on pp.8–9 and 263, there was a demand for Russia's presence in the energy sectors of other states.

State–company relations and institutional change

The legacies of the Soviet economy were from the beginning used, and shaped, by Russian elites in a general struggle for power and resources. State–company relations did not progress as a neat negotiation process between two clearly delineated sides. State fragmentation and incapacity in the 1990s opened opportunities for elites, regardless of nominal affiliations with the state or a company, to influence policy and shape property relations. Control of the state's mechanisms for control and coercion was the ultimate weapon against any rival group. Weak state organisations would be employed as fronts for business interests, whereas the stronger would compete with each other for influence. State bodies and new private organisations informally related to state organisations, were available for hire and protection. As the saying went, "the red roof is the tallest and most influential" (Veligzhanina, 2000).

Change in the state, the economy and state–company relations is analysed building on the conceptual framework of social order, introduced by Douglass North, John Wallis and Barry Weingast (North et al., 2009). State–company relations generally reflect the capacity of the state to uphold companies (North et al., 2009, p.47). Companies rely on the state for their very existence, and the state relies on companies to create economic resources for it to extract and redistribute. State regulation of the economy includes overall support for the existence of companies, fundamentally the basic institutions of property rights and contract enforcement, and the institutions that extract resources, such as taxation, and redistribute them through different channels for spending. Institutions are here defined as the rules of the game devised by humans but constraining human interaction (North, 1990, p.4), while state organisations and economic organisations like companies are here all seen to be the players in the game (North, 1990, pp.4–5).

Like many other states, Russia is a limited access order (Connolly, 2013), where access to valuable resources and activities, such as the formation of significant political and economic organisations, is a restricted privilege (North et al., 2009, p.21). In turn, the privileged form a ruling coalition and control the state. The alternative is an all-out war for control of the state. There is no division between economic and political power. Instead, the distribution of political and economic power must correspond for the social order to be stable. Limited access orders are different from open access orders, where the access to start or acquire a company, or stand for political office, is an impersonally enforced right and political and economic power are strictly delineated (North et al., 2009, pp.11–12). In limited access orders, institutions constrain differently, as rules are enforced according to privilege, not rights. Relations between the Russian state and large companies have been shaped by a social order that maintains privileges, from the dependence of big companies on particularistic treatment from the state for business development (Hanson and Teague, 2005, p.674), to state actors' privilege to take control of companies (Gans-Morse, 2012; Hanson, 2014; Rochlitz, 2014), to the persistent difficulties of Russian business in using collective action to resist predation and violence from the state (Yakovlev et al., 2014). Without impersonal protection of property rights, reasonable and transparent taxation and open access to markets, companies need to pursue close relations with the state in order to operate and survive. In practise, top managers need to interact with the state's top politicians. In return for the privilege of property right protection and access to economic resources, managers and owners often willingly accept obligations to serve the state. They share their rents with members of the ruling coalition, here called the regime. Rent sharing plays a significant role in increasing state capacity. In result, the regime is relatively stable and in a position to rule.

Resource abundance and institutional development

Close and personal elite relations place resource-rich energy companies in a powerful position towards the state. Comparative political science has long discussed the challenge that resource abundance, and more specifically, oil wealth, poses for political development (Karl, 1997; Ross, 1999; 2001; Jensen and Wantchekon, 2004; Ross, 2012). This effect has been pinned down more narrowly as one of oil wealth on institutions (Luong and Weinthal, 2006; 2010; Weber, 2018). What matters for regime survival or collapse is the level of institutional development at the moment when resources increase (Smith, 2007). However, the concern here is not collapse, but institutional change in relation to the very industries that control abundant resources. It is reasonable to expect that the wider economic and political effects of wealth, especially increasing wealth, matter. Increased rent streams affect the potential gains of privilege, and may create vested interests that resist change, or have an interest in specific changes.

This is well known from Russia, where there are powerful vested interests favouring the status quo (Yakovlev, 2006; Rochlitz, 2015; Mau, 2016; 2017). There are simply too many groups in the elite with too much to lose from change. Clifford Gaddy and Barry Ickes argue that one economic legacy of the Soviet system is a societal addiction to energy rents. Rents from energy export were in the Soviet period turned into cheap and abundant energy and used to alleviate the effects of, and expand production in, inefficient sectors of the economy (Gaddy and Ickes, 2010, p.293). As a consequence, Russia's economic structure was altered, and the interruption of rents will incur potentially disruptive shocks to the system (Gaddy and Ickes, 2013). The elites are aware of this, as illustrated by their priority of keeping factories open during the 2009–2010 crisis, and of accessing more rents from the resource industries after 2014. Rent addiction furthermore extended across the former Soviet Union, with the abundant flow of cheap energy mostly directed from Russia to the other republics. This inherited energy dependence on Russia created rent claimants across the post-Soviet region.

Institutional development: formality and informality

Returning to the question of how resource abundance affects institutions, Pauline Jones Luong and Erika Weinthal (2010) argue that considerations of power maximisation among leaders result in different types of petroleum ownership. Ownership arrangements in turn shape institutions. Indirect resource management and private ownership speed the development of institutions and state capacity, as in the case of the Russian oil sector before 2005. Direct management through state ownership, as in the case of Gazprom, lets the state access rents directly, but its capacity does not develop as much and the state by necessity acquires a greater role in managing the economy (Luong and Weinthal, 2010, pp.121–180).

However, institutional change cannot be studied without taking into account how ownership is exercised. Resource management institutions may change independent of ownership changes like nationalisation or privatisation. For example, specialisation in the shape of market making strengthened the state and built state capacity in the Russian electricity sector (Wengle, 2012; 2014). Privatisation was only one part of this process, and the institutional framework established during the electricity reform exists regardless of ownership structure. On the other hand, formal rules are not applied impersonally in Russia, neither in law enforcement (Paneyakh, 2014) nor in relation to major companies (Sharlet, 2001; Hanson and Teague, 2005; Sakwa, 2008; Kluge, 2017). The informal rules of the game complement, but also undermine, formal institutions, to the point where informality is seen to represent the "normal" in society from the point of view of e.g. owners of smaller businesses (Vasileva, 2018). At the very top of the elite, informality places opaque constraints on political leaders (Monaghan, 2012, p.8). This impedes the emergence of impartiality, the constant codification, modification and specialisation in institutions that are essential to institutional development.

To capture overall institutional development, institutional variation is approached as a continuum from perfect formality, where rules and rights are applied uniformly and perfectly impersonally, to complete informality, where there are no rules and no property rights, apart from those established through privilege and personal connections. While neither extreme exists in the real life of modern states, the balance between informality and formality indicates a level of overall institutional development, both with regard to a specific industry, and at the aggregate level, in the social order.

Oversight and control: access and participation

Returning to the institutional framework, ownership and markets are analytically distinct from the extent to which the state can implement rules and exercise oversight. Informality and its opaque constraints weaken the state's capacity for policymaking and industry control. Instead, policymaking and oversight are likely to be undercut, but also underpinned, by informal relations between state representatives and representatives of the companies. Regulation and policymaking for major companies and their industries turn into a matter of discretion for high-level state actors (Easter, G.M., 2012, p.169), showing how big economic organisations in a limited access order are "necessarily also political ones" (North et al., 2009, pp.268–269). A lack of differentiation between state and private interests also occurred in companies nominally controlled and owned by the state. Formal ownership diverged from de facto, informal control.

This dimension of the institutional framework is often referred to as informality, but the complex reality of weakly enforced institutions and informal privilege demands a more precise description of inclusion and exclusion among elites and their organisations. To capture it, I apply two simple concepts, access and participation.[1] Access includes opportunities available to top company managers to approach key Russian state officials and top politicians, the regime, and the possibilities available to the state to exercise oversight and extract resources from the companies. The extent of state access reflects its capacity to support more complex economic organisations with less direct ties to the government. The companies' responses reflect their adaptation to the changing state. On occasion, company managements used relations with the state to initiate change. Often company managements resisted the state.

Participation is the extent to which companies influenced government policymaking, and the state could influence sector development. Could the companies influence their institutional environment? From the state's point of view, it is participation in company development and an opportunity to influence company strategies, including foreign operations. In this way, access and participation in formal and informal channels of interaction complemented the formal and informal rent streams described below. In the analysis, these concepts are used to gauge how state capacity to support economic activity, extract and redistribute resources developed over the period under study.

Formal and informal rents

Finally, resource extraction and redistribution are central to the relationship between the state and companies. Gaddy and Ickes argue that Russia's rent management system is an institutional framework for state–business ties (Gaddy and Ickes, 2010, p.292). They define oil and gas rents in Russia as the surplus obtained from oil and gas production (Gaddy and Ickes, 2005, pp.560–561). Often defined as "excess payment above that required to induce supply" (Pomfret, 2013, p.415), rent is a common feature and economic challenge of resource-rich economies.

The importance of petroleum rents to the Russian economy increased over the post-Soviet period. In 1992, crude and refined petroleum and petroleum products represented 45 per cent of all Russian exports, which totalled 34 billion US$ (UN Comtrade database harmonised by Gaulier and Zignago, 2010, accessed through Simoes and Hidalgo, 2011).[2] While this share fluctuated through the 1990s, it was back at 45 per cent in 2000, with the total at 102 billion US$. Overall export increased through the 2000s and peaked at 418 billion US$ in 2008, of which petroleum and petroleum products represented 58.3 per cent. In 2015, Russia's exports totalled 222 billion US$, and the share of petroleum and petroleum products was 42.5 per cent (UN Comtrade database harmonised by Gaulier and Zignago, 2010, accessed through Simoes and Hidalgo, 2011).[3] The changes in the value of petroleum export in this period reflect not only fluctuations in the oil price, such as the period of high oil prices from 2003 to 2015, but also the decline of Russia's non-oil producing industries in the period under study.

Informal rent sharing is of particular relevance here, because it gives political leaders more discretion to redistribute rents according to their preferences outside the formal channels of taxation and state budget. In turn, this requires the deliberate weakening of property rights (Gaddy and Ickes, 2005, p.571). Accordingly, the rent management system includes an informal complement to the state's formal relationship with companies. The particular structure of rents is significant. Nominal costs to Russian companies are inflated by excess extraction costs and informal taxes like bribes, while revenues are deflated by price subsidies (Gaddy and Ickes, 2005, p.561). Rent accordingly comes in many forms: excess costs, informal tax, price subsidies, formal tax, and formal profit. Excess extraction costs are claimed by producers, subcontractors and suppliers, but also by employees on inflated staff rosters. Insofar as staff numbers are inflated by the dispensation of (mandatory) favours to privileged recipients, this is related to bribes and other types of informal taxation. General price subsidies relieve consumers and industrial sectors of part of their energy spending in the short term, while stabilising both society and the regime. In terms of the state budget, these are quasi-fiscal arrangements (Luong and Weinthal, 2010, pp.39–40). Quasi-fiscal arrangements have persisted in Russia, even as typical price subsidies of e.g. gas prices to consumers were reduced in the late 2000s and 2010s (IMF, 2014, p.63). There is little transparency on the extent and especially the cost of such arrangements (IMF, 2014, p.63).

Informal taxes are often couched in the language of voluntary contributions, but from the companies' point of view, they are no less mandatory than formal taxes, because they are essential for property rights protection and company survival. This may also apply to bribes, inflated corporate spending on social services and healthcare, politically recommended corporate social responsibility (CSR) spending (Guriev and Tsyvinskii, 2011), culture, sports (Müller, 2015; Rutland, 2015, p.74) and philanthropy. Charity contributions in particular are understood to channel rents towards a wide variety of causes, which may include the development of residences and sports complexes used also for private leisure. Again, little is known on the cost of non-commercial services extended by many companies. A very incomplete estimate for 2012 arrived at a cost corresponding to 0.1 per cent of GDP (IMF, 2014, p.64). CSR programmes, generous healthcare provisions and spending on sports in part relieve the state and regional budgets of the burden of public services, or contribute towards achieving developmental goals set by the government. They can be seen as a substitute for welfare provision by the state. In contrast, formal after-tax profits are generally distributed among owners (shareholders), and in the case of state ownership represent a formal rent stream shared between companies and the state as an owner. In this way, formal and informal resource streams, and formal and informal relations of control, bind the state and companies together and secure political stability.

State capacity and institutional development

The constraints of informality, the formal and informal channels of access and participation, limit state autonomy from society. This is a brake on Russia's economic and societal development. State and business are both weak because informal institutions, informal rent sharing and weakly protected property rights inhibit the development of state capacity and of financially healthy companies. But as an all-out war among elites remains a likely outcome in the case of regime breakdown, both the state and the companies maintain the status quo.

In the 1990s, the combination of a weak state and weak companies led to the enrichment of a part of the elite, often called the "oligarchs", at the expense of everyone else. This also affected the state. The state fragmented into constituent sectors and regions, with energy remaining closely linked to central state organisations. The fruits of enrichment, the rents, were however not all siphoned off to private coffers. Some were distributed through informal rent sharing, even reaching selected sections of the general population (Ledeneva, 2013, p.278). In return, the elites became reliant on political machines (Hale, 2010, pp.35–37) that delivered votes and stabilised the wider population.

In this way, state and society are linked through formal and informal institutions. The state can rely on both formal and informal channels of rent to extract resources from the economy and redistribute them to various claimants in the elite and wider population. The constraints of informal channels like patronage networks are interlinked with and embedded in the formally articulated institutional context of the state. In for example tax collection in 1991–1992, the discretionary powers of formerly Soviet tax collectors were undermined by both formal institutional changes and widespread elite bargaining in informal networks (Easter, G., 2006, pp.32–33). Bargaining remained important in tax collection through the 1990s. However, even after the introduction of a far more formalised, transparent and enforceable taxation system in 2001, exemptions are granted and tax-related coercion distributed in a context where real property rights depend upon informal, personal relations with the regime, and in the regions, with regional elites (Rochlitz, 2014; Yakovlev et al., 2014; Gans-Morse, 2017; Vasileva, 2018).

The state is more than institutional context. States are also defined by their power, or capacity, exercised by state organisations according to an institutional framework. Here, state power is seen to consist of policymaking power and infrastructural power. Policymaking power is the range of actions that state organisations can undertake without routine negotiation with society (Mann, 2012, p.59). Infrastructural power is the institutional capacity of a state to "penetrate its territories and logistically implement decisions" (Mann, 2012, p.59). Infrastructural power has a central place in analyses of post-Soviet Russia (e.g. in Colton and Holmes, 2006; Stoner-Weiss, 2006), which is not surprising considering how infrastructural weakness has limited its capacity. Both dimensions of state capacity are related to institutional development. Without institutions that are to some extent stable, at least somewhat regularised and formalised, state actors will find it difficult to develop policy, let alone implement decisions.

The Russian state was lower in both policymaking and infrastructural power in the 1990s than in the Soviet period. The relatively rapid weakening of the Soviet state during the break-up of the Union left the new Russian state so weak that it lost real, as opposed to nominal, control of state companies and enterprises. This led to a downward spiral of state capacity in the early 1990s. Its capacity in the energy industries was further weakened by frequent changes in the Fuel and Energy Ministry (1992–2000) and its successor, the Energy Ministry (2000–2004). From August 1996 to June 2001, the longest period served by any Fuel and Energy minister was 12 months. As the system eroded from within, existing channels of access and participation were disrupted without new ones emerging, and companies became insulated from the state. They may even have developed into a state within the state, operating beyond the reach of an impotent state apparatus.

In the 2000s, both policymaking and infrastructural power increased. When Putin came to power, he subordinated the fragmented public sector and its constituent political machines to himself and his supporting coalition, thereby strengthening the state both with respect to policymaking and infrastructural power. State actors gained access to resources that under Yeltsin were subject to negotiation with company managers or regional governors. Where the state's reach ended, it could compel for example energy companies to fund services and thereby substitute state welfare. Informal channels of rent management, access and participation persisted, but they were now as likely to reinforce the formal institutional framework as to undercut it. As a result, the state could penetrate its territory and energy sectors better, and more effectively. Institutional frameworks were upheld and implemented to a greater extent.

Changes in state capacity reflect the development from a fragile state to a basic state and then to a mature state, while remaining a limited access order. A fragile state can uphold only itself, and a basic state can support organisations that it controls (North et al., 2009, p.21). As state capacity increases further, the state can support organisations outside its immediate reach. It can at least temporarily enforce and protect some contracts and property rights, extract resources from companies not just by owning them, but also through the less direct method of taxation, and regulate market access for at least some companies. As it matures even more, the state can protect property rights more completely and permanently, extract taxes more indirectly, transparently and predictably, and open up and regulate more markets (North et al., 2009, pp.11–12). The depth of specialisation among state organisations, private companies and political groups indicates the level of development, but in a limited access order, any division into "state" and "private" organisations remains conditional and non-distinct, even as state organisations and companies become more specialised and delineated (Zudin, 2013, pp.16–17). The state cannot impersonally protect property rights and enforce contracts that involve members of the ruling coalition, because the imperative to protect privileges is more important for social and political stability. Still, during the change from a fragile to a mature order, institutions become more important for relations among elite groups. Intra-elite relations develop from constant and personal interaction to interaction regulated by (increasingly) formal institutions. Institutions are enforced more impersonally, regardless of privilege. Organisations depend less directly on the personal influence of their top managers (Zudin, 2013, p.17). But there are limits to how impersonal institutions can become in a limited access order before the stability of the regime is threatened.

Elites in the limited access order

State–company relations at this level are by definition elite relations. This is especially true of Russia, where elites form a top layer in public affairs, while the general population has only limited influence on how, and whether, its interests are represented in politics at all (Levada, 2010, p.85). As such, the analysis is concerned with a limited set of relations among a few elite groups. Business elites are expected to be prominent. The book shows how company managers, top state bureaucrats and some parts of the ruling coalition were all important to institutional development for and within these industries. While government priorities, also in national security or foreign policy, mattered for overall national development, industrial policies and institutions that regulate the economy in Russia have been shaped, primarily, among elites from those industries, and second, among elites with a more general managerial or political background. This broader elite is crucial for regime stability (Rivera and Rivera, 2006). As discussed throughout, and particularly in Chapter 5 on Lukoil, company managers are often aware of this role and loath to rock the boat of current property right arrangements and privileges, even when that reality does not serve their business all that well.

The people in this book are state and company actors, sometimes both. All the companies' predecessors were production units and ministries in the Soviet economy. Their original top managers were industry specialists first and Soviet managers second, typical of the so-called "Red Directors" who had made their careers as enterprise directors before continuing to climb the hierarchy within only one industry (Fortescue, 2006, p.24). Over time, many of Russia's "Red Directors" were replaced by general managers, younger men with a more diverse managerial background. Among the protagonists in this book, the most typical successor to the "Red Director" is a state bureaucrat or technocratic politician, with or without prior knowledge of the industry in question. These people all had close relations with the government, and often with the president when they were appointed to top company positions. In the case of Minatom/Rosatom, they are government members or heads of agencies, although the relations are more complicated than indicated by formal positions. Among the state actors, ministers and otherwise, we find typical reformers in the 1990s as well as trusted, loyal and experienced technocrats in the 2000s.

While the composition of Russia's elites underwent change, how infighting, not consensus, characterised elite relations did not. From the beginning, the breakdown of the Soviet system, reforms and economic crisis were accompanied by elite fragmentation. Personal connections and the sharing of informal rent streams were integral to elite relations under Yeltsin, also when they concerned policy formation and implementation. Elite networks certainly mattered in state–company relations. In the 1990s, financial and operational control over Gazprom in particular was almost tantamount to control of the state via the state budget. Added to this was the possibility of accessing rent streams through companies. The larger the company, and the greater its potential as a source of rents, the more central an object it became in conflicts over control of the state.

Under Putin, these mechanisms changed, and they became less visible. Following his accession to power, he had sufficient support among elites and population alike for a conditional and temporary agreement to emerge. This study confirms Peter Rutland's finding that this was not consensus, but a widespread support for stability over chaos and infighting (Rutland, 2018, p.282). Below this truce on the ruling coalition, infighting in a divided elite remained an essential feature of Russian policy- and decision-making: a feature shaping Russia's political economy. To rule Russia, it was still important to master, and dominate, informal relations, personal relationships and informal rent sharing (Baturo and Elkink, 2016). Any regime stability is precarious, because it hinges on balancing among groups of interest. In relatively stable periods between election seasons, elite conflicts around the companies studied here often revolved around modifications of the institutional framework in a way that maximised rents, either to the state, to the companies, or both. But more fundamentally, state–company relations in the energy sphere remained significant because control of any major company had the potential to influence political survival in post-Soviet Russia.

To many elite groups, including state actors, the companies studied here were important for their resources first, and by extension for their political influence. Other company contributions to the economy, for example innovation, appear to have been seen as less significant, even uninteresting. The elites' generally positive view of the nuclear energy industry, which is more research intensive and more dependent on the state than other energy industries, is an exception in this respect.[4] Russia's elites are in general oriented towards the state (Levada, 2010, p.83). This is evident in how economic power and business development is conceptualised in the case of the energy companies outside the nuclear energy industry. Companies' challenges and opportunities are not widely discussed or even understood in many elite groups. The importance for the national economy of these companies is often approached through concepts like national backwardness (Rutland, 2015, p.83). Putin's use of the term "energy superpower" or "hydrocarbon superpower", discussed in Chapter 2, represents both a departure from this general state of affairs, in emphasising the value of energy resources, and a continuation, in relating this value to the power of the state (Bouzarovski and Bassin, 2011).

The institutions that made it possible to access those resources were fundamental to such power projection. In Chapter 2, I discuss the role of energy in Russian foreign policy towards the post-Soviet region. In the case chapters that come afterwards, I return to institutional development in the energy industries and how it related to the foreign policy role of each company.

Notes

1 These concepts are also used in education and social studies, where they capture social inclusion.
2 Data available from the Observatory of Economic Complexity (https://atlas.media.mit.edu/en/). Values are calculated using current US dollars to exchange rates provided by the reporting nation.
3 Data available from the Observatory of Economic Complexity (https://atlas.media.mit.edu/en/). Values are calculated using current US dollars to exchange rates provided by the reporting nation.
4 For example, as demonstrated by public displays on the historic and current technological advances of this industry, such as those observed by the author in Moscow in April 2018.

References

Aalto, P. et al. (2012) "How are Russian energy policies formulated? Linking the actors and structures of energy policy" in Aalto, P. ed., *Russia's Energy Policies. National, Interregional and Global Levels* (Cheltenham, UK/Northampton, USA: Edward Elgar), pp.20–42

Åslund, A. (1999) "Russia's collapse", *Foreign Affairs*, 78 (5): 64–77

Baev, P.K. (2013) "Diversification, Russian-style: Searching for security of demand and transit" in Godzimirski, J.M. ed., *Russian Energy in a Changing World. What is the Outlook for the Hydrocarbons Superpower?* (Farnham: Ashgate), pp.111–129

Balmaceda, M.M. (2012) "Russia's central and eastern European energy transit corridor: Ukraine and Belarus" in Aalto, P. ed., *Russia's Energy Policies. National, Interregional and Global Levels* (Cheltenham, UK/Northampton, USA: Edward Elgar), pp.136–155

Balmaceda, M.M. (2013) *The Politics of Energy Dependency. Ukraine, Belarus and Lithuania between Domestic Oligarchs and Russian Pressure* (Toronto: University of Toronto Press)

Barkanov, B. (2018) "Natural Gas" in Tsygankov, A.P. ed., *Routledge Handbook of Russian Foreign Policy* (Abingdon/New York: Routledge), pp.138–152

Baturo, A. and Elkink, J.A. (2016) "Dynamics of regime personalization and patron–client networks in Russia, 1999–2014", *Post-Soviet Affairs*, 32 (1): 75–98

Bouzarovski, S. and Bassin, M. (2011) "Energy and identity: Imagining Russia as a hydrocarbon superpower", *Annals of the Association of American Geographers*, 101 (4): 783–794

Brada, J.C. (2013) "The Exchange Rate and Foreign Direct Investment" in Hare, P. and Turley, G. ed., *Handbook of the Economics and Political Economy of Transition* (London/New York: Routledge), pp.181–189

Bradshaw, M. (2008) "The geography of Russia's new political economy", *New Political Economy*, 13 (2): 193–201

Bukkvoll, T. (2003) "Putin's strategic partnership with the West: The domestic politics of Russian foreign policy", *Comparative Strategy*, 22 (3): 223–242

Busygina, I. and Filippov, M. (2013) "'Resource curse' and foreign policy: Explaining Russia's approach to the EU" in Godzimirski, J.M. ed., *Russian Energy in a Changing World. What is the Outlook for the Hydrocarbons Superpower?* (Farnham: Ashgate), pp.91–109

Closson, S. (2014) "Subsidies in Russia's gas trade" in Oxenstierna, S. and Tynkkynen, V.-P. ed., *Russian Energy and Security up to 2030* (London/New York: Routledge), pp.61–76

Colton, T.J. and Holmes, S. (ed.) (2006) *The State after Communism. Governance in the New Russia* (Langham: Rowman & Littlefield)

Connolly, R. (2013) *The Economic Sources of Social Order Development in Post-Socialist Eastern Europe* (London/New York: Routledge)

Connolly, R. and Hanson, P. (2012) "Russia's accession to the World Trade Organization", *Eurasian Geography and Economics*, 53 (4): 479–501

Cooper, J. (2013) "The Russian economy twenty years after the end of the socialist economic system", *Journal of Eurasian Studies*, 4 (1): 55–64

Drabek, Z. and Benacek, V. (2013) "Trade Reorientation and Global Integration" in Hare, P. and Turley, G. ed., *Handbook of the Economic and Political Economy of Transition* (London/New York: Routledge), pp.167–180

Easter, G. (2006) "Building fiscal capacity" in Colton, T.J. and Holmes, S. ed., *The State after Communism. Governance in the New Russia* (Lanham: Rowman & Littlefield), pp.21–52

Easter, G.M. (2012) *Capital, Coercion, and Postcommunist States* (Ithaca/London: Cornell University Press)

Ericson, R.E. (2013) "Command economy and its legacy" in Alexeev, M. and Weber, S. ed., *The Oxford Handbook of the Russian Economy* (Oxford: Oxford University Press), pp.51–85

Fish, M.S. (2005) *Democracy Derailed in Russia. The Failure of Open Politics* (Cambridge/New York: Cambridge University Press)

Fortescue, S. (2006) *Russia's Oil Barons and Metal Magnates. Oligarchs and the State in Transition* (Basingstoke/New York: Palgrave Macmillan)

Frye, T. (2002) "Capture or exchange? Business lobbying in Russia", *Europe-Asia Studies*, 54 (7): 1017–1036

Gaddy, C.G. and Ickes, B.W. (2005) "Resource rents and the Russian economy", *Eurasian Geography and Economics*, 46 (8): 559–583

Gaddy, C.G. and Ickes, B.W. (2010) "Russia after the Global Financial Crisis", *Eurasian Geography and Economics*, 51 (3): 281–311

Gaddy, C.G. and Ickes, B.W. (2013) *Bear Traps on Russia's Road to Modernization* (London/New York: Routledge)

Gans-Morse, J. (2012) "Threats to property rights in Russia: From private coercion to state aggression", *Post-Soviet Affairs*, 28 (3): 263–295

Gans-Morse, J. (2017) "Demand for law and the security of property rights: The case of post-Soviet Russia", *American Political Science Review*, 111 (2): 338–359

Gaulier, G. and Zignago, S. (2010) *BACI: International Trade Database at the Product-Level. The 1994–2007 Version*. CEPII Working Paper. (Paris: CEPII)

Gel'man, V. (2015) *Authoritarian Russia. Analyzing Post-Soviet Regime Changes* (Pittsburgh: University of Pittsburgh Press)

Guriev, S. and Rachinsky, A. (2005) "The role of oligarchs in Russian capitalism", *Journal of Economic Perspectives*, 19 (1): 131–150

Guriev, S. and Tsyvinskii, O. (2011) "Guriev, Tsyvinskii: Pered kem v otvete biznes [Guriev, Tsyvinskii: to whom is business accountable]", *Vedomosti*, 12 September 2011, Available from: https://www.vedomosti.ru/opinion/articles/2011/09/13/kompanii_i_filantropy [Accessed 25 March 2020]

Gvosdev, N.K. and Marsh, C. (2014) *Russian Foreign Policy. Interests, Vectors, and Sectors* (Thousand Oaks/London: SAGE/CQ Press)

Hale, H.E. (2010) "Eurasian polities as hybrid regimes: The case of Putin's Russia", *Journal of Eurasian Studies*, 1 (1): 33–41

Hale, H.E. (2015) *Patronal Politics. Eurasian Regime Dynamics in Comparative Perspective* (New York/Cambridge: Cambridge University Press)

Hanson, P. (2003) *The Rise and Fall of the Soviet Economy. An Economic History of the USSR from 1945* (Harlow: Pearson Education)

Hanson, P. (2014) *Reiderstvo: Asset-grabbing in Russia*. Programme papers on Russia and Eurasia. 3. (London: Chatham House)

Hanson, P. and Teague, E. (2005) "Big Business and the State in Russia", *Europe-Asia Studies*, 57 (5): 657–680

Hellman, J. (1998) "Winners take all: The politics of partial reform in postcommunist transitions", *World Politics*, 50 (2): 203–234

Hellman, J.S., Jones, G. and Kaufmann, D. (2000) *"Seize the State, Seize the Day". State Capture, Corruption, and Influence in Transition*. Policy Research Working Paper. 2444. (Washington, DC: The World Bank)

Huskey, E. (2014) "Legacies and Departures in the Russian State Executive" in Beissinger, M.R. and Kotkin, S. ed., *Historical Legacies of Communism in Russia and Eastern Europe* (New York: Cambridge University Press), pp.111–127

IMF (2014) *Russian Federation. Fiscal Transparency Evaluation*. IMF Country Report. (Washington, DC: International Monetary Fund)

IMF et al. (1990) *The Economy of the USSR. Summary and Recommendations*. Report for Group of Seven Countries. (Washington, DC: World Bank)

Jensen, N. and Wantchekon, L. (2004) "Resource wealth and political regimes in Africa", *Comparative Political Studies*, 37 (7): 816–841

Kaczmarski, M. (2014) "Domestic power relations and Russia's foreign policy", *Demokratizatsiya*, 22 (3): 383–409

Karl, T.L. (1997) *The Paradox of Plenty: Oil Booms and Petro-States* (Berkeley: University of California Press)

Kivinen, M. (2012) "Public and business actors in Russia's energy policy" in Aalto, P. ed., *Russia's Energy Policies. National, Interregional and Global Levels* (Cheltenham, UK/Northampton, USA: Edward Elgar), pp.45–62

Kluge, J.N. (2017) "Foreign direct investment, political risk and the limited access order", *New Political Economy*, 22 (1): 109–127

Kotkin, S. and Beissinger, M.R. (2014) "The historical legacies of Communism: An empirical agenda" in Beissinger, M.R. and Kotkin, S. ed., *Historical Legacies of Communism in Russia and Eastern Europe* (New York: Cambridge University Press), pp.1–27

Ledeneva, A.V. (2006) *How Russia Really Works. The Informal Practices That Shaped Post-Soviet Politics and Business* (Ithaca and London: Cornell University Press)

Ledeneva, A.V. (2013) *Can Russia Modernise? Sistema, Power Networks and Informal Governance* (Cambridge: Cambridge University Press)

Levada, I. (2010) "Ruling authority, the elite, and the masses", *Sociological Research*, 49 (2): 82–94

Luong, P.J. and Weinthal, E. (2006) "Rethinking the resource curse: Ownership structure, institutional capacity, and domestic constraints", *Annual Review of Political Science*, 9: 241–263

Luong, P.J. and Weinthal, E. (2010) *Oil Is Not a Curse. Ownership Structure and Institutions in Soviet Successor States* (Cambridge: Cambridge University Press)

Malcolm, N. (1996) "Foreign policy making" in Malcolm, N. et al. ed., *Internal Factors in Russian Foreign Policy* (Oxford: The Royal Institute for International Affairs/Oxford University Press), pp.101–168

Malle, S. (2013) "Economic modernisation and diversification in Russia. Constraints and challenges", *Journal of Eurasian Studies*, 4 (1): 78–99

Mann, M. (2012 [1993]) *The Sources of Social Power* (Cambridge: Cambridge University Press)

Marten, K. (2015) "Informal political networks and Putin's foreign policy", *Problems of Post-Communism*, 62 (2): 71–87

Mau, V. (2016) "Between crises and sanctions: Economic policy of the Russian Federation", *Post-Soviet Affairs*, 32 (4): 350–377

Mau, V. (2017) "Russia's economic policy in 2015–16: The imperative of structural reform", *Post-Soviet Affairs*, 33 (1): 63–83

Meister, S. (ed.) (2013) *Economization Versus Power Ambitions: Rethinking Russia's Policy Towards Post-Soviet States* (Berlin: Deutsche Gesellschaft für Auswärtige Politik e.V.)

Melville, A., Stukal, D. and Mironyuk, M. (2014) "'King of the Mountain', or why post-communist autocracies have bad institutions", *Russian Politics and Law*, 52 (2): 7–29

Miller, C. (2018) *Putinomics. Power and Money in Resurgent Russia* (Chapel Hill: University of North Carolina Press)

Monaghan, A. (2012) "The vertikal: Power and authority in Russia", *International Affairs*, 88 (1): 1–16

Müller, M. (2015) "After Sochi 2014: Costs and impacts of Russia's Olympic Games", *Eurasian Geography and Economics*, 55 (6): 628–655

North, D.C. (1990) *Institutions, Institutional Change and Economic Performance* (Cambridge/New York: Cambridge University Press)

North, D.C., Wallis, J.J. and Weingast, B. (2009) *Violence and Social Orders. A Conceptual Framework for Interpreting Recorded Human History* (Cambridge: Cambridge University Press)

Paneyakh, E. (2014) "Faking performance together: Systems of performance evaluation in Russian enforcement agencies and production of bias and privilege", *Post-Soviet Affairs*, 30 (2–3): 115–136

Peregudov, S.P., Lapina, N.Yu. and Semenenko, I.S. (1999) *Gruppy interesov i rossiiskoe gosudarstvo* [*Interest groups and the Russian state*] (Moscow: Editorial URSS)

Pirani, S. (ed.) (2009) *Russian and CIS Gas Markets and their Impact on Europe* (Oxford: Oxford Institute for Energy Studies/Oxford University Press)

Pomfret, R. (2013) "Resource-rich transition economies" in Hare, P. and Turley, G. ed., *Handbook of the Economics and Political Economy of Transition* (London/New York: Routledge), pp.406–417

Popov, V. (2013) "Transformational recession" in Alexeev, M. and Weber, S. ed., *The Oxford Handbook of the Russian Economy* (Oxford: Oxford University Press), pp.102–131

Poussenkova, N. (2012) "'The went East, they went West...': The global expansion of Russian oil companies" in Aalto, P. ed., *Russia's Energy Policies. National, Interregional and Global Levels* (Cheltenham: Edward Elgar), pp.185–205

Rivera, S.W. and Rivera, D.W. (2006) "The Russian elite under Putin: Militocratic or bourgeois?", *Post-Soviet Affairs*, 22 (2): 125–144

Rochlitz, M. (2014) "Corporate raiding and the role of the state in Russia", *Post-Soviet Affairs*, 30 (2–3): 89–114

Rochlitz, M. (2015) "At the crossroads: Putin's third presidential term and Russia's institutions", *Political Studies Review*, 13 (1): 59–68

Ross, M.L. (1999) "The political economy of the resource curse", *World Politics*, 51 (2): 297–322

Ross, M.L. (2001) "Does oil hinder democracy?", *World Politics*, 53 (3): 325–361

Ross, M.L. (2012) *The Oil Curse. How Petroleum Wealth Shapes the Development of Nations* (Princeton/Oxford: Princeton University Press)

Rutland, P. (ed.) (2001) *Business and the State in Contemporary Russia* (Boulder, CO: Westview Press)

Rutland, P. (2015) "Petronation? Oil, gas and national identity in Russia", *Post-Soviet Affairs*, 31 (1): 66–89

Rutland, P. (2018) "The political elite in post-Soviet Russia" in Best, H. and Higley, J. ed., *The Palgrave Handbook of Political Elites* (London: Palgrave Macmillan), pp.273–294

Sakwa, R. (2008) "Putin and the Oligarchs", *New Political Economy*, 13 (2): 185–191
Sharlet, R. (2001) "Putin and the politics of law in Russia", *Post-Soviet Affairs*, 17 (3): 195–234
Simoes, A.J.G. and Hidalgo, C.A. (2011) "The Economic Complexity Observatory: An analytical tool for understanding the dynamics of economic development" in Workshops at the Twenty-Fifth AAAI Conference on Artificial Intelligence
Smith, B. (2007) *Hard Times in the Lands of Plenty. Oil Politics in Iran and Indonesia* (Ithaca/London: Cornell University Press)
Stern, J.P. (2005) *The Future of Russian Gas and Gazprom* (Oxford: Oxford University Press/Oxford Institute for Energy Studies)
Stoner-Weiss, K. (2006) *Resisting the State. Reform and Retrenchment in Post-Soviet Russia* (Cambridge: Cambridge University Press)
Stulberg, A.N. (2007) *Well-Oiled Diplomacy. Strategic Manipulation and Russia's Energy Statecraft in Eurasia* (Albany, New York: State University of New York Press)
Stulberg, A.N. (2015) "Out of gas? Russia, Ukraine, Europe, and the changing geopolitics of natural gas", *Problems of Post-Communism*, 62 (2): 112–130
Sutela, P. (2012) *The Political Economy of Putin's Russia* (London/New York: Routledge)
Torbakov, I. (2013) "Understanding Moscow's conduct: The analysis of the domestic-foreign policy nexus in Russia" in Meister, S. ed., *Economization Versus Power Ambitions: Rethinking Russia's Policy Towards Post-Soviet States* (Berlin: Deutsche Gesellschaft für Auswärtige Politik e.V.), pp.19–33
Vasileva, A. (2018) "Trapped in informality: The big role of small firms in Russia's statist-patrimonial system", *New Political Economy*, 23 (3): 314–330
Veligzhanina, A. (2000) "Krasnaya 'krysha' vsekh kruche i vyshe [The red 'roof' is the most influential and tallest]", *Komsomol'skaya pravda*, 14 June 2000
Weber, Y. (2018) "Petropolitics" in Tsygankov, A.P. ed., *Routledge Handbook of Russian Foreign Policy* (Abingdon/New York: Routledge), pp.99–117
Wenger, A., Perovic, J. and Orttung, R.W. (ed.) (2006) *Russian Business Power. The Role of Russian Business in Foreign and Security Relations* (London/New York: Routledge)
Wengle, S.A. (2012) "Engineers versus managers: Experts, market-making and state-building in Putin's Russia", *Economy and Society*, 41 (3): 435–467
Wengle, S.A. (2014) *Post-Soviet Power. State-led Development and Russia's Marketization* (Cambridge/New York: Cambridge University Press)
Yakovlev, A. (2006) "The evolution of business–state interaction in Russia: From state capture to business capture?", *Europe-Asia Studies*, 58 (7): 1033–1056
Yakovlev, A., Sobolev, A. and Kazun, A. (2014) "Means of production versus means of coercion: Can Russian business limit the violence of a predatory state?", *Post-Soviet Affairs*, 30 (2–3): 171–194
Zudin, A.Yu. (2013) "Biznes i gosudarstvo v Rossii: opyt primeneniya podkhoda Norta-Uollisa-Vaingasta. Stat'ya 1. Etapy razvitiya rossiiskikh biznes-assotsiatsii [Business and the state in Russia: an attempt at applying the approach of North-Wallis-Weingast. Article 1. Stages in the development of Russian business associations]", *Obshchestvennye nauki i sovremennost'*, 2013 (2): 15–31

2 Energy and Russia's foreign policy towards post-Soviet states

State–business relations in Russia placed energy companies in positions where they could become foreign policy tools. That is the supply side of Russian foreign economic policy. There is also a demand side. Without energy companies, Russian foreign policy would have been qualitatively different, especially in the post-Soviet region. Company operations were crucial to wider economic power projection. In the 2000s, Russia aimed to exploit regional influence in the energy sector to develop as a great power.

This chapter discusses how energy policy towards other post-Soviet states developed within the context of overall Russian foreign policy. It is instructive to look at the post-Soviet period in terms of the constraints on Russian foreign economic policy. The constraints mattered, and in the 1990s, they were of a domestic nature. Overall foreign policy was rhetorically ambitious, but Russia lacked in real power in global and regional affairs. The use of energy tools in the post-Soviet region stood out, because they were based on real economic power. It demonstrated a potential for influence that could be used coercively as well as for cooperative ends, even as Russia in practice often prioritised dominance. Still, domestic constraints mattered. In the 1990s, either economic weakness or a lack of policy priority and consensus limited Russia's use of energy power. The following boom in global energy markets increased activity in the global energy industries, also in the post-Soviet region, and contributed to growing Russian economic power.

In the 2000s, Russia became a genuinely attractive partner and investor, and foreign economic policy was highly prioritised. But as it started to use regional energy power to claim a global great power position, the limits to what energy power did and could potentially achieve began to show. This was a general foreign policy challenge (Rutland, 2008; Orttung and Øverland, 2011) visible in relations with Europe (Finon and Locatelli, 2008; Stent, 2008; Stegen, 2011; Closson, 2014), and post-Soviet states (Closson, 2011; Meister, 2013). This chapter shows that where in the 1990s, Russian foreign policy distinguished between a regional and an international level, in the late 2000s and 2010s it was no longer possible to isolate relations with its western post-Soviet neighbours from those with other European states. Moreover, it shows how a foreign policy based on economic power in interconnected energy markets is subject to market-related constraints. As any energy producer, Russia depended on global energy markets and on maintaining good working relations with energy consuming states (Rutland, 2008, pp.207–208; Orttung and Øverland, 2011, p.76; Closson, 2014, p.72). This was particularly salient for Russia due to its position as a price taker in global energy markets, and its role in supplying Europe with pipeline gas. Russia was in an interdependent energy relationship with European customers, and subject to the ups and downs of the oil price. These constraints were less consequential for Russian power projection as long as the oil price and the demand for gas and nuclear power were high. When market conditions changed, they had immediate effects.

Foreign policy fragmentation

In 1992 it was difficult to foresee that the energy sector's foreign policy lobbying power would become unsurpassed, comparable to that of the defence industry in the Soviet period (Pravda, 1996, p.183). During the break-up of the Soviet Union, policymakers were more preoccupied with the new possibilities that opened for Russia once it became free of what was perceived as the Soviet burden. Integration into the global economy, and above all, with the West, was a central aim of Boris Yeltsin's first government (November 1991 to December 1992). The intention was to support economic development aims – becoming a normal civilised country with a market economy, in short, a "normal great power" integrated into the global economy, as articulated by Foreign Minister Andrei Kozyrev (1992–1995) (Kozyrev, 1992, p.10). Energy relations with Europe and the rest of the world were important to integration. Especially in the Ministry of Foreign Affairs (MFA), relations with the other post-Soviet states had lower priority than those with the "far abroad" (Arbatov, 1993, p.20). When the "near abroad" was discussed, it was to emphasise that bilateral and multilateral relations would be reformed based on Russian interests (*Diplomaticheskii vestnik*, 1992). There was little attention to energy relations, with the crucial exception of the possibility of using them to influence other post-Soviet states.

This early period was characterised by a lack of foreign policy coordination and coherence within the government, and between government and the Presidential Administration. Combined with a lack of interest on the part of the Ministry of Foreign Affairs, this opened relations with post-Soviet states to other actors, from political factions and regional politicians to security agencies, military commanders, and industrialists. These groups maintained relations with bases of support, old colleagues and contacts, suppliers and markets in the region. Fragmentation was exacerbated by a difficult relationship between Foreign Minister Kozyrev and key elite groups, like the foreign policy committee in the State Duma (hereafter the Duma), from December 1993. In addition, responsibility for foreign economic policy was shared between two new ministries, the Ministry of Foreign Economic Relations (1992–1997) and that of relations with the Commonwealth of Independent States (CIS) (1992–1997).

Duality was maintained until the formation of the Ministry of Economic Development and Trade in May 2000. As a result, overall relations with the post-Soviet region deteriorated in the 1990s, and company priorities shaped foreign economic policy.

From mid-1992, parts of Russia's foreign policy elite began to perceive Russia as strategically weakened in the region (Sovet po vneshnei i oboronnoi politike—SVOP, 1992). Overall foreign policy priorities changed somewhat in December 1992, when Yeltsin replaced Yegor Gaidar's reform government with that of Viktor Chernomyrdin. Chernomyrdin's government[1] was far more attuned to the interests of sectoral lobbies, and was, as this book shows, closely related to the energy industries. It was a conservative government in the sense that it emphasised Russia's position in the region and abandoned the idea that Russia's interests could be subsumed into any broadly Western community. This increased consensus on foreign policy, with a more widely shared priority on the post-Soviet region (Light, 1996, pp.77–78). The consensus comprised an understanding that Russia's position in the region should be defended "in extreme cases by the use of force", especially when responding to "one-sided actions" on the part of the other states (Ministry of Foreign Affairs, 1993, pp.4, 8).

The new policy priorities also reflected popular discontent with economic reform, and with it, the policy of comprehensive economic and political integration with the West. The population had begun to yearn for a more active Russian policy towards the post-Soviet region as a whole (Dunlop, 1997, pp.55–57). This was articulated at the ballot box in December 1993, when nationalist and Communist candidates enjoyed great success in the Duma elections. However, actual foreign policy making remained fragmented, and priorities in the post-Soviet region remained divisive, until the end of Kozyrev's period as foreign minister in 1995.

Regional disintegration: Russia as a "leading force"?

At the regional level, the ties that bound the post-Soviet economies together were loosening. Post-Soviet elites disagreed over the speed of economic change, leading to the collapse of the ruble zone in 1993 (Dabrowski, 1993, pp.29–30). The trade patterns of the Soviet period ceased to exist, in part due to Russia's priority to integrate with the global economy (Michalopoulos and Tarr, 1994; Drabek and Benacek, 2013). While in 1989, Soviet trade had been overwhelmingly internal, by 1995, the CIS members had diversified their trade. For five member states (Armenia, Azerbaijan, Russia, Tajikistan, Uzbekistan) the regional CIS share of total export more than halved from 1989 to 1995 (Freinkman et al., 2004, pp.12–13). For six member states (Belarus, Georgia, Kazakhstan, Moldova, Turkmenistan, Ukraine) the share of export destined for other CIS states decreased from 85 per cent or more of all export in 1989, to 63 per cent or less in 1995 (Freinkman et al., 2004, pp.12–13). Only for Kyrgyzstan did the CIS share of all export remain at a relatively high level, 73 per cent in 1995, compared to 98 per cent in 1989 (Freinkman et al., 2004, pp.12–13).[2] This reorientation of trade towards states outside the region was accompanied by a "precipitous decline" in total international trade (Freinkman et al., 2004, p.7). The post-Soviet economies went through a serious crisis.

The economic effects of post-Soviet economic disintegration came as a serious political shock to elites in all the states (Light, 1996, p.83). The 1993 Russian policy turn in relation to the post-Soviet region was therefore part of a broader yearning in the region for selective post-Soviet reintegration, combined with policy coordination within the CIS framework. But unlike the other states, Russia approached the CIS as a framework within which it could assert regional hegemony. This ambition was tempered by a realisation that regional economic integration would come with drawbacks for the Russian economy. This ambiguous approach, lack of consistent implementation, and especially, Russian attempts to assert hegemony, met with a mix of selective engagement and disengagement by the other states. As a result, Russia's ties with other post-Soviet states were mainly managed in bilateral fashion. There was no regional strategy.

Another gap emerged between rhetoric and capacity for implementation in Russian policy towards the other states. The first policy document on Russia's approach to the region, the Strategic Course towards the Participant States in the Commonwealth of Independent States (hereafter the "Strategic Course"), was issued in September 1995. A brief, general outline, its central objective was to integrate the CIS countries economically and politically with Russia as a "leading force". This would create a region capable of "claiming a worthy place in global society" (Decree No. 940, 1995). In light of the transformational recession in the Russian economy, and unresolved security issues throughout the region, this was a proposition for the very long term at best. The other post-Soviet states were opening to the world and amidst a process of developing relations with European states, Turkey, the US and China. The Baltic states pursued integration with the EU and NATO. In some states, especially in Georgia, Azerbaijan and Turkmenistan, there was a profound scepticism towards Russia's policies. Other states, like Belarus and Kazakhstan, were closer to Russia in terms of strategic orientation, but still had reservations regarding the scope of integration. To all post-Soviet elites, escaping from Russian dominance was an integral part of state-building. The implementation of a Russian claim to leadership in the region was bound to be difficult, especially if that claim would include attempts to establish hegemony. The somewhat aggressive tone, emphasis only on Russian interests, and lack of mention of any potential for mutual advantage in the Strategic Course, appeared to confirm that this was indeed the aim. Russia's haphazard approach to the region in 1992–1993 and its decreasing attractiveness complicated its strategic return. In consequence, the gap between a rhetoric of undisputed regional leadership and weakening real control persisted through the 1990s.

Asymmetric energy dependence

Energy dependence on Russia was a Soviet legacy and a given for most post-Soviet leaders. Even with substantial oil and gas production in other union republics, 80 per cent was in the Russian Soviet Republic (Dodsworth et al., 2002, pp.9, 12). There had been few ties to international markets for oil, gas and nuclear fuel, and they were under central control. Within the post-Soviet region, energy supply was not easily transferred from existing suppliers in Russia to others. In 1992, the other post-Soviet states were highly dependent on imports for both oil and gas supply. Eleven of fourteen states depended on import for 80 to 100 per cent of their oil supply, and for 77 to 100 per cent of their gas supply (author's calculation based on IEA, 2016). Russia was their main source of energy.[3] The oil and gas producing Central Asian states, on their side, depended on Russian markets, or on transit through Russia to international markets. The nuclear energy industry in Kazakhstan and Ukraine depended on access to Russian technology for further development, including market access. In all cases, non-delivery, subsidy withdrawal, or a lack of development would threaten political legitimacy across the region.

Following the break-up of the Soviet Union, the Russian energy sector suffered from economic crisis, falling oil production and low hydrocarbon prices. The government decided on serious cuts to energy exports, especially of oil and oil products, to the CIS from 1993 (Becker, 1996, p.125). The aim was to make larger volumes available for export to global markets, at market prices, instead of supplying set quotas for CIS states in return for barter goods (Konoplyanik et al., 1992, p.44). The cuts were effective. In 1993, more than 50 per cent of Russia's crude oil export and 18 per cent of its oil products went to CIS states, while in 1997, 90 per cent of all oil and oil products export went to other parts of the world (Nekrasov and Sinyak, 2001, p.94).

Oil trade within the CIS transferred to market principles. This change contributed to an energy crisis, especially serious in Armenia and Moldova, and exacerbated tendencies towards fuel poverty across post-Soviet countries (Anex, 2002, p.400; Gentile, 2015, pp.585–586). In light of such consequences, gas and electricity trade remained non-market based and a matter of political negotiation. Russia continued to subsidise gas prices. All the western post-Soviet states were also transit states for Russian oil and gas, and their economies depended in part on the income generated by transit. This was often paid in kind, on barter terms. To post-Soviet governments, continued subsidies in gas pricing, acceptance of barter payment and soft payment terms reduced the cost of energy dependence on Russia, while at the same time increasing the cost of reducing it.

To Russia, the economic cost of regional energy trade remained substantial. Even with reduced oil trade, energy was less affected than other sectors by the overall trade collapse. In 1996, the first year for which there is data available in the UN Comtrade database, exports of fuel, electricity and nuclear reactors constituted 39.4 per cent of Russia's total exports to the post-Soviet states.[4]

To ease the terms for post-Soviet customers, price subsidies in energy sales were from 1992–1993 combined with loss-incurring loans ("technical credits") to CIS members to help them pay. But this exacerbated the problem, resulting in mounting debts. CIS energy trade burdened Gazprom and RAO UES in particular (Becker, 1996, p.125).

Nevertheless, Russia's foreign policymakers saw the benefits of maintaining relations as they were. Asymmetric energy dependence was an attractive lever of economic power towards other post-Soviet states. Russia's energy policy prioritised the development of what was rather vaguely referred to as "mutually advantageous energy relations with CIS states" (Decree No. 472, 1995), and emphasised that energy export should facilitate Russia's integration into the global economy (Korsun, 1994). The Strategic Course, on the other hand, contained the foundations of an instrumental approach to energy relations. Economic relations were not only a foundation for "non-compulsory" integration "at different speeds", they were also described as instrumental (Decree No. 940, 1995). They were tools for lifting Russia out of economic crisis and sources of Russian influence, including through "the formation of joint equity". In particular, post-Soviet states' willingness to pursue closer relations with Russia would be "an important factor in deciding the extent of Russian economic, political and military support". Russia's interests in bilateral relations included "the prevention of indebtedness in trade (…); the most favourable regime for transit of Russian goods" (Decree No. 940, 1995). In the energy sector, Russia had the capabilities to match these phrases. Energy trade and transit could, and would, be used to influence, reward and punish individual states, as a response to their foreign policy towards Russia.

In the beginning, debt was exchanged for equity in the gas industry. The state allowed Gazprom to recover debts through equity acquisitions, in the Baltic states and Moldova in 1994 and 1995, respectively. This was also the case with Belarus in 1993, except that the process took many years to accomplish (Chapter 7). But debt was exchanged for equity in Belarus's oil sector, creating the jointly owned company Slavneft. It was promised that Rosneft and Lukoil would acquire stakes in Belarusian oil refineries upon privatisation, but in the event this did not happen. By 1997, debt-for-equity deals were found useful in relation to Armenia, whose foreign policy position was also close to Russia. This policy was a rational business strategy, providing at least some compensation to e.g. Gazprom when it was otherwise difficult to obtain full debt repayment. To the government, debt for equity deals fitted well also with the idea of mutually advantageous energy relations. The practice spread to the electricity and nuclear industries in the 2000s, becoming a universal approach that could coerce and reward post-Soviet states regardless of their policy towards Russia.

Another characteristic of the instrumental approach to energy ties, Gazprom and Transneft's transit avoidance policies, appeared in the mid to late 1990s. They entailed the development of alternative routes, sometimes with excess export capacity, in avoidance of existing pipelines inherited from the Soviet period. The aim was to minimise the risk in relation to what from the Russian point of view were troublesome transit states like Belarus, Ukraine, Latvia and Lithuania. To elites in post-Soviet states, policies like these signalled that Russia pursued regional integration on its own terms, and that they would need to balance Russia in order to make room for strategic manoeuvre.

Outside the energy industries, Russia's integration policies in the post-Soviet region continued to display a gap between rhetoric and reality. Economic integration with Belarus, including a free trade zone from 1995, a Commonwealth of Belarus and Russia from 1996 and a Union State from 1997, went far on paper. Belarus's complete dependence on subsidised oil and gas from Russia made it willing to agree to integration. When Russia proposed terms that reinforced its dominance and subjected Belarus to further pressure, implementation stalled. One of Russia's aims with the Union State was to attract other states, Ukraine and Kazakhstan in particular, to closer integration. When this failed, Russia was left to observe how its influence began to erode in Central Asia and the South Caucasus. The Baltic states developed closer relations with, and eventually acceded to the EU and NATO. Ukraine and Moldova tried to maintain as balanced a foreign policy as they could, not committing to close integration with Russia.

Russia's foreign policy towards the post-Soviet region continued to develop based neither on assessments of neighbouring states' interests, nor on analysis of its overall effectiveness in promoting Russia's influence in the longer term. The changing international relations in the region were in the late 1990s increasingly perceived as a function of a global multipolar system. Now, Russia saw itself as a weakened great power facing competition in its regional sphere of influence from other great powers, above all the US. From 1996, the new Foreign Minister Evgenii Primakov's[5] multilateral foreign policy aimed at improving Russia's global position and advancing Russia's interests in what had become a far more conflictual relationship with the West (Katz, 2006, p.145). Russia's foreign policy in the region aimed to maintain control and hegemony in order to preserve some of its previous global influence. Under Primakov, foreign policy articulated a broader political consensus, but policy in the post-Soviet region remained incoherent.

A new approach: expansion and commercialisation

In the late 1990s, Russia's economic ties with the post-Soviet region were changing. Following the 1998 financial crisis, Russian recovery and catch-up growth entailed that companies accumulated the capital necessary for regional expansion (Crane et al., 2005, p.414). Russia's vertically integrated corporations and holdings were no longer muddling through. Instead they were consolidated entities pursuing bottom-up regional economic integration, at the very time when politically motivated top-down integration projects were failing (Libman, 2007; Libman and Kheifets, 2007, p.19). By the turn of the century, the importance of economic ties for foreign policy and Russia's international position was increasing, and the gap between bold rhetoric and real capabilities narrowed.

From the beginning of Vladimir Putin's presidency in 2000,[6] Russian companies' business operations were given a more central place in foreign policy. Ahead of the 2000 presidential election, Putin emphasised the need to rebuild and develop the state, not just in terms of internal capacity, but as a great power in the international system (Putin, 1999; 2000). In his view, this would be achieved through economic power projection across the post-Soviet region. This was a continuation of Primakov's foreign policy, especially its emphasis on Russian interests. The domestic constraints on foreign policy implementation were now reduced. The political landscape had changed. During Putin's first period, the Russian state went through a period of recentralisation. The scope for sectoral policy initiatives in foreign policymaking diminished. Compared to the 1990s, state capacity for policy formation and power projection increased. The elites, many of whom now had a reduced influence on foreign policy, in general saw this in a positive light. Part of Putin's attraction was that he seemed capable of delivering on Russia's return as a global great power, with a regional position that underpinned this aim. The 1998 financial crisis had demonstrated the dangers of elite infighting, and how this weakened the state. A stronger Russian state appealed to many elite groups, whether they understood it in terms of state capacity and economic development, or of national pride and great power status.

The economic realities began to change: there was more power to project. In part this was due to increasing oil production in the post-crisis recovery period. In addition, developments in global energy markets, and in oil markets in particular, had a substantial impact on Russia's economy. Oil prices recovered from a low of nine to ten US$/barrel in the winter of 1998–1999, to 30 US$/barrel in summer 2000, above 40 US$/barrel four years later and then 70 in 2006. The oil price boom was followed by substantial increases in gas prices, and beginning in 2003 increasing prices for uranium and other commodities. From 2001 to 2006, oil revenue increased from three per cent of GDP to 11.2 per cent (IMF, 2007, p.10; 2016, p.28). Russia's increased means, in relative and absolute terms, made a difference to its regional influence.

An energy strategy in pursuit of power

Strategic documents were revised. A comprehensive Energy Strategy appeared in 2003. In the previous energy strategy, issued in 1995, a major aim was to "support the export potential of the Russian fuel and energy complex and broaden its export potential" (Decree No. 472, 1995). There was also a need to attract foreign investment to the energy industries, especially to facilitate reorganisation based on market principles (Korsun,

1994). In 2003, circumstances had changed, and so had policy priorities. The new Energy Strategy was more specific, and reflected a new political reality. The energy sector should now be used to strengthen the state (Ministry of Industry and Trade, 2003). In 1995, there was an emphasis on "mutually advantageous cooperation with CIS states (...) [and] widening the mutually advantageous cooperation with other states" (Decree No. 472, 1995). Integration at the regional level was mentioned, referring to electricity, but this was not an immediate task (Korsun, 1994). In 2003, this gave way to a forthright description of the energy industries as a "core element of Russia's diplomacy", which could be used to deliver benefits to pro-Russian states (Ministry of Industry and Trade, 2003, Ch.7). The new Energy Strategy thus applied the foreign policy line from the Strategic Course of 1995 to the energy industries. The emphasis on their instrumental role in relation to foreign policy, which had appeared there, was now expanded to give them a more explicit political role. Great power, in this approach, meant economic power.

The context was a more assertive foreign policy, intended to bolster Russia's power in the post-Soviet region, and its international position as a counterweight to the US. In October 2003, several statements by Putin and Defence Minister Sergei Ivanov[7] highlighted the link between the state and foreign energy operations (RFE/RL, 2003; Suslov, 2003). Russia now reserved the right to intervene militarily in the CIS to settle disputes as a means of last resort, and the prerogative to maintain the natural gas and oil pipelines to the West in order to protect Russian interests, even "beyond Russia's borders" (RFE/RL, 2003). In this way, a sphere of influence in the post-Soviet region, aimed at protecting Russian national interests, would be supported by energy relations. Maintaining close relations with post-Soviet states gradually became more highly prioritised, also in practice. This change of priorities was further strengthened following the "colour revolutions" in Georgia (2003), Ukraine (2004–2005) and Kyrgyzstan (2005). Ukraine's Orange Revolution in 2004–2005 especially demonstrated to Russian foreign policymakers that their attempts at wielding influence had a limited impact (Kuzio, 2005; Wilson, 2010, pp.28–29). Regional integration processes, with Russia as the region's great power, came to the fore, and energy relations were a foundation for integration (Ministry of Foreign Affairs, 2007; 2008). The emphasis on integration in the post-Soviet region was to remain central to foreign policy in the coming years (Ministry of Foreign Affairs, 2013).

In the 2000s, strengthening Russian companies' positions abroad became a more pronounced priority (Ministry of Energy, 2009, p.9; Ministry of Foreign Affairs, 2013). The state offered the companies support in return for their role in foreign policy. This resulted in, for example, that the government from 2005 supported Gazprom's adoption of a commercially based pricing policy towards post-Soviet customers (called "European netback prices" by Gazprom). Making this change had long been anathema to the Russian government. A commercially based pricing policy reduced subsidy costs to Gazprom, but appeared to deprive Russia of the possibility of using price subsidies as a tool of influence. As will be discussed in Chapter 7, the use of carrots and sticks in post-Soviet gas trade continued, only now with price increases as a new stick and temporary postponement as a carrot. The exact terms and timing of the transition to "European netback prices" was used to expand Gazprom's control of post-Soviet gas sectors, through more exchanges of debt, or price subsidies, for equity. Russia's economic dominance in the energy sector increased further in the states that obtained a slower schedule towards European netback prices. In some cases, Russian dominance in the electricity and nuclear industries complemented Gazprom's position in the gas sector. In terms of overall Russian foreign policy, the implication was that Russia refused to underwrite regional integration. Other post-Soviet gas importers had little choice but to pay for Russian hegemony, either through equity transfers or in cash. In practise, post-Soviet gas prices continued to be differentiated on a scale of dependence/independence in their political positions towards Russia. The novelty was that, compared to the 1990s, states that were closer to Russia politically now found it difficult to resist Russia's economic dominance in the energy industries.

In the view of Russia's top leadership, energy power would increase Russia's international leverage, above all in Europe. Energy power enabled international action independent of other great powers. In August 2006, oil revenue was used to repay Soviet-era debts to international creditors ahead of schedule. When asked about his main achievements during his time in power, Putin made a point of this at the 2006 meeting of the Valdai Club (Kremlin.ru, 2006). Oil revenue made it possible to accumulate a Stabilisation Fund from 2004, in 2008 split into the Reserve Fund and the National Welfare Fund.[8]

Energy wealth could be channelled into local communities to develop and expand energy infrastructure and production, and support other economic sectors and the state. Before the financial crisis hit Russia in early 2009, energy was a wealth generator that increased the attractiveness and influence of the energy industries in the post-Soviet region. The high oil price, and debt-for-equity exchanges in non-petroleum industries, opened business opportunities for Russian companies in the post-Soviet region. The additional investment needed to take advantage of existing assets was not always large, but made a major difference to communities and elites in the region. Energy resources, it seemed, were an asset which Russia could continue to use to influence other states, to accumulate financial resources, and to support its claim to great power status.

The problems of energy power

Relations with the US and the European Union, Russia's most significant international partners, turned more complicated. The popular protests and "colour revolutions" in Georgia (2003), Ukraine (2004) and Kyrgyzstan (2005) were met with American and European engagement and support.

Georgia in particular began to pursue closer relations with the West, looking to NATO for a Membership Action Plan (MAP) and to the European Union for a more comprehensive European Neighbourhood Policy than the one launched in 2003. To Russian policymakers, these events combined two wholly undesirable developments, popular protest leading to a change of government, and increased western influence in the post-Soviet region. They were seen to be instigated by the West, with the US as the main culprit. Much of Russia's elites shared a zero-sum approach to great power politics, and concluded that Russia's influence in the post-Soviet region would disappear if left undefended.

But Russia's moves towards a strategy of dominance in the region further complicated relations with the EU. The strategy, intended as a basis for great power status, was founded on a distinction between major states and smaller ones, where the former dominated and competed for influence over the latter. The European liberal principle of equally valid claims to national sovereignty was incompatible with the introduction of distinctions among European states on the basis of their proximity to Russia. Particular attention was paid in Europe to how Russia used energy relations with regard to other post-Soviet states, since this had direct consequences for its European customers. Moreover, when Russia used energy power to claim great power status, it was seen as indicative of its overall approach to energy customers, especially weaker ones (Harsem and Claes, 2013, p.8). To the EU, Russia's energy policies were particularly important because Russia was its largest supplier.

Russia began to face market-related constraints in Europe also with regard to its energy relations with post-Soviet states, at least in gas. The problem became apparent when a dispute over gas transit terms between Russia and Ukraine reached crisis point in January 2006, leading to temporarily reduced gas supply to several European countries. In response, Gazprom and Russia blamed Ukraine. Following the crisis, governments across Europe started to question Gazprom's reliability of supply and to discuss how to reduce, or mitigate, dependence on Russian gas. Trust in Russia as a gas supplier was weakened (Finon and Locatelli, 2008). The reaction was particularly strong in Poland and Hungary. But Germany and Italy, too, expressed concern over the crisis.

When in August 2008 war broke out in Georgia, both the Russian state and energy companies carefully distinguished between state policy and business operations, insisting that business considerations dominated in relationships with customers and transit states. Inter RAO and Gazprom, the two Russian energy companies with significant operations in Georgia, were relatively unaffected by the brief war. The relatively limited European and American reactions that followed did not directly target Russian energy companies. However, only months later, another gas transit crisis soured relations between Russia and Ukraine. This crisis was to have much greater impact on Russia's position as energy supplier to Europe.

At this point, Gazprom began to face reduced demand and increased competition in European gas markets. It was slow to respond to those changes, insisting that everyone, including its European customers, gained from the status quo of long-term contracts tied to the oil price. To many in Europe, the Ukrainian transit crisis in 2009 indicated otherwise. Russia's proposed terms to Ukraine, and rhetoric during the crisis and subsequent negotiations to settle it, exploited Ukraine's weak position to the maximum and escalated the crisis. The European public and political elites were shocked by the implication, that by using gas transit to settle political scores with Ukraine and Viktor Yushchenko's government, Russia had jeopardised security of supply to Europe. By also using the crisis to promote the Nord Stream project as an alternative transit route (Stegen, 2011, p.6509), Russia played up the political side of the conflict. To many in Europe, this indicated that Russia was using the interdependence inherent in pipeline gas on long-term contracts to press for a greater market share, just as the market was turning in Gazprom's disfavour. In consequence, the established image of Russian energy companies in Europe as reliable and non-politicised suppliers suffered. They were seen as more closely connected to the government, and in consequence, as sources of Russian influence.

Increasingly, the dividing line between Russia's relations with post-Soviet states and other states, especially in Europe, began to blur. The strategy of re-establishing Russia as a great power based on energy had linked the post-Soviet level in Russian foreign policy to its global position. Around 2008–2009, the international reactions to that strategy affected both levels of Russian foreign policy. For example, Gazprom's projects to bypass Ukraine and Belarus as transit states occasioned alternative European proposals to reduce dependence on Russian gas. The Nabucco pipeline project[9] was one project that, in spite of uncertainties over supply and a lack of willing investors, attracted political support in Europe (Guillet, 2011). Gazprom's return proposal, South Stream, again bypassed Ukraine[10] and further reinforced the European perceptions that Russia aimed to use gas export as a tool to pressure Ukraine and take European markets captive. Russian efforts to control infrastructure and influence economic development in the post-Soviet region resulted in policies to balance Russia on the part of Georgia, Ukraine, Moldova and later Armenia. When in 2008 the EU engaged with Georgia, Ukraine and Moldova through the Eastern Partnership, Russian foreign policy towards these countries became entangled with its relations with the EU. This reinforced Russian perceptions of a zero-sum competition for influence over post-Soviet states.

The great power project backfires

Oil prices remained high to 2014. But in 2008–2012, the financial crisis and the "shale revolution" in global oil and (especially) gas markets profoundly affected the outlook for Russia as an energy-based great power. In the post-

Soviet region, policies of integration continued, finally with some success. Regional economic integration, which for so long had existed largely on paper, moved forward in 2010 with the establishment of the Customs Union of Russia, Kazakhstan and Belarus.

One reason for this was that Russia had changed its approach to integration with the global economy. The international financial crisis in 2008–2009 hit Russia particularly hard. Russia, like many other states, responded with increased protectionism (Solanko, 2016, p.5). Part of the response was to halt the pursuit of integration into the global economy, in favour of limited, regional economic integration within the Customs Union. Russia unexpectedly paused the World Trade Organization (WTO) accession negotiations in June 2009, at a point when they were close to completion. Russia would now pursue accession jointly with Kazakhstan and Belarus within the framework of the Customs Union. In 2012, the Customs Union was complemented by the foundations of a single market, the Eurasian Economic Space. But Russia's foreign policy aims in the post-Soviet region remained ambiguous. Tangible, selective, and possibly successful integration in the post-Soviet region seemed to indicate that Russian foreign policy could become based on shared interests and mutually advantageous terms. However, the means by which Russia pursued this goal were not mutually advantageous. By pausing WTO negotiations in favour of joint accession, all three Customs Union members were slowed down in their WTO accession process. And within the Eurasian Economic Space and from 2015 the Eurasian Economic Union (EEU), Russia was reluctant to take steps that could limit its room for manoeuvre. For example, it postponed the introduction of a single market for trade in oil, gas and petrochemicals.

The backdrop to this spurt of integration was nevertheless one of centrifugal tendencies and weakening Russian influence in the post-Soviet region. China dominated investment in Central Asia, and Central Asian governments in various ways balanced the two great powers. Russia did not have the economic resources to match Chinese investment. After the 2008 war with Georgia, Russia's engagement in the South Caucasus was by necessity more selective. In Ukraine, the approach of using economic ties for political influence, combined with selective engagement with pro-Russian politicians, made its real influence contingent on the prevailing forces in Ukrainian politics. A similar situation obtained in Moldova. Belarus was a partner and ally, but also adept at maximising overall returns from its alliance with Russia.

As Russia aimed to dominate the region, and saw its relationship with the West in terms of competition, its approach to the post-Soviet states was increasingly one of "either–or", driven by the approach that states had to choose, and pursue integration in one direction only (Samokhvalov, 2015, p.1372). Russia's view of the post-Soviet region was framed by competition with the West. Above all, the centrality of competition with the West was visible in the importance attached to attracting Ukraine as a member of the

Customs Union and the Eurasian Economic Space. In bilateral negotiations, Russia exerted pressure on Ukraine to join the Customs Union, reflecting its hegemonic position (Socor, 2010). With Ukraine, the potential for a regional economic and political bloc would be realised.

Euromaidan

The Euromaidan crisis in Ukraine in 2013–2014, and Russia's response to it, intensified the centrifugal tendencies in post-Soviet international relations. Energy relations played a part in the long run-up to the crisis, and Russian energy companies were considerably affected in the fall out. In 2010, the Kharkiv Accords between Russia and Ukraine exchanged a gas price discount in return for an advantageous deal for Russia on the terms of its military presence in Ukraine. According to this deal, the Russian Black Sea Fleet would be based in Crimea to 2042, possibly 2047. However, the returns disappointed Ukraine. The gas price discount turned out to be insubstantial. In addition, Russia did not follow up on its side of accompanying plans for closer nuclear energy cooperation. Russia's continued pursuit of bypass pipelines placed Ukraine in a disadvantageous position. Moreover, other post-Soviet examples of economic, and energy, integration with Russia, particularly pertaining to Belarus, demonstrated how energy integration with Russia could erode economic independence. Therefore, while April 2010 appeared as a high point in Russian–Ukrainian bilateral relations, it was followed by further erosion of trust in Russia's intentions amongst the Ukrainian elite (Moshes, 2013; Samokhvalov, 2015, pp.1379–1380). Energy played a part in the immediate run-up to Euromaidan in November 2013, when Putin offered the Ukrainian President Viktor Yanukovych a substantial package of economic incentives, including 15 US$ billion in economic aid, reduced gas prices and continued cooperation in the nuclear sector, in return for pausing Ukraine's integration with the EU and not signing the Association Agreement. Similar pressure had been employed in September, when Serzh Sargsyan, the Armenian president, called off the signing of Armenia's Association Agreement with the EU and embarked on accession to the Customs Union, and later the Eurasian Union (Ter-Matevosian et al., 2017). But in the Ukrainian case, popular protests followed, and they were met with violence. In late February 2014, Yanukovych departed from Ukraine and was subsequently removed from office. Russia's reaction, covert military intervention and illegal annexation of Crimea, provided yet another confirmation of post-Soviet elites' worst fears as to how Russia viewed its role in the region. To other post-Soviet capitals, Crimea and then Donbas demonstrated that the war in Georgia was not a one-off. To the contrary, Russia had shown itself willing to use military means to assert regional hegemony.

This was a watershed for the post-Soviet region. Russia now met with far lower levels of trust among its neighbours (Guedes Vieira, 2016), alienating even the potentially more Russia-friendly "inner circle" of EEU partners.

Ukraine's rejection of integration with Russia was comprehensive, and the ties that continued to exist were much reduced. Selective regional integration continued within the Eurasian Economic Space and then the EEU. But Belarus, Kazakhstan and Kyrgyzstan took balancing precautions (Kudaibergenova, 2016; Nurgaliyeva, 2016) and opposed Russia's aim to use integration in the EEU as a precursor to political integration (Smith, 2016, p.180). Russia's own policies were also a brake on EEU integration, for example, by continuing to postpone the introduction of a single market for oil, gas and petrochemicals in the EEU. Energy relations continued to matter within existing bilateral frameworks. During Russia's economic crisis in 2015–2017, Russian companies found it more difficult to deliver on their investment promises and scaled down their presence across the post-Soviet region. Russia became less important to regional economies, especially in Central Asia. A major company like RusHydro stalled the Kambarata and Naryn hydropower plants in Kyrgyzstan, both important projects. Its agreements with the Kyrgyz government were nullified in 2016. The same year, Gazprom terminated its gas relationship with Turkmenistan, due to a fall in European gas demand. In Armenia, household tariff increases spurred the "Electric Yerevan" protests in summer 2015, leading to Inter RAO's exit from the country. The protests raised the question of how EEU membership benefited ordinary Armenians. When more political protests led to a peaceful change of government in April 2018, Russia's role was reduced to that of an onlooker. Russia's declining economic power in the post-Soviet region exposed its lack of broader engagement with post-Soviet societies (cf. Just, 2016).

Sanctions

The annexation of Crimea and war in Donbas caused the greatest setback for Russian foreign policy after 2000. European states and the US jointly isolated Russia, and its international prestige was considerably reduced also among non-western states (Rutland and Kazantsev, 2016, p.409). Before March 2014, Putin regularly met with Western leaders, both bilaterally and in multilateral settings like the Group of Eight (G8). After the annexation of Crimea, the level of contact was markedly reduced. Russia was suspended from the G8, with the 2014 summit in Russia replaced by a scaled down G7 meeting in Brussels.

This change in Russia's international position was accompanied by concerted economic sanctions. They targeted the energy industries, in particular investment and prospects for development. The first and second rounds of European, US and Canadian sanctions, imposed in March and April 2014, restricted the possibilities of a number of individuals, including Gennadiy Timchenko and Igor Sechin from the energy sector, to visit the US and Europe and hold accounts there. The third round of sanctions imposed from July 2014 had wider implications. Financial measures against several companies curtailed access to long-term financing in European and US financial markets. The sectoral sanctions affected all oil and gas companies' access to equipment and technology for development of deep water and Arctic offshore oil fields, and unconventional shale oil formations.

The sanctions had considerable effects. As global companies, banks, and financial markets rigorously assessed them and potential consequences of breaches, costs mounted, and some decisions inevitably went in favour of staying out altogether. The prospects of further sanctions, and the intentionally vague formulations of the US sanctions, heightened the sense of risk attached to transactions and investment connected to Russian companies. In addition, Russia's rating with international agencies slipped below investment grade. In a risk-averse period for international financial markets, this amounted to a quasi-closure of global finance to Russia.

Conclusion

In the initial period after the break-up of the Soviet Union, integration with the global economy was an important foreign policy aim. As this became less central, economic relations were increasingly perceived as instruments of Russian foreign policy, especially in relations with the other post-Soviet states. From around 2003, Russia aimed to return to great power status through its position as regional energy supplier, using relations with post-Soviet states in support of its ambitions. This was possible as long as market conditions were relatively stable. It was more difficult when changing markets began to constrain the possibilities to project energy power. As external reactions mattered relatively little in Russian foreign energy policy formation, Russia was less inclined to respond to such rapid changes in international markets and changing policies among its customers.

Russia's approach to power projection made a difference to its possibilities of becoming a great energy power. The 2003 Energy Strategy linked Russia's policy towards post-Soviet states more closely to relations with other energy markets. Trust in Russia as a supplier would demand that it maintain a strategic, more consistent approach to energy relationships. This was at variance with Russia's use of post-Soviet energy relations as tools of coercion. A consistent policy towards all energy customers demanded that Russia compromise on its aim of creating and dominating a regional bloc in the post-Soviet space. As the difficulties associated with integration into the global economy increased, opting for post-Soviet integration appeared to be the easier route for Russia as a great power. The latter years under study in this book show how Russia's foreign economic policy has failed to resolve the tension between two views of Russian power in the world. On the one hand, post-Soviet economic integration remained attractive because it came with a promise of making Russia a regional great power. On the other hand, Russia could project power in global energy markets in a beneficial way, if it restrained its regional power projection. Energy power and regional power, which seemed to be so closely related in the early 2000s, turned out to be irreconcilable aims for Russian foreign policy.

Notes

1 First government December 1992 to August 1996, second government August 1996 to March 1998.
2 As discussed in some detail in the cited report, there are some deficiencies in the data used for these calculations (Freinkman et al., 2004, pp.1–5). The unavailability of consistent price data is particularly relevant to the discussion here.
3 Due to deficiencies in trade reporting, it is generally difficult to estimate the exact value and volume of foreign trade flows among CIS member states in the period from 1992 to 1996. The UN Comtrade Database contains data from 1996 onwards. Deficient reporting and very high inflation in some states make it difficult to estimate precise values for CIS energy trade before 1996 (Belkindas and Dikhanov, 1994). For energy, widespread barter payment complicates the picture further. On this background, this chapter does not include calculations for Russia's share in energy imports for other CIS states.
4 Author's calculation based on data from the UN Comtrade Database. Energy exports calculated on the basis of export flows from Russia as reported by Russia to Armenia, Azerbaijan, Belarus, Georgia, Estonia, Kazakhstan, Kyrgyzstan, Latvia, Lithuania, Moldova, Tajikistan, Turkmenistan, Ukraine and Uzbekistan of goods reported under the commodity codes 2709 Petroleum oils, oils from bituminous minerals, crude; 2710 Oils petroleum, bituminous, distillates, except crude; 271121 Natural gas in gaseous state; 2716 Electrical energy; 8401 Nuclear reactors, fuel elements, isotope separators. Calculations in US$.
5 Foreign minister January 1996 to September 1998, prime minister September 1998–May 1999.
6 Acting president 31 December 1999 to March 2000, president 2000–2008 and 2012–.
7 Defence Minister March 2001 to February 2007.
8 At its peak in September 2008, the Reserve Fund held 142.6 billion US$, while the National Welfare Fund exceeded 80 billion US$ in 2009. The Reserve Fund was established to offset future shortfalls in oil revenue. Having been used to cover deficits during the 2015–2017 economic crisis, the Fund was depleted by the end of 2017. In January 2018, what remained was merged with the National Welfare Fund. This Fund had been designed to cover national pensions in the mid-term. This did not prevent the government from resorting to the National Welfare Fund to meet income shortfalls.
9 Early proposals were for a pipeline through Turkey, Bulgaria, Romania and Hungary to the gas hub at Baumgarten in Austria. A later proposal, Nabucco West, included only the part from Bulgaria's border with Turkey to Baumgarten.
10 Across the Black Sea to Bulgaria, Serbia, and Hungary to Baumgarten and Slovenia, with a second leg to Greece and Italy.

References

Anex, R.P. (2002) "Restructuring and privatizing electricity industries in the Commonwealth of Independent States", *Energy Policy*, 30 (5): 397–408

Arbatov, A.G. (1993) "Russia's foreign policy alternatives", *International Security*, 18 (2): 5–43

Becker, A.S. (1996) "Russia and economic integration in the CIS", *Survival*, 38 (4 (Winter 1996–1997)): 117–136

Belkindas, M. and Dikhanov, Y. (1994) "Appendix: Foreign trade statistics in the Former Soviet Union" in Michalopoulos, C. and Tarr, D.G. ed., *Trade in the New Independent States* (Washington, DC: The World Bank/UNDP), pp.21–27

Closson, S. (2011) "A comparative analysis on energy subsidies in Soviet and Russian policy", *Journal of Communist and Post-Communist Studies*, 44 (4): 343–356

Closson, S. (2014) "Subsidies in Russia's gas trade" in Oxenstierna, S. and Tynkkynen, V.-P. ed., *Russian Energy and Security up to 2030* (London/New York: Routledge), pp.61–76

Crane, K., Peterson, D.J. and Oliker, O. (2005) "Russian investment in the Commonwealth of Independent States", *Eurasian Geography and Economics*, 46 (6): 405–444

Dabrowski, M. (1993) *Two Years of Economic Reform in Russia. Main Results.* (Warsaw: CASE – Center for Social and Economic Research)

Decree No. 472 (07/05/1995) *Ob osnovnykh napravleniyakh energeticheskoi politiki i strukturnoi perestroiki toplivno-energeticheskogo kompleksa Rossiiskoi Federatsii na period do 2010 goda [On the basic directions of energy policy and structural reorganisation for the fuel and energy complex of the Russian Federation to 2010]* (Moscow: President of the Russian Federation)

Decree No. 940 (14/09/1995) *Ob utverzhdenii strategicheskogo kursa Rossiiskoi Federatsii s gosudarstvami-uchastnikami Sodruzhestva Nezavisimykh Gosudarstv [In confirmation of the Russian Federation's strategic course towards the participant states in the Commonwealth of Independent States]* (Moscow: President of the Russian Federation)

Diplomaticheskii vestnik (1992) "Kolonka redaktora [From the Editor]", *Diplomaticheskii vestnik*, 1992 (1): 2

Dodsworth, J.R., Mathieu, P.H. and Shiells, C.H. (2002) *Cross-Border Issues in Energy Trade in the CIS Countries.* IMF Policy Discussion Paper. (Washington, DC: International Monetary Fund)

Drabek, Z. and Benacek, V. (2013) "Trade reorientation and global integration" in Hare, P. and Turley, G. ed., *Handbook of the Economic and Political Economy of Transition* (London/New York: Routledge), pp.167–180

Dunlop, J.B. (1997) "Russia: In search of an identity?" in Bremmer, I. and Taras, R. ed., *New States, New Politics. Building the Post-Soviet Nations* (Cambridge/New York: Cambridge University Press), pp.29–95

Finon, D. and Locatelli, C. (2008) "Russian and European gas interdependence: Could contractual trade channel geopolitics?", *Energy Policy*, 36 (1): 423–442

Freinkman, L.M., Polyakov, E. and Revenco, C. (2004) *Trade Performance and Regional Integration of the CIS Countries.* World Bank Working Paper, 38 (Washington, DC: World Bank Publications)

Gentile, M. (2015) "The Post-Soviet urban poor and where they live: Khrushchev-era blocks, "bad" areas, and the vertical dimension in Luhansk, Ukraine", *Annals of the Association of American Geographers*, 105 (3): 583–603

Guedes Vieira, A.V. (2016) "Eurasian integration: Elite perspectives before and after the Ukraine crisis", *Post-Soviet Affairs*, 32 (6): 566–580

Guillet, J. (2011) "How to get a pipeline built: Myth and reality" in Dellecker, A. and Gomart, T. ed., *Russian Energy Security and Foreign Policy* (London/New York: Routledge), pp.58–73

Harsem, Ø. and Claes, D.H. (2013) "The interdependence of European–Russian energy relations", *Energy Policy*, 59: 784–791

IEA (2016) *Online Data Services*, Issue date [online]. Published by International Energy Agency. Available from: http://www.iea.org/statistics/ [Accessed 13 October 2016]

IMF (2007) *Russian Federation. Staff Report for the 2007 Article IV Consultation.* IMF Country Report No. 351. (Washington, DC: International Monetary Fund)

IMF (2016) *Russian Federation. Staff Report for the 2016 Article IV Consultation.* IMF Country Report No. 16/229. (Washington, DC: International Monetary Fund)

Just, T. (2016) "Promoting Russia abroad: Russia's post-Cold war national identity and public diplomacy", *Journal of International Communication*, 22 (1): 82–95

Katz, M.N. (2006) "Primakov redux? Putin's pursuit of 'multipolarism' in Asia", *Demokratizatsiya*, 14 (1): 144–152

Konoplyanik, A. et al. (ed.) (1992) *Neft' i gaz vo vneshnei politike Rossii* [*Oil and gas in Russia's foreign policy*] (Moscow: Fond vneshnei politiki)

Korsun, Yu. (1994) "Energeticheskaya strategiya Rossii do 2010 g [Russia's energy strategy until 2010]", *Obozrevatel'* [*Observer*], 1994 (16–17 and 19–20)

Kozyrev, A. (1992) "Russia: A chance for survival", *Foreign Affairs*, 71 (2): 1–16

Kremlin.ru (2006) *Stenograficheskiy otchet o vstreche s uchastnikami tret'ego zasedaniya Mezhdunarodnogo diskussionnogo kluba "Valdai"* [*Shorthand report from meeting with participants in the third meeting of the International Discussion Club Valdai*] (Moscow: Kremlin.ru)

Kudaibergenova, D. (2016) "Eurasian Economic Union integration in Kazakhstan and Kyrgyzstan", *European Politics and Society*, 17 (S1): 97–112

Kuzio, T. (2005) "Russian policy towards Ukraine during elections", *Demokratizatsiya*, 13 (4): 491–517

Libman, A. (2007) "Regionalisation and regionalism in the post-Soviet space: Current status and implications for institutional development", *Europe-Asia Studies*, 59 (3): 401–430

Libman, A. and Kheifets, B.A. (2007) "Korporativnaya model' regional'noi ekonomicheskoi integratsii [The corporate model of regional economic integration]", *Mirovaya ekonomika i mezhdunarodnye otnosheniya*, 2007 (3): 15–22

Light, M. (1996) "Foreign policy thinking" in Malcolm, N. et al. eds., *Internal Factors in Russian Foreign Policy* (Oxford: The Royal Institute for International Affairs/ Oxford University Press), pp.33–100

Meister, S. (ed.) (2013) *Economization Versus Power Ambitions: Rethinking Russia's Policy Towards Post-Soviet States* (Berlin: Deutsche Gesellschaft für Auswärtige Politik e.V.)

Michalopoulos, C. and Tarr, D.G. (1994) *Trade in the New Independent States.* Studies of Economies in Transformation (Washington, DC: The World Bank/UNDP)

Ministry of Energy (2009) *Energeticheskaya strategiya Rossii na period do 2030 goda* [*Russia's Energy Strategy for the period to 2030*] (Moscow: Institute of Energy Strategy)

Ministry of Foreign Affairs (1993) *Kontseptsiya vneshnei politiki Rossiiskoi Federatsii* [*Foreign policy concept of the Russian Federation*] (Moscow: Diplomaticheskii vestnik)

Ministry of Foreign Affairs (2007) *Obzor vneshnei politiki Rossiiskoi Federatsii* [*An overview of the foreign policy of the Russian Federation*] (Moscow: Ministerstvo Inostrannykh Del (MID))

Ministry of Foreign Affairs (2008) *Kontseptsiya vneshnei politiki Rossiiskoi Federatsii* [*Foreign policy concept of the Russian Federation*], (Moscow: Ministerstvo Inostrannykh Del (MID))

Ministry of Foreign Affairs (2013) *Kontseptsiya vneshnei politiki Rossiiskoi Federatsii* [*Foreign policy concept of the Russian Federation*], (Moscow: Ministerstvo Inostrannykh Del (MID))

Ministry of Industry and Trade (2003) *Energeticheskaya strategiya Rossii na period do 2020 goda* [*Russia's Energy Strategy for the period to 2020*] (Moscow: Ministerstvo promyshlennosti i torgovli)

Moshes, A. (2013) *A Marriage of Unequals: Russian–Ukrainian Relations under Yanukovych* (Berlin: Deutsche Gesellschaft für Auswärtige Politik e.V.)

Nekrasov, A.S. and Sinyak, Yu.V. (2001) "Problemy i perspektivy rossiiskoi energetiki na poroge XXI veka [Problems and perspectives for Russian energy on the threshold to the 21st century]", *Problemy prognozirovaniya*, 2001 (1): 86–101

Nurgaliyeva, L. (2016) "Kazakhstan's economic soft balancing policy vis-à-vis Russia: From the Eurasian Union to the economic cooperation with Turkey", *Journal of Eurasian Studies*, 7 (1): 92–105

Orttung, R.W. and Øverland, I. (2011) "A limited toolbox: Explaining the constraints on Russia's foreign energy policy", *Journal of Eurasian Studies*, 2 (1): 74–85

Pravda, A. (1996) "The public politics of foreign policy" in Malcolm, N. et al. eds., *Internal Factors in Russian Foreign Policy* (Oxford: Oxford University Press), pp.169–229

Putin, V. (1999) "Rossiya na rubezhe tysyacheletiya [Russia at the turn of the millennium]", *Nezavisimaya gazeta*, 30 December 1999, p.4

Putin, V. (2000) "Otkrytoe pis'mo Vladimira Putina k rossiiskim izbiratelyam [Vladimir Putin's open letter to Russian voters]", *Kommersant*, 25 February 2000, p.3

RFE/RL (2003) "RFE/RL Newsline", *Radio Free Europe/Radio Liberty*, 3 October

Rutland, P. (2008) "Russia as an energy superpower", *New Political Economy*, 13 (2): 203–210

Rutland, P. and Kazantsev, A. (2016) "The limits of Russia's 'soft power'", *Journal of Political Power*, 9 (3): 395–413

Samokhvalov, V. (2015) "Ukraine between Russia and the European Union: Triangle revisited", *Europe-Asia Studies*, 67 (9): 1371–1393

Smith, H. (2016) "Statecraft and post-imperial attractiveness: Eurasian integration and Russia as a Great Power", *Problems of Post-Communism*, 63 (3): 171–182

Socor, V. (2010) "Salient issues in Ukraine–Russia Relations and Yanukovych's Moscow Visit", *Eurasia Daily Monitor*, 10 March

Solanko, L. (2016) *Opening up or Closing the Door for Foreign Trade? Russia and China Compared.* BOFIT Policy Brief. (Helsinki: Bank of Finland Institute for Economies in Transition)

Sovet po vneshnei i oboronnoi politike (SVOP) (1992) "Strategiya dlya Rossii [A Strategy for Russia]", *Nezavisimaya gazeta*, 19 August

Stegen, K.S. (2011) "Deconstructing the 'energy weapon': Russia's threat to Europe as a case study", *Energy Policy*, 39: 6505–6513

Stent, A.E. (2008) "An energy superpower? Russia and Europe" in Campbell, K. and Price, J. ed., *The Global Politics of Energy* (Washington, DC: Aspen Institute), pp.76–96

Suslov, D. (2003) "Rossiya ob"yavlyaet NATO kholodnuyu voinu [Russia declares a cold war on NATO]", *Nezavisimaya gazeta*, 10 October, p.5

Ter-Matevosian, V. et al. (2017) "Armenia in the Eurasian Economic Union: Reasons for joining and its consequences", *Eurasian Geography and Economics*, 58 (3): 340–360

Wilson, J.L. (2010) "The legacy of the color revolutions for Russian politics and foreign policy", *Problems of Post-Communism*, 57 (2): 21–36

3 The electricity industry
RAO UES and Inter RAO

This chapter analyses relations between the Russian electricity monopoly (RAO UES 1992–2008), its subsidiary, Inter RAO (1997–), and the state. The chapter shows how the Russian state and RAO UES/Inter RAO developed foreign policy guidelines and foreign electricity operations, as part of their interaction on institutional development. In an early phase, the Soviet legacy with an integrated electricity sector was a channel for sharing rents through a subsidised power supply system, where electricity was often not paid for. RAO UES in this way stabilised society and the state through the 1990s' transformational recession. In the 2000s, changing state–company interaction drove institutional development at home, and boosted state capacity. RAO UES had better opportunities to expand foreign operations, and established a new subsidiary for that purpose, Inter RAO. Its operations were significant for other post-Soviet economies, and the company could in turn be used as a foreign policy tool. In 2008, after the electricity reform, Inter RAO changed its business profile and turned into a leaner successor to RAO UES. In 2012–2018, it came under the control of Rosneftegaz and Igor Sechin, with closer ties to the regime as a result.

Like all the case chapters, this chapter starts with a brief outline of the power industry. The rest of the chapter is structured chronologically according to the milestones of Russia's contemporary development outlined in Chapter 1. For each period, domestic state–company interaction is discussed first, followed by interaction abroad.

The electricity industry

Unlike the other energy industries investigated here, the electric power industry is organised around a utility, and not a primary energy commodity. The power industry generates electricity from primary energy (e.g. coal, gas, fuel oil, nuclear fuel), for subsequent transmission, distribution and marketing to consumers. Due to economies of scale, generation is concentrated, while transmission and distribution disperse the utility often at long distance, through extensive grids. Establishing this infrastructure requires considerable investment, which benefits the economy as a whole. The power industry was traditionally organised into vertically integrated companies operating in different countries or regions.

Electricity production must correspond exactly to demand, and it is expensive to store electricity in large quantities. The larger the electricity grid, the more stable it is, provided it is well maintained and technologically up to date. To cover base and peak demand and reserve capacity, multiple sources of supply make economic sense. Hours of peak demand vary across different regions, facilitating more rational utilisation.

The development of the electric power industry goes hand in hand with economic development. It represents progress and hope for the future. Even so, electricity held special significance in the Soviet Union, beginning with the ideological emphasis provided by Vladimir Lenin's 1920 slogan "Communism is Soviet government plus the electrification of the whole country".[1] Seventy years later, the United Energy System (UES)[2] was the largest integrated power distribution system in the world, operating synchronously with the systems of Central and Eastern Europe.[3] The Russian part of the system was impressive enough on its own. Before unbundling,[4] RAO UES was the largest integrated power company in the world, measured by installed generation capacity. But Soviet power grids were not designed to operate in isolation. Systematic under- and overcapacity criss-crossed republican boundaries (Anex, 2002, p.401), leaving a complicated infrastructural legacy after the break-up of the USSR.

The break-up of the Soviet Union and Soviet legacies

In the Soviet period, the power sector, excluding nuclear energy, was organised under the Ministry of Electric Power. The distribution system, UES, united nine of eleven Soviet electricity systems (Museum of the Urals Power Industry, 2018).[5] A Russian Fuel and Electricity Ministry was created in February 1991, while Minatom remained responsible for nuclear power generation. When the Soviet Ministry of Electric Power was abolished in November 1991, the Russian ministry took its place, along with responsibility for UES. At the same time, a reformer without industrial experience, Vladimir Lopukhin, was appointed Fuel and Energy Minister (Gustafson, 2012, pp.63–64). As the state hierarchy weakened, established institutions failed to constrain actors lower down in the hierarchy. Momentum passed from the Ministry to a subordinate committee appointed to manage UES. This committee was headed by a former Soviet, now Russian, deputy minister, Anatolii Dyakov, an experienced insider in the power industry who had started as an electrical fitter. He was well positioned to recognise that UES, the grid, was the central infrastructural legacy of the Soviet Union. Reliable electricity supply would enable the industry to carry on, interacting with the government as before.

During 1992, UES re-emerged as a holding company, in three stages. In July, a presidential decree established privatisation procedures (Decree No. 721, 1992). Electricity was exempted along with the rest of the fuel and energy complex in August (Decree No. 922, 1992). Next, the generation and distribution system was divided into shareholding companies (Decree No. 923, 1992). In November, a final decree established the holding company RAO UES, supposed to include the entire electricity sector (Decree No. 1334, 1992). At least 50 per cent of RAO UES was to remain in state hands. The rest would be privatised in stages, in a process open to industry employees. Dyakov became head of RAO UES in December and soon after was made Board Chairman (Museum for the History of the Northwest Power Industry, 2014). An opportunity arose for him with the collapse of the old institutional framework to maximise sector autonomy, but also to ensure as far as possible the survival, stability and integrity of UES itself.

Keeping afloat and muddling through

RAO UES did not consolidate as planned. The breakdown of the central planning system sparked a process of regionalisation. By 1992, this process was well underway (Engoian, 2006, p.3241). In the weeks between the decrees of July and August 1992, several regional power companies fell partially or wholly under regional control; in some places this was done to reward loyal governors (Berger and Proskurnina, 2008, pp.69–71). The government reformers had planned a consolidation from below. This policy was however undercut by the need to maintain a ruling coalition with regional support. At the time, RAO UES controlled 72 per cent of Russia's generation and 96 per cent of the transmission network (Patel, 2013, p.45). But RAO UES held only minority stakes in nine of the regional subsidiaries (Tompson, 2004, p.5). Some of these were crucial to general power supply.

Thus the regions came to hold considerable power in the holding company RAO UES. The process of regional autonomy progressed apace throughout the 1990s, contributing to the fragmentation of the public sector and of RAO UES. Power companies and power industry service companies fell into creditors' hands for defaulting on real debts, or debts imagined by creative local managements (Berger and Proskurnina, 2008, pp.68–70; 74–79). Yeltsin handed out stakes in regional power companies to governors who supported his ruling coalition. Regional power companies were political assets. Thirty per cent of the government votes were exercised by the regions (Decree No. 1334, 1992). The institutional framework gave local directors more power than the RAO UES top management, which in turn depended on the goodwill of subsidiary managements. In this way, decentralised decision-making permeated the ownership structure and created a powerful group of owners in favour of the status quo (Tompson, 2004, pp.4–5). Dividends on state-held shares were to be reinvested in RAO UES (Decree No. 1334, 1992), producing a disincentive for transparency. In late 1994, 25 per cent of RAO UES was in non-state hands (Gray, 1995, p.39). In mid-1996, the state reduced its stake from 60 to 52 per cent.

The power industry continued in a semi-reformed state. The government controlled tariffs which grew at only half the rate of industrial producer prices, lagging behind fuel prices (IEA, 2003, p.22; Tompson, 2004, p.7). The result was a negative spiral of under-investment in power infrastructure, falling power supply reliability, and fixed capital depletion. By the mid-1990s, non-payments and arrears were the rule rather than the exception in regional power companies bringing them to the brink of bankruptcy (Nevezhin, 1996). Indeed, the entire economy was plagued by debts and non-payments due to the absence of real budget constraints. This became an acute problem for the electricity industry after the government made it illegal to turn off power supply to state-owned enterprises in October 1995 (Murtazaev, 1995). RAO UES's subsidiaries became the largest creditors in their respective regional economies. The regional electricity sector was plunged into debt, most of it owed to Gazprom and the coal companies. When electricity companies failed to pay, primary energy suppliers like Gazprom were obliged to extend credit, thereby sharing their rents with the electricity industry. By the second half of 1996, electricity consumers owed the industry 71 trillion rubles in unpaid tariffs, while industry employees had 1.5 trillion rubles in outstanding pay (*Ekonomika i zhizn'*, 1996). By that year's end, enterprises in federal ownership owed the electricity sector 8.7 trillion rubles (Nevezhin, 1996). The sums were largely offset against regional tax claims on the power companies. In comparison, RAO UES, the holding company, had a turnover of only 8.9 billion rubles that year (RAO UES, 1997). Tariff collection rates fell below 85 per cent, only 15–20 per cent of which was paid in cash (Berger and Proskurnina, 2008, p.59). The rest was barter involving all kinds of goods, and other forms of nonmonetary payments, including promissory notes (Gaddy and Ickes, 2002, p.25).

Barter trade and promissory exchanges created ample opportunities for enrichment through a flourishing intermediary sector (Bekker, 1997; Nevezhin, 1997), which channelled rents to regional and federal elites. Dyakov himself established a company, RAO EEK, which did very well as an intermediary in the promissory note trade (Ivanov, 1998; *Rossiiskaya gazeta*, 1999; Berger and Proskurnina, 2008, p.67). Unchecked by central state control, the holding company grew at the expense of its subsidiaries, which in turn lost much of their value. The holding company made a profit and paid dividends (RAO UES, 1997), while the regional power companies had to look to the state budget for investments (Babich, 1997).

At the same time, the semi-reformed electricity system was useful to the state. By making it possible for unprofitable enterprises to survive, RAO UES stabilised many regions. Central state organisations, however, failed to take an interest in its development, let alone conduct audits (Babich, 1997). But people and factories continued as before, regardless of failing tariff payments. RAO UES buoyed the economy by softening budget constraints for non-profitable companies. As long as power companies failed to pay for their own gas, Gazprom had to provide gas for free. This was in practice financed by Gazprom's profits from export to Europe, and RAO UES therefore acted as a channel for Gazprom's rents to entire regions. This reduced human suffering and preserved a modicum of political stability, but it also reduced the pressure to accelerate structural reform. RAO UES channelled rents from barter trade, as by 1998, around 80 per cent of payments were in barter, promissory notes and setoffs (Federal'naya Setevaya Kompaniya—FSK, 2018). Regional economies depended on the electricity subsidy, and regional authorities depended on the rent streams. RAO UES's top management joined other monopolies, especially Gazprom, to keep reform off the agenda (Bekker, 1997). Unlike Gazprom, RAO UES had no access to foreign markets that could shield it completely from the hazards of playing the economic stabiliser role and distributing rents through subsidies to consumers. This weakened the company considerably as a result.

The trade collapse

Electricity trade in the post-Soviet region fell significantly after 1991. Between 1991 and 1997, Russia's import of electricity, all from the post-Soviet region, decreased from 35 to 7 TWh, or by 80 per cent (OECD/IEA, 2005, p.24). Russian exports were halved between 1991 and 2000 (OECD/IEA, 2005, p.24). The trade decline reflected reduced consumption. Overall utilisation of installed generation capacity in the post-Soviet region fell from 61 per cent in 1990 to 50 per cent in 1994 (Gray, 1995, p.21).

RAO UES continued to export power to other post-Soviet states. This was desirable from the company's point of view (Kommersant, 1994), as it mitigated some of the pervasive instability caused by the disintegration of previously connected grids. People in the region got used to frequent, hour-long power cuts, breakdowns and electricity rationing. While tariffs were high, payment rates were low, and the debts accumulated. Belarus, Kazakhstan, Ukraine and Georgia by 1998 owed RAO UES 647 million US $, as shown in Table 3.1. In volume, export to places outside the post-Soviet region stood at only 10 per cent of the export to post-Soviet states, but export to the "far abroad" generated 1.23 times more cash revenue (RAO UES, 1999). Barter payment and non-payments were the general rule inside the post-Soviet region, as illustrated by Table 3.2. Negotiating debt-for-equity swaps to recover debts was complicated, particularly with Kazakhstan (Stalker, 1995).

Reform and financial crisis

Reform of the natural monopolies, including electricity, came back onto the political agenda in Yeltsin's second presidential period (1996–1999). RAO UES, Gazprom, the railways and the post and telecommunications systems were targeted. Reformers in the new government, led by Fuel and Energy Minister Boris Nemtsov, drafted the decree, which was detailed on RAO UES (Decree No. 426, 1997; Gotova, 1997; Berger and Proskurnina, 2008, pp.43–44). Reform, it was said, would attract investment. By 2003, a wholesale electricity

Table 3.1 Accumulated electricity debts to Russia, 1998–2000

	1998	1999	2000
Ukraine	129.4	83.8	54.7
Kazakhstan	419.1	413.5	414.3
Belarus	53.6	39.5	22.2
Georgia	45.6	46.4	46.5
Total	647.7	583.2	537.7

Million US$/end of year. Author's compilation based on RAO UES annual reports

market would appear together with a spot market, a market operator and a stable regulatory environment, several competing, fuel-based generating companies and one state-owned hydropower-based generating company (Kurronen, 2006; Skyner, 2010; Solanko, 2011). Payment discipline would be enforced, cross-subsidies abolished, the tariff system restructured (Decree No. 426, 1997). The tasks were monumental. The reform was modelled on similar reforms in Brazil, Mexico and South Africa, but RAO UES was the largest electricity monopoly ever put up for unbundling.

Dyakov was vehemently opposed to reform, but he failed to understand the changing political context of Yeltsin's second presidential period (Nevezhin, 1996; Gotova, 1997; Berger and Proskurnina, 2008, pp.58–59). As the new government reinterpreted and enforced RAO UES guidelines, Dyakov was told in early 1997 that his positions as top manager and Board Chairman were incompatible (Bekker, 1997). Boris Brevnov, a young manager and former colleague of Nemtsov's, was hired in from outside the electricity sector, and appointed as top manager in March 1997, with Dyakov remaining Board Chairman. Brevnov was unprepared for the job of heading RAO UES, let alone reforming it (Berger and Proskurnina, 2008, pp.29–35). He began by ordering a comprehensive audit of RAO UES, a move boycotted by the incumbent management (Wengle, 2014, p.198). This made it difficult to proceed with the reform. When Anatolii Chubais succeeded Brevnov in April 1998, his predecessor had already fallen out of favour with his erstwhile patrons. Dyakov, on his side, had marginalised himself with his resistance to reform and handling of Brevnov, which included an exchange of compromising material between them (Ivanov, 1998). Chubais could therefore embark on the reform with a clean slate.

Chubais had experience. He was deputy prime minister from 1992 to 1996 and one of Russia's leading privatisation and reform advocates. He had co-authored the 1990 market reform programme, headed the State Property Committee (1991–1994), the Presidential Administration (1996–1997), served as Finance Minister in 1997 and headed Yeltsin's electoral campaign in 1996. When he came to RAO UES in 1998 to reform it, it was apparently at his own request; it was, in his opinion, a key sector (Berger and Proskurnina,

Table 3.2 Non-payment and barter in Russia's electricity trade, 1998–2001

	1998			1999			2000			2001		
	Export value	Total paid	Paid in cash	Export value	Total paid	Paid in cash	Export value	Total paid	Paid in cash	Export value	Total paid	Paid in cash
Ukraine	84.4	9	1.1	0	20.5	0.9	0	17.2	0.2	2.6	16.3	1.1
Kazakhstan	64.1	29.8	17.7	41.35	46.2	18.8	28	27.2	25.8	27.3	31.3	31.3
Belarus	121	67.3	0	122.27	136.4	0	108.7	126	15.3	84.5	85.5	54.3
Georgia	4.7	2	2	1.4	0.1	0.1	4.7	4.6	4.6	7.3	5.9	5.9
Total	274.2	108.1	20.8	165	203.2	19.7	141.4	175	45.9	121.9	139	92.5

Million US$/end of year. Author's compilation based on RAO UES annual reports

2008, pp.17–18; 23–24). At this point, he had become a Russian household name. He was wildly unpopular due to his role in the reforms, and was associated with the economic deprivation that many people had experienced over recent years.

By August 1998, when Russia defaulted on its debts and entered the financial crisis, the ground was well prepared for reform. With Dyakov gone as Board Chairman, Chubais and his team had compiled a reform manual (Berger and Proskurnina, 2008, pp.36–39), and they were determined to see it pushed through. A presidential decree and a compromise with Gazprom enabled them to launch a campaign against non-payers, in which regional companies could, and did, turn off electricity to non-paying power users (Decree No. 889, 1998). Collection rates and the share of barter improved slightly in the last months of 1998, reducing informal rent streams somewhat (RAO UES, 1999). Throughout the entire organisation, old industry hands were being replaced by younger managers (Wengle, 2012, p.442).

The RAO UES reform was unusual at the time for being pushed through by a management that gradually took over control of the industry. This was well understood by Chubais and his team (Gaidar and Chubais, 2008, p.134). After 2000, attracting investment to the sector was no longer controversial. Power demand was projected to rise rapidly during the post-crisis recovery, a point often emphasised by Chubais. Rouble devaluation had made export beyond the post-Soviet region competitive. Even as previously underutilised generation capacity could cover some of the demand increase, it would be difficult to meet it without new investment. But still, the sheer scale of the reform repeatedly delayed it. The regions lined up against a reform designed to disempower them (Knyazev and Reznik, 2000). Many regional power company managers were unfavourably disposed to working in radically different conditions. The final period of reform was pushed forward from 2003 to 2004, later to 2007–2008.

A new approach to the post-Soviet region

With reform underway, Chubais also brought a new approach to the post-Soviet region. In 1998, RAO UES sold about two-thirds of Russia's electricity exports (RAO UES, 1999). The company now sought to restructure the debts it was owed, and in 1999 ceased to accept barter on current payments (RAO UES, 2000). Hard budget constraints were extended to the post-Soviet region as well. The Ukrainian grid was cut off in 1999, and supply to Georgia reduced (RAO UES, 1998; 1999; 2000). Even in Kazakhstan, whose northern regions were completely integrated with Russia, non-paying customers had their supply reduced (Klasson, 2000; RAO UES, 2000; 2001). RAO UES established the subsidiary Inter RAO to effectuate cross-border trade (Gubenko, 2002). Inter RAO started in 2000, first recovering Belarusian electricity debts and then facilitating transmission to Kaliningrad. Performing what was essentially a barter operation, it cleared electricity debts country by country. In Georgia and Kazakhstan, Inter RAO used unannounced blackouts as a form of pressure (Berger and Proskurnina, 2008, pp.211–212; 216). Where old debts could not be paid in cash, exchanging debt for equity in the power industry became the preferred strategy (RAO UES, 1999).

Inter RAO was intended as more than a vehicle for market-based cross-border trade. It gradually began to act as a trade monopoly. Starting in 2000, RAO UES excluded other companies from cross-border trade. From 2001 Inter RAO was the export–import operator on delegation from RAO UES. The function could be performed on behalf of third parties, i.e. other exporters (Zvyagin, 2004, p.52). *De jure*, there was no monopoly on cross-border electricity trade. The legal stipulation was that RAO UES organised and conducted cross-border electricity trade (Melkumyan, 2002). In 2001, Rosenergoatom, the state nuclear power plant company, planned electricity exports to both Georgia and Ukraine (Gorelov, 2001; Rybal'chenko and Razumovskii, 2001). Instead of agreeing to effectuate trade for Rosenergoatom, RAO UES offered it a 15 per cent stake in Inter RAO. Rosenergoatom refused to accept less than 50 (Maksimov, 2001; Melkumyan, 2002). The export–import conflict went to the Anti-Monopoly Ministry for arbitration. Rosenergoatom settled for a 40 per cent share of Inter RAO in mid-2002, and sought a corresponding share in electricity exports (Gorelov, 2006). The latter was unsuccessful, apparently due to resistance from within RAO UES (Siluyanova, 2003b).

The new coalition

Anatolii Chubais was an old acquaintance of Putin's from the St. Petersburg City Administration, and he headed Putin's first election campaign in 2000. He was also close to Finance Minister Aleksei Kudrin (2000–2011). Chubais combined personal political clout and network with formal mechanisms to drive reform forward. He was consistently rated as one of Russia's three or four most influential businessmen (e.g. in Turanov, 2006). When Putin became president in 2000, he distanced himself from Chubais as he did from many others, especially businessmen, or "oligarchs". All the same, relations between Chubais and Putin remained relatively close (Smirnov, 2000), and Chubais was not worried about his own position. When asked whether his loyalty to Putin protected him from arrest, he replied "Unlike the oligarchs ... I built this power" ("*V otlichie ot oligarkhov ... ya stroil etu vlast*") (Tregubova, 2000). He identified with public service and the pursuit of state interests, rather than those of the business community (Berger and Proskurnina, 2008, p.138).

When the reform legislation was passed by the Duma in February 2003, it was a political victory for Chubais and his team, and for the government (Federal Law No. 35, 2003; Federal Law No. 36, 2003).[6] With the support of the Duma and state organisations, especially the Presidential Administration led by Aleksandr Voloshin (1999–2003), Chubais and his team enjoyed wide-ranging powers in how the reform was implemented, leading one observer to comment that RAO UES "substitut[ed] itself for the state on the issue of reform" for as long as a decade (Engoian, 2006, p.3241). One interpretation would be that state organisations were not sufficiently supportive of reform to secure its irreversible completion. But, more persuasively, by farming out reform to the RAO UES management, the state indicated the seriousness of its commitment. The RAO UES reform planners seem to have learnt from other electricity reforms the importance of "demonstrat[ing] the viability and robustness of the new regulation", especially in case of changes in government (Newbery, 1994, p.311). Arguably, RAO UES did not so much substitute itself for the state as manage reform in a way that emphasised the state's commitment to implementing it. State access to RAO UES was ensured through the Board, chaired in 1998–1999 by Deputy Fuel and Energy Minister Viktor Kudryavyi and after that, by Voloshin (1999–2008). The new institutional framework in turn obliged the state to enforce institutions, or face great costs in the event of failing to do so (Gaidar and Chubais, 2008, pp.138–139).

There was also informal access at the very top of the state. Right up until 2008, Chubais and Putin are known to have met alone at least twice a year. Meetings with third parties, or in preparation for group meetings, often included an element of mediation. Putin on these occasions had to conciliate opposing parties, conciliation being one of the most important informal institutions of the presidency, especially in Putin's first term. Conciliation was necessary in the early 2000s when Chubais and Rem Vyakhirev or Aleksei Miller of Gazprom clashed on gas prices and deliveries to power generation, and between Chubais and Putin's own senior economic advisor, Andrei Illarionov, over the electricity reform. When Chubais and Putin met on their own, they would discuss wider political concerns, too (Smirnov, 2002; Kornysheva, 2003).

Expansion in the post-Soviet region: Building a "liberal empire"

In 2003, RAO UES and Inter RAO embarked on a programme of expansion in the post-Soviet electricity sector. Remarkably, it was underpinned by a coherent mission statement. In September 2003, just as RAO UES/Inter RAO completed this first wave of expansion, Chubais advocated a policy of "liberal empire" in the post-Soviet region (Chubais, 2003). This became the heart of the expansion project. In the eyes of Chubais, Russia's mission in the 21st century was to become the centre of an integrated post-Soviet region. The liberal empire would be based on economic power, used for the benefit of all states in the region. He emphasised the need to support Russian culture in the post-Soviet region, along with freedom and human rights. Significantly, he gave the state the role of supporting Russian businesses abroad. His proposals also justified RAO UES's foreign operations, particularly Inter RAO's recent expansion wave.

52 The electricity industry

The expansion programme had three widely articulated goals: to make a profit from electricity trade; to stabilise power supplies; and export to countries outside the post-Soviet region. The potential markets were Romania and Bulgaria, Turkey and Afghanistan. Exports from Azerbaijan to Iran, and from Kyrgyzstan to China, were also a possibility (Gorelov, 2004; Blagov, 2006). A fourth, connected aim, to synchronise UES with the continental European grid,[7] was frequently mentioned; it was one of Chubais's pet projects.[8] It was postponed indefinitely after the 2008 financial crisis. Reuniting the post-Soviet electricity grids was an essential first step, but this was already well underway. By 2003, only the grids of Armenia, Azerbaijan and Turkmenistan were isolated from the region's wide area synchronous transmission grid, UPS/IPS. Inter RAO could expand operations in the region (Startseva, 2003). Resynchronisation and trade improved power supplies; investing in dilapidated assets helped further. To turn a profit, RAO UES used its understanding of post-Soviet business cultures to make the end customer pay (Crane et al., 2005, pp.424–425).

Making use of investment opportunities where Western companies had failed was one of Inter RAO's two routes to expansion. The other was debt-for-equity deals that recovered outstanding electricity bills from the 1990s. Inter RAO leant on the creditworthiness of RAO UES to acquire equity for a low price, financed by short-term loans without collateral (Bekker, 2003).

In the early period until 2005, Inter RAO was run almost as a department of RAO UES. Andrei Rappoport, a trusted member of RAO UES's management, headed Inter RAO's Board of Directors (Medvedeva, 2007a). The five-member Board was largely a formality, conducting most of its business through correspondence (Kommersant, 2008). Important decisions were made by the RAO UES board, rather than Inter RAO's. The addition of Rosenergoatom as minority owner in 2002 does not seem to have altered this situation significantly. If anything, it led to even closer supervision from RAO UES. The formal institutional design was unaffected, with the composition of the Board as the sole exception. Working with Chubais, Rappoport authored Inter RAO's development and managed the company's political support and media profile. The company's young and efficient manager, Evgenii Dod (2000–2009), kept a lower profile. Part of the new cohort who brought a market-centred approach to the power industry, he owed Rappoport and Chubais his position (Petlevoi et al., 2015).

Building on its good relations with Belarus, in 2002–2003 Inter RAO worked with the Belarusian company Belenergo on exports to Poland (Grib, 2003). In 2002, RAO UES established a trading company, Tsentr realizatsii energii (TsRE), to export power to Russia and Belarus. In 2003 Inter RAO was put in charge of electricity exports to Belarus in place of RAO UES, and the price increased by 28 per cent for 2004 (Mazaeva, 2004), in response, apparently, to government pressure on RAO UES (Gorelov, 2008b). Belarus could substitute domestic electricity for imported Russian power, but at a higher price (Grib, 2004). It preferred instead to buy expensive Ukrainian electricity, and later Lithuanian electricity. In Lithuania, however, Inter RAO was the only exporter with spare capacity, and Belarus was therefore forced to accept Inter RAO's terms (Grib, 2004; Mazaeva, 2004; Naumova and Grivach, 2004). Belarus subsequently reduced its overall electricity import (Gorelov, 2008b). When the issue came up again in 2008, Inter RAO gave Belarus a more flexible contract (Gorelov, 2008b).

Re-synchronisation of the Russian and Ukrainian electricity grids proved problematic (Vorotynskii, 2000). The synchronisation agreement did not regulate electricity trade, which would be negotiated afterwards (Stepanenko and Gorelov, 2001). RAO UES aimed to export to Ukraine and to work with Ukraine on exports to Moldova. But Ukraine linked Russian electricity export to Moldova to Russia's ratification of the EU Energy Charter Treaty, terms it would be impossible for Russia to fulfil (Stepanenko, 2003). Ukraine was not eager to compete with Russia for the Moldovan market, where the South Ukraine nuclear power plant (NPP) was directing its surplus (Grishkovets and Dar'in, 2006; Grishkovets and Gavrish, 2006). Synchronisation was eventually completed in August 2001 (Klasson, 2001).

Expansion through equity seemed a promising strategy. In November 2003, RAO UES participated in a Russian–Ukrainian consortium that came close to acquiring stakes in ten (of 27) regional power distribution companies undergoing privatisation. The timing was good and the price quite low, according to a minority representative on RAO UES's Board, Seppo Remes (Egorova et al., 2003). Prime Minister Viktor Yanukovych and President Leonid Kuchma were positive to RAO UES participation, and the consortium included Kuchma's son-in-law, Viktor Pinchuk (Egorova et al., 2003; Siluyanova, 2004c). However, the consortium met with resistance from Ukrainian competitors (Siluyanova, 2004b) and from Verkhovna Rada, Ukraine's parliament, due to RAO UES's participation. The privatisation process was delayed in December 2003, and halted in January 2004 (Butrin et al., 2003; Egorova and Gavrish, 2003). Dmitrii Medvedev, at that point head of the Presidential Administration, travelled to Kyiv to support RAO UES and other Russian energy companies, like Gazprom. He was unable to influence the process (Zaets, 2003). One of the Russian businessmen in the consortium, Konstantin Grigorishin, had his property in Ukraine confiscated in March 2004 (Butrin and Rudenko, 2004; Siluyanova, 2004b).

In the event, Kuchma established a public company that owned the regional companies (Mishneva et al., 2004). Chubais is alleged to have suggested this solution (Ivzhenko, 2005). When a possible privatisation came up after the Orange Revolution in 2005, Inter RAO was seen as a likely buyer (Ivzhenko, 2005). Chubais had supported Viktor Yushchenko during the Revolution. But Inter RAO did not invest in Ukraine, possibly due to the difficult political environment and the fierce competition among Ukraine's oligarchs.

The gigantic Moldova thermal power plant (TPP)[9] in Dnestrovsk dominated Moldova's electricity generation. It was located in the secessionist republic of Transnistria and controlled by its authorities in Tiraspol. Up to

2000, the Moldovan government in Chisinau was the formal owner. By then, the TPP operated at reduced capacity and needed modernisation and repairs estimated at 120 million US$ (Prikhodko, 2000).

Inter RAO first tried to acquire control of the plant in 2000 in a joint effort with Moldova's Moldelektrika and a Transnistrian company, Moldavskaya GRES (Prikhodko, 2000). They failed. In 2003, Tiraspol allowed privatisation in Transnistria, apparently to prevent the local economy from coming under control of the government in Chisinau. Several large enterprises came under Russian control, directly or indirectly (Solov'ev, 2006). Gazprom and Inter RAO submitted a joint bid for Moldova TPP, proposing a debt-for-equity deal (Gudim et al., 2003, p.15). Gazprom would write off Moldova's more than 600 million US$ gas debts, mostly incurred by Transnistria, in return for Russian investments in Moldova TPP. Inter RAO would manage the plant (Siluyanova, 2004c). However, an unknown Belgian company, St. Guidon Invest, won the tender in late 2003, paying 29 million US$ for the plant and offering 161 million in investments (Gamova, 2004). Clearly a front company, St. Guidon was rumoured to be connected to the Tiraspol government (Suvorova, 2004; cf. Levinskii, 2005), and possibly backed by Russian money (Gamova, 2004; Burlak, 2005). Chisinau and Tiraspol's tense relationship complicated the situation further (Siluyanova, 2004c), especially as Chisinau had recently refused to sign a Russian conflict resolution proposal for Transnistria, the Kozak plan.

Unlike Gazprom, Inter RAO remained interested in Moldova TPP (Bruce and Yafimava, 2009, p.174), as electricity export to Romania was a possibility. A subsidiary, RAO Nordic, acquired 51 per cent of Moldova TPP in March 2005. In August, Inter RAO acquired the remaining 49 per cent by buying St. Guidon Invest. The estimated price for both deals was 85–100 million US$, giving both the Transnistrian authorities and St. Guidon's owners a good share in the proceeds (Vin'kov, 2005; Grishkovets, 2008c). The Moldovan government was not pleased by this *fait accompli*. A legal transfer required its prior approval. In addition, Inter RAO had been advised on the deal by Valerii Pasat, a former Moldovan official who had served as defence minister, head of special services and ambassador to Moscow (Gamova, 2007). Reportedly, Putin had recommended Pasat to Chubais (Kolesnikov, 2008, p.64). Following the deal, Pasat was arrested on arrival in Moldova and convicted in January 2006 (Solov'ev and Popov, 2007). Chubais followed up with a campaign against Moldova's president, Vladimir Voronin, targeting Moldova's relations with EU governments (RFE/RL, 2006; Kolesnikov, 2008, pp.66–68). Whether with or without the tacit approval of the Russian government, Chubais had assumed a foreign policy role.

Inter RAO and the Moldovan government were now in conflict on all fronts. In November 2005, Inter RAO cut electricity supplies to right-bank Moldova, which had refused to accept a price increase (Kiselev and Panfilova, 2005). Moldova imported electricity from Ukraine. The Moldovan government outlawed transmission from Moldova TPP to Romania, on account of the dilapidated state of the Moldovan grid (Gorelov, 2007a). The prospect of making a profit from Moldova TPP evaporated. RAO Nordic then sold 49 per cent of Moldova TPP to an unknown offshore company, FREECOM, for 38 million US$ (Grishkovets, 2008c). In early 2006, Chisinau kept Inter RAO from participating in privatisation tenders for sections of the Moldovan grid (Gamova and Krashakov, 2006; RFE/RL, 2006), offering Gazprom instead a controlling stake in the national power grid in exchange for lower gas prices until the end of 2009 (Reznik and Egorova, 2006). But Gazprom declined non-gas equity (Grib and Dar'in, 2006). The pressure worked, and in return for a discounted gas price from April to and including July 2006, the Moldovan government withdrew its demand for a review of the privatisation deals in Transnistria (Reznik and Egorova, 2006; Solov'ev, 2006), and Inter RAO retained its 51 per cent share in Moldova TPP. In July 2007, the presidents of Russia and Moldova agreed on a compromise in the electricity conflict. The compromise included plans for cooperation on electricity transit to Romania, possible future supplies to right-bank Moldova (Embassy Chisinau, 2007) and Pasat's release from prison (Gamova, 2007).

When Inter RAO in mid-2003 acquired power generation and distribution assets in Georgia and Armenia, it was a major breakthrough for the company in the South Caucasus. The lack of control with generation and transmission in Georgia had in 2002 hampered electricity exports to Turkey (Klasson, 2003). After privatisation in 1998, much of Georgia's electricity generation and distribution was owned by the US-based AES Corporation (Gularidze, 2003b; 2003c; Siluyanova, 2004c). Non-payments, generally around 50–60 per cent across the CIS (Fankhauser and Tepic, 2007, p.1042), were a serious problem in Georgia.

AES pulled out in spring 2003. Two electricity plants, Tbilisi's distribution grid, and 50 per cent of the Turkish energy trading company Transenerji, came up for sale (Gotova, 2003). The subsequent deal with Inter RAO was made public in Georgia in July 2003, four months before general elections (Sikamova and Efimov, 2003; Siluyanova, 2003a). The Georgian government and President Eduard Shevardnadze first claimed not to have been informed of the deal beforehand (Bekker, 2003). In the light of AES's longstanding problems, and the general energy crisis in Georgia in the preceding months, their ignorance is not very credible. Chubais and Rappoport argued that the investment made sense as an entry into the Georgian market, emphasising their commercial intentions, including the possibilities of electricity trade with Turkey (Bekker, 2003; Gularidze, 2003a). The Georgian opposition criticised the government over the deal and forced the resignation of Energy Minister Davit Mirtskhulava (Vignanskii, 2003). After the November 2003 Rose Revolution, Mirtskhulava was arrested and convicted (Civil.ge, 2004). In February 2004 Ilya Kutidze, RAO UES's market director in Georgia, was interrogated as well. Rappoport responded by instituting a sudden blackout in order to pressure the Georgian government to stop interrogations and release Kutidze (Berger and Proskurnina, 2008, pp.213–214).

Inter RAO paid 25 million US$ for the Georgian electricity assets (Siluyanova, 2004c), and acquired accumulated non-payments as outstanding debt. AES had recorded a 129 million US$ net loss in the second quarter of 2003 (Civil.ge, 2003). The Georgian government now committed to a debt payment schedule (Bekker, 2003). Following the Rose Revolution, the new government and RAO UES developed normal working relations, reflecting the extent of Georgia's dependence on Inter RAO for electricity.

Later, Chubais complained of a lack of support from the Russian embassy in Tbilisi, referring to the acquisition of AES not in terms of its commercial rationale, but as an important deal for Russia (Berger and Proskurnina, 2008, p.213). The narrative had changed from 2003. Inter RAO's expansion in Georgia revealed how the company relied on informal support for its operations. Inter RAO and AES concluded the deal through subsidiaries based abroad and Inter RAO had used RAO Nordic, which operated in the Nordic electricity market. There was therefore no obligation to inform Inter RAO's Board ahead of the deal. The minority shareholder, Rosenergoatom, and RAO UES appear to have disagreed on the need for expansion and how it should be carried out (Gotova, 2003). Using RAO Nordic as investment vehicle allowed money earned abroad to stay abroad, avoiding Russian taxation. Information on its expansion had very likely passed from Chubais to Putin in advance, to secure presidential approval (Gotova, 2003; Kornysheva, 2003; Siluyanova, 2003a). This was necessary for any Russian state-owned company branching out into a neighbouring state. It was more important to use informal mechanisms of participation in foreign operations, going straight to the president, than to ensure formal institutional oversight within RAO UES and the hierarchy of state organisations.

Inter RAO expansion in Armenia caused far less controversy. The Armenian electricity sector had a tariff collection rate of 60–80 per cent (Kaiser, 2000, p.464; Anex, 2002, p.404). The Armenian nuclear power station, Metsamor, had incurred debts for nuclear fuel supplied after 1995. Russia in 2001 proposed an exchange of Armenia's 40 million US$ debt for stakes in Armenia's nuclear and electricity sectors, and cooperation on electricity exports to Iran (Polyanskii, 2001). Armenia swapped surplus electricity from Metsamor for Iranian gas on a seasonal basis (Anex, 2002, p.403). In early 2003, Russia and Armenia reached a deal, leading to equity transfers beginning in July. In the first transfer, Inter RAO assumed control of the Hrazdan[10] hydropower plants (Hakobyan, 2003; Kravchenko, 2003). In the second transfer, Metsamor's management rights were transferred to Inter RAO on a five-year renewable basis. TVEL, Metsamor's creditor, could not own equity outside Russia (Hakobyan, 2003; Kravchenko, 2003). According to RAO UES's management, Inter RAO would not have acquired control of Metsamor without having Rosenergoatom as a minority shareholder (Egorova, 2006a). The arrangement was extended for five more years in 2008 (WNA, 2018).

RAO UES had been expected to win the privatization tender for the Armenian power grid in 2002, but it went to Midland Resources Holding, a

British company run by two Russian expats (Urikhanyan, 2001). Midland specialised in initial privatisation deals in the post-Soviet region and made its profits from their resale (Avakyan, 2014). In early 2005, Inter RAO acquired the grid, paying Midland 73 million US$ for a 99-year lease (Movsesyan, 2005; Zhelenin, 2005). Ideas of expanding the electricity and gas trade with Iran surfaced regularly in Armenia. Inter RAO's acquisitions gave Russia a lever in this relationship. By 2005, Inter RAO controlled around 70 per cent of Armenia's generation (Table 3.3.). The deal between Inter RAO and Midland attracted criticism for having been carried out without the Armenian government's approval (Gordienko and Orlova, 2005). The Armenian State Regulatory Commission demanded clarifications from the National Grid Company about Inter RAO's lease, but the matter was later dropped (Gordienko and Orlova, 2005). Armenia was politically close to Russia and attracted few alternative investors.

In Azerbaijan, Inter RAO had tried several times to acquire a stake in transmission on the Absheron peninsula, where Baku is located (cf. Mirkadyrov and Gordienko, 2004; Kjærnet, 2007; Sabonis-Helf, 2007). In 2005, Russia and Azerbaijan began to trade electricity. Within the framework of the emerging North–South transport corridor,[11] Russia, Azerbaijan and Iran synchronised electricity grids and expanded cross-border lines from 2006.

RAO UES began negotiating with Kazakhstan in 1995 on a restructuring package for Kazakhstan's electricity debt to RAO UES (Stalker, 1995), which stood at 419 million US$ by the end of 1998 (RAO UES, 1999). In January 2000, the prime ministers agreed on a debt-for-equity swap in principle (Pulina, 2000). Agreeing on content was more difficult. A detailed deal was reached in September 2004, and the swap took place in 2005 (Gleason, 2004). Industry and Energy Minister Viktor Khristenko and President Putin both played an important role in finalising the swap to the benefit of RAO UES (Berger and Proskurnina, 2008, pp.215–217). Under the final deal, Kazakhstan and RAO UES formed a 50/50 joint venture (JV) for ownership of Ekibastuz-2 TPP, which was already exporting electricity to Russia (Gleason, 2004).

In 2003, negotiations started on a debt-for-equity swap involving Tajikistan's debts to Russia. The final package strengthened Russia's military and strategic presence in Tajikistan, but also included two billion US$ of Russian investments in Tajikistan's hydropower sector (Panfilova, 2009). Sangtuda-1, a hydropower project from the Soviet period, was included in the deal, possibly a result of Chubais's and Rappoport's respective efforts (Gorelov, 2008c). By July 2004, RAO UES/Inter RAO was set to receive a 51 per cent share of Sangtuda-1 to settle 50 million US$ of Tajikistan's debt, while undertaking a 50 million US$ investment obligation (Berger and Proskurnina, 2008, p.226). From August, Tajikistan and Kyrgyzstan exported electricity by swaps to Kazakhstan and Russia in anticipation of a final agreement. In September, however, Tajikistan's President Imomali Rakhmon declared that Iran was joining Sangtuda-1 with 250 million US$, thereby jeopardising the Russian–Tajik deal. The deal was settled in a last-minute call between Rakhmon and Putin (Berger and Proskurnina, 2008, p.226). In this final deal, the Russian side undertook to invest 200 million US$ at Sangtuda-1, while the 50 million US$ debt settlement was retained (Glumskov and Grib, 2004). The Russian share of Sangtuda-1 was set at 75 per cent (Litvinov, 2004). The Russian government guaranteed Inter RAO's investments in the project, emphasising the state's involvement in the deal (Libman and Kheifets, 2007, p.22). Construction on Sangtuda-1 recommenced in 2005, and the first part of the power plant opened in January 2008 (Berger and Proskurnina, 2008, pp.218–226).

Implementing the "liberal empire"

As Inter RAO expanded its business, Chubais concentrated on strategic development and overall business strategy. He managed the politics of Inter RAO's business through his network, securing government support for Inter RAO operations. There was little state interference in Inter RAO's development before the end of the monopoly came closer, in late 2006. Rappoport managed some aspects of Inter RAO's operations subordinated to Chubais (Berger and Proskurnina, 2008, pp.211–217; 218–222). Electricity exports and import deals remained his responsibility (RAO UES, 2003; Grib et al., 2006). The formal institutional framework for cross-border trade was underdeveloped and tied to RAO UES. The arrangement that allowed Inter RAO to assume day-to-day responsibilities was based on personal trust. This kept Rosenergoatom away from cross-border trade. Dod was in charge of Inter RAO's now substantial business, but his position remained somewhat junior to Rappoport's.

The legal status of the foreign trade monopoly remained unclear. According to the electricity reform legislation, there was no monopoly on foreign trade. It was regulated like trade in general (Federal Law No. 35, 2003). RAO UES's trade monopoly was a practical consequence of its domestic transmission monopoly. The grid would remain a state monopoly post reform. But access to it, and thereby to foreign trade, would be open to market participants (Federal Law No. 35, 2003, para.30–31). In 2006, the Audit Chamber highlighted the absence of a legal basis for the transfer of foreign trade from RAO UES to Inter RAO (Gorelov, 2006; Medvedeva, 2006). Rappoport's dual role in charge of foreign trade at RAO UES and as Board Chairman of Inter RAO occasioned doubts on whether RAO UES had formally granted Inter RAO a foreign trade monopoly, or simply informally allowed it to effectuate such trade. Upon RAO UES's dissolution, the effectuation of foreign trade automatically passed not to Inter RAO, but to the Federal Grid Company (FSK) (Gorelov, 2008a). This indirectly confirmed that the previous arrangement had been informal. As for Inter RAO itself, it had been included on a decree with a list of strategic companies in 2004. This enabled the state to take its strategic value into account in case of privatisation

Table 3.3 Inter RAO's investments in CIS member states

	Equity	Part of power industry	Ownership (management) period	Installed generation capacity or grid size	Vehicle for ownership or control	Share of supply/distribution/market in country*
Armenia	Armenian Nuclear Power Plant (Metsamor)	Nuclear power generation	2003–2011	815 MW	Management rights	35–45 per cent
Armenia	Electricity network of Armenia (ENA)	Transmission and distribution	2005–2016	29600 km	Interenergo BV, originally 99-year lease	100 per cent
Armenia	Hrazdan River Power Plants/cascade of 7 units	Hydropower generation	2003–2011**	560 MW	Management rights	10 per cent
Armenia	Hrazdan TPP	Thermal power generation	2005–2016	1100 MW	Inter RAO BV (Netherlands)	Variable (seasonal and reserve), average 10–15 per cent
Georgia	Mtkvari energetika/2 units of Tbilisi power plant	Thermal power generation	2003–2016	2 x 300 MW	RAO Nordic OY	12 per cent (2015)
Georgia	Khrami GES/2 units of plant	Hydropower generation	2003–	2 x 110 MW	Management rights	4.3 per cent (2017)
Georgia	Telasi power distribution/75% share	Transmission and distribution (Tbilisi)***	2003–	5658 km (in 2003)	RAO Nordic OY	35 per cent
Moldova	Moldova GRES	Thermal power generation	2005–	2520 MW	RAO Nordic OY, direct ownership from 2010	85 per cent
Kazakhstan	Ekibastuz GRES-2 (50 percent)	Thermal power generation	2005–	2 x 500 MW	Direct	12 per cent
Tajikistan	Sanguda-1 (75 percent, combined Russian share)	Hydropower generation	2004–	670 MW	2.18 per cent direct share, operator	15 per cent

* Armenia: As share of real generation. Where no date is given, the higher number refers to earlier years, while lower numbers apply to later years. Georgia, Moldova, Kazakhstan, Tajikistan: as share of installed capacity
** Sold to RusHydro. In 2017–2018, RusHydro looked for a buyer for Hrazdan HPP.
*** Telasi later branched out to water supply and waste management.
Author's compilation based on RAO UES and Inter RAO annual reports and webpages

(Decree No. 1009, 2004). In 2006 things were left as they were, both with regard to foreign trade and to ownership. Informal political support for RAO UES's management preserved the monopoly. The state's increasing control of the energy sector during Putin's second term reinforced this support. To both state representatives and market participants, foreign trade was relatively insignificant and based anyway on long-term contracts.

Chubais and other management representatives were always careful to point out that Inter RAO's expansion had a commercial, not political, motive. Rappoport at one point denied that Inter RAO's Board had even discussed the political implications of the South Caucasus investments (Siluyanova, 2004a). According to another source, the question of commercial gains from post-Soviet expansion was raised by RAO UES's board, but brushed aside by the chairman, Voloshin (Siluyanova, 2005). However, Chubais clearly saw Inter RAO as fulfilling a geopolitical mission in its South Caucasus acquisitions, and indicated that the investments in Georgia and Armenia were made in cooperation with the Kremlin (Egorova, 2005). Informal contacts were used to cut across the formal institutional framework, also when RAO UES was formally authorised to make decisions. The balance between formal and informal channels of access and participation was tilted towards the informal. Representatives of the state repeatedly viewed Inter RAO expansion in light of foreign policy. This caused worries around the question of "to whom they will belong after restructuring, and how much has been paid for them" (Egorova et al., 2003).

The end of the monopoly

Chubais remained an independent state company leader, and critic of Putin. Russian business leaders generally took Mikhail Khodorkovskii's arrest in October 2003 as a signal to keep quiet (discussed in Chapter 5), but Chubais was not deterred (Vardul', 2003; Kommersant-Vlast', 2005). This continued in Putin's second term, when criticism of Putin was a less frequent phenomenon (Derbilova and Panyushkin, 2007). At this point, RAO UES had become a "refuge" for Yeltsin-era liberals (Wengle, 2012, p.449). In his pre-election speech in Luzhniki stadium in November 2007, Putin invoked the image of domestic and foreign enemies, and "oligarchs" in particular. Chubais replied by calling Medvedev the better choice for president and criticised Putin for "spitting on his predecessors" (Latukhina, 2007). After this incident, the two ceased to pursue contact (Kolesnikov, 2008, pp.183; 300–301).

Nevertheless, the RAO UES reform progressed as planned. Chubais seemed to have an informal guarantee of RAO UES's autonomy as well as overall support for the reform, giving him a carte blanche in implementation. Chubais's position was further strengthened when it became apparent that the reform would be a success. The electricity market grew by 19 per cent annually in the period 2004–2008 (Datamonitor, 2009). Growth and reform attracted private investment, enabling Russia to escape an impending shortfall in power generation capacity (Derbilova et al., 2012). Even though Putin and Chubais by 2007 disagreed about most things, the former refrained from interfering (Kolesnikov, 2008, p.264). Chubais was supported by the liberals in Putin's government (Wengle, 2012, p.449), and Board Chairman Voloshin was another effective advocate of reform (Gazeta, 2003; Gorelov, 2003; Smirnov, 2004). To all state representatives, the reform's great advantage was that it increased state capacity in the sector by establishing functioning market mechanisms (Wengle, 2012, pp.436–437). Stalling the reform would have brought back the old problem of a sector beyond state control, and starved of investment. The electricity reform, like the reform of Rosatom, restored state capacity in a previously insulated sector and made it governable, and potentially profitable. But it was different from Rosatom's reform in consisting of the dissolution of a monopoly and the privatisation of state property (cf. Vin'kov, 2008). A related, major attraction was that the reform process undercut the power of regional governors. This served Putin's centralising project well (Wengle, 2012, pp.451–452).

RAO UES was dissolved on 19 June 2008, just a month into Medvedev's presidential term. The establishment of a competitive electricity market depended on the implementation of key elements in the coming months. The timing turned out to be unfavourable, as the global financial crisis began to spread from September. At the time, however, it seemed more important that Chubais had lost some of his influence over reform implementation in the final months before June 2008. This was in part a consequence of the reform design, which vested the Energy Ministry with considerable regulatory power after RAO UES's dissolution (Derbilova et al., 2012). Chubais lost formal and informal influence over key appointments. Members of the reform team, such as Rappoport (Medvedeva, 2007a; Mazneva, 2008) and Voloshin (Kommersant, 2008), began to lose their positions. Yurii Udaltsov, *the* key RAO UES reform manager, was relegated to the government's expert group on electricity reform (Dokukina, 2012). Crucial new organisations like the Market Council,[12] the self-regulating sectoral organisation responsible for monitoring prices, were headed by people closer to the Kremlin (Vedomosti, 2008; Skyner, 2010, pp.1399–1400). As the complete picture emerged, it appeared that Igor Sechin, head of the Presidential Administration until May and deputy prime minister afterwards, had placed trusted people in crucial positions.

Sechin, who was also chairman of Rosneft's Board, was critical of the electricity reform and would have preferred a vertical consolidation under state control (Petlevoi et al., 2015). Chubais and Sechin had very different views on the role of the state in the economy, particularly in the resource sectors. Sechin was no liberal reformer, but a proponent of state intervention in strategic sectors (Gustafson, 2012, pp.248–249). In Sechin's view, this was of course oil, but also the energy industries more widely (Tovkailo et al., 2012). In 2008, as Sechin moved with Putin into government, he took on responsibility for the fuel and energy sector. He was one of Putin's closest advisors and had known him since the early 1990s, i.e. much longer than Chubais.

With RAO UES gone, and the financial crisis unfolding, completion of the power industry reform became more difficult. Electricity demand contracted, followed by stagnation. Attracting investment was critical to reform success. Without investment, it would be difficult to create competition in wholesale and spot markets, because they depended on participation from several large generating companies. But the new, private owners of the generating companies were less eager to keep their investment obligations, undertaken during reform, during the economic slowdown (Solanko, 2014, pp.138–139). Some complained that the obligations were based on excessively high projected growth rates on the part of RAO UES's last management (Wengle, 2014, p.258). In these adverse circumstances, it did not help that Chubais was ensconced in Rusnano, in a different industry, and no longer in a position to influence the reform process (Skyner, 2010; Solanko, 2014). Electricity prices once again became subject to politics, as when the Federal Anti-Monopoly Service (FAS) introduced price caps on wholesale prices in the election year 2011. This happened just as the wholesale market was supposed to complete its transition towards floating prices. Both foreign and Russian executives in the generating companies reacted strongly, as they had entered the sector on the assumption of reform completion (Peretolchina and Derbilova, 2011). Price caps hit the privately owned thermal generation companies disproportionately hard, while state-owned hydropower (RusHydro) and nuclear power (Rosatom) were allowed to charge extra for safety and investment costs. Key market actors called the reform incomplete (Peretolchina and Derbilova, 2011; Dokukina, 2012). As Chubais commented in 2012, the Energy Ministry was not up to the task of putting its regulatory powers to use (Derbilova et al., 2012). The Energy Ministry had been strengthened, and formal institutions became more important in interactions within the elite, but there were limits. When faced with demands by members of the ruling coalition, such as Sechin, the Energy Ministry was overruled.

Inter RAO on its own

According to Theresa Sabonis-Helf, Inter RAO was created "so that foreign generation holdings of RAO-UES will not be affected by the electricity reform currently under way in Russia" (Sabonis-Helf, 2007, pp.430–431). This was also flagged in the Russian press to explain why Inter RAO's expansion occurred so close to RAO UES's planned dissolution (Gotova, 2003; Sikamova and Efimov, 2003; Khrennikov, 2006).[13] Sometimes, one purpose of Inter RAO's seemed to be in ensuring that RAO UES's top management, especially Rappoport, retained lucrative positions in the future. This assumption was not baseless, as subsequent events would show.

But Inter RAO was useful to different elite groups. Representatives of the state and of RAO UES/Inter RAO agreed on the priority of keeping Inter RAO's assets in one company and protecting the de facto export–import monopoly. To Chubais, it was essential to maintain Inter RAO's monopoly until neighbouring, post-Soviet markets developed to a level where they could reliably predict electricity demand (Gaidar and Chubais, 2008, p.141). State representatives connected state ownership of Inter RAO to post-Soviet influence. In 2007, a representative of the Industry and Energy Ministry commented on a possible sale of Inter RAO: "It's a strategic stake. As the company sells electricity abroad, it influences the policies of many states, above all in the CIS" (Medvedeva, 2007b). Another government source called Inter RAO a "knife switch"[14] and a "serious argument in dialogues with neighbouring states" (Egorova, 2006b).

While everyone agreed that Inter RAO would remain in state hands, the details of the ownership structure were subject to intense negotiation. In 2006, Chubais preferred a 100 per cent sale to Gazprom. Rosenergoatom naturally preferred a complete transfer to Rosatom (Grib and Kornysheva, 2006). In May 2007, Chubais advised Putin to retain Inter RAO's pre-reform management, but to no avail (Gorelov, 2007b). Only in late 2007 was an unequivocal decision taken to let Rosatom become a majority shareholder in Inter RAO (Medvedeva, 2007a). Throughout 2006 and 2007, Inter RAO's management, with Chubais's support, sought the RAO UES Board's approval for a management stock option (Gorelov, 2007b). They first demanded a 15 per cent stake in Inter RAO's ordinary shares, which would reduce the state's stake. A second demand was for 9.9 per cent (Gorelov, 2007b). In the end, the management was awarded one-off bonuses and no ownership in Inter RAO.[15] The struggle revealed the hostility of state representatives, and representatives of Rosatom, to the current management as future minority owners of Inter RAO. As Chapter 6 shows, previous experiences with former managers as minority owners were not positive. But in this case, the government was firmly against having reform advocates as minority owners.

On Chubais's advice, Inter RAO was reorganised as an open-stock shareholding company, and enlarged with equity in Russia's most modern generation (Gorelov, 2007b; OAO Inter RAO (OAO Sochinskaya GES), 2008; Dzaguto, 2010c). Now a larger company with more of its business in Russia, the new Inter RAO was transferred to Rosatom. With most of the previous management and Board gone, Inter RAO became subject to more direct state control. The role and interest of minority shareholders diminished (Grishkovets, 2008b; 2009).

Unusually for a RAO UES top manager, Dod seemed to have acquired Sechin's confidence and remained head of Inter RAO (*The Moscow Times*, 2009; Petlevoi et al., 2015). In October, Sechin became a member of Inter RAO's Board, and in December, he was elected chairman. Energy Minister Shmatko also joined the Board in 2008 (Grishkovets et al., 2008b). Dod remained Inter RAO's head only until November 2009, when he became head of the hydropower company RusHydro,[16] apparently not of his own volition (Petlevoi et al., 2015). He retained a position on Inter RAO's Board until 2012.

Inter RAO Group

The new acting Director General, Boris Kovalchuk, had joined Inter RAO's Board in June 2009. This was after a short stint in Rosatom's top management, but he had earlier been responsible for national priority projects in the government apparatus (*The Moscow Times*, 2009). He was the son of the well-known businessman Yurii Kovalchuk, Board Chairman of the Rossiya Bank and a friend of Putin's.

In 2010–2011, Inter RAO Group, as it was now known, integrated vertically through acquisitions in Russian generation and retail supply, and power engineering. The result was a RAO UES-like structure, only leaner and without electricity grids (Fialko et al., 2010; Ispolatov, 2010a; 2010b). The circumstances were favourable, as many of its competitors had had their margins squeezed by the price caps and stock prices were low. A major part of the acquisitions were stakes in generation that the state had reserved for later privatisation, which were now transferred to Inter RAO at market price (Dzaguto, 2010a). This idea was floated by Sechin in October 2009, as he joined the Board, and the plans were realised only a year later. The acquisitions were financed by a private placement with the Russian state, Russian state energy companies and private investors, increasing Inter RAO's capital stock threefold. Rosneft, RusHydro and Norilsk Nikel became shareholders (Inter RAO, 2011a). In this way, reduced direct state ownership opened for ownership by state-owned companies and companies close to the regime (Ispolatov, 2010a; Dzaguto and Grishkovets, 2011). Inter RAO became the third-largest electricity company in Russia, controlling 10 per cent of generation (Solanko, 2014, p.135). With Rosatom, RusHydro and GazpromEnergo, the state now controlled over half of Russia's generation capacity (Solanko, 2014, p.146).

In 2011, Sechin and Shmatko left the Board, following President Medvedev's decree to reduce government representation on Russian company boards (Sterkin and Mazneva, 2011). Medvedev's aims were to gradually decrease the role of the state in the economy, and for the state to manage its equity at arm's length until market conditions were beneficial for privatisation. Inter RAO's acquisitions made it an attractive, but also quite large company.

Regime control with Inter RAO's foreign operations increased from 2011. Its management participated in official delegations to India, and opened offices in Cuba and Abu Dhabi (Inter RAO, 2011e). There were investments in Laos (Skorlygina and Dzaguto, 2012). A new expansion plan for Latin America and Asian states, several of which had notoriously unprofitable electricity sectors, indicated that foreign policy considerations weighed more than commercial opportunities (Grishkovets, 2008b; Kommersant, 2009). China was a strategic priority. New interconnectors completed in 2011 and 2012 made it possible to increase exports fourfold (Vostochnaya energeticheskaya kompaniya, 2018). China became the second largest importer of

Russian electricity, after Finland. Inter RAO became an instrument of foreign policy also outside the post-Soviet region. To coordinate all its development projects, a new subsidiary, Inter RAO Eksport, was established in October 2011 (Inter RAO, 2018c). However, the days of a complete foreign trade monopoly were over (Grishkovets, 2010b). TGK-1, owned by Gazprom and Fortum, and ENEL's electricity subsidiary, Rusenergosbyt, pursued a limited cross-border electricity trade in 2011 (TGK-1, 2012, p.33; Vasil'ev, 2012, p.61), but Inter RAO remained the dominant exporter (TGK-1, 2012, p.33). After RAO UES's dissolution, there was still a lack of detail in formal regulatory framework for cross-border electricity trade (Gorelov, 2008a). Inter RAO continued in a monopoly position due to its market share.

But the state also changed its relations with Inter RAO with respect to its foreign operations, tying them more closely to foreign policy. In September 2012, a decree that primarily aimed to support and strengthen Gazprom's position, made it compulsory for strategic companies to obtain prior state approval in all relations with their foreign customers (Decree No. 1285, 2012). In addition, it reduced their overall independence in relations with foreign bodies. Inter RAO was now obliged to act as an agent of the state in foreign economic policy.

The post-Soviet region: Ubiquitous Inter RAO

Meanwhile, Inter RAO's foreign operations continued more or less as before. With commercially based business principles, broad industry experience, and a good political network in Moscow and other capitals, it was the ideal post-Soviet company. In 2008–2012 it reached the height of its powers, a mature company which had used most of the good possibilities for expansion outside Russia. But now it was affected by changing economic realities. The financial crisis reduced electricity demand, growth projections, and the viability of new projects.

In a more difficult environment, Inter RAO had to choose between expanding its business in Russia or outside. At stake was not foreign operations as such, but the extent to which investment would go into established and new non-Russian generation, complemented by synchronisation, transmission and trade. The alternative would be to retain existing foreign assets, but invest in generation in Russia. The annual reports for 2009 and 2010 placed equal priorities on growth within Russia and without Russia (Inter RAO, 2010b, p.50; 2011b, p.63). The 2009 business strategy prioritised reliable service in Russia at the expense of synchronisation with neighbours (Inter RAO, 2010b, p.50). However, in 2010, the goal of integrating electricity markets and opening up for transnational trade was back (Inter RAO, 2011b, p.64). At this point, it remained an open question whether Inter RAO would continue to develop parts of the liberal empire, or concentrate all its efforts on vertical integration and empire-building at home. The expansion in Russia in 2010–2011 was in effect a decision to pursue the second option, but the post-Soviet operations remained a cornerstone in the company business.

Relations with Ukraine diminished. Ukraine's share in Russian electricity import fell from 27.9 per cent in 2005 to 0.2 per cent in 2009 (Inter RAO, 2006; 2010a). By 2008, Ukraine received 5 per cent of Russia's exports (Inter RAO, 2009a, p.68). Relations with Belarus deteriorated. In 2010, Belarus tried to increase electricity transit tariffs to pressure Russia in an oil transit dispute (Chapter 6) (Grishkovets, 2010a). But transit volumes were too small for the ploy to yield any result. As the dispute unfolded and Belarus faced liquidity problems, debts accumulated. In 2011, Inter RAO disconnected Belarus (Dzaguto and Dyatel, 2017). Exports resumed only after President Medvedev had intervened, following what appeared to be a political signal conveyed by Inter RAO (Grishkovets, 2011).

Things went better in Moldova. In July 2008, Inter RAO again consolidated complete control of Moldova TPP in a 63 million US$ deal with FREECOM, leaving its owners with 125 million US$ for its two-and-a-half-year-long ownership (Embassy Chisinau, 2008; Grishkovets, 2008c). A Hungarian company, EMFESZ, belonging to the Ukrainian businessman Dmytro Firtash, was possibly involved in the deal (Zateichuk, 2007; Grishkovets, 2008c; Peretolchina, 2008). From 2009, Moldova again had Moldova TPP supply following problems with Ukrainian suppliers (Grishkovets et al., 2008a).

Inter RAO's position in Georgia was solid, but always subject to political controversy. It generated around 35 per cent of the country's electricity, and had avoided interruptions during the war. Its business expansion in Georgia seemed to continue in 2009, when both the Abkhazian de facto authorities and the Georgian government pursued contact with it over a new management arrangement for the Enguri hydropower plant (HPP) (Civil.ge, 2009; Grishkovets et al., 2009; Simonyan, 2009). Enguri, the largest hydropower plant in the South Caucasus, straddled the boundary between the Zugdidi region and the secessionist republic Abkhazia, with Abkhazian control of operations. Inter RAO was sceptical of the political risk, in light of its existing engagement in Georgia. In the event, the plans were quietly shelved, and Georgia in 2011 attracted finance from the European Investment Bank, EBRD and the European Neighbourhood Facility to rehabilitate and modernise Enguri HPP (Civil.ge, 2011). Inter RAO also turned down a later offer of Russia's 50 per cent stake in the company SakRosEnergo[17] that controlled grids in parts of Russia, Georgia and Abkhazia (Dzaguto and Grishkovets, 2011). This stake was eventually transferred to Russia's FSK.

Inter RAO's operations in Armenia changed less, but were used as tools to shape energy relations with Iran (discussed in Chapter 7). Seventy per cent of Armenia's electricity exports went to Iran in 2010 (Oganesyan, 2009; Polyakova, 2010). Armenia's room for manoeuvre was limited by the expansion of Russia's energy relations with Azerbaijan and Iran in the North–South Transport Corridor. By 2009, the plans for trilateral cooperation were expanding (Inter RAO, 2010b, p.12).

In Kazakhstan, the package deal from 2004 also included plans to expand the Ekibastuz-2 thermal power plant with two new units. In late 2009, financing for one of them was included in the credit line Russia opened for Kazakhstan during the financial crisis. The financial package from Vneshekonombank was finalised in 2010 (Granik, 2010; Gabuev and Konstantinov, 2011) and construction work started in 2011 (Inter RAO, 2014, p.84). Also in 2010, Inter RAO came close to acquiring 50 per cent of Ekibastuz-1 (Bol'shakov and Ishmukhammetov, 2007). Instead, however, Kazakhstan strengthened state ownership in the electricity sector (Grishkovets and Dzaguto, 2009; Mazneva, 2010).

In Tajikistan, Sangtuda-1 was completed in 2009 and opened by the two presidents. The Russian government now owned 83.5 per cent of Sangtuda-1: 66.4 per cent directly, 14.9 through FSK, and 2.24 per cent through Inter RAO (Dzaguto, 2009a). Inter RAO planned a shares emission to take over some of the government shares (Inter RAO, 2009b), but this did not happen. Tajikistan quickly ran up electricity debts to Sangtuda. Exporting to Russia through swaps was proposed as a means of debt recovery (Dzaguto, 2009b). In August 2011 Sangtuda started exporting to Afghanistan.

Inter RAO's success at Sangtuda-1 opened up other possibilities for the company. Rogun, a much larger unfinished Soviet project, was included in the 2004 deal, with the aluminium company RusAl as Russian partner (Marat, 2010). By 2007, RusAl and Tajikistan disagreed over Rogun, and Tajikistan abrogated the agreement (Marat, 2008a; Panfilova, 2008a). Russia, Chubais then declared, was not going to abandon the Rogun project, implying Inter RAO participation (Solov'ev and Grishkovets, 2008). This was approved by all parties, but negotiations stalled. Sergei Naryshkin, head of the Presidential Administration, took part in the negotiations (Gorelov, 2008c; Panfilova, 2008b). Tajikistan's government tried to attract Iran and Pakistan to join the project, to no avail (Grishkovets, 2008a). The government broached other possibilities, such as an international consortium with Russian participation. But Inter RAO and the Presidential Administration demanded a 50 per cent share for Russia in return for Russian finance for Rogun. A minority stake was unacceptable to Tajikistan (Grishkovets and Ravinskii, 2008; Grishkovets and Solov'ev, 2008). By now, the financial crisis complicated negotiations (Gabuev, 2009; Panfilova, 2009). The Tajik government proceeded without Russian participation (Marat, 2008b; 2010).

Chubais had in 2004 declared an interest in an expansion at the Kyrgyz HPP Kambarata, but this was delayed by the 2005 Tulip Revolution. The tender for Kambarata-1 came in 2007, while Kyrgyzstan would complete Kambarata-2 on its own (Panfilova, 2008a). Kazakhstan participated in the Kambarata-1 tender (Zhelenin, 2007). Russia's bid succeeded, and Inter RAO proceeded jointly with a Kyrgyz partner in June 2009. Riots and regime change in 2010 further delayed Kambarata-1, but also put Kambarata-2 back into the contest. Cost estimates then stood at 1.7–3 billion US$, to be financed by Russian credits (Gabuev and Karabekov, 2011; Panfilova, 2011).

In 2010, Russia was invited to participate in the Central Asia-South Asia-1000 (CASA-1000) project. Originally a project involving Tajikistan,

68 *The electricity industry*

Afghanistan and Pakistan, it would construct high-voltage lines from Central Asia to Peshawar in Pakistan. Inter RAO proposed supplies from Kambarata-1 and Rogun (Dzaguto, 2010b). Russia later offered 500 million US$ in project funding in return for Inter RAO control of the line (Dzaguto, 2011).

Inter RAO and the reorganised coalition

Boris Kovalchuk remained head of Inter RAO. From 2012, he developed its business along the strategic priorities outlined in the next sub-chapter, with greater ambitions in Russian electricity generation and more selective aims abroad. He was generally seen as an influential energy industry manager, rated among the 25 or even 20 most influential energy industry managers in Russia (Oilcapital.ru, 2012; 2016). The change of strategic priorities was however connected to changes of state company in charge of Inter RAO, and the influence of Igor Sechin.

Sechin was known to be unhappy to be removed from Inter RAO's Board in 2011, but grasped the opportunity when Putin returned to the Presidency in May 2012. This return was the beginning of a consolidation of power among a narrower group of trusted associates, who had already benefitted from concentration in the economy during the financial crisis. Putin revoked Medvedev's decision on state representatives on corporate boards. From 2012 president of Rosneft, Sechin returned as Board Chairman in mid-2013 (Inter RAO, 2014, p.96). He was elected not as representative of the state, but of the Inter RAO subsidiary Inter RAO-Kapital, relieving him of any obligation to vote on behalf of the state (Dzyadko, 2013).

Upon Putin's return to the Presidency in May 2012, Sechin immediately proposed to use Rosneftegaz's dividends from Rosneft and Gazprom to consolidate the state's stakes in energy. Rosneftegaz had been created as a temporary holding company in 2004 to facilitate the Rosneft–Gazprom merger, essentially to acquire and hold state-owned stocks until the process was completed (Chapter 7). When the merger failed, Rosneftegaz held Rosneft's state-owned controlling stake and then acquired a significant minority in Gazprom. However, in spite of intentions to subsequently liquidise Rosneftegaz and transfer the stocks to direct state ownership, the company was there to stay. The small entity was housed in Rosneft's head office in Moscow, with Sechin as head of the Board of Directors. Rosneftegaz's sole purpose was to hold stocks for the state. State demands for dividend payment had steadily increased, but during the financial crisis, the Ministry of Finance had allowed companies to retain dividends. Now, the issue was back with full force, and Rosneftegaz, too, was expected to contribute higher dividends to the budget. Sechin's proposal entailed that much of Rosneft's and Gazprom's profits would be used to increase Rosneftegaz's role in the sector on behalf of the state.

The necessary decree was passed before the end of May (Decree No. 695, 2012; Mel'nikov, 2012). But the policy change had not been agreed with

Medvedev's incoming government, especially not with Deputy Prime Minister Arkadii Dvorkovich, in charge of overseeing the fuel and energy complex including Inter RAO and Rosneftegaz. The government, as Rosneftegaz's owner, did not agree that its role should increase, and most importantly, it preferred that the profits from state-owned stock accrue to the state budget. Dvorkovich was likely irked by an accompanying decree, issued on the day of his own appointment, that had lengthened the list of strategic enterprises in the fuel and energy sector (Decree No. 688, 2012; Stanovaya, 2016). Policy for state-owned strategic companies was made by the government, under its general responsibility for the economy. But due to such companies' strategic status, major decisions also required the president's approval. Decision-making routines had evolved in a way that subjected an even broader range of decisions to routine agreement by both the government and the president (Dzaguto et al., 2012). In this first major conflict over policy in Putin's third term, Dvorkovich succeeded in restricting Rosneftegaz's reach in the fuel and energy sector. However, Sechin won the battle with regard to Inter RAO in late 2012, enabling Rosneftegaz to invest in the company (Dzyadko and Ivankina, 2014). The deal was complete a year later, when Rosneftegaz acquired Rosatom's stake. Shortly thereafter Rosneftegaz took over the stake previously directly held by the state (Inter RAO, 2014, p.131). In this way, Rosneftegaz acquired control of 27.63 per cent of Inter RAO (Dzyadko and Ivankina, 2014; Rosneftegaz, 2014, p.4; 2015, p.22; Inter RAO, 2018b). Rosatom may have sold at a rather high price. From the point of view of the state, money was just being moved around. According to one analyst, the directors in charge therefore decided on price based on "who needed the money most" (Dzaguto et al., 2013).

In 2014, Rosneftegaz was reorganised into a non-public shareholding company, and became exempt from disclosing its finances publicly. Instead, Putin was informed directly of its financial development and investment programmes (Panchenkova and Starinskaya, 2016; Yakoreva, 2016). The government, Rosneftegaz's owner, did not receive this information. When the Ministry of Finance and Rosimushchestvo in autumn 2016 requested it to contribute between 50 per cent of its dividends from Rosneft, Gazprom and Inter RAO to the budget, as a reply Rosneftegaz asked Putin to allow a reduced contribution (Panchenkova and Starinskaya, 2016). Putin granted his approval and allowed the company to contribute 25 per cent as before (Podobedova and Milyukova, 2016). Furthermore, Putin allowed Rosneftegaz to accumulate funds to spend on "the kind of things for which the government, at the end of the day, does not have the money" (Dzaguto, 2016). In this way, Inter RAO's rent streams were partly channelled towards developmental aims at Sechin's discretion, such as shipyards and icebreakers (Vedeneeva, 2018). While Inter RAO had remained a relatively transparent company, the government was deprived of influence on its business plans.

A reduced liberal empire

In 2011–2012, Inter RAO's business strategy changed once more. Expanding foreign operations, especially market presence and trade, remained a priority (Inter RAO, 2011d). However, it was unclear how this could be combined with aims like obtaining a leading role in the Russian power industry, developing a leading global vertically integrated company, or promoting energy security in Russia. In practice, foreign operations were streamlined under a narrower business profile. Later changes to the strategy prioritised to maintain a leading role in the Russian power industry, and increase Inter RAO's presence only in selected foreign markets, "promoting Russian practices and solutions in the power industry" (Inter RAO, 2018a).

Belarus remained among the top four destinations for Inter RAO's electricity export, behind Finland, China and Lithuania, but this was likely to cease on the opening of the Belarusian NPP in 2019 or 2020 (Chapter 4). Inter RAO's subsidiaries in the Baltic states, held through Inter RAO Lietuva, branched out to Poland and started trading directly on the Nordic power exchange, NordPool, in 2011. The same year, it acquired a wind park in Lithuania. Electricity trade with Ukraine had almost ceased by 2013, but increased in the wake of the annexation of Crimea in 2014. As Crimea depended for its electricity supply on mainland Ukraine, Ukraine tried to use this as a bargaining chip with Russia. Nevertheless, Ukraine faced electricity shortfalls in autumn 2014. Russia proposed a swap of electricity from Russia to Ukraine and from mainland Ukraine to Crimea (Varfolomeyev, 2015). This was effectuated by a subsidiary of Inter RAO, *Tsentr osushchestvleniya raschetov* (TsOR), which seems to have been established solely for this purpose in June 2014 (Inter RAO, 2015, p.239; Fadeeva and Serkov, 2018). When Karina Tsurkan, Inter RAO's head of trade from 2012, was arrested on espionage charges in summer 2018, media leaks from the investigation centred on her role in organising electricity supply to Crimea and possibly also Donbas (Fadeeva, 2018; Fadeeva and Serkov, 2018).

Inter RAO remained the owner of Moldova TPP. It competed with Ukrainian suppliers for the Moldovan market only to lose it in 2017 when a trading company controlled by the Ukrainian oligarch Rinat Akhmetov submitted a lower bid (Popşoi, 2017; Solov'ev and Dzaguto, 2017). Well-connected intermediary trading companies were a regular feature in Moldova's electricity trade, whether generation was located in Transnistria or Ukraine (Ul'yanov, 2015; Popşoi, 2016). At some point, Moldova TPP's gas supply ceased to come directly from Gazprom, but from an organisation close to the de facto president of Transnistria, Evgenii Shevchuk (2011–2016) (Popşoi, 2016). Media leaks from the Tsurkan investigation raised the question of whether trade in electricity from Moldova TPP had been used to defraud Inter RAO (Yur'ev, 2018). In light of the ongoing process to integrate Ukraine and Moldova's grids with the continental European grid (Varfolomeyev, 2017), Moldova TPP's market situation was likely headed for substantial change.

In Georgia, Inter RAO held on to its hydropower generation (Khrami HPP) and the Telasi grid, but sold the Mtkvari TPP to the Georgian Industrial Group in 2016 (Georgian Industrial Group, 2016). There were no plans for business expansion in Georgia.

In Armenia, Inter RAO ceased to act as manager of Metsamor at the end of 2011 (ARKA News Agency, 2012b; 2012a), and sold its stake in Hrazdan HPP to RusHydro the same year (Inter RAO, 2011c). Its third asset, the Armenian grid ENA, developed in a stable and profitable way until 2012. Following years of draught, it had begun to rely more on thermal generation, and especially on the 5th unit of the Hrazdan TPP (not to be confused with Hrazdan HPP). This was a new facility with high production costs, owned by Gazprom (Elektricheskie seti Armenii, 2013, p.17). From then on, ENA, one of Armenia's largest taxpayers, accumulated debts to the Armenian state, banks and suppliers, even as the regulated tariffs were increased (Grigoryan, 2015b). In 2014, rumours began to circulate about a possible Gazprom takeover of ENA (Avakyan, 2014). That rumours could circulate was understandable, considering that Gazprom had by then obtained full control of Armenia's gas market (Chapter 7).

ENA's position was complicated in 2015 due to water shortage and planned maintenance at Metsamor, which meant that Armenia would have to rely on gas-fired generation (Dzaguto and Dyatel, 2017). To improve its financial situation, ENA requested a 40 per cent tariff hike for retail customers, later reduced to 17 per cent by the State Regulatory Commission. When this became known in early June, people protested in the streets. While the increases were decidedly unpopular, a general perception of mismanagement and unjustified expenses at ENA, especially connected to electricity purchases from gas-fired plants, raised questions about ENA's relations with Gazprom and politicised the issue further (Grigoryan, 2015a; 2015c). The parliament launched tariff hearings, but ENA's managers while refusing to participate again requested a 40 per cent tariff increase. At this point, protests increased in scale (Grigoryan, 2015c), and became known as "Electric Yerevan" in English.[18] In late June, the tariff hike was postponed.

A later audit showed that the price hike was justified, but also revealed serious structural problems in the Armenian electricity sector (ARKA News Agency, 2015). Inter RAO was already leaving Armenia. In an only partially transparent deal, Tashir Group, connected to the Moscow-based Armenian businessman Samvel Karapetyan, acquired Inter RAO's equity in Armenia (Grigoryan, 2015a). Karapetyan, who had no previous experience from the electricity industry, later admitted that he had been asked by Boris Kovalchuk, and by the Armenian government, to come to Inter RAO's rescue (Grigoryan, 2016b). While Inter RAO exited Armenia's electricity industry in 2015, it was not the end of bilateral contact over electricity. The same year, saw the beginning of a four-partite regional energy cooperation between Russia, Georgia, Armenia and Iran. This included plans for new transmission lines between Armenia and Georgia, and Armenia and Iran, which would`enable grid synchronisation between all the four countries (Grigoryan, 2016a).

The exit from Kyrgyzstan was different. There was no progress on Kambarata-1 after 2009. In this period, when Inter RAO modified its strategy and streamlined its foreign holdings, it was not a worthwhile investment, with a low commercial potential (Skorlygina, 2014). In particular, the project was vehemently opposed by Uzbekistan, and therefore carried high political risk (Hashimova, 2017). In 2012, the project came back on the table as part of a Russian government investment package to persuade Kyrgyzstan to finally close the US transit centre Manas[19] (Recknagel, 2013). But it was still not prioritised by Inter RAO, even after considerable government pressure (Dzaguto and Skorlygina, 2013). At the beginning of 2016, Kyrgyzstan nullified both the Kambarata-1 deal and Upper Naryn, supposed to be built by RusHydro (Orozobekova, 2016). When the regional transmission line CASA-1000 was inaugurated later that year, Russia did not attend. Ekibastuz-2 was now Inter RAO's only asset in Central Asia.

Conclusions

The Russian electricity monopoly emerged unreformed from the Soviet period. By 1993, RAO UES was a semi-reformed holding company under nominal state control. It had little clout over regional power companies and informal rent streams were siphoned off at every level. The Russian state did not have, and appears not to have sought, full regulatory access to the electricity system beyond perfunctory formal meetings. RAO UES did not participate in limited attempts made at institutional development or policymaking, and there was little of either. In terms of the structure of interaction, the electricity industry had extensive autonomy.

As the formal channels of access and participation atrophied, the state was left incapacitated and fragmented. Informal access and participation dominated state–company interaction, the basis of which was an exchange of mutual support and rent sharing between regional and industrial elites and the ruling coalition. This preserved elite stability, especially in the regions, where elites constituted select circles of claimants. Wider rent sharing in the form of cheap electricity and non-payments stabilised society. It also cultivated dependence on the state, but in particular on Yeltsin's ruling coalition.

Electricity trade in the post-Soviet region declined rapidly. Barter, soft payment constraints, and informal channels of participation and rent sharing proliferated where some trade remained. In this way, dependence on Russia was cultivated among post-Soviet elites and populations. However, RAO UES was unable to shoulder this burden at length, and customer relations in the post-Soviet states transformed into hard constraints and real payment terms after the 1998 financial crisis. This was subsequently also the case with domestic customers.

When Chubais took over at RAO UES in 1998, structural reform was long overdue. The reform was prepared during Yeltsin's second presidential period and pushed through in the early years of Putin's first. It was a political project aimed at increasing state capacity and creating electricity markets. The state gained real regulatory powers and real, formalised access to the electricity industry. Regional authorities and sector insiders were marginalised. Arrears and debts were cleared. While formal channels were used to boost state capacity in this way, Chubais and his team complemented them with informal channels of access and participation to achieve results. At the highest level, Putin supported both reform and foreign operations. The state reduced its direct engagement in electricity and increased its indirect regulatory powers through market institutions. To the extent that the reform gave companies almost free access to electricity markets in substantial parts of the country, the state now had far greater capacity to support complex economic organisations. For the state, electricity reform was a process resulting in an indirect relationship, structured through market regulation, with the electricity industry. State organisations became more specialised, with a clearer delineation between policymaking and administrative functions. This extended to ownership, which in the electricity sector was now more specialised, also among state companies. But while markets and companies were now further removed from the state's reach, the state retained control of a substantial part of the sector indirectly via ownership ties.

Inter RAO passed to Rosatom in the course of the reform, but it also came into the orbit of the regime through Sechin's involvement. The later reform stages, after the dissolution of RAO UES and the creation of a wholesale market for electricity, progressed only slowly and partially. The financial crisis reduced the prospects for further growth, and for private investment. The crisis delayed privatisation of state-owned companies like Inter RAO. But state control and oversight also changed, as a result of policy change. When Chubais in 2012 commented on the Energy Ministry's weakness in putting its regulatory powers to use, he unwittingly provided an example of precisely the type of regime influence exercised through the state-owned majors in the electricity sector after 2010. The 2008 reform had enabled the state to exert property rights, and thereby empowered the regime. Subsequent developments showed that the government's ability to create and implement policy was again undercut by informal networks at the top of the elite. Between 2012 and 2015, state access to Inter RAO became more complicated, due to the increasing power of Rosneftegaz. Sechin and Rosneftegaz had direct access to Putin, while the government had fewer channels to Rosneftegaz. Because of this, it was difficult for the government to participate in the development of the company. To a considerable extent, dividends were channelled into economic development projects outside the state budget.

The electricity switch was used as a tool at an early stage to recover post-Soviet electricity debts. With a subsidiary for cross-border electricity trade, Inter RAO, RAO UES's management ensured that foreign operations continued relatively unaffected by reform. Inter RAO expanded, partly shielded from formal hierarchies within and without RAO UES. Informality and personal trust were at the heart of the company's operations until well into

2006. Informality seems to have enabled a sharing of electricity rents with host country businessmen, in Moldova almost openly. When Inter RAO survived intact in the post-reform era, it was because it was a state tool in the post-Soviet region. For a few more years, it maintained dependence on Russia in the post-Soviet electricity sector, by virtue of its ubiquitous role in enabling electricity development across the region. At times, Inter RAO acted as the carrot and enabler to Gazprom's stick (see Chapter 7). Inter RAO seemed to accept its role as instrument of foreign policy, after 2008 as well, when it directed some of its rents at foreign policy goals to invest in distant electricity sectors of variable commercial merit. But this lasted only until Rosneftegaz gained access to its dividends. From then on, Russia was first priority for Inter RAO.

Notes

1 Put into use following the 8th All-Russian Congress of Soviets in Moscow on 22–23 December 1920, which passed the plan for electrification of the whole country (Plan GOELRO).
2 UES is used here, as it corresponds to the most frequent English name for the company RAO UES. *Edinaya energeticheskaya sistema* is abbreviated EES in Russian. United Power System (UPS) is the most frequent translation of EES in the electricity industry.
3 Electricity grids that are connected operate synchronously, meaning that their speed and frequency match. After disconnection, they have to be brought back to exact synchronisation to exchange power.
4 Unbundling refers to the separation of different business lines of a previously integrated company. Ownership unbundling occurs when a company, often a monopoly, is divested of previously integrated assets through legislation. The aim is usually to create more competitive markets.
5 Two electricity grids operated in isolation: the Central Asian grid, which included southern, but not northern Kazakhstan, and the (Far) Eastern grid.
6 An overview of reform legislation is found at http://www.fsk-ees.ru/about/reform/ (in Russian).
7 The synchronous grid of Continental Europe was known as UCTE until 1 July 2009, when it was reorganised as the European network of Transmission System Operators (ENTSO-E).
8 As electricity trade can be effected through high-voltage, synchronous or non-synchronous DC interlinks/interconnectors, export does not necessarily depend on synchronisation.
9 Moldova TPP is sometimes known as Cuciurgan/Kuchurgan, like the adjacent lake. The Russian term for thermal power plant is GRES, originally an abbreviation of *gosudarstvennaya raionnaya elektrostantsiya*, meaning state regional power plant. The correct modern term is *gidroretsirkulyatsionnaya elektrostantsiya*, meaning hydro-recycling power plant. Many thermal power plants are designed for more than one fuel, with different boilers and the possibility of switching fuels depending on price and availability.
10 Razdan in Russian.
11 Initialised by Russia, Iran and India in 2002. Azerbaijan joined in 2005.
12 In Russian: NP Sovet rynka, https://www.np-sr.ru/
13 The date for unbundling and privatisation was at the time of Inter RAO's expansion in the process of being pushed forward to 2007–2008.

14 An open switch for high current circuits, now generally replaced by closed safety switches.
15 As it later emerged, they were well placed to acquire other assets. In particular, Rappoport and Vladimir Avetisyan, upon unbundling director of a substantial part of RAO UES's generation assets, took control of lesser companies in non-core industries (in e.g. power engineering). Before reform such assets appeared less interesting. After reform they were merged into major companies in their own right. RAO UES's financial advisor, Troika Dialog, organized the financial side of the equity transfers (Shmagun et al., 2019).
16 Gidro-OGK was established in 2004 as part of the electricity reform and later renamed to RusHydro (RusGidro in Russian). Dod left RusHydro unexpectedly, and again involuntarily, in August 2015. He was arrested on charges of fraud, connected to subsequent work with a RusHydro subsidiary, in July 2016.
17 GruzRosEnergo in Russian.
18 In Armenian the slogan was "Voch t'alanin", meaning "No robbery".
19 Manas was an airbase until 2009, when a renewed bilateral agreement between the US and Kyrgyzstan changed its status to a transit centre.

References

Anex, R.P. (2002) "Restructuring and privatizing electricity industries in the Commonwealth of Independent States", *Energy Policy*, 30 (5): 397–408

ARKA News Agency (2012a) "Pravitel'stvo Armenii odobrilo dosrochnoe prekrashchenie dogovora s 'INTER RAO EES' o doveritel'nom upravlenii AES [The government of Armenia approved early termination of the agreement on management of the NPP by 'Inter RAO UES']" [online]. 1 March (Yerevan: ARKA News Agency). Available from: http://arka.am/ru/news/business/pravitelstvo_armenii_odo brilo_dosrochnoe_prekrashchenie_dogovora_s_inter_rao_ees_o_doveritelnom_upra/ [Accessed 25 October 2018]

ARKA News Agency (2012b) "Glava Rosatoma ne schitaet neobkhodimym uchastie Rossii v upravlenii Armyanskoi AES [The head of Rosatom does not find it necessary for Russia to take part in the management of the Armenian NPP]" [online]. 7 February (Yerevan: ARKA News Agency). Available from: http://arka.am/ru/news/economy/gla va_rosatoma_ne_schitaet_neobkhodimym_uchastie_rossii_v_upravlenii_armyanskoy_ aes_/ [Accessed 25 October 2018]

ARKA News Agency (2015) "Deloitte & Touche says the rise of electricity in Armenia is justified" [online]. 30 September (Yerevan: ARKA News Agency). Available from: http://arka.am/en/news/technology/deloitte_touche_says_rise_of_electricity_ in_armenia_is_justified/ [Accessed 22 October 2018]

Avakyan, S. (2014) "Odisseya ZAO 'Elektricheskie seti Armenii' [The Odyssey of the private limited company 'Electric networks of Armenia']" [online]. 10 March (Yerevan: Hetq.am). Available from: https://hetq.am/ru/article/33072 [Accessed 22 October 2018]

Babich, D. (1997) "Boris Nemtsov razbiraetsya s RAO 'EES Rossii' [Boris Nemtsov investigates RAO EES of Russia]" *Nezavisimaya gazeta*, 9 April, p.1

Bekker, A. (1997) "Gosudarstvo reabilitiruet sebya v pravakh na RAO 'EES' [The state reinstates its entitlement to RAO EES]" *Segodnya*, 15 January

Bekker, A. (2003) "V pol'zu RAO EES [To the benefit of RAO UES]" *Vedomosti*, 7 August

Berger, M. and Proskurnina, O. (2008) *Krest Chubaisa [Chubais's Cross]* (Moscow: KoLibri)

Blagov, S. (2006) "China eyes Russia, Central Asian states as source of cheap electricity" *Eurasia Daily Monitor*, 26 June
Bol'shakov, S. and Ishmukhammetov, F. (2007) "Kazakhstan prizval AES k rasplate [Kazakhstan calls on AES for payment]" *Kommersant*, 6 October, p.5
Bruce, C. and Yafimava, K. (2009) "Moldova's gas sector" in Pirani, S. ed., *Russian and CIS Gas markets and their impact on Europe* (Oxford: Oxford University Press for the Oxford Institute for Energy Studies), pp.170–202
Burlak, S. (2005) "Voina kak sposob otvlecheniya ot revolyutsii. Voiska i voennaya tekhnika styagivayutsya po obe storony Dnestra [War as a distraction from revolution. Troops and military equipment assemble on both sids of the Dnestr]" *Nezavisimaya gazeta*, 21 February, p.12
Butrin, D. and Rudenko, G. (2004) "Ukrainskikh energetikov sberegut ot rossiiskikh kolleg putem aresta imushchestva [Ukrainian energy business is protected from Russian colleagues through property confiscation]" *Kommersant*, 17 March, p.16
Butrin, D. et al. (2003) "Ukraina pozhertvovala vitse-prem'erom posle ego vystupleniya protiv rossiiskogo TEKa [Ukraine sacrifices the deputy prime minister after his statements on the Russian energy sector]" *Kommersant*, 8 December, p.13
Chubais, A. (2003) "Missiya Rossii v XXI veke [Russia's mission in the 21st century]" *Nezavisimaya gazeta*, 1 October, p.1
Civil.ge (2003) "AES sells Telasi to Russian UES" [online]. 1 August (Tbilisi: Civil.ge). Available from: https://old.civil.ge/eng/article.php?id=4685 [Accessed 25 October 2018]
Civil.ge (2004) "Ex-energy minister on trial" [online]. 3 November (Tbilisi: Civil.ge). Available from: https://old.civil.ge/eng/article.php?id=8249 [Accessed 25 October 2018]
Civil.ge (2009) "Russia, Georgia to jointly manage Enguri Power Plant" [online]. 12 January (Tbilisi: Civil.ge). Available from: http://old.civil.ge/eng/article.php?id=20257 [Accessed 12 October 2018]
Civil.ge (2011) "EIB Lends Georgia EUR 20 mln for Enguri HPP" [online]. 7 January (Tbilisi: Civil.ge). Available from: http://old.civil.ge/eng/article.php?id=23025 [Accessed 12 October 2018]
Crane, K., Peterson, D.J. and Oliker, O. (2005) "Russian Investment in the Commonwealth of Independent States", *Eurasian Geography and Economics*, 46 (6): 405–444
Datamonitor (2009) *Electricity in Russia – October 2009*. Industry Profile. (New York/London/Frankfurt/Sydney: Datamonitor)
Decree No. 426 (28/04/1997) *Ob osnovnykh polozheniyakh strukturnoi reformy v sferakh estestvennykh monopolii [On the basic provisions for structural reform in the spheres of the natural monopolies]* (Moscow: President of the Russian Federation)
Decree No. 688 (21/05/2012) *O vnesenii izmenenii v perechen' strategicheskikh predpriyatii i strategicheskikh aktsionernykh obshchestv, utverzhdennii Ukazom Prezidenta Rossiiskoi Federatsii ot 4 avgusta 2004 g. No. 1004 [On changes to the list of strategic enterprises and shareholding companies, established by Presidential Decree no. 1004 from 4 August 2004]* (Moscow: President of the Russian Federation)
Decree No. 695 (22/05/2012) *O merakh po privatizatsii nakhodyashchikhsya v federal'noi sobstvennosti paketov aktsii krupneishikh kompanii toplivno-energeticheskogo kompleksa [On measures for the privatisation of state-held stocks in the largest companies of the fuel and energy complex]* (Moscow: President of the Russian Federation)
Decree No. 721 (01/07/1992) *Ob organizatsionnykh merakh po preobrazovaniyu gosudarstvennykh predpriyatii, dobrovol'nykh ob"edinenii gosudarstvennykh predpriyatii v aktsionernye obshchestva [On the organisational measures to convert state enterprises,*

The electricity industry 77

voluntary associations of state enterprises into shareholding companies] (Moscow: President of the Russian Federation)

Decree No. 889 (25/07/1998) *O merakh po snizheniyu tarifov na elektricheskuyu energiyu* [*On measures to reduce electricity tariffs*] (Moscow: The President of the Russian Federation)

Decree No. 922 (14/08/1992) *Ob osobennostyakh preobrazovaniya gosudarstvennykh predpriyatii, ob"edinenii, organizatsii toplivno-energeticheskogo kompleksa v aktsionernye obshchestva* [*On the specificities of the conversion of state enterprises, associations and organisations in the fuel and energy complex into shareholding companies*] (Moscow: The President of the Russian Federation)

Decree No. 923 (15/08/1992) *Ob organizatsii upravleniya elektroenergeticheskim kompleksom Rossiiskoi Federatsii v usloviyakh privatizatsii* [*On the organisation of management of the electricity complex of the Russian Federation during the privatisation process*] (Moscow: President of the Russian Federation)

Decree No. 1009 (04/08/2004) *Ob utverzhdenii perechnya strategicheskikh predpriyatii i strategicheskikh aktsionernykh obshchestv* [*On the approval of a list of strategic enterprises and strategic shareholding companies*] (Moscow: President of the Russian Federation)

Decree No. 1285 (11/09/2012) *O merakh po zashchite interesov Rossiiskoi Federatsii pri osushchestvlenii rossiiskimi yuridicheskimi litsami vneshneekonomicheskoi deyatel'nosti* [*On measures to protect the interests of the Russian Federation when foreign economic activity is carried out by a Russian juridical person*] (Moscow: President of the Russian Federation)

Decree No. 1334 (05/11/1992) *O realizatsii v elektroenergeticheskoi promyshlennosti Ukaza Prezidenta Rossiiskoi Federatsii ot 14 avgusta 1992 g. N 922 "Ob osobennostyakh preobrazovaniya gosudarstvennykh predpriyatii, ob"edinenii, organizatsii toplivno-energeticheskogo kompleksa v aktsionernye obshchestva"* [*On the realisation of Decree no. 922, issued on 14 August 1992 by the President of the Russian Federation "On the specificities of the conversion of state enterprises, associations and organisations in the fuel and energy complex into shareholding companies" in the electricity industry*] (Moscow: President of the Russian Federation)

Derbilova, E. and Panyushkin, V. (2007) "'Khochu na pensiiu' – Anatolii Chubais, predsedatel' pravleniya RAO 'EES Rossii' ['I would like to retire' – Anatolii Chubais, head of management at RAO UES of Russia]" *Vedomosti*, 4 October

Derbilova, E., Tsukanov, I. and Pis'mennaya, E. (2012) "'Ne vozvrashchaites' k bylym vozlyublennym' – Anatolii Chubais, predpravleniya 'Rusnano', eks-predpravleniya RAO 'EES Rossii' ['Don't return to old sweethearts', says Anatolii Chubais, CEO of Rusnano and former CEO of RAO UES]" *Vedomosti*, 15 November, p.5

Dokukina, K. (2012) ""Rezervov dlya rosta tsen uzhe net" – Aleksandr Starchenko, predsedatel' nablyudatel'nogo soveta "Soobshchestva pokupatelei rynkov elektronenergii" ['There are no longer reserves for price increases', says Aleksandr Starchenko, head of the Association of Buyers in Electricity Markets' Monitoring Council]" *Vedomosti*, 13 August

Dzaguto, V. (2009a) "Igor' Sechin vzyskal dolg s Tadzhikistana [Igor Sechin recovers debt from Tajikistan]" *Kommersant*, 27 April, p.11

Dzaguto, V. (2009b) "Tadzhikistan vklyuchil Ural v elektricheskuyu skhemu [Tajikistan includes the Urals in its electricity schedule]" *Kommersant*, 7 April, p.11

Dzaguto, V. (2010a) ""Inter RAO" pogloshchaet gosudarstevennye aktivy [Inter RAO swallows state equity]" *Kommersant*, 1 October, p.9

Dzaguto, V. (2010b) "Rossiya tyanet seti k Pakistanu [Russia draws lines to Pakistan]" *Kommersant*, 19 August, p.9

Dzaguto, V. (2010c) "'Inter RAO' vozvrashchaetsya na Blizhnyi Vostok [Inter RAO returns to the Middle East]" *Kommersant*, 2 June, p.11

Dzaguto, V. (2011) "Rossiya tyanet LEP na sebya [Russia draws a power line for itself]" *Kommersant*, 24 January, p.9

Dzaguto, V. (2016) "Pravila igry v suverennye fondy Rossii menyayutsya [The rules of the game of Russia's sovereign wealth funds are changing]" *Kommersant*, 27 December, p.7

Dzaguto, V. and Grishkovets, E. (2011) "'Inter RAO' otkazalos' ot malogo [Inter RAO denies itself little]" *Kommersant*, 13 May, p.12

Dzaguto, V. and Skorlygina, N. (2013) "Den'gi 'Inter RAO' otpravyat v Kirgiziyu [Inter RAO's money will be sent to Kyrgyzstan]" *Kommersant*, 18 February, p.11

Dzaguto, V. and Dyatel, T. (2017) "'Rusgidro' slivaetsya iz armyanskikh GES [Rushydro flows away from Armenian hydropower plants]" *Kommersant*, 23 April, p.11

Dzaguto, V., Netreba, P. and Zanina, A. (2012) "Igoryu Sechinu otklyuchayut elektrichestvo [Electricity is turned off for Igor Sechin]" *Kommersant*, 21 September, p.1

Dzaguto, V., Fomicheva, A. and Mel'nikov, K. (2013) "Igor' Sechin nachal sborku 'Inter RAO' [Igor Sechin begins to assemble Inter RAO]" *Kommersant*, 6 December, p.11

Dzyadko, T. (2013) "Sechin vozvrashzhetsya v energetiku [Sechin return to electricity]" *Vedomosti*, 13 May

Dzyadko, T. and Ivankina, E. (2014) "Sechin blokiruet 'Inter RAO' [Sechin blocks Inter RAO]" *RBK Daily*, 20 January, p.1

Egorova, T. (2005) "Interv'yu: Anatolii Chubais, predsedatel' pravleniya RAO 'EES Rossii': 'Gosudarstvo – plokhoi sobstvennik' [Interview: Anatolii Chubais, chairman of RAO UES's management: 'The state is a poor owner']" *Vedomosti*, 22 November

Egorova, T. (2006a) "Interv'yu: Andrei Rappoport, predsedatel' pravleniya Federal'noi setevoi kompanii [Interview. Andrei Rappoport, general manager of the Federal Grid Company]" *Vedomosti*, 14 February

Egorova, T. (2006b) "Rubil'nik dlya 'Gazproma' [A knife switch for Gazprom]" *Vedomosti*, 14 February

Egorova, T. and Gavrish, O. (2003) "Kuchma ispugalsya RAO UES [Kuchma scared of RAO UES]" *Vedomosti*, 22 December

Egorova, T., Gavrish, O. and Nikol'skii, A. (2003) "RAO idet po provodam [RAO follows the power lines]" *Vedomosti*, 5 December

Ekonomika i zhizn' (1996) "Zerkalo [Mirror]" *Ekonomika i zhizn'*, 24 August

Elektricheskie seti Armenii (2013) *Godovoi otchet 2012 [Annual report 2012]*. (Yerevan: ENA/Electric Networks of Armenia)

Embassy Chisinau (2007) Moldovan energy woes, 07CHISINAU1520/Wikileaks #135844. Issue date 28 December 2007. *Cablegate* [online]. (Published by Wikileaks 1 September 2011). Available from: https://search.wikileaks.org/plusd/cables/07CHISINAU1520_a.html [Accessed 30 June 2019]

Embassy Chisinau (2008) Russian energy giant completes takeover of Moldovan Power Plant In Transnistria, 08CHISINAU846/Wikileaks #166724. Issue date 20 August 2008. *Cablegate* [online]. (Published by Wikileaks 1 September 2011). Available from: https://search.wikileaks.org/plusd/cables/08CHISINAU846_a.html [Accessed 30 June 2019]

Engoian, A. (2006) "Industrial and institutional restructuring of the Russian electricity sector: Status and issues" *Energy Policy*, 34 (17): 3233–3244
Fadeeva, A. (2018) "Dolgie provoda [Long lines]" *RBK Daily*, 4 July, p.12
Fadeeva, A. and Serkov, D. (2018) "Popalas' na donbasskikh setyakh [Caught on the Donbass grids]" *RBK Daily*, 25 June, pp.1, 3
Fankhauser, S. and Tepic, S. (2007) "Can poor consumers pay for energy and water? An affordability analysis for transition countries" *Energy Policy*, 35 (2): 1038–1049
Federal Law No. 35 (26/03/2003) *Ob elektroenergetike* [*On electricity*] (Moscow: The Federal Assembly)
Federal Law No. 36 (26/03/2003) *Ob osobennostyakh funktsionirovaniya elektroenergetiki v perekhodnyi period i o vnesenii izmenenii v nekotorye zakonodatel'nye akty Rossiiskoi Federatsii i priznanii utrativshimi silu nekotorykh zakonodatel'nykh aktov Rossiiskoi Federatsii v svyazi s prinyatiem Federal'nogo zakona 'Ob elektroenergetike'"* [*On the specificities of the functioning of the electricity system in the transition period and on the entering of alterations in some legislative acts of the Russian Federation and the declaration as invalid of some legislative acts of the Russian Federation in connection with the passing of the Federal law 'On electricity'*] (Moscow: The Federal Assembly)
Fialko, A., Mazneva, E. and Chechel', A. (2010) "Koval'chuk sobiraet aktivy [Kovalchuk gathers assets]" *Vedomosti*, 26 May
FSK (Federal'naya Setevaya Kompaniya) (2018) "*Istoriya otrasli* [*The history of the sector*]" [online]. (Moscow: Federal'naya setevaya kompaniya). Available from: http://www.fsk-ees.ru/about/history_industry/ [Accessed 10 October 2018]
Gabuev, A. (2009) "Predvaritel'naya nedogoverennost' [A preliminary lack of agreement]" *Kommersant*, 25 February, p.8
Gabuev, A. and Konstantinov, A. (2011) "Poka idet zaderzhka v otnosheniyakh, mesto zanimayut drugie [While [our] relations are held up, others take [our] place]" *Kommersant*, 4 August, p.6
Gabuev, A. and Karabekov, K. (2011) "Otnosheniya s Kirgiziei postavleny na zhidkuyu osnovu [Relations with Kyrgyzstan on a liquid basis]" *Kommersant*, 18 November, p.8
Gaddy, C.G. and Ickes, B.W. (2002) *Russia's Virtual Economy* (Washington, DC: Brookings Institution Press)
Gaidar, E. and Chubais, A. (2008) *Ekonomicheskie zapiski* [*Notes on the economy*] (Moscow: Rossiiskaya politicheskaya entsiklopediya ROSSPEN)
Gamova, S. (2004) "Pereuchet [Stocktaking]" *Novye izvestiya*, 18 October, p.1
Gamova, S. (2007) "Obmenyali Pasata na kilovatty [Pasat exchanged for kilowatts]" *Nezavisimaya gazeta*, 18 July 2007, p.1
Gamova, S. and Krashakov, A. (2006) "Kompromissnyi kilovatt. Moldaviya gotova ustupit' "Gazpromu" elektroseti v obmen na deshevyi gaz [Kilowatt compromise. Moldova ready to give up its power grid to Gazprom in return for cheap gas]" *Nezavisimaya gazeta*, 5 April, p.3
Gazeta (2003) "Chubais predlozhil Voloshinu postoyannuyu rabotu [Chubais offered Voloshin a regular job]" *Gazeta*, 31 October, p.2
Georgian Industrial Group (2016) "*International company, affiliated with the Georgian Industrial Group, as a part of international investors consortium has acquired shares in the holding company of energy company 'Mtkvari'*" [online]. 2 June (Tbilisi: Georgian Industrial Group). Available from: http://www.gig.ge/?newsid=17 [Accessed 12 October 2018]
Gleason, G. (2004) "Russian companies propose debt-equity swaps in Central Asia" *Eurasia Daily Monitor*, 11 October

Glumskov, D. and Grib, N. (2004) "Tadzhikistan ne rastratil energiyu vpustuyu [Tajikistan did not spend its energy unnecessarily]" *Kommersant*, 18 October, p.13

Gordienko, A. and Orlova, N. (2005) "Kocharyan izmenyaet Rossii. Chast' svoego otpuska neprimirimyi borets s Kremlem Mikhail Saakashvili provedet na Sevane v kompanii armyanskogo prezidenta [Kocharyan betrays Russia. The uncompromising campaigner against the Kremlin, Mikhail Saakashvili, will spend part of his holiday on the Sevan in the company of the Armenian president]" *Nezavisimaya gazeta*, 19 August, p.1

Gorelov, N. (2001) "MAP interesuetsya provodami. Atomshchiki prodolzhayut sporit' s RAO 'EES Rossii' [MAP is interested in grids. The nuclear business continues its conflict with RAO UES]" *Vremya novostei*, 22 August, p.5

Gorelov, N. (2003) "Energeticheskii kart-blansh [Carte blanche in energy]" *Vremya novostei*, 15 January, p.1

Gorelov, N. (2004) "Elektrichestvo v obmen na vodu. RAO 'EES' zhelaet postroit' elektrostantsii v Kirgizii [Electricity in return for water. RAO UES wants to build power stations in Kyrgyzstan]" *Vremya novostei*, 23 August, p.8

Gorelov, N. (2006) "Eksportno-importnoe napryazhenie [Export-import tension]" *Vremya novostei*, 19 December, p.8

Gorelov, N. (2007a) "Moldavskii transit [Moldavian transit]" *Vremya novostei*, 16 July, p.8

Gorelov, N. (2007b) "Premiya s chetvertoi popytki [Bonus at fourth attempt]" *Vremya novostei*, 25 June, p.8

Gorelov, N. (2008a) "Pro eksport zabyli [They forgot about export]" *Vremya novostei*, 3 July, p.7

Gorelov, N. (2008b) "Elektricheskoe bratstvo [Electric brotherhood]" *Vremya novostei*, 5 March, p.8

Gorelov, N. (2008c) "Tadzhikskie nepriyatnosti [Tajik troubles]" *Vremya novostei*, 21 January, p.8

Gotova, N. (1997) "Anatolii D'yakov, kazhetsya, smirilsya s MVF [Anatolii D'yakov is apperently reconciled with IMF]" *Segodnya*, 9 April

Gotova, N. (2003) "Gruzinskii pokhod Chubaisa [Chubais's Georgian campaign]" *Profil'*, 11 August, pp.28–29

Granik, I. (2010) "Rossiya i Kazakhstan zaklyuchili atomnye soglasheniya [Russia and Kazakhstan conclude nuclear agreements]" *Kommersant*, 6 July

Gray, D. (1995) *Reforming the energy sector in transition economies*. World Bank Discussion Papers. 296. (Washington, DC: The World Bank)

Grib, N. (2003) "Belorusskie energetiki perekinuli most v Evropu [The Belarussian power sector throw out a bridge to Europe]" *Kommersant*, 4 February, p.15

Grib, N. (2004) "'Belenergo' torgovalsya nedolgo [Belenergo did not bargain for long]" *Kommersant*, 13 April, p.16

Grib, N. and Dar'in, A. (2006) "Moldaviyu rasschitali po-evropeiski [Moldova given a European bill]" *Kommersant*, 29 May, p.14

Grib, N. and Kornysheva, A. (2006) "'Inter RAO EES' gotova pereimenovat'sya v 'Gazpromenergo' [Inter RAO ready to change name to Gazpromenergo]" *Kommersant*, 29 June, p.14

Grib, N., Grishkovets, E. and Gavrish, O. (2006) "'Inter RAO EES' kupit elektroenergiyu na Ukraine v obmen na turkmenskii gaz [Inter RAO buys electricity in Ukraine in return for Turkmen gas]" *Kommersant*, 2 October, p.17

Grigoryan, A. (2015a) "Sale of Armenia's monopoly electricity distributor confirmed" *Eurasia Daily Monitor*, 14 October

Grigoryan, A. (2015b) "Planned electricity fee increase may revive protest movement in Armenia" *Eurasia Daily Monitor*, 12 June

Grigoryan, A. (2015c) "Yerevan electricity protests reach Climax" *Eurasia Daily Monitor*, 29 June

Grigoryan, A. (2016a) "Armenia, Georgia, Russia and Iran plan to expand energy cooperation" *Eurasia Daily Monitor*, 4 January

Grigoryan, A. (2016b) "Russian factor remains critical for Armenia's regional projects" *Eurasia Daily Monitor*, 1 March

Grishkovets, E. (2008a) "Pravila igry [The rules of the game]" *Kommersant*, 30 April, p.13

Grishkovets, E. (2008b) "'Inter RAO' gotovo torgovat'sya [Inter RAO is ready to trade]" *Kommersant*, 7 May, p.9

Grishkovets, E. (2008c) "'Inter RAO' voshlo v Moldavskuyu GRES dvazhdy [Inter RAO entered Moldova GRES twice]" *Kommersant*, 31 July 2008, p.10

Grishkovets, E. (2009) "Moi vnutrennii golos davno uzhe ne obmanyvaet menya" [My inner voice has not failed me for a long time]" *Kommersant*, 26 June, p.1

Grishkovets, E. (2010a) "Pravila igry pereklyuchaet rukovoditel' gruppy TEK Ekaterina Grishkovets [The rules of the game as interpreted by the head of the Fuel and Energy Group Ekaterina Grishkovets]" *Kommersant*, 12 January, p.7

Grishkovets, E. (2010b) "Ne bylo takogo, chtoby nas ne slyshali [It hasn't happened that we weren't heard]" *Kommersant*, 21 December, p.13

Grishkovets, E. (2011) "Dmitrii Medvedev vklyuchil svet Belorussii [Dmitrii Medvedev turns the light on for Belarus]" *Kommersant*, 4 July, p.5

Grishkovets, E. and Gavrish, O. (2006) "'Inter RAO EES' vyshlo na Ukrainu [Inter RAO goes to Ukraine]" *Kommersant*, 21 August, p.6

Grishkovets, E. and Dar'in, A. (2006) "Moldaviya oboidetsya bez rossiiskoi energii [Moldova makes do without Russian electricity]" *Kommersant*, 7 June, p.15

Grishkovets, E. and Ravinskii, V. (2008) "'Inter RAO EES' podryadilas' na stroiku Rogunskoi GES [Inter RAO contracts to the building of Rogun hydropower plant]" *Kommersant*, 2 July, p.10

Grishkovets, E. and Solov'ev, V. (2008) "Rossiya vozvrashchaetsya na Rogunskuyu GES [Russia returns to Rogun hydropower plant]" *Kommersant*, 6 June, p.14

Grishkovets, E. and Dzaguto, V. (2009) "Glava 'RusGidro' pomozhet 'Inter RAO' potratit' $2 mlrd [The head of RusHydro helps Inter RAO to spend $2 bn]" *Kommersant*, 24 November, p.9

Grishkovets, E., Dzaguto, V. and Popov, V. (2008a) "'Inter RAO' vernulo moldavskii rynok [Inter RAO recovers the Moldavian market]" *Kommersant*, 24 December, p.17

Grishkovets, E., Dzaguto, V. and Solov'ev, V. (2009) "'Inter RAO' voidet v gruzinskie vody [Inter RAO enters Georgian waters]" *Kommersant*, 13 January, p.11

Grishkovets, E. et al. (2008b) "Igor' Sechin pribavil v moshchnosti [Igor Sechin puts on power]" *Kommersant*, 6 October, p.1

Gubenko, O. (2002) "Svet – na prodazhu. RAO 'EES Rossii' sostavilo eksportnye plany [Light for sale. RAO UES assembles export plans]" *Izvestiya*, 28 December, p.5

Gudim, A. et al. (2003) *Research paper on Transnistria* (Chisinau: Center for Strategic Studies and Reforms)

Gularidze, T. (2003a) "Georgian authorities, UES Chief pledge for cooperation" [online]. 7 August (Tbilisi: Civil.ge). Available from: http://old.civil.ge/eng/article.php?id=4724 [Accessed 9 October 2018]

Gularidze, T. (2003b) "Tbilisi would have electricity, for the time being…" [online]. 11 February (Tbilisi: Civil.ge). Available from: https://old.civil.ge/eng/article.php?id=3167 [Accessed 25 October 2018]

Gularidze, T. (2003c) "AES, Georgian government locked in battle" [online]. 28 February (Tbilisi: Civil.ge). Available from: https://old.civil.ge/eng/article.php?id=3264 [Accessed 25 October 2018]

Gustafson, T. (2012) *Wheel of Fortune. The battle for oil and power in Russia* (Cambridge, MA/London: The Belknap Press of Harvard University Press)

Hakobyan, A. (2003) "Armenia's light and protection?" *Transitions Online*, 7 November

Hashimova, U. (2017) "Uzbekistan and Kyrgyzstan undertake resolving their water disputes" *Eurasia Daily Monitor*, 17 October

IEA (2003) *Regulatory reform review of Russia: Background on the electricity sector* (Paris: International Energy Agency)

Inter RAO (2006) *Godovoi otchet 2005 [Annual report 2005]* (Moscow: Inter RAO)

Inter RAO (2009a) *Godovoi otchet 2008 [Annual report 2008]* (Moscow: Inter RAO)

Inter RAO (2009b) "*Sobranie aktsionerov OAO 'Inter RAO EES' rassmotrit vopros provedeniya dopemissii v pol'zu Vneshekonombanka, FAUGI i GK 'Rosatom'* [*Inter RAO's shareholder meeting will consider the question of an additional share issuing in favour of Vneshekonombank, FAUGI and Rosatom State Corporation*]" [online]. 1 June 2009 (Moscow: Inter RAO). Available from: http://www.interrao.ru/press-center/news/?ELEMENT_ID=659 [Accessed 29 November 2011]

Inter RAO (2010a) "*Import elektroenergii [Electricity import]*" [online]. n.d. (Moscow: Inter RAO). Available from: http://www.interrao.ru/activity/traiding/exporteng/ [Accessed 12 January 2010]

Inter RAO (2010b) *Godovoi otchet 2009 [Annual report 2009]* (Moscow: Inter RAO)

Inter RAO (2011a) "Struktura aktsionernogo kapitala [Capital structure]" [online]. n.d. (Moscow: Inter RAO). Available from: http://www.interrao.ru/company/capital/ [Accessed 28 November 2011]

Inter RAO (2011b) *Godovoi otchet OAO "Inter RAO EES" za 2010 god [Annual report for Inter RAO UES in 2010]* (Moscow: Inter RAO)

Inter RAO (2011c) "INTER RAO UES and RusHydro close Sevan-Razdan cascade sale in Armenia" [online]. 24 March (Moscow: Inter RAO). Available from: http://www.interrao.ru/en/press-center/news/detail.php?ID=441 [Accessed 22 October 2018]

Inter RAO (2011d) "INTER RAO UES Board of Directors approves corporate development Strategy till 2015 with an outlook till 2020" [online]. 20 January (Moscow: Inter RAO). Available from: http://www.interrao.ru/en/press-center/news/detail.php?ID=387 [Accessed 22 October 2018]

Inter RAO (2011e) "Inter RAO establishes representative office in the Middle East" [online]. 13 February (Moscow: Inter RAO). Available from: http://www.interrao.ru/en/press-center/news/detail.php?ID=385 [Accessed 15 October 2018]

Inter RAO (2014) *Godovoi otchet OAO "Inter RAO EES" za 2013 god [Annual report for Inter RAO UES in 2013]* (Moscow: Inter RAO)

Inter RAO (2015) *Godovoi otchet OAO "Inter RAO EES" za 2014 god [Annual report for Inter RAO UES in 2014]* (Moscow: Inter RAO)

Inter RAO (2018a) "Strategiya razvitiya Gruppy 'Inter RAO' na period do 2020 g. [Inter RAO Group's development strategy to 2020]" [online]. (Moscow: Inter RAO). Available from: http://www.interrao.ru/strategy/ [Accessed 22 October 2018]

Inter RAO (2018b) *Inter RAO EES. 2017. Godovoi otchet* [*Inter RAO UES. 2017. Annual report*] (Moscow: Inter RAO)
Inter RAO (2018c) "Zarubezhnyi biznes [Foreign business]" [online]. (Moscow: Inter RAO). Available from: http://www.interrao.ru/activity/foreignact/ [Accessed 15 October 2018]
Ispolatov, S. (2010a) "Vpered v proshloe [Forward to the past]" *RBC Daily*, 26 May
Ispolatov, S. (2010b) "'Inter RAO' zaberet ne vse [Inter RAO does not get it all]" *RBC Daily*, 11 August
Ivanov, N. (1998) "Boris Brevnov i Anatolii D'yakov – kvity [Boris Brevnov and Anatolii D'yakov are quits]" *Segodnya*, 30 January
Ivzhenko, T. (2005) "Kiev boitsya prodeshevit'. Rossiiskie oligarkhi nachali bor'bu za ukrainskuyu energetiku [Kyiv is afraid of selling too cheap. Russian oligarchs have started their fight for Ukrainian electricity]" *Nezavisimaya gazeta*, 27 April, p.3
Kaiser, M.J. (2000) "Pareto-optimal electricity tariff rates in the Republic of Armenia" *Energy Economics*, 22 (4): 463–495
Khrennikov, I. (2006) "Imperiya na vydan'e [A marriageable empire]" *Forbes*, 3 January
Kiselev, V. and Panfilova, V. (2005) "Konets sveta v otdel'noi vzyatoi strane. Rossiiskie energetiki ne soshlis' s moldavskimi kollegami v tsene [The end of light in a single country. The Russian energy people did not agree about a price with their Moldovan colleagues]" *Nezavisimaya gazeta*, 11 November, p.5
Kjærnet, H. (2007) "En smak av egen medisin: Aserbajdsjans russlandsstrategi [A taste of its own medicine: Azerbaijan's Russia strategy]", *Nordisk Øst-Forum*, 21 (4): 457–474
Klasson, M. (2000) "Energeticheskaya tyaga [The thrust of energy]" *Vremya MN*, 25 October, p.4
Klasson, M. (2001) "Chubais vvodit za Uralom osoboe polozhenie [Chubais introduces a state of emergency on the other side of the Urals]" *Vremya MN*, 8 February, p.3
Klasson, M. (2003) "Chubais podnimaet energetiku Gruzii [Chubais raises Georgia's energy]" *Vremya MN*, 7 August, p.1
Knyazev, V. and Reznik, I. (2000) "Tyumenskaya oblast'. Poltora milliarda pod zemlei [Tymen' oblast'. One and a half billion under the turf]" *Kommersant-Vlast*, 5 December, p.59
Kolesnikov, A. (2008) *Anatolii Chubais. Biografiya* [*Anatolii Chubais. A biography*] (Moscow: AST)
Kommersant-Vlast' (2005) "Fevral' bez revolyutsii [February without revolution]" *Kommersant-Vlast'*, 31 January
Kommersant (1994) "Press-konferentsiya RAO [RAO's press conference]" *Kommersant*, 16 December
Kommersant (2008) "Aleksandr Voloshin pokinul energetiku [Aleksandr Voloshin leaves energy]" *Kommersant*, 6 October
Kommersant (2009) "Plany 'Inter RAO' [Inter RAO's plans]" *Kommersant*, 26 June
Kornysheva, A. (2003) "Prezident prinyal otchet Anatoliya Chubaisa o zime [The president received Anatolii Chubais's winter report]" *Kommersant*, 8 December, p.2
Kravchenko, E. (2003) "'Mirnyi atom' v rukakh Chubaisa. Armyanskuyu AES peredayut v upravlenie rossiiskomu energokholdingu ['The peaceful atom' in Chubais's hands. The Armenian nuclear power plant is being transferred to the Russian power holding's management]" *Izvestiya*, 8 July, p.5
Kurronen, S. (2006) "Russian electricity sector – reform and prospects", *BOFIT Online*, 2006 (6). Available from: https://helda.helsinki.fi/bof/bitstream/handle/123456789/12518/128145.pdf [Accessed 5 April 2020]

Latukhina, K. (2007) "Chubais dal otvet Putinu [Chubais replies to Putin]" *Vedomosti*, 18 December
Levinskii, R. (2005) "RAO EES i 'Gazprom' snova vmeste [RAO UES and Gazprom back together]" *Vedomosti*, 6 April
Libman, A. and Kheifets, B.A. (2007) "Korporativnaya model' regional'noi ekonomicheskoi integratsii [The corporate model of regional economic integration]", *Mirovaya ekonomika i mezhdunarodnye otnosheniya*, 2007 (3): 15–22
Litvinov, A. (2004) "Alyuminievye sapogi [Aluminium boots]" *Gazeta*, 18 October, p.2
Maksimov, V. (2001) "RAO EES sdaet eksport [RAO UES hands over export]" *Vedomosti*, 31 October
Marat, E. (2008a) "Need for more transparency in Kyrgyz and Tajik energy sectors to avoid future crises" *Eurasia Daily Monitor*, 19 December
Marat, E. (2008b) "Tajik government asks for contributions to build Rogun hydropower station" *Eurasia Daily Monitor*, 1 May
Marat, E. (2010) "Will Tajikistan successfully construct Rogun?" *Eurasia Daily Monitor*, 26 January
Mazaeva, O. (2004) "Kuplyu elektroenergiyu bez posrednikov. Minsk ishchet al'ternativnykh postavshchikov v obkhod Moskvy [I will buy electricity without intermediaries. Minsk is looking for alternative suppliers to Moscow]" *Nezavisimaya gazeta*, 18 February, p.5
Mazneva, E. (2008) "Glavnyi po setyam [The head of the grids]" *Vedomosti*, 2 December
Mazneva, E. (2010) "Doroga v Kazakhstan [The road to Kazakhstan]" *Vedomosti*, 3 March
Medvedeva, E. (2006) "'Inter RAO' vne zakona [Inter RAO outside the law]" *Vedomosti*, 19 December
Medvedeva, E. (2007a) "'U nas nastoyashchaya tekhnicheskogo revolyutsiya' – Andrei Rappoport, predsedatel' pravleniya Federal'noi setevoi kompanii ['We are undergoing a genuine technological revolution' – Andrei Rappoport, management chair at the Federal Grid Company]" *Vedomosti*, 27 December
Medvedeva, E. (2007b) "'Dochka' na vyrost [A 'daughter' to bring up]" *Vedomosti*, 17 January
Mel'nikov, K. (2012) "Gosudarstvo rasprodast TEK sebe [The state will sell the fuel and energy complex to itself]" *Kommersant*, 25 May, p.1
Melkumyan, S. (2002) "Ottok energii [Energy exodus]" *Novye izvestiya*, 1 August, p.4
Mirkadyrov, R. and Gordienko, A. (2004) "Predprodazhnyi vzryv. Nakanune vizita Chubaisa v Baku Azerbaidzhan okazalsya na grani energeticheskogo krizisa [A presell burst. Before Chubais's visit to Baku, Azerbaijan finds itself on the border of a power crisis]" *Nezavisimaya gazeta*, 25 May, p.1
Mishneva, R., Grib, N. and Butrin, D. (2004) "'EES Rossii' ne nashlos' mesta na Ukraine [No room for Russia's UES in Ukraine]" *Kommersant*, 29 January, p.13
Movsesyan, G. (2005) "S Chubaisom na vek. RAO 'EES' budet upravlyat' armyanskimi energosetyami 99 let [With Chubais for a century. RAO UES will manage the Armenian electricity grid for 99 years]" *Vremya novostei*, 25 July, p.7
Murtazaev, E. (1995) "Dolgi energetikam rastut so skorost'yu 700 mln dollarov v mesyats [Electricity debts rise by 700 million dollars a month]" *Segodnya*, 20 December
Museum for the History of the Northwest Power Industry (2014) "D'yakov Anatolii Fedorovich" [online]. *Muzei istorii energetiki severo-zapada (OAO TGK-1)*. Available from: http://energomuseum.ru/persons/dyakov_anatoliy_fyedorovich_/ [Accessed 26 September 2014]

Museum of the Urals Power Industry (2018) "Tsentral'noe dispetcherskoe upravlenie EES SSSR [The central control authority of the United Power System of the USSR]" [online]. *Muzei energetiki Urala*. Available from: http://musen.ru/chronicle/1969/ [Accessed 9 October 2018]

Naumova, A. and Grivach, A. (2004) "Opasnyi tranzit. Eksport gaza cherez Belorussiyu vyshel na pik riska [Dangerous transit. Gas export through Belarus reaches highest risk]" *Vremya novostei*, 18 February, p.7

Nevezhin, Yu. (1996) "Obrashchenie energetikov k pravitel'stvu [The electricity sector employees' address to the government]" *Izvestiya*, 20 December

Nevezhin, Yu. (1997) "Chto budet s RAO EES? [What will become of RAO EES?]" *Izvestiya*, 10 April

Newbery, D.M. (1994) "Restructuring and privatizing electric utilities in Eastern Europe", *Economics of Transition*, 2 (3): 291–316

OAO Inter RAO (OAO Sochinskaya GES) (2008) *Godovoi otchet 2007 [Annual Report 2007]* (Sochi: Inter RAO)

OECD/IEA (2005) *Russian electricity reform. Emerging challenges and opportunities.* (Paris: The Organisation for Economic Co-operation/the International Energy Agency)

Oganesyan, L. (2009) "Elektroenergiya – eto i valyuta, i politicheskie dividendy [Electricity is hard currency as well as political dividends]" *Golos Armenii*, 10 November

Oilcapital.ru (2012) "Reiting vliyaniya krupnykh predprinimatelei i top-menedzherov toplivno-energeticheskogo kompleksa v dekabre 2012 g. [Rating of the influence of major businessmen and top managers in the fuel and energy complex, December 2012]" [online]. 6 December (Moscow: IG Industriya). Available from: https://oilcapital.ru/news/companies/06-12-2012/reyting-vliyaniya-krupnykh-predprinimateley-i-top-menedzherov-tek-v-dekabre-2012-g [Accessed 18 March 2019]

Oilcapital.ru (2016) "Reiting vliyaniya krupnykh predprinimatelei i top-menedzherov toplivno-energeticheskogo kompleksa v marte 2016 g. [Rating of the influence of major businessmen and top managers in the fuel and energy complex, March 2016]" [online]. 29 March (Moscow: IG Industriya). Available from: https://oilcapital.ru/news/companies/29-03-2016/reyting-vliyaniya-krupnykh-predprinimateley-i-top-menedzherov-toplivno-energeticheskogo-kompleksa-v-marte-2016-g [Accessed 20 February 2019]

Orozobekova, C. (2016) "Kyrgyzstan's capacity to meet its CASA-1000 obligations comes under question" *Eurasia Daily Monitor*, 26 May

Panchenkova, M. and Starinskaya, G. (2016) "Nevedomoe bogatstvo [Unknown riches]" *Vedomosti*, 25 October, pp.1, 12

Panfilova, V. (2008a) "Privatizatsiya po-kirgizski [Privatisation Kyrgyz style]" *Nezavisimaya gazeta*, 4 February, p.17

Panfilova, V. (2008b) "Moskva sdelala predlozhenie Dushanbe [Russia gave Dushanbe an offer]" *Nezavisimaya gazeta*, 28 November, p.5

Panfilova, V. (2009) "Dushanbe pred'yavit Moskve schet [Dushanbe gives Russia the bill]" *Nezavisimaya gazeta*, 20 February, p.1

Panfilova, V. (2011) "Predvybornyi triuk Bishkeka [Bishkek's pre-election trick]" *Nezavisimaya gazeta*, 12 April, p.6

Patel, S. (2013) "The Russian Power Revolution" *Power*, 157 (1): 44–49

Peretolchina, A. (2008) "Po puti v Rumyniyu [On the road to Romania]" *Vedomosti*, 31 July

Peretolchina, A. and Derbilova, E. (2011) "Prigovor reforme [A sentence for reform]" *Vedomosti*, 18 March, p.1

Petlevoi, V., Derbilova, E. and Peschinskii, I. (2015) "Igor' Sechin – eto moi starshii tovarishch [Igor Sechin is my older friend]" *Vedomosti*, 4 July, p.12

Podobedova, L. and Milyukova, Ya. (2016) "Investitsii vmesto dividendov [Investment instead of dividends]" *RBK Daily*, 15 April, p.16

Polyakova, A. (2010) "Baku i Tbilisi khotyat soedinit' Vostok s Zapadom [Baku and Tbilisi want to unite East and West]" *Georgia Times*, 26 July

Polyanskii, N. (2001) "Svet i teni energosistemy Armenii. Pochemu vlasti respubliki otvergayut vygodnye predlozheniya rossiiskoi storony [The light and shadows of Armenia's energy system. Why the republic's authorities reject the Russian side's profitable offers]" *Nezavisimaya gazeta*, 7 April, p.5

Popşoi, M. (2016) "Are Moldovan consumers financing Transnistrian separatism?" *Eurasia Daily Monitor*, 21 April

Popşoi, M. (2017) "Moldova-Ukraine energy deal upsets Russia by cutting Transnistria out" *Eurasia Daily Monitor*, 3 April

Prikhodko, N. (2000) "Elektroenergiya kak energiya mirotvorchestva. Kishinev i Tiraspol' sposobny sovmestno reshat' ekenomicheskie voprosy [Electricity as peacemaking power. Chisinau and Tiraspol can decide on economic issues together]" *Nezavisimaya gazeta*, 19 December, p.5

Pulina, N. (2000) "Astana i Moskva dogovorilis' [Astana and Moscow have made a deal]" *Nezavisimaya gazeta*, 20 January

RAO UES (1997) *Godovoi otchet OAO RAO EES 1996 [RAO UES Annual Report 1996] [electronic version]* (Moscow: RAO UES)

RAO UES (1998) *Godovoi otchet OAO RAO EES 1997 [RAO UES Annual Report 1997] [electronic version]* (Moscow: RAO UES)

RAO UES (1999) *Godovoi otchet OAO RAO EES 1998 [RAO UES Annual Report 1998] [electronic version]* (Moscow: RAO UES)

RAO UES (2000) *Godovoi otchet OAO RAO EES 1999 [RAO UES Annual Report 1999] [electronic version]* (Moscow: RAO UES)

RAO UES (2001) *Godovoi otchet OAO RAO EES 2000 [RAO UES Annual Report 2000] [electronic version]* (Moscow: RAO UES)

RAO UES (2003) *Godovoi otchet OAO RAO EES 2002 [RAO UES Annual Report 2002]* (Moscow: RAO UES)

Recknagel, C. (2013) *"Promises, promises: Moscow's record of broken aid pledges"* [online]. 17 December (Prague: Radio Free Europe/Radio Liberty). Available from: https://www.rferl.org/a/russia-promises-aid-unfilled/25203488.html [Accessed 15 October 2018]

Reznik, I. and Egorova, T. (2006) "'Gazprom' vmesto RAO EES [Gazprom instead of RAO UES]" *Vedomosti*, 10 April

RFE/RL (2006) "RFE/RL Newsline" 26 January

Rosneftegaz (2014) *Godovoi otchet otkrytogo aktsionernogo obshchestva "Rosneftegaz" za 2013 god [Annual Report for the open shareholding company Rosneftegaz for 2013]* (Moscow: OAO Rosneftegaz)

Rosneftegaz (2015) *Godovoi otchet otkrytogo aktsionernogo obshchestva "Rosneftegaz" za 2014 god [Annual Report for the open shareholding company Rosneftegaz for 2014]* (Moscow: OAO Rosneftegaz)

Rossiiskaya gazeta (1999) "Dokhodov – nul', zato Mersedesov – kucha [Zero income and a heap of Mercedeses]" *Rossiiskaya gazeta*, 17 November

Rybal'chenko, I. and Razumovskii, K. (2001) "Ukraina khochet poluchat' energiyu RAO 'EES Rossii' [Ukraine wishes to rceive energy from Russia's RAO UES]" *Kommersant*, 16 August, p.4

Sabonis-Helf, T. (2007) "The unified energy systems of Russia (RAO-UES) in Central Asia and the Caucasus: nets of interdependence", *Demokratizatsiya*, 15 (4): 429–444

Shmagun, O. et al. (2019) "Koshelek rossiiskoi elity. Kak ustroena ofshornaya imperiya 'Troiki Dialog'. Rassledovanie OCCRP [The wallet of the Russian elite. How Troika Dialog's offshore empire was set up. An OCCRP investigation]" *Meduza.io*, 4 March

Sikamova, A. and Efimov, A. (2003) "Chubaisa v Gruzii ne zhdali. Pokupka RAO 'EES Rossii' znachtel'noi chasti gruzinskoi energosistemy vyzvala volnu protestov v Tbilisi [Chubais was not expected in Georgia. RAO UES's acquisitions of a considerable share of the Georgian power system caused a wave of protest in Tbilisi]" *Nezavisimaya gazeta*, 7 August, p.3

Siluyanova, P. (2003a) "Elektroshok dlya Eduarda Shevardnadze [An electric shock for Eduard Shevardnadze]" *Gazeta*, 7 August, p.8

Siluyanova, P. (2003b) "Bor'ba. 'Rosenergoatom' snizhaet eksport [Struggle. Rosenergoatom decreases export]" *Gazeta*, 11 August, p.8

Siluyanova, P. (2004a) "Plany. 'My igraem v kapitalizatsiyu' [Plans. 'We are working on capitalisation']" *Gazeta*, 7 September, p.11

Siluyanova, P. (2004b) "Oblom. Anatolii Chubais proigryvaet match [Failure. Anatolii Chubais loses a game]" *Gazeta*, 17 March, p.10

Siluyanova, P. (2004c) "Ekspansiya. Politicheskii rubil'nik [Expansion. A political knife-switch]" *Gazeta*, 7 September, p.11

Siluyanova, P. (2005) "Sdelka. Na svoi strakh i risk [Deal. At one's own risk]" *Gazeta*, 2 February, p.9

Simonyan, Yu. (2009) "Nepriznannaya Inguri GES [The unrecognised Enguri hydropower plant]" *Nezavisimaya gazeta*, 20 January, p.1

Skorlygina, N. (2014) "'Rosneftegaz' zaplatit za Kirgiziyu v obmen na aktsii 'RusGidro'" *Kommersant*, 14 March, p.12

Skorlygina, N. and Dzaguto, V. (2012) "'Inter RAO' slivaet dolgi Laosa [Inter RAO merges Laos's debts]" *Kommersant*, 22 February, p.9

Skyner, L. (2010) "The reform of the Russian power sector: the rhetoric and reality", *Europe-Asia Studies*, 62 (8): 1383–1402

Smirnov, K. (2000) "Dvenadtsat' [The twelve]" *Kommersant-Vlast'*, 11 July, p.16

Smirnov, K. (2002) "Prezident predlozhil zamorozit' zakon [The president suggested to freeze the law]" *Kommersant*, 14 January 2002, p.3

Smirnov, K. (2004) "Ot administratsii k elektrifikatsii [From administration to electricification]" *Kommersant-Den'gi*, 29 March

Solanko, L. (2011) *How to succeed with a thousand TWh reform? Restructuring the Russian power sector*. FIIA Working Paper. 68. (Helsinki: The Finnish Institute of International Affairs)

Solanko, L. (2014) "Securing electricity supply for a growing economy" in Oxenstierna, S. and Tynkkynen, V.-P. ed., *Russian energy and security up to 2030* (Abingdon: Routledge) pp.129–149

Solov'ev, V. (2006) "Respublika Polurussiya [The Semirussian republic]" *Kommersant-Vlast'*, 10 April, pp.52–56

Solov'ev, V. and Dzaguto, V. (2017) "Moldaviya perekhodit na ukrainskie vatty [Moldova transfers to Ukrainian watts]" *Kommersant*, 3 April, p.1

88 The electricity industry

Solov'ev, V. and Grishkovets, E. (2008) "Vakhsh vlivaetsya v rossiiskuyu energetiku [Vakhsh flows into Russian electricity]" *Kommersant*, 23 July, p.6

Solov'ev, V. and Popov, V. (2007) "Nevol'nik mesti [A slave of revenge]" *Kommersant*, 10 July, p.10

Stalker, A. (1995) "Ekonomicheskaya integratsiya v SNG [Economic integration in the CIS]" *Kommersant*, 27 May

Stanovaya, T. (2016) "Ideal'naya zhertva: kto stoit za presledovaniem Doda? [The ideal victim: Who is behind the persecution of Dod?]" *Republic*, 23 June

Startseva, A. (2003) "Chubais Plans 'Aggressive' Expansion in CIS" *The Moscow Times*, 9 September, p.5

Stepanenko, S. (2003) "Chem bol'she svyazuyushchikh zven'ev, tem krepche sotrudnichestvo [The more connecting links, the stronger the cooperation]" *Vremya novostei*, 18 July, p.5

Stepanenko, S. and Gorelov, N. (2001) "I vashim i nashim. Rossiiskie i ukrainskie energetiki nikak ne dogovaryatsya [For yours and ours. Russian and Ukrainian power sector people cannot agree in any way]" *Vremya novostei*, 5 April, p.5

Sterkin, F. and Mazneva, E. (2011) "Ravnoudalenie kompanii [The equidistancing of companies]" *Vedomosti*, 4 April

Suvorova, N. (2004) "Rossiya pokupaet SSSR [Russia is buying the USSR]" *Versiya*, 6 September

TGK-1 (2012) *Godovoi otchet OAO TGK-1 2011 [Annual report OAO TGK-1 2011]* (St. Petersburg: TGK-1)

The Moscow Times (2009) "Inter RAO's Dod tapped for RusHydro" *The Moscow Times*, 23 November

Tompson, W. (2004) *Restructuring Russia's Electricity Sector: Towards Effective Competition or Faux Liberalisation?* OECD Economics Department Working Papers. 403. (Paris: OECD Publishing)

Tovkailo, M., Derbilova, E. and Lyutova, M. (2012) "Sechin protiv Medvedeva [Sechin against Medvedev]" *Vedomosti*, 12 January

Tregubova, E. (2000) "Vlast' dolzhna byt' zhestkoi [The powers should be tough]" *Kommersant-Vlast'*, 1 August

Turanov, S. (2006) "50 naibolee vliyatel'nykh predprinimatelei i investorov [The 50 most influential businessmen and investors]" *Nezavisimaya gazeta*, 28 July, p.11

Ul'yanov, V. (2015) "Tainy pridnestrovskogo dvora [The secrets of the Transistrian Court]" *Voenno-promyshlennyi kur'er*, 25 November, p.4

Urikhanyan, A. (2001) "Pereraspredelenie topliva i kapitala v pol'zu Rossii [The redistribution of fuel and capital in favour of Russia]" *Vremya MN*, 24 October, p.3

Vardul', N. (2003) "Molchat' [Stay silent]" *Kommersant*, 28 October, p.1

Varfolomeyev, O. (2015) "Ukraine turns to Russia in energy crisis" *Eurasia Daily Monitor*, 12 January

Varfolomeyev, O. (2017) "Ukraine moves to integrate its power grid with European network" *Eurasia Daily Monitor*, 12 July

Vasil'ev, I.V. (2012) "Otchet o rezul'tatakh kontrol'nogo meropriyatiya 'Proverka organizatsii tamozhennogo kontrolya pri peremeshchenii cherez tamozhennuyu granitsu Rossiiskoi' Federatsii tovarov po liniyam elektroperedachi, formirovaniya kontraktnykh tsen, pravil'nosti ischisleniya, polnoty i svoevremennosti uplaty tamozhennykh platezhei v 2009–2010 godakh i istekshem periode 2011 goda' [Account of the results of the control measure 'Control of the organisation of customs control of the movement of goods across the customs border of the Russian

Federation on electricity transmission lines, of contract price formation, correct calculation, full and timely duty payments in 2009–10 and to date in 2011']" *Byulleten' Schetnoi' palaty Rossii'skoi' Federatsii*, February, pp.45–69

Vedeneeva, A. (2018) "'Lider' posylayut na 'Zvezdu' [Lider will be sent to Zvezda]" *Kommersant*, 28 July, p.1

Vedomosti (2008) "Vektor. Svobodnyi vybor [Vector. Free choice]" *Vedomosti*, 28 July

Vignanskii, M. (2003) "Chubais snyal ministra energetiki Gruzii. David Mirtskhulava ne vyderzhal obvinenii v prorossiiskoi orientatsii [Chubais removed the Georgian energy minister. David Mirtskhulava could not stand up to accusations of being pro-Russian]" *Vremya novostei*, 13 August, p.2

Vin'kov, A. (2005) "Attraktsion shchedrosti [The attraction of generosity]" *Ekspert*, 31 October, pp.28–30

Vin'kov, A. (2008) "Gosudarstvo – eto ty! [You are the state]" *Ekspert*, 14 January, pp.28–31

Vorotynskii, I. (2000) "Sto dnei dlya energetiki [A hundred days in energy]" *Nezavisimaya gazeta*, 15 February

Vostochnaya energeticheskaya kompaniya (2018) "*Istoriya [History]*" [online]. (Blagoveshchensk: Vostochnaya energeticheskaya kompaniya). Available from: http://eastern-ec.ru/about_company/history/ [Accessed 12 October 2018]

Wengle, S.A. (2012) "Engineers versus managers: experts, market-making and state-building in Putin's Russia" *Economy and Society*, 41 (3): 435–467

Wengle, S.A. (2014) *Post-Soviet power. State-led development and Russia's marketization* (Cambridge/New York: Cambridge University Press)

WNA (2018) "Nuclear power in Armenia" [online]. March 2018 (London: World Nuclear Association). Available from: http://www.world-nuclear.org/information-library/country-profiles/countries-a-f/armenia.aspx [Accessed 12 October 2018]

Yakoreva, A. (2016) "Chernaya dyra s polovinoi trilliona. Skol'ko deneg skopil 'Rosneftegaz' [A black hole with half a billion. How much money Rosneftegaz accumulated]" *Republic (Slon)* 1 November

Yur'ev, S. (2018) "Shpionskie igry Kariny Tsurkan [Karina Tsurkan's espionage games]" *Moskovskii Komsomolets*, 24 July, p.1

Zaets, I. (2003) "Medvedev v perevode na ukrainskii – eto Medvedchuk. Zachem glava putinskoi administratsii ezdil v Kiev i vstrechalsya s Kuchmoi? [Medvedev in Ukrainian is Medvedchuk. Why did the head of Putin's administration travel to Kyiv and meet Kuchma?]" *Nezavisimaya gazeta*, 18 December, p.1

Zateichuk, M. (2007) "Firtashu nuzhna energiya [Firtash needs energy]" *Vedomosti*, 7 November

Zhelenin, A. (2005) "Tushi svet! [Turn off the lights!]" *Russkii kur'er*, 25 July, p.6

Zhelenin, A. (2007) "Astana proshchaet Bishkeku dolgi [Astana remits Bishkek's debts]" *Nezavisimaya gazeta*, 13 July, p.8

Zvyagin, V. (2004) "Raznost' potentsialov ili potentsial raznykh [Differences in potential or the potential of being different]", *Mirovaya energeticheskaya politika*, 2003 (4): 50–54

4 The nuclear energy industry
Minatom/Rosatom

This chapter analyses the relations of the Russian nuclear energy industry, organised under the umbrella of Minatom (1992–2004)/Rosatom (2004–), and the state. The study of the electricity sector in Chapter 3 shows how, in the 1990s, informal rent sharing and informal institutions in Russia continued to have bearings on relations with the post-Soviet region. When, in the 2000s, the state initiated formal institutional change towards indirect management and increased formal rent sharing, this also extended into the post-Soviet region. The increases in state capacity that followed reform made it possible to maintain an asymmetric energy dependence on Russia and use it as a foreign policy tool. In the nuclear energy industry, too, the Russian state and companies in the industry interacted over foreign policy and foreign operations to the extent that they participated in institutional development at home. Once post-Soviet states placed nuclear energy development back on the agenda following the post-Chernobyl, post-breakup downturn, they faced the reality of depending on Russia for technological development. Nuclear industry development in Ukraine and Kazakhstan was not a Russian priority. However, as Russia's state capacity increased, it was possible to use asymmetric dependence to influence, and limit, nuclear industry development in those states. When they undertook to broaden their range of international industry contacts in response, Russia's approach was to minimise their possibilities to pursue such cooperation. Dependence on Rosatom for nuclear energy, and for technological development, was a foreign policy tool that could be harnessed in the aim of promoting Russia as a great power.

Rosatom is a holding company for the Russian nuclear energy industry. Rosatom's civilian side, the nuclear energy industry, comprises several companies united under Atomenergoprom, a subsidiary holding company.[1] The Rosatom subsidiaries relevant to this study are those involved in the nuclear fuel cycle (overview below) and the construction and operation of nuclear power plants (NPP) in post-Soviet states: Atomredmetzoloto/ARMZ, Uranium One (from 2013), Tekhsnabeksport/Tenex, TVEL, and Atomstroieksport (from 2016 ASE). The uranium holding ARMZ[2] is one of the world's five leading uranium mining companies and unites all of

Rosatom's uranium and raw materials assets in Russia. Uranium One in 2013 became Rosatom's subsidiary for uranium mining outside Russia. Tekhsnabeksport[3] is the world's largest supplier of uranium conversion services and enriched uranium, and holds a 40 per cent share of the global market in enrichment services for fuel purposes. The fuel company TVEL has 17 per cent of the world nuclear energy market, producing and selling nuclear fuel to many countries. Russia holds approximately 45 per cent of global enrichment capacity (EURATOM Supply Agency, 2018). Atomstroieksport/ASE[4] is a leading supplier of nuclear power stations to the world market.[5]

Following the consolidation of Rosatom as a state corporation in 2007, it went through a period of significant growth. Turnover[6] increased from 498 billion rubles in 2010 to 967.4 billion rubles in 2017 (Rosatom, 2013, p.309; 2018b, p.11), and in 2017 Rosatom was Russia's 13th largest company by turnover (RBK, 2018). Export is important to overall turnover, and increasingly so. While in 2010, nuclear energy exports contributed approximately 29 per cent to Rosatom's overall turnover, this had increased to 33 per cent in 2012 (Dzaguto, 2011a; Rosatom, 2013, p.134). In 2016, all foreign operations, including, but not restricted to those related to energy, contributed 47 per cent of Rosatom's turnover (Rosatom, 2017, p.43). Energy is the most important part of Rosatom's civilian production. In 2010, the nuclear energy industry contributed 78.4 per cent of Rosatom's turnover (Dzaguto, 2011a). Increasing domestic electricity tariffs and an increasing share of global uranium production, as well as international sales of nuclear power plants and their fuel, were the main contributors to Rosatom's revenue. State funding through the budget has always been important to Minatom/Rosatom, but other incomes contribute. In the 1990s, this was the sale of stockpiled uranium to global markets. In the 2000s, nuclear fuel and technology exports mattered. Following the electricity reform in 2008, electricity tariffs became more important, and especially the mandatory surcharges earmarked for the nuclear energy industry.

The nuclear fuel cycle and the nuclear energy industry

The nuclear fuel cycle refers to all the stages of nuclear energy production. Natural uranium is mainly U-238, with a small concentration of the fissile U-235. Following the mining and purification of uranium ore, natural uranium is processed into U_3O_8 (yellowcake), then converted to uranium hexafluoride (UF_6 or hex). This is followed by enrichment. Low enriched commercial uranium (LEU) usually has a 3–5 per cent concentration of U-235 sufficient for use in NPPs, while highly enriched uranium (HEU) has a 20 per cent or higher concentration of U-235, though weapons grade uranium has even higher concentrations. Fuel production follows, when the fuel is pressed into pellets and stacked inside rods. The rods are assembled and placed inside nuclear reactors[7] at NPPs, where they generate steam for the turbines to generate electricity. In the last stage of the cycle, spent nuclear fuel (SNF) is most often stored as waste (open cycle), but it can also be reprocessed (closed cycle). In the latter case, fissile material is recovered and reprocessed into fresh fuel. While this reduces the amount of high-level waste, the resulting fuel is expensive. Five per cent of the world's natural uranium is currently (2016 and 2017) produced in Russia.

The nuclear energy industry is skills and research intensive, extremely risk averse, and requires substantial investment (Stulberg and Fuhrmann, 2013, p.2). Establishing or phasing out nuclear power is a major political decision with long-term implications. The industry's origins, in parallel with the development of nuclear weapons, has served to further amplify its political significance. For this reason, as well as reasons of safety, it is highly controlled and subject to strict monitoring. Uranium trade was traditionally opaque and cartel-like. This began to change in the 1990s, but markets remain fragmented and different from that of other commodities. The global nuclear energy industry is highly concentrated, with very few suppliers of the full range of services from construction and fuel to waste disposal. Fuel is often obtained directly from producers using long term contracts. Many utilities acquire uranium directly from producers, contracting different companies for different stages of the fuel cycle.

The break-up of the Soviet Union and Soviet legacies

Until 1986, the Soviet military and civilian nuclear industries belonged to Minsredmash, the Ministry for Medium Machine-Building[8] (Cooper, 1991, p.7, 17; Perera, 1997, pp.14–16, 35–40). Following the Chernobyl disaster of May 1986, there were attempts to restructure the nuclear industry, but it remained overblown, inefficient, and unsafe (Kudrik et al., 2004, pp.25–26). When foreign trade was reorganised in 1988, the nuclear industry acquired control of official foreign trade in nuclear materials, conducted through Tekhsnabeksport. In 1992, the Russian segments of the civilian nuclear industry were reconstituted by decree as the Nuclear Energy Ministry, Minatom (Decree No. 61, 1992). Minatom had ministerial policy-making, planning and executive powers, with no clear delineation of military and civilian divisions of the nuclear sector (Decree No. 61, 1992; Bukharin, 1995). Minatom had little ability to design specific policies for the different parts of the nuclear industry. Enterprises involved in the nuclear fuel cycle formed specialised companies directly subordinate to Minatom. Until around 2000, personnel from the Soviet period dominated industry development. For example, the Minister for Medium Machine-Building for 1986–1989, Lev Ryabev, returned as first deputy minister in 1993 and remained there until 2002.

Keeping afloat and muddling through

The new nuclear industry companies, including TVEL, ARMZ, Tekhsnabeksport and Atomstroieksport, evaded the disruptive privatisations of the early 1990s. Nuclear power plants also remained on state hands (Palamarchuk et al., 2001, p.53). This was a close escape. From 1993, a select number of enterprises subordinate to Minatom could be partially privatised, apart from sensitive institutes and factories (Decree No. 446, 1993). In this process, licensing requirements and state stakes or golden shares[9] benefited company directors and industry insiders (Kudrik et al., 2004, p.26; Jeppesen, 2006, pp.20–25; Pappe and Drankina, 2007). TVEL and Atomredmetzoloto, state "concerns" from 1991, were ripe for privatisation (Kadosov, 1992b). Their subsidiaries were slipping out of their control, often as a result of local action to take control of export streams (Kuznetsov et al., 2006, p.25). Even in the nuclear energy industry, where the state had an obvious interest in retaining control, fragmentation and insider privatisation had an impact.

In this situation, privatisation could have started a process of differentiation of state and private organisations. The reality in the nuclear energy sector became instead a grey zone at the state's fringes, with only partial access for central state organisations and a struggle for control between industry hands and regions. This struggle, not government policy, shaped institutional development. The hierarchy of state institutions was upended. Private gain and informal relations proliferated, blurring the boundaries between state and non-state.

Tekhsnabeksport provides one example of a privatisation effort that did not in the event succeed. In 1995, a handful of major banks and investors were allowed to take control of state-owned minority stakes as collateral for fresh loans to the Russian state. The arrangement was known as "loans for shares" (Treisman, 2010), and it was to have a lasting impact on Russia's political economy. Importantly here, it allowed major businessmen, or in some cases company insiders, to obtain a share of the companies' informal rent streams. In the event, they acquired the actual stakes when the state defaulted on its debts in 1996. The fuel service export company Tekhsnabeksport was placed on the first list of companies up for auction (*Segodnya*, 1995b). This may have been the result of efforts by Oneksimbank, which belonged to Mikhail Prokhorov and Vladimir Potanin. The bank was seen to be close to Chubais (Pelekhova, 1998b). Due to its control of export streams, Tekhsnabeksport channelled significant rent streams. After an auction without bidders, possibly due to Minatom's effort to reverse the process (Pelekhova, 1998b), Tekhsnabeksport was placed on a list of strategic enterprises and withdrawn from further auctions (*Segodnya*, 1995a).

Insiders could pursue informal privatisation in other ways, as seen in the case of TVEL. Vitalii Konovalov, the former Soviet nuclear energy industry minister (1989–1991), was central to TVEL's establishment in 1991–1992. However, along with other insiders, he also created a duplicate, the TVEL

Concern (Belyaninov, 2001; Kuznetsov et al., 2006, pp.25, 35). It positioned itself as the legal successor to the state-owned TVEL (Proskuryakov and Buran, 1994, p.51). TVEL was at this point being reorganised from a Minatom department into a joint-stock company (Decree No. 166, 1996). Ahead of its incorporation in 1996, it experienced severe cash-flow constraints (Perera, 1997, p.115), creating a need for the TVEL Concern's services. Notwithstanding the incorporation of the state-owned TVEL, the private company survived until Konovalov was forced to resign in September 2000 (Proskuryakov and Buran, 1994; Belyaninov, 2001). The TVEL Concern supplied Ukraine and other states with nuclear fuel for several years (Osetinskaya and Shcherbakova, 2001). By taking control of export, TVEL Concern could coordinate uranium sales and associated rent streams. This channelled rents from exports back into the industry and made it possible to keep it afloat. But some of these rent streams were likely channelled to a diverse group of claimants, creating vested interests in the arrangement. Central actors in this process, including Konovalov, emphasised how this situation resulted from their efforts to save nuclear fuel production from disintegration from below and foreign takeover (Proskuryakov and Buran, 1994; Kuznetsov et al., 2006, pp.25, 35, 38). Konovalov came under investigation by the Public Prosecutor in the mid-1990s, but was never charged (Belyaninov, 2001). The Security Ministry was unable to ascertain the full extent of the illegal trade in uranium in the early 1990s, according to then Deputy Prime Minister Sergei Stepashin (Belyaninov, 2001). Konovalov remained important in TVEL and within the industry also after his resignation.

The state's lack of control of the nuclear energy industry in the 1990s reflected the lack of state capacity. Minatom, like Minsredmash before it, was not wholly under government control, and ruled by protective industry veterans. It survived on informal rent streams. Several subsidiaries, especially TVEL and Tekhsnabeksport, enjoyed considerable autonomy. There was a hierarchical relationship between ministry and enterprises, but less real control. This was somewhat mitigated by the presence of company directors, i.e. of TVEL, on the Minatom collegium (Government Order No. 775, 1992; Government Resolution No. 175, 1992 (1993)).

The industry's informal rent streams came from uranium sales. The Soviet Union officially entered international uranium markets in 1990. Scientists and other insiders were then already engaged in an informal trade of nuclear material, often bartered in exchange for laboratory equipment, or for a cut of proceeds. In 1991 and 1992, foreign trade relations multiplied, officially through Tekhsnabeksport, and unofficially through minor channels (Mikhailin, 1995). Foreign trade companies in the nuclear industry started doing deals outside the sector (Zotova, 1992; Kravchenko, 1994). Due to the absolute nature of the nuclear non-proliferation regime, a state's nuclear energy relations can come into doubt if there is suspicion of any grey areas in contacts with other states. This lack of state control became a foreign policy problem. Contact with Iran, established in 1992, was initiated by the nuclear industry (*Kommersant*, 1992). It got out of hand in 1995, when Nuclear Energy Minister Viktor Mikhailov (1992–1998) signed a protocol of intent with Teheran on a Russian-built Iranian centrifuge plant for uranium enrichment (Orlov, V.A. and Vinnikov, 2005, p.52). Neither the president nor the Ministry of Foreign Affairs (MFA) had been consulted. The protocol was quickly cancelled (Orlov, V.A. and Vinnikov, 2005, p.52). An uncontrolled establishment of contacts between the Russian nuclear industry followed under Mikhailov's successor, Evgenii Adamov (1998–2001), and Iran (Stenin, 2005). Similar situations occurred with India, Syria and Libya (Khripunov, 2001, p.54).[10]

By 1994, non-payments and deferred salary payments were a regular occurrence in the Russian nuclear industry (*Segodnya*, 1994; Popov, 1995; Alieva, 1998), as well as in Ukraine (Kovynev, 2017). To address nuclear safety and non-proliferation, it was essential to retain trained personnel in their jobs and provide them with income. To this end, the Russian nuclear energy industry pursued a wide range of partnerships with foreign agencies and companies (Serov, 1997; Yamshchikov et al., 1998; Kudrik et al., 2004). There was a sense of urgency, which gave Russia an unexpected competitive advantage amid global industry difficulties. Global demand for uranium, enrichment services and nuclear fuel remained depressed after Chernobyl. But Russian stockpiled uranium was relatively cheap, and even more so Russian labour and expertise.

International collaboration, and especially the significant US–Russian Megatons to Megawatts programme,[11] saved the industry from collapse at a time when "people weren't paid their wages", as Mikhailov remarked (Perera, 1997, p.42; Koroleva, 2006). According to Konovalov, nuclear fuel sales abroad were the sector's only source of income and covered "less than half" of its costs (Alieva, 1998). In 1997, Minatom earned 2.2 billion US$ on its foreign (hard currency) contracts (Volchko, 1998). Megatons to Megawatts alone was worth 8 billion US$ over its lifetime (Centrus Energy Corp., 2018). To avoid US anti-dumping procedures, Russia's foreign trade in nuclear materials and uranium often involved middlemen (Kadosov, 1992a; Lavr, 1992). But when the uranium trade, including what was conducted under international collaboration programmes, was effectuated by Minatom's subsidiaries, there was a danger of undermining government control of the industry. There was ample opportunity for informal rent streams and embezzlement (Pavlov, 1998), including in Tekhsnabeksport (Kats, 1999). Minatom under Mikhailov refused to put a stop to this, in defiance of government orders (Bogatykh, 1999). Minatom's informal rent streams protected it from central state interference. The state lacked the capacity to upend this arrangement.

The trade collapse

Within the Soviet Union, all enrichment enterprises and a significant share of the nuclear fuel cycle enterprises were located on Russian territory. Russia had about 80 per cent of former Minsredmash enterprises. However, the most profitable uranium reserves were in Kazakhstan[12] and Uzbekistan, and there was some production in Ukraine. Yellowcake and fuel pellet production took place in Kazakhstan. Intra-regional trade in nuclear cycle goods collapsed with the Soviet break-up.

Demand for nuclear fuel declined as economies contracted, and planned projects were put on hold. Ukraine, Armenia and Lithuania remained dependent on Russia for nuclear fuel, storage services for spent fuel, and they were heavily dependent on nuclear energy to cover domestic needs. Armenia shut down its reactors completely between 1989 and 1993, reopening one in 1993 using Russian fuel. Economic transition in Central Europe reduced demand for Russian nuclear fuel there, too.

Ukraine represented up to a third of the international market for Russian nuclear fuel, but its financial situation was constantly difficult. While the Chernobyl disaster in 1986 led to a slow reduction of nuclear power generation, the disaster and the 1989 moratorium on NPP commissioning and construction also increased overall power demand. Ukraine closed some reactors in 1992, and initially fuelled the rest from stocks (Voskresenskii, 2000). This was only a temporary arrangement, and in 1993–1995 Ukraine exchanged its nuclear warheads for Russian fuel. This began as a bilateral arrangement. From 1994 it included the US, in anticipation of Ukraine's commitment to denuclearise and accede to the Treaty on Non-Proliferation of Nuclear Weapons (NPT) later that year (Garnett, 1995).[13] The management of spent nuclear fuel (SNF) was expensive, and connected to fuel acquisition. Ukraine continued to rely on Russia for SNF storage, at a market-based price (Kovynev, 2017). To minimise the cost, Ukraine developed some domestic storage facilities, and reduced its reliance on Russian storage (WNA, 2018c).

Nuclear power expansion returned to the agenda in Ukraine relatively quickly, with the moratorium lifted in 1995 (Kovynev, 2017). Fuel was first procured commercially in 1995, when the TVEL Concern won the tender for the period from 1996 to 2010 (Voskresenskii, 2000). The TVEL Concern was an attractive supplier to Ukraine due to its low prices, but also because it accepted nuclear cycle goods as payment (Vaganov, 1999; Voskresenskii, 2000). As the TVEL Concern rather than TVEL the Minatom subsidiary was the Russian counterparty, and this was barter trade, the resource streams on the Russian side, too, probably went though both formal and informal channels. The arrangement appeared under bilateral agreements, but bore some resemblance to payment scams in nuclear fuel deliveries to Lithuania in 1995 (Perera, 1997, p.86) as well as to similar arrangements in the Ukrainian gas sector at the time (Balmaceda, 2013, pp.107–111). Ukraine ran up debts for nuclear fuel, and Russia withheld part of the supply for 1998 (Vaganov, 1999). In an effort to regulate the debt, in 1997 the trade was channelled through a multilateral Russian–Ukrainian joint venture (JV), created for the purpose. The founding companies included the Ukrainian state property fund, a

Ukrainian and a Russian bank, the TVEL Concern and a Ukrainian–Andorran entity (Prime-TASS, 1997). The payment arrangement benefited the Russian state less than private companies. It persisted for several years (Vaganov, 1999; Voskresenskii, 2000).

Ukraine sought to diversify fuel supplies and maintained contact with Westinghouse, a major US nuclear energy company which had participated in the 1995 tender. By means of further diversification, Ukraine conducted a tender for the construction of a nuclear fuel plant in 1995, narrowly won by TVEL (Zamyatin, 1996). Further development of the project was shelved at this point, for unknown reasons (Vaganov, 1999). But Ukraine remained well prepared to develop a fuel plant, with established uranium mining and modest, but significant recoverable uranium reserves, zirconium production suitable for rod casings, and domestic demand for fuel in an established nuclear energy industry.

To the Russian nuclear energy industry, ties with customers were difficult, but still easier to maintain than those with suppliers. In 1993, post-Soviet uranium producers agreed to develop their production under an integrated organisation, with the aim of creating a transnational company (Kadosov, 1993). Accessing finance was a fundamental problem. States left with minor components of the Minsredmash system, like Kyrgyzstan's Kara-Balta Mining Combine, lacked resources and sought Russian support. Russia lacked the resources and also a strategic planning capacity to make use of such opportunities.

Differing views of the priorities ahead slowed post-Soviet integration. It was exacerbated by the difficulty of navigating in a non-transparent international uranium market. Kazakhstan in particular was interested in expanding uranium production and looked to Russia for partnership and customers. But Russia had stopped importing uranium ore from Kazakhstan when the Soviet Union was dissolved. Uranium processed in Kazakhstan at the time was stranded (Koretskii, 1994). Views on the uranium market also differed. When Kazakhstan's experts warned about an impending uranium shortage, Russian experts disagreed (Sidorenko, 1997, p.19). Minatom did not expand its nuclear ties with Kazakhstan; it left it to its subsidiaries. Atomredmetzoloto, Russia's partner for an integrated uranium industry in the CIS, saw Kazakhstan only as a competitor on the international market. TVEL's vision for post-Soviet reintegration was to see Russia become a dominant partner. It had little understanding of how circumstances had changed, however (Alieva, 1998). Atomredmetzoloto and TVEL maintained ties with Ulba, Kazakhstan's only nuclear industry plant, due to the companies' total inter-dependence. The Ulba plant processed uranium ore into yellowcake and produced fuel pellets from uranium enriched in Russia. Fuel pellet production was the only part of the nuclear cycle that was not located on Russian territory. In 1996 Atomredmetzoloto and TVEL ceased payments, forcing Ulba to diversify its customer base (Perera, 1997, pp.150, 153; Shmidke, 2006). Kazakhstan's uranium production in 1997 was only 25 per cent of what it had been in 1991 (WNA, 2011a).

Out of the shadows and into the financial crisis

By the mid-1990s, Minatom and its subsidiaries had weathered the post-breakup crisis. International uranium sales generated resources and allowed ministers and company heads to retain sector control. Non-payments at nuclear power stations were connected to problems in the wider economy. The government, especially Deputy Prime Ministers Chubais and Nemtsov, worked from 1997 to widen its control of the nuclear sector (Volchko, 1998). Minatom resisted structural reform, its autonomy protected by its considerable resources. Informal rent streams shielded it from interference, including oversight within the hierarchy of state organisations. In late 1997, Minatom secured government support for an expansion programme in the domestic nuclear energy sector, and the reorganisation of nuclear power production into a Minatom holding company (Volchko, 1998). This programme, which envisaged the construction of 16 new reactor units before 2010, was eventually passed by the government in July 1998 (Government Resolution No. 815, 1998; Kasperski, 2015, p.63). Four weeks later, the government devaluated the ruble and defaulted on its debts. Nuclear expansion was off the table again, and with it any potential improvement of government access to the industry.

Meanwhile, the sector's top leadership changed. Mikhailov's resignation in early March 1998 was a surprise. A major scandal connected to the Megatons to Megawatts programme was just unravelling, and there was speculation that Mikhailov had tried to save the industry by resigning (Pavlov, 1998), or conversely that the scandal was used as an excuse to get rid of an independent-minded minister (Emel'yanenko, 1998). His first deputy, Aleksandr Belosokhov, also resigned (Pavlov, 1999). However, at the time several banks were fighting for the control of Minatom's income streams from abroad (Gotova, 1998; Pelekhova, 1998b). Two banks, Oneksimbank and Menatep, were in a position to influence outcomes at the level of the president via Chubais and the prominent businessmen Boris Berezovskii and Roman Abramovich, all of whom had connections with the ruling coalition. A third bank, Natsional'nyi rezervnyi, was vying for the position of insider bank with the established sector bank, Konversbank (Gotova, 1998; Pelekhova, 1998b). The stakes in gaining control of Minatom were increasing.

Mikhailov's most likely successors in Minatom were Konovalov of TVEL and the prominent nuclear scientist Evgenii Adamov. Konovalov had proposed in 1991 an integration of the nuclear fuel cycle companies into one organisation (Pelekhova, 1998a). He now proposed to restructure the industry into a military, a civilian and a scientific branch (Pelekhova, 1998a). He was known to have a dismal view of outside influence in the sector. In particular, he was hostile to Oneksimbank's and Menatep's advances into the sector's financial streams (Pelekhova, 1998b). Adamov was less politically experienced but was supported by Abramovich (Gotova, 1998; Pelekhova, 1998b), and appointed in the end (Pelekhova, 1998b; Vaganov, 1998). Following the financial crisis in August, he selected Konversbank as Minatom's overall banker (Gotova, 1998).

Konovalov continued to push for a reorganisation of the nuclear energy industry divorced from the military and science branches (Pelekhova, 1998b). This included a proposal to Gazprom, in which he offered Gazprom a prominent role, possibly equity control, in a partially privatised nuclear energy industry, in return for financial support for TVEL (Oganesyan, 1998; Pelekhova, 1998a; Agentstvo ekonomicheskikh novostei, 1999).

Under both Mikhailov (1992–1998) and Adamov (1998–2001), the government's efforts to introduce contemporary management and financial practices and turn Minatom into a "team player" were perceived as attacks on the industry (Khripunov, 2001, pp.50, 57; cf. Sotnik, 2001). The state was regularly denied access to the industry and its rent streams. Adamov was popular within the sector. He followed government orders (Bogatykh, 1999), and had Chubais's and Berezovskii's support (Gotova, 1998). He would have been well positioned to launch a reform. But the onset of financial crisis meant that the timing was inauspicious. It was difficult to see how the federal budget and the nuclear industry would support the ambitious plan for expansion. In addition, Adamov's efforts to create a market-economy version of Minsredmash met with resistance in the military nuclear industry (Khripunov, 2001, p.55). After his resignation in 2001, he was credited within the nuclear sector for the nuclear revival that followed the crisis years (Atomnaya strategiya, 2009). But real structural reform of the sector was postponed, with lack of progress at home and a wide variety of foreign activities beyond government control. Before March 1998, Minatom had operated somewhat autonomously of other state organisations, including of the cabinet ministers directly in charge of its oversight. The lack of a channel to central state actors hindered institutional development. The state's difficulties in overseeing and accessing the industry made it more complicated to overcome the problem of strong inter-company competition.

A new approach to the post-Soviet region

The most profitable section of the post-Soviet nuclear industry, uranium mining in Kazakhstan, was the first to initiate programmes of renewal and expansion. Kazakhstan in 1997 reorganised its nuclear industry into a state company, Kazatomprom. At the time, Kazakhstan produced less than 900 tonnes of uranium annually, and the industry was struggling. Nevertheless, Kazatomprom in 2005 made it a strategic priority to become the world's leading uranium extractor by 2010 (*NEI Magazine*, 2005; Grudnitskii, 2006b; 2006a). In 2000, Kazatomprom announced that increased extraction would be a starting point for a full nuclear fuel cycle, and began to expand its ties with Western, Japanese, Chinese and Russian companies. Before 2004, Kazatomprom aimed for maximum reintegration with Russia (Grudnitskii, 2006b). Russian companies and Minatom were interested in Kazakhstan's fuel pellet production and future uranium supplies, but did not consider Kazakhstan a partner in the nuclear fuel cycle (Grudnitskii, 2006b). Giving Kazakhstan a stake in enrichment was off the Russian agenda well into the 2000s, even if the enrichment process were to remain under Russian control. Kazatomprom's overtures on cooperation and partnership in enrichment found little response in Russia (Grudnitskii, 2006b).

Instead, Russia from 1996–1997 promoted tripartite cooperation with Kazakhstan and Ukraine in nuclear fuel production in the JV Ukrtvel, dominated by Russia (Koretskii, 1997). Kazakhstan would supply fuel pellets, Ukraine would make zirconium casing for the fuel rods, and Russia would enrich the uranium and assemble fuel rods (Koretskii, 1997; Voskresenskii, 2000; Shmidke, 2006; *Delovaya stolitsa*, 2008a). Progress was slow. Ukraine was financially constrained and would have preferred a barter agreement to a JV. Ukrainian decision makers disagreed over a partnership with Russia (Koretskii, 1997). Russia took Kazakhstan's participation for granted (Koretskii, 1997), and while a cooperation was interesting to Kazatomprom, the negotiations were still tough. The JV was established in 2003 (Starostin, 2003). However, technical difficulties in Ukraine initially slowed production (*Delovaya stolitsa*, 2008a; Ivzhenko, 2010).

Ukraine continued to explore diversification in nuclear fuel supply, a factor it made use of in negotiations with Russia (Rubtsov, 1999). In 2000, the two agreed to exchange uranium concentrate and zirconium alloy for nuclear fuel, with only 35 per cent of Ukraine's fuel paid for in cash (Perera, 1997, pp.146–147; Vaganov, 1999; Voskresenskii, 2000).

The new coalition

By 2000, progress in Russia's nuclear energy sector was held back by a lack of mutual access and participation with state organisations. The state still had less than complete access to Minatom's foreign contacts. One of Rosatom's key reformers, Anna Belova, later remarked that Russia's nuclear sector had been less modern compared to other nuclear powers (Turanov, 2004; Belova, 2008). The nuclear energy industry was unable to address issues like future uranium supply, decommissioning of old NPPs and safe long-term SNF storage (Kudrik et al., 2004). The latter was highlighted during the legislative process in 2000–2001 that facilitated import of SNF for storage, supposed to give Russia a commercial advantage internationally. The legislation was adopted amidst widespread popular and regional political protest (Katys, 2001). There was an accumulated lack of investment for every stage of the fuel cycle, including SNF management. Considering the failure of Minatom's leaders to implement change, successful reform seemed to require new leaders.

Adamov left Minatom in 2001 after a Duma anti-corruption investigation concluded he had breached the law (RFE/RL, 2001). Together with three subordinates, he was later convicted of fraud, and Adamov was charged with embezzlement in the US (Sokovnin, 2008; Sergeev, N. and Sokovnin, 2011). Adamov's successor at Minatom was Aleksandr Rumyantsev (2001–2005). He was expected to bring the industry into line and subject it to reform, and he subscribed to Adamov's reform and expansion plans (Khripunov, 2001, p.57). The government and the new president saw it as a priority to modernise and develop the industry (Kasperski, 2015, p.63). Putin also tasked Rumyantsev with regaining control over Minatom's considerable cash flows (Leskov, 2006), that is, make its rent streams available to the state.

Despite all this, under Rumyantsev, the nuclear energy industry was vulnerable to creeping privatisation in the struggle among elites. In 2003, the Russian–Georgian businessman Kakha Bendukidze attempted to gain control over Atomstroieksport by taking a stake in the partly privatised company Atomenergoeksport (Aleksandrov, 2004; Pappe and Drankina, 2007). When Putin and Minatom became aware of this, Bendukidze was pressured out of business in Russia. Gazprombank acquired his stakes (Aleksandrov, 2004; Pappe and Drankina, 2007). In the state's effort to regain control, Minatom lost its supra-ministerial powers and became a Federal Agency for Nuclear Energy early in 2004. It lost policymaking powers and was placed organisationally directly under the new Energy and Industry Ministry, established as part of a government reform. Some of its powers and its direct participation in policymaking were restored in July, but Rosatom, as it was now known, had become a second-tier organisation (Kudrik et al., 2004, p.27).

It remained a government priority to gain access to the nuclear energy industry and restructure it to support expansion. To a government and a president eager to promote economic development and return Russia to great power status, nuclear energy industry expansion ticked many boxes. The industry was technologically advanced, creating high hopes for export markets. As discussed in Chapter 3, between 1999 and 2009, forecasters expected rising electricity demand. However, as Russian electricity prices still remained regulated while export markets for oil and gas were highly profitable, increasing oil and gas supply to Russian electricity generation was not desirable for Russia's oil and gas producers, and did not create revenue to the state. The possibility of increasing nuclear generation and releasing a greater share of oil and gas for export became one of the nuclear energy industry's arguments for an expansion of NPPs (Nigmatulin and Nigmatulin, 2006). This now became an attractive alternative also outside the industry (Orlov, V., 2008; Oxenstierna, 2010, pp.21, 37).

NPPs already generated 16 per cent of Russia's electricity (Ministry of Industry and Trade, 2003, p.96), up from 13 per cent in 1997 (Government Resolution No. 815, 1998). Following the grand plans from 1998, one reactor became operational in 2001, another would come online in 2004. Capacity utilisation at NPPs had increased (Kasperski, 2015, p.63). The Russian government now planned to add 26 completely new reactors before 2020, to bring the nuclear share of total generation capacity to 23 per cent. Uranium demand would almost double (Ministry of Industry and Trade, 2003, p.96). But the industry faced challenges that made such projections appear unrealistic. By 2005, 15 of Russia's 31 reactors in operation would have ten years or less left of their licensed service life,[14] and would have to undergo expensive refurbishment for lifetime extensions from 2006 (WNA, 2008). The plan was that extensions would add 15 years to most reactors' service life, necessitating major new investment by 2015–2020. To replace existing reactors as well as bring new capacity online, the industry would have to go through a massive expansion affecting everything from recruitment to machine-building and construction.

Domestic expansion potentially supported the export business, as innovations could be tested in the home market. Russian nuclear technology export was already a success in the growing international market. TVEL experienced a 20 per cent increase in profits from international sales from 2003 to 2004 (Siluyanova and Kovalevskii, 2004). Russian nuclear fuel exports now accounted for around 17 per cent of the world market, but the government envisioned a 30 per cent share by 2020 (Vakhmenin, 2007; Omelchenko, 2008; Ministry of Energy, 2009, p.69). In the eyes of Rosatom's reformers, domestic and international concerns drove the reform (Belova, 2008; Orlov, V., 2008). Without reform, investment, manpower and uranium shortages would inhibit growth, including international growth. The government also found it necessary to control the industry through a working "power vertical" (Belova, 2008). The nuclear energy industry could only develop on terms that enabled state management and control of the sector (Belova, 2008). This was emphasised by the US reactions to the construction of the Bushehr NPP in Iran (Kornysheva et al., 2006). By 2005–2006, the industry and the government both saw reform as a matter of urgency.

Expansion and renewal?

Uranium stockpiles and reprocessed Soviet-era warheads and spent fuel cells still made up for some of the discrepancy between Russian uranium demand and supply. Imports covered the rest. With increasing demand, imports would have to increase. The post-Soviet region had good uranium sources close to home (Ministry of Industry and Trade, 2003, pp.53, 58; Ministry of Energy, 2009, p.41). From a low point of 7 US$/lb. in 2001, uranium prices increased to 10 US$/lb. in 2002–2003. With several years needed to develop new uranium fields, and rising international demand, the Russian nuclear energy industry found itself in a new situation. As a consequence, Kazakhstan now appeared as an attractive source of uranium.

In 2002–2003, relations in the nuclear energy field between Russia and Kazakhstan began to change. TVEL acquired a "golden share", nominally 32 per cent, of the Ulba plant in 2000 (Voskresenskii, 2000; Stulberg, 2007, p.208).[15] This was subsequently converted into an ordinary minority stake.[16] It was a first step towards further integration. But according to Mukhtar Dzhakishev, head of Kazatomprom, it was still difficult to organise a substantial degree of cooperation between Russia and Kazakhstan until 2003–2005, because there was no political will in Russia to support a reform agenda (Grudnitskii, 2006b). Kazatomprom found Russia's terms insufficiently advantageous, moreover (cf. Stulberg, 2007, pp.177–209). Russia wanted Ulba to process uranium from Russian stockpiles, while under Kazatomprom's plan Ulba would receive newly mined uranium from the Zarechnoe uranium wellfield (Kucherenko, 2000; Shmidke, 2006).

Armenia's debt to TVEL for nuclear fuel in the 1990s had long been subject to negotiation. In 2003, the debt was included in the large debt-for-equity swap with Inter RAO (Chapter 3). Ukraine, on the other hand, took steps in 2005 to limit its dependence on Russian nuclear fuel, but this was set to be a long process. Ukraine's overall demand for nuclear power was only going to increase, as in 2004 two new units became operational, at Khmelnytskyi-2 and Rivne-4, respectively. It was likely to remain an important nuclear fuel market for Russia also in the coming decades. Nevertheless, trials of Westinghouse fuel at the South Ukraine NPP began in 2005 (Dye et al., 2015).

Reform and growth

When Minatom was downgraded in spring 2004, it marked the beginning of a turbulent period in the nuclear energy industry. Rumyantsev tried to push the reform through. He was confident that Minatom's organisational successor, Rosatom, would hold the nuclear energy industry, through Rosenergoatom, as a shareholding company in one hundred per cent state ownership (Emel'yanenkov, 2006; Nikol'skii, 2006a; Vaganov, 2006). This much was decided by the State Council in December 2004 (Kornysheva, 2005a). Rosenergoatom would be included on the list of strategic enterprises, thereby precluding privatisation except if by presidential decree (Kornysheva, 2005b). The hierarchy of its subsidiaries was not clear, with three alternatives on the table (Butrin et al., 2006; Proskurnina and Nikol'skii, 2006). However, while the involvement of the State Council signified that Putin took a personal interest in reform, responsibility for oversight and policy for the industry rested with the government. The proposal to organise Rosenergoatom as a shareholding company met resistance from the Economic Development Ministry and ecology NGOs (Vaganov, 2005; Slivyak et al., 2010, p.7). This had financial implications for Rosatom, which suffered from a lack of funds (Nikol'skii, 2005). The continued absence of a shareholding entity precluded the possibility of attracting finance in the form of credit, and the government was not prepared to fully finance the industry's proposed expansion programme (Nikol'skii, 2005). Towards the end of Rumyantsev's period in Rosatom, the impetus for reform and expansion seemed to disappear again.

But now, experienced government hands took over the reform process. Presidential Aide Sergei Prikhodko, an experienced trouble-shooter, had been appointed chairman of TVEL's Board of Directors in October 2004 (Chereshnev, 2004; Siluyanova and Kovalevskii, 2004). Another sign of impending change came in February 2005 when Pyotr Shchedrovitskii, advisor to the presidential envoy to the Volga Federal District, Sergei Kirienko, became director of the nuclear management institute, TsNIIatominform (Antonov et al., 2005). And then, Sergei Kirienko himself was appointed to head Rosatom in November 2005. Sergei Sobyanin, appointed head of the Presidential Administration in November 2005, was also involved and chaired TVEL's board from May 2006 to November 2007 (Butrin et al., 2006; Melikova, 2006). That position had previously been held by a deputy minister in Minatom/Rosatom. In December 2007, Sobyanin became head of the Supervisory Board for Rosatom, the state corporation (Tovkailo, 2007).

Kirienko was the first nuclear sector top manager from outside the industry. He was a loyal state manager who knew Putin well, although he was not among his closest associates. After his arrival at Rosatom, Kirienko continued to bring in his own team (Koroleva, 2006). Along with Sobyanin, he installed loyal managers from outside in crucial positions, apparently to ensure that changes to formal institutions would be followed by changes in informal constraints. Kirienko's former deputy, Sergei Obozov, became head of Rosenergoatom before its conversion into a shareholding entity (Kudryashov, 2006; Malkova, 2006; Nikol'skii, 2006b). Vladimir Travin, Kirienko's deputy at Rosatom and head of Atomenergoprom, had a nuclear sector background, but came with Kirienko from Nizhnii Novgorod (Embassy Moscow, 2007a). A few years later, Kirienko's earlier critics had left Rosatom's top echelons. A key reformer later remarked that people and enterprises in the wider industry should have been included during the reform (Belova, 2008, p.145), in addition to the already large team of experts from the Presidential Administration and the sector (Bovt, 2007). The wider industry was subjected to, not involved in, a reform process. In return, however, the state was now committed to a massive expansion programme, creating an incentive for reform. This time, the timing and management finally seemed auspicious.

Kirienko duly emphasised the expansion side of the impending reform in the first months after coming to Rosatom (Naumov, 2006), but preparing and passing the legislation took two years. The federal programme for development of the nuclear energy industry was presented to the Cabinet in October 2006. By then, its critics in the industry and the Duma were drawing attention to weaknesses, like how to draw the line between the civilian and commercial side of the industry on the one hand and the military side on the other (Ivanov and Rogozhin, 2006). The crucial law on property in the nuclear energy industry reached the Duma in November, with the urgency emphasised by its being forwarded by the Presidential Administration. It passed through the committee stage almost immediately (Rodin, 2006), and promptly passed by the legislature in the first reading only a month later (Belyakov, 2006; Federal Law No. 13, 2007). It was signed by the President in February 2007.

The law stipulated that the military and civilian parts of the industry be separated, although Rosatom would remain the common umbrella. Crucially, the President would have the final say in each stage of the property reorganisation (Federal Law No. 13, 2007). At the lower level, the industry became more specialised. The state's shareholding company for the nuclear energy industry, Atomenergoprom, was established by decree in April 2007 (Emel'yanenkov, 2007a). Final legislation on Rosatom passed the Duma quickly, in October–November 2007 (Belyakov and Sokolovskaya, 2007; Emel'yanenkov, 2007b). As with the other proposed laws, it was forwarded by the President, not the government. Throughout the 12 months when all these laws were passed, it appeared that Putin, rather than risk a lengthy and substantial political debate, threw his "most powerful support" behind the reform (Kornysheva, 2007b; Orlov, V., 2008). By early 2008, most of the new structures were in place, just in time for the presidential election.

The reform's great surprise came in the final legislation package, when it was announced that Rosatom would become a state corporation. This outcome was not foreseen, as the reform programme, also under Kirienko, had stipulated shareholding entities (Neimysheva et al., 2006; Vaganov, 2006). One reason was that this was a rare type of organisation re-invigorated by Putin in 2007 (Butler, 2008, p.310). Throughout 2007, Putin promoted it as a vehicle of state participation in the economy (Putin, 2007). The organisational outcome of state corporation, closer to a foundation than a truly state-owned company, indicated that Putin had the final say on this issue. Rosatom became vested with wide-ranging policymaking, regulatory, oversight and financial powers. Observers took this as proof that the state would no longer take a hands-off, commercial approach to the economy, but act as manager as well as owner (Embassy Moscow, 2007b).[17] In October 2009, President Medvedev criticised state corporations because, he said, they had got out of control; as a result no more state corporations were established (Filatova, 2009). By then, Rosatom's organisational form was secured by stable, but rather non-transparent institutions.

Rosatom the state corporation

State corporations were subject to less public oversight, mandatory transparency and budgetary control than other state companies. They were "non-state, non-private, administrative-commercial entities" (Krasavin, 2007), with considerable freedom to dispose of their means through non-commercial funds. Their position did not amount to state ownership, but something closer to foundations, or self-ownership with far less state control (Kluge, 2019, p.34). The ambiguity was fundamental. State corporations were tasked with the implementation of government policy, while excluded from regular state budget documentation (IMF, 2014, p.32). Resources transferred from the state budget to state corporations ceased to belong to the state and were at the state corporations' disposal, as were any profits (Krasavin, 2007). State corporations could also attract private investors in public–private partnerships. In short, they were a potential channel for rents in their own right. The boundaries of the state remained blurred, and this benefited Rosatom. Its Supervisory Board controlled the state corporation's primary funds and four reserve funds that were intended to function as guarantee and collateral for all Rosatom's subsidiaries (Malkova and Mazneva, 2007). The institutional set-up enabled cross-subsidisation among Rosatom subsidiaries, with profitable activities subsidising loss-making ones (Cooper, 2013, pp.59–60). In effect, soft budget constraints returned to the industry, as state corporations could not be bankrupted. Loss-making entities would be sustained on rents.

State corporations were exempt from many of the usual state enforcement and oversight mechanisms and requirements of mandatory disclosure of information (e.g. on suspicion of money laundering, etc.) that applied to other state controlled entities. In particular, state corporations were exempt from audits by the Audit Chamber (Krasavin, 2007), and were only required to report to it annually. Crucially in the nuclear sector, Rosatom took on greater responsibility for its own safety, security and anti-terrorism measures. Between 2004 and 2008, reorganisations among other state agencies with oversight responsibility for safety and security reduced their ability to perform their tasks effectively (Kasperski, 2015, p.61). In other matters, Rosatom was overseen by the Supervisory Board, with members appointed by the president (Federal Law No. 317, 2007). The Supervisory Board and the general director had more independence from the state than did state-owned shareholding companies.

The outcome of reform was re-centralisation of the nuclear sector, and Rosatom the state corporation had wide powers and tasks (Kasperski, 2015, p.59). One crucial advantage of the state corporation as an organisation type was that Rosatom maintained management control of Atomenergoprom, obstructing any attempts at establishing autonomy in the nuclear energy industry. Rosatom was the first state organisation apart from the Federal Agency for State Property Management (Rosimushchestvo) allowed to hold state-controlled companies as 100 per cent state property (Kornysheva, 2007b). Rosatom now had greater control over subsidiaries. At the same time, it functioned as a ministry, performing regulatory and budget tasks. Subsidiary holding companies, like Atomenergoprom, were protected from privatisation by the new strategic sectors law that restricted private, especially foreign, investment in sectors like the electricity grid, subsoil companies and the nuclear industry (Federal Law No. 57, 2008; Heath, 2009). For practical purposes, the dividing line between Atomenergoprom and Rosatom was thin. They were both housed in the old ministry building and responded to outside inquiries, also by this author,[18] as an integrated entity.

The government saw it as an efficient setup. With Atomenergoprom a wholly state-owned shareholding company, government control further down in the hierarchy was secured (Emel'yanenkov, 2007a). As observed by Belova, one wanted to avoid a situation in which.

> the whole holding company [khozyaistvuyushchii sub"ekt] Atomenergoprom would start living a life of its own, and problems connected to e.g. nuclear radiation safety, or a lack of unified, coordinated management would have negative consequences for the development of all parts of the nuclear industry.
>
> (Belova, 2008, p.146)

Indeed, Rosatom's subsidiaries did what they could to retain some autonomy and resist change. In November 2006, the long-standing rivals, TVEL and Tekhsnabeksport, formed a JV, the Uranium Mining Company (UGRK), intended to become Rosatom's uranium mining subsidiary (Butrin et al., 2006; Kornysheva, 2006b; 2006a). It was a non-starter. There were licensing problems, perhaps compounded by unwillingness in Rosatom to allow an audit of the involved assets (Yur'eva, 2007). Importantly, UGRK did not fit into Rosatom's final structure. In 2008–2009, with the central organisational features in place, Tekhsnabeksport ceded gas centrifuge production to TVEL, which incorporated the nuclear fuel cycle, while uranium assets were now wholly organised under ARMZ (Kiselev, 2011).

Uniquely among state corporations, Rosatom was endowed with the right to conclude treaties with foreign states (Butler, 2008, p.310). This institutionalised Rosatom's practice of entering into relationships with other states on nuclear matters without the MFA's knowledge, as happened with Burma in 2007 (Embassy Moscow, 2007c). In this respect, there was a lack of coordination in the state also with the new institutional framework. According to Kirienko, the "legendary Minsredmash was reconstructed, only in the new market environment" (Emel'yanenkov, 2007b). Post-reform Rosatom incorporated several direct successors of Minsredmash entities, reorganised them, and added control of foreign trade. There were similarities, Kirienko argued, because Minsredmash had proven to be an efficient type of organisation in the Soviet Union (Orlov, V., 2008). In the nuclear energy industry, the Soviet period was the golden age, and Soviet institutions were adapted to fit Russia's contemporary needs.

Rosatom's new strategy under Kirienko was to embark on an expansion of nuclear power in Russia, providing 25 per cent of Russia's electricity by 2030 (Government Resolution No. 605, 2006). This would mean a new golden age, as the proportion of nuclear in Russian generation at the time remained 16 per cent as before. While Rosatom's expansion projections continued to increase, the government later reduced the targets (Kasperski, 2015; WNA, 2018b). The 2009 Energy Strategy foresaw that the role of nuclear-based and renewable generation combined would increase two to 2.5-fold (Ministry of Energy, 2009, p.60). The nuclear energy industry did increase in size in the years that followed, to a considerable extent due to Kirienko's effectiveness in advancing the industry's interests. This included plans to double Rosatom's size, launched internationally as part of a globalisation strategy (Gorst and Simon, 2010). Due to the political priority on nuclear energy as a technologically advanced, modern export industry, Kirienko found a receptive audience in the Kremlin and the government. Even as Rosatom's projections were more optimistic than those of the government, the belief in a nuclear renaissance (Stulberg and Fuhrmann, 2013, pp.4–8) was shared by the wider elite (Kasperski, 2015, p.64).

The clouds on the horizon were less discussed. The planned expansion was from the beginning unlikely to lead to increases in the nuclear energy industry beyond the medium term, as a large share of Russia's nuclear reactors would reach the end of their extended service life around 2030. In 2010 the projections for decommissioning of nuclear generation capacity by 2030 stood at 70 per cent of total installed capacity at the time (WNA, 2018b). This was not yet a topic in public discussions on industry development. Optimism prevailed among Rosatom's subsidiaries. It was easier to bring them on board the reform when the promise of increased funding served as a carrot. This carrot was also implicated in reform implementation, as increasing funds could alleviate the internal competition for funding.

The financial side of expansion was off the public agenda, even though it was achieved with state and public finance. In the period 2009–2014, new nuclear energy investments were 65 per cent financed by the federal budget (Milov, 2015). The rest was covered by mandatory investment surcharges on electricity tariffs, earmarked for nuclear generation (Milov, 2015). The surcharges were considerable, generating 59 billion rubles in 2010 (Dzaguto, 2009). This was a contrast to the situation for non-nuclear electricity generating companies, which were not privileged with a similar surcharge,[19] as discussed in Chapter 3. When the mandatory investment charges were reduced during the 2011–2012 election cycle, to further curb the growth in electricity tariffs, the nuclear generation subsidiary Rosenergoatom ran substantial losses (Rosenergoatom, 2013, p.5). Investment was however not reduced (Skorlygina, 2012). In effect, the state's effort to expand nuclear power generation gave the industry privileged access to state finance. Nuclear power generation was promoted over other, more economically efficient fuels. The industry received a substantial share of the federal budget. Rosatom received 826 billion rubles in budget funding over the 2009 to 2014 period (Milov, 2015). It was found important enough to receive crisis support in 2009, amounting to 65.3 billion rubles (Rosatom, 2010, p.55). Rosatom's plan was to fund investment from its own revenues by 2015 (WNA, 2018b), but in the 2009–2010 crisis, it was supported by the state. In contrast to a decade earlier, the state had the means and the capacity to buoy up the economy through crisis.

Rosatom was now subject to less public scrutiny and state oversight than it had been as a federal agency, and the channels for rent sharing between Rosatom and the state were opaque. There were opportunities for corruption, and occasionally, indications in the media that factory-level kickbacks were channelled upwards as rent (Kotlyar, 2012). Rosatom now reported directly to the president. In this way, complex state mechanisms for access to Rosatom were replaced by a personal connection to the president. This was not necessarily an improvement of state oversight and policymaking capabilities. Arguably, informal enforcement mechanisms were turned into an important part of the institutional framework. There was a possibility that Rosatom's direct access to the president could undercut other efforts on the part of the state to get access to the company. A few years later in 2011, embezzlement charges against Rosatom's deputy head, Evgenii Evstratov (2008–2011) seemed to suggest that Rosatom's earlier problems with a lack of oversight and control might be reproducing themselves (*The Moscow Times*, 2012). At the very least, considering that the charges were withdrawn at a much later point,[20] the lack of transparency in Rosatom's institutional set-up made the corporation vulnerable to such charges. The complexity and vastness of Rosatom and its subsidiaries could potentially counteract external control mechanisms and deny real access to the industry. That being the case, it would replicate the problem of an autonomous sector.

In Rosatom's relations with the state, it was the actors that mattered. Kirienko and Sobyanin were loyal to Putin and owed their positions to him. They were not just state managers, but Putin's personal representatives. Kirienko's authority outside and within the industry increased further as he delivered on the expansion programme and improved the sector's standing in government circles. Sobyanin provided additional oversight on Putin's behalf. When Dmitrii Medvedev took over as president in 2008, Sobyanin followed Putin from the Kremlin to the Cabinet. When Sobyanin ceded his place on the Board on becoming Mayor of Moscow in October 2010, Igor Shuvalov, a Board representative from the Presidential Administration known to be close to Putin, took over as chairman. No less importantly, the appointment of Sergei Shmatko as Energy Minister in May 2008 may have reassured nuclear energy industry leaders. Shmatko had a background from Rosenergoatom in the 1990s and Atomstroieksport from 2002, including Bushehr construction. While loyal to Putin, Shmatko was known also to be close to Igor Sechin (Embassy Moscow, 2008). A combination of loyalty and connections towards the regime promised to maintain high priority for the sector in the years ahead, while ensuring that the state would not again have difficulties in controlling the sector. However, the formal institutional framework could potentially be used to replicate sectoral autonomy, and therefore, personal loyalties would be instrumental in increasing state capacity. The implementation of formal institutions strengthened by reform still ultimately depended on informal constraints.

The reassertion

After Rosatom was recreated as a market version of Minsredmash, Russia made it a foreign policy priority to revive as much as possible of the old Minsredmash structures (Belkina, 2006). Rosatom's efforts to increase its international foothold came during a period of relative optimism in the global nuclear energy industry, particularly in the US and Europe. While the economic fundamentals of nuclear energy remained challenging, especially due to high investment and decommissioning costs and long lead times, the expectation of a nuclear renaissance persisted (Bradford, 2009). Still, the realities failed to deliver. A key reason was the fierce competition from gas and coal accompanied by risk aversion in financial markets (Ferguson, 2009), and from late 2008 also the financial crisis. To Rosatom, however, the expectation of a renaissance for nuclear power created a heightened sense of urgency in maintaining its competitive advantages among customers and prospective partners. There remained a strong sense of pride in the nuclear energy industry in Russia, which now extended to the industry's export potential.

Kazakhstan and Uzbekistan: careful balancing

Kirienko's vision was to integrate the nuclear sectors in Russia, Kazakhstan and Ukraine in a vertically integrated holding company (Humber, 2006; Yermukanov, 2006). Kazakhstan was very positive towards the idea, with a generally cooperative stance towards Russia. Kazakhstan faced competition from Australia and Namibia in the international uranium market (Humber, 2006). In this situation, cooperation in fuel production with Russia promised to improve market access above and beyond what could be achieved by its competitors.

A strategic nuclear energy partnership between Russia and Kazakhstan was established in 2006. Kazakhstan was now an attractive uranium supplier and Russia only one of several rivals for partnership (Vinokurov, 2007; Muzalevsky, 2010). Kazakhstan had developed relations with Japan (Sergeev, M., 2007a), Canada and France (Shmidke, 2006; Ibragimova, 2010), and in 2007 acquired ten per cent of Westinghouse. In one decade, Kazatomprom had acquired stakes in all parts of the nuclear fuel cycle (Ibragimova, 2010). Dzhakishev was careful to rebuff any suggestions that Kazatomprom competed with Rosatom (RFE/RL, 2007).

With a strategic partnership established with Russia, Kazatomprom was willing to compromise over uranium supplies to the Ulba uranium processing and fuel pellet plant. Production began in 2006 (Yermukanov, 2006). The same year, Tekhsnabeksport and Kazatomprom began to explore the Budenovskoe 1 and 2 wellfields, where production began in 2008 (WNA, 2011a). Kazakhstan also planned to develop nuclear power production jointly with Atomstroieksport. The project, scheduled from 2006, failed to take off until 2009. This was apparently due to funding problems, but possibly also to Russian reluctance to share intellectual property rights (WNA, 2011a).

The International Uranium Enrichment Centre (IUEC), set up in 2006–2007, completed the expansion of bilateral nuclear energy ties.[21] Strongly promoted by Putin (Blagov, 2007), it was a Russian–Kazakhstani JV open to other states. Initially, the cooperation included plans for a joint Tekhsnabeksport–Kazatomprom enrichment facility next to the IUEC, but this was later decided to be uneconomic (WNA, 2011a). The centre was set up to provide enrichment services and access to enriched uranium to states that were new to nuclear power, or those with small nuclear programmes (WNA, 2018e). Iran was an important target (Rykovanova, 2006; Sindelar, 2006; Loukianova, 2008), but it also served Kazakhstan's purpose of obtaining a stake in uranium enrichment (Ibragimova, 2010, p.82). To Russia, profits mattered, too (Sindelar, 2006; Torbakov, 2006). Offering a ten per cent stake to new participants, a minimum of 51 per cent of the IUEC would remain with Tekhsnabeksport (Kornysheva, 2007a).

In May 2009, Dzhakishev, long-serving president of Kazatomprom, was unexpectedly arrested along with eight of his deputies, on embezzlement charges connected to the establishment of uranium mine JVs with foreign partners.[22] He was convicted and sentenced to 14 years in prison in March 2010 (Gorst, 2010). He was replaced by Vladimir Shkolnik, former trade and industry minister whose background was from the nuclear industry. Shkolnik was assumed to be more pro-Russian than Dzhakishev, but he continued Kazatomprom's ambitious expansion strategy (Pannier, 2009; Ibragimova, 2010).[23] After the arrest of the senior management, the decision process in Kazatomprom slowed down. It was speculated that Russia would want to reduce the position of Kazatomprom to that of just a uranium producer instead of a well-positioned competitor to Rosatom in the nuclear fuel cycle (Embassy Astana, 2009). With reduced access to Australian uranium after the war in Georgia, Rosatom had to rely more on uranium from Kazakhstan, among others.

Dzhakishev's arrest imperilled the balanced business partnership between Kazatomprom and its international partners (Emel'yanenkov, 2009).[24] In Dzhakishev's own opinion, his arrest was connected to Rosatom's attempts to acquire shares in Uranium One, a Canadian company that had acquired stakes in uranium mines in Kazakhstan in 2007 (Gorst, 2010). What followed was a major change in the relations between Rosatom and Kazatomprom. ARMZ subsequently did acquire control of Uranium One in a series of acquisitions and equity exchanges from June 2009 to December 2010 (Varaksin, 2009; Atomredmetzoloto, 2011, pp.15–17, 32–33, 36–37). There was a business rationale on both sides. Uranium One's overall production was falling and investor confidence was low. Rosatom faced an impending overstretch, as it possessed considerable enrichment capacity, while its order books for enriched uranium threatened to exceed its access to easily mined uranium (Belton, 2009). However, Kazakhstan's elite struggle for political and economic power had intensified during the financial crisis (Gorst, 2009). Uranium One clearly found it difficult to manage the political risk of doing business in Kazakhstan after Dzhakishev's arrest. Whatever the background, what began as a strategic partnership quickly turned into a much closer relationship in the years that followed.

It is not possible to say whether Kazatomprom's temporary weakening in the nuclear fuel cycle after May 2009 had anything to do with Russian influence on Kazakh state organisations. There was discussion on a possible "Russian lobby" in Kazakhstan's uranium and nuclear industry (Regnum.ru, 2013). As Kazatomprom established JVs in fuel production and marketing with Areva in 2009 (*NEI Magazine*, 2009), central elements of its international strategy continued unaffected. In 2010–2011, the bilateral strategic partnership reached a second stage, with progress in both uranium exploration and nuclear power plant plans. Kazatomprom was expected to acquire a share in the enrichment plant at Novouralsk from Russia in 2011 (WNA, 2011a; 2011b). In addition to this, Kazatomprom continued to develop cooperation with Japan and China. However, the progress in uranium exploration and nuclear power indicated that Russia now emerged as Kazakhstan's main nuclear energy partner.

On the expiration of the US–German uranium trader Nukem's contract with Uzbekistan's uranium-producing Navoi Mining & Metallurgy Combinat (NMMC) in 2005, Uzbekistan aimed to diversify uranium sales (Faizullaev, 2009, p.29). Russia had for several years wanted to return to Uzbekistan's uranium sector and now tried to capitalise on its support of Uzbekistan's repressive regime after the 2005 massacre in Andijon (Torbakov, 2006). In 2006, Uzbekistan and Tekhsnabeksport agreed to develop the Aktau deposit jointly (Faizullaev, 2009, p.30). But Uzbekistan baulked at allowing privatisation or outside investment in NMMC, precluding further integration in the uranium industry (Faizullaev, 2009, p.29). Following ARMZ's acquisition of Uranium One, Uzbekistan's government held off from closer ties with Russia on nuclear energy (Faizullaev, 2009, p.30). Negotiations on a JV in Aktau gave no result, and Tekhsnabeksport withdrew in 2010 (WNA, 2018a). Complexity in the ore may have played a part in Tekhsnabeksport's decision. NMMC renewed its contract with Nukem in 2013, but in parallel pursued a careful diversification of its customer base to South Korea, Japan and later China (Panfilova, 2009; Hashimova, 2011; WNA, 2018a).

Ukraine: dependence and balancing

Ukraine remained rather positive to tripartite cooperation with Russia and Kazakhstan, but progress was much slower in comparison to Kazakhstan (Humber, 2006). In 2007, Russia and Ukraine concluded a cooperation protocol covering nuclear equipment, uranium exploration and fuel production (Angelova, 2008; Davydov, 2008). Cooperation on uranium production development failed to materialise. Ukraine was expanding its production, and disagreed with Russia over funding and equity (WNA, 2018c). In 2008, Westinghouse[25] secured a three-year commercial contract for larger fuel deliveries from 2009 (Kurdov, 2007; Sergeev, M., 2007b). Deliveries under the commercial contract commenced in 2010 (Energoatom, 2010). Some of the fuel was supposed to be produced from Ukrainian uranium (*Delovaya stolitsa*, 2008b; 2010b). Westinghouse's price was allegedly 10 to 30 per cent higher than TVEL's, but it was fixed (Ivanitskaya et al., 2008; Ravinskii, 2008). TVEL's price was determined in the annual Russian–Ukrainian negotiations for all the energy industries (Gorelov, 2007; Kornysheva, 2007c; Kornysheva and Chernovalov, 2007). However, in this period Rosatom offered Ukraine a substantial discount if it would sign up for 20 years of exclusive TVEL supply (WNA, 2018c). Exclusive supply was problematic, as it went against the trend of increasing attention in Europe towards fuel supply diversification. Ukraine depended on fuel storage and reprocessing in Russia. Russia's fees for this service rose considerably between 2005 and 2008. A further increase would bring TVEL's fuel price up to Westinghouse's level

(Embassy Kyiv, 2008). While Ukraine had signed a contract on development of its own SNF storage facility with a US company already in 2004, this process was several times placed on hold due to the political situation in Ukraine, with little progress before 2014 (*NEI Magazine*, 2017a).

Ukraine had also developed relations with the Australian uranium company Uran Ltd. (Ivzhenko, 2009b), and built up a strategic uranium reserve (*Delovaya stolitsa*, 2010b). In late 2008, Ukraine decided to join the IUEC effective from 2010 (IUEC, 2019). This would give Ukraine access to enrichment facilities, thus opening the possibility of enriching its own uranium. In 2009, Rosatom made progress on comprehensive cooperation contingent on increased fuel deliveries for TVEL and that Rosatom become Ukraine's sole provider of enrichment services (Ivzhenko, 2009b; Kosharnaya, 2009). This had the effect of halting progress in projects like the completion of the two final reactors at the Khmelnytskyi NPP, and its financial package in particular (Ivzhenko, 2009a). Internal Rosatom documents leaked to the Ukrainian press in 2009 indicated that Rosatom was pursuing a strategy to force Ukraine to abandon the Westinghouse supply option and agree instead to a comprehensive and exclusive cooperation deal with Russia (Kosharnaya, 2009). Ukraine's dependence on Rosatom would be used to that company's maximum advantage. The danger of eroding Ukrainian trust in Rosatom as a partner in the nuclear energy industry seems not to have been discussed.

After Viktor Yanukovych became Ukraine's president in January 2010, relations with Russia improved in all energy industries. In April, the Agreement between Ukraine and Russia over the Black Sea Fleet in Ukraine (the Kharkiv Accords, see also Chapter 7) in effect extended the lease for Russia's Black Sea Fleet base in Sevastopol in return for gas price discounts for Ukraine. When visiting Kyiv later in April 2010, Putin proposed that the two states integrate their operations in the nuclear fuel cycle, nuclear machine building and power generation in one holding. This, in effect, would recreate a modern Russian–Ukrainian Minsredmash. If the suggestion was "too revolutionary" for Ukraine, Putin proposed carrying out the integration "in stages" (Dzaguto, 2010b; Ivzhenko, 2010). The projects under discussion had been put on hold by Yushchenko, but a joint holding company would be a further step towards integration (Emel'yanenkov, 2010; Dzaguto, 2011c). Yanukovych was most enthusiastic towards the modernisation of Ukraine's NPPs and establishing the nuclear fuel assembly plant in cooperation with Russia. It would replace the Ukrtvel JV, according to Energoatom's president, Yurii Nedashkovskyi (*Delovaya stolitsa*, 2008a; Ivzhenko, 2010). Yushchenko had preferred Westinghouse, while Yanukovych now preferred to go with TVEL (Emel'yanenkov, 2010). Putin wanted to see cooperation in nuclear machine building and uranium production, especially with regard to the Turboatom turbine factory in Kharkiv and the Novokostyantynivka[26] uranium basin (Emel'yanenkov, 2010). Ahead of the negotiations on nuclear cooperation, there were some indications that the design of the tender for the nuclear fuel plant would favour Rosatom more than Westinghouse (Embassy Kyiv, 2010).

The Kharkiv Accords gave a new impetus to bilateral cooperation plans that had become stuck. Atomstroieksport and Energoatom agreed on reactors 3 and 4 at Khmelnytskyi NPP in June 2010, and the contract was agreed by February 2011 (Dzaguto, 2010a). Later in 2010, TVEL was awarded the long-term contract for Ukraine's complete nuclear fuel supply for the remaining lifespan of all reactors. Rosatom had by then specified the fuel supply discount for a 25-year contract to more than 1 billion US$ (WNA, 2018c). Energoatom also agreed on a service contract for Ukraine's VVER reactors with a new Rosatom subsidiary, Rusatom Service (*NEI Magazine*, 2012b). But further progress was again slow. The agreement on Khmelnytskyi 3 and 4 met resistance in Verkhovna Rada, Ukraine's parliament, for its non-transparency, and more generally, for constructing generation capacity in excess of demand (Ivzhenko, 2011). Finance was another problem. Russia would provide credit for 85 per cent of the costs, but following the first tranche, the effectuation of the financial package was slow (Dzaguto, 2010a; *NEI Magazine*, 2010c).

TVEL also finally secured the contract for Ukraine's fuel plant as agreed by the two presidents (Dzaguto, 2011b; WNA, 2018c). The Ukrainian company Yaderne Palyvo would have 50 per cent plus one share, while TVEL would control the rest (Dzaguto, 2011b). This ownership arrangement was not proportional to the investment on each side. The agreement provided for technology transfer, joint intellectual property rights, and a financial package from Russia equivalent to 60 per cent of the plant's total cost (*Delovaya stolitsa*, 2010a; Ivzhenko, 2010; *NEI Magazine*, 2010b). According to the World Nuclear Association, it represented as much as 70 per cent of the total investment (WNA, 2018c). The final agreement likely reflected that Energoatom was TVEL's most important foreign customer, taking 55 per cent of its exports (WNA, 2018c). Westinghouse had not been prepared to invest its own funds in the project, and this was decisive for the outcome in favour of TVEL (*NEI Magazine*, 2010a). The initial plans foresaw that the plant would be complete in 2013 (Vakarelska, 2017). Again, implementation was slow. The real difficulty with the fuel plant was to implement joint intellectual property rights. There was no progress on the feasibility study until the Rosatom institute GSPI became subcontractor (UNIAN, 2011). As in the case of Khmelnytskyi 3 and 4, Rosatom and Energoatom disagreed on the terms of the financial package (*Delovaya stolitsa*, 2011). Ukraine had no means of forcing Rosatom to implement agreements, so plans and projects materialised when it suited Rosatom.

The delays in the fuel plant project in 2010–2011 suited TVEL's plans. The company was in a process of integrating other parts of the nuclear fuel cycle into its own structure. Only after reorganisation would it be possible to maximise production based on enrichment capacity, and consolidate in Ukraine (Gorbenko, 2010, p.22). In October 2011, the project was declared on time according to a revised schedule, with completion in 2015 (Shtaltovnyi, 2011), and construction started in October 2012 (*NEI Magazine*, 2012a). The new factory would cover half of Ukraine's nuclear fuel demand by 2016–2017. At this point, Ukraine became even more dependent on Russia for fuel. Westinghouse fuel had performed as expected during trials in South Ukraine NPP. But upon regular reloading in 2012, some assemblies showed scratching and even damage to the grid that surrounded the fuel rods (Dye et al., 2015). Nedashkovskyi was promptly dismissed from Energoatom (*NEI Magazine*, 2015a). TVEL and Rosatom were now in a historically good position in their most significant market.

Armenia and Belarus: new NPPs

Armenia had planned to close the Metsamor NPP in 2017 and build a new plant. After a feasibility study in 2008, financed by the US government, a tender was announced in 2009 (Danielyan, 2009). Rosatom and Atomstroieksport were in contact with Armenian officials over the project from 2007, starting with a visit from Kirienko (Danielyan, 2007). Rosatom was the only potential contractor that offered a financial package. Armenia and Atomstroieksport set up the JV Metsamorenergoatom as owner and operator of the plant, in December 2009, and Atomstroieksport was designated contractor (Melikova, 2008; Danielyan, 2009). Construction of the new, larger NPP was planned to commence in 2018 (ARKA News Agency, 2014). Russia would finance much of the cost of the new NPP and the extensions to the old NPP's service life (RIA Novosti, 2014). The plans were for the new NPP to export power to Georgia, Turkey (through Georgia) and, possibly, Iran, in accordance with Inter RAO's strategic plans (Khachatrian, 2008; Danielyan, 2009). In 2008, ARMZ and Armenia agreed also on cooperation in exploring Armenia's uranium reserves (Avoyan, 2008; Kudrin, 2008). Exploration started in 2009 (Atomredmetzoloto, 2010, p.15) and Armenia joined the IUEC in March 2012 (IUEC, 2019).

In the years 2005–2008, the Baltic region had copious plans to expand its nuclear energy capacity. Russia constructed a new NPP in Kaliningrad. Lithuania began to develop plans for a new plant at Visaginas to replace the Ignalina plant, which was decommissioned from 2009. The first plans for a Belarusian NPP had emerged in Soviet times, and in 2006, rising gas prices brought the project back on the agenda (Marples, 2006). In late 2008, President Aleksandr Lukashenko announced that the project NPP be located at Astravets,[27] with intended completion of two reactors planned for 2016 and 2018. After some back and forth with other suppliers, only Atomstroieksport submitted a substantial offer (Marples, 2009; Thomas, 2018, p.241). A politically important project in Belarus, planning for the NPP proceeded despite protests among the Belarusian public, criticism from Lithuania's government and the financial expense (Marples, 2008; 2010). There were delays from the beginning.

Belarus, the Russian government and Russian banks negotiated the financial package in 2007–2010. Belarus initially aimed to secure 9 billion US$

from the Russians to cover the full cost of construction. Russia offered 6 billion. If Belarus let Inter RAO have a 50 per cent stake in the plant, Russia was prepared to offer more (Emel'yanenkov, 2007c; Sandler, 2010). At this point, bilateral disagreements over oil transit and gas trade affected progress also in the negotiations over the NPP (Marples, 2010). In 2011, Belarus conditioned Gazprom's takeover of Beltransgaz (Chapter 7) on Russian finance for the NPP (Ioffe, 2011). Russia then offered a package deal with a preferential 10 billion US$ loan to cover up to 90 per cent of the cost (WNA, 2015; Thomas, 2018). This removed the major hurdle in the process, meaning that the NPP could now be built.

No nuclear renaissance

The Fukushima Daiichi disaster in March 2011 effectively ended the general sense of optimism in the global nuclear energy industry, and was to have profound consequences for Rosatom's international competitors (*NEI Magazine*, 2018b; 2018d). But Rosatom and the government retained expansive plans. In the 2006 programme, ten new reactors had been supposed to come online in the period to 2015 (Government Resolution No. 605, 2006). In 2014, two of these had been brought online and another two were close to completion (Kasperski, 2015, p.63; WNA, 2018b). The 2006 plans had been based on a "relatively optimistic development model", as stated in the programme, but projections were not scaled down when it was time to update it (Government Resolution No. 605, 2006, Appendix 2). Optimism prevailed, and plans were to a considerable extent rolled over. The new programme for the period to 2020, approved in June 2014, contained plans and finance for 13 new reactors (Government Resolution No. 506–12, 2014, Appendix 2). In the event, only three new reactors became operational in 2017 and 2018, in addition to the two that had opened to plan in 2015 and 2016 (WNA, 2018b). By the time Russia entered a new economic crisis in 2015, it was already clear that the earlier expectations of a nuclear renaissance had been too optimistic.

One problem was structural, with a lack of resources due to lower demand than anticipated. Expectations of growth in electricity demand, including demand for new nuclear capacity, were revised down in 2013 and again in 2015 (WNA, 2018b). Domestic competition played a part, with the high cost and long lead times of nuclear power reducing its attractiveness compared to gas and hydro. New nuclear generation was simply too expensive for Russia's electricity market (Fadeeva, 2014; Peschinskii, 2017). There was also political problems connected to Russia's own foreign policy. International sanctions following the annexation of Crimea and war in east Ukraine also contributed, especially by increasing interest rates and thereby technology costs (*NEI Magazine*, 2015d).

No less importantly, there were ample reasons to question Rosatom's effectiveness and its development strategy (Milov, 2015). Rosatom's lack of funds was not a new occurrence. Predictably, during the general budget sequestration in spring 2015, Rosatom had to reduce its investment, especially in nuclear generation (Fomicheva, 2015). Unlike in the previous crisis in 2009–2010, the state did not have sufficient funds to shield nuclear energy through economic crisis. It was difficult to sustain high investment costs with less money to spend in the short term, particularly in light of lower electricity demand projections. In 2011, the freeze of the compulsory investment surcharge on electricity tariffs ahead of Duma and presidential elections had a negative effect on Rosatom's incomes, with the shortfall financed by credits (Audit Chamber, 2014, p.170). However, Rosatom had continued to pursue its expansion plans, on the basis of overblown projections for new nuclear generation capacity. There was a marked contrast between the state corporation's plans, and reasonable expectations based on what its subsidiaries had delivered before. Tellingly, the state had reduced Rosatom's budget before 2014. Compared with the plan, the budget was reduced by 181.1 billion rubles, or 30 per cent, in the years 2011–2013, significantly delaying unit completion (Audit Chamber, 2014, pp.152–153). Apparently, this was the immediate cause of its problems. However, reduced state finance seems to have reflected that Rosatom's results in nuclear power station construction were already lagging behind the development programme (Audit Chamber, 2014, pp.154–160). Its reduced budget appeared to be the consequence, not the cause, of its underperformance.

After almost 11 years as head of Rosatom, Kirienko left to become first deputy chief of staff at the Presidential Administration in October 2016 (RIA Novosti, 2016). There was a general rotation of cadres there following the 2016 Duma elections, and Kirienko was given the key role of overseeing domestic politics ahead of the 2018 presidential election. The new general director, Aleksei Likhachev, came from several years and two deputy ministerial posts at the Economic Development Ministry, but he also knew Kirienko well from Nizhnii Novgorod (Peschinskii and Nikol'skii, 2016). Within months, Kirienko became the head of Rosatom's Supervisory Board (cf. Dzaguto, 2016). Since its establishment, the Supervisory Board had gradually taken on a less active role compared to Kirienko as general director. This had especially been the case from 2012, when the prominent United Russia politician and previous Duma Speaker, Boris Gryzlov, became its chair (Dzaguto, 2016). Observers expected this to change, and that Kirienko would exert considerable influence on Rosatom also after 2016 (Dzaguto et al., 2016b; *RBK Daily*, 2016).

Rosatom under Likhachev by and large maintained the development strategy from the Kirienko years. In particular, much emphasis was placed on acting as a domestic technological powerhouse. The corporation maintained a high profile at events like the 2017 Moscow exposition "Rossiya ustremlennaya v budushchee" ("Russia towards the future"). Likhachev, like Kirienko before him, was rated among the top ten energy industry managers in terms of influence (cf. Oilcapital.ru, 2016; APEK, 2017). Nevertheless, the economic realities of the nuclear energy industry remained the same. In 2017, it became clear that the projections for new NPPs would have to be further reduced. Up to 11 planned new NPPs were shelved (Dyatel, 2017). Some of the demand reduction was due to the Belarusian NPP, which would not be able to break into electricity markets in Poland and Lithuania, and therefore would have to export to Russia (Dyatel, 2017). Rosatom seemed to reach the limits of its potential for expansion in this core activity.

Limits to foreign expansion?

The wave of expansion in 2009–2010 changed Rosatom's business profile, internationalising new NPP construction in particular. Presence in foreign markets remained a priority in the difficult period after Fukushima. To some extent, Rosatom's relative international position improved, as the reaction to the disaster was most severe among other companies' customers in Europe and the US. In political terms, the positive image of Rosatom, compared to for example Gazprom, was an advantage in international markets. To Russian foreign policy this was a soft diplomacy asset, ensuring state support for Rosatom's foreign operations (Aalto et al., 2017). Foreign sales were even more important for the Russian industry during and after the economic crisis of 2015–2016 (*NEI Magazine*, 2016a). Towards the end of the period covered here, Rosatom faced a challenge of maintaining the expected quality and fulfilling its order book from the wave of expansion in 2009–2010.

Throughout the last decade under study, Rosatom's main competitive advantage was its offers of tailored financial packages for new construction. Initially very attractive, these packages may to some extent have served to create an interest in nuclear power in markets that would not necessarily have embarked on plant construction otherwise (Thomas, 2018). At least in one case, Akkuyu NPP in Turkey, the Audit Chamber found that funds from the financial package were dispensed ahead of the elaboration of the financial plan, and without Rosatom exercising necessary oversight (Audit Chamber, 2014, pp.164–166). More than 70 per cent of the financial package went to advance payments for equipment, services and licences in Turkey (Audit Chamber, 2014, p.167). As discussed in Chapter 3, some of the proceeds from the sale of Rosimushchestvo and Rosatom's stakes in Inter RAO in 2013 and 2014 would be spent on Akkuyu NPP (Dzyadko and Ivankina, 2014).

The downturn after the Fukushima disaster changed the international uranium industry and uranium supply. Share prices were affected by low demand and decreasing prices for uranium. Rosatom used this to its advantage. After obtaining control of Uranium One in 2010, in 2013 it acquired the remainder of the company, turning it into its 100 per cent subsidiary (Uranium One Group, 2018). In the global uranium business, sole ownership is not unusual. Uranium One already had a Russian management, led by Vadim Zhivov, and it now moved its headquarters to Moscow. With this acquisition, Rosatom significantly increased its access to easily exploited deposits of uranium, and could reduce the mining of relatively expensive ore in Russia. In 2018, Rosatom restructured its subsidiaries, concentrating the profitable uranium trade in Tekhsnabeksport. Uranium One was turned into a mining company without market access of its own (Dzaguto and Dzhumailo, 2018).

Construction of the first unit at the Belarusian NPP at Astravets began in 2013, with an intended start-up date in 2018. In 2016, three accidents during the construction and installation process delayed completion (Dzaguto et al., 2016a; Ioffe, 2016; Thomas, 2018, p.241). In 2018 the start-up was planned for November 2019 (Barsukov and Dzaguto, 2018; WNA, 2018f). Following Poland and Lithuania's declarations that they would not import electricity from Astravets, Belarus's main gain was in the potential to reduce its reliance on gas-fired power generation and on Gazprom. When Astravets came online, gas demand in Belarus would go down by between 18 per cent and a third (Barsukov and Dzaguto, 2018; WNA, 2018f). The other market within reach was Russia, where it would offer competition for Russia's own generation (Dyatel, 2017). However, overall dependence on Russia for fuel supply did not change, even as it remained an option to acquire nuclear fuel from other suppliers in the future, if relations with the rest of Europe would improve (Marples, 2012). The Russian credits for Astravets significantly increased Belarus's financial dependence on Russia, which in 2016 held 48 per cent of its external debt (*RBK Daily*, 2017).

Uzbekistan had little contact with Rosatom between 2009 and 2016, but it broadened its ties with South Korea, Japan and India (Hashimova, 2011; Weitz and Choi, 2014; Voloshin, 2015). Following the death of President Islam Karimov in September 2016, the new president, Shavkat Mirziyoyev, embarked on a more open foreign policy and pursued economic modernisation. This included opening discussions on economic cooperation with Rosatom. Russia and Uzbekistan signed a cooperation agreement on nuclear energy in December 2017 (WNA, 2018a). Subsequently, Uzbekistan proceeded to develop plans for an NPP supplied by Rosatom (Mashrab, 2018). Putin and Mirziyoyev opened the geological and engineering survey phase in October 2018 (Rosatom, 2018a). Russia was expected to finance most of the cost, projected to around 13 billion US$ (WNA, 2018a), possibly through the Russian Export Centre, which had been established in 2015 (Podrobno.uz, 2018).

Following the Dzhakishev affair, it was more challenging for Kazakhstan to balance cooperation with Russia in the nuclear fuel cycle with that of other partners. Shkolnik was the target of accusations of maintaining an overly pro-Russian line as head of Kazatomprom (Regnum.ru, 2012a). He retained the position until August 2014, remaining on the Board for another year. In 2012, Kazakhstan's aim of acquiring a stake in fuel enrichment finally materialised when Kazatomprom acquired a stake in the Novouralsk plant through a JV with TVEL (Regnum.ru, 2012b). To Rosatom, Kazakhstan was an important partner for uranium and in the fuel cycle, as well as an important producing country for its international uranium production, with equity held through Uranium One. There were also plans under consideration for a new NPP in Kazakhstan. Kazatomprom was the largest global uranium producer, and the only one with all its supply in its country of origin. It was now a swing producer with decisive influence on the price of uranium (Regnum.ru, 2017a), with Russia, China, the US, France and Japan among its five largest customers (Kazatomprom, 2016, p.27). Unusually for a uranium producing company, Kazatomprom in November 2018 conducted an IPO to open the company to minority shareholders and become a public company, thus aiming to improve the company's attractiveness and extend its global network further.[28]

After Russia's annexation of Crimea, Ukraine in summer 2014 began to review its nuclear energy relations with Russia. Yurii Nedashkovskyi returned as Energoatom's CEO already in early March.[29] The review included all stages of the nuclear fuel cycle – uranium supply, enrichment services and the fuel plant project, nuclear power development, and SNF management. Nuclear power, which already covered almost half of Ukraine's electricity demand, was especially important in the effort to reduce overall energy dependence on Russia. As the next few years demonstrated, nuclear power could compensate for lost coal-fired generation, where supply was seriously affected by the war in Donbas (*NEI Magazine*, 2017b). Due to Ukraine's uranium reserves and established relations with Rosatom's international competitors, it was feasible to increase nuclear fuel supply from producers other than Russia. This could be done while expanding nuclear generation in electricity supply, thereby reducing reliance on gas, coal, and on Gazprom in particular. The sources of this policy were not only in Russia's policies towards Ukraine. The new European Energy Security Strategy from 2014 strengthened the EU's recommendation that nuclear power generators diversify fuel supply to have at least two suppliers, to enhance energy security. But indirectly, Russia mattered also here. Another new EU policy alerted members to the need of avoiding excessive reliance on Russian fuel (EURATOM Supply Agency, 2015, p.35). While formally it applied only to EU member states, the recommendation shaped Ukraine's nuclear energy strategy after 2014 (*NEI Magazine*, 2018a).

To Rosatom, and particularly to TVEL, it was even more important than before to maintain its position in the Ukrainian market and good relations with this large customer. As the domestic economic crisis began to unfold, service and supply contracts with foreign customers were again key to maintaining profit margins and production (*NEI Magazine*, 2015d). Ukraine was especially important to corporate survival because of the protracted crisis in the global nuclear industry after Fukushima. But TVEL's politically most important project, the fuel plant, was significantly delayed by the annexation of Crimea and the war in Donbas. In March 2015, Nedashkovskyi declared that TVEL had not fulfilled its contractual obligations. The contract would be transferred to the company that came second in the tender, Westinghouse (Vakarelska, 2017). In a parallel development, the contract with Atomstroieksport for Khmelnytskyi 3 and 4 came under review in December 2014 and the facilitating legislation repealed in September 2015. In August 2016, Ukraine entered into a new contract with the company that came second in the tender, Korea Hydro & Nuclear Power (WNA, 2018c). The finance for this project was to come from electricity trade between Khmelnytskyi 2 and the EU, itself a new project (*NEI Magazine*, 2018e). Rosatom's hold on the Ukrainian market was likely to decrease further.

In 2015–2016, Energoatom began to transfer Zaporizhzhya NPP and South Ukraine NPP entirely to Westinghouse fuel (Energoatom, 2018). It was expected that Rivne NPP, too, would begin to use Westinghouse fuel (Regnum.ru, 2017b). The aim was to reduce TVEL's overall share of Ukrainian fuel supply from 94–95 per cent in 2015 to 60 per cent in 2016, and this did indeed happen (*NEI Magazine*, 2016d). TVEL threatened to treat this as a breach of the terms of the 2010 contract (*NEI Magazine*, 2016d).[30] The Russian MFA accused Ukraine of turning Ukraine into "a testing ground for experimental US fuel assemblies" (*NEI Magazine*, 2016c). Ukraine continued its course unabated.

At the other end of the nuclear fuel cycle, Ukraine further increased its domestic uranium production. Already up from 830 tonnes annually in 2010, in 2015 Ukraine produced 1200 tonnes, and planned to reach self-sufficiency (approximately 1880 tU/year) within a few years (WNA, 2018c). It developed comprehensive relations with Areva and later Urenco for enrichment (*NEI Magazine*, 2015c; 2016b). After three years of negotiations, Ukraine and Areva's successor Orano agreed on a feasibility study for fuel assembly recycling in 2018 (*NEI Magazine*, 2015b; 2018c). This was in addition to Ukraine's own SNF storage facility at Chernobyl, for which the development process finally moved forward again in 2014 (*NEI Magazine*, 2017a). The former meant that independence from Rosatom's enrichment services would come within reach, as Ukraine's own uranium was not enriched at the IUEC (*NEI Magazine*, 2016e). The latter would be a prerequisite for further limiting dependence on Russia for nuclear fuel, as the existing contract with Rosatom did not cover SNF from Westinghouse.

Rosatom and Armenia in 2013 and 2014 agreed that Rosatom would undertake the work on upgrading Metsamor to extend its service life to 2026, with Russian finance of 300 million US$ (WNA, 2018d). Planning was then underway for a new NPP to replace Metsamor, with an anticipated construction start in 2018–2019 (ARKA News Agency, 2018). However, the new government that came to power in spring 2018 declared that it would reconsider the need to replace Metsamor with a new NPP (ARKA News Agency, 2018; Khvostik et al., 2018).

Conclusions

Minatom in the 1990s had extensive autonomy vis-à-vis the central state, and this extended into its foreign operations. The lack of mutual adaptation to facilitate access and participation in institutional development in the relations between the state and Minatom inhibited development on both sides. This status quo was sustained by informal rent sharing. The extent to which rent was channelled outside Minatom is not known. The ruling coalition under Yeltsin was only loosely integrated; moreover it was characterised by infighting. The squabble among the banks in 1995 and 1997–1998 to acquire a share of the rents most likely reflected that Minatom until then retained a considerable share itself, and was not channelling its rent towards any one part of the ruling coalition. In the end, the outcome of that struggle was that Minatom continued to take care of its own rent streams and decide where they were channelled.

Until 1998, it was difficult to exercise real state control and oversight over Minatom and the companies in the nuclear fuel cycle. Other state organisations were in effect denied access to crucial sides of Minatom's decision making and development. This situation could only continue with the informal support of representatives of state organisations and the ruling coalition. Its extensive autonomy allowed Minatom to disregard formal institutions and establish a de facto privilege to enter into transactions with international parties on behalf of the Russian state. Informality and personal ties were accordingly decisive in interactions between the state and Minatom in the 1990s. State capacity remained low as a result.

Thanks to informal rent streams, the industry managed to muddle through in splendid isolation. Increasingly however, this inhibited its development. The industry was ill equipped to compete internationally. Without coordination at the top state level, the institutional framework for international cooperation was insufficiently developed to support strategic partnerships. When the oil price boom and the electricity reform increased the state's capacity to invest, also in nuclear energy, the industry was more inclined to give the state access. Expansion served as a carrot for the industry, ensuring that it supported a wide-ranging reorganisation.

The nuclear sector reform of 2005–2007 modernised the nuclear energy industry and forged a higher degree of specialisation among its organisations. Oversight within the industry was institutionalised and implemented through Atomenergoprom. But at the top level, state oversight of Rosatom, conducted through the Supervisory Board, depended in practice on personal loyalty in a regime context. Here, the informal mechanisms similar to those of Yeltsin's ruling coalition were found also in the now more developed state, but they were formalised. On paper, oversight of Rosatom was an impersonal arrangement between the president and representatives of the state, but informally, personal loyalty mattered when vacancies were filled. With time, informal constraints could eventually enable implementation of formal institutions, but this would still be at the president's discretion. The restoration of state capacity in the sector did not progress to a level where it would take precedence over regime stability. Oversight would therefore depend on the regime.

The reform proceeded much faster than the reform of RAO UES (Chapter 3), although the several false starts to Rosatom reform added a very long lead time to the process. The legislation phase was in any case much quicker, and designed to minimise public discussion and industrial and political attempts to derail and influence it. There was no Duma debate and subsequent amendments, no minority owners to placate, no regional governors to get on board or marginalise in the process. There was however one major similarity in how Putin placed Kirienko in charge of the reform on behalf of the state, while throwing his full support behind the endeavour. This was sustained throughout the process.

With regard to the outcome, RAO UES reform implementation and the subsequent trajectory of the electricity industry fell short of the plans for reform. However, the Russian electricity industry and markets were transformed, even if incompletely. Similarly, Rosatom was reorganised and modernised with a new and more functional institutional framework. But the reform only partially addressed the nuclear energy industry's persistent problems. An institutionalised lack of transparency was to some extent reproduced. Informal institutions were put onto paper, but not substantially changed. The problem of funding the industry did not go away, as shown in the last part of this chapter. A lack of overall state participation in industrial policymaking meant that costly plans were developed and then partially implemented following government cuts. There was little sense, or discussion, of priority and purpose at the outset and at the level of the state. The industry was left to set priorities. In consequence, improvements to efficiency and capacity utilisation were secured, but nobody had any interest in discussing whether the way ahead was to maintain only the status quo.

The process that formed a new institutional framework for the nuclear energy industry extended to international operations. It became possible to offer a real strategic partnership to Kazakhstan, and make further nuclear cooperation with Ukraine contingent on a greater role for Russia. Without the necessary coordination and financial muscle, support for Armenia's and Belarus's nuclear energy development would have been difficult. The reform had shaped the expansion of nuclear energy operations abroad in a direction that was desirable for the state, and made nuclear energy companies integral to foreign policy. The industry became far more accessible as an instrument of foreign policy, which could be applied to slow the independent technological development of Ukraine and Kazakhstan, and cultivate regional dependence on Russia for nuclear energy. Dependence was used as a tool of foreign policy in Kazakhstan. In Ukraine, financial weakness and dependence on Russia for nuclear fuel were used to maximise outcomes in favour of Russia in bilateral negotiations. This was most visible in the Kharkiv Accords of 2010, but also in routine negotiations where it brought real market advantages to the Russian nuclear energy industry. In this way, Russia retained Ukraine's captive nuclear fuel market in the short term. However, the subsequent lack of industry development in Ukraine contributed to eroding the Ukrainian elites' shaky trust in Russia's willingness to deliver. Ukraine's relatively fast change of partners in the nuclear energy industry after 2014 happened because of Russia's aggression towards Ukraine, but it was technologically and commercially possible because other partnerships had been established and maintained, and used to balance Russia for many years. Kazakhstan also pursued a handful of comprehensive international partnerships in the nuclear energy industry, using them to balance Russia. In the case of Belarus, which had little alternative than to rely on Rosatom to supply an NPP, much care was taken to make Russian offers of credit and technology binding and consequential. This appeared to come at the cost of greater dependence on Russia in the gas sector. However, as will be seen in Chapter 7, that process was long under way. It was Minsk's determined negotiation that delivered an NPP in return.

The political commitment to nuclear industry expansion connected domestic development, and especially the concern of maintaining a technologically advanced industry, to a foreign policy rationale. The industry was seen as important to Russia's great power status. It was also a source of influence in post-Soviet states, and an export business in its own right. The issue of overstretch was not raised on the domestic agenda, possibly for such reasons. It remains to be seen whether the industry will have to adopt more modest strategies in the years to come.

Notes

1 Rosatom holds enterprises in the nuclear military complex directly. Nuclear construction was in 2011 incorporated in the Atomenergomash holding.
2 ARMZ was until 2008 Atomredmetzoloto, when it became Uranovyi kholding ARMZ (Uranium holding ARMZ).
3 Tekhsnabeksport operates as Tenex internationally.
4 Between 2011 and 2016, Rosatom's nuclear engineering companies NIAEP, Atomenergoproekt, Atomproekt, and Atomstroieksport were reorganized into Rosatom's engineering division ASE.
5 An overview of Russian-produced reactors, in Russia and elsewhere, can be found at http://www.world-nuclear.org/information-library/country-profiles/countries-o-s/russia-nuclear-power.aspx
6 From civilian production and services. Rosatom's share of military expenditure is part of the non-disclosed part of the state budget.
7 An overview of reactor types, including pressurized water reactors like the Russian VVER, is found at the website of the World Nuclear Association: http://www.world-nuclear.org/
8 Minsredmash existed from 1953 to 1986. Its predecessor was Pervoe glavnoe upravlenie pri SNK (Sovet narodnykh kommissarov) SSSR, in English the First Chief Directorate. PGU was founded in 1945.
9 A golden share is a nominal share that gives an owner, often a government, direct influence over company development and an opportunity to outvote other owners on specific issues. It is an instrument associated with privatisation processes and with sectors of strategic interest to states.
10 At the time of writing, there is no indication that Russia does not keep its obligations within the international regime on non-proliferation regime in relations with Iran, but at that time, there were serious international worries about Russia's interpretation of the non-proliferation regime.

The electricity industry 125

11 Also known as HEU-LEU in English and VOU-NOU in Russian. Under the programme, which lasted from 1993 to 2013, 500 tonnes of weapons-grade Russian HEU were downblended to LEU using US natural uranium, then transported to the US for use in NPPs. This fuel supplied up to ten per cent of all US electricity in the 20-year period. The two partners in the commercial agreement were Tekhsnabeksport (Tenex) and USEC (from 2014 Centrus Energy Corp.). In an unintended consequence of the programme, the American partner USEC became dependent on Rosatom for enrichment, leaving global primary enrichment services in the hands of three companies, Rosatom, the UK–Netherlands–German company Urenco, and the French company Areva (from January 2018 Orano).
12 Orebodies in Kazakhstan are larger and the ore can be more easily extracted than in Russia's deposits. They are therefore more commercially viable.
13 Ukraine acceded to the NPT in December 1994, following the signing of the Budapest Memorandum on Security Assurances. The Memorandum provided security assurances against threats or use of force against the territorial integrity or political independence of Ukraine, Belarus and Kazakhstan on the part of the US, UK and Russia. As a consequence, Ukraine, Belarus and Kazakhstan gave up their nuclear weapons stockpiles in 1994–1996.
14 Most reactors had a licensed service life of 30 years from first power.
15 The golden share gave TVEL a veto over "unfavourable business decisions" including closure, ownership change, management change, change of business direction and decreases in production.
16 Initially, 45 per cent held by ARMZ, in 2010 49.67 per cent held by Uranium One.
17 Other state corporations were Vneshekonombank/VEB (foreign investment financial organisation), Rosnano (nanotechnology industry development, shareholding company from 2010), Rostekhnologii (advanced technology development), Olimpstroi (The 2014 Olympic Games in Sochi), and the Corporation for housing reform.
18 In February 2009.
19 Hydropower generation was privileged in a similar way.
20 Evstratov was later released on bail, and the court returned the case to further investigation in 2012 and again in 2014 (Barinov, 2014). The charges were withdrawn in 2016 when the investigating authority, the Central Board of Economic Security and Anti-Corruption of the Interior Ministry, was itself charged with corruption. That trial ended with convictions in 2017. This is also known as the Sugrobov case.
21 The IUEC is not to be confused with the two international nuclear fuel banks. Under the auspices of IAEA, Russia established a nuclear fuel reserve near Angarsk in 2010. Nuclear fuel is available at market rates, to any IAEA member of good standing unable to procure nuclear fuel for political reasons. In addition, IAEA controls a bank of low-enriched uranium in Kazakhstan (Ulba), operational from 2017, which can be made available to any IAEA member that finds it difficult to secure supply of LEU.
22 Dzhakishev had been cleared of similar charges in 2007.
23 Shkolnik was born in Russia, and his son was married to the daughter of Vadim Zhivov, then head of ARMZ (now Uranium One) and responsible for Rosatom's contacts with Kazatomprom.
24 Following Dzhakishev's arrest, Uranium One shares traded down by a third before being suspended from the Toronto stock exchange.
25 From October 2006 Westinghouse-Toshiba following the acquisition of 77 per cent of Westinghouse's shares by Toshiba. This was reduced to 67 per cent in 2007, when a 10 per cent stake was sold to Kazatomprom.
26 Novokonstantinovka in Russian.
27 Ostrovets in Russian.

28 Cameco is the only other uranium producer that is a public company.
29 The acting CEO in 2013–2014, Nikita Konstantinov, in 2015 took up a position in the Rosatom subsidiary Rusatom International.
30 Had this happened, it would have been a similar development to relations between Gazprom and Naftogaz at the same time. Interestingly, TVEL did not pursue this course of action.

References

Aalto, P. et al. (2017) "Russian nuclear energy diplomacy in Finland and Hungary", *Eurasian Geography and Economics*, 58 (4): 386–417

Agentstvo ekonomicheskikh novostei (1999) "Vypusk 'Biznes-fakt. Privatizatsiya' [Edition 'Business news. Privatization']", *Agentstvo ekonomicheskikh novostei*, 23 April

Aleksandrov, Yu. (2004) "Monopolii. Ottsy i deti 'Gazproma' [Monopolies. Gazprom's fathers and sons]", *Novoe vremya*, 14 November, pp.20–22

Alieva, N. (1998) "Estestvennoi monopolii – OAO 'TVEL', po mneniyu ego prezidenta Vitaliya Konovalova, est' chto skazat' [OAO Tvel has something to say for the natural monopoly, according to president Vitalii Konovalov]", *Vek*, 29 January

Angelova, A. (2008) "AES 'Druzhba': Rossiya na rynke stran tsentral'noi i vostochnoi Evropy [NPP Friendship: Russia on the Central and East European market]", *Indeks bezopasnosti*, 14 (2): 97–116

Antonov, V., Bocharova, S. and Vaganov, A. (2005) "Dorvalsya do atomnykh milliardov. Kirienko stal khozyainom Rosatoma [Got hold of the nuclear billions. Kirienko head of Rosatom]", *Nezavisimaya gazeta*, 16 November, p.1

APEK (2017), *Reiting vliyaniya krupnykh predprinimatelei i top-menedzherov toplivno-energeticheskogo kompleksa v iyune 2017 g. [Rating of the influence of major businessmen and top managers in the fuel and energy complex, June 2017]* [online]. 29 June (Moscow: Agentstvo politicheskikh i ekonomicheskikh kommunikatsii). Available from: http://apecom.ru/projects/item.php?SECTION_ID=102&ELEMENT_ID=3803 [Accessed 18 March 2019]

ARKA News Agency (2014) "Rossiya pokroet chast' raskhodov na stroitel'stvo novoi AES v Armenii stoimost'yu v $4,5 mlrd. – ministr [Russia will cover partial costs for construction of the new Armenian NPP up to 4.5 bn. US$, says minister]" [online]. 4 July (Yerevan: ARKA News Agency). Available from: http://www.arka.am/ru/news/economy/rossya_pokroet_chast_raskhodov_na_stroitelstvo_novoy_aes_v_armenii_stoimostyu_v_4_5_mlrd_ministr/ [Accessed 1 July 2019]

ARKA News Agency (2018) "Glava Minenergo ne vidit nasushchnoi neobkhodimosti v stroitel'stve novoi AES [The Head of the Energy Ministry does not see any urgent need to build a new NPP]" [online]. 25 May (Yerevan: ARKA News Agency). Available from: http://arka.am/ru/news/economy/glava_minenergo_ne_vidit_nasushchnoy_neobkhodimosti_v_stroitelstve_novoy_aes/ [Accessed 9 November 2018]

Atomnaya strategiya (2009) "K 70-letiyu Evgeniya Olegovicha Adamova [To Evgenii Olegovich Adamov's 70th birthday]", *Atomnaya strategiya*, June 2009, pp.3–6

Atomredmetzoloto (2010) *OAO "Atomredmetzoloto". Godovoi otchet za 2009 god [Atomredmetzoloto. Annual report for 2009]* (Moscow: Atomredmetzoloto)

Atomredmetzoloto (2011) *2010 OAO "Atomredmetzoloto" godovoi otchet [2010 Annual report for Atomredmetzoloto]* (Moscow: Atomredmetzoloto)

Audit Chamber (2014) *Otchet o rezul'tatakh kontrol'nogo meropriyatiya "Proverka tselevogo i effektivnogo ispol'zovaniya byudzhetnykh sredstv, vydelennykh v 2011–2013 godakh na realizatsiyu meropriyatii po stroitel'stvu energoblokov na deistvuyushchikh atomnykh elektrostantsiyakh, svyazannykh s razvitiem atomnogo energopromyshlennogo kompleksa v ramkakh programmy deyatel'nosti gosudarstvennoi korporatsii po atomnoi energii "Rosatom" na dolgosrochnyi period (2009–2015 gody)"* [*Report on the results of the control activity "Verification of targeted and effective utilisation of budgetary funds issued in 2011–2013 to implement measures to construct units at operating atomic power plants in connection with the development of the atomic energy industrial complex within the activity programme of the state corporation for atomic energy Rosatom in the long term period (2009–2015)"*] (Moscow: Byulleten' Schetnoi Palaty Rossiiskoi Federatsii)

Avoyan, S. (2008) "Armenia: Yerevan, Moscow set up uranium venture", *Radio Free Europe/Radio Liberty*, 25 April

Balmaceda, M.M. (2013) *The Politics of Energy Dependency. Ukraine, Belarus and Lithuania between Domestic Oligarchs and Russian Pressure* (Toronto: University of Toronto Press)

Barinov, V. (2014) "'Atomnye den'gi peredali po sledstvennoi linii [The atomic money were returned to the line of inquiry]", *Kommersant*, 22 September, p.4

Barsukov, Yu. and Dzaguto, V. (2018) "Belorussiya ukhodit ot Gazproma [Belarus goes away from Gazprom]", *Kommersant*, 5 September, p.9

Belkina, O. (2006) "Sovmestnye usiliya [Joint efforts]", *Megapolis*, 31 July

Belova, A. (2008) "Itogi reformirovaniya atomnoi otrasli Rossii [A summary of the reforms in Russia's nuclear industry]", *Indeks bezopasnosti*, 14 (2): 141–146

Belton, C. (2009) "Rosatom agrees deal for stake in Uranium One", *The Financial Times*, 15 June

Belyakov, E. (2006) "'Atomprom' ostanovil svoi poluraspad ['Atomprom' stops its half-disintegration]", *Gazeta*, 7 December, p.13

Belyakov, E. and Sokolovskaya, M. (2007) "Metamorfozy Rosatoma [Rosatom's metamorphoses]", *Gazeta*, 9 October, p.9

Belyaninov, K. (2001) "Strana nepuganykh i.o. [The country of fearless acting heads]", *Novye Izvestiya*, 31 August, p.1

Blagov, S. (2007) "Russia and Kazakhstan pursue energy partnership", *Eurasia Daily Monitor*, 4 April

Bogatykh, M. (1999) "Minatom dozrel. I vypolnil postanovlenie pravitel'stva [Minatom grew up. And carried out the government's decision]", *Segodnya*, 26 March

Bovt, G. (2007) "'Anna Belova: Loshchad' mozhno privesti k vode, no ee nel'zya zastavit' pit'" [Anna Belova: You can take the horse to the water, but you cannot force her to drink]", *Profil'*, 26 February, p.44–50

Bradford, P.A. (2009) "The nuclear renaissance meets economic reality", *Bulletin of the Atomic Scientists*, 65 (6): 60–64

Bukharin, O. (1995) "Integratsiya voennogo i grazhdanskogo yadernykh toplivnykh tsiklov v Rossii [Integration of the military and civilian nuclear fuel cycles in Russia]", *Yadernyi kontrol'*, 1995 (9): 10–13

Butler, W.E. (2008) "Treaty capacity and the Russian state corporation", *The American Journal of International Law*, 102 (2): 310–315

Butrin, D., Kornysheva, A. and Kiseleva, E. (2006) "Atomokhod Sobyanina [Sobyanin's atomic move]", *Kommersant*, 29 May, p.1

Centrus Energy Corp. (2018) "Megatons to Megawatts" [online]. (Bethesda, Maryland: Centrus Energy Corp.). Available from: https://www.centrusenergy.com/who-we-are/history/megatons-to-megawatts/ [Accessed 2 November 2018]

Chereshnev, S. (2004) "Yadernoe toplivo dlya Kremlya. Pomoshchnik prezidenta vozglavil kompaniyu 'TVEL' [Nuclear fuel for the Kremlin. The presidential aide heads the TVEL Company]", *Izvestiya*, 26 October, p.7

Cooper, J. (1991) *The Soviet Defence Industry: Conversion and Reform* (London: The Royal Institute of International Affairs/Pinter Publishers)

Cooper, J. (2013) "The Russian economy twenty years after the end of the socialist economic system", *Journal of Eurasian Studies*, 4 (1): 55–64

Danielyan, E. (2007) "U.S. moves to help Armenia build new nuclear power plant", *Eurasia Daily Monitor*, 28 November

Danielyan, E. (2009) "Armenia presses ahead with nuclear power plant construction", *Eurasia Daily Monitor*, 29 May

Davydov, I. (2008) "Voznya vokrug yadernoi energetiki [The troubles of nuclear energy]", *Nezavisimaya gazeta*, 15 January, p.19

Decree No. 61 (29/01/1992) *O Ministerstve Rossiiskoi Federatsii po atomnoi energii* [*On the Ministry for atomic energy of the Russian Federation*] (Moscow: President of the Russian Federation)

Decree No. 166 (08/02/1996) *O sovershenstvovanii upravleniya predpriyatiyami yaderno-toplivnogo tsikla* [*On the improvement of management of enterprises in the nuclear fuel cycle*] (Moscow: President of the Russian Federation)

Decree No. 446 (15/04/1993) *Ob osobennostyakh privatizatsii predpriyatii, nakhodyashchikhsya v vedenii Ministerstva Rossiiskoi Federatsii po atomnoi energii, i upravleniya imi v usloviyakh razvitiya rynochnoi ekonomiki* [*On the particularities of privatisation of the enterprises that fall under the authority of the Ministry of atomic energy of the Russian Federation, and on management in the circumstances of the development of a market economy*] (Moscow: President of the Russian Federation)

Delovaya stolitsa (2008a) "Vremya obogashchat'. Ukraina yaderno kooperiruetsya s Rossiei i Kazakhstanom [It's time to enrich. Ukraine in nuclear cooperation with Russia and Kazakhstan]", *Delovaya stolitsa*, 9 July

Delovaya stolitsa (2008b) "Gruppa kontaktov. Ukraina vplotnuyu vzyalas' za diversifikatsiyu istochnikov postavok yadernogo topliva [Contact group. Ukraine has begun in earnest to diversify supply sources for nuclear fuel]", *Delovaya stolitsa*, 7 April

Delovaya stolitsa (2010a) "Geny sovetskogo atoma. Ukraina doverila svoyu atomnuyu energetiku rossiyanam [The Soviet atom's genes. Ukraine entrusts its nuclear power sector to the Russians]", *Delovaya stolitsa*, 1 November

Delovaya stolitsa (2010b) "Rezerv nakachali uranom. Ukrainskie atomshchiki popytayutsya sokratit' zavisimost' ot Rossii [A reserve pumped up on uranium. The Ukrainian nuclear sector try to limit the dependence on Russia]", *Delovaya stolitsa*, 18 January

Delovaya stolitsa (2011) "CHAO, atom. Ukraina peredaet korporativnye prava na svoe yadernoe budushchee Rossii [Ciao, atom. Ukraine transfers its corporate rights to a nuclear future to Russia]", *Delovaya stolitsa*, 18 September

Dyatel, T. (2017) "Mirnyi atom otkladyvayut v dolgii yashchik [The peaceful atom is shelved]", *Kommersant* 25 October, p.1

Dye, M., Höglund, J. and Benjaminsson, U. (2015) "Diversification of the VVER fuel market" [online]. 30 September Nuclear Engineering International). Available from: https://www.neimagazine.com/features/featurediversification-of-the-vver-fuel-ma rket-4682502/ [Accessed 1 July 2019]

Dzaguto, V. (2009) "Energetikam ogranichili investsostavlyayushchuyu [The investment surcharge is reduced for the electricity sector]", *Kommersant*, 23 December, p.11

Dzaguto, V. (2010a) "Rossiya dostroit Khmel'nitskuyu AES i sama za eto zaplatit [Russia completes the Khmelnitskyy NPP and also pays for it]", *Kommersant*, 10 June, p.11

Dzaguto, V. (2010b) "Rossiya i Ukraina ob"edinyatsya na atomnom urovne [Russia and Ukraine will unite at the atomic level]", *Kommersant*, 28 April, p.9

Dzaguto, V. (2011a) "'Rosatom" vyros v "renessanse" i nadeetsya uderzhat'sya na fone padeniya rynka [Rosatom grew during the "renaissance" and hopes to hold its ground in the falling market]", *Kommersant*, 29 September, p.11

Dzaguto, V. (2011b) "'Rosatomu" ukazali ego mesto na rynke yadernogo topliva Ukrainy [Rosatom is shown its place in Ukraine's nuclear fuel market]", *Kommersant*, 22 August, p.9

Dzaguto, V. (2011c) "Rossiya i Ukraina razzhigayut yadernoe toplivo [Russia and Ukraine kindle the nuclear fuel]", *Kommersant*, 3 February, p.9

Dzaguto, V. (2016) "Atom tak prosto ne otpuskaet [The atom does not let go that easily]", *Kommersant*, 6 October, p.4

Dzaguto, V. and Dzhumailo, A. (2018) "'Rosatom' slivaet dokhody [Rosatom merges its incomes]", *Kommersant*, 11 January, p.9

Dzaguto, V., Barsukov, Yu. and Kozlov, D. (2016a) "Belorusskaya AES mozhet podvinutsya [The Belarusian NPP may move further]", *Kommersant*, 2 August, p.9

Dzaguto, V. et al. (2016b) "Isotop Sergeya Kirienko [Sergei Kirienko's isotope]", *Kommersant*, 6 October, p.1

Dzyadko, T. and Ivankina, E. (2014) "Sechin blokiruet "Inter RAO" [Sechin blocks Inter RAO]", *RBK Daily*, 20 January, p.1

Embassy Astana (2009) Kazakhstan: Russian hand in Kazatomprom drama?, 09ASTANA2197/Wikileaks #241141. Issue date 22 December 2009. *Cablegate* [online]. (Published by Wikileaks 1 September 2011). Available from: https://search.wikileaks.org/plusd/cables/09ASTANA2197_a.html [Accessed 14 November 2018]

Embassy Kyiv (2008) Ukraine's dependence on Russian energy, 08KYIV2358/Wikileaks #180940. Issue date 2 December 2008. *Cablegate* [online]. (Published by Wikileaks 1 September 2011). Available from: https://search.wikileaks.org/plusd/cables/08KYIV2358_a.html [Accessed 1 July 2019]

Embassy Kyiv (2010) Ukraine's Deputy PM on money laundering, elections, IMF, 10KYIV193_a. Issue date 5 February 2010. *Cablegate* [online]. (Published by Wikileaks 1 September 2011). Available from: https://wikileaks.org/plusd/cables/10KYIV193_a.html [Accessed 16 November 2018]

Embassy Moscow (2007a) Russia: Vladimir Travin named to head Atomenergoprom, 07MOSCOW3407/Wikileaks #115159. Issue date 12 July 2007. *Cablegate* [online]. (Published by Wikileaks 1 September 2011). Available from: https://search.wikileaks.org/plusd/cables/07MOSCOW3407_a.html [Accessed 1 July 2019]

Embassy Moscow (2007b) Russia: Ambassador's April 26 meeting with Audit Chamber Chairman Stepashin, 07MOSCOW1960/Wikileaks #106069. Issue date 27 April 2007. *Cablegate* [online]. (Published by Wikileaks 1 September 2011). Available from: https://search.wikileaks.org/plusd/cables/07MOSCOW1960_a.html [Accessed 1 July 2019]

Embassy Moscow (2007c) Russia: MFA caught off guard by Burma nuclear deal, 07MOSCOW2316/Wikileaks #108794. Issue date 18 May 2007. *Cablegate* [online]. (Published by Wikileaks 1 September 2011). Available from: https://search.wikileaks.org/plusd/cables/07MOSCOW2316_a.html [Accessed 1 July 2019]

Embassy Moscow (2008) Commentators underscore continuity in assessing new government, 08MOSCOW1336/Wikileaks #153704. Issue date 13 May 2008. *Cablegate* [online]. (Published by Wikileaks 1 September 2011). Available from: https://search.wikileaks.org/plusd/cables/08MOSCOW1336_a.html [Accessed 1 July 2019]

Emel'yanenko, V. (1998) "Ukroshchenie stroptivogo [The taming of the obstinate]", *Moskovskie novosti*, 10 March, p.9

Emel'yanenkov, A. (2006) "Renessans po Kirienko [A renaissance according to Kirienko]", *Rossiiskaya gazeta*, 5 July, p.1

Emel'yanenkov, A. (2007a) "Megatonny - nalevo, megavatty - napravo [Megatonnes to the left, megawatts to the right]", *Rossiiskaya gazeta*, 3 May, p.6

Emel'yanenkov, A. (2007b) "Krylatyi 'Rosatom' [Winged Rosatom]", *Rossiiskaya gazeta*, 14 November, p.4

Emel'yanenkov, A. (2007c) "Usloviya diktuet zakazchik [The customer sets the conditions]", *Rossiiskaya gazeta*, 25 October, p.1

Emel'yanenkov, A. (2009) "Kazakhskii atom otdali Shol'niku [The Kazakh atom is transferred to Shkol'nik]", *Rossiiskaya gazeta*, 4 June, p.6

Emel'yanenkov, A. (2010) "Nedelimyi atom [The indivisible atom]", *Rossiiskaya gazeta*, 30 April, p.6

Energoatom (2010) *NAEK "Energoatom" NNEGC "Energoatom"* (Kiyv: Energoatom)

Energoatom (2018) "Presidents of Energoatom and Westinghouse discussed the progress of implementation of Westinghouse nuclear fuel at Ukrainian nuclear power plants" [online]. 30 May (Kyiv: Energopatom). Available from: http://www.energoatom.kiev.ua/en/actvts/international/international_activities/53881-presidents_of_energoatom_and_westinghouse_discussed_the_progress_of_implemenation_of_westinghouse_nuclear_fuel_at_ukranian_nuclear_power_plants/ [Accessed 15 November 2018]

EURATOM Supply Agency (2015) *Annual Report 2014*. (Luxembourg: EURATOM/European Union)

EURATOM Supply Agency (2018) "Nuclear Fuel Cycle - Front End" [online]. n.d. (Luxembourg: EURATOM/European Union). Available from: http://ec.europa.eu/euratom/observatory_segments_e.html [Accessed 22 November 2018]

Fadeeva, A. (2014) "Atomnaya peregruzka [Atomic overload]", *Vedomosti*, 2 October, p.13

Faizullaev, D.A. (2009) "Tsentral'noaziatskii atomnyi "renessans" [The Central Asian nuclear 'renaissance']", *Aziya i Afrika segodnya*, 2009 (8): 25–31

Federal Law No. 13 (05/02/2007) *Ob osobennostyakh upravleniya i rasporyazheniya imushchestvom i aktsiyami organizatsii, osushchestvlyayushchikh deyatel'nost' v oblasti ispol'zovaniya atomnoi energii, i o vnesenii izmenenii v otdel'nye zakonodatel'nye akty Rossiiskoi Federatsii* [*On the peculiarities of management and direction of property and shares by organisations that carry out their business in the field of atomic energy, and on changes to separate acts of legislation of the Russian Federation*] (Moscow: The Federal Assembly)

Federal Law No. 57 (29/04/2008) *O poriadke osushchestvleniya inostrannykh investitsii v khozyaistvennye obshchestva, imeyushchie strategicheskoe znachenie dlya natsional'noi bezopasnosti Rossiiskoi Federatsii* [*On the realisation of foreign investments in entities with a strategic significance for the Russian Federation's national security*] (Moscow: The Federal Assembly)

Federal Law No. 317 (01/12/2007) *O Gosudarstvennoi korporatsii po atomnoi energii "Rosatom"* [*On the State corporation for atomic energy "Rosatom"*] (Moscow: The Federal Assembly)

Ferguson, C.G. (2009) "A nuclear renaissance?" in Luft, G. and Korin, A. ed., *Energy Security Challenges for the 21st Century* (Santa Barbara/Denver/Oxford: Praeger Security International), pp.295–307

Filatova, I. (2009) "Clock ticking on state corporations", *The Moscow Times*, 22 October, p.1

Fomicheva, A. (2015) "Byudzhet perevedut na bystrye neitrony [The budget is transferred to fast neutrons]", *Kommersant*, 8 April, p.9

Garnett, S.W. (1995) "Ukraine's decision to join the NPT", *Arms Control Today*, 25 (1): 7–12

Gorbenko, P. (2010) "Ukrainskaya simfoniya dlya TVELa [A Ukrainian symphony for TVEL]", *Vestnik Atomproma*, October, p.20–24

Gorelov, N. (2007) "Rynok s 'dopolnitel'nymi soglasheniyami' [A market with 'extra agreements']", *Vremya novostei*, 17 January, p.8

Gorst, I. (2009) "Kazakhs charge ex-head of atomic power", *The Financial Times*, 28 May

Gorst, I. (2010) "Former Kazakh nuclear chief given jail term", *The Financial Times*, 12 March

Gorst, I. and Simon, B. (2010) "Rosatom launches global charm offensive", *The Financial Times*, 1 September

Gotova, N. (1998) "Gryaznye tantsy na reaktore [Dirty dancing on the reactor]", *Moskovskii Komsomolets*, 10 December

Government Order No. 775 (22/04/1992) *O chlenakh kollegii Ministerstva Rossiiskoi Federatsii po atomnoi energii* [*On members of the collegium of the Ministry of atomic energy of the Russian Federation*] (Moscow: The Government of the Russian Federation)

Government Resolution No. 175 (19/03/1992 (22/09/1993)) *Voprosy Ministerstva Rossiiskoi Federatsii po atomnoi energii* [*On the question of the Ministry of atomic energy of the Russian Federation*] (Moscow: The Government of the Russian Federation)

Government Resolution No. 506-12 (02/06/2014) *Ob utverzhdenii gosudarstvennoi programmy Rossiiskoi federatsii "Razvitie atomnogo energopromyshlennogo kompleksa"* [*On the confirmation of the state programme of the Russian Federation "Development of the atomic energy industry complex"*] (Moscow: The Government of the Russian Federation)

Government Resolution No. 605 (06/10/2006) *O Federal'noi tselevoi programme "Razvitie atomnogo energopromyshlennogo kompleksa Rossii na 2007–2010 gody i na perspektivu do 2015 goda"* [*On the Federal development programme 'Development of the Russian atomic energy industry complex in 2007 to 2010 and towards 2015*] (Moscow: The Government of the Russian Federation)

Government Resolution No. 815 (21/07/1998) *Ob utverzhdenii Programmy razvitiya atomnoi energetiki Rossiiskoi federatsii na 1998–2005 gody i na period do 2010 goda* [*On the confirmation of a Development programme for the atomic energy industry of the Russian Federation in 1998 to 2005 and the period to 2010*] (Moscow: The Government of the Russian Federation)

Grudnitskii, P. (2006a) "Uranovyi tandem [A tandem in uranium]", *Ekspert*, 23 October, pp.54–55

Grudnitskii, P. (2006b) "Uran – nashe vse [Uranium is our everything]", *Ekspert Kazakhstan*, 21 May

Hashimova, U. (2011) "East-West diplomacy of the Uzbek President", *Eurasia Daily Monitor*, 17 February

Heath, J.R. (2009) "Strategic protectionism? National security and foreign investment in the Russian Federation", *George Washington International Law Review*, 41 (2009): 101–137

Humber, Y. (2006) "Putin revives nuclear alliance", *The Moscow Times*, 13 January, p.1

132 *The nuclear energy industry*

Ibragimova, G. (2010) "Atomnaya energetika v Tsentral'noi Azii: Est' li perspektivy? [Nuclear energy in Central Asia: is there a future?]", *Indeks bezopasnosti*, 16 (4): 77–103

IMF (2014) *Russian Federation. Fiscal Transparency Evaluation*. IMF Country Report. (Washington, DC: International Monetary Fund)

Ioffe, G. (2011) "Washington struggles to formulate strategy on Belarus", *Eurasia Daily Monitor*, 12 December

Ioffe, G. (2016) "Possible nuclear plant accident in Belarus sheds light on Minsk's internal political process", *Eurasia Daily Monitor*, 1 August

IUEC (2019) "Key dates" [online]. n.d. (Angarsk: International Uranium Enrichment Center,). Available from: http://eng.iuec.ru/about/dates/ [Accessed 1 July 2019]

Ivanitskaya, N. et al. (2008) "Nesvoevremennyi vizit [An untimely visit]", *Vedomosti*, 28 April

Ivanov, V. and Rogozhin, Yu. (2006) "Energetika: Kak postroit' atom [Energy: How to build the atom]", *Vedomosti*, 28 September

Ivzhenko, T. (2009a) "Kiev rasschityvaet na rossiiskii atomnyi kredit [Kyiv counts on Russia's atomic credit]", *Nezavisimaya gazeta*, 25 September, p.6

Ivzhenko, T. (2009b) "V Kieve tyanut vremya [Kyiv plays for time]", *Nezavisimaya gazeta*, 14 July, p.6

Ivzhenko, T. (2010) "Trekhmernyi atom Viktora Yanukovicha [Viktor Yanukovich's three-dimensional atom]", *Nezavisimaya gazeta*, 17 September, p.1

Ivzhenko, T. (2011) "Mirnyi atom mozhet razdelit'sya [The peaceful atom may split]", *Nezavisimaya gazeta*, 25 March, p.6

Jeppesen, M. (2006) *Russland og arbeidet med kjernefysisk ikke-spredning: en kartleggingsstudie [Russia and the nuclear non-proliferation process: An exploratory study]*. FFI Rapport (Kjeller, Norway: Norwegian Defence Research Establishment)

Kadosov, D. (1992a) "Rossiya boretsya za rynki urana [Russia fights for uranium markets]", *Kommersant*, 27 November

Kadosov, D. (1992b) "Sozdaetsya AO 'Atomredmet' [Atomredmet stock company is founded]", *Kommersant*, 11 December

Kadosov, D. (1993) "Soglashenie proizvoditelei urana [Agreement among uranium producers]", *Kommersant*, 25 February

Kasperski, T. (2015) "Nuclear dreams and realities in contemporary Russia and Ukraine", *History and Technology: An International Journal*, 31 (1): 55–80

Kats, E. (1999) "Ubytochnyi biznes 'generalov ot radiatsii' [The 'radiation generals' unprofitable business]", *Segodnya*, 9 February

Katys, M. (2001) *"Vvoz otrabotavshikh yadernykh otkhodov [The import of spent nuclear waste]"* [online]. 21 February 2001 (Prague: Radio Svoboda). Available from: https://www.svoboda.org/a/24197716.html [Accessed 31 January 2019]

Kazatomprom (2016) *Godovoi otchet. 2015 [Annual Report. 2015]* (Astana: Kazatomprom)

Khachatrian, H. (2008) "Armenia: Contemplating life as a regional electricity exporter", *Eurasianet.org*, 30 October

Khripunov, I. (2001) "MINATOM: Time for crucial decisions", *Problems of Post-Communism*, 48 (4): 49–58

Khvostik, E. et al. (2018) "Bryussel' stavit blok Armyanskoi AES [Brussels puts on the Armenian NPP's reactor]", *Kommersant Daily*, 31 January, p.7

Kiselev, S. (2011) "Rossiiskie atomshchiki zakreplyayutsya v Evrope [The Russian nuclear sector gains positions in Europe]", *Nezavisimaya gazeta*, 12 September, p.4

The electricity industry 133

Kluge, J. (2019) *Mounting Pressure on Russia's Government Budget. Financial and Political Risks of Stagnation.* SWP Research Paper (Berlin: Stiftung Wissenschaft und Politik)

Kommersant (1992) "Vizit rossiiskikh atomshchikov v Iran [Russian nuclear specialists' visit to Iran]", *Kommersant*, 27 October

Koretskii, A. (1994) "Uranovaya sdelka mezhdu Kazakhstanom i SShA [An uranium deal between Kazakhstan and US]", *Kommersant*, 25 November

Koretskii, A. (1997) "Rossiiskie atomnye 'tabletki' vyzyvayut v Kieve allergiyu [Russian nuclear 'pills' cause allergy in Kiev]", *Segodnya*, 3 April

Kornysheva, A. (2005a) "V 'Rosenergoatome' smenilsya rukovoditel'. Stanislav Antipov naznachen otvetsvennym za aktsionirovanie kontserna [Change of hands in Rosenergoatom. Stanislav Antipov placed in charge of incorporation of the concern]", *Kommersant*, 7 May, p.5

Kornysheva, A. (2005b) "Reforma energetiki. Rosatom gotov k aktsionernoi sobstvennosti [Electricity reform. Rosatom is ready for shareholding property]", *Kommersant*, 4 April, p.15

Kornysheva, A. (2006a) "'TVEL' i 'Tekhsnabeksport' ostanutsya samostoyatel'nymi yurlitsami" ['TVEL' and 'Tekhsnabeksport' will remain independent juridical persons]", *Kommersant*, 11 September, p.5

Kornysheva, A. (2006b) "Atomnaya promyshlennost'. TVEL i 'Tekhsnabeksport' sozdayut gornorudnuyu kompaniyu [Atomic industry. TVEL and 'Tekhsnabeksport' will create a mining company]", *Kommersant*, 18 July, p.10

Kornysheva, A. (2007a) "Rossiiskii uran budet bogache [Russian uranium will become richer]", *Kommersant*, 23 June, p.5

Kornysheva, A. (2007b) "Rosatom razgonyayut na apparatnom uskoritele [Speeding up Rosatom on the bureaucratic accelerator]", *Kommersant*, 5 October, p.14

Kornysheva, A. (2007c) "Ukraina zasvetila atomnye tseny [Ukraine illuminates nuclear prices]", *Kommersant*, 8 May, p.11

Kornysheva, A. and Chernovalov, A. (2007) "Ukraina vybila iz Rossii atomnuyu skidku [Ukraine manages to get an atomic discount from Russia]", *Kommersant*, 17 January, p.12

Kornysheva, A., Yambaeva, R. and Grib, N. (2006) "Rosatom sdaet aktivy v 'Atomprom' [Rosatom will place its equity in 'Atomprom']", *Kommersant*, 9 February, p.15

Koroleva, N. (2006) "Viktor Mikhailov: Sergeya Kirienko naznachal Predsedatel' Pravitel'stva, a ego reshenie nuzhno uvazhat' [Viktor Mikhailov: The Prime Minister appointed Sergei Kirienko, and we should respect the decision]", *Atomnaya Strategiya*, March, p.3

Kosharnaya, O. (2009) "Plan 'ponuzhdeniya' k sotrudnichestvu [A plan for 'forced' cooperation]", *Zerkalo Nedeli*, 9 October

Kotlyar, E. (2012) "Oboronosposobnost' strany, prevrashchennaya v zoloto [The country's defence capacity is converted to gold]", *Moskovskaya pravda*, 10 August, p.9

Kovynev, A. (2017) "Nuclear power in Ukraine – 40 years of unease", *Nuclear Engineering International*. Available from: https://www.neimagazine.com/features/featurenuclear-power-in-ukraine-40-years-of-unease-5956752/ [Accessed 5 April 2020]

Krasavin, A. (2007) "Gosmonopol'zovanie [State monopoly-utilization]", *Itogi*, 8 October

Kravchenko, E. (1994) "Krupnyi kontrakt 'Tekhsnabeksporta' [A major contract for Tekhsnabeksport]", *Kommersant*, 12 January

Kucherenko, V. (2000) "Kirgiziya vstupaet v 'uranovyi proekt' s Rossiei [Kyrgyzstan enters a 'uranium project' with Russia]", *Rossiiskaya gazeta*, 23 December, p.7

Kudrik, I. et al. (2004) *The Russian nuclear industry*. Bellona Report. 4 (Oslo, Norway: The Bellona Foundation)

Kudrin, Yu. (2008) "S Rossiei nadezhnee [It is safer with Russia]", *Rossiiskaya gazeta*, 24 March, p.3

Kudryashov, D. (2006) "Kirienko naznachaet 'svoikh' [Kirienko appoints loyal hands]", *Gazeta*, 17 March, p.16

Kurdov, D. (2007) "Tupikovaya diversifikatsiya [Blind alley diversification]", *Kievskii Telegraf*, 2 July

Kuznetsov, A. et al. (2006) *Korporatsiya "TVEL": pervye desyat' [The TVEL Corporation: The first decade]* (Moscow: TVEL/OOO Izdatel'skii tsentr "Atompressa")

Lavr, S. (1992) "Problema uranovoi torgovli ne snyata [The uranium trade problem remains]", *Kommersant*, 26 October

Leskov, S. (2006) "Smert' Sredmasha [The death of Sredmash]", *Profil'*, 20 November, p.100

Loukianova, A. (2008) "The International Uranium Enrichment Center at Angarsk: A step towards assured fuel supply?", *Nuclear Threat Initiative* [online]. Available from http://www.nti.org/analysis/articles/uranium-enrichment-angarsk/ [Accessed 8 September 2014]

Malkova, I. (2006) "Nizhegorodskii universal [The universalist from Nizhnii Novgorod]", *Vedomosti*, 17 March

Malkova, I. and Mazneva, E. (2007) "Sozdaetsya atomnaya goskorporatsiya [An atomic state corporation is being formed]", *Vedomosti*, 5 October

Marples, D. (2006) "Lukashenka opts for nuclear power", *Eurasia Daily Monitor*, 6 December

Marples, D. (2008) "New revelations concerning nuclear power plant in Belarus", *Eurasia Daily Monitor*, 10 January

Marples, D. (2009) "Protests planned against Belarus nuclear plant", *Eurasia Daily Monitor*, 20 April

Marples, D. (2010) "Surge in nuclear power projects imperils Belarusian program", *Eurasia Daily Monitor*, 4 August

Marples, D. (2012) "Is Nuclear Power The Panacea For Belarusian Energy Problems?", *Eurasia Daily Monitor*, 5 March

Mashrab, F. (2018) "Uzbekistan and Russia reach agreement on construction of new nuclear power plant", *Eurasia Daily Monitor*, 10 July

Melikova, N. (2006) "Fenomen Sobyanina [The Sobyanin phenomenon]", *Nezavisimaya gazeta*, 13 November, p.7

Melikova, N. (2008) "Zheleznaya doroga za prezidentskii privet [A railway in return for the president's greetings]", *Nezavisimaya gazeta*, 7 February, p.5

Mikhailin, M. (1995) "Delo o khishchenii izotopov [The isotope theft case]", *Kommersant*, 25 February

Milov, V. (2015) "'Rosatom': itogi desyatiletiya [Rosatom: summing up a decade]", *Forbes*, 15 October

Ministry of Energy (2009) *Energeticheskaya strategiya Rossii na period do 2030 goda [Russia's Energy Strategy for the period to 2030]* (Moscow: Institute of Energy Strategy)

Ministry of Industry and Trade (2003) *Energeticheskaya strategiya Rossii na period do 2020 goda [Russia's Energy Strategy for the period to 2020]* (Moscow: Ministerstvo promyshlennosti i torgovli)

Muzalevsky, R. (2010) "Japanese-Kazakh nuclear energy cooperation: a partnership for the future", *Eurasia Daily Monitor*, 2 August

Naumov, I. (2006) "Kirienko zastryal na starte. Reforma Rosatoma probuksovyvayut na normativno-pravovom pole [Kirienko gets stuck on the start line. The reform of Rosatom is spinning on the normative-legal field]", *Nezavisimaya gazeta*, 17 April, p.4

NEI Magazine (2005) "Kazakhstan to become uranium player" [online]. 23 November (London: Nuclear Engineering International). Available from: https://www.neimagazine.com/news/newskazakhstan-to-become-uranium-player [Accessed 1 February 2019]

NEI Magazine (2009) "Areva and Kazatomprom to create fuel JV" [online]. 8 October (London: Nuclear Engineering International). Available from: https://www.neimagazine.com/news/newsareva-and-kazatomprom-to-create-fuel-jv/ [Accessed 15 November 2018]

NEI Magazine (2010a) "Russia picked to build fuel fabrication plant in Ukraine" [online]. 6 October (London: Nuclear Engineering International). Available from: https://www.neimagazine.com/news/newsrussia-picked-to-build-fuel-fabrication-plant-in-ukraine/ [Accessed 16 November 2018]

NEI Magazine (2010b) "TVEL wins tender to build fuel plant in Ukraine" [online]. 1 November (London: Nuclear Engineering International). Available from: https://www.neimagazine.com/news/newstvel-wins-tender-to-build-fuel-plant-in-ukraine/ [Accessed 16 November 2018]

NEI Magazine (2010c) "Russia to pay for 85% of costs to complete Khmelnitsky 3&4 " [online]. 12 November (London: Nuclear Engineering International). Available from: https://www.neimagazine.com/news/newsrussia-to-pay-for-85-of-costs-to-complete-khmelnitsky-34/ [Accessed 20 November 2018]

NEI Magazine (2012a) "Russia-Ukraine nuclear fuel plant begins construction" [online]. 11 October (London: Nuclear Engineering International). Available from: https://www.neimagazine.com/news/newsrussia-ukraine-nuclear-fuel-plant-begins-construction/ [Accessed 19 November 2018]

NEI Magazine (2012b) "Russia signs VVER service agreement with Energoatom" [online]. 6 November (London: Nuclear Engineering International). Available from: https://www.neimagazine.com/news/newsrusatom-signs-vver-service-agreement-with-energoatom/ [Accessed 19 November 2018]

NEI Magazine (2015a) "Ukraine pushes ahead with fuel diversification" [online]. 16 November (London: Nuclear Engineering International). Available from: https://www.neimagazine.com/news/newsukraine-pushes-ahead-with-fuel-diversification-4720393/ [Accessed 20 November 2018]

NEI Magazine (2015b) "Ukraine looks to reduce nuclear fuel supplies from Russia" [online]. 24 August (London: Nuclear Engineering International). Available from: https://www.neimagazine.com/news/newsukraine-looks-to-reduce-nuclear-fuel-supplies-from-russia-4653681/ [Accessed 19 November 2018]

NEI Magazine (2015c) "AREVA wins enrichment contract in Ukraine" [online]. 27 April (London: Nuclear Engineering International). Available from: https://www.neimagazine.com/news/newsareva-wins-enrichment-contract-in-ukraine-4562812/ [Accessed 19 November 2018]

NEI Magazine (2015d) "Russia: Surviving sanctions" [online]. 4 June (London: Nuclear Engineering International). Available from: https://www.neimagazine.com/features/featurerussia-surviving-sanctions-4592602/ [Accessed 19 November 2018]

NEI Magazine (2016a) "Profits for TVEL" [online]. 5 July (London: Nuclear Engineering International). Available from: https://www.neimagazine.com/news/newsprofits-for-tvel-4941492/ [Accessed 21 November 2018]

NEI Magazine (2016b) "Urenco to supply enriched uranium to Ukraine" [online]. 23 August (London: Nuclear Engineering International). Available from: https://www.

neimagazine.com/news/newsurenco-to-supply-enriched-uranium-to-ukraine-4986122/ [Accessed 22 November 2018]

NEI Magazine (2016c) "More Westinghouse fuel for Ukraine" [online]. 5 July (London: Nuclear Engineering International). Available from: https://www.neimagazine.com/news/newsmore-westinghouse-fuel-ukraine-4941497/ [Accessed 21 November 2018]

NEI Magazine (2016d) "Continued Ukraine-Russia tensions over fuel" [online]. 7 June (London: Nuclear Engineering International). Available from: https://www.neimagazine.com/news/newscontinued-ukraine-russia-tensions-over-fuel-4915829/ [Accessed 21 November 2018]

NEI Magazine (2016e) "Ukraine resumes nuclear fuel trade with Russia" [online]. 9 August (London: Nuclear Engineering International). Available from: https://www.neimagazine.com/news/newsukraine-resumes-nuclear-fuel-trade-with-russia-4974528/ [Accessed 21 November 2018]

NEI Magazine (2017a) "Ukraine presses on with used storage facility" [online]. 19 May (London: Nuclear Engineering International). Available from: https://www.neimagazine.com/news/newsukraine-presses-on-with-used-fuel-storage-facility-5819651/ [Accessed 22 November 2018]

NEI Magazine (2017b) "Ukraine increases nuclear share as power shortage looms" [online]. 22 February (London: Nuclear Engineering International). Available from: https://www.neimagazine.com/news/newsukraine-increases-nuclear-share-as-power-shortage-looms-5744263/ [Accessed 22 November 2018]

NEI Magazine (2018a) "Ukraine's fuel priorities" [online]. 8 August (London: Nuclear Engineering International). Available from: https://www.neimagazine.com/features/featureukraines-fuel-priorities-6703002/ [Accessed 22 November 2018]

NEI Magazine (2018b) "Canada's Brookfield to buy Westinghouse" [online]. 8 January (London: Nuclear Engineering International). Available from: https://www.neimagazine.com/news/newscanadas-brookfield-to-buy-westinghouse-6021321/ [Accessed 4 December 2018]

NEI Magazine (2018c) "Orano signs contract with Ukraine on fuel reprocessing" [online]. 5 June (London: Nuclear Engineering International). Available from: https://www.neimagazine.com/news/newsorano-signs-contract-with-ukraine-on-fuel-reprocessing-6175810/ [Accessed 22 November 2018]

NEI Magazine (2018d) "Areva NP becomes Framatome and Atmea is reorganised" [online]. 8 January (London: Nuclear Engineering International). Available from: https://www.neimagazine.com/news/newsareva-np-becomes-framatome-and-atmea-is-reorganised-6021305/ [Accessed 4 December 2018]

NEI Magazine (2018e) "Turboatom and Westinghouse extend nuclear cooperation" [online]. 9 November (London: Nuclear Engineering International). Available from: https://www.neimagazine.com/news/newsturboatom-and-westinghouse-extend-nuclear-cooperation-6843967/ [Accessed 22 November 2018]

Neimysheva, N., Mazneva, E. and Nikol'skii, A. (2006) "Teplaya voda [Tepid water]", *Vedomosti*, 7 February

Nigmatulin, R.I. and Nigmatulin, B.I. (2006) "Neft', gaz, energiya, mir, Rossiya: sostoyanie i perspektivy [Oil, gas, energy, the world, Russia: the state of affairs and the perspectives]", *Atomnaya strategiya*, January, p.11–13

Nikol'skii, A. (2005) "'Rosenergoatom' obmanuli [Rosenergoatom has been fooled]", *Vedomosti*, 27 June

Nikol'skii, A. (2006a) "Edinyi atom [United atom]", *Vedomosti*, 10 November

Nikol'skii, A. (2006b) "Interv'yu: Sergei Obozov, gendirektor FGUP 'Rosenergoatom' [Interview: Sergei Obozov, general director of the federal enterprise 'Rosenergoatom']", *Vedomosti*, 27 September

Oganesyan, T. (1998) "Atomnye igry [Nuclear games]", *Ekspert*, 11 May

Oilcapital.ru (2016) "*Reiting vliyaniya krupnykh predprinimatelei i top-menedzherov toplivno-energeticheskogo kompleksa v marte 2016 g.* [*Rating of the influence of major businessmen and top managers in the fuel and energy complex, March 2016*]" [online]. 29 March (Moscow: IG Industriya). Available from: https://oilcapital.ru/news/companies/29-03-2016/reyting-vliyaniya-krupnyh-predprinimateley-i-top-menedzherov-toplivno-energeticheskogo-kompleksa-v-marte-2016-g [Accessed 20 February 2019]

Omelchenko, S. (2008) "Spornyi atom [The disputed atom]", *Ekonomika i zhizn'*, 8 March, p.36

Orlov, V. (2008) "Sergei Kirienko. 'Pri sushchestvuyushchei seichas konkurentsii nevozmozhno byt' vtorym' [Sergei Kirienko. 'In the current competition, it is impossible to come second']", *Indeks bezopasnosti*, 14 (2): 11–14

Orlov, V.A. and Vinnikov, A. (2005) "The Great Guessing Game: Russia and the Iranian Nuclear Issue", *The Washington Quarterly*, 28 (2): 49–66

Osetinskaya, E. and Shcherbakova, A. (2001) "Piterskie kadry idut v Minatom [The Petersburg people are coming to Minatom]", *Vedomosti*, 8 June

Oxenstierna, S. (2010) *Russia's Nuclear Energy Expansion*. Defence Analysis (Stockholm: FOI Swedish Defence Research Agency)

Palamarchuk, S.I., Podkovalnikov, S.V. and Voropai, N.I. (2001) "Getting the electricity sector on track in Russia", *The Electricity Journal*, October 2001, pp.52–58

Panfilova, V. (2009) "Uzbekskii ryvok na zapad [An Uzbek dash to the West]", *Nezavisimaya gazeta*, 11 November, p.1

Pannier, B. (2009) "*Link to Iran Spoils Kazatomprom Party*" [online]. 30 December (Prague: Radio Free Europe/Radio Liberty). Available from: http://www.rferl.org/content/Link_To_Iran_Spoils_Kazatomprom_Party/1917808.html [Accessed 1 July 2019]

Pappe, Ya. and Drankina, E. (2007) "Kak natsionaliziruyut Rossiyu: atomnaya promyshlennost' [How Russia is being nationalised: the nuclear industry]", *Kommersant-Den'gi*, 24 September

Pavlov, D. (1998) "Skandal v Minatome [Scandal in Minatom]", *Kommersant*, 12 March, p.1

Pavlov, D. (1999) "Za rossiiskii uran zaplatyat strany NATO [Nato states will pay for Russian uranium]", *Kommersant*, 26 March, p.2

Pelekhova, Yu. (1998a) "Gazpromu predlozhili mirnyi atom [Gazprom is offered the peaceful atom]", *Kommersant*, 7 May, p.9

Pelekhova, Yu. (1998b) "Rasshcheplenie Minatoma [The splitting of Minatom]", *Kommersant*, 28 April, p.1

Perera, J. (1997) *The Nuclear Industry in the Former Soviet Union. Transition from Crisis to Opportunity.* Vol I. 2 (London: Financial Times Energy Publishing)

Peschinskii, I. (2017) "Dorogoi mirnyi atom [The expensive peaceful atom]", *Vedomosti*, 26 September, p.14

Peschinskii, I. and Nikol'skii, A. (2016) "Likhachev vozglavil "Rosatom" [Likhachev heads Rosatom]", *Vedomosti*, 6 October, p.12

Podrobno.uz (2018) "*Rossiiskii eksportnyi tsentr mozhet profinansirovat' stroitel'stvo AES v Uzbekistane* [*The Russian Export Centre may finance the construction of an NPP in Uzbekistan*]" [online]. 25 April (Tashkent: Podrobno.uz). Available from: https://podrobno.uz/cat/uzbekistan-i-rossiya-dialog-partnerov-/rossiyskiy-eksportnyy

-tsentr-mozhet-profinansirovat-stroitelstvo-aes-v-uzbekistane-/ [Accessed 9 November 2018]

Popov, A. (1995) "AES mogut ostanovit'. Terpenie personala rossiiskikh atomnykh stantsii istoshchaetsya [NPPs may be closed. Nuclear plant personnel's patience is becoming exhausted]", *Nezavisimaya gazeta*, 2 December

Prime-TASS (1997) "Ukraina i Rossiya sozdayut SP dlya obespecheniya yadernym toplivom ukrainskikh AES [Ukraine and Russia create JV to supply Ukrainian NPPs with fuel]", *Prime-TASS*, 22 October 1997

Proskurnina, O. and Nikol'skii, A. (2006) "Atom obrel reformatora [The atom has found its reformer]", *Vedomosti*, 9 February

Proskuryakov, L. and Buran, V. (1994) "TVEL Concern: Road to Amalgamation", *International Affairs (Moscow)*, 1994 (9): 51–55

Putin, V. (2007) "Poslanie Federal'nomu Sobraniyu Rossiiskoi Federatsii Prezidenta Rossii Vladimira Putina [Address to the Federal Assembly of the Russian Federation by President Vladimir Putin]", *Rossiiskaya gazeta*, 27 April, p.3

Ravinskii, V. (2008) "Ukraina rasshchepila mirnyi atom [Ukraine splits the peaceful atom]", *Kommersant*, 10 April, p.14

RBK (2018) "RBK 500: Reiting rossiiskogo biznesa [RBK 500: The Russian Business Rating]" [online]. Moscow. Available from: https://www.rbc.ru/rbc500/ [Accessed 23 November 2018]

RBK Daily (2016) "Kto vmesto Kirienko [Who, instead of Kirienko]", *RBK Daily*, 6 October, p.5

RBK Daily (2017) "Kreditnaya zavisimost' [Credit dependence]", *RBK Daily*, 16 June, p.7

Regnum.ru (2012a) "Kazakhstanskomu obshchestvu nasazhdaetsya obraz vraga v litse Rossii: glava "Kazatomprom" [Kazakhstani society is is being inculcated with the image of Russia as an enemy - Kazatomprom's head]" [online]. 15 August (Moscow: Regnum). Available from: https://regnum.ru/news/polit/1561532.html [Accessed 15 November 2018]

Regnum.ru (2012b) "'Kazatomprom; sovmestno s 'TVEL' sozdayut sovmestnye moshchnosti po obogashcheniyu urana [Kazatomprom and TVEL establish joint capacities in uranium enrichment]" [online]. 23 November (Moscow: Regnum). Available from: https://regnum.ru/news/polit/1596706.html [Accessed 15 November 2018]

Regnum.ru (2013) "'Tikhoe razmezhevanie' s Rossiei: Kazakhstan za nedelyu [A quiet demarcation with Russia: Kazakhstan this week]" [online]. 10 April (Moscow: Regnum). Available from: https://regnum.ru/news/polit/1646997.html [Accessed 15 November 2018]

Regnum.ru (2017a) "V povyshenii mirovykh tsen na uran vinovat Kazakhstan [Kazakhstan is to blame for the rise in the global uranium price]" [online]. 15 May (Moscow: Regnum). Available from: https://regnum.ru/news/economy/2274747.html [Accessed 15 November 2018]

Regnum.ru (2017b) "Ocherednaya AES na Ukraine perekhodit na amerikanskoe toplivo [Another NPP in Ukraine transfers to American fuel]" [online]. 11 December (Moscow: Regnum). Available from: https://regnum.ru/news/economy/2355822.html [Accessed 15 November 2018]

RFE/RL (2001) "RFE/RL Newsline", *Radio Free Europe/Radio Liberty*, 23 March

RFE/RL (2007) "RFE/RL Newsline", *Radio Free Europe/Radio Liberty*, 13 April

RIA Novosti (2014) "Rossiya predostavit Armenii $270 mln. na prodlenie sroka raboty AES [Russia extends $270 million credit to prolong NPP operational period]" [online]. 26 December (Moscow: RIA Novosti). Available from: https://ria.ru/20141226/1040277548.html [Accessed 1 July 2019]

RIA Novosti (2016) "Rosatom v 2016 godu: k strategicheskim tselyam s novym rukovodstvom [Rosatom in 2016: towards strategic goals under a new management]" [online]. 30 December (Moscow: RIA Novosti). Available from: https://ria.ru/20161230/1484960036.html [Accessed 28 November 2018]

Rodin, I. (2006) "Rosatom dvinulsya k privatizatsii [Rosatom got its privatization going]", *Nezavisimaya gazeta*, 7 November, p.1

Rosatom (2010) *Publichnyi godovoi otchet 2009 [Annual report for the public 2009]* (Moscow: Rosatom)

Rosatom (2013) *Publichnyi godovoi otchet 2012 [Annual report for the public 2012]* (Moscow: Rosatom)

Rosatom (2017) *Publichnyi godovoi otchet 2016 [Annual report for the public 2016]* (Moscow: Rosatom)

Rosatom (2018a) "Prezident RF V. Putin i Prezident Uzbekistana Sh. Mirzieev dali start proektu stroitel'stva pervoi AES v Uzbekistane [The president of the Russian Federation, V. Putin, and the president of Uzbekistan, Sh. Mirziyoyev, gave the start signal for the construciton project for the first NPP in Uzbekistan]" [online]. 19 October (Moscow: Rosatom). Available from: https://www.rosatom.ru/journalist/news/prezident-rf-v-putin-i-prezident-uzbekistana-sh-mirzieev-dali-start-proektu-stroitelstva-pervoy-aes-/ [Accessed 9 November 2018]

Rosatom (2018b) *Publichnyi godovoi otchet 2017 [Annual report for the public 2017]* (Moscow: Rosatom)

Rosenergoatom (2013) *Godovoi otchet 2012 [Annual report 2012]* (Moscow: Rosenergoatom)

Rubtsov, A. (1999) "Rossiisko-amerikanskii yadernyi konflikt [The Russian-American nuclear conflict]", *Kommersant*, 24 November

Rykovanova, E. (2006) "Rossiiskaya initsiativa po sozdaniyu sistemy mezhdunarodnykh tsentrov po predostavleniyu uslug yadernogo toplivnogo tsikla [The Russian initiative to create a system of international centres to provide nuclear fuel cycle services]", *Voprosy bezopasnosti*, 2006 (May)

Sandler, Yu. (2010) "Bratskii atomnyi soyuz [The brotherly atomic union]", *Vestnik Atomproma*, October, pp.30–33

Segodnya (1994) "Provintsial'naya khronika [The provincial chronicle]", *Segodnya*, 9 August

Segodnya (1995a) "El'tsin otmenyaet zalogovye auktsiony po aktsiyam 8 strategicheskikh predpriyatii [El'tsin revokes collateral auctions for shares of 8 strategic enterprises]", *Segodnya*, 9 December

Segodnya (1995b) "El'tsin utverzhdaet spisok predpriyatii, aktsii kotorykh peredayutsya v zalog bankam [El'tsin confirms list of enterprises whose shares will be transferred to banks as collateral]", *Segodnya*, 27 September 1995

Sergeev, M. (2007a) "Rossiyu ottesnyayut ot kazakhstanskogo urana [Russia is being pushed out of Kazakhstani uranium]", *Nezavisimaya gazeta*, 10 July, p.1

Sergeev, M. (2007b) "Kiev ishchet zamenu Rosatomu [Kiev looks for a substitute for Rosatom]", *Nezavisimaya gazeta*, 20 July, p.1

Sergeev, N. and Sokovnin, A. (2011) "Den'gi Evgeniya Adamova priznany chistymi [Evgenii Adamov's money are found to be clean]", *Kommersant*, 28 September, p.4

Serov, A. (1997) "Megadollary [Megadollars]", *Itogi*, 5 May

Shmidke, A. (2006) "Atomnaya promyshlennost' Kazakhstana: Sovremennoe sostoyanie i perspektivy razvitiya [Kazakhstan's nuclear industry: current situation and development perspectives]", *Resursy po stranam - Tsentral'naya Aziya - Analiz*

Shtaltovnyi, O. (2011) "Rosiya zberezhe monopoliyu na yaderne palyvo [Russia retains the monopoly on nuclear fuel]" [online]. 7 October (Kyiv: BBC Ukrainian). Available from: http://www.bbc.co.uk/ukrainian/news/2011/10/111007_russia_nuclear_it.shtml [Accessed 1 July 2019]

Sidorenko, V.A. (1997) "Nuclear power in the Soviet Union and in Russia", *Nuclear Engineering and Design*, 173: 3–20

Siluyanova, P. and Kovalevskii, A. (2004) "Stop, kadr. Atomnyi prikhod [Freeze. A nuclear appointment]", *Gazeta*, 25 October, p.9

Sindelar, D. (2006) *"Russia: Moscow seeks to reignite nuclear power industry"* [online]. 14 February Radio Free Europe/Radio Liberty). Available from: http://www.rferl.org/content/article/1065754.html [Accessed 1 July 2019]

Skorlygina, N. (2012) "'Rosenergoatom' stal ubytochnym [Rosenergoatom at a loss]", *Kommersant*, 12 March, p.11

Slivyak, V. et al. (2010) *Mify ob atomnoi energii. Pochemu razvitie atomnoi energii vedet nas v tupik [Myths on atomic power. Why the development of atomic energy leads us down a cul-de-sac]*. (Moscow: Heinrich Böll Stiftung)

Sokovnin, A. (2008) "Devyat' let odnogo dela [One case for nine years]", *Kommersant*, 25 January, p.5

Sotnik, A. (2001) "Ekonomika. Atom tyanetsya k alyuminii [Economy. The nuclear sector extends to aluminium]", *Moskovskie novosti*, 10 April

Starostin, A. (2003) "'Troistvennyi' yadernyi soyuz v deistvii [The 'triple' nuclear union in action]", *Delovaya stolitsa*, 12 May

Stenin, A. (2005) "Peretyagivanie Adamova [The tug-of-war for Adamov]", *Gazeta.ru*, 19 May

Stulberg, A.N. (2007) *Well-oiled Diplomacy. Strategic Manipulation and Russia's Energy Statecraft in Eurasia* (Albany, New York: State University of New York Press)

Stulberg, A.N. and Fuhrmann, M. (2013) "Introduction: Understanding the nuclear renaissance", in Stulberg, A.N. and Fuhrmann, M. eds, *The Nuclear Renaissance and International Security* (Stanford: Stanford Security Studies/Stanford University Press), pp.1–16

The Moscow Times (2012) "Ex-Rosatom deputy head granted $160,000 bail", *The Moscow Times*, 13 November

Thomas, S. (2018) "Russia's nuclear export programme", *Energy Policy*, 121: 236–247

Torbakov, I. (2006) "Russia welcomes Uzbekistan into its Eurasian energy empire", *Eurasia Daily Monitor*, 27 January

Tovkailo, M. (2007) "Sergei Kirienko raskolol yadro atoma [Sergei Kirienko splits the atomic nucleus]", *Gazeta*, 13 December, p.13

Treisman, D. (2010) "'Loans for shares' revisited", *Post-Soviet Affairs*, 26 (3): 207–227

Turanov, S. (2004) "Rukovoditeli gosudarstvennykh bankov ukreplyayut svoi pozitsii", *Ekonomika i zhizn'*, 24 July, p.21

UNIAN (2011) "TEO zavoda po proizvodstvu yadernogo topliva v Ukraine gotovo na 80% [The feasibility study for a nuclear fuel factory in Ukraine is 80% ready]" [online]. 14 September (Kyiv: UNIAN News Agency). Available from: http://energy.unian.net/oilandgas/542093-teo-zavoda-po-proizvodstvu-yadernogo-topliva-v-ukraine-gotovo-na-80.html [Accessed 1 July 2019]

Uranium One Group (2018) "Uranium One: About us" [online]. (Toronto: Uranium One Group,). Available from: http://www.uranium1.com/about-us/#history [Accessed 13 November 2018]

Vaganov, A. (1998) "Smena rukovodstva Minatoma [Leadership succession in Minatom]", *Nezavisimaya gazeta*, 3 March, p.1

Vaganov, A. (1999) "Ukraina ssorit'sya s Rossiei nevygodno [Ukraine stands to lose from quarreling with Russia]", *Nezavisimaya gazeta*, 11 November

Vaganov, A. (2005) "'Rosenergoatom" aktsioniruyetsya. Atomnaia energetika zhazhdaet kreditov, investitsii i drugikh atributov rynka [Rosenergoatom is being incorporated. The atomic energy industry thirsts for credits, investment and other market attributes]", *Nezavisimaya gazeta*, 19 September, p.1

Vaganov, A. (2006) "Atomnuyu energetiku privatiziruyut. No Atomprom budet stoprotsentno gosudarstvennym, uveryayut v Rosatome [The atomic energy industry is being privatised. But Atomprom will be 100% state owned, Rosatom assures]", *Nezavisimaya gazeta*, 10 February, p.3

Vakarelska, R. (2017) "Ukraine's power game" [online]. 2 February Nuclear Engineering International). Available from: https://www.neimagazine.com/features/featureukraines-power-game-5730089/ [Accessed 20 November 2018]

Vakhmenin, A. (2007) "Koloss na atomnykh nogakh [A colossus with atomic feet]", *Moskovskie novosti*, 21 December

Varaksin, D. (2009) "Uranovyi obmen [Uranium exchange]", *Vedomosti*, 16 June

Vinokurov, E. (2007) "Perspektivy integratsii atomno-energeticheskikh kompleksov Rossii i Kazakhstana [Perspectives for integration between Russia's and Kazakhstan's nuclear energy complexes]" [online]. 15 June Proatom.ru). Available from: http://www.proatom.ru/modules.php?name=News&file=article&sid=1014 [Accessed 1 July 2019]

Volchko, D. (1998) "Minatom spokoen [Minatom is calm]", *Russkii Telegraf*, 4 March

Voloshin, G. (2015) "India covets comprehensive reengagement with Central Asia", *Eurasia Daily Monitor*, 28 July

Voskresenskii, G. (2000) "Yadernyi poluraspad integratsionnogo protsessa. Diktuet li logika razvitiya atomnoi energetiki svoi zakony politikam [The integration process's nuclear semi-collapse. Do nuclear energy development logics set their own laws to the politicians]", *Vek*, 3 November, p.8

Weitz, R. and Choi, D. (2014) "Seoul seeks Central Asian partners", *Eurasia Daily Monitor*, 14 July

WNA (2008) "Nuclear power in Russia" [online]. August (London: World Nuclear Association). Available from: http://world-nuclear.org/info/inf45.html [Accessed 27 August 2008]

WNA (2011a) "Uranium and Nuclear Power in Kazakhstan" [online]. 1 October 2011 (London: World Nuclear Assosiation). Available from: http://www.world-nuclear.org/info/Country-Profiles/Countries-G-N/Kazakhstan/ [Accessed 7 October 2011]

WNA (2011b) "Russia's nuclear fuel cycle" [online]. 2 September 2011 (London: World Nuclear Association). Available from: http://www.world-nuclear.org/info/inf45a_Russia_nuclear_fuel_cycle.html [Accessed 10 December 2011]

WNA (2015) "Nuclear power in Russia" [online]. January 2015 (London: World Nuclear Association). Available from: http://world-nuclear.org/info/Country-Profiles/Countries-O-S/Russia–Nuclear-Power/ [Accessed 13 February 2015]

WNA (2018a) "Uranium in Uzbekistan" [online]. October World Nuclear Association). Available from: http://www.world-nuclear.org/information-library/country-profiles/countries-t-z/uzbekistan.aspx [Accessed 9 November 2018]

WNA (2018b) "Nuclear power in Russia" [online]. October (London: World Nuclear Association). Available from: http://www.world-nuclear.org/information-library/country-profiles/countries-o-s/russia-nuclear-power.aspx [Accessed 28 November 2018]

WNA (2018c) "Nuclear power in Ukraine" [online]. August World Nuclear Association). Available from: http://www.world-nuclear.org/information-library/country-profiles/countries-t-z/ukraine.aspx [Accessed 16 November 2018]

WNA (2018d) "Nuclear power in Armenia" [online]. March (London: World Nuclear Association). Available from: http://www.world-nuclear.org/information-library/country-profiles/countries-a-f/armenia.aspx [Accessed 9 November 2018]

WNA (2018e) "Russia's nuclear fuel cycle" [online]. May (London: World Nuclear Association). Available from: http://www.world-nuclear.org/information-library/country-profiles/countries-o-s/russia-nuclear-fuel-cycle.aspx [Accessed 7 November 2018]

WNA (2018f) "Nuclear power in Belarus" [online]. June World Nuclear Association). Available from: http://www.world-nuclear.org/information-library/country-profiles/countries-a-f/belarus.aspx [Accessed 8 November 2018]

Yamshchikov, S. et al. (1998) "Yadernyi eksport: period poluraspada [Nuclear export: the semi-collapse period]", *Obshchaya gazeta*, 24 December

Yermukanov, M. (2006) "Astana opts for Russian assistance in nuclear energy development", *Eurasia Daily Monitor*, 8 November

Yur'eva, E. (2007) "Rossiya vklyuchilas' v uranovuyu gonku [Russia joins the uranium race]", *Ekspert*, 8 October, pp.30–36

Zamyatin, V. (1996) "Tender na stroitel'stve zavoda [A tender to construct a factory]", *Kommersant*, 7 February, p.17

Zotova, I. (1992) "Dzhokhar Dudaev i Ruslan Utsiev zaklyuchili ekonomicheskii soyuz [Dzhokhar Dudaev and Ruslan Utsiev enter into economic union]", *Kommersant*, 6 January

5 The oil industry
Lukoil

This chapter analyses the relations between the oil company Lukoil (1992–) and the state. The two previous chapters show how Russia's domestic development influenced which tools the state could use in the post-Soviet region. At home, informality in institutions and rent sharing, and a lack of development in the 1990s, were followed by more formalised relations, institutional change and international expansion in the 2000s. Abroad, both electricity and nuclear energy companies engaged in often profitable operations that also served as tools of the state. Lukoil is different. Lukoil's relationship with the state is characterised by more formal institutions and less personal relations, and private ownership. But also in this case, relations changed over time from informal and personal in the early 1990s to more formal and impersonal towards the end of the period covered here. In the 2000s, the state's growing capacity placed limitations on Lukoil's possibilities for development in Russia. Its foreign operations, already significant, became important to the company because they enabled it to expand outside a restrictive Russian business environment. The chapter shows how the Russian state only occasionally influenced Lukoil's foreign operations in the post-Soviet region. All the same, the support it received abroad was conditioned on its acceptance of and support for the state at home.

The petroleum industry

The petroleum or oil and gas industry is global. Oil and oil products are traded globally and in dollars. Large petroleum companies operate in more than one region of the world. There are several petroleum company types, from international oil companies (IOCs), the largest are often dubbed super-majors (Yergin, 2012 (1993)), through national oil companies (NOCs), independent producers and service companies (Hilyard, 2012, pp.226–232). IOCs are publicly owned, while NOCs are state-owned. Some companies, like Petrobras and Equinor,[1] have a background similar to that of NOCs, but are partially publicly traded and are therefore sometimes dubbed "hybrid" (Hilyard, 2012, p.229). Others approach them as NOCs (Victor et al., 2012). Most IOCs and NOCs are vertically integrated, meaning that they have upstream and downstream control from oilfield to market, and hold oilfield exploration and production services. Upstream covers exploration and production activities, while downstream usually includes refining of crude oil and sales and distribution of gas and products derived from crude oil.[2] Independent producers are often small or medium-sized and have a lesser share of their activity in the downstream sector, while service companies specialise in exploration, drilling and production activities. Similarly, there exists a variety of specialised companies that provide services in e.g. refining, transportation and storage of crude oil and products.

The Soviet oil industry performed the same tasks as the rest of the global industry, and it had international customers. Enterprises were of course organised differently. Uniquely in a global industry context, oil and gas were separate industries, with different production associations,[3] supply chains, and ministries (until 1989).[4] Like all other Soviet industries, the oil industry was connected to the outside world only through organisations specialised in foreign trade. The Soviet oil industry was in many respects technically advanced, but it was isolated from its international peers. When the Soviet economy opened up towards the world, the oil industry was among the first to take advantage of the opportunity. Even more than the other fuel industries, the oil industry had an internationally competitive product to market, with considerable profits to be made.

Lukoil has always been among Russia's largest companies, developing oil production and at times outperforming its peers (Moser, 2016). In 2018, it was Russia's second largest company by turnover, and number three by profit (RBK, 2018). Throughout its lifetime, it has developed from having strong similarities to an NOC into a private company, and from a first among equals in the private sector to the most significant private company among many state-controlled holdings. In 2017, 11.6 per cent of Lukoil's oil and gas reserves, 12.7 per cent of its production, and 28.9 per cent of retail sales were located outside Russia, in line with its profile as a Russia-based IOC (Lukoil, 2018a, pp.51–52). Compared to its international peers, Lukoil's production is tilted more towards liquid hydrocarbon production (mostly oil) than to gas, even as gas had grown to 20.5 per cent of overall production in 2017 (Lukoil, 2018a, p.51).

The break-up of the Soviet Union and Soviet legacies

Lukoil was founded by then Deputy Minister for Oil and Gas Vagit Alekperov, in 1991. Alekperov had spent most of his career in the West Siberian oilfields. He had seen oil production decline and the Soviet oil sector disintegrate as perestroika legislation empowered enterprises but failed to free prices. In 1990, Alekperov made an effort to keep the entire oil industry together in a state-owned concern, much like Viktor Chernomyrdin did with the gas industry (Chapter 7). Alekperov and Chernomyrdin knew each other from working at the Ministry for Oil and Gas. Remarkably, Alekperov saw the IOCs BP, Chevron and Agip/Eni as organisational models for the Russian oil industry (*Neft' i Kapital*, 1999). The initial plan failed: disintegration had progressed too far and only a third of industry heads supported the idea (Gustafson, 2012; Neftegazovaya vertikal', 2016d, p.21). Alekperov's second-best strategy was to create a vertically integrated company based on parts of the industry (Gustafson, 2012, p.72; Neftegazovaya vertikal', 2016d). Alekperov had been head of the production association Kogalym in West Siberia. With his old colleagues, he planned a loose organisation consisting of the large and modern production associations Kogalym, Langepas and Urai, with their traditional downstream partners, the oil refineries in Perm, Volgograd, Ufa and Mažeikiai.[5] A Russian government resolution to this effect was passed in late 1991 (Government Order No. 18, 1991), establishing LangepasUraiKogalymNeft, Lukoil's predecessor.

The new Russian government was bent on furthering the disintegration of the oil industry as part of its market reforms. The formation of LangepasUraiKogalymNeft demonstrated the viability of a vertical integration combined with autonomy from the state, as an alternative to horizontal and vertical disintegration along with immediate privatisation (Gustafson, 2012, pp.104–107). By 1992, key members of the government, in particular First Deputy Prime Minister (from June Prime Minister) Egor Gaidar and Deputy Prime Minister Anatolii Chubais were convinced that further disintegration and privatisation would bring chaos to the oil industry (Gustafson, 2012, pp.71–72). Alekperov, who left government for LangepasUraiKogalymNeft in 1992, and other oil managers remained in close contact with the government. The appointment of Chernomyrdin as deputy prime minister with special responsibility for the fuel and energy complex in late May signified a priority on reintegration and the creation of viable, vertically integrated structures in the oil industry. A November decree institutionalised the emerging structure of the oil industry (Decree No. 1403, 1992). LUKoil (here Lukoil) and two other vertically integrated companies were authorised and would remain at least 45 per cent state owned for the following three years (Decree No. 1403, 1992; Moser, 2016).[6] Disintegration from below became more difficult.

Lukoil appeared as the result of individual agency, especially Alekperov's. Existing constraints on the oil industry crumbled under perestroika. Alekperov was better informed than many others, and occupied a central position in Moscow. He and his peers responded to uncertainty by acting on self-interest to prevent the industry from disintegrating further. The most vital parts of the Soviet industry were moulded into new structures, taking Western companies as models. Faced with crisis, Alekperov adapted his goals, used his government access for what it was worth, and settled for a concern composed of only parts of the industry. Along with other oil managers, he kept in close contact with the government's young reformers, who had no experience with the oil sector. As an experienced insider, Alekperov insisted on participating in the industry's institutional development.

Keeping afloat: a new beginning

Alekperov remained head of Lukoil throughout the period under study. He and other Lukoil managers maintained close contact with a former Langepas colleague, Yurii Shafranik, Fuel and Energy Minister in the first Chernomyrdin government (1992–1996). Alekperov wielded considerable influence over the oil sector reform of the early 1990s (Khnychkin, 1992; Alekperov, 2011a). By participating in the development of a formal institutional framework for the oil sector, Alekperov made sure that key legislative acts and regulations for oil sector development and privatisation suited the needs of Lukoil, a pioneer in the sector. This applied to privatisation auctions in 1994 (Gustafson, 2012, p.115), and the decree that allowed oil companies to convert into single stock companies (Decree No. 327, 1995; *Neft' i Kapital*, 2011c). In light of later developments, two traits of the property consolidation process in the industry are particularly interesting. Firstly, the fierce competition over the state's remaining stakes in the oil industry, organised under the umbrella of Rosneft. A decade later, Rosneft emerged as a fully fledged NOC, but at this point, it was a weak structure of little promise (Gustafson, 2012, pp.320–324). As to Lukoil, it did exceptionally well in that competition, expanding into the Volga-Urals region using its considerable production base in West Siberia as a platform (cf. Rogers, 2015, p.108; Neftegazovaya vertikal', 2016b, pp.12–13). And secondly, in this process, the position of regional authorities and regional elites mattered (Rogers, 2015, pp.106–114). While regional authorities were deftly manipulated into obedience in the case of Transneft (Chapter 6), in oil production and supply they held significant power, in a parallel to the electricity industry. Again, there is a contrast between the regions' significance in the struggle for property and corporate control in the 1990s and their lesser significance for property relations after 2000.

Lukoil's close relations with the state went to the highest levels. It had secured tax exemptions worth more than one trillion rubles by 1995 (Easter, 2012, p.67). In return, Alekperov supported Yeltsin against political challengers, and canvassed for him in Tyumen, an oil region, in the 1996 presidential election campaign (Davydov, 1996; RFE/RL, 1996). It was an open secret that the tax exemptions had been granted, in an act of discretionary regulation, in return for support for Yeltsin.

Institutional development allowed Lukoil and other companies to grow. Private ownership proliferated throughout the oil sector. The gradual privatisation of Lukoil began early, in 1994, with the state gradually reducing its minority stake until its last remaining share was sold in 2004.[7] Lukoil was the first oil company to convert holdings into a single stock (1995–1997), expand into international stock markets (1997) and attract a foreign shareholder, ARCO. It was the first Russian company to open its own petrol stations. It acquired another vertically integrated oil company, KomiTEK, in 1999, the first acquisition of its kind in Russia (*Neft' i Kapital*, 2004e; 2004d; 2006b).

Lukoil was a giant among Russian oil companies. Its original production was around 14 per cent of Russia's total production and it consolidated ahead of the others. Lukoil's development went hand in hand with the process of creating institutions for the oil industry.

Collapse of the Soviet Union: New opportunities for oil companies

The disintegration of the Soviet Union had two major consequences for the oil industry. The loss of Soviet home markets and reliance on transit to reach global markets applied to all industries. The impact on the oil industry had a further dimension, since oil was a competitive commodity. The 1990s brought fierce competition for market access to the oil industry, not paralysis and stagnation. The second consequence came in the form of an opportunity – one that Lukoil's management were quick to grasp. Soviet priorities in resource development promoted Russian petroleum production while much non-Russian hydrocarbon development was put on hold. This no longer applied. At different speeds, post-Soviet governments opened new regions to the international oil industry.

Alekperov knew all the likely producing regions from his time at the Soviet Ministry for Oil and Gas (Romanova, 1999). He cultivated ties with post-Soviet presidents in every possible way (*Upstream*, 1998a; Neftegazovaya vertikal', 2016c) and obtained licences in Azerbaijan, Kazakhstan, Iraq, Egypt and Uzbekistan in return. Chernomyrdin supported Lukoil's international expansion. The government put its weight behind Lukoil when it mattered, as in Lukoil's relations with Kazakhstan and other post-Soviet states (Burchilina, 1995; Ivanov, A., 1997; Narzikulov, 1997).

Lukoil did not hesitate to act independently of official Russian foreign policy where its economic interests were concerned (Tutushkin, 1996b). Fragmentation of central state organisations and in the elite made it difficult for the state to influence Lukoil's post-Soviet operations abroad (Tutushkin, 1999). In consequence, Lukoil enjoyed a measure of independence abroad, supported by parts of the government. This applied in particular to the issue of delimitation of the Caspian Sea.

The MFA's Caspian policy under Andrei Kozyrev (1992–1995) was to wait for an agreement between all the littoral states and then develop the Sea's resources jointly (Cockburn, 1994; Aleksandrovich, 2000). If successful, this would play to Russia's interest. The MFA aimed to exclude the involvement of IOCs and preserve a sphere of influence for Russia around the Caspian Sea (Bolukbasi, 1998, p.399). To conform to this policy, Lukoil would have to refrain from competing in Azerbaijan's and Kazakhstan's offshore zones, which they had opened to international companies. The Russian MFA was alone in its view of the Caspian, however, and Lukoil preferred to participate in the development of the de facto national zones. Also at the level of the Russia government, there was little support for the MFA's line. Prime Minister Chernomyrdin and Fuel and Energy Minister Shafranik held positions close to Lukoil's, and stated as much when meeting their international partners (Cockburn, 1994; Smirnov, A., 1995; Tutushkin, 1995; Vardul', 1995; Aleksandrovich, 2000). One industry observer remarked that Lukoil and the Fuel and Energy Ministry "tried to establish their policy [as regards the Caspian shelf] based on economic interests" at a time when there was little official interest, and what there was, was based on "abstract geopolitical daydreams" (Aleksandrovich, 2001). Familiarity with the global oil business may have mattered to the strategic approach on Lukoil's and the Fuel and Energy Ministry's part. When states open new regions for production, what matters in the long run is joining the game, not keeping others out. The MFA's lack of strategic foresight placed it on the side lines of Russia's actual engagement in the Caspian Sea. Under Evgenii Primakov (1996–1998), the MFA was more forthcoming towards the other Caspian littoral states (Bolukbasi, 1998, pp.408–409). The government was also more united. However, the Russian state remained on the side lines of developments until its policy changed more fundamentally in 2001.

Azerbaijan opened its well-explored shelf to foreign investment earlier than other Caspian states. Azeri–Chirag–Gunesli (ACG), a giant field estimated to hold around 700 million tonnes of oil, opened first. In September 1994, a production sharing agreement (PSA)[8] awarded ACG to an international, Western-dominated consortium, the Azerbaijan International Operating Company (AIOC). It was called "the deal of the century". Lukoil was well placed to seize the opportunity. Azerbaijan initially held 30 per cent of ACG, but ceded 10 per cent to Lukoil early on (Fuller, 1995).

Lukoil entered the project at a time when the MFA was especially negative to Russian participation in Caspian development (Cockburn, 1994). The official Russian line on transportation of ACG oil to global markets was to get the parties to use Russian routes or risk Russia's participation. Lukoil's share in AIOC persuaded the consortium to choose a Russian route for early oil, which was exported out of Novorossiisk. Alekperov saw this as positive for Russia in both economic and geopolitical terms (Tutushkin, 1999). Transit through this route (Baku–Novorossiisk) continued at a moderate level of 1.5–2.5 million tonnes per annum (tpa) after the opening of ACG's primary export pipeline, the BTC pipeline from Baku via Tbilisi to Ceyhan in Turkey.

Kazakhstan's government released licences more slowly than Azerbaijan, but Lukoil was again in a good position to participate in the development of local fields. With considerable support from the Russian government, in 1995 Lukoil obtained a frame agreement and a 50 per cent stake in the Kumkol oil field (Stalker, 1995; Vardul', 1995). Lukoil's persistent lobbying and strong support from the Russian government resulted in invitations to Lukoil to participate at the giant Tengiz field (Burchilina, 1995; Neftegazovaya vertikal', 2016c). Lukoil joined the transport consortium (the Caspian Pipeline Consortium, CPC) in 1996 and the production consortium (TengizChevroil) in 1997. Lukoil's participation was instrumental in resolving the deadlock around the CPC pipeline, turning the complicated project in Russia's favour.

In the process of getting the project off the ground, it also managed to outmanoeuvre Transneft (cf. Chapter 6) (Neftegazovaya vertikal', 2016c, p.37). While the government's line on the delineation of the Caspian was fragmented, and Transneft handled oil transit from Kazakhstan with a heavy hand, Lukoil's forthcoming approach gave it a prominent role in relations with Kazakhstan (Shumilin, 1997). It was interested in developing production in Uzbekistan (Novolodskaya, 2001), but there, foreign companies found it almost impossible to operate before 2001 due to unfavourable PSA legislation (*Neft' i Kapital*, 2002c).

Russia's western neighbours were central to Lukoil's expansion of downstream activities and market access. Its activities soon included petrol stations, refining and petrochemicals.

Ukraine was a particularly important market and transit state. Alekperov had been interested from the beginning in acquiring one of its large oil refineries (Gavrish and Lysova, 1999). When Ukraine privatised its refineries in the late 1990s, Russian companies were well prepared. They had consolidated production and were developing their downstream sectors (Tutushkin, 1999; Balmaceda, 2008, p.60). Lukoil's position was particularly good, given the strong support of the Russian government (Razumovskii, 1998). Alekperov wielded considerable influence in Ukraine as well. During Leonid Kuchma's presidency (1994–2005), he was one of the Russian businessmen with close ties to the leading figures in the Ukrainian executive (Moskovskii Komsomolets, 1998; Vandenko, 1999; Timoshchenko, 2001; *Kommersant*, 2004b). In 1999, Lukoil acquired 51 per cent of the Odesa refinery, Ukraine's fourth largest. It paid 7.9 million US$ plus 41.2 million US$ in promised investments and debt relief, and guaranteed a minimum workload (Gavrish and Lysova, 1999). Not long after, the Ukrainian government accused Lukoil of breaching these terms, and raised the issue with the Russian government (Shiryaev, 1999). The Russian government could not, or would not interfere in the company's operations in Ukraine. In 2000, Lukoil acquired full control of the refinery (*Neft' i Kapital*, 2004c).

Lukoil also exported oil via Belarus and from Baltic ports. In Belarus it awaited privatisation of the two refineries Naftan[9] and Mozyr. Alekperov's wish list for the 1990s with regard to Lithuania and Latvia included a stake in the Mažeikiu refinery and in one of the two oil ports Klaipėda or Ventspils (*Kommersant*, 1996).

When Lukoil was founded it enjoyed close ties with the government, and positioned itself in the market as a Russian company first and foremost. In the 1990s, Lukoil was the flagship of the Russian oil industry abroad (Stolyarov, 1999) and a giant at home. Good relations with the Russian government helped the company to develop. This was complemented by considerable efforts to stay on good terms with host governments in the post-Soviet region. Lukoil's good relations with the Russian state shielded it from the predictable criticism it received from e.g. Duma politicians for investing abroad while industrial capacity in Russia was under-utilised. Foreign investment had become synonymous with the exodus of capital, and Russian companies often bought rundown plants abroad. Lukoil stood out because it had plans to modernise and expand its foreign operations. There were important push-factors in Lukoil's pursuit of opportunities abroad. As Alekperov admitted, in the 1990s international growth reduced the negative effects of the unpredictable and complicated tax regime in Russia (Tutushkin, 1999).

Financial crisis and reform

The tax system was a brake on economic development. It was at the core of the crisis of the Russian state in the 1990s. The patchwork of old and new regulations, often mutually contradictory, was complicated by arbitrary, exorbitant rates decreed at the federal level, and local and regional demands for services over and above the formal tax burden. Many companies would have gone bankrupt if they had paid all their taxes, so they tended to conceal profits in legal and semi-legal ways. Mutual offsets and negotiations over actual tax payments emerged as an informal solution (Easter, 2012, pp.114–116). The state in the 1990s collected only about half of projected revenue from the sector (Luong and Weinthal, 2004, p.140).

When on 17 August 1998 the Russian government devalued the ruble and defaulted on its debts, oil prices had been falling for a year. In the double crisis of oil prices and state capacity, there were several confrontations over oil taxation between the oil companies and the governments of Evgenii Primakov (1998–1999), Sergei Stepashin (1999) and Vladimir Putin (1999–2000) (Gustafson, 2012, p.261). The state was unable to access much of the rents from oil production. The oil industry boosted production during the crisis, following several years of declining output (Gustafson, 2012, pp.188–192). From 1999, oil production increased. The devaluated ruble and rising global prices for oil combined to make oil export particularly profitable. Russia experienced a genuine oil price boom.

Alekperov was now one of the sector's most influential executives. His opinion mattered at the highest level of the state (RFE/RL, 1996; Lysova, 1999). Energy Minister Viktor Kalyuzhnyi (1999–2000) was particularly close to Lukoil (Ivanov, N., 1999). The state's minority stake institutionalised formal interaction with Lukoil. But the management also prioritised participation in economic development. It responded to requests for societal stabilisation. When domestic oil prices surged in 1999, Lukoil acquiesced to government requests to limit exports (Boiko, 1999; Lysova, 1999). Alekperov often professed that his main duty was towards the state, "the Fatherland", and to "fulfil the tasks that a company should resolve" (*Neft' i Kapital*, 1999). Lukoil's staff and shareholders were his other priorities. But his sense of duty went together with a preference for indirect relations between the state and oil companies. Alekperov took care to reject suggestions of direct state ownership and management of the oil industry (Romanova and San'ko, 1999).

One typical example came in autumn 1999, and this time Alekperov was rather veiled. Putin had recently been appointed prime minister, and the government, particularly the Property Ministry,[10] considered establishing a golden share[11] in Lukoil and other partially state-owned oil companies so as to gain direct influence over management decisions (*Vedomosti*, 1999). This could easily restore direct state control of Lukoil. Alekperov replied, ahead of Duma elections, that he was willing to consider the proposal, depending on what he was offered in return. An appropriate compensation for weaker property rights, he suggested in an interview with the independent *Novaya gazeta* newspaper, was guaranteed standing orders from several large state organisations (Stolyarov, 1999). When he was asked for his opinion about state ownership in general, Alekperov said he would be interested in managing state shares in smaller oil companies (Stolyarov, 1999). In short, Lukoil was willing to have a closer relationship with the state, but it would incur costs. In the interview Alekperov made his terms public. In the event, neither the golden share, nor Lukoil control of state-held shares materialised. In the 1999 elections, Alekperov supported Fatherland – All Russia (OVR), led by Yurii Luzhkov, Evgenii Primakov and Vladimir Yakovlev. Well ahead of polling day, it appeared a pretty safe bet, and a promising option. Primakov was a better choice than candidates with plans to increase the state's control of the oil sector. But the subsequent impressive election outcome for the recently established Unity bloc, which Putin supported, demonstrated that Russian politics were about to change.

By 2000, Lukoil was one of the world's largest private oil companies by reserves and production (Tutushkin, 1996b; Lukoil, 2000; 2001, p.10; 2004, p.13). In 2002, it was the Russian company with the largest annual turnover irrespective of sector (Lukoil, 2003). It emerged from the financial crisis as one of the five most profitable companies in the Russian oil and gas sector (Meshcherin, 2011a). Lukoil's management had always aimed at turning it into a truly international company (Neftegazovaya vertikal', 2006b). Now, their aim was to turn it into a Russian ExxonMobil, a supermajor (Golubkova et al., 2007).

A new approach to the post-Soviet region

In June 2000, Alekperov published an op-ed in *Izvestiya* discussing the place of the post-Soviet region and eastern Europe in Russia's energy strategy (Alekperov, 2000). In his view, Russia could, and should, return to these regions only as an investor. What Russian energy companies needed to do was to pursue investment programmes before the arrival of Western companies. The post-Soviet region was united by language, mentality, and a multitude of ties, he maintained. In effect, it was the basis of a new economic system that could "speak like an equal to other transnational blocs" (Alekperov, 2000). He urged the Russian government to support energy companies like Lukoil in the post-Soviet region, just like the US government supported

American corporations. Alekperov articulated sentiments that were gaining foothold in the debate on Russian foreign policy towards the post-Soviet region. For example, on the question of the status of the Caspian Sea, Lukoil's approach now began to resonate with Russia's official policy. Russia began to engage the Caspian littoral states and looked more positively on Russian companies' participation in the development of the Caspian, undergoing a change of line that was complete by 2001 (Shumilin, 1997; *Upstream*, 1997; Krivorotov, 1998; Sborov, 2000). Russia began to engage Kazakhstan and Azerbaijan in a process of border delimitation in the Caspian Sea.

Lukoil received government support abroad, especially in Uzbekistan, and by 2001 also in Azerbaijan and Kazakhstan. Its engagement in the post-Soviet region and position in the Caspian Sea had given Lukoil a say in Russian foreign policymaking. This was to its own advantage, as well, especially in Kazakhstan. But in return it had to go along with the wishes of the state concerning its opportunities for development abroad. As discussed both below and in Chapter 6, the Russian government limited Lukoil's range of export options by sanctioning Transneft's reduced support for export through Baltic ports. The state was now in a better position to regulate market access for Lukoil. Lukoil chose to initiate new routes in regions where they would not directly compete with Transneft's pipeline network. In this way, Lukoil's challenge to Transneft was slightly less open than that of Yukos, which was not inclined to toe the government's line. And in and around the Caspian Sea, Lukoil's status as the major Russian oil company with well-developed international operations gave it an advantage. After the change in Russian foreign policy, Lukoil was ready to benefit.

Lukoil's new projects in Azerbaijan were not a commercial success, like most of the projects that followed the "deal of the century". ACG and the giant gas project Shah Deniz were exceptions in a region where the geological risks were abundant. Kazakhstan was more promising. In 1996, President Nursultan Nazarbaev agreed in principle to reserve around 20 per cent of operations on the Kazakhstan shelf for Lukoil (Tutushkin, 1996a). After Russia's policy change regarding the Caspian Sea, Russia and Kazakhstan in 2002 completed the delimitation of cross-border hydrocarbon fields on the shelf. This released several new projects. Lukoil's projects in Kazakhstan grew from five in 1997 to nine in 2004, and 13 in 2010 (Kravets, 2004), even as it lost one licence after the border agreement (*Upstream*, 1998b). Two cross-border fields were awarded to Russia, but with joint exploration. Lukoil was designated Russia's entrusted company; KazMunayGaz was in charge on Kazakhstan's side (Glumskov and Skorobogat'ko, 2003; *Neft' i Kapital*, 2011b).

Uzbekistan introduced new PSA legislation in 2001 to attract international oil and gas companies (Makarkin, 2008a). In May, President Islam Karimov met Putin and invited Russian companies to participate in developing Uzbekistan's hydrocarbon sector. Two months later, Lukoil signed a PSA with the Russian gas company Itera and Uzbekneftegaz to explore and develop three large gas fields: Kandym, Khauzak and Shady (*Neft' i Kapital*, 2002c). Also in this case, Lukoil was Russia's flagship abroad. By 2004, 6.1 per cent of Lukoil's reserves were in Uzbekistan (Lukoil Overseas Holding Ltd., 2005, p.14).

Privatisation programmes in Ukraine opened for substantial Russian ownership in many sectors. By 2002, Russian companies controlled three of the six Ukrainian oil refineries, three quarters of the market for oil products, and were strong in petrochemicals, too (*Kommersant*, 2002). Lukoil invested in petrochemicals and established Lukor, a JV with the Ukrainian government in 2000 (Rybal'chenko, 2001). There was considerable uncertainty around the company's privatisation, and Lukoil's property rights remained weakly protected. However, until the end of Kuchma's presidency (2004), Alekperov could counter attacks by talking to him and promising additional investments. He would thus dispel any claims Ukraine might be considering against Lukoil (Gorelov, 2001, Razumovskii, 2001; *Neft' i Kapital*, 2004c).

Lukoil remained interested in further expansion and acquiring stakes in the Baltic states (*Neft' i Kapital*, 2002b), either in the Ventspils oil terminal (Pravosudov, 2003) or the Mažeikiu refinery (Tutushkin, 1999; Rybal'chenko, 2000). As discussed in Chapter 6, around 2000 Russia planned to cut transit volumes through Latvian and Lithuanian ports. Yukos acquired Mažeikiu in 2002. Transneft's policy towards Ventspils deterred Lukoil from acquiring a stake there (Chapter 6).

The new coalition

Relations between oil companies and the government changed with the ascent of Vladimir Putin in 1999–2000. The government's overtures to establish golden shares in Lukoil and other companies indicated a preference for greater state control. In his 2000 presidential election campaign, Putin stated his intention to keep all "oligarchs" equally distant from the Kremlin. It was a popular policy, in promising to reduce the considerable political influence of certain businessmen, in particular Boris Berezovskii (a joint owner of the oil company Sibneft), in the years 1995–1999 (Fortescue, 2006, pp.101–111). Putin's main aim, however, was to make oil companies pay their taxes in full (Gustafson, 2012, pp.260–262). After his inauguration in May, together with Finance Minister Aleksei Kudrin he initiated a campaign to recover taxes, in effect, to capture oil rents for the state budget (Gustafson, 2012, pp.260–262). The state would now strengthen its weakest spot, resource extraction through taxation.

In the *Izvestiya* op-ed from June 2000 discussed on p. 151, Alekperov deliberated on state–business relations in the energy sector in considerable detail. In his view, they were far from optimal. Criticising the oligarchs' influence on the state, he also chastised a common view among state officials, that private interests by their very nature were antithetical to state interests (Alekperov, 2000). In particular, he criticised the taxation system, which made investment difficult and tax compliance costly. He called for structural reforms, encompassing legislation, taxation, banking and land ownership regulations, to improve the business climate and in effect improve institutional quality, thereby reducing the demand for personalised relations between state and business. In Alekperov's view, the oligarchs would have less influence if the state carried out structural reform, and opened for real dialogue with business leaders.

But Alekperov was vulnerable, too. Ahead of the annual shareholder meeting in June 2000, the government initially nominated 11 candidates for Lukoil's 11 member Board. The state's stake was around 16 per cent at the time. Its list of 11 candidates had political implications, and it was interpreted as a political signal (Tutushkin, 2000). Alekperov's *Izvestiya* article, released on the day of the shareholder meeting, was part of Lukoil's response. In the end, Lukoil's management persuaded the government to nominate only two candidates (Tutushkin, 2000). At the meeting, the management obtained shareholder support for a change to Lukoil's statutes, making it more difficult to remove the company's president before his term expired. The presidential term was extended from two years to five, and the right to hire senior staff transferred from the Board Chairman to Lukoil's president (Tutushkin, 2000). The position of Lukoil's president was thus strengthened relative to that of the Board. But the Board's independence was also strengthened. It was reduced from 13 members to 11, at the expense of management representatives. Independent board members, in particular foreigners, were important as a cushion against government influence, and their number increased steadily from two in 1999 to eight ten years later.[12] In 2005, after the state sold its last remaining stake in Lukoil, the members of the Board regained their influence over business decisions (*Vedomosti*, 2005). The implication was that the measures taken in 2000 to strengthen the President's direct control were no longer necessary.

A few weeks later in July 2000, Lukoil, Alekperov personally, and Lukoil's chief accountant, were indicted for tax evasion. It was a warning shot, according to some observers, to dissuade Lukoil from taking part in the imminent privatisation of ONAKO, a state-owned company with a refinery that would fit Lukoil's profile. Lukoil and Yukos had just announced joint plans to bid for ONAKO (Khartukov, 2000). Whatever the ulterior motives (and Lukoil did not participate in the ONAKO auction[13]), the indictment showed that no company, not even Lukoil, was above the (tax) law. It also showed that Putin and Kudrin meant business with their taxation campaign. The allegations against Alekperov were withdrawn after he requested, and was granted, an immediate meeting with Putin (Igorev et al., 2000; Jensen, 2000; Heil, 2008). Most of the charges against Lukoil were later thrown out by the court (*Kommersant*-Vlast', 2002). When major businessmen met Putin in late July at their first plenary meeting ("oligarch meeting"), Putin refused to back down on taxation (Germanovich, 2000; Gustafson, 2012, pp.262, 564). Regular meetings later improved the state–

business dialogue somewhat, alleviating fears of re-nationalisation (Smirnov, K., 2002). The meetings institutionalised and formalised involvement with the state, but also limited informal contact and business participation in state decisions. This was precisely what the government had intended. Compared to Yeltsin's frequent, and private, meetings with prominent businessmen, dealings were now less arbitrary and personal. State–business interaction changed also at a more fundamental level, as the state prepared to enforce legislation and increase its capacity.

Over the following year, the government drafted a new taxation system for natural resources. There was little broad consultation with oil companies, but the government started from a draft proposed by Yukos (Yermakov, 2001, cited in Gustafson, 2012, p.264). The legislation passed the Duma, with considerable opposition, in the summer of 2001 (Lyapunova, 2001; Sidorov, 2001; Gustafson, 2012, pp.263–266). The new system, effective from 1 January 2002, introduced a new consolidated production tax (*nalog na dobychu poleznykh iskopaemykh*—NDPI). It was tied to the export price and therefore difficult to manipulate (Gustafson, 2012, p.264). It became impossible to make deductions, including deductions for investments, from the tax on profit (Konoplyanik, 2001). A commission, chaired by Kudrin, determined rates in accordance with oil price changes (Gustafson, 2012, p.265). The final version of another oil tax, a tax on additional incomes (popularly called super profits), remained under elaboration (Konoplyanik, 2001). The new system was simple. It enabled the state to access rents from oil production to the extent desired by the government. State representatives considered its considerable negative effects on investment and sector development to be of secondary importance (Bradshaw, 2012, pp.208–209).

In 2000–2002, Lukoil adopted a more neutral position in intra-elite politics. The first sign came in autumn 2000, when Lukoil, as the only major company, refused a seat on the new presidium of the Russian Union of Industrialists and Entrepreneurs (*Rossiiskii soyuz promyshlennikov i predprinimatelei*—RSPP) (Pravosudov, 2000). Alekperov kept his distance from the political elite and reduced his engagement in institutional development. His previous political preferences, in particular his ties to Chernomyrdin and support for OVR and Primakov, were a liability (Jensen, 2000; *Neft' i Kapital*, 2004d). Lukoil also kept a distance from the state-owned companies. A strategic partnership with Gazprom, started in 1999, naturally included some cooperation, but it was intensified only in 2002. The competition with Rosneft was much more intense, and open in the case of licences in the north (Gustafson, 2012, pp.333–334).

On several occasions in Putin's first term, Lukoil was in conflict with Transneft. Lukoil reduced its reliance on Transneft's pipelines, not least by opening the temporary export terminal Varandei on the Barents Sea coast, in 2001. It was served by its own, non-Transneft, pipeline. Lukoil pursued another plan for a non-Transneft route, the Murmansk pipeline, but this fell through (Chapter 6). In 2003, Alekperov suggested that Transneft's pipeline monopoly could be abolished (Alekperov, 2003; Bolshoi biznes, 2003). Lukoil's management frequently expressed impatience with Transneft's lack of response to the industry's need for more pipeline capacity (Tutushkin, 2003; Zagorodnaya, 2003; Vin'kov et al., 2004; Yakovleva-Ustinova, 2004). Export through Varandei gradually expanded and Lukoil opened a permanent terminal there in 2008 (Lukoil-Trans, 2014). This was in contradiction to government policy, which was neatly summed up by First Deputy Prime Minister Sergei Ivanov when he insisted that Lukoil had legal access to one crude oil port, Vysotsk on the Baltic Sea, where Lukoil had established its own export terminal (Sivakov and Vin'kov, 2007). Criticism of Transneft and the development of an independent export capacity increased the political risk to Lukoil. Alekperov prioritised business development whenever possible. It helped that Varandei served fields located far from Transneft's pipeline network, and was located some 1,700 km from Vysotsk.

There were visible continuities in Lukoil's relationship with the state in the 1990s and 2000s. Lukoil was always close to the government and leading state representatives. Under Yeltsin, such relations were personal and non-transparent. Alekperov's longstanding relations with key government figures were an advantage. In the early 2000s, Lukoil had a mixed approach to state organisations and preferred to keep its distance, especially from state-owned companies. Lukoil's management modified the terms of access and participation that applied to the state to protect the property rights in Lukoil. State–Lukoil relations grew more distanced by the state's new approach under Putin. The state became unambiguously more powerful than oil companies, which it now kept at arm's length. Interaction became based on formal procedures, compliance and plenary business meetings. Business associations flourished (Zudin, 2013). But transparent rent collection through taxation also strengthened oil companies' property rights. The rising oil price, and increasing rent collection from the oil sector, enabled the state to develop capacity and infrastructural power to provide services to the population.

A foreign energy strategy

In 2002, Lukoil started a restructuring programme to increase profits and efficiency. Foreign operations played an important part. Exploration and production outside Lukoil's traditional producing regions, and export to global markets, were set to expand. From 2001 to 2006, the number of international upstream projects increased from seven to 26 (*Neft' i Kapital*, 2002a; Lukin, 2007).

Beginning in 2000, foreign policy gradually became more coherent and more targeted towards the post-Soviet region. A new Energy Strategy made it a government priority to support Russian energy companies in world markets (Ministry of Industry and Trade, 2003, pp.41–42). From Alekperov's point of view, it was a step in the right direction. In the 1990s, Lukoil's management had often invoked the image of the company as a pioneer. Under Putin, priorities of Russian foreign policy took precedence over Lukoil's business interests. In return for loyalty, Lukoil enjoyed the government's continued support to expand its international operations, particularly in the post-Soviet region. It put Lukoil's Russianness abroad in a different light. There was no difference, Alekperov said on several occasions, between Lukoil's interests abroad and those of the Russian state (Butrin, 2003). These were not just words. Lukoil's "state-mindedness" (*gosudarstvennoe myshlenie*) was carefully emphasised when Lukoil, naturally for a vertically integrated oil company, supported the Russian government's resistance to the EU's Energy Charter Treaty. "State-mindedness" is prominent in Alekperov's writings on the Russian oil industry (Alekperov, 2009; 2011a). As far as the government stake in Lukoil was concerned, Alekperov stated that it brought a small, but tangible advantage to operations in Central Asia and the Middle East (Zagorodnaya, 2003; *Vedomosti*, 2005).

In Azerbaijan, Russian foreign policy came first. After AIOC's choice of BTC as the main export route from ACG to global markets, Lukoil's Investor Relations Director, Leonid Fedun, stated that Lukoil participation in BTC was a political question, and that oil from Azerbaijan and Kazakhstan should transit via Russia (Interfax, 2001). BTC was the main alternative to Russian routes, and the international companies preferred establishing a non-Russian route. In 2001–2002, as the start of BTC construction drew near, Lukoil considered acquiring a 7.5 per cent stake in the transport consortium. In late 2001, the management tried to obtain government and Transneft approval of an acquisition (Butrin, 2001; *Upstream*, 2001; Useinov, 2002). It would be contrary to Russia's interests, the government responded. The acquisition proposal was ditched by April 2002 (*Vedomosti*, 2002a). Lukoil also proposed that Transneft could develop a connection to BTC as an additional export route (Useinov, 2001; 2002). Again, this was ruled out by Transneft and the Russian government (Butrin, 2001; *Upstream*, 2001; Egorova, 2004; Useinov, 2002). ACG was politically important in Russia's relations with Azerbaijan, but not important enough when up against the priorities of controlling export routes from the Caspian Basin. The decision was costly to Lukoil, as it increased the costs of its transport options for ACG oil. Without a stake in BTC, it would have to access the pipeline on unfavourable third party terms. As it was in a minority position in AIOC, it lacked influence on the choice of export routes, with no possibility of tilting outcomes in favour of Russia. But it could not disregard the government's preferences for transport routes. In consequence of these difficulties, Lukoil in November sold its stake in the ACG field for 1.375 billion US$, in a highly profitable and timely transaction (Sapozhnikov, 2002; Sapozhnikov et al., 2002; Ignatova, 2003; *Neft' i Kapital*, 2003b). Its new strategy, Lukoil explained, was to prioritise exit from projects in which it was not an operator, and to concentrate on projects where it had more influence. But ACG was not the only project in which Lukoil was not operator. The released capital did not find any new investment opportunity soon. For Russia, the result was a shrinking place in Azerbaijan's energy sector, and reduced influence on oil transport routes from the region.

What applied to oil did not apply to gas, however. The giant Shah Deniz gas field and its export pipeline seemed to have fewer political connotations in Russia. It was certainly strategically important to Lukoil, even more so than what in the end had applied to ACG. Lukoil, through LukAgip, held 5 per cent of Shah Deniz, which was planned to export gas to Turkey through the Baku–Tbilisi–Erzurum (BTE) gas pipeline. In 2004, Lukoil increased its stake to 10 per cent. Lukoil's share of the South Caucasus Pipeline Company, which owned the BTE pipeline, increased to 10 per cent, and its share of the Azerbaijan Gas Supply Company to 8 per cent (Sapozhnikov and Khvostik, 2004). Acquiring a significant presence in gas was a strategic priority of Lukoil's. Non-Russian gas projects were all the more important as they enabled the company to market its own gas. At home, of course, its options were severely limited by Gazprom's export monopoly.

By 2003, Lukoil was the largest Russian investor in Kazakhstan, and an experienced operator (Glumskov and Skorobogat'ko, 2003). In the following years, it became the fourth largest petroleum producer in the country (Alekperov, 2006; Neftegazovaya vertikal', 2011c). This reflected the position of Kazakhstan as Lukoil's most significant production region outside Russia. In 2004, 19.9 per cent of its reserves and 27.4 per cent of its oil and gas production were in Kazakhstan (Lukoil Overseas Holding Ltd., 2005, p.14). For comparison, Azerbaijan held only 2.4 per cent of Lukoil's reserves and no production at that point (Lukoil Overseas Holding Ltd., 2005, p.14). Lukoil's connections to Kazakhstan's leaders remained excellent (Kravets, 2004; *Kommersant*, 2006).

Uzbekistan's gas export depended entirely on Russian transit, and Western companies were less interested in its gas projects. Russia and Uzbekistan concluded a strategic partnership agreement in 2004 (Gotova, 2004; *Neft' i Kapital*, 2004a). In 2003, Itera was forced out of the gas transit market from Central Asia when Gazprom acquired the management rights to the Uzbek gas grid (Butrin, 2004). Lukoil took over Itera's shares in Kandym–Khauzak–Shady (Vinogradova, 2003). By 2004, Lukoil controlled 90 per cent of this PSA (Lukin, 2006; Neftegazovaya vertikal', 2007). The gas was sold to Gazprom at the Uzbek border (*Neft' i Kapital*, 2004a) at the same price as other Uzbek gas, and much higher than Gazprom's price for Lukoil's Russian gas.[14] Contrary to standard business practice, Lukoil shared its profits from the PSA with Uzbekneftegaz before having recovered costs, thereby far exceeding the obligations of the PSA. This was probably expected, possibly demanded, by the Uzbek government (Makarkin, 2008a). After Kandym–Khauzak–Shady, Lukoil entered into a series of exploration projects and advantageous PSAs. By 2010, 74 per cent of Lukoil's gas reserves outside Russia were in Uzbekistan (Lukoil Overseas Holding Ltd., 2011, p.20).

Lukoil no longer acted independently of the government line on foreign policy as a matter of routine. Decisions that could be perceived as contrary to Russian foreign policy were approached with care, and there was more "state-mindedness" in its operations. While others saw Lukoil as a conformist in this period (Vahtra and Liuhto, 2004, p.95), the analysis here reveals a more nuanced picture. Lukoil took the written and unwritten rules of Russian foreign policy into account, but it did pursue its most prioritised projects.

As oil prices rose, Russia could more easily achieve its aims in international politics. After 2001, Kremlin and government support of and interest in Lukoil abroad seemed more pronounced than before, according to Alekperov (Drankina and Fadeev, 2001; *Neft' i Kapital*, 2002d; Zagorodnaya, 2003). He was included in the business delegation when Putin travelled to countries in which Lukoil operated, or had an interest. When Lukoil signed agreements or opened facilities abroad, members of the Russian government were usually present. Lukoil's dealings with the state on foreign policy issues included advice to policymakers, as Lukoil had expertise and knowledge from operations in many countries (Butrin, 2003). It ensured that Lukoil's interests would be taken into account in Russian foreign policy.

The new stability: Loyalty and limits for private companies

The state now increased its capacity in the oil sector, but the government was impatient with oil companies' efforts to minimise tax payments. In 2003, Putin and the government clashed with Mikhail Khodorkovskii of Yukos on the subject of oil sector regulation. The case included tax optimisation, especially through domestic offshore havens, but also the extent to which the state should influence production methods. Yukos's attempts to develop export options with China but without Transneft, and its lobbying of the Duma, especially with regard to taxation, were other issues of contention (Gustafson, 2012, pp.294–295). When Khodorkovskii was arrested on tax claims in October, the campaign against Yukos, underway for some time, moved up a gear into expropriation. The heads of other companies kept quiet at this point. In Thane Gustafson's analysis, Alekperov's previous alignment with some of Khodorkovskii's views on industry development disappeared at the first public hint of a confrontation with Putin (Gustafson, 2012, pp.335–336). As discussed here, Alekperov had long seen it as imperative to maintain good working relations with the state. Because of that, he quickly grasped the implications and potential damage to other companies of the Yukos affair. A few weeks ahead of Khodorkovsky's arrest, Alekperov emphasised that any challenge to the current order would have to come from somewhere else (Butrin, 2003).

In the period from October 2003 to the end of 2005, Yukos's production company, Yuganskneftegaz, was sold off and eventually acquired by Rosneft. In the same period, the major private oil company Sibneft came under Gazprom's control. The state undertook an extensive control mission of oil industry operations in West Siberia (Gustafson, 2012, pp.308–309). The private oil sector seemed under threat of renationalisation. Rosneft and Gazprom acquired several large oil companies in the years that followed. As a result, the playing field was tilted in favour of the state (Bradshaw, 2009, p.5).

Lukoil complied with the new formal and informal requirements, and remained a successful company. Even more than before, Alekperov was prone to describing Lukoil as "state-minded". There was no difference, in principle, he insisted, between the Russian oil companies. They were all Russian (e.g. in Tutushkin, 2008). The subject often came up in the context of licensing on the continental shelf, suspended in 2005, and access to new offshore fields. This was of particular interest to Lukoil, because it was the next frontier of its development and important to its strategy.

The Yukos case illustrated the importance of political loyalty and adherence to informal convention to avoid being targeted for selective rule enforcement. In exemplifying the selective application of formal rules, the Yukos affair reinforced a system of personal privileges. Alekperov learnt this lesson. Perhaps most importantly, once he understood that Putin was promoting state-owned Rosneft, still a company of lesser significance than his own, he settled all ongoing disputes with that company (Gustafson, 2012, pp.334–335). Lukoil quickly eliminated its legal tax optimisation schemes like those employed by Yukos (Skorobogat'ko, 2004). In December 2004, when the Kremlin asked the oil companies to cut petrol prices, Lukoil was the first to be asked. It complied, and others followed (Levinskii, 2004). When prices started rising again in September 2005, Lukoil initiated a renewed price freeze (Neftegazovaya vertikal', 2006a). When a new request came in 2008, and Lukoil acquiesced, Alekperov approached the matter in the following way: "Do you have any other option? Have you seen anyone else who disagrees with the state? What is the point? If it is required to help the state at any time, you have to help" (Shevel'kova, 2008).

This highlighted a central lesson to be drawn from the Yukos affair. To Putin, the long process of increasing revenue collection in the oil sector, or rather, to force the companies to share more of their rents, was not just about accessing rent streams through formal taxation. It was also about the state's right to access informal rent streams and use oil companies as tools of the state through direct control. Oil companies could not ignore suggestions of regional development in the form of corporate social responsibility (CSR), charity and sports contributions. Douglas Rogers argues that the Yukos affair "enhanced" the significant existing corporate–regional cooperation over cultural and social projects, and was also a state-building exercise (Rogers, 2015, pp.145–146, 158–160). From the perspective of a company like Lukoil, such cooperation at the regional level anchored business activity in the community where it took place, by facilitating desired cultural and social activities. Close cooperation with regional authorities may have been an end in itself, as it made Lukoil a partner in regional development. Crucially to regional authorities, cooperation ensured that the activities fulfilled regional and national priorities.

CSR as infrastructural power

From the perspective of the central state, there is more to this cooperation. At the system level, the extent and depth of welfare provision strengthened the state and its top representatives, the regime. Nationally, following up on government plans for a national, oil-driven development policy was now part of what significant oil and gas companies were expected to do. Compliance reduced their vulnerability to state predation. Informal rent extraction by demanding voluntary contributions became a staple of the state's relations with the oil sector and big business in general (Meshcherin, 2010). The division between state-owned and privately held organisations became more conditional, less distinct. Lukoil promoted regional museums, supported veterans, invalids, orphanages and hospitals, funded university programmes and sponsored a wide variety of regional and youth sports, as well as teams and clubs on the national level. While some of this is typical of many large corporations, in the Russian context, these tasks were traditionally and in the public perception the responsibility of the state. During the transformational recession and after, state funding had ceased. Now the void was filled by companies like Lukoil. In its own way, Lukoil now substituted for some of the state's traditional public welfare obligations and supplied infrastructural power as well. As long as the priorities were in line with those of the central state, one may see this as a development that multiplied state capacity. The state could indirectly harness the strengths of Russia's energy companies to fulfil its tasks. On the other hand, if sports and cultural activity were so important for the state, why could it not to a greater extent redistribute taxes through regional and national budgets? In this sense, the practice did not enhance state capacity in general, only by proxy using companies like Lukoil, and not uniformly across the country, only in regions and industries with significant company CSR programmes.

For Lukoil, broad contact with state organisations opened for small-scale participation in, and access to information about, policymaking. State organisations regularly asked Alekperov, among other prominent businessmen, to advise them on policy and support social projects in everything from the North Caucasus to education. At the national level, the opportunity to consult with Putin on the side lines of roundtables and conferences held considerable attraction (cf. Nikolaeva and Bekker, 2006). According to media reports, Alekperov was one of the Russian managers to meet Putin most frequently (*Kommersant*, 2004a; 2005). One study from this period claims that Alekperov spent up to 80 per cent of his time studying changes in the Kremlin's balance of power (Gorst, 2007, p.3). As Lukoil was no longer state owned, this appears partly as compensation, through informal interaction, for formal access and participation. It was important to keep abreast of state plans for the oil sector, and to pursue closer relations with the state now that property rights in the oil sector had less protection. Alekperov claimed never to have been denied access to the prime minister or other government members (Butrin, 2003). Other members of the senior management, like Vice President Fedun, did not enjoy the same level of access (Mazneva et al., 2008).

Participation in business roundtables became more important as a channel of access to the state following the end of state ownership in Lukoil. The state sold its remaining 7.59 per cent stake in Lukoil to ConocoPhillips in 2004 (*Kommersant*, 2004c). Lukoil had valued having the state as a shareholder. The decision to divest the state of its stake was the Kremlin's, moreover against Alekperov's wishes and with little prior consultation (Tutushkin, 2004; *Vedomosti*, 2005). The new shareholder, ConocoPhillips, was selected on the basis of Lukoil's strategic priorities. In advance of the deal, Alekperov and James Mulva of ConocoPhillips sought Putin's approval. Their meeting covered the terms of the deal, including guarantees against political attacks, and future business plans (*Neft' i Kapital*, 2004b; Tutushkin et al., 2004). The final deal reflected Kremlin priorities, especially a restriction on direct ConocoPhillips partnerships in projects inside Russia (Makarkin, 2008b). This was particularly important in light of the Yukos affair, which had been ongoing for a year by then. Ahead of Khodorkovskii's arrest, Yukos had pursued merger talks with Sibneft, Chevron and ExxonMobil. In addition to ConocoPhillips's stake, Lukoil's managers increased their ownership control of the company substantially in the mid to late 2000s.[15] Consultations with the president involved seeking his approval of new upstream projects and entry into new downstream markets before acting on the plans. In February 2006, Alekperov received Putin's approval to acquire more petrol stations in Europe (*Neft' i Kapital*, 2007d; Mazneva, 2008). Such consultations shielded Lukoil from criticism of, for example, causing a capital flight when investing abroad (*Vedomosti*, 2002b). This was another sensitive topic after the Yukos affair.

Limits to business development in Russia

Lukoil's leadership in production output in the Russian sector was overtaken by Yukos in 2003 (only) and by Rosneft, which acquired Yukos's production assets, in 2007 (*Neft' i Kapital*, 2007a). That fact in itself said more about Rosneft than Lukoil: from 2003 through 2009 its share of Russian oil production varied between 18 and 19 per cent, and its absolute oil and condensate production in Russia increased gradually.[16] Lukoil was the second largest exporter of crude oil from Russia in 2001, barely surpassed by Yukos at approximately 23 million tonnes. By 2005, both Rosneft and TNK-BP exported more, and Lukoil's exports peaked at just above 34 million tonnes. In 2009, Lukoil was the fourth largest exporter at just below 25 million tonnes (Neftegazovaya vertikal', 2010c).[17] This was partly explained by Lukoil's relatively high share in domestic refining and oil products export, but output had stagnated (Neftegazovaya vertikal', 2010a; *Neft' i Kapital*, 2011c). The company now maximised profits, not output volume (Meshcherin, 2011c). Lukoil maintained its position through innovation and modernisation (Mel'nikov, 2011; Vin'kov et al., 2011), and by increasing exploitation rates in oil reservoirs (O'Cinneide, 2011). Many of Lukoil's Russian oil reserves were now in fields under production, and past their peak (Neftegazovaya vertikal', 2011b).

The reasons for Lukoil's difficulties in bringing new fields into production were both structural and political. Lukoil's Russian fields were maturing and most of the attractive onshore fields were in production. Geological exploration was expensive. There was a lack of incentives for new developments. The administrative barriers remained high and legislation unsatisfactory. This problem by 2010 affected all the major Russian companies (Neftegazovaya vertikal', 2010b; Mandrik, 2011; Meshcherin, 2011b). The oil taxation system of 2001 contributed to their woes. Following adjustments in 2004, 80 per cent of the profits from the years of the oil price boom were directed into the federal budget. The taxation system discouraged investment, including investment to sustain future production levels (Aleksashenko, 2012, p.36 fn. 34, 46; Bradshaw, 2012, p.209). As the problem went from chronic to acute with the financial crisis, a federal law allowed companies to apply for exemptions, but only as tax breaks for individual fields. Some projects were also allowed to drop the oil export duty (*Ekonomika i zhizn'*, 2009; Oilcapital. ru, 2010). This initially worked to Rosneft's advantage (Gudkov, 2010). Alekperov later successfully lobbied for lower oil export duties for two fields in the Caspian Sea, by speaking with Prime Minister Putin directly at the opening of one of them (Meshcherin, 2010).

In addition, Lukoil's participation in auctions of new licences in Russia declined, for several reasons. There were fewer licences to bid for. The major Russian oil provinces were maturing, and new ones remained undeveloped. Some licences were withheld from auction until Rosneft and Gazprom could afford them. Yukos's remaining assets were tacitly reserved for the state-controlled companies (Neftegazovaya vertikal', 2006b). Some auctions included licences that, in light of business strategy and existing assets, appeared particularly attractive to Lukoil, but where it refrained from bidding (*Neft' i Kapital*, 2005b). Lukoil did not challenge the situation (Savushkin, 2005; *Neft' i Kapital*, 2006b), and thereby maintained its working relations with Gazprom and Rosneft. It was unfair, said Lukoil's management, but would not "recommend anyone to enter into conflict with Gazprom" (Sivakov and Vin'kov, 2007; Mel'nikov, 2011). While the new informal rules placed the state companies in advantageous positions, Lukoil in particular butted against a glass ceiling as far as new licences were concerned (Neftegazovaya vertikal', 2006b; Malkova, 2010). The ConocoPhillips ownership stake incurred informal restrictions. This was later supplanted by formal regulations when the restrictions on foreign ownership were formalised in the law on Strategic Stakes from 2008 (Heath, 2009; Golubkova and Ershov, 2010). In consequence, ConocoPhillips was not allowed into Lukoil's most profitable operations. It eventually sold its stake in Lukoil in 2010 (Embassy Vilnius, 2005b; Neftegazovaya vertikal', 2011d, p.56).

In 2008, Lukoil and other private companies were barred by new legislation from seeking new offshore licences, following a major change to the Law on the Subsoil (Federal Law No. 2395, 1992; cf. Fortescue, 2009). Lukoil criticised the legal change during the lengthy policy process from

2005 to 2008 (Graifer, 2005; Nekrasov, 2007; Sivakov and Vin'kov, 2007; Tutushkin et al., 2007). The law amendment was actively lobbied through by Sechin, now chair of Rosneft's Board (2004–2011) (Mel'nikov, 2015). When passed, the revised law only allowed state companies with a minimum of five years offshore experience in Russia to seek new licences on the continental shelf (Federal Law No. 2395, 1992; *Kommersant*, 2008; Malkova, 2010). Lukoil held offshore licences already, in Russia and abroad, and would have been the most serious contender for new ones. Lukoil's management openly criticised the new arrangement (*Vedomosti*, 2012). Their misgivings notwithstanding, Lukoil's management had accepted the balance of power, it said, between Russia's largest oil companies as a Kremlin decision. When privately owned Bashneft invited Lukoil in 2010 to join in the development of the giant strategic Trebs and Titov fields, which Lukoil had previously contested, it was a major exception to the general rule in the sector (Orekhin, 2010; Neftegazovaya vertikal', 2012b). The project later ran into considerable licensing problems.

The changing regulation of the oil and gas industries, which privileged state-owned companies over privately owned ones, was promoted and supported by Sechin (Meshcherin, 2010, pp.17, 20). Energy Minister Shmatko acquiesced. In the view of oil industry actors, he was a weak minister who left difficult decisions, especially decisions that affected the state-owned companies' privileges, to Sechin, Medvedev or Putin (Starinskaya et al., 2010). Reportedly, Putin, too, preferred to leave sector development to Sechin, and general economic questions to Medvedev (Meshcherin, 2010). By 2012, the lack of sector policy and strategic planning seriously hampered the oil industry's development (Neftegazovaya vertikal', 2012a). The state was weakened in its capacity to respond to industry demands. Instead of strategies for development, the state regulated the industry at a more detailed level. Oil company representatives regularly complained about micro-legislation and enforced monitoring, which the state could use to reach each company in case of non-compliance with its priorities at any time (Nikitin, 2010; Vinogradova, 2010; Nikitin, 2011). Lukoil was no exception (Mel'nikov, 2011).

Private companies could become Rosneft and Gazprom's partners or expand abroad (Zotova, 2008). Lukoil did both. It renewed and expanded its partnership with Gazprom in 2005 (Firsova, 2005; Afanasiev, 2011), and took steps to build a partnership with Rosneft (Vinogradova, 2011). Gas production became an important business segment, again a first for a Russian oil company (Neftegazovaya vertikal', 2005; Rebrov and Skorlygina, 2006). From a single-digit share in overall hydrocarbon production, gas in 2006 reached a 10.2 per cent share of Lukoil's overall production (Lukoil, 2007, p.3). From 2005 to 2006, gas production increased by 141.6 per cent as the first gas was produced at Shah Deniz, and the Nakhodkinskii field in Russia began to peak (Lukoil, 2007, pp.3, 32, 34). The plan was to increase gas production to around 30 per cent of overall production by 2016.[18]

Challenges notwithstanding, Alekperov continued to see it as Lukoil's responsibility to develop the Russian oil sector. He even asked, indirectly referring to the difficulties foreign investors encountered in Russia, "if companies like Lukoil and Gazprom start orienting themselves on projects outside Russia – who would come here if [Russia's own] companies leave?" (Rebrov, 2010a). Alekperov and heads of other private companies remained critical of the preferential treatment of state companies, particularly on the shelf (Alekperov, 2011b; Astakhova and Basvain, 2011; Derbilova and Mazneva, 2011). When the issue was reopened in 2012, the Ministry of Natural Resources shared that view, to no avail (Mel'nikov, 2015). Alekperov's pursuit of greater Lukoil participation (Tutushkin, 2008) resulted in 2011 in an alliance, and a partnership for Russian shelf development, with Rosneft (Neftegazovaya vertikal', 2011a; 2011b). A junior role like this was a considerable achievement for a private company at the time. In practice, it proved difficult to agree on the working format for the shelf partnership (Interfaks-ANI, 2011). In spring 2012, when international majors were concluding "shelf alliances" with Rosneft, Russian private companies were offered similar terms (Barsukov, 2012; Tovkailo, 2012).

Loyalty to the state, to formal and informal rules, became increasingly important in the mid-2000s. In the context of the 2011 post-election demonstrations, Alekperov stated that he always voted for United Russia, but otherwise was not "a political figure" (Derbilova and Mazneva, 2011). His was the position of an ideal, loyal businessman under Putin (Babaeva, 2001; cf. Rachkov, 2001). This allowed the company to adapt to changes wrought by the state to the institutional framework, first in the form of informal constraints and then formal regulations. The turn towards greater asymmetry in power relations between Lukoil and the state was tangible. State companies had privileges, such as participation in policymaking, that were unavailable to a private company like Lukoil.

Expansion?

Lukoil now developed upstream projects in Egypt, West Africa and Iraq in addition to the post-Soviet region, and outside Russia, 40 per cent of its hydrocarbon production was gas (Lukoil Overseas Holding Ltd., 2011, p.14). It established petrol stations in the US and many European countries, and acquired refineries by the Black Sea, on Sicily and in the Netherlands (Mazneva et al., 2008; Socor, 2009). In 2008, Lukoil also considered acquiring a strategic stake in the Spanish oil company, Repsol. In this case, it seems that the support of the Russian state was withheld at the highest level (Granik and Gabuev, 2009). There was no acquisition. However, it is difficult to know how much price, or political considerations, mattered in the final decision.

Relations with the Russian state in connection with operations abroad remained on the whole supportive – in exchange for Lukoil's loyalty at home. In addition, Lukoil was occasionally involved in the state-led development of

166 *The oil industry: Lukoil*

foreign energy ties, when Russian energy companies teamed up and pledged participation in bilateral energy deals with partner states. This type of involvement became more important in Russian foreign policy after 2003. Sometimes, Lukoil engaged in well-targeted CSR activity abroad. This happened for example in 2006 when Lukoil offered to build a textile factory, supermarket and business centre in Dushanbe, which it promised would generate around 1 billion US$ in investments for Tajikistan (Petrachkova, 2006). Tajikistan was not an oil and gas producing region, but possibly a future market. Still, Lukoil here seemed to join the state-owned companies RAO UES and Gazprom in sharing its rents with Tajikistan's elites ahead of presidential elections there (Blagov, 2006). The provision of economic support and help to stabilise Russia-friendly regimes in Central Asia was a foreign policy priority.

Participation in cooperation with a foreign policy rationale could extend beyond the post-Soviet region. In 2008, Lukoil was a co-founder of the National Oil Consortium (NOC). NOC was headed by Sechin, and in addition to Rosneft, TNK-BP, Gazprom and Surgutneftegaz also participated. The consortium was put together to develop fields in Venezuela's Orinoco belt jointly with the Venezuelan national oil company, Petróleos de Venezuela, S.A. (PdVSA) (RIA Novosti, 2009; Finam, 2010). The presence was clearly based on a foreign policy priority, as Venezuela under Hugo Chávez was emerging as a more important partner for Russia in Latin America. The oil production engagement was part of a bilateral package that included military cooperation and Transneft's participation in oil pipeline development in Venezuela. The participants, including Lukoil, seem to have found it politically expedient in domestic Russian terms to join the consortium, and they may even have felt some pressure towards participation (Lowe and Sagdiev, 2019). The Russian partners seem not to have gained any returns from the JV with PdVSA, and it is doubtful whether the investment was recoverable (Lowe and Sagdiev, 2019). By 2014, political relations seemed to be the sole rationale behind the continued presence of the Russian consortium, which was now also engaged in Cuba and Nicaragua. Following the exit of Surgutneftegaz in November 2012, Lukoil terminated its participation in December 2014 and sold its 20 per cent share in NOC to Rosneft (Lukoil, 2015, p.146).

A lesser flagship

In its traditional international upstream around the Caspian Sea, the mid-2000s presented Lukoil with new challenges. Host governments gave foreign companies less generous terms in response to fewer operational risks, wider profit margins, along with NOCs' increasing experience and financial strength. Chinese companies became significant competitors.

Support from the Russian state regarding Lukoil's business in Kazakhstan became increasingly conditional on loyalty at home. When Lukoil in 2004 stopped using tax optimisation schemes altogether in Russia, it was rewarded with Putin's presence at the signing of a major cooperation agreement with KazMunayGaz, significantly named the Dostyk ("Friendship") agreement (*Kazakhstan Business Magazine*, 2004; Kravets, 2004). The new circumstances reflected the changing power balance in the Russian oil and gas industries, where the state's policy of supporting state companies led to setbacks for other companies. This happened, for example, when Kulalinskaya, a longtime Lukoil project, came under Kazakhstan's jurisdiction following the delineation of the Russian–Kazakhstani sea border. The Russian government designated Rosneft and Zarubezhneft as its entrusted companies in the field (now Kurmangazy) with a 25 per cent share each (*Neft' i Kapital*, 2006a). Lukoil also planned, with KazMunayGaz, to expand gas-based petrochemicals and refinery capacity either in Russia or Kazakhstan. In 2005, the proposal included resources from two offshore fields, Khvalynskoe and Tsentralnoe (*Neft' i Kapital*, 2006c; 2011a). The Russian government postponed finalisation of Lukoil's involvement in both fields, referring to the 2008 Subsoil Law and its restrictions on offshore participation of non-state companies (*Neft' i Kapital*, 2011b). As Lukoil went ahead with plans for a polypropylene factory in Budennovsk, which would process gas from Lukoil's offshore fields on both sides of the border, Gazprom withheld guarantees in 2010–2011 for Lukoil's access to the Russian gas pipeline system in this particular region (*Neft' i Kapital*, 2011a). The Russian tax system placed the profitability of the project in question (Rebrov, 2010b). There was some progress in the development of Khvalynskoe after 2011. Plans for Tsentralnoe, where Lukoil and Gazprom were partners on the Russian side, remained pending for a long time. In 2015, the international sanctions on the Russian oil and gas industry created capacity bottlenecks that delayed exploratory drilling (Oilcapital.ru, 2015c). In 2018, Tsentralnoe awaited final inter-agency approval (Oilcapital.ru, 2018).

Nevertheless, Lukoil did well in Kazakhstan with less support from the Russian state. It sometimes functioned as a counterweight to Chinese companies. This seems to have been understood in Lukoil, and appreciated, perhaps encouraged, by Kazakhstan's government (Skorlygina, 2006). The same thing happened in the case of the large oilfield Kumkol, part of which was operated by Turgai Petroleum, of which Lukoil held 50 per cent. The Chinese state company China National Petroleum Corporation (CNPC) acquired PetroKazakhstan, which owned the other half of Turgai Petroleum in 2005 (Suleimenov, 2005; Marten, 2007). Lukoil protested against the sale to CNPC, claiming that its right of first refusal to PetroKazakhstan's share had been denied (Skorlygina and Rebrov, 2007; Rebrov and Konstantinov, 2008). After a lengthy process involving arbitration and negotiations, Lukoil was compensated in August 2010 (Today.kz, 2010). However, between 2005 and 2010, Lukoil's claims towards PetroKazakhstan and CNPC gave Kazakhstan an opportunity to reduce CNPC's share in PetroKazakhstan and award 33 per cent to KazMunayGaz (Suleimenov, 2005; Marten, 2007). This was undoubtedly appreciated in Moscow. Also in other cases, such as Lukoil's acquisition of Caspian Investment Resources (CIR) in 2005 (Savushkin, 2005; Alekperov, 2006), Kazakhstan's government clearly treated Lukoil preferentially. CIR's previous owner was Timur Kulibaev, Nazarbaev's son-in-law (Neftegazovaya vertikal', 2016c, p.38). Lukoil closed the deal just when CNPC displayed an interest (Savushkin, 2005; Skorobogat'ko, 2005; Neftegazovaya vertikal', 2006a).

From around 2006, Lukoil and other foreign companies faced a far more assertive Kazakh government (Lukin, 2010b; 2010a). This new stance also affected the Karachaganak Petroleum Operating consortium (KPO), in which Lukoil held 15 per cent. Beginning in 2009, Kazakhstan's government pressured KPO in a variety of ways. In 2011, the conflict was resolved when Lukoil and the other KPO partners sold parts of their stakes to KazMunayGaz at a third of the market price (Mel'nikov, 2010; Mazneva, 2011).[19] In return, Kazakhstan's government relinquished all its claims against KPO. Having the support of the Russian government now made no difference to disputes in Kazakhstan.

In this business environment, foreign companies needed to work together. Following the conflict with CNPC over PetroKazakhstan, maximising cooperation and minimising conflict with Chinese companies turned into an aim of its own. In 2007, Lukoil entered into a strategic partnership with CNPC in Central Asia (Gorshkova, 2007; Kezik, 2007). In 2010 the companies signed a comprehensive partnership accord during President Medvedev's visit to Beijing (Grib and Mel'nikov, 2010; *Upstream*, 2010). It was a priority to maintain good relations with Lukoil's main international competitor in Kazakhstan and Uzbekistan. Cooperation was also important in the context of Russia and China's expanding energy relations. Lukoil offered Rosneft competition in the Russian–Chinese energy relationship. This was best done outside the immediate bilateral energy relationship, where Rosneft was the Russian state's designated oil supplier and China's partner.

Lukoil's Uzbekistan ventures were a major success. By 2010, after three years of production in Uzbekistan, 14.8 per cent of Lukoil's non-Russian hydrocarbon production was located in the country (Lukoil Overseas Holding Ltd., 2011, p.15). The same year, gas production there was estimated to represent half the company's profits from gas, even as the production volume was only around 31 per cent of Lukoil's overall gas production (*Neft' i Kapital*, 2010). The company had the solid support of the Russian government; indeed, Lukoil seemed integral to Russia's policy in Central Asia (*Neft' i Kapital*, 2007c; 2008). In 2009, Uzbekistan's President Islam Karimov promised Medvedev that by 2015, all of Uzbekistan's gas exports would go to Russia (*Neft' i Kapital*, 2009). However, in 2008–2009 bilateral relations deteriorated. Uzbekistan suspended its membership of the Eurasian Economic Community.[20] Gazprom scaled down its activities in Uzbekistan (Grib and Mel'nikov, 2010; *Neft' i Kapital*, 2011a). Uzbekistan set stricter terms for foreign oil and gas companies to operate in its petroleum sector, and Chinese companies, eager to expand their business in the Central Asian state, were the quickest to respond (Lukin, 2010b; *Neft' i Kapital*, 2011d). Lukoil was somewhat constrained by Gazprom's reluctance, as demand decreased, to buy gas from other producers (*Neft' i Kapital*, 2011d). Lukoil's gas production in Uzbekistan now targeted the Chinese market (*Neft' i Kapital*, 2011a; 2011b; Lukin, 2012, p.19). However, when there was an opportunity to increase its presence in the country, Lukoil seized the opportunity and increased its stake in the Aral Sea Operating Company to 26.6 per cent (Sharip, 2012). In Turkmenistan, however, Lukoil could not compete with Chinese companies. After Russian–Turkmen relations deteriorated in 2008, a situation to which Gazprom contributed greatly (Chapter 7), Lukoil's chances of gaining a foothold disappeared.

Limits to expansion

After the Orange Revolution of 2004, the business climate for Russian companies in Ukraine worsened (Makarkin, 2005b; *Vedomosti*, 2005). The influence of Chernomyrdin, then Russia's ambassador to Ukraine (2001–2009), may have compensated a little. During Viktor Yushchenko's presidency (2005–2010) the Russian state did sometimes force the Russian companies to show solidarity with each other, as in 2007, like when the Kremlin appears to have compelled Russian oil companies not to supply crude oil to the Kremenchug refinery, where Tatneft had problems with its partners (*Neft' i Kapital*, 2007b). Lukoil and several other Russian companies halted supplies to the refinery.

There were limits to the Russian government's readiness to lend its support. In April 2005, Prime Minister Yuliya Tymoshenko (January to September 2005, 2007–2010) accused refinery owners, Lukoil and TNK-BP in particular, of creating a Russian-controlled petrol monopoly (*Neft' i Kapital*, 2005a). Lukoil was threatened with the renationalisation of its holdings in Ukraine. Russian oil companies tried to get the Russian government to intervene, to no avail (Orekhin et al., 2005). The situation improved with President Yushchenko's intervention (Gavrish, 2005; Gavrish and Chernovalov, 2005; Makarkin, 2005a), but another crisis followed in 2006 (Gavrish, 2006). In October 2009, Lukoil again ran into problems when operations at the Odesa refinery came in the way of the most influential business conglomerate in Ukraine, the Privat group (Grivach, 2009; Mordyushenko and Gavrish, 2009; Eremenko, 2011). Odesa later closed for repairs and was sold to a Ukrainian company in 2013 (*Neft' i Kapital*, 2013).

In 2010, Ukraine began to release shelf exploration licences. This was attractive to Gazprom and Lukoil for commercial reasons, but obtaining licences could also pre-empt competition at an early stage and keep options open later when Russian production would drop. Lukoil was a likely partner in the Bezymyannyi, Odesa and Subbotinskii blocks (Vinogradova, 2011), and competed – unsuccessfully – for the Skyfska gas field (Socor, 2013). Along with Gazprom, it was designated a partner on the Russian side on the

Pallas oil and gas field in the north eastern part of the sea, and negotiations took place in late 2013 and early 2014 (Bugriy, 2016). Russia's annexation of Crimea in March 2014 stopped all these processes. Lukoil concentrated its Black Sea exploration on the Romanian shelf.

Like all major Russian oil exporters, Lukoil depended partly on transit through Belarus to reach the European crude oil market. Lukoil was one of the companies that profited from refining crude oil in and exporting oil products from Belarus to avoid domestic bottlenecks and export duties (Chapter 6). In 2007, Lukoil supplied around a quarter of all oil delivered to Belarus (Rebrov et al., 2006). This volume declined slowly after the 2007 and 2010 oil transit crises. Lukoil remained interested in stakes in the Naftan and Mozyr refineries, in the event of privatisation (*Neft' i Kapital*, 2003a). Meanwhile, Lukoil and Naftan formed a joint venture in oil product additives in 2006 (Rebrov et al., 2006). Belarusian authorities repeatedly declared the privatisations of Naftan and Mozyr imminent, but this seemed unlikely (Khodasevich, 2010; Slavinskaya, 2011).

In 2005, a new opportunity arose to acquire the Mažeikiu refinery in the sale of Yukos's holdings. The Lithuanian government clearly preferred non-Russian ownership. Lukoil remained interested, but was disadvantaged by the political climate (Embassy Vilnius, 2005a; 2005b). However, the final signal to refrain from acquiring Mažeikiu appears to have come from the Russian government (Embassy Moscow, 2006; cf. Embassy Vilnius, 2006). Shortly thereafter, Transneft phased out non-Russian Baltic ports (Chapter 6), and Mažeikiu ceased to be a commercially viable option for Lukoil.

In the 2010s, Russian foreign policy placed some limitations on Lukoil's development in the post-Soviet region. To Lukoil, as to any IOC, the possibilities and business environment offered by host governments would always matter much to major business decisions. By definition, the Russian government had limited possibilities to influence Lukoil's international business. The exceptions were few, as illustrated by Lukoil's business development in Kazakhstan and Belarus. But in the post-Soviet region, and sometimes outside it, Lukoil needed to relate to the priorities of Russian foreign policy. In Ukraine, both governments contributed towards a deteriorating bilateral relationship, but until 2014, Lukoil's problems above all had to do with the difficult business environment in Ukraine. In relation to Baltic export routes, however, Lukoil's commercial interests came up against new Russian foreign policy priorities, carried out by Transneft. Lukoil faced the same problems in Turkmenistan with Gazprom. Lukoil's opportunity, and resolution, to take part in Russian foreign policymaking on the post-Soviet region were limited. Russian foreign policy priorities would now sometimes limit its options for development, if not the development itself.

Lukoil, the sanctions and the reorganised ruling coalition

The annexation of Crimea and the introduction of international sanctions against Russian oil and gas companies influenced the conditions for Lukoil's business development, particularly in Russia. Alekperov, like other business leaders, refrained from commenting on the annexation of Crimea. Lukoil's arm's length relations with the state shielded it from the first and second round of sanctions in March and April. But over the first months after the annexation, uncertainty regarding possible future sanctions increased and began to affect financial decisions (Oilcapital.ru, 2014b). The third round of sanctions in August and September targeted Russia's development of offshore oil and gas in the Arctic, offshore projects in deep waters further south, and deep shale deposits. The restrictions affected access to Western technological equipment as well as finance. According to Alekperov in 2015, the impact on Lukoil was limited, as it had not been allowed access to shelf licences of the targeted type (Oilcapital.ru, 2015b). Its Russian offshore projects were located in shallower waters and outside the Arctic. But the sanctions effectively shelved a new onshore deep shale project with the French IOC Total, which had depended on access to specific technology and equipment (Oilcapital.ru, 2019a). Lukoil had been well prepared to operate challenging projects in Russia that would depend on access to Western technology. Now, the technological and financial possibilities for such future development were more limited.

While adaptation to the sanctions incurred some costs, the overall picture was one of a lesser impact on Lukoil compared to Gazprom Neft and Rosneft. New projects that depended on international finance, or highly developed technological equipment, were most affected. Lukoil was in a good financial position, with a low debt ratio, but the sanctions still affected its financial options for the medium term (Starinskaya and Serov, 2015a). In terms of politics, the sanctions revealed some of the costs of the unequal playing field for oil and gas companies. The government again reopened the discussion on a central issue to Lukoil, the lack of access to the shelf for private companies, in 2015 (Analiticheskii Tsentr, 2015, p.28). This time, it reached the level of the Presidential Administration (Mel'nikov, 2015). However, the slow process that followed did not open the shelf to private companies during the period under study (*The New Times*, 2019). In the period after 2014, Alekperov concentrated his efforts on influencing policies for the petroleum industry on issues of taxation, but also transport tariffs (Oilcapital.ru, 2014a; 2015a; Mordyushenko and Barsukov, 2017). A natural priority for the head of a Russian oil company in this period, this reflected that other major issues in the state–company relationship, particularly the distinction between state-owned and private companies, were not up for change.

Tellingly, geopolitics entered Lukoil's risk assessment in the 2015 Annual Report, and remained a staple among financial risks thereafter (Lukoil, 2016, p.158; 2017, p.28; 2018a, p.32 Appendix 2). Until 2014, only political risks connected to certain operating regions and countries in Africa and the Middle East were included in the risk assessment. From 2014, the international sanctions resulted in "virtually closed capital markets", in Lukoil's own assessment (Lukoil, 2015, p.56). Lukoil still managed to attract external finance, but the costs increased. While in 2013, the average weighted interest rate on its long-term loans and credits was 2.94 per cent, in 2014, this indicator of the cost of borrowing was 4.65 per cent (Lukoil, 2015, p.119). Like all major Russian companies, Lukoil was affected by Russia's falling credit rating, which suffered from the Russian financial crisis and the impact of the financial sanctions. Russian companies began to look to Asia, particularly China, for credits. Alekperov was not optimistic, finding it an expensive source of finance (Starinskaya and Serov, 2015b). Lukoil was known to always adhere to its business strategy when making investment decisions, for example, staying out of projects with an internal rate of return below a cut-off rate of 16 per cent (Neftegazovaya vertikal', 2017b, p.30).

In 2017, Alekperov said that Lukoil planned for sanctions remaining in place for a decade (Barber and Foy, 2017). Russia, and with it the Russian oil and gas industries, had by then adapted to the sanctions (Connolly, 2018). Lukoil, too, had adapted to the sanctions. For example, it had succeeded in replacing much of its previous Western technology import. In five years, the share of Russian-produced equipment had increased from 42 per cent to 70 per cent (Oilcapital.ru, 2019a). However, the sanctions regime had increased uncertainty for the company in the longer term. This was highlighted by the Countering America's Adversaries Through Sanctions Act of 2017 (abbreviated to CAATSA; US Congress, 2017). Under CAATSA, the US Treasury released a report with a list of 114 senior political figures and 96 oligarchs, including Alekperov, in January 2018 (US Department of the Treasury, 2018). The list did not impose any restrictions on its own; rather, it listed Russia's most powerful individuals and indicated that the US was prepared to initiate sanctions against them. The general nature of the list of oligarchs was emphasised by the fact that the criterion for their inclusion was a net worth of 1 billion US$ or more.

Sanctions created some challenges for Lukoil's further development, but oil price volatility mattered much more. Like many others in the oil business, Alekperov was very sceptical of Russia's possibilities of reaching a deal with OPEC on oil production cuts in 2016 (Oilcapital.ru, 2016b). When it did, this illustrated well how state capacity had changed over the course of 20 years (Anokhin, 2017, pp.31–32). In contrast to Russia's earlier efforts to align with OPEC production cuts and influence the oil price, Russia in 2017 did carry through its proposed cuts.[21] Lukoil followed up on the deal and later extensions (Krasovskaya, 2017).

Lukoil made a point of staying on good working terms with its peers and partners, including the state-controlled Rosneft and Gazprom. The state continued to favour Rosneft and support its development. This sometimes made it difficult for Lukoil to develop. This was the case when the state's 50 per cent stake in Bashneft, Lukoil's partner in the Trebs and Titov licence, came up for privatisation in summer 2016. Lukoil was among the nine interested buyers, and clearly a favourite (Kozlov et al., 2016). Rosneft declared an interest, in spite of being owned by the state and the fact that it, too, was put up for partial privatisation (Oilcapital.ru, 2016c). Following criticism of Rosneft's potential role, the government postponed Bashneft's privatisation in August. However, in the beginning of October the government reopened the sale,[22] ordering Rosneft to acquire Bashneft at a price below 330 billion rubles (Dzyadko and Podobedova, 2016). This in effect allowed Rosneft to pay a price substantially above the company's market value, and 20 to 30 per cent above the price that Lukoil would have been prepared to pay (Kozlov et al., 2016; Kupfer and Jardine, 2016; Neftegazovaya vertikal', 2016a). Following Rosneft's acquisition of Bashneft, the cooperation in the Trebs and Titov fields continued (Neftegazovaya vertikal', 2016a; Oilcapital.ru, 2017b).

On the Russian energy industries' non-level playing field, Lukoil managers were generally seen as very influential (Oilcapital.ru, 2016a). Alekperov vied with Igor Sechin of Rosneft and Aleksei Miller of Gazprom at the very top of influence ratings, and Lukoil altogether had seven or eight managers on the list of 80 or so managers, compared to Rosneft's two or three (Oilcapital.ru, 2012b; 2016a, APEK, 2017). Its pursuit of commercial success and emphasis of commercial goals set it apart from companies like Rosneft or Gazprom, which would be expected to take on projects that were important to the state, or politically expedient. This also enabled its international expansion, and it was a source of strength and influence in relation to the state.

A Russian IOC

In the last few years discussed here, Lukoil's international projects began to play a greater role in its overall production, delivering 12.7 per cent of its total hydrocarbon production in 2017 (Lukoil, 2018a, p.8). Along with Egypt and Iraq, Azerbaijan, Kazakhstan and Uzbekistan remained important producing regions. Its exploration activities outside Russia were now in Nigeria, Ghana, Cameroon, Mexico, Egypt and Norway, as well as Uzbekistan. Lukoil had refineries in Russia, Bulgaria, Italy, the Netherlands and Romania, and a petrochemicals plant in Ukraine. It had a market presence in 17 countries, including ten European countries, Turkey and the US, and also Azerbaijan, Georgia, Belarus and Moldova. The company's upstream activities now included solar and hydro, several offshore and other technology-driven projects in oil and gas production, and enhanced recovery of oil and gas in fields already under production was a priority. In short, it remained at the forefront among Russia's oil and gas companies, and developed along the lines of an international IOC. It was a commercial success and highly profitable to its owners.

In addition to the effect of sanctions, Russia's annexation of Crimea changed the context also for Lukoil's foreign operations. As shown below, its business in Ukraine was affected within months. There were indirect effects, especially as Lukoil had most of its markets and other downstream operations in Europe, where the perception of Russian companies turned more negative than before. Until 2017, the sanctions did not really affect Lukoil's international business. But this changed as the US expanded its sectoral sanctions. A revision of the 2014 sectoral sanctions in October 2017 extended the restrictions to include any international oil project in which the major Russian oil and gas companies held a share above 33 per cent (Barsukov, 2017). Furthermore, the publication of the list of 96 oligarchs from January 2018 had a negative effect on how Lukoil was perceived in capital markets (Reuters, 2018). The implications were clearly illustrated when in April, sanctions were introduced against seven businessmen and their companies, and 17 senior government officials, from the list (Weaver et al., 2018). This had an immediate effect on the share values of the companies in question.

Lukoil's international operations continued, and Azerbaijan, Kazakhstan and Uzbekistan remained the primary upstream regions. In Azerbaijan, Lukoil did not participate in any of the new medium-sized "next-generation" Caspian projects, but concentrated on gas. It retained the ten per cent stake in the two interlinked consortia that controlled Shah Deniz production and the Southern Gas Corridor. Shah Deniz headed into a phase 2 stage of production combined with further exploration (Socor, 2014). It was not engaged in oil or oil transport in Azerbaijan. Following the decision not to participate in BTC, and the sale of its ACG stake, in 2001–2002, Lukoil shipped its oil from the Caspian on other routes. In 2012, Alekperov ruled out oil shipments through BTC. Oil from the Yurii Korchagin field in the North Caspian, where production had started in 2010, would go through the CPC pipeline (Oilcapital.ru, 2012a). Russia's annexation of Crimea changed the priorities somewhat. Beginning in May 2014, Lukoil shipped some of its oil through the BTC pipeline (Daly, 2014). The implication was that Azerbaijan, Georgia and Turkey would lose business in the event of sanctions being introduced against Lukoil. Shipments continued on a regular, but short-term basis until 2017, when SOCAR planned to offer Lukoil's oil trader Litasco longer-term contracts (Oilcapital.ru, 2017a). SOCAR also tried to attract additional volumes of oil from Lukoil's North Caspian fields, as the BTC pipeline was utilised at 58–59 per cent of capacity (Oilcapital.ru, 2017a).

In Kazakhstan, the business environment changed further as the opportunities for a non-Kazakh company like Lukoil were less lucrative (Neftegazovaya vertikal', 2016c, p.38). Lukoil remained important, but the additional advantage of being a Russian company in Kazakhstan had decreased. Fundamentally for an oil company, the replacement rate in the country's onshore fields was low (Neftegazovaya vertikal', 2016c, p.38; 2017c, p.54). Due to falling production, Lukoil sold its 50 per cent share of Caspian Investment Resources to Sinopec in August 2015 after a difficult process (Oilcapital.ru, 2015d). Sinopec did not abide by the original agreement from late 2014, and Lukoil intended to recover the loss through the London Court of International Arbitration. However, both the Russian and the Chinese government requested the companies to resolve the dispute without taking it to court, and the companies duly settled (Tret'yakov, 2015). Lukoil remained the biggest Russian investor in Kazakhstan after the sale, expanding its share of the downstream sector as the upstream sector gradually turned less profitable (Neftegazovaya vertikal', 2016c, p.38).

Uzbekistan remained a key gas and condensate producing region for Lukoil. Many experienced investors in the country's petroleum sector left or downscaled their engagement following the 2008–2010 financial crisis. The potential for further development of existing production was lower than expected (Neftegazovaya vertikal', 2017a, p.60). Some companies left due to the challenging investment climate before 2016 and the ascent to the presidency of Shavkat Mirziyoyev (Kim, 2014). Unlike Gazprom, Lukoil stayed clear of the Uzbek intra-elite conflict over economic assets in the last decade under Islam Karimov. It was well-placed to benefit when new opportunities opened in 2016 and 2017. Lukoil moved into the Uzbek high-end petrol station market in 2017–2018 (Neftegazovaya vertikal', 2017a; Lukoil, 2018b). In *Upstream*, it pursued further development at both the Gissar field and in the Kandym-Khauzak-Shady region (Lukoil – PJSC "Lukoil", 2019). It also completed a gas processing complex in Kandym in April 2018 (Lukoil, 2018c).

Lukoil's business in Ukraine continued as usual in the first few months after the annexation of Crimea (Oilcapital.ru, 2014d). But its market presence was increasingly met by protests (Oilcapital.ru, 2014e). In July, the Ukrainian nationalist organisation Pravyi Sektor instigated blockades against some of the company's petrol stations (Oilcapital.ru, 2014f). Shortly thereafter, Lukoil sold its petrol stations in Ukraine to Austrian AMIC (Oilcapital.ru, 2014e). Later in the year, it exited the Czech, Slovak and Hungarian retail markets. The Russian Federal Technical and Export Control Service in practice restricted Russian companies from supplying diesel to Ukraine in September the same year (Oilcapital.ru, 2016d). But Lukoil gained approval from same Federal Service in March 2016 to supply diesel to Ukraine again (Oilcapital.ru, 2016d). To avoid sanctions, Lukoil in May 2014 sold its petrol station network in Crimea to the Ukrainian businessman Sergei Kurchenko (Oilcapital.ru, 2014c; Kudinov, 2016).

Conclusions

Lukoil started as an insider project, and it participated in, even drove, institutional change in the Russian oil industry in the 1990s. In this period, its early incorporation and consolidation as a company meant that it was possible to focus on developing both its upstream and downstream, instead of being weakened by struggles for control of the company. Development of state organisations and policies and Lukoil as a private company went hand in hand. At times, Lukoil seemed to have evolved into a more advanced company, than the state had developed on its side as a state. Its access to central state organisations was informal and personal along with the more formal relations, but rents were shared formally with the state as well as informally. Lukoil had a stake in the development and implementation of formal institutions, insofar as its existence as an organisation depended on property rights upheld by the state. Formal rent sharing was negotiated with the state, while informal rent sharing tied Lukoil to the ruling coalition and offered further protection of property rights. As its foreign operations grew, Lukoil could turn divisions among state representatives on the issue of the Caspian Sea to its advantage, shaping foreign policy in the process.

In 2000–2003, Lukoil's relations with the state grew increasingly formal and impersonal. Access to senior figures and participation in policy and decision making took place now on more generalised terms, embodied in collective oligarch meetings. Putin's ruling coalition now used the state's coercive infrastructure to increase its despotic power. Rent extraction and distribution were increasingly institutionalised as taxation, to give the state a greater advantage over oil companies and society. For Lukoil, the beginning of the Putin regime meant loss of access to government figures and participation in developing policy and the institutional framework. Yet it was also a turn towards greater formality and impersonal relations, insofar as oil companies were now treated more equally, on more transparent terms. Had this lasted, it might have been the beginning of a stronger protection of property rights throughout the oil industry, because informality could have yielded to formality in rent sharing and property rights protection. The turn towards greater asymmetry in power between Lukoil and the state indicated that Russia's social order developed somewhat, but the strengthening of the state did not work out in favour of Lukoil as a private company.

Increased state capacity affected Lukoil's foreign operations in Azerbaijan and the Baltic states. But Lukoil did not itself control integrated infrastructure that extended into the post-Soviet region, and state–company interaction did not make Lukoil a tool that could be used for coercion. As shown in Chapter 6, Transneft was here the coercive tool of the state. Khodorkovskii's arrest represented the highpoint in the conflict between the state and the oil industry. "State-minded" Lukoil inevitably accepted state regulation in the oil industry. During the forced sale of Yukos's assets, Lukoil's management watched as the state regulated property relations among oil companies, and privileged Rosneft and Gazprom over other companies. The oil sector stagnated. In Lukoil's case, there was a glass ceiling in licence acquisitions in Russia.

Informality returned as the basis of state–company interaction. Informal relations were again of the essence for a private company like Lukoil to gain access to the state. Whether intended or not, the Yukos affair weakened property rights in the oil industry and Lukoil's owners could not afford the luxury of refraining from informal rent sharing in return for property rights protection. This was most notably in the form of extensive CSR programmes. Among state organisations, some were more important than others. Rosneft took the lead in sector development, and may well have sidelined the Energy Ministry. This indicates that the regime's interest in staying in power may have been more important than considerations of state and societal development. State–company relations became the province of an inner circle. In this period, Lukoil stands apart from the other cases in this study. Its executive manager remained on the periphery of that circle, and had to compensate by paying greater attention to Putin's every move. Lukoil had a fundamentally supportive and loyal role in relation to the regime, but it was further removed and therefore more autonomous than the other cases.

Support for Lukoil's foreign operations became, around 2003, conditional on loyalty to the state at home. Its fundamentally subordinate and remote relationship with the state was carried over into foreign operations. From 2006–2007, there are a few instances in which Lukoil seems to have acted as an instrument of the state, at home and abroad, on a small scale. Private ownership clearly played a part in limiting such practices. The state had no direct access to Lukoil's resources. In the case of Lukoil's taking on more significant investment responsibilities, this would have to be negotiated at some level, and include at least a modest prospect for making a profit, as in the case of Venezuela. The main form of quasi-fiscal activities engaged in by Lukoil seems to have been CSR and regional development in line with state priorities, by extension supplying the state with infrastructural power. To Lukoil, it seemed important that such projects deliver business advantage in some way, and demonstrate its commitment to the regions and communities where it operated. There were no mandatory undertakings that acted as brakes on its commercial operations. Private ownership may have shielded the company from the two great informal taxation drains of mandatory loss-making investment in core business areas, and artificially inflated staff rosters.

By the end of the period covered here, Lukoil had turned into an outlier. Only on a few occasions did it act as a tool of Russian foreign policy. When it did, this seemed to be on the basis of a negotiated understanding, or even a responsibility accepted voluntarily. Lukoil did not maintain or cultivate dependence on Russia in the post-Soviet region. At home, Lukoil had lesser informal access to state officials and had to adapt to the state, and its preference for supporting state-owned companies, while losing influence on state policies. In this context, the imposition of international sanctions against the Russian petroleum industry was far less significant for the company's development. It remained one of Russia's greatest corporate successes.

Notes

1 The Norwegian company Statoil (est. 1972) in 2018 changed its name to Equinor.
2 In the petroleum industry, storage and transport are designated as "midstream" activities. Here, only the terms "upstream" and "downstream" are used, and storage and transport are included with downstream activities.
3 Production associations formed the operational level in the Soviet oil and gas industries. A production association could be comprised of one or more fields, with often substantial production.

4 An all-union Oil Industry Ministry was established in 1939, while the all-union Gas Industry Ministry was established in 1965. The two were merged to become the Ministry for the Oil and Gas Industries in 1989.
5 Mažeikiu dropped out of the project when it became clear that the Soviet Union would break up, and the refinery became Lithuanian property. It did not figure in the government resolution. Ufa did not remain with Lukoil after it became vertically integrated in 1993.
6 Yukos and Surgutneftegaz were the two others.
7 The state's share was 53.2 per cent until 1995, 26.2 per cent by 1999, 15.5 in 2000 and 7.59 in 2002–2004.
8 In a production sharing agreement (PSA) or production sharing contract (PSC), a government awards a company the right to explore and produce a resource from a given field or region, at the company's own risk. If and when costs are recovered, subsequent profits are divided between the government and the company according to the contract. PSAs are used by many governments, especially those new to the global petroleum industry, or in countries associated with high (political) risk. Unlike concessions, they are seen to create a legal enclave in which the contract regulates all relations between the parties. Once signed, they are subject to change only by mutual consent, and therefore alleviate risk for the company. In practise, they are often governed by general legislation, and disputes tend to arise when a specific contract does not align with other legislation. The term PSA is best known outside the industry and is used here.
9 Situated in Navapolatsk (Belarusian)/Novopolotsk (Russian).
10 In 2004, this ministry became a federal agency, Rosimushchestvo.
11 With a government prerogative to veto important management decisions, have a designated place on the Board, and access all internal documents.
12 The Russian government had three representatives on the Board in 1999–2000 (elections were held at shareholder meetings in June), two in 2000–2003 and one in 2003–2005.
13 ONAKO ended up with TNK, later TNK-BP (from 2013 Rosneft).
14 In 2007, Uzbek gas fetched 100 US$ per thousand cubic metres, while Lukoil's Russian gas fetched 40 US$.
15 In 2005, Alekperov held a share of approximately 13%. In the following four to five years, the combined management share increased to above 32 per cent, around 20 of which were held by Alekperov. In 2017, the top management of 14 people, including Alekperov, owned 23.97 per cent of the company, while the members of the Board of Directors, including Alekperov, controlled 33.79 per cent of the company. Alekperov owned 23.13 per cent (Lukoil, 2018a, pp.36–39).
16 In 2003, Lukoil produced 78.6 million tonnes of oil and gas condensate in Russia, and in 2009 91.9 million tonnes, with a gradual increase in the years in between (numbers from combined annual reports).
17 Numbers exclude exports to the CIS.
18 In the event, it reached 20.5 per cent in 2017 (Lukoil, 2018a, p.15).
19 Lukoil's stake was reduced from 15 to 13.5 per cent. The financial compensation from KazMunayGaz for its new 10 per cent stake was to be paid out over three years.
20 The other members were Russia, Belarus, Kazakhstan, Kyrgyzstan and Tajikistan.
21 According to Energy Minister Aleksandr Novak, the deal brought Russia an estimated 6 trillion rubles in additional revenue over its two years' duration in 2017–2018, in addition to 2 to 2.5 trillion rubles to Russia's oil companies in the same period (Oilcapital.ru, 2019b). For comparison, Russia's actual total revenue in 2017 was 15.26 trillion rubles.
22 This turn of events would later in 2016 serve as the background for the corruption accusations against then Minister of Economic Development, Aleksei Ulyukaev, for which he was convicted in 2017.

References

Afanasiev, V. (2011) "Lukoil to broaden horizons" *Upstream*, 28 October, p.37

Alekperov, V. (2000) "My slishkom dolgo zapryagali? [Did we prepare for too long?]" *Izvestiya*, 8 June

Alekperov, V. (2003) "Preimushchestva konkurentsii. Demonopolizatsiya neftyanogo sektora prevratila resursnyi potentsial Rossii v lokomotiv ee ekonomicheskogo razvitiya [The advantages of competition. The de-monopolization of the oil sector turned Russia's resource potential into a locomotive for its economic development]" *Izvestiya*, 7 March, p.6

Alekperov, V. (2006) *Vystuplenie V. Yu. Alekperova na sobranii aktsionerov [V. Yu. Alekperov's speech at the annual general meeting]* (Moscow: Lukoil)

Alekperov, V. (2009) *Vystuplenie prezidenta OAO "Lukoil" V. Yu. Alekperova na evropeiskom biznes sammite, Bryussel' [Speech of Lukoil's president, V. Yu. Alekperov, at the European Business Summit, Brussels]* (Moscow: Lukoil)

Alekperov, V. (2011a) *Oil of Russia. Past, Present & Future* (Minneapolis: East View Press)

Alekperov, V. (2011b) "Bazis integratsii [The basis of integration]" *Izvestiya*, 18 November, p.1

Aleksandrovich, S. (2000) "'Lukoil' formiruet novuyu rossiiskuyu politiku na Kaspii [Lukoil forms the new Russian policy in the Caspian]" *Neft' i Kapital*, April 2000

Aleksandrovich, S. (2001) "Moskva-Baku: soobshchenie vozobnovlyaetsya [Moscow–Baku: contact is renewed]" *Neft' i Kapital*, January

Aleksashenko, S. (2012) "Russia's economic agenda to 2020", *International Affairs*, 88 (1): 31–48

Analiticheskii Tsentr (2015) *Inertsiya elektroenergetiki [The inertia of electricity]*. Energeticheskii byulleten'. (Moscow: Analiticheskii Tsentr pri Pravitel'stve Rossiiskoi Federatsii/Analytical Center for the Government of the Russian Federation)

Anokhin, K. (2017) "Produktivnaya energodiplomatiya [Productive energy diplomacy]" *Neftegazovaya vertikal'*, Nos 1–2, pp.30–33

APEK (2017) "*Reiting vliyaniya krupnykh predprinimatelei i top-menedzherov toplivno-energeticheskogo kompleksa v iyune 2017 g. [Rating of the influence of major businessmen and top managers in the fuel and energy complex, June 2017]* [online]. 29 June 2017 (Moscow: Agentstvo politicheskikh i ekonomicheskikh kommunikatsii). Available from: http://apecom.ru/projects/item.php?SECTION_ID=102&ELEMENT_ID=3803 [Accessed 18 March 2019]

Astakhova, O. and Basvain, D. (2011) "LUKOIL zhdet rosta dobychi posle 2012 g., zhazhdet rabotat' v RF [Lukoil expects a rise in production after 2012, is longing to work in Russia]" *Reuters*, 31 August

Babaeva, S. (2001) "Vagit Alekperov: Neftyanaya otrasl' vyzdorovela [Vagit Alekperov: The oil sector has recovered]" *Izvestiya*, 28 June, p.1

Balmaceda, M.M. (2008) *Energy Dependency, Politics, and Corruption in the Former Soviet Union. Russia's Power, Oligarchs' Profits and Ukraine's Missing Energy Policy, 1995–2006* (London/New York: Routledge)

Barber, L. and Foy, H. (2017) "Lukoil chief says sanctions may last a decade" *The Financial Times*, 12 October

Barsukov, Yu. (2012) "FAS predlagaet otkryt' shel'f [FAS proposes to open the shelf]" *Kommersant*, 2 August, p.7

Barsukov, Yu. (2017) "Neftyanikov zapirayut v Rossii [The oilmen are locked in Russia]" *Kommersant*, 1 November

Blagov, S. (2006) "Russia renews diplomatic-economic offensive" *Eurasianet.org*, 18 April

Boiko, B. (1999) "Eksport ob"yavlen politicheski vrednym [Export is announced to be politically harmful]" *Kommersant*, 30 July 1999, p.7

Bolshoi biznes (2003) *Interv'yu V. Yu Alekperova zhurnalu Bolshoi Biznes, noyabr' 2003 goda* [*Interview by V. Yu. Alekperov to Bolshoi Biznes magazine, November 2003*] (Moscow: Lukoil)

Bolukbasi, S. (1998) "The controversy over the Caspian Sea mineral resources: Conflicting perception, clashing interests", *Europe-Asia Studies*, 50 (3): 397–414

Bradshaw, M. (2009) "The Kremlin, national champions and the international oil companies: The political economy of the Russian oil and gas industry", *Geopolitics of Energy*, 31 (5): 2–14

Bradshaw, M. (2012) "Russian energy dilemmas: Energy security, globalization and climate change" in Aalto, P. ed., *Russia's Energy Policies. National, Interregional and Global Levels* (Cheltenham: Edward Elgar), pp.206–229

Bugriy, M. (2016) "Russia's moves to gain dominance in the Black Sea" *Eurasia Daily Monitor*, 17 February

Burchilina, T. (1995) "Situatsiya vokrug Tengizskogo mestorozhdeniya. Za odnogo bitogo predlozhili dvukh nebitykh [The situation around the Tengiz deposit.Two unconquered ones proposed to replace one vanquished]" *Kommersant*, 15 November 1995, p.9

Butrin, D. (2001) "Baku-Dzheikhan dotyanetsya do Rossii [Baku–Ceyhan reaches into Russia]" *Kommersant*, 24 November, p.4

Butrin, D. (2003) "'Na yuge Evropy nas interesuet vse' ['In southern Europe, everything interests us']" *Kommersant*, 8 September 2003, p.1

Butrin, D. (2004) "Gazprom menyaet Yamal na Uzbekistan [Gazprom exchanges Yamal for Uzbekistan]" *Kommersant*, 16 April 2004, p.16

Cockburn, P. (1994) "Russia and US in tussle over oil in Caspian" *The Independent*, 3 November 1994, p.14

Connolly, R. (2018) *Russia's Response to Sanctions* (Cambridge: Cambridge University Press)

Daly, J.C.K. (2014) "Russian oil to feature in Baku–Tbilisi–Ceyhan Pipeline: Circumventing possible sanctions?" *Eurasia Daily Monitor*, 30 May

Davydov, A. (1996) "Novoe soglashenie LUKOILa. Dazhe uidya iz politiki, ne izbezhat' vstrech s politikami [Lukoil's new agreement. Even when you leave politics, it's difficult to avoid meeting politicians]" *Kommersant*, 6 July 1996, p.9

Decree No. 327 (01/04/1995) *O pervoocherednykh merakh po sovershenstvovaniyu deyatel'nosti neftyanykh kompanii* [*On first measures to perfect the operations of oil companies*] (Moscow: President of the Russian Federation)

Decree No. 1403 (17/11/1992) *Ob osobennostyakh privatizatsii i preobrazovaniya v aktsionernye obshchestva gosudarstvennykh predpriyatii, proizvodstvennykh i nauchno-proizvodstvennykh ob"edinenii neftyanoi, neftepererabatyvayushchei promyshlennosti i nefteproduktoobespecheniya* [*On the specificities of privatisation and conversion into shareholding companies of enterprises, production and scientific production associations in the oil and oil refinery industries and oil product distribution*] (Moscow: President of the Russian Federation)

Derbilova, E. and Mazneva, E. (2011) "'Moya lyubov' na vsyu zhizn' – eto neft' ['Oil is the love of my life']" *Vedomosti*, 22 December 2011, p.5

Drankina, E. and Fadeev, V. (2001) "Formula nefti [The oil formula]" *Ekspert*, 16 April 2001, pp.22–27
Dzyadko, T. and Podobedova, L. (2016) "'Bashneft' v odni ruki [Bashneft in the same hands]" *RBK Daily*, 7 October, p.1
Easter, G.M. (2012) *Capital, Coercion, and Postcommunist States* (Ithaca/London: Cornell University Press)
Egorova, T. (2004) "Vse v Baku-Dzheikhan [Everyone to Baku–Ceyhan]" *Vedomosti*, 18 March
Ekonomika i zhizn' (2009) "Nulevaya stavka NDPI dlya nefti [A zero mineral extraction tax for oil]" *Ekonomika i zhizn'*, 9 October 2009, p.8
Embassy Moscow (2006) Russian oil to Lithuania – Mixing revenge and business, 06MOSCOW9482/Wikileaks #76658. Issue date 30 August 2006 [online]. (Published by Wikileaks 8 September 2011). Available from: https://wikileaks.org/plusd/cables/06MOSCOW9482_a.html [Accessed 13 February 2019]
Embassy Vilnius (2005a) Adamkus upset about Conocophillips-lukoil bid on the Baltics' only oil refinery, Issue date 23 September 2005 [online]. (Published by Wikileaks 1 September 2011). Available from: https://wikileaks.org/plusd/cables/05VILNIUS1007_a.html [Accessed 13 February 2019]
Embassy Vilnius (2005b) Conocophillips set to request Usg advocacy on bid with Lukoil for refinery, 05VILNIUS1186/Wikileaks #44450. Issue date 4 November 2005 [online]. (Published by Wikileaks 1 September 2011). Available from: https://wikileaks.org/plusd/cables/05VILNIUS1186_a.html [Accessed 13 February 2019]
Embassy Vilnius (2006) Two Russian oil suppliers cancel July crude shipments to Lithuanian refinery, 06VILNIUS618/Wikileaks #70128. Issue date 3 July 2006 [online]. (Published by Wikileaks 1 September 2011). Available from: https://wikileaks.org/plusd/cables/06VILNIUS618_a.html [Accessed 13 February 2019]
Eremenko, A. (2011) "Energorynok: 20 let (ne) zavisimosti [The energy market: 20 years of (in) dependence]" *Zerkalo nedeli*, 26 August
Federal Law No. 2395 (21/02/1992) *O nedrakh* [*On the subsoil*] (Moscow: The Federal Assembly)
Finam (2010) "'Natsional'nyi neftyanoi konsortsium'" mozhet investirovat' $900 mln v razrabotku bloka Khunin-6 v Venesuele [The National Oil Consortium may invest $900 million in the development of the Junin-6 block in Venezuela]" [online]. 26 January 2010 (Moscow: Finam). Available from: http://www.finam.ru/analysis/news item45C28/default.asp [Accessed 13 February 2019]
Firsova, A. (2005) "Edinaya skvazhina dlya investora [A unified borehole for investors]" *Finam.ru*, 30 March
Fortescue, S. (2006) *Russia's Oil Barons and Metal Magnates. Oligarchs and the State in Transition* (Basingstoke/New York: Palgrave Macmillan)
Fortescue, S. (2009) "The Russian law on subsurface resources: A policy marathon", *Post-Soviet Affairs*, 25 (2): 160–184
Fuller, L. (1995) "Azerbaijan: The 'Near Abroad'" *Transitions Online*, 28 April
Gavrish, O. (2005) "Viktor Yushchenko preodolel benzinovyi krizis [Viktor Yushchenko overcomes the petrol crisis]" *Kommersant*, 21 May 2005, p.5
Gavrish, O. (2006) "Vlasti Ukrainy zastavili neftyanikov samoogranichit'sya [Ukraine's powers forces the oilmen to restrain themselves]" *Kommersant*, 15 August 2006, p.10
Gavrish, O. and Lysova, T. (1999) "Nesamostiinyi benzin [Dependent petrol]" *Ekspert*, 26 July

Gavrish, O. and Chernovalov, A. (2005) "'Lukoil-Neftekhim' zanes v 'Lukor' den'gi vmesto aktsii [Lukoil-Neftekhim contributes money instead of shares to Lukor]" *Kommersant*, 5 December 2005, p.15

Germanovich, A. (2000) "Trebuetsya novoe slovo [A new word is needed]" *Vedomosti*, 31 July

Glumskov, D. and Skorobogat'ko, D. (2003) "LUKOIL ne zhaleet deneg na Kazakhstan [Lukoil does not spare any money in Kazakhstan]" *Kommersant*, 14 October 2003, p.13

Golubkova, E. and Ershov, A. (2010) "Interv'yu prezidenta OAO 'Lukoil' V.Yu. Alekperova agentstvu Reiter [Interview with Lukoil president V.Yu. Alekperov by Reuters agency]" *Reuters*, 31 August 2010

Golubkova, E., Sapozhnikov, P. and Lyrchikova, A. (2007) "'Nam komfortno v proektakh s goskapitalom', – Vagit Alekperov [Vagit Alekperov: 'We are comfortable in projects with state capital']" *RBC Daily*, 26 February

Gorelov, N. (2001) "Ukrainskie stradaniya. LUKOILu razreshili postavlyat' v Odessu malo nefti [Ukrainian sufferings. Lukoil is allowed to supply little oil to Odesa]" *Vremya novostei*, 27 September 2001, p.4

Gorshkova, A. (2007) "Kompromiss dlya kitaitsev [A compromise for the Chinese]" *Vremya novostei*, 13 September 2007, p.8

Gorst, I. (2007) *Lukoil: Russia's Largest Oil Company* (Houston: The James A. Baker III Institute for Public Policy, Rice University)

Gotova, N. (2004) "Plov i vyshka [Pilau and derrick]" *Profil'*, 21 June 2004, pp.30–32

Government Order No. 18 (25/11/1991) *Ob obrazovanii neftyanogo kontserna "LANGEPASURAIKOGALYMNEFT" ("LUKOIL") [On the creation of the oil concern "LANGEPASURAIKOGALYMNEFT" (LUKOIL)* (Moscow: The Government of the RSFSR (Russian Soviet Federative Socialist Republic))

Graifer, V.I. (2005) *Vystuplenie V.I. Graifera na s"ezde gornopromyshlennikov [V.I. Graifer's speech at the Miners' Convention]* (Moscow: Lukoil)

Granik, I. and Gabuev, A. (2009) "Rossiiskii gaz rasshirilsya do Ispanii [Russian gas has been extended to Spain]" *Kommersant*, 4 March 2009, p.6

Grib, N. and Mel'nikov, K. (2010) "LUKOIL pustit gaz v Kitai [Lukoil sends gas to China]" *Kommersant*, 20 September 2010, p.9

Grivach, A. (2009) "Berkut-shou v 'Ukrtransnafte' [Golden eagle show in Ukrtransnafta]" *Vremya novostei*, 23 June 2009, p.8

Gudkov, A. (2010) "LUKOIL pognalsya za 'Rosneft'yu' [Lukoil ran after Rosneft]" *Kommersant*, 9 November 2010, p.6

Gustafson, T. (2012) *Wheel of Fortune. The Battle for Oil and Power in Russia* (Cambridge, MA/London: The Belknap Press of Harvard University Press)

Heath, J.R. (2009) "Strategic protectionism? National Security and Foreign Investment in the Russian Federation", *George Washington International Law Review*, 41 (2009): 101–137

Heil, A. (2008) "5 + 2 = 42 million" [online]. Posted to the blog 'Transmission' on 22 July. Available from: http://www.rferl.org/content/Moldova/1185425.html [Accessed 13 June 2019]

Hilyard, J.F. (2012) *The Oil & Gas Industry. A Nontechnical Guide* (Tulsa: PennWell)

Ignatova, M. (2003) "Leonid Fedun, vitse-prezident 'LUKOILa': Ideya pobol'she obobrat' neftyanikov segodnya uspeshno realizuetsya [Leonid Fedun, Lukoil's vice president: The idea of grabbing the oil sector as much as possible is being implemented]" *Finansovye Izvestiya*, 10 October 2003, p.5

Igorev, A. et al. (2000) "Prishli za Alekperovym [They came for Alekperov]" *Kommersant*, 12 July 2000, p.1

Interfaks-ANI (2011) "Ya ne veryu v $200 za barrel', no i ne veryu v $50 [I don't believe in $200 a barrel, but neither do I believe in $50]" *Interfaks-ANI*, 18 November 2011

Interfax (2001) "Lukoil requires more information to purchase Hellenic shares" *Interfax Business Report*, 2 November

Ivanov, A. (1997) "Pekin perekhvatil u LUKOILa kazakhskuyu neft' [Beijing intercepts Kazakh oil from Lukoil]" *Kommersant*, 7 October 1997, p.2

Ivanov, N. (1999) "Svoi chelovek v Mintope [One of our own in the Fuel and Energy Ministry]" *Segodnya*, 26 May

Jensen, D. (2000) "End Note: Putin to meet oligarchs" *Radio Free Europe/Radio Liberty Newsline*, 28 July

Kazakhstan Business Magazine (2004) "Kazakhstan's oil sector: Events and facts" *Kazakhstan Business Magazine*, 38 (1). Available from: http://www.investkz.com/en/journals/38/159.html [Accessed 5 April 2020]

Kezik, I. (2007) "Lukoil i 'Rosneft' podelili kitaiskuyu druzhbu [Lukoil and Rosneft share Chinese friendship]" *Gazeta*, 11 September 2007, p.9

Khartukov, E. (2000) "Russia's oil privatization is more greed than fear" *Oil & Gas Journal*, 3 July 2000, p.30

Khnychkin, Yu. (1992) "Na neftyanom nebosklone Rossii voskhodit zvezda 'Luk oil' [Luk oil rises on Russia's oil horizon]" *Kommersant*, 13 July

Khodasevich, A. (2010) "Lukashenko obeshchaet novuyu privatizatsiyu [Lukashenka promises a new privatisation]" *Nezavisimaya gazeta*, 13 April 2010, p.6

Kim, A. (2014) "Political scandal in Uzbekistan harms investment climate" *Eurasia Daily Monitor*, 3 February

Kommersant-Vlast' (2002) "Prem'er v sostoyanii voiny [The premier in a state of war]" *Kommersant-Vlast'*, 28 May, p.9

Kommersant (1996) "'YUKOS' i 'LUKOIL' priobretut sobstvennost' v Litve [Yukos and Lukoil acquire equity in Lithuania]" *Kommersant*, 13 November 1996, p.8

Kommersant (2002) "Chem vladeyut rossiiskie kompanii na Ukraine [What Russian companies own in Ukraine]" *Kommersant*, 21 December, p.1

Kommersant (2004a) "Statistika vstrech prezidenta s oligarkhami [Statistics of the president's meetings with the oligarchs]" *Kommersant*, 2 July 2004, p.2

Kommersant (2004b) "Prezident LUKOILa vstretilsya s prezidentom Ukrainy [Lukoil's president meets Ukraine's president]" *Kommersant*, 22 October 2004, p.16

Kommersant (2004c) "Kak sozdavalsya LUKOIL [How Lukoil was formed]" *Kommersant*, 23 July, p.6

Kommersant (2005) "Kto chashche vsekh poseshchal prezidenta [Who visited the president most often]" *Kommersant*, 25 March 2005, p.1

Kommersant (2006) "Segodnya [Today]" *Kommersant*, 11 January, p.5

Kommersant (2008) "'Nashi blagie namereniya chasto razbivayutsya o kharakter administrirovaniya'" ['Our good intentions are often crushed against the nature of administration']" *Kommersant*, 24 January 2008, p.20

Konoplyanik, A. (2001) "Povyshenie denezhnogo davleniya. Nalogovaya reforma v neftyanoi otrasli: pervye rezul'taty [Increased pressure for money. The tax reform in the oil sector: first results]" *Izvestiya*, 21 November 2001, p.7

Kozlov, D., Barsukov, Yu. and Butrin, D. (2016) "Neft' bez chastnykh primesei [Oil without private additives]" *Kommersant*, 3 October, p.1

Krasovskaya, E. (2017) "LUKOIL vypolnit reshenie OPEK o prolongatsii sokrashcheniya neftedobychi [Lukoil will fulfil OPEC's decision on prolonged production cuts]" [online]. 25 May (Moscow: IG Industriya). Available from: https://oilcapital.ru/news/companies/25-05-2017/lukoyl-vypolnit-reshenie-opek-o-prolongatsii-sokrascheniya-neftedobychi [Accessed 21 March 2019]

Kravets, M. (2004) "Pol'za ot udvoeniya VVP [The utility of doubling the GDP]" *Neftegazovaya vertikal'*, No. 2, 9 February

Krivorotov, A. (1998) "Delit'sya budem bystro, no chestno [We will divide quickly, but honestly]" *Neft' i Kapital*, May 1998

Kudinov, I. (2016) "Kurchenko zazhil 'po-novomu' [Kurchenko started a 'new life']" *Nefterynok*, 29 June

Kupfer, M. and Jardine, B. (2016) "Russia's Bashneft: A very public privatization" *The Moscow Times*, 5 October

Levinskii, R. (2004) "Tsepnaya reaktsiya [Chain reaction]" *Vedomosti*, 21 December

Lowe, C. and Sagdiev, R. (2019) "How Russia sank billions of dollars into Venezuelan quicksand" [online]. 14 March (London: Reuters). Available from: https://www.reuters.com/investigates/special-report/venezuela-russia-rosneft/ [Accessed 14 March 2019]

Lukin, O. (2006) "Tashkent zastavit potesnit'sya [Tashkent forces them closer together]" *Neftegazovaya vertikal'*, No. 4, 21 March

Lukin, O. (2007) "Vybor strategii opredelit budushchee TEK Rossii [The choice of strategy decides the future of Russia's energy industry]" *Neftegazovaya vertikal'*, No. 1, 20 January

Lukin, O. (2010a) "Bog dal, Bog vzyal [The Lord giveth and the Lord taketh away]" *Neftegazovaya vertikal'*, No. 8, pp.79–81

Lukin, O. (2010b) "Ostorozhno, dveri zakryvayutsya [Please mind the closing doors]" *Neftegazovaya vertikal'*, No. 18, pp.62–64

Lukin, O. (2012) "Tsentral'naya Aziya: Usilenie gazovoi konkurentsii [Central Asia: The gas competition strengthens]" *Neftegazovaya vertikal'*, No. 9, pp.18–20

Lukoil-Trans (2014) "OOO 'Varandeiskii terminal' [The Varandei Terminal]" [online]. (Moscow: Lukoil). Available from: http://trans.lukoil.ru/ru/About/Structure/VarandeyTerminal [Accessed 1 July 2019]

Lukoil – PJSC "Lukoil" (2019) "Oil Company Lukoil" [online]. (Moscow: Lukoil). Available from: http://www.lukoil.com/ [Accessed 21 February 2019]

Lukoil (2000) *Neftyanaya kompaniya Lukoil. Godovoi otchet 1999 [Oil company Lukoil. Annual report 1999]* (Moscow: Lukoil)

Lukoil (2001) *Lukoil. Neftyanaya kompaniya. Godovoi otchet 2000 [Lukoil, oil company. Annual report 2000]* (Moscow: Lukoil)

Lukoil (2003) *Neftyanaya kompaniya Lukoil. Otchet o deyatel'nosti 2002 [Oil company Lukoil. Annual report 2002]* (Moscow: Lukoil)

Lukoil (2004) *Lukoil. Otchet o deyatel'nosti kompanii v 2003 godu [Lukoil. Annual report for 2003]* (Moscow: Lukoil)

Lukoil (2007) *Lukoil. Otchet o deyatel'nosti 2006 [Lukoil. Annual report 2006]* (Moscow: Lukoil)

Lukoil (2015) *OAO Lukoil. Annual report 2014* (Moscow: Lukoil)

Lukoil (2016) *Lukoil. Always moving forward. Annual report 2015* (Moscow: Lukoil)

Lukoil (2017) *Lukoil. The sea of opportunities. Annual report 2016* (Moscow: Lukoil)

Lukoil (2018a) *Lukoil. Unlocking the potential. Annual report 2017* (Moscow: Lukoil)

Lukoil (2018b) *Lukoil otkryl pervuyu AZS v Uzbekistane [Lukoil opens first petrol station in Uzbekistan]* (Moscow: Lukoil)

Lukoil (2018c) *Lukoil commissions gas processing complex in Uzbekistan ahead of schedule* (Moscow: Lukoil)
Lukoil Overseas Holding Ltd. (2005) *Korporativnyi otchet 2004* [*Corporate report 2004*] (Moscow: Lukoil Overseas)
Lukoil Overseas Holding Ltd. (2011) *Korporativnyi otchet 2010* [*Corporate report 2010*] (Moscow: Lukoil Overseas)
Luong, P.J. and Weinthal, E. (2004) "Contra coercion: Russian tax reform, exogenous shocks, and negotiated institutional change", *American Political Science Review*, 98 (1): 139–152
Lyapunova, G. (2001) "Deputaty ukhodyat v nedra [Deputies go to the subsoil]" *Kommersant*, 7 June 2001, p.1
Lysova, T. (1999) "Lukoilu 'nuzhny ne aktsii, a den'gi' [Lukoil does not need shares, but money]" *Vedomosti*, 13 September
Makarkin, A. (2005a) "Revolyutsiya i proza zhizni [Revolution and the prose of life]" *Neft' i Kapital*, October
Makarkin, A. (2005b) "Ukraina pri Viktore Yushchenko i interesy rossiiskogo TEK [Ukraine under Viktor Yushchenko and the interests of the Russian energy complex]" *Neft' i Kapital*, January–February
Makarkin, A. (2008a) "V Tashkente vse stabil'no [In Tashkent, all is stable]" *Neft' i Kapital*, May
Makarkin, A. (2008b) "Vosem' let prezidenta Putina [Eight years of President Putin]" *Neft' i Kapital*, April
Malkova, I. (2010) "Otkryt' shel'f [Opening up the shelf]" *Vedomosti*, 31 March
Mandrik, I. (2011) "OAO 'LUKOIL': problemy razvitiya mineral'no-syr'evoi bazy [Lukoil: the problems of development of its mineral and raw materials base]" *Neftegazovaya vertikal'*, 5, pp.40–44
Marten, K. (2007) "Russian efforts to control Kazakhstan's oil: The Kumkol case", *Post-Soviet Affairs*, 23 (1): 18–37
Mazneva, E. (2008) "Daite otsrochku [Give a deferment, please]" *Vedomosti*, 1 November
Mazneva, E. (2011) "Kazakhskaya arifmetika [Kazakh arithmetics]" *Vedomosti*, 16 December, p.7
Mazneva, E., Zhelobanov, D. and Tutushkin, A. (2008) "'Net pokupatelei i adekvatnoi tseny' – Leonid Fedun sovladelets 'Lukoila', IFD 'Kapital', FK 'Spartak-Moskva' [No buyers and no adequate price – Leonid Fedun, co-owner of Lukoil, Kapital and Spartak-Moscow]" *Vedomosti*, 18 December
Mel'nikov, K. (2010) "Plata za spokoistvie [A charge for peace of mind]" *Vremya novostei*, 4 June 2010, p.8
Mel'nikov, K. (2011) "'Rebyata, my vozvrashchaemsya v Sovetskii Soyuz, u nas reguliruemaya tsena na benzin' ['Guys, we're returning to the Soviet Union, the petrol price is regulated']" *Kommersant*, 14 April 2011, p.14
Mel'nikov, K. (2015) "Arkticheski reshennyi vopros [An Arctically decided question]" *Kommersant*, 26 March, p.1
Meshcherin, A. (2010) "Energeticheskii duumvirat [The energy duumvirate]" *Neftegazovaya vertikal'*, 13–14, pp.16–23
Meshcherin, A. (2011a) "Dividendy: eto vam ne el'dorado [Dividends: no Eldorado]" *Neftegazovaya vertikal'*, 15–16, pp.32–37
Meshcherin, A. (2011b) "Oglushitel'nyi prirost zapasov [A deafening growth in reserves]" *Neftegazovaya vertikal'*, 2, pp.12–15

Meshcherin, A. (2011c) "Fasadnoe blagopoluchie neft' i gaz Rossii 2010: predvaritel'nye itogi [Facade prosperity in Russian oil and gas in 2010: a preliminary summary]" *Neftegazovaya vertikal'*, 4, pp.26–47

Ministry of Industry and Trade (2003) *Energeticheskaya strategiya Rossii na period do 2020 goda [Russia's Energy Strategy for the period to 2020)* (Moscow: Ministerstvo promyshlennosti i torgovli)

Mordyushenko, O. and Gavrish, O. (2009) "Neft' LUKOILa ostanovilas' v Odesse [Lukoil's oil stopped in Odesa]" *Kommersant*, 2 October 2009, p.11

Mordyushenko, O. and Barsukov, Yu. (2017) "Problemy strategicheskogo naznacheniya [Problems of strategic purpose]" *Kommersant*, 26 January, p.1

Moser, N. (2016) "Ownership and enterprise performance in the Russian oil industry, 1992–2012", *Post-Communist Economies*, 28 (1): 72–86

Moskovskii Komsomolets (1998) "Non-stop. Politika. Berezovskii zaviduet Kuchme [Non-stop. Politics. Berezovskii envies Kuchma]" *Moskovskii Komsomolets*, 11 August

Narzikulov, R. (1997) "'Neft' – eto vsegda politika' ['Oil is always politics']" *Nezavisimaya gazeta*, 14 January 1997, p.1

Neft' i Kapital (1999) "Interv'yu V.Yu. Alekperova zhurnalu *Neft' i Kapital* [Interview with V. Yu. Alekperov in *Neft' i Kapital* magazine]" *Neft' i Kapital*, November

Neft' i Kapital (2002a) "Sebestoimost' – sokrashchat', eksport – narashchivat' [Reduce cost, increase export]" *Neft' i Kapital*, June

Neft' i Kapital (2002b) "'Lukoil Baltija R' gotova prodavat' toplivo v Evrope [Lukoil Baltija R is ready to sell fuel in Europe]" *Neft' i Kapital*, September

Neft' i Kapital (2002c) "Tyazhelye razdumki pered reshitel'nym shagom [Difficult considerations before the decisive step]" *Neft' i Kapital*, October

Neft' i Kapital (2002d) "Vagit Alekperov: 'My s optimizmom smotrim i na segodnyashnyuyu situatsiyu, i na dal'nyuyu perspektivu' [Vagit Alekperov: 'We're optimistic in our view of both the present situation, and when looking at the longer perspective']" *Neft' i Kapital*, June

Neft' i Kapital (2003a) "'Famil'noe serebro' belorusskoi promyshlennosti [Belarusian industry's 'family silver']" *Neft' i Kapital*, April

Neft' i Kapital (2003b) "Rim Bagmanov: "Yalama – zadacha strategicheskaya" [Rim Bagmanov: 'Yalama is a strategic task']" *Neft' i Kapital*, May

Neft' i Kapital (2004a) "Lakmusovaya bumazhka [Litmus paper]" *Neft' i Kapital*, September

Neft' i Kapital (2004b) "Tochka rosta [A point of growth]" *Neft' i Kapital*, September

Neft' i Kapital (2004c) "Ukrainskie NPZ [The Ukrainian refineries]" *Neft' i Kapital*, October

Neft' i Kapital (2004d) "Vagit Alekperov" *Neft' i Kapital*, October

Neft' i Kapital (2004e) "Lukoil" *Neft' i Kapital*, October

Neft' i Kapital (2005a) "Ukrainskaya revolyutsia trebuet zhertv [The Ukrainian revolution claims victims]" *Neft' i Kapital*, May

Neft' i Kapital (2005b) "Netraditsionnyi podkhod [An untraditional approach]" *Neft' i Kapital*, December

Neft' i Kapital (2006a) "Dvukhletnii taim-aut [A two-year time-out]" *Neft' i Kapital*, September

Neft' i Kapital (2006b) "Pervomu – 15! [The first-born is 15!]" *Neft' i Kapital*, November

Neft' i Kapital (2006c) "Knutom i pryanikom [With stick and carrot]" *Neft' i Kapital*, September

Neft' i Kapital (2007a) "'Rosneft" – samaya neftyanaya kompaniya [Rosneft, the oiliest company]" *Neft' i Kapital*, May

Neft' i Kapital (2007b) "Po vremennoi skheme [Temporary measures]" *Neft' i Kapital*, December

Neft' i Kapital (2007c) "Ustupaya, nastupai [Advance while conceding]" *Neft' i Kapital*, December

Neft' i Kapital (2007d) "Plody strategicheskogo al'yansa [The fruits of a strategic alliance]" *Neft' i Kapital*, January–February

Neft' i Kapital (2008) "'LUKOIL' prinyal estafetu [Lukoil takes on the baton]" *Neft' i Kapital*, May

Neft' i Kapital (2009) "Kontekst. Gunvor konsolidiruet nefteperevalku v Ust'-Luge [Context. Gunvor is consolidating oil transhipment at Ust-Luga]" *Neft' i Kapital*, April

Neft' i Kapital (2010) "Kak dym ot papirosy [Like smoke from a cigarette]" *Neft' i Kapital*, March

Neft' i Kapital (2011a) "Polimery bez polumer [Polymers without half measures]" *Neft' i Kapital*, October

Neft' i Kapital (2011b) "Uzbekskaya 'sinitsa' [The Uzbek 'bird']" *Neft' i Kapital*, July

Neft' i Kapital (2011c) "Chetyre pyatiletki 'LUKOILa'" [Lukoil's four five-year plans]" *Neft' i Kapital*, September

Neft' i Kapital (2011d) "Iz Tashkenta s nadezhdoi [From Tashkent with hope]" *Neft' i Kapital*, March

Neft' i Kapital (2013) "Zhdem peremen [Waiting for changes]" *Neft' i Kapital*, June

Neftegazovaya vertikal' (2005) "LUKOIL: po materialam godovogo otcheta [Lukoil: an analysis of the annual report]" *Neftegazovaya vertikal'*, No. 11, 8 August

Neftegazovaya vertikal' (2006a) "Individual'nyi pocherk. Chast' 1 [Individual style. Part 1]" *Neftegazovaya vertikal'*, No. 5, 10 April

Neftegazovaya vertikal' (2006b) "NK 'Lukoil': strategiya udvoeniya [Lukoil: a strategy for doubling]" *Neftegazovaya vertikal'*, No. 16, 16 November

Neftegazovaya vertikal' (2007) "Lukoil v Uzbekistane: Igraet po-krupnomu [Lukoil plays a serious game in Uzbekistan]" *Neftegazovaya vertikal'*, No. 1, 16 January

Neftegazovaya vertikal' (2010a) "Eksport nefti i nefteproduktov [Oil and oil products export]" *Neftegazovaya vertikal'*, No. 5, pp.73–89

Neftegazovaya vertikal' (2010b) "Resursnaya baza: 'Slivki' konchilis' [The resource base: no cream left]" *Neftegazovaya vertikal'*, No. 5, pp.40–53

Neftegazovaya vertikal' (2010c) "TNK-BP 2000–2010 v tsifrakh [TNK-BP 2000–2010 in numbers]" *Neftegazovaya vertikal'*, No. 22, pp.22–27

Neftegazovaya vertikal' (2011a) "Rosneft': Osvoenie shel'fa [Rosneft: opening up the shelf]" *Neftegazovaya vertikal'*, Nos 15–16, pp.28–30

Neftegazovaya vertikal' (2011b) "Podarok sud'by [A gift of fortune]" *Neftegazovaya vertikal'*, Nos 15–16, pp.4–15

Neftegazovaya vertikal' (2011c) "Neftyanaya otrasl' Respubliki Kazakhstan [The oil industry in the Republic of Kazakhstan]" *Neftegazovaya vertikal'*, No. 20, pp.28–33

Neftegazovaya vertikal' (2011d) "Spekulyanty ne veryat v neftyanku [The speculants do not believe in oil business]" *Neftegazovaya vertikal'*, No. 3, pp.52–59

Neftegazovaya vertikal' (2012a) "Antisobytiya goda. Reitingovyi obzor 'Neftegazovoi vertikali' [The non-events of the year. Neftegazovaya vertikal's rating survey]" *Neftegazovaya vertikal'*, No. 1, pp.17–21

Neftegazovaya vertikal' (2012b) "Tendentsii goda. Reitingovyi obzor 'Neftegazovoi vertikali' [The trends of the year. Neftegazovaya vertikal's rating survey]" *Neftegazovaya vertikal'*, No. 1, pp.22–26

Neftegazovaya vertikal' (2016a) "'Lukoil' ne vidit riskov dlya SP s 'Bashneftyu' posle privatizatsii etoi kompanii – Alekperov [Alekperov: Lukoil does not see any risks for the JV with Bashneft after the privatisation of the company]" [online]. 12 October. Moscow. Available from: http://www.ngv.ru/news/lukoyl_ne_vidit_riskov_dlya_sp_s_bashneftyu_posle_privatizatsii_etoy_kompanii_alekperov_/ [Accessed 22 March 2019]

Neftegazovaya vertikal' (2016b) "Pyat' pyatiletok Lukoila [Lukoil's five five-year plans]" *Neftegazovaya vertikal'*, No. 22, pp.12–18

Neftegazovaya vertikal' (2016c) "Mirnaya ekspansiya [Peaceful expansion]" *Neftegazovaya vertikal'*, No. 22, pp.32–39

Neftegazovaya vertikal' (2016d) "Valerii Graifer: Vertikal'naya integratsiya nachinalas' s Lukoila [Valerii Graifer: Vertical integration started with Lukoil]" *Neftegazovaya vertikal'*, No. 22, pp.20–25

Neftegazovaya vertikal' (2017a) "Vyekhat' na gaze. V Srednei Azii problemy s dobychei nefti probuyut kompensirovat' pererabotkoi gaza [Going out on gas. Central Asia tries to compensate oil production problems with gas processing]" *Neftegazovaya vertikal'*, No. 11, pp.58–62

Neftegazovaya vertikal' (2017b) "Mikhail Krutikhin: Sozdanie VINK – men'shee iz zol [Mikhail Krutikhin: The creation of the vertically integrated oil companies was the lesser evil]" *Neftegazovaya vertikal'*, No. 21, pp.28–34

Neftegazovaya vertikal' (2017c) "Ne tol'ko megaproekty [Not just mega-projects]" *Neftegazovaya vertikal'*, No. 9, pp.52–56

Nekrasov, V.I. (2007) "Vystuplenie pervogo vitse-prezidenta OAO "Lukoil" V.I. Nekrasova na zasedanii "kruglogo stola" po neftepererabotke i neftekhimii v Sovete Federatsii RF [Testimony of Lukoil's first vice president V.I. Nekrasov at the meeting of the Roundtable on oil refining and the petrochemical industry in the Federation Council of the Russian Federation]" [online]. 4 July 2007 (Moscow: Lukoil). Available from: http://www.lukoil.ru/press.asp?div_id=2&id=1123&year=2007 [Accessed 23 January 2012]

Nikitin, N. (2010) "Benefitsiar neftyanoi perepisi [The beneficiary of the oil inventory]" *Neftegazovaya vertikal'*, No. 21, p.56

Nikitin, N. (2011) "Ogosudarstvlenie v zakone [Transfer into state ownership by law]" *Neftegazovaya vertikal'*, No. 8, p.4–12

Nikolaeva, A. and Bekker, A. (2006) "Pokhod na Kavkaz [Caucasian campaign]" *Vedomosti*, 2 October

Novolodskaya, S. (2001) "'LUKOIL' ob"edinyaetsya s 'Iteroi' [Lukoil unites with Itera]" *Vedomosti*, 24 July

O'Cinneide, E. (2011) "Lukoil plans $48bn splurge" *Upstream*, 1 December

Oilcapital.ru (2010) "Lukoil prizyvaet Pravitel'stvo RF rasprostranit' nalogovye l'goty na novye neftyanye provintsii [Lukoil calls on the Russian government to extend tax breaks to new oil provinces]" 29 January

Oilcapital.ru (2012a) "LUKOIL budet transportirovat' dobytuyu na Kaspii neft' po sisteme KTK – Alekperov [Alekperov: Lukoil will transport its Caspian oil through the CPC system]" [online]. 16 May (Moscow: IG Industriya). Available from: https://oilcapital.ru/news/companies/16-05-2012/lukoyl-budet-transportirovat-dobytuyu-na-kaspii-neft-po-sisteme-ktk-alekperov [Accessed 20 February 2019]

Oilcapital.ru (2012b) "Reiting vliyaniya krupnykh predprinimatelei i top-menedzherov toplivno-energeticheskogo kompleksa v dekabre 2012 g. [Rating of the influence of major businessmen and top managers in the fuel and energy complex, December 2012]" [online]. 6 December (Moscow: IG Industriya). Available from: https://oilcapital.ru/news/companies/06-12-2012/reyting-vliyaniya-krupnyh-predprinimateley-i-top-menedzherov-tek-v-dekabre-2012-g [Accessed 18 March 2019]

Oilcapital.ru (2014a) "Glava 'LUKOILa' Alekperov prosit pravitel'stvo zamorozit' tarify 'Transnefti', RZhD i portovye sbory v usloviyakh sanktsii [Lukoil head Alekperov asks government to freeze Transneft, RZhD tariffs and port rates due to sanctions]" [online]. 6 November 2014 (Moscow: IG Industriya). Available from: https://oilcapital.ru/news/transport/06-11-2014/glava-lukoyla-alekperov-prosit-pravitelstvo-zamorozit-tarify-transnefti-rzhd-i-portovye-sbory-v-usloviyah-sanktsiy [Accessed 18 March 2019]

Oilcapital.ru (2014b) "'LUKOIL' poka ne vidit ostroi neobkhodimosti v privlechenii sredstv s vneshnikh rynkov [Lukoil does not yet see any urgency in attracting finance from external markets]" [online]. 5 June (Moscow: IG Industriya). Available from: https://oilcapital.ru/news/companies/05-06-2014/lukoyl-poka-ne-vidit-ostroy-neobhodimosti-v-privlechenii-sredstv-s-vneshnih-rynkov [Accessed 20 March 2019]

Oilcapital.ru (2014c) "'Vnuchka' 'Gazproma' uidet iz Kryma iz-za ugrozy sanktsii [Gazprom's granddaughter leaves Crimea due to the threat of sanctions]" [online]. 25 August (Moscow: IG Industriya). Available from: https://oilcapital.ru/news/companies/25-08-2014/vnuchka-gazproma-uydet-iz-kryma-iz-za-ugrozy-sanktsiy [Accessed 20 March 2019]

Oilcapital.ru (2014d) "Situatsiya na Ukraine nikak ne skazalas' na rabote predpriyatiy LUKOILa v strane [The situation in Ukraine has not affected Lukoil's business in the country in any way]" [online]. 17 April (Moscow: IG Industriya). Available from: https://oilcapital.ru/news/companies/17-04-2014/situatsiya-na-ukraine-ne-skazalas-na-rabote-predpriyatiy-lukoyla-v-strane [Accessed 20 March 2019]

Oilcapital.ru (2014e) "Roznichnyi biznes 'LUKOILa' na Ukraine pokupaet avstriiskaya AMIC [Lukoil's retail business in Ukraine acquired by Austrian AMIC]" [online]. 31 July (Moscow: IG Industriya). Available from: https://oilcapital.ru/news/companies/31-07-2014/roznichnyy-biznes-lukoyla-na-ukraine-pokupaet-avstryskaya-amic [Accessed 20 March 2019]

Oilcapital.ru (2014f) "Zapravki 'LUKOILa' na Ukraine blokiruyut – OBSE [OSCE: Lukoil's petrol stations in Ukraine are blockaded]" [online]. 29 July (Moscow: IG Industriya). Available from: https://oilcapital.ru/news/companies/29-07-2014/zapravki-lukoyla-na-ukraine-blokiruyut-obse [Accessed 20 March 2019]

Oilcapital.ru (2015a) "'LUKOIL' predlagaet prodlit' l'goty po NDPI dlya mestorozhdeniya Kaspiya na 10 let. Ob etom zayavil v Gosdume glava NK 'LUKOIL' Vagit Alekperov [Lukoil proposes to extend mineral extraction tax reductions for Caspian deposits by 10 years, as declared by Lukoil head Vagit Alekperov in the State Duma]" [online]. 2 June (Moscow: IG Industriya). Available from: https://oilcapital.ru/news/companies/02-06-2015/lukoyl-predlagaet-prodlit-lgoty-po-ndpi-dlya-mestorozhdeniy-kaspiya-na-10-let [Accessed 18 March 2019]

Oilcapital.ru (2015b) "Sektoral'nye sanktsii okazali neznachitel'noe vliyanie na deyatel'nost' LUKOILa – Alekperov [Alekperov: The sectoral sanctions have had little impact on Lukoil's business]" [online]. 25 June (Moscow: IG Industriya). Available from: https://oilcapital.ru/news/companies/25-06-2015/sektoralnye-sanktsii-okazali-neznachitelnoe-vliyanie-na-deyatelnost-lukoyla-alekperov [Accessed 25 February 2019]

Oilcapital.ru (2015c) "'Lukoil' i 'Gazprom' otlozhili burenie na Tsentral'nom mestorozhdenii do snyatiya sanktsii [Lukoil and Gazprom delay drilling on the Tsentral'noe field until sanctions are lifted]" [online]. 24 December (Moscow: IG Industriya). Available from: https://oilcapital.ru/news/*Upstream*/24-12-2015/lukoyl-i-gazprom-otlozhili-burenie-na-tsentralnom-mestorozhdenii-do-snyatiya-sanktsiy [Accessed 20 February 2019]

Oilcapital.ru (2015d) "'Lukoil'" vygodno prodal aktiv v Kazakhstane kitaitsam [Lukoil sold its active in Kazakhstan to China, at a profit]" [online]. 21 August (Moscow: IG Industriya). Available from: https://oilcapital.ru/news/companies/21-08-2015/lukoyl-vy godno-prodal-aktiv-v-kazahstane-kitaytsam [Accessed 21 February 2019]

Oilcapital.ru (2016a) "Reiting vliyaniya krupnykh predprinimatelei i top-menedzherov toplivno-energeticheskogo kompleksa v marte 2016 g. [Rating of the influence of major businessmen and top managers in the fuel and energy complex, March 2016]" [online]. 29 March (Moscow: IG Industriya). Available from: https://oilcapital.ru/news/compa nies/29-03-2016/reyting-vliyaniya-krupnyh-predprinimateley-i-top-menedzherov-topliv no-energeticheskogo-kompleksa-v-marte-2016-g [Accessed 20 February 2019]

Oilcapital.ru (2016b) "Alekperov nadeetsya na OPEK, no ne verit v realistichnost' 'Soglasiya' [Alekperov places hopes on OPEC, but does not believe in the realism of a 'deal']" [online]. 16 November (Moscow: IG Industriya). Available from: https:// oilcapital.ru/news/companies/16-11-2016/alekperov-nadeetsya-na-opek-no-ne-ver it-v-realistichnost-soglasiya [Accessed 21 March 2019]

Oilcapital.ru (2016c) "'Bashneft': Prodano! 'Rosneft" kupila kompaniyu s premiei k rynku [Bashneft: Sold! Rosneft buys the company above the market price]" [online]. 2 December (Moscow: IG Industriya). Available from: https://oilcapital.ru/news/compa nies/02-12-2016/bashneft-prodano-rosneft-kupila-kompaniyu-s-premiey-k-rynku [Acce ssed 21 March 2019]

Oilcapital.ru (2016d) "'Lukoil' poluchil razreshenie na postavki diztopliva grazhdanskim potrebitelyam Ukrainy [LUkoil allowed to supply diesel to civilian customers in Ukraine]" [online]. 30 March (Moscow: IG Industriya). Available from: https:// oilcapital.ru/news/export/30-03-2016/lukoyl-poluchil-razreshenie-na-postavki-diztop liva-grazhdanskim-potrebitelyam-ukrainy [Accessed 18 February 2019]

Oilcapital.ru (2017a) "Azerbaidzhan predlagaet 'LUKOILu' ispol'zovat' nefteprovod BTD dlya nefti s mestorozhdeniya Filanovskogo [Azerbaijan offers use of BTC pipeline to Lukoil to use for oil from the Filanovsky field]" [online]. 13 October (Moscow: IG Industriya). Available from: https://oilcapital.ru/news/transport/13-10-2017/azerba ydzhan-predlagaet-lukoylu-ispolzovat-nefteprovod-btd-dlya-nefti-s-mestorozhdeniya-filanovskogo [Accessed 20 February 2019]

Oilcapital.ru (2017b) "'LUKOIL' ne planiruyet prodavat' dolyu v SP po razrabotke mestorozhdenii Trebsa i Titova [Lukoil does not plan to sell its share of the JV for development of the Trebs and Titov fields]" [online]. 19 January (Moscow: IG Industriya). Available from: https://oilcapital.ru/news/companies/19-01-2017/lukoyl-ne-planiruet-prodavat-dolyu-v-sp-po-razrabotke-mestorozhdeniy-trebsa-i-titova [Accessed 22 March 2019]

Oilcapital.ru (2018) "Kaspiiskaya konventsiya: uzh luchshe takaya, chem nikakaya [The Caspian Convention: better still this one than none]" [online]. 1 August (Moscow: IG Industriya). Available from: https://oilcapital.ru/article/general/01-08-2018/kaspiyskaya -konventsiya-uzh-luchshe-takaya-chem-nikakaya [Accessed 18 February 2019]

Oilcapital.ru (2019a) "Negativno vliyayut sanktsii na 'Lukoil', odnako adaptatsiya vozmozhna [The sanctions impact Lukoil negatively, but adaptation is possible]" [online]. 12 March (Moscow: IG Industriya). Available from: https://oilcapital.ru/news/companies/12-03-2019/negativno-vliyayut-sanktsii-na-lukoyl-odnako-adaptatsiya-vozmozhna [Accessed 13 March 2019]

Oilcapital.ru (2019b) "6 trln rublei zarabotala Rossiya za vremya sdelki OPEK+ [Russia earned 6 trillion rubles for the duration of OPEC+]" [online]. 13 February (Moscow: IG Industriya). Available from: https://oilcapital.ru/news/markets/14-02-2019/6-trln-rubley-zarabotala-rossiya-za-vremya-sdelki-opek [Accessed 21 March 2019]

Orekhin, P. (2010) "Bol'shoi priz [The big prize]" *Profil'*, 27 September 2010, pp.6–11

Orekhin, P., Naumov, I. and Ivzhenko, T. (2005) "Fradkov otkazalsya zashchishchat' neftyanikov. Rost tsen na benzin prodolzhaetsya [Fradkov declined to defend the oilmen. The petrol price rise continues]" *Nezavisimaya gazeta*, 21 April 2005, p.1

Petrachkova, A. (2006) "Interes k Tadzhikistanu [An interest in Tajikistan]" *Vedomosti*, 18 September

Pravosudov, S. (2000) "Interv'yu L.A. Feduna zhurnalu Russkii Fokus [Interview with L. A. Fedun with the magazine Russkii Fokus]" *Russkii Fokus*, 5 December

Pravosudov, S. (2003) "Vagit Alekperov: 'Otkuda vy znaete, chto Kukuru ukrali beznakazanno?' [Vagit Alekperov: 'How do you know that Kukura was kidnapped with impunity?'" *Russkii Fokus*, 14 April

Rachkov, B. (2001) "U biznesa i vlasti zaboty obshchie [The business sector and the authorities have common worries]" *Ekonomika i zhizn'*, 23 June

Razumovskii, K. (1998) "Privatizatsiya 'Linosa': Vtoraya popytka [The privatisation of Linos: a second attempt]" *Kommersant*, 16 January 1998, p.11

Razumovskii, K. (2001) "Novaya strategiya LUKOILa na Ukraine [Lukoil's new strategy in Ukraine]" *Kommersant*, 27 September 2001, p.4

RBK (2018) "RBK 500: Reiting rossiiskogo biznesa [RBK 500: The Russian Business Rating]" [online]. Moscow: Available from: https://www.rbc.ru/rbc500/ [Accessed 23 November 2018]

Rebrov, D. (2010a) "Nashi aktsionery riskuyut [Our shareholders take a risk]" *Kommersant*, 24 June 2010, p.10

Rebrov, D. (2010b) "LUKOILu ne khvataet gaza na polipropilenovyi zavod v Budennovske [Lukoil does not have enough gas for a polypropylene factory in Budennovsk]" *Kommersant*, 24 June 2010, p.9

Rebrov, D. and Skorlygina, N. (2006) "LUKOIL vyrastet na gaze [Lukoil will grow on gas]" *Kommersant*, 19 October 2006, p.13

Rebrov, D. and Konstantinov, A. (2008) "LUKOIL ne srabotalsya s CNPC [Lukoil and CNPC did not work well together]" *Kommersant*, 23 June 2008, p.9

Rebrov, D., Naumova, A. and Tomashevskaya, O. (2006) "Bez nefti vinovatyi [Guilty of no oil]" *Vremya novostei*, 19 January, p.7

Reuters (2018) "Russia's Lukoil says banks stricter with it after US 'oligarch list'" [online]. 15 February (London: Reuters). Available from: https://www.reuters.com/article/us-russia-lukoil-banks-sanctions/russias-lukoil-says-banks-stricter-with-it-after-u-s-oligarch-list-idUSKCN1FZ19A [Accessed 14 March 2019]

RFE/RL (1996) "RFE/RL Newsline" *Radio Free Europe/Radio Liberty*, 17 April

RIA Novosti (2009) "Russia, Venezuela sign raft of energy, military deals" [online]. (Moscow: RIA Novosti). Available from: http://en.rian.ru/russia/20090910/156088746.html [Accessed 16 February 2019]

Rogers, D. (2015) *The depths of Russia. Oil, power, and culture after socialism* (Ithaca/London: Cornell University Press)

Romanova, L. (1999) "Interesy 'neftyanoi diplomatii' [The interests of 'oil diplomacy']" *Nezavisimaya gazeta – Sodruzhestvo*, 24 February

Romanova, L. and San'ko, V. (1999) "Vagit Alekperov: 'Vse nado schitat" [Vagit Alekperov: 'Everything must be taken into account']" *Nezavisimaya gazeta*, 27 August, p.4

Rybal'chenko, I. (2000) "Mazeikiu Nafta rasschitivaet na rossiiskuyu neft' [Mazeikiu Nafta counts on Russian oil]" *Kommersant*, 9 December 2000, p.5

Rybal'chenko, I. (2001) "'LUKoil' menyaet investitsii na tarify [Lukoil exchanges investments for tariffs]" *Kommersant*, 10 February 2001, p.3

Sapozhnikov, P. (2002) "LUKOIL vygodno prodal nedra Azerbaidzhana [Lukoil sold Azerbaijan's mineral wealth profitably]" *Kommersant*, 21 December 2002, p.4

Sapozhnikov, P. and Khvostik, E. (2004) "LUKOIL kupil ital'yanskuyu polovinu [Lukol buys the Italian half]" *Kommersant*, 1 July 2004, p.1

Sapozhnikov, P., Sborov, A. and Mamaev, S. (2002) "LUKOIL rasprodaet nedra Azerbaidzhana [Lukoil sells out Azerbaijan's mineral wealth]" *Kommersant*, 18 November 2002, p.1

Savushkin, S. (2005) "Kremlevskii kapitalizm na marshe [Kremlin capitalism marches ahead]" *Neft' i Kapital*, October

Sborov, A. (2000) "Kalyuzhnyi poshel po delu 'LUKoila' v Baku [Kalyuzhnyi goes to Baku on the Lukoil case]" *Kommersant*, 14 July, p.3

Sharip, F. (2012) "Uzbekistan's quest for Aral Sea oil may weaken Kazakhstan's position in the Caspian" *Eurasia Daily Monitor*, 2 February

Shevel'kova, O. (2008) "'Padenie dobychi – eto uzhe tendentsiya' [Falling production is already a tendency]" *SmartMoney*, 12 May 2008, p.24

Shiryaev, V. (1999) "'LUKoil' mogut poprosit' s Odesskogo NPZ, esli on ne budet vypolnyat' svoikh obyazatel'stv [Lukoil may be asked to leave the Odesa oil refinery if it does not fulfil its obligations]" *Novye izvestiya*, 23 December

Shumilin, A. (1997) "Sergei Markov: LUKOIL sil'nee MIDa [Sergei Markov: Lukoil is stronger than the MFA]" *Kommersant*, 23 July 1997, p.4

Sidorov, E. (2001) "'Takoi nalog nam ne nuzhen…' 'Starye' neftyanye kompanii nadeyutsya na ponimanie deputatskogo korpusa ['We don't want this tax…' The 'old' oil companies hope for understanding from deputies]" *Nezavisimaya gazeta*, 3 July 2001, p.4

Sivakov, D. and Vin'kov, A. (2007) "Prosto ne nado zhadnichat' [Just don't be greedy]" *Ekspert*, 12 November 2007, pp.32–39

Skorlygina, N. (2006) "LUKOIL stolknulsya s kitaiskoi ugrozoi [Lukoil clashes with the Chinese threat]" *Kommersant*, 27 October 2006, p.17

Skorlygina, N. and Rebrov, D. (2007) "LUKOIL obmenyaetsya aktivami s CNPC [Lukoil will exchange equity with CNPC]" *Kommersant*, 13 September 2007, p.13

Skorobogat'ko, D. (2004) "LUKOIL zarabotal na nalogi [Lukoil has worked on taxes]" *Kommersant*, 14 January 2004, p.16

Skorobogat'ko, D. (2005) "Minoritarii Nelson soglasilis' na tsenu LUKOILa [Nelson's minority shareholders agree to Lukoil's price]" *Kommersant*, 21 October 2005, p.15

Slavinskaya, L. (2011) "Geopoliticheskii afront: Rossiya protiv vsekh? [Geopolitical affront: Russia against all?]" *Neftegazovaya vertikal'*, No. 20, pp.44–47

Smirnov, A. (1995) "Neftyanye kompanii delyat resursy nepodelennogo Kaspiya [The oil companies divide the resources of the undivided Caspian]" *Kommersant*, 10 November 1995, p.1

Smirnov, K. (2002) "Zachem oni tuda khodyat [Why they go there]" *Kommersant-Vlast'*, 21 May

Socor, V. (2009) "Lukoil acquires major stake in Netherlands refinery and marketing" *Eurasia Daily Monitor*, 26 June
Socor, V. (2013) "Ukraine launches major gas extraction projects with Western companies" *Eurasia Daily Monitor*, 8 November
Socor, V. (2014) "Beyond Shah Deniz: Azerbaijan's next-generation gas" *Eurasia Daily Monitor*, 29 January
Stalker, A. (1995) "Rossiiskie neftyaniki zakreplyayutsya v Srednei Azii [Russian oilmen consolidate their hold in Central Asia]" *Kommersant*, 14 April
Starinskaya, G. and Serov, M. (2015a) "'U nas ni razu ne bylo udachi v peregovorakh s kitaiskimi bankami" ['We never had any luck in negotiations with Chinese banks']" *Vedomosti*, 7 September. Available from: https://www.vedomosti.ru/business/video/2015/09/07/607775-u-nas-ne-bilo-udachi-s-kitaiskimi-bankami [Accessed 31 March 2020]
Starinskaya, G. and Serov, M. (2015b) "'Kitaiskie kredity – samye dorogie v mire' ['Chinese credits are the most expensive in the world']" *Vedomosti*, 6 September
Starinskaya, G., Kashevarova, A. and Korytina, E. (2010) "Glava 'Rosnefti' mozhet stat' ministrom energetiki [The head of Rosneft may become energy minister]" *RBC Daily*, 26 August 2010
Stolyarov, B. (1999) "Professiya: oligarkh. A za chto, skazhite, nas ne lyubit'?! Prezident LUKOILa o svoikh vzaimootnosheniyakh s gosudarstvom [Profession: oligarch. And why, please, should we not be loved? Lukoil's president on his mutual relations with the state]" *Novaya gazeta*, 29 November
Suleimenov, M. (2005) "Kazakhstanskaya dolya [Kazakhstan's share]" *Neft' i Kapital*, December
The New Times (2019) "Vitse-prem'er Yurii Trutnev: investoram v Arktike nuzhny nalogovye kanikuly i l'goty [Vice-premier Yurii Trutnev: Investors in the Arctic need tax breaks and deductions]" *The New Times/Novoe Vremya*, 4 March
Timoshchenko, V. (2001) "Do Novogo goda eshche daleko, a god Ukrainy uzhe nachinaetsya. Protsessom sblizheniya dvukh bratskikh gosudarstv budut upravlyat' 'kapitany' rossiiskoi ekonomiki [New Year is still far off, but the Year of Ukraine is already starting. The 'captains' of the Russian economy are in charge of the rapprochement process between the two brotherly states]" *Nezavisimaya gazeta*, 29 November 2001, p.5
Today.kz (2010) "'PetroKazakhstan' i LUKOIL uregulirovali spor po 'Turgai Petroleum' [PetroKazakhstan and Lukoil have regulated their dispute over Turgai Petroleum]" *Today.kz*, 24 August
Tovkailo, M. (2012) "Propusk na shel'f [Admission to the shelf]" *Vedomosti*, 3 August
Tret'yakov, P. (2015) "Kitaiskie investory ne speshat vkhodit' v rossiiskie aktivy [Chinese investors are in no haste to acquire Russian equity]" *Vedomosti*, 5 May
Tutushkin, A. (1995) "'LUKoil' stal liderom mezhdunarodnogo proekta v Azerbaidzhane [Lukoil becomes the leader of an international project in Azerbaijan]" *Kommersant*, 14 November 1995, p.9
Tutushkin, A. (1996a) "LUKOIL metit territorii benzokolonkami [Lukoil marks territories with petrol pumps]" *Kommersant*, 11 July 1996, p.9
Tutushkin, A. (1996b) "Vagit Alekperov: My ne khotim teryat' svyaz' s gosudarstvom [Vagit Alekperov: We do not want to lose our ties to the government]" *Kommersant*, 6 February 1996, p.10
Tutushkin, A. (1999) "Vagit Alekperov: 'Esli by ne Lukoil…' [Vagit Alekperov: 'If not for Lukoil…']" *Vremya MN*, 5 November

Tutushkin, A. (2000) "Zashchita Alekperova [Alekperov's defence]" *Vedomosti*, 9 June

Tutushkin, A. (2003) "Interv'yu: Vagit Alekperov, prezident neftyanoi kompanii 'Lukoil' [Interview: Vagit Alekperov, president of the oil company Lukoil]" *Vedomosti*, 20 June

Tutushkin, A. (2004) "Interv'yu: Vagit Alekperov, prezident NK 'Lukoil' [Interview. Vagit Alekperov, president the oil company Lukoil]" *Vedomosti*, 23 June

Tutushkin, A. (2008) "'U menya prochnoe sovetskoe vospitanie', – Vagit Alekperov, prezident 'Lukoila' ['I have a solid Soviet upbringing', says Vagit Alekperov, Lukoil's president]" *Vedomosti*, 1 September

Tutushkin, A., Ivanitskaya, N. and Kramnets, G. (2007) "'Lyudi ne dolzhny boyat'sya' ['People should not be scared']" *Vedomosti*, 10 October

Tutushkin, A. et al. (2004) "Putin dal dobro. Na investitsii ConocoPhillips v aktsii 'LUKOILa' [Putin approved. Of ConocoPhillips's investments in Lukoil shares]" *Vedomosti*, 23 July

US Congress (02/08/2017) *Countering America's adversaries through Sanctions Act* (Washington, DC: Congress of the United States.)

US Department of the Treasury (2018) *Report to Congress Pursuant to Section 241 of the Countering America's Adversaries Through Sanctions Act of 2017 Regarding Senior Foreign Political Figures and Oligarchs in the Russian Federation and Russian Parastatal Entities* (Washington, DC: US Dept of the Treasury)

Upstream (1997) "Russians shift on Caspian carve-up" *Upstream*, 25 October

Upstream (1998a) "Lukoil's boss bows to the Kazakhs" *Upstream*, 24 January

Upstream (1998b) "Caspian Sea thaw" *Upstream*, 31 January

Upstream (2001) "Lukoil eyes Baku-Ceyhan stake" *Upstream*, 26 December

Upstream (2010) "Lukoil, CNPC talk team up" *Upstream*, 28 September

Useinov, A. (2001) "Diskussiya o truboprovodakh [A discussion on pipelines]" *Vremya novostei*, 16 November, p.2

Useinov, A. (2002) "'Bol'she blagozhelatel'nosti, bol'she dobrososedstva'. Geidar Aliev opyat' stal drugom Rossii ['More goodwill, more good-neighbourliness'. Heydar Aliev is again friends with Russia]" *Vremya novostei*, 24 January, p.2

Vahtra, P. and Liuhto, K. (2004) *Expansion or exodus? – Foreign operations of Russia's largest corporations.* Electronic Publications of Pan-European Institute. 8/2004. (Turku, Finland: Turku School of Economics and Business Administration)

Vandenko, A. (1999) "Prezident Ukrainy Leonid KUCHMA: Ya 38 let zhenat na russkoi, o chem nikogda ne zhalel [Ukraine's president Leonid Kuchma: I've been married to a Russian woman for 38 years, and never regretted]" *Komsomol'skaya Pravda*, 29 September

Vardul', N. (1995) "Azartna lyubaya igra v karty. Osobenno v geograficheskie [Any card game is a game of chance. Especially a geography game]" *Kommersant-Vlast'*, 29 August 1995, p.12

Vedomosti (1999) "Zolotaya reviziya [Golden revision]" *Vedomosti*, 15 November

Vedomosti (2002a) "Baku-Dzheikhan postroyat bez Rossii [Baku-Ceyhan will be built without Russia]" *Vedomosti*, 17 April

Vedomosti (2002b) "Pogovorili [Someone had a chat]" *Vedomosti*, 12 April

Vedomosti (2005) "Interv'yu: Vagit Alekperov, prezident NK 'LUKOIL' [Interview: Vagit Alekperov, president of the oil company Lukoil]" *Vedomosti*, 11 July

Vedomosti (2012) "Vkrattse [In brief]" *Vedomosti*, 4 June

Victor, D.G., Hults, D.R. and Thurber, M.C. (ed.) (2012) *Oil and Governance. State-owned Enterprises and the World Energy Supply* (Cambridge: Cambridge University Press)

Vin'kov, A., Rubanov, I. and Sivakov, D. (2011) "Zametit' korovu v korovnike [To notice the cow in the cowshed]" *Ekspert*, 28 March 2011, pp.36–44

Vin'kov, A. et al. (2004) "Tsena bezdeistviya [The cost of doing nothing]" *Ekspert*, 11 October, pp.38–43

Vinogradova, O. (2003) "Kozyrnaya karta uzbekskogo gaza [The trump card of Uzbek gas]" *Neftegazovaya vertikal'*, 6 December 2003

Vinogradova, O. (2010) "Total'nyi kontrol' pridet vmeste s zakonom o nefti [Total control will come with the Law on oil]" *Neftegazovaya vertikal'*, pp.52–57

Vinogradova, O. (2011) "Nastuplenie na Chernoe more [An offensive on the Black Sea]" *Neftegazovaya vertikal'*, pp.70–74

Weaver, C., Hille, K. and Seddon, M. (2018) "US imposes toughest Russian sanctions to date" *The Financial Times*, 6 April

Yakovleva-Ustinova, T. (2004) "Interv'yu. Andrei Gaidamaka, nachal'nik upravleniya investitsionnogo analiza i otnoshenii s investorami LUKOILa: 'My vynuzhdeny izobretat' novye transportnye skhemy' [Interview. Andrei Gaidamaka, head of the Department for investment analysis and investor relations in Lukoil: 'We have to devise new transport plans']" *Kommersant*, 26 October 2004, p.20

Yergin, D. (2012 (1993)) *The Prize. The epic quest for oil, money and power* (London/ New York: Simon & Schuster)

Yermakov, V. (2001) *New Russian oil taxes: A World of the Second Best?* Cambridge Energy Research Associates Decision Brief. (Cambridge, MA: Cambridge Energy Research Associates)

Zagorodnaya, E. (2003) "Vagit Alekperov: 'My gotovy k tomu, chtoby dinamichno razvivat'sya' [Vagit Alekperov: 'We are ready for dynamic development']" *Izvestiya*, 26 June 2003, p.7

Zotova, E. (2008) "Zapasnoi platsdarm Lukoila. Ekspansiya za rubezh – edinstvennaya vozmozhnost' razvitiya dlya negosudarstvennykh neftegazovykh kompanii [Lukoil's reserve base. Expanding abroad is the only possibility to develop for non-state oil and gas companies]" *Business & FM*, 25 January 2008

Zudin, A.Yu. (2013) "Biznes i gosudarstvo v Rossii: opyt primeneniya podkhoda Norta-Uollisa-Vaingasta. Stat'ya 1. Etapy razvitiya rossiiskikh biznes-assotsiatsii [Business and the state in Russia: an attempt at applying the approach of North-Wallis-Weingast. Article 1. Stages in the development of Russian business associations", *Obshchestvennye nauki i sovremennost'*, 2013 (2): 15–31

6 The oil industry
Transneft and pipeline transport

In this chapter, we return to a close state–company relationship characterised by considerable informality. Transneft, the oil pipeline monopoly in Russia, had a close relationship with the state from the beginning, and was a readily available tool for foreign policy purposes. Its relationship with the state is characterised more by continuity than by change. But still, there is a difference between the 1990s and the 2000s. In the first period studied here, the state–company relationship was characterised by informality and personal relations, with institutional and company development suffering. With a more formal relationship, and improved state access to Transneft, there is more modernisation – albeit not necessarily with an overall aim of improving effectiveness. This chapter shows how improved state access to Transneft gave the company, and indirectly the state, access to oil producers' resources. In this respect, it was central to state capacity in the oil industry. With respect to foreign policy, Transneft's priority was control over export pipelines and minimisation of reliance on non-Russian transit pipelines. With improved state control of Transneft in the 2000s, maximum control of export became a central priority in Russia's foreign economic policy.

Pipeline transport of oil

Pipelines are natural monopolies. Their economies of scale and high investment costs create high barriers to entry for newcomers. Most often, they are owned and operated by one oil producing company or a consortium of producers, for whom the pipeline forms part of an integrated chain from production to markets (Dodsworth et al., 2002; Stevens, 2009, p.18). In contrast, Transneft started as an integrated pipeline system and has remained a pipeline company only, with a formalised monopoly on oil transport by pipeline. Russian pipelines owned and used by one company only, such as feeder pipelines for refineries, are excepted and may have private ownership.

Transneft (1993–) is the world's largest oil pipeline company. Its pipelines extend more than 68,000 km, and it currently transports around 83 per cent of all oil produced in Russia. The main quality exported through its system is the blend Urals.[1] Transneft employs 114,000 people, and its turnover in 2018 was 854 billion rubles. In 2018, it was number 12 on the list of Russian companies by turnover (RBK, 2018).

The break-up of the Soviet Union and Soviet legacies

Crude and oil product transport in the Soviet Union was effectuated by Glavtransneft, the Directorate for Oil Transport and Deliveries. By 1991, it controlled an extensive and completely integrated 94,000 km pipeline network (Transneft, 2014b). While the Soviet oil industry disintegrated, Glavtransneft remained intact. Glavtransneft's management had few options to develop the organisation at the time. As oil production declined, by 1990 the pipeline system was operating below capacity (Gustafson, 2012, pp.83–84). Glavtransneft owned and sold the oil in the pipelines (Gustafson, 2012, p.82). Amid perestroika and reform, the regulated domestic oil prices increased more slowly than purchase prices. With low demand and a selling price below the buying price, Glavtransneft ran up debts. The entity was too weak to serve as a platform for a quest for market power along the lines of Gazprom (Gustafson, 2012, pp.83–84).

The head of Glavtransneft and Deputy Minister for Oil, Valerii Chernyaev, therefore refrained from taking control of large-scale oil trading, staying out of the battle for control and markets in the oil industry. Chernyaev, who stayed on as head of post-Soviet Transneft (*Neft' i Kapital*, 2004c), instead introduced a standard tariff for Transneft's services, serving oil producers on a neutral basis. Moreover, Transneft no longer owned the oil in the pipelines. The process was quick, finalised in late 1991, and in effect from 1992 (Gustafson, 2012, p.84). This was a significant change to the institutional framework, which altered Transneft's role in the transportation of crude oil. Paradoxically, by ceasing to act as an intermediary in the oil market, Transneft retained a major role as oil transporter and thereby maintained a stability. In the turmoil affecting Russia's oil industry at the time, this was a lesser change. A year later in November 1992, the state of affairs was preserved for the future when Transneft, still a loosely integrated association of pipeline enterprises was formalised as state property. Transneft was split off from the oil product pipelines, which turned into the wholly state-owned Transnefteprodukt (Decree No. 1403, 1992). In August 1993, Transneft was reorganised as a wholly state-owned shareholding company, and a de facto monopoly "for the duration of the prohibition on private oil pipeline transport" (Government Resolution No. 810, 1993). In this way, Transneft remained a state-owned monopoly, separate from the new oil companies that would become vertically integrated corporations. The Soviet legacy in oil pipeline transport was therefore a state-owned 48,000 km de facto monopoly (Transneft, 2014b).[2] With a natural monopoly, many actors will tend to favour the status quo. However, had the endeavour to create one integrated company in the oil industry succeeded, like it did in the gas industry, the pipeline monopoly would have been its backbone.

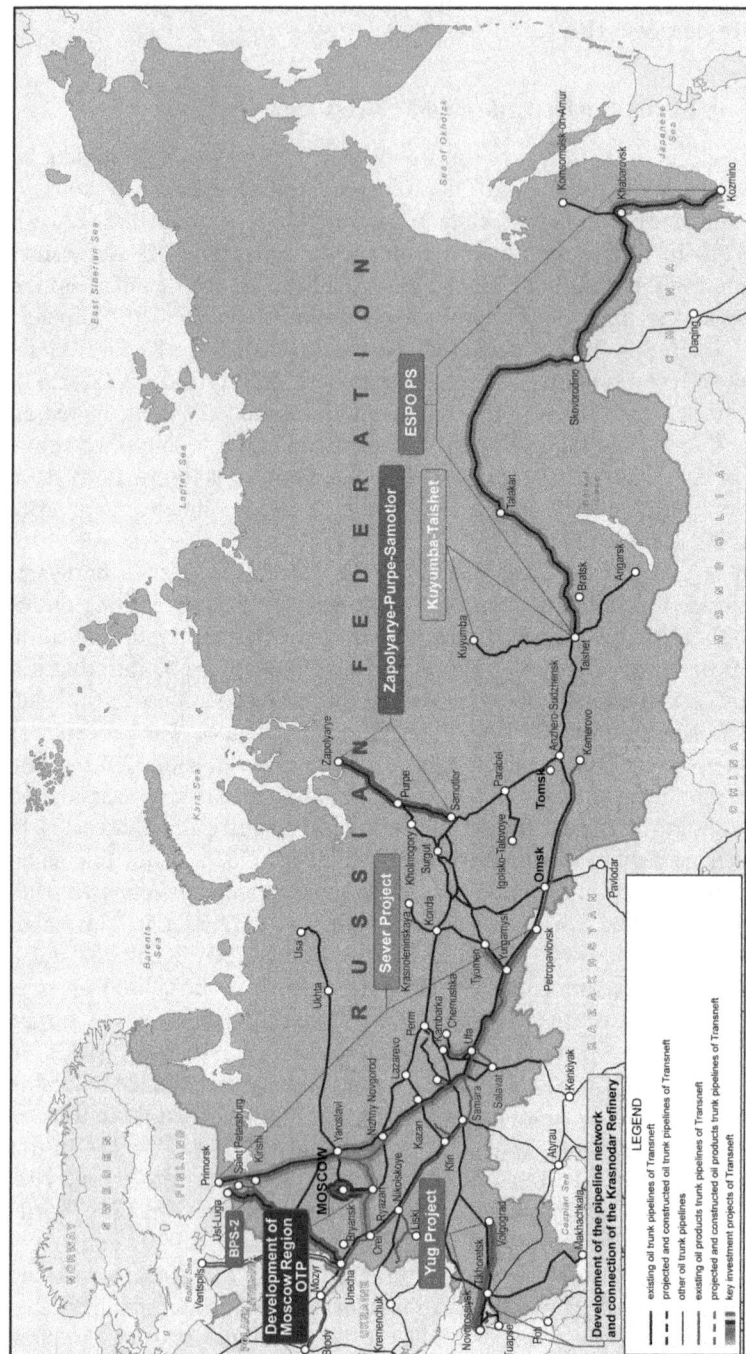

Figure 6.1 Map of oil pipelines of Transneft. (c) Transneft. Printed with permission.

Keeping afloat and muddling through

Transneft's services were essential for the Russian oil industry. Amidst industry restructuring, nobody supported lifting the moratorium on private pipelines. Transneft's conditions and tariffs were the same for everyone. It brought oil to market, and kept companies and the state budget afloat. Meanwhile, the tariffs gave Transneft a predictable income. There was little need to build pipelines between 1985 and 1999. Pipeline capacity was reduced as demand contracted. Older pipelines were repaired.

A dedicated professional, Chernyaev had succeeded his father in Glavtransneft in 1980. Externally, Chernyaev's personal friendship with Prime Minister Chernomyrdin protected Transneft's position (Verezemskii, 1998b). Internally, Chernyaev demanded and enforced complete loyalty throughout Transneft's regional subsidiaries (Verezemskii, 1998b). The subsidiaries were financed by the basic ruble tariff. The top management controlled Transneft's income from a temporary hard-currency surcharge on tariffs, introduced in 1993 (Verezemskii, 1998b). This was intended to cover pipeline repairs. A preference for repairs over replacement went hand in hand with the development of an affiliated repair organisation, lavishly furnished with imported equipment and controlled by Chernyaev's son (Smirnov, 1998; Verezemskii, 1998b). The surcharge extracted rent from the oil companies, and directed a share of it towards pipeline maintenance. In this way, Transneft's central position in the oil industry was used also for private gain.

By early 1996, oil company managers were impatient with the no longer very temporary surcharge. However, afraid of upsetting the status quo, they refrained from making an open complaint (Smirnov, 1998). The managers were not alone. Government ministers, too, were irked by Transneft's wealth, wanting a greater share of the rents from what was, after all, a state-owned company (Verezemskii, 1998b). In order to force Transneft to share rents, the Fuel and Energy Ministry tried to reduce the hard-currency surcharge. To this end, it obtained a government order supposed to make Chernyaev choose between his posts as Transneft's Board Chairman and its head (Government Resolution No. 1333, 1997). Prime Minister Chernomyrdin signed the order, but allowed it to remain dormant, protecting Chernyaev (Verezemskii, 1998b). With such discretionary regulation by the prime minister, central state organisations could not implement formal institutions. Transneft was by now a rather autonomous entity.

Even as oil pipeline transport came through the oil industry privatisation process largely unaffected, the latter stages had some impact on Transneft and Transnefteprodukt. In April 1995, the state authorised the creation of privileged, non-voting shares in these companies (Decree No. 327, 1995). These shares would be distributed among employees, and give them a generous share of profits. Transneft's statutes reserved 10 per cent of the annual profits for the privileged shares, to be paid out before dividends on ordinary, state-held shares (Transneft, 2014a). Failure to heed this obligation would convert the privileged shares into ordinary, voting shares, thereby diluting state control.

200 The oil industry: Transneft

By 1995, many a company management had lost control first over subsidiaries, or a minority of the shares, and subsequently over the entire company. State ownership was no guarantee against such developments, as seen in Chapters 3 and 4. One may approach what happened next as the Transneft management's effort to avoid losing insider control in a gradual, hostile privatisation (Verezemskii, 1998a). In the process, they maintained their own control over Transneft and its rent streams, as opposed to government control.

In the summer of 1996, a privileged share package (25 per cent of all shares) was distributed among Transneft's employees and pensioners. On management orders, shareholder lists remained secret (Verezemskii, 1998a). Then followed a series of secret processes, carried out by Transneft's top 22 managers. There was no consultation with central state organisations. Transneft's subsidiaries first acquired most of the privileged shares from employees, possibly under some pressure. This was not very unusual at the time. The argument was that share consolidation would prevent a hostile takeover and bolster state control (Verezemskii, 1998a). Further consolidation of share packages in the head company would, however, be difficult to accomplish within the law. The shares were instead consolidated by another affiliate, which in turn sold most of them to a private holding company (Verezemskii, 1998a). The holding company, in which Chernyaev appears to have held a significant stake, had been established by Transneft's managers for that purpose (Verezemskii, 1998a). Unusually for the mid-1990s, Chernyaev did not give any representative of central state organisations a stake in the private company. Such informal rent sharing with a patron could have shielded the semi-legal share consolidation from investigation.

When oil prices began to fall in early 1997, the revenue shortfall made the state and oil companies less inclined to let Transneft continue to accumulate funds. However, Transneft's management became vulnerable after Chernomyrdin's dismissal in March 1998. Chernyaev was left without friends in government, and there was no informal rent stream tying Transneft to the ruling coalition. By diverting Transneft's informal rent streams away from the ruling coalition, he had breached the informal constraints. When refusing the government access to the company, he had also breached the formal rules. Chernyaev had failed to protect Transneft's autonomy. Sergei Kirienko's government, in place in April, acted resolutely. In late May, Chernyaev and another manager were dismissed, and Transneft ordered to conduct an audit to international standards (Government Resolution No. 512, 1998). Chernyaev was replaced by a former colleague of Kirienko's from Nizhnii Novgorod, Dmitrii Savelev (Sokolov, 1999). Savelev proceeded to change Transneft's auditor, who had participated in the transfer of privileged shares to the private holding company (*Neft' i Kapital*, 1998; Verezemskii, 1998a). The scandal broke and started a series of lawsuits. In the end, Transneft employees could not retrieve their shares, and the state and the new Transneft management could not reverse the share consolidation and sale (*Neft' i Kapital*, 2004h). In the absence of a solution in favour of the state, the next years brought protracted conflict over the issue of annual dividends to the privileged shareholders.

Trade collapse and system break-up

Transneft lost control of oil pipelines outside Russia, but the system continued to function as an integrated one (Siddiky, 2012, p.72). The difference was that Russia depended on transit to reach established markets. The main route was the 4,000 km Druzhba pipeline system. It crossed Belarus, Ukraine, Latvia and Lithuania, and extended into Poland, Germany, the Czech Republic, Slovakia and Hungary, taking 30 per cent of Russian oil exports to Europe. The three largest ports for Russian oil, Ventspils, Klaipėda and Odesa, were now abroad. Only the fourth largest, Novorossiisk on the Black Sea, was in Russia. Russia was in turn a transit country for oil from Azerbaijan and Kazakhstan to old customers in Ukraine and Belarus, and to Europe. In contrast, Transnefteprodukt's oil product pipelines were of lesser significance. Transnefteprodukt's grid was developed for fuel supplies to Soviet troops at the Union's western borders (*Neft' i Kapital*, 2003e). Therefore, it did not extend far beyond Russia's post-Soviet borders, and played an insignificant role in export. Transnefteprodukt's share of domestic oil products transport was low, too.

Bargaining power now shifted to transit state governments, which had become owners of a monopoly (Stevens, 2009, p.2). Transit pipelines were not regulated according to any overarching jurisdiction, and host governments held the key to continued operation. Post-Soviet host governments negotiated over transit terms, like tariffs, and saw pipelines as sources of rent.

The Russian elite gradually came to see Russia's own transit dependence as a problem. With relatively low oil prices and export volumes, oil companies were reluctant to invest in new export pipelines. Established routes are always more cost efficient than new ones. As transit fees rose, so did Russian discontent. On some routes, especially the Baltic branch of Druzhba and the Lysychansk route, where the pipeline crossed Ukraine en route to Novorossiisk, transit fees increased more quickly than in other places. Significantly, a Lysychansk bypass was discussed from 1993 (*Neft' i Kapital*, 2004i).

Throughout the 1990s, around 24 per cent of Russian sea bound oil export was shipped out of Ventspils (Khikmatov, 2001). The idea of a Russian export route, a Baltic Pipeline System (BPS), originated around 1994. Different proposals were supported by Transneft, Russian companies, IOCs and regional authorities (Rutland, 1999, p.169; Pynnöniemi, 2008, pp.196–199; Zimin, 2012, pp.224–225). But the IOCs were reluctant to rely on Transneft and preferred to wait (Ivanov, 1997; *Neft' i Kapital*, 2004b). Regional rivalry over routes and ports also delayed development (Gustafson, 2012, pp.244–245). The project moved forward from late 1996 (Azarova, 1997; Government Resolution No. 1325, 1997), but stalled until it received a new impulse in April 1998. Amid Russian protests over the situation for Latvia's Russian population, Latvia increased its oil transit fees. In retaliation, the Russian government asked oil companies to reduce their export through Ventspils (Sysoev and Gankin, 1998; *Neft' i Kapita*l, 2004e). The prospect of BPS became a tool for pressuring Latvia.

From 1995, transit relations with Belarus were regulated in the Russia–Belarus Customs Union. This was far from a comprehensive and detailed document, but rather a political settlement intended to relieve Belarus of some of the pressure of its chronic energy crisis and mounting oil and gas debts to Russia (Markus, 1995; 1996). The Customs Union exempted Belarus from Russian oil export duties, but obliged it to return 85 per cent of its oil products' export duty to Russia. Belarus failed to comply (Yafimava, 2011, p.250). The Belarusian refineries imported 19 million tonnes of Russian crude oil annually, paying the Russian domestic price and no duties. Their refined oil products were re-exported to Europe. Most Russian oil producers participated in the re-export business. They gained access to refinery capacity, in short supply in Russia, and they paid the lower Belarusian export duties. These duties supported the Belarusian budget. This "unique system of sharing of oil rents" was an informal institution that de facto undermined the Customs Union (Balmaceda, 2012, p.151). By the 2000s, this Russian subsidy annually transferred around four billion US$ to Belarus. Oil products from Belarus undercut the price of Russian oil products in the European market.

In transit from the Caspian Basin, Transneft was the monopolist. Preserving this position as production there expanded became a goal of Russia's foreign policy, and of Transneft, with the additional aim of maximising control over resource development in the region (Fuller, 1995).

In relation to Azerbaijan, Russia would have a hard time in maintaining transit control. Azerbaijan's priority of relations with Turkey, its distrust of Russia after the war in Nagorno-Karabakh, and its openness to IOCs contributed to its search for alternatives to Russian transit. To Russia, any oil transit routes from the Caspian not on Russian territory threatened Transneft's pursuit of maximum control. It was therefore paramount to secure the early oil stream for Transneft's system and export from Novorossiisk (Bolukbasi, 1998, p.404). In Azerbaijan's effort to balance between Russia and Turkey, in 1995 two existing routes were selected for early oil from its new fields in the Caspian Sea, Baku–Novorossiisk and Baku–Supsa, on Georgia's Black Sea coast. A year later, Baku–Tbilisi–Ceyhan (BTC) emerged as the preferred route of both Azerbaijan and Turkey for the primary new export pipeline (Bolukbasi, 1998, p.405). Its advantage was in avoiding Russia. Lukoil's participation in the project was important, as it enabled Azerbaijan to balance also Russia's interests somewhat.

Transneft continued to pursue maximum control on export routes from the Caspian, in attempts to spoil the emerging consensus around the BTC as an export route. The early oil transit agreement for Baku-Novorossiisk stipulated an annual export of 2.5 million tonnes each by the State Oil Company of Azerbaijan (SOCAR) and Azerbaijan International Operating Company (AIOC) until 2007. Instability in Chechnya regularly disrupted this transit (Romanova, O. et al., 1997; Useinov and Klasson, 1999a; Useinov and Tutushkin, 1999). From SOCAR's point of view, the route was not sufficiently reliable. On its side, Transneft demanded unrealistically high guarantees for throughput, minimum 12 million tonnes per annum (tpa), to make the construction of a bypass economically viable. AIOC and SOCAR's combined exports stood at around 7.4 million tonnes at the time (Osetinskaya, 1999).

Kazakhstan, too, prioritised the development of alternative export routes. Transneft responded slowly to Kazakhstan's need for increased capacity (Nazarbaev, 1997; Embassy Astana, 2008), including on Kazakhstan's main export route, Atyrau–Samara (Babali, 2009). Kazakhstan developed alternatives as production increased. Crude was shipped across the Caspian Sea to Iran for swapping,[3] or to Baku and by pipeline to Supsa on the Black Sea. From 1997, Kazakhstan and China also pursued contact over the project of a pipeline that could bring Kazakh oil to China.

However, Kazakhstan's main new export route was to be the Caspian pipeline, intended to bring oil from Tengiz and Kashagan, both supergiant[4] fields, to Novorossiisk on Russia's Black Sea shore. Kazakhstan, Oman, and Russia were the original partners from 1992. Their plan was to attract Chevron, which held the Tengiz license, to join and take on a considerable financial role, in excess of its proposed share of pipeline equity (Bolukbasi, 1998, p.406). In the initial agreements, Transneft was designated pipeline operator, but it was unenthusiastic about the prospect of having to operate a pipeline under consortium control. Its refusal to allocate priority transit quotas to any oil from Kazakhstan on the Atyrau–Samara route added another brake on the further development of Tengiz. In return, Chevron put its participation and finance for CPC on hold in 1995 (Bolukbasi, 1998, p.406). The deadlock was resolved in 1996 when several oil companies joined the CPC along with Chevron (*Neft' i Kapital*, 2005b; *Neftegazovaya vertikal'*, 2016b). This included Lukoil, which appears to have been generally welcomed as a Russian company that could also balance Transneft's position (*Neftegazovaya vertikal'*, 2016b). The consortium remained plagued by internal divisions. Western IOCs, especially Chevron and ExxonMobil, were often on opposite sides of the table from Russia, while Kazakhstan took care not to antagonise Russia.

Financial crisis and reform

Savelev was closely associated with Prime Minister Kirienko, and pursued a tough line with oil companies. After Kirienko's dismissal as Prime Minister in August 1998, few thought Savelev would last long in Transneft. But by refusing to compromise with the previous management over the privileged shares, Savelev discredited his predecessor sufficiently to remain in his position. After his failure to revert the privileged share consolidation, Savelev tried to stop, or at least reduce, payments to the privileged shareholders. He minimised profits. But this reduced dividends to the state, and he was accused of denying the state of revenue (Vodyanova, 1999).

Savelev seized the BPS as an opportunity to improve his standing. He moved it forward to project stage, thus trying to strengthen his position with Evgenii Primakov's (September 1998 to May 1999), and then Sergei

Stepashin's government (May to August 1999). This was only a partial success for Savelev, but it was crucial for BPS. In early 1999, the Primakov government proceeded with plans for two oil ports on the Gulf of Finland, Primorsk and Ust-Luga, and a new pipeline from Kirishi south of St Petersburg, to Primorsk on the north shore of the Bay of Finland (*Delovoi Peterburg*, 1999a; 1999b; Slyusarenko, 1999; SPB *Vedomosti*, 1999). This was the start of the BPS, which would later also include pipeline refurbishment and expansion of existing pipelines from Kirishi back to the producing regions of West Siberia. Transneft followed up with recommendations to reduce transit through post-Soviet states. In a report, Transneft estimated that Russian infrastructure would reduce the transit cost by up to ten US$/tonne (Strel'tsov, 1999). Oil prices were at a historical low point, below 20 US$ a barrel. The estimate assumed that post-Soviet transit fees would remain significantly higher than the cost of Russian transit. But as he was strongly against direct oil company ownership in BPS, Savelev found it difficult to attract finance. Lukoil was particularly reluctant to finance BPS without minority ownership, especially as Transneft would not consider reduced tariffs for prospective consortium members, a widespread industry practice outside Russia (Reznik and Binchuk, 2000).

Then, in September 1999, Savelev was abruptly dismissed by First Deputy Prime Minister Nikolai Aksenenko and Fuel and Energy Minister Viktor Kalyuzhnyi. The newly appointed prime minister, Vladimir Putin, was abroad and not informed. Kalyuzhnyi had made a previous attempt at dismissing Savelev shortly after his own appointment in May, without success. Transneft and the Fuel and Energy Ministry were not in agreement on further pipeline development, with Kalyuzhnyi apparently unhappy about the priority on BPS above all other new projects. The conflict most likely involved many issues, including rent streams. This next turn of events was nevertheless a complete surprise to everyone. Quite unexpectedly, Savelev barricaded himself in his office. The door was allegedly opened with an angle grinder to let the new Transneft president, Semyon Vainshtok, in (*Kommersant-Vlast'*, 1999; Osetinskaya and Velikanov, 1999). The lack of consultation with Putin cost Aksenenko his job when Putin became president a few months later, and Kalyuzhnyi did not last much longer (Bekker, 1999a; Vodyanova, 1999). Savelev in turn stood as a Duma candidate from Nizhnii Novgorod in the December elections, a decision he may have contemplated for some time. He was later accused of economic misconduct (Protsenko, 1998; Chernitskii, 1999; Romanova, L., 1999; Martynov, 2007).

During his year as energy minister (May 1999 to May 2000), Kalyuzhnyi attempted to increase ministry control in the oil industry (Osetinskaya, 2000b). Savelev's dismissal was only part of this. Control of oil export was at stake. On that account, interest towards Kalyuzhnyi's role centred on his relations with Lukoil, especially in light of Lukoil's well-known scepticism towards BPS (Poluektov, 1999; *Vedomosti*, 1999). And predictably enough, a few weeks after Savelev's dismissal, Kalyuzhnyi declared that a bypass of

Chechnya, by now highly prioritised also by Russian companies, had higher priority than BPS (RFE/RL, 1999). However, control of Transneft and its rent streams was not an issue only of which pipelines to build first. There were wider political implications of some significance ahead of the Duma elections in December and the anticipated presidential elections in June 2000 (Bekker, 1999b).[5] Relatively accessible rent streams, like Transneft's, could be used to influence voting (Petrov and Titkov, 1999; Zhulebin, 1999). It is difficult to assess the motives behind this course of events.

The rents connected the central state, regions and companies. At the time, the Fuel and Energy Ministry allocated oil export quotas according to a complicated system, with a multitude of export quotas (Osetinskaya, 2001). Several export quotas financed federal programmes and initiatives directly, in spite of a 1997 presidential decree supposed to end the practice (Davydova, 2000; Osetinskaya, 2000c; Davydova, 2001). The direct finance mechanism undermined budget unity and control. The export quotas, and the rent streams, were under the ministry's control, not that of the cabinet or prime minister. Oil companies received additional export quotas depending on their relations with the minister in question (Stolyarov, 2000). Transneft, meanwhile, set pipeline quotas. In practice, the major oil companies were in charge of different export routes, dividing responsibilities in an oligopolistic manner (Reznik, 2002b). Any changes to this system were fraught with potential conflict on both political and economic accounts.

However, Vainshtok, an experienced Lukoil top manager, got along well with Putin. After his appointment in August 1999, Putin had become a strong supporter of the new oil export routes (Gustafson, 2012, pp.268–269; Marochkin, 2012). In case Vainshtok remained too much an oil company man, Putin appointed two former colleagues, Nikolai Tokarev as Transneft's vice president and Aleksei Miller as chief of the Baltic Pipeline System Corporation responsible for BPS (Government Resolution No. 1325, 1997; Gustafson, 2012, pp.269–270). But Vainshtok turned out to be an efficient advocate of both the Chechnya bypass and the BPS. When Putin became president a few months later, Tokarev became head of the unremarkable state-owned oil company Zarubezhneft.[6] Miller later became the head of Gazprom.

In Transneft, Vainshtok first undertook an inventory of oil in the pipelines, followed by inventories of the transport subsidiaries extending back to 1992 (*Vremya MN*, 1999). Transneft had never conducted inventories. For the first time, it was possible to quantify technical losses in the pipeline system (Samoilova, 2000). Oil companies had long been dissatisfied with Transneft's loss volumes, whether of technical oil – oil used to keep the system going – or just ordinary losses due to faults and theft. The inventory provided the state with better access to information about Transneft's infrastructure. Inventories were a basis for more modern management practices in Transneft. In the months that followed, the new government's changes to export routes and their management further strengthened Transneft as well as the state. The development of BPS was crucial here.

Transit avoidance

Oil prices picked up after the financial crisis, and oil production and export increased. The domestic market was flooded with crude, due to insufficient export capacity. The most cost efficient route was pipeline transport to the oil terminals at Butinge in Lithuania (opened 1999) and Ventspils in Latvia (Paramonov, 2001). But Ventspils operated to capacity. Transport by rail through Estonia and Tallinn port was another important, but expensive option. The Russian government now began to plan for new export routes, developing them in a way that avoided transit and decreased reliance on routes that were perceived to be troublesome. Transit avoidance would reduce transit risks and costs and increase Russia's bargaining power. The government took regional development into account, and aimed to capture more of the transport fees for the Russian state. To the oil companies, cost-efficiency and their own incomes mattered. New pipelines would cost more. Accordingly, the development of new pipelines became an instrument to make Russian oil companies invest more in Russia, and extract more of their resources. The effect on company investment costs was of secondary importance to the government. Developing new pipelines required considerable state capacity for policymaking and regulation in the oil sector. To preserve Transneft's monopoly, the best solution from the state's point of view would be to keep oil companies from owning pipelines. This would underpin their dependence on Transneft for transport services. Transneft was now a source of infrastructural power to the state.

Putin supervised the BPS project in person, and Vainshtok implemented it. He began by resolving the deadlock over its financing. In early 2000, he offered the oil companies stakes in the BPS Corporation, with Transneft holding the majority share (Osetinskaya, 2000a; Reznik and Binchuk, 2000; Gustafson, 2012, pp.269–270). With this ownership model, BPS would be a pipeline consortium like other major pipelines. CPC was the closest example, but not an altogether positive one. Only a few months later, the model was rejected. Transneft took direct charge of BPS, apparently again at Putin's initiative (Sapozhnikov and Ovchinnikov, 2000). Vainshtok then obtained government consent to a surcharge on all its tariffs to finance BPS. It was levied on companies regardless of their eventual use of the pipeline (Osetinskaya, 2000a; IEA, 2002, pp.90, 97). Only strong government support could neutralise the oil company resistance that ensued. The surcharges were paid. Media outlets close to the government condemned criticism of BPS and the surcharge, and presented such criticism as counter to Russia's strategic interests (Inozemtsev, 1999). Nevertheless, oil managers frequently complained about opaque tariff hikes (Druzenko et al., 2002; Oliphant, 2010): the increase in Transneft's operating costs could not fully justify these tariff hikes (IEA, 2002, p.89). However, over the next few years, the rising oil prices cushioned their adjustment to the rising tariffs.

In relation to Ukraine, Transneft promoted projects that would diminish the oil stream through the congested Bosporus Straits, but also jeopardise competing Ukrainian projects. Transneft's preferred route, a connection from the Druzhba system in Hungary to the Croatian oil port Omisalj on the Adriatic Sea (referred to as Druzhba–Adria), called for the reversal of an existing import pipeline from Omisalj to Hungary. It would be reversed and repurposed for Russia's export of Urals to European and global markets (Solov'ev, 2000). Russia first advanced the proposal in late 1996 (Bolukbasi, 1998, p.403). This plan competed with a Ukrainian plan. From 1996, Ukraine sought to develop a pipeline for light Caspian crudes from the Odesa oil terminal to the western Ukrainian hub of Brody. Brody was on the Druzhba system and near Lviv and the Polish border. A pipeline from Odesa to Brody would provide Eastern European markets with an alternative to Urals. The two projects, Druzhba–Adria and Odesa–Brody, competed for capacity in Druzhba, and potentially for markets. When in 2000 Ukraine withdrew initial approval of the Druzhba–Adria plan, Transneft urged the earliest possible construction of the Lysychansk bypass (*Neft' i Kapital*, 2004i). Vainshtok now tried to pressure Ukraine over Druzhba–Adria (Dmitriev, 2000; Aleksandrov and Orlov, 2001). The Ukrainian government refused to budge. In retaliation, the Lysychansk bypass was opened in September 2001. Russian oil transit fell by 43.7 per cent from 48 million tonnes in 2001 to 27.4 million in 2002 (*Neft' i Kapital*, 2004i). On its side, Ukraine completed the Odesa–Brody pipeline in 2001, without any prospects of filling it with oil, as discussed later in this chapter. The Druzhba–Adria plan later failed due to environmental objections in Croatia. Russia relaunched the project again in 2009 and 2013 as part of proposals for deepening energy cooperation with Croatia, but nothing came of this.

On the oil products side, the main pipelines from Russia into Ukraine[7] were transferred to Transnefteprodukt in 1993. Russia would occasionally interrupt deliveries to Ukraine's oil refineries to retaliate when Ukraine siphoned off Russian gas in transit to Europe (Romanova, L., 2000). In addition, Ukrainian refineries suffered from Transnefteprodukt's inferior pipeline maintenance. Rail transport was the only alternative to get oil products to market. This deflated refinery value during privatisation, and Russian companies acquired the refineries on the cheap (Eremenko, 2011). Dependence on Russia in Ukraine's oil products sector increased.

The new coalition

After 2000, Transneft's development was driven by a stronger state. Transneft became more important as a tool of the state, and it was used both to facilitate national development and keep oil companies under control. It represented infrastructural power that compelled oil companies to share rents, and complicated their pursuit of strategies that were in conflict with government policies.

Table 6.1 Selected Transneft proposed and completed pipeline projects in Russia and abroad

Name	Route	Length (km)	Idea floated	Proposal/plan	Construction started	Construction completed	Projected/initial throughput (tpa)	Expanded throughput (year) (tpa)
Chechnya bypass	Sulak–Trudovaya (RF)	312			Dec. 1999	April 2000		
Druzhba–Adria	Százhalombatta (Hungary)–Omisalj (Croatia)	127	1996	2000	NA	NA	NA	
Ukraine (Lysychansk) bypass	Sukhodolnaya–Rodionovskaya (RF)	262	1993	2000	April 2001	Sept. 2001	28 mill.	
Burgas–Aleksandroupolis	Burgas (Bulgaria)–Aleksandroupolis (Greece)	280	1997	1999–2007	NA	NA	35 mill.	50 mill.
BPS-1	Yaroslavl–Kirishi–Primorsk and Primorsk terminal and port (RF)	1300	1993–1994	1996–2000	June 2000	Dec. 2001	12 mill.	50 mill. (2004) 67 mill. (2006) 75 mill. (2009)
BPS-2	Unecha–Ust-Luga/Kirishi refinery and Ust-Luga terminal and port (RF)	998 and 172	2007–2009		June 2009	March 2012	30 mill.	50 mill./12 mill. to Kirishi and 38 mill. for exports
Khar'yaga–Indiga (the Northern Route)	Khar'yaga–Indiga	430	(2002 (Murmansk pipeline) 2003	2005	NA	NA	12 mill.	

Name	Route	Length (km)	Start	Completion	Capacity	Notes
Sever (oil products)	Kstovo (Vtorovo)–Yaroslavl–Kirishi–Primorsk (RF)	1067		May 2008	8.5 mill.	25 mill. (2018), achieved partly by converting crude oil pipelines serving BPS 1&2 to oil products
YUg (diesel)	Syzran–Saratov–Volgograd–Novorossiisk (RF)	1465	2007–2008	2010 Samara–Volgograd delayed to 2023	8.7 mill (plan), actual 2018 capacity 6 mill.	2018 (Volgograd–Novorossiisk)
Purpe–Samotlor	Purpe–Samotlor (RF)	429	2008	March 2010	25 mill.	Oct. 2011
Zapolyar'e–Purpe	Purpe–Zapolyar'e (RF)	490	2010–2011	2012 (plan)	32 mill.	2014–16
VSTO-1	Taishet–Ust-Kut–Lensk–Olekminsk–Aldan–Skovorodino, and Kozmino port (RF)	2694	(1999–2003) 2004–2006	April 2006	30 mill.	50 mill. (2012–14) 80 mill. (to be completed in 2019); Oct. 2009
Skovorodino–China border	Skovorodino–China border (Dzhalinda/Mohe)	64	2009	April 2009	15 mill.	20 mill. (2015) 30 mill. (2017); Sept. 2010

(*Continued*)

Table 6.1 (Cont.)

Name	Route	Length (km)	Idea floated	Proposal/plan	Construction started	Construction completed	Projected initial throughput (tpa)	Expanded throughput (year) (tpa)
VSTO-2	Skovorodino–Blagoveshchensk–Birobidzhan–Khabarovsk–Kozmino, and expansion of VSTO-1 (RF)	2046		2010	Sept 2011	(2014)	20+ mill	50 mill. (to be completed in 2019)
Samsun–Ceyhan	Samsun–Tokat–Ceyhan (Turkey)	550		2008–2012	NA	NA	50 mill.	
Orinoco (Venezuela)				2009	NA	NA		
CPC expansion	Tengiz–Novorossiisk (pumping stations and pipeline repairs) (Kazakhstan–RF)	1510	2001	2008–2010		(2001 for CPC) 2015 for expansion	28.8 mill	67–76 mill.
Baku–Tikhoretsk expansion	Baku–Tikhoretsk (pumping stations and repairs) (Azerbaijan–RF)	1051				(2012)		11 mill
Kuyumba–Taishet	Kuyumba–Taishet			2012–2016		2016	8.6 mill	Possible to 15. mill

Author's compilation based on Transneft's annual reports and webpages
The list is not exhaustive, and does not include investments in the refurbishment of existing pipelines.

By 2001–2002, Russian oil companies faced a capacity deficit on their main export routes. Transneft turned into a source of frustration. Its new pipeline projects developed slowly, while oil companies were not allowed to build their own. They had little influence on route design and development. The allocation of transport volumes to each company was non-transparent and unpredictable (Tutushkin, 2008), and the capacity deficit contributed to opacity. Changes to export administration complicated the situation.

In autumn 2000, a new government commission chaired by Vice Premier Viktor Khristenko took over responsibility for export quota allocation. To improve transparency and government control further, Khristenko proposed to auction off export quotas instead of allocating them (Osetinskaya, 2001). The oil companies protested vigorously (Osetinskaya, 2000d). The idea was postponed after they complained to Prime Minister Kasyanov (Osetinskaya, 2000d; 2001). This conflict placed Transneft in a good position to strengthen its role. In late 2000, with a new energy minister, Aleksandr Gavrin, in place, Transneft succeeded in taking control of the export terminals in Novorossiisk and Tuapse, as a temporary arrangement (Reznik, 2002b). It was also in full control of the new BPS export terminal at Primorsk, due to open only months later. However, in June 2001, the next energy minister, Igor Yusufov, changed export stream management yet again (Chernitskii, 2001b). Transneft was firmly subordinated to the Energy Ministry. Oil companies were marginalised from control over export routes.

In 2002, Lukoil proposed a new pipeline to the Barents Sea, attracting interest from Sibneft, TNK and Yukos (*Neft' i Kapital*, 2002f). The plan was to bring West Siberian crude to Murmansk. Unlike other ports in European Russia, Murmansk could accommodate large tankers for direct exports to North America. Transneft's support was essential to the project (*Neft' i Kapital*, 2002f). Transneft reacted negatively. A private Russian pipeline consortium would infringe on its monopoly. In Transneft's view, the Murmansk project would undermine its possibility of financing new pipelines through special tariffs imposed equally on all customers, because it would provide an example of how to avoid the entire system. Transneft's top management emphasised that all oil companies had equal access to its network. This was only guaranteed if all companies participated. A pipeline that suited the four largest exporters' needs therefore undermined the smaller companies. By extension, letting the four major oil companies, all private, expand their profits and independence could lead to a slippery slope and challenge the current ruling coalition. Transneft's vice president, Sergei Grigorev, accused the participants of attempting to "evade state control", which would lead to "the disintegration of Transneft, a catastrophe for the country [because] the state would inevitably lose control with the oil sector" (*Neft' i Kapital*, 2003f). Vainshtok was also dismissive: "Why would they want a private pipeline?" (*Neft' i Kapital*, 2005a). The issue was settled. Energy Minister Yusufov requested further project elaboration in Transneft, where it was buried (Vin'kov et al., 2004). In late 2005, the project resurfaced as a much shorter and smaller pipeline from Kharyaga in Komi to Indiga on the Barents Sea shore. This project faltered in 2007 due to market changes and Transneft's priority on the East Siberia—Pacific Ocean pipeline (ESPO)[8] (Rosbalt, 2007).[9] Russian oil exporters had to use BPS and the export terminal at Primorsk to reach European and US markets.

The most serious challenges to Transneft's monopoly came from the Murmansk project and from the pipeline proposed by Yukos from Siberia to Daqing in China. In both cases, Transneft promoted alternatives, to Primorsk not Murmansk, and Nakhodka (Kozmino) instead of Daqing, maximising pipeline length on Russian territory (Sim, 2008, p.70). The management made a serious effort to ensure that these would be the last challenges to its monopoly. Vainshtok and other top managers used every occasion to declare that state-owned pipelines guaranteed equal access for all, and served wider industry interests. On this, Transneft had the government's support. In 2002–2003, Mikhail Kasyanov's government (2000–2004) protected Transneft as a matter of principle and to an extent not previously seen (Kanevskaya, 2003). The continued need for a pipeline monopoly was enshrined in the new Energy Strategy (Ministry of Industry and Trade, 2003, p.43). In this context, Sergei Grigoriev's warning against the perils of non-Transneft pipelines served to underline that the government needed Transneft. Like the new oil industry taxation system discussed in Chapter 5, Transneft was a direct level of control for the state. By maintaining the monopoly, the government protected the privileged extraction of rents through Transneft.

But the state did not have complete access to Transneft, and especially not to its rent streams. The most contentious issue remained the dividends on the state-owned ordinary shares. The issue was repeatedly reopened by the conflict over the privileged shares. These were sequestrated, partially or wholly, by the General Procurator several times after 1999. The conflict abated only after most of the privileged shares changed hands in 2001 from Transneft's old management to people closer to the ruling coalition (*Neft' i Kapital*, 2004h). With that problem solved, Vainshtok tried to reduce dividend payments to the state, too, to increase investment. The Audit Chamber protested (Reznik, 2003; *Neft' i Kapital*, 2004k). In turn, government representatives on Transneft's Board argued for re-investing as much of the profit as possible in the company (*Neft' i Kapital*, 2003a). Disagreement among state organisations prolonged the conflict for several years (Prime-TASS, 2006; Transneft, 2006, pp.42–43; 2007, pp.40–41; 2008, pp.26–27).

Even so, Transneft's rent streams were increasingly formalised. Pipeline inventories had quantified the volume of technical oil in the system. It appears to have been Transneft's regular practice to sell this oil, which the oil companies counted as lost. Transneft later claimed that the income derived from sales of technical oil from 2001 was invested in new pipelines (Ivanova et al., 2008). From 2005, it was donated to charity, as discussed on p.222.

In this period, Vainshtok took care to emphasise how Transneft was only a loyal instrument of the state, in statements like "If we are told tomorrow [by state agencies] that [the public lottery] Sportloto will do this [assign export quotas to oil exporters], then it will be that way" (Reznik, 2002a). By placing responsibility for energy policy firmly with the government, Vainshtok understated Transneft's influence, and emphasised the significance of the formal institutional framework. This was supplemented with declarations of personal loyalty to Putin. It became difficult for oil company managers to criticise Transneft.

A foreign energy strategy: Control of transit to Europe

From 2000, the global demand for oil increased, leading to a historic boom in oil prices. Over the years 2000 to 2016, Russia's oil exports increased by an impressive 76 per cent, and that of oil products more than doubled (Analiticheskii Tsentr, 2017b, p.20). For crude oil, the curve was even steeper. Most of the increase took place between 2000 and 2004, when export increased from 145 to 258 million tonnes, including transit from other countries (IEA, 2015). Overall export capacity followed suit, beginning in 2001 with the opening of BPS and Primorsk. Even in the face of considerable competition from rail transport, Transneft retained the bulk of domestic oil transport and crude export within its network, as seen in Table 6.2. This bolstered the monopoly's legitimacy and demonstrated its relevance as state-owned infrastructure.

Export through transit states continued during the export boom. The Druzhba pipeline, the non-Russian ports on the Baltic Sea, and the Odesa terminal were important export routes in the 2000s. In 2003, crude oil export from Primorsk (17.7 million tonnes) was roughly comparable to non-Russian ports on the Baltic Sea (16 million tonnes) (Transneft, 2006, pp.32–33). The same year, 10.8 million tonnes of Russian crude was exported through Odesa and the nearby Pivdennyi[10] terminal on Ukraine's Black Sea coast, compared to 47.7 million tonnes from the more important oil port of Novorossiisk in Russia (Transneft, 2006, pp.32–33). Druzhba, however, was the main export route, taking 73.9 million tonnes of Russia's oil exports to Central European countries (Transneft, 2006, pp.32–33). However, implementation of the policy of transit avoidance began in earnest in the early 2000s. New oil terminals appeared in Russia, and opening more was a prime concern in the Energy Strategy published in 2003 (Ministry of Industry and Trade, 2003, pp.42–43). By 2006, the result was to reduce the importance of other routes, and especially the non-Russian Baltic ports. However, what went largely unnoticed was that transit avoidance in practice undermined another aim of Russia's foreign energy policy, the promotion of a single transport infrastructure with non-discriminatory access in the post-Soviet region (Ministry of Industry and Trade, 2003, pp.42–43). In the post-Soviet context, the pursuit of bypass pipelines under Transneft's control was by a discriminatory, not an integrational endeavour.

The oil industry: Transneft

Table 6.2 Transneft share of Russian crude oil export, 2004–2017

Year	Share
2004	93
2005	91
2006	91
2007	90
2008	89
2009	88
2010	88
2011	88.5
2012	89
2013	88.1
2014	87.6
2015	86.4
2016	85
2017	84

Export through Transneft's pipeline system as share of total export.
Exclusive of oil of non-Russian origin
Author's compilation based on Transneft's annual reports

Russian government spokespeople often said that BPS and Primorsk terminal were not intended to displace existing export routes. Yet in practice, every opportunity was used to mention how BPS and Primorsk could increase Russia's revenue (Vasil'ev and Suchkov, 1999). After BPS opened in December 2001, the emphasis shifted. Ventspils and Butinge's owners came under pressure from Transneft to allow Russian control of export infrastructure at reduced prices. The government now differentiated among export routes according to their share of Russian involvement in ownership (Kravchenko, 2003). This policy was echoed by Transneft's vice president, Sergei Grigorev (Dmitriev, 2003). With time, the emphasis on avoiding transit became increasingly pronounced.

The Latvian and Lithuanian Druzhba branches, with a parallel diesel pipeline, were 66 per cent owned by Ventspils Nafta and 34 per cent by Transnefteprodukt. Ventspils Nafta also owned the Ventspils terminal and a shipping company. When BPS opened, crude export through the Baltic ports fell by about 10 per cent (*Neft' i Kapital*, 2002e). Primorsk was less expensive now, as the oil companies received a rebate on terminal charges in return for their compulsory surcharge payments (Oilcapital.ru, 2002). The next year in 2002, Transneft first reduced, then turned off the flow of crude to Ventspils. Ventspils Nafta's transshipment of crude oil decreased from 15 million tonnes in 2001 to approximately 3 million in 2003 (*Neft' i Kapital*, 2004g). This was first blamed on technical limitations, but later, a lack of Russian capital interest in Ventspils emerged as a rationale for the decision (*Neft' i Kapital*, 2003d; 2005d).

Ventspils now had to rely on oil products. In the 2000s, approximately half of Russia's oil products export was shipped through the diesel pipeline (*Neft' i Kapital*, 2003b; 2007d). Transneft offered to invest more in the branch pipeline in return for 50 per cent of Ventspils Nafta. The Latvian government, which controlled 34 per cent of Ventspils Nafta, found the offer too low (Dmitriev, 2003; *Vedomosti*, 2003; *Neft' i Kapital*, 2006c), and in the end rejected it (*Neft' i Kapital*, 2006h). Russian oil companies like Lukoil, which previously had seen Ventspils Nafta as an attractive terminal, now lost their interest in a minority stake (Pravosudov, 2003).[11] After the Ventspils route was discontinued, more oil was shipped through Butinge, which had a lower throughput capacity of ten million tpa (*Neft' i Kapital*, 2004j). Butinge had been established to import North Sea oil to the Mažeikiu refinery, but refining and exporting Urals from pipeline was more profitable. Lukoil and Yukos were the main suppliers. Yukos obtained a 53.7 per cent stake of Mažeikiu Nafta in mid-2002 (*Neft' i Kapital*, 2002c; 2003c) and had control of forwarding there (Oilcapital.ru, 2002).

As for BPS, its capacity expanded from 12 million tpa in 2001 to 75 million in 2009. This was costly: 460 million US$ was spent on the first and most expensive part of the project (*Neft' i Kapital*, 2002d; 2011d). BPS became a model for transit avoidance also in oil products export. Transnefteprodukt embarked on a new export pipeline in 2003, Sever ("North").[12] Opened in 2007, it delivered oil products to Primorsk and reduced the flow of oil products to Ventspils (*Neft' i Kapital*, 2003e; 2007d; 2012c). By 2006, Primorsk was the largest oil terminal on the Baltic Sea. While only 26 per cent of all goods in the Baltic region were shipped from Russian ports in 2000, this had increased to 55.2 per cent in 2007 and 61.6 per cent in 2015 (Analiticheskii Tsentr, 2017a, p.9). When Transneft terminated its use of Butinge as an oil export route in 2006, a consequence was that the volume of oil exports out of Primorsk jumped from 66 to 74 million tonnes from 2006 to 2007 (Transneft, 2009b, p.30). By 2014, 88.7 per cent of the Russian crude oil exported outside the post-Soviet region was shipped from Transneft's system (Vinogradova, 2015, p.58).

The opening of BPS applied pressure to Belarus, too. When Russia in 2001 withdrew from the bilateral free trade agreement, this increased the pressure, as BPS strengthened Russia's position in the negotiations that followed. The end of transit to Ventspils in 2002 reduced the flow also to Belarus. This affected exports from Lukoil, Surgutneftegaz, Rosneft and Yukos. In a letter to Prime Minister Kasyanov, company heads urged him to keep the route open (Nikolaev, 2003). This had no effect. Alekperov called the abrogation of the free trade agreement "mistaken" (Pravosudov, 2003). However, the free trade arrangement for oil, which shared rents between Belarus and Russian companies, was extended through 2006.

Ukraine's Odesa–Brody pipeline was also completed in 2001 (Balmaceda, 2008, p.92). It offered a bypass of both Transneft and the Bosporus (*Neft' i Kapital*, 2004f), but the Ukrainian government had departed from standard practice and failed to secure oil supply of any kind before it opened. There was little effort to divert existing flows (Balmaceda, 2008, p.93). Azerbaijan and Kazakhstan expressed some interest, but did not commit oil (*Neft' i Kapital*, 2002a; Savushkin, 2003; *Neft' i Kapital*, 2004f). Eastern European refineries were anyway not geared to their lighter qualities, but ran on Urals. A planned connection between Brody and Plock in Poland failed to materialise. In consequence, the main trunk of the Odesa–Brody line stood empty in 2001–2004 (Savushkin, 2003). In 2003, Russia suggested to reverse Odesa–Brody in order to take oil from Druzhba at Brody to the Odesa terminal. The Ukrainian government was against this (Gavrish, 2003; Ignatova, 2003). Reversing the pipeline made some sense to Russian oil companies, especially TNK-BP. But the high cost of reversal accentuated the political overtones in Russia's machinations (*Neft' i Kapital*, 2004d). As a result, a stalemate ensued (Butrin and Sapozhnikov, 2004).

A foreign energy strategy: Control of east–west transit

In the late 1990s, involvement by IOCs in petroleum projects in the Caspian Sea made it harder for Russia to monopolise Caspian transit. However, it did remain a foreign policy priority to establish control over transit routes from the region. Transit route control became part of a strategy to integrate Eurasia and tie the post-Soviet economies closer to Russia (Zhiznin, 2010). However, especially from 2000, Russia's priority of control often undercut integration. In oil transport, the pursuit of transit route dominance pushed post-Soviet states and IOCs to develop non-Russian routes. Kazakhstan aimed to achieve balance in export routes; in practice this meant establishing alternatives to Russian routes. Azerbaijan avoided Transneft wherever possible.

Transneft's domestic monopoly, too, worked to the disadvantage of non-Russian companies. Its fundamental operating principles were not suited to promote industry integration and international cooperation. Russian companies were allocated transport quotas on the basis of their domestic production rates. This was an essential component of Transneft's policy of equal access to the pipelines. As a consequence, non-Russian shippers had lower priority, limiting their access to the best routes. Another drawback of transit through Russia was in Transneft's organisation of oil quality in the pipelines. Transneft did not operate a quality bank. A quality bank arrangement sets a benchmark quality for oil in the pipeline, and shippers of higher quality oil are compensated for reduced oil quality and market price.[13] Without such an arrangement, crude oil of a higher quality improves the oil in the pipeline and contributes to an inflated higher price for lower-grade oil, without compensation. In practice, higher-grade Kazakh and Azeri oil transited by Transneft was discounted (Useinov and Klasson, 1999b). As the price differential was absorbed by Russia, Azeri and Kazakh producers were in effect obliged to share their rents with Transneft. Oil from Kazakhstan was discounted by up to 10 per cent by the time it had reached Europe (Dodsworth et al., 2002, pp.10, 24).

Transneft's relations with Azerbaijan were particularly fraught. In the second half of the 1990s, Transneft declined to accommodate Azerbaijan's requests for a bypass of Chechnya on the Baku–Novorossiisk pipeline. Eventually, in 2000, Transneft built the bypass (Osetinskaya, 1999), but then refused to expand pipeline capacity to meet Azerbaijan's needs. Transneft made expansion contingent on Azerbaijan's commitment of large volumes to the pipeline. Such a guarantee would threaten the viability of the BTC project, which was under development, and Azerbaijan predictably rejected the terms (Sborov, 2000). Transit relations continued to deteriorate (Mishin, 2000; *Vedomosti*, 2000), and Azerbaijan exported less oil through Novorossiisk than previously agreed (Buyantseva, 2000; Buyantseva and Osetinskaya, 2000). The construction of the BTC pipeline proceeded to plan. As discussed in Chapter 5, Lukoil would have liked Russia to participate in BTC and to retain its stake in the pipeline consortium, but failed to muster support for the idea, both with the government and in Transneft.

Kazakhstan, in contrast, could to a certain extent develop new routes while maintaining established ones. Around the turn of the century, Kazakhstan's oil production was rising by 10 per cent annually (*Neft' i Kapital*, 2002a). But even as Transneft made more of a priority of maintaining good relations with Kazakhstan than with Azerbaijan, Kazakhstan's government found it complicated to develop new routes without antagonising Russia. In 2000, Kazakhstan still had two main oil export routes, Atyrau–Samara and tanker freight to Baku and the Baku–Supsa pipeline to the Black Sea. As production increased, most was transported through Russia, by rail or pipeline to the Baltic and Black Seas. By 2000, the expansion of the Atyrau–Samara pipeline had become a matter of urgency to Kazakhstan. Insufficient export capacity would soon slow down oil industry development. Additives and extra maintenance increased capacity to 15–17 million tpa, but to increase it to 25–30 million tpa, Atyrau–Samara would need investment and expansion. To ensure Russia's goodwill, Kazakhstan delayed development of the China pipeline project as long as Yukos's Angarsk–Daqing pipeline project was on the table in 2000–2003 (*Neft' i Kapital*, 2006f). If the Angarsk–Daqing project were realised, instead of Transneft's proposed alternative to Nakhodka, there was a remote possibility that Kazakhstan could develop a feeder pipeline to this project. Its own China pipeline project therefore competed with Angarsk–Daqing. But in 2002, Russia preliminarily agreed to expand Atyrau–Samara. However, Transneft then made implementation contingent on Kazakhstan's reserving a corresponding volume for the route (Vainshtok, 2000; Vin'kov and Rubanov, 2006). If Kazakhstan had complied, that would have complicated the pursuit of other routes. Kazakhstan proceeded to develop non-Russian routes, especially from 2003 the China pipeline project, establishing a project organisation and developing a plan in 2004.[14] KazTransOil, a subsidiary of KazMunayGaz, proposed that the Russian oil companies with suitable production, Yukos, Lukoil and Rosneft, could join the project (*Neft' i Kapital*, 2003g). They stayed out.

Kazakhstan's first new route, the Caspian Pipeline, ran into a string of problems. Construction costs soared, and the consortium members issued additional loans to CPC. The pipeline opened in 2001 with maximum throughput of 20 million tpa. A planned expansion would raise throughput to 67 million tpa, of which 50 million tonnes would come from Kazakhstan, and 17 from Russia (*Neft' i Kapital*, 2002b). In light of the CPC members' different interests, in 2000 they decided to retain joint operatorship and thereby collective command and control (*Neft' i Kapital*, 2002f). As a result, Russia lost control over pipeline tariffs. Transneft remained the operator, but it was a technical function (Reznik, 2000b). It had also lost control of the CPC terminal's operations to Lukoil (Reznik, 2000a). Now, Russia and Transneft made expansion contingent on a tariff increase and reduced interest rates on the consortium members' loans to the consortium. Russia accused the oil producing CPC members of using low tariffs (paid by themselves as customers) and high interest rates (paid to themselves as lenders) to prevent the consortium from accumulating taxable profits in Russia (Mazneva, 2007; Surzhenko, 2007). From this point of view, the Russian state lost a revenue source. To get the point across to the consortium members, Transneft stalled the expansion process.

In another power demonstration, Transneft stalled the process of connecting the Caspian pipeline to its own system inside Russia. The intention was to construct a connection, the Tikhoretsk–Kropotkin leg, which would maximise capacity utilisation, giving Russian producers access to the Caspian pipeline. Beginning in 2000, Transneft refused to finance the leg from its own pocket. In turn, Russian producers refused to pay Transneft's suggested surcharge to fund the connection. The connection was not built, and CPC operated below capacity in the first years of operation (Druzenko et al., 2002). By 2004, Russian producers in need of additional export capacity would use an expensive rail connection instead (Aleksandrovich, 2001; *Neft' i Kapital*, 2005b; 2005c).

Vainshtok openly campaigned against the Caspian pipeline (Chernitskii, 2001a; Dmitriev, 2002a). If successful, the Caspian pipeline would show that it was possible and attractive to develop private pipelines in Russia. It operated a quality bank, and was already a success in the competition for export of light Kazakh crude, at a time when higher-grade producers were moving away from Transneft's pipelines (Reznik, 2001). But while CPC was a commercial success, from the Russian government's view it was a loss-making consortium that did not pay taxes (*Neft' i Kapital*, 2004a). It was compared with BPS, which finished on time and budget (Bekker, 2002). In this light, Vainshtok's campaign raised the stakes for Russian oil companies in search of independent control of export routes.

The new stability: A stronger monopoly

The Yukos affair strengthened state support for Transneft, and Transneft's position in general. Its leverage over oil companies increased. The remaining companies challenged the institutional framework less. Yukos had been a vocal opponent of the pipeline monopoly. It had tried to undermine it when pursuing the Angarsk–Daqing route for export to China, and by participating in the Murmansk project. Its equity and interest in Mažeikiu Nafta posed a challenge for BPS. A Russian equity stake in the terminal undermined one argument for BPS, namely, the aim of establishing Russian control over export infrastructure.

The monopoly was further strengthened in 2007 when Transnefteprodukt was reorganised as a Transneft subsidiary. The merger took place against Vainshtok's wish (*Neft' i Kapital*, 2008b). Transneft received 16,400 km of oil product trunk pipeline in Russia, and pipelines in Ukraine, Belarus and Kazakhstan (Transnefteprodukt, 2009, p.23). As a result, Transneft in Russia resembled an updated version of Glavtransneft, and it increased in relevance as a foreign policy tool.

The state now demanded better access to Transneft. In 2001, the Finance Ministry had made it obligatory for state-owned companies to adopt international financial reporting standards (IFRS) by 2005. This contributed to transparency, and institutionalisation, of Transneft's informal rent stream. Transneft began publishing annual reports under IFRS, the first in 2005. Transparency entailed sharing some information on what happened to the proceeds from the sale of technical oil. From 2005, it appeared that this rent stream was donated to charity. More transparency went hand in hand with changes to formal rent streams. In 2005, the Federal Agency for Property Management, Rosimushchestvo, prevented dividends being paid for 2004 to force an increase over the 2003 level (Fokina, 2006). In effect, it now claimed a greater share of Transneft's rents for the state. Transneft was left without a functioning Board for over six months as a consequence (Fokina, 2006). Rosimushchestvo backed down at the last minute to avoid a situation in which the privileged shares would be converted into ordinary shares, and dilute state control (Fokina, 2006).

Transneft now began to minimise profit by retaining much of it in its subsidiaries (Derbilova, 2006; Fokina, 2006). The argument was that the subsidiaries owned the pipelines, but the aim was clearly to reduce dividends (Surzhenko and Reznik, 2008). This irritated Rosimushchestvo, which again found dividends payments to the state short of target (*Neft' i Kapital*, 2004h). Their irritation may have grown when they learned that the privileged shares were most likely held by people close to the ruling coalition. However, in the struggle with Rosimushchestvo, Transneft had support from the Ministry for Economic Development and the Industry and Energy Ministry. Transneft prevailed, and began in 2006 to channel more of its profits into business development (Transneft, 2008; Bloomberg/*The Moscow Times*, 2009; Transneft, 2009b; 2010; 2011b). As seen in Table 6.3, in the following years the state showed less interest in extracting higher dividends from the company. Relations with the minority shareholders, too, seemed to take a turn for the ordinary. More of the privileged shares were also traded on the Moscow Stock Exchange between 2008 and 2012 than in the periods before or after.

Table 6.3 Dividends and taxes paid by Transneft, 2001–2018

Year	Dividends on ordinary shares held by the state	Taxes	For comparison: Dividends on privileged (non-voting) shares
2002	1 272		1 396
2003	1 300		1 345
2004	2 377		1 584
2005	250		500
2006	860		461
2007	472	21 778	350
2008	750	22 118	402
2009	0	29 794	368
2010	584	29 248	389
2011	734	58 139	489
2012	1 671	15 638	1 114
2013	3 800	11 772	1 065
2014	6 774	76 136	1 126
2015	1 767	56 656	1 178
2016	11 521	89 877	1 280
2017	30 600	182 000	
2018	55 000		

Million rubles. By payment year.
Note on taxes: The numbers may not reflect all taxes paid. Comparison over time should only be carried out with regard for changes in tax regulations. For 2003 and 2004, consolidated financial reports state only tax paid on profits, and for 2005 and 2006, annual reports state only taxes not paid by the end of the year. Numbers for these years are therefore not included here. Beginning in 2007, annual reports state total consolidated tax payments for the entire year, and the numbers are therefore understood to reflect the real level of taxation levied off Transneft's head organisation, even as some taxes, like VAT, may have been partially returned later. From 2012, Transneft paid taxes on a consolidated basis as an integrated organisation, and the changes here reflect real changes in taxes paid.
Note on dividends: Dividends are paid out based on results for the preceding year. Dividends paid out in 2017 and 2018 are for both ordinary and privileged shares, according to Transneft's revised dividends policy.
Author's compilation based on Dmitriev (2002b), Transneft's consolidated financial reports for 2003 and 2004, and Transneft's annual reports for 2005–2017. Numbers for 2018 are from Bazanova and Petlevoi (2019).

There was increasing openness around tariff calculation. Transneft asked the recently established Federal Tariff Service (FST)[15] to approve a transparent formula for price formation (Transneft, 2006, p.25; 2007, p.23). This applied only to the base price. The cumulative surcharges were excepted; they appeared frequently and at short notice (Transneft, 2006, p.25; 2007, p.23;

Oilcapital.ru, 2009). But the introduction of quarterly transport schedules improved transparency further (Surzhenko and Reznik, 2008).

The issue of oil quality in the pipelines was contentious, also among Russian oil producers. Before 2005, Transneft had government support for its unwillingness to introduce a quality bank in its pipelines. This was emphasised when Deputy Prime Minister Viktor Khristenko stated in 2003 that "the quality of crude has not deteriorated from being mixed" (*Neft' i Kapital*, 2003f). This rather surprising statement aside, there was widespread support for the status quo. Producers of lower-grade crude were mostly state or regionally owned, while producers of higher-grade oil were privately owned. But in 2005, the pressure to adopt a quality bank strengthened. The state-owned Rosneft had by now acquired Yukos's main production company Yuganskneftegaz, which produced higher quality oil. At this point, President Putin complained that Urals regularly traded at a 4–5 US$ discount compared to Brent blend (Stratfor, 2005). A quality bank in Transneft's system could make the price gap narrower. Vainshtok argued the case against: "if we say we have a unitary state, why should Tatneft and Bashneft (...) suffer?" (*Neft' i Kapital*, 2007f). In the end, Transneft prevailed over Rosneft, and there was no quality bank.

The project of a Russian pipeline to China progressed from 2003 in an altered form, the ESPO pipeline. The two alternatives, a China route overland to Daqing and a more general export route with a terminal and port at Kozmino, were at this point joined in one project, at the government's order (Bradshaw, 2014, pp.200–201). Developing the Kozmino route was first priority, but construction would proceed from East Siberia. Putin and government ministers followed the project closely. Construction was supposed to begin in April 2006. Two days before, Putin, spontaneously and in public, ordered the pipeline route moved to the north of Lake Baikal, thereby lengthening it by 500 km (Kolesnikov, 2006). Inevitably, the pipeline's cost almost doubled, from 6.65 billion US$ to 11.2 billion, not least because Vainshtok asserted that the pipeline would still be delivered on schedule. Construction proceeded in a rush (Martynov, 2008). Cost estimates continued to rise, to 14.45 billion US$ by November 2010 (Gavshina and Reznik, 2010). Vainshtok failed to get his contract in Transneft renewed in September 2007 (Rebrov, 2009b). In October, Nikolai Tokarev was appointed head of Transneft, announcing early on that the ESPO pipeline would be completed a year behind schedule (*Neft' i Kapital*, 2008c).

Tokarev came to Transneft from Zarubezhneft, where he had remained after his short stint in the BPS pipeline project and Transneft in 1999–2000. He had modernised Zarubezhneft from an unreformed Soviet-style company to a state-owned shareholding entity on the list of strategic companies. According to media reports, in the earlier parts of his career he had risen to the rank of major general in the KGB. He had worked with Putin in the KGB's Dresden office in the 1980s, and in the Presidential Administration in the mid-1990s (Shvedko, 2002; Gordeev, 2007; Makarkin, 2007b). In the latter position he had been in charge of state companies (Surzhenko and Reznik, 2008). Tokarev was seen as close to First Deputy Prime Minister and

Rosneft Board Chairman Igor Sechin (Makarkin, 2007b), and he knew Gennadii Timchenko of the oil trader Gunvor quite well (Surzhenko and Reznik, 2008). Timchenko was rumoured to manage Putin's private business interests in oil and gas, but no business link was substantiated at that point (Bernstein, 2007; Harding, 2007; Quiring, 2007; Bernstein, 2008).[16] Tokarev brought his management team from Zarubezhneft to Transneft (Makarkin, 2007b; Transneft, 2008, pp.11–14).

In 2008, the Audit Chamber began investigations of ESPO expenditures (Butrin, 2008). It concluded that a substantial part of ESPO contracts had been awarded without tender, but the misuse of funds on Transneft's part was less significant than previously alleged (Audit Chamber, 2009; Rebrov, 2009b; Bratersky, 2010). The audit did not lead to charges at first, but its full text was not disclosed (*Neft' i Kapital*, 2010a). It remains difficult to know how much informal rent was extracted through ESPO construction.

Charity and infrastructural power

Following the onset of the financial crisis, it became increasingly difficult to attract finance for ESPO. Much of it came from the China Development Bank as loans to Transneft (10 billion US$) and Rosneft (15 billion US$). This had the effect of moving the overland route to China higher up on the list of priorities (Bradshaw, 2014, p.201). In addition, Transneft issued bonds. This had the side effect of improving company transparency further. In 2009 it issued ruble-denominated bonds, in the largest-ever offering by a Russian company until then, totalling 35 billion rubles or 1.1 billion US$ (Bloomberg/*The Moscow Times*, 2009; Oilcapital.ru, 2009). The investor information package included information on Transneft's charity donations from the sale of technical oil in 2005–2008. They were enormous in the Russian context, over a billion rubles annually, reaching 7.2 billion in 2007 (Malkova, 2009). They were larger than the dividends issued to shareholders in the same years, as seen in Tables 6.3 and 6.4.

In addition to charity, in 2009 Transneft sponsored the new Continental Ice Hockey League with 100 million rubles (Transneft, 2010, p.39). Several major companies, most of them state owned, had founded the League in 2008, and Transneft owned an 11.76 per cent stake (Dospekhov, 2008; Transneft, 2010, p.39).

In the years that followed, more light was shed on the extent of Transneft's donations and their beneficiaries. Transneft was Russia's largest corporate charity donor in 2007 (Kaz'min, 2012). This informal rent had been channelled into charities like a fund for veterans of the Federal Guards Service (Malkova, 2009). In May 2010, the transparency campaigner and Transneft shareholder Aleksei Navalnyi obtained a court order to force the police to investigate undisclosed beneficiaries (Malkova, 2010; Oliphant, 2010). In 2011, Transneft disclosed comprehensive information on charity donations (Transneft, 2011a), while it is more difficult to obtain detailed information for later years.

Table 6.4 shows that Transneft contributed just above 8.5 billion rubles to charity, or around 208 million Euro/289 million US$, in 2011.[17] Donations went to a range of organisations and individuals across Russia, but more than half of recipients were located in Moscow, and many were ordinary organisations that provided healthcare, or welfare for orphaned children (Transneft, 2011a). However, of the 8.5 billion rubles, 7.3 billion went to a charity, the Konstantinovskii charity fund,[18] which restored historic monuments, and developed them for various purposes (Transneft, 2011a). Many of these were state residences. In 2011, Transneft donated 5.5 billion rubles to the fund's science park development, an ocean and sea life centre, on Russkii Island in Vladivostok (Transneft, 2011a; Archi.ru, 2019). Vladivostok at this point underwent considerable development as the venue for the September 2012 APEC summit (Lee, 2013). The summit was preceded by considerable showcase development intended to increase Russia's international prestige.[19] Arguably, such charity amounted to a CSR programme that channelled informal rent to enhance the state's infrastructural power. Transneft performed a quasi-fiscal service for the state, by collecting considerable rents through excess transportation costs extracted from oil companies, and directing them into selected groups and individuals in the elite and the wider population.

The status quo in Transneft benefited many people, in the elite and across the country. To preserve it, Tokarev fended off a 2010 government proposal to privatise 25 per cent of Transneft (Butrin, 2010; Kommersant, 2010; Korytina, 2010; Oliphant, 2010; Tovkailo and Biryukov, 2010). There were, however, indications of financial overstretch in Transneft, as shown when the idea of a JV model was floated for a new pipeline in West Siberia, Zapolyarye–Purpe (Starinskaya, 2010). In the event, it was easier to find the means for the new pipeline in Transneft's investment programme (*Neft' i Kapital*, 2011b). This would again minimise oil company influence on pipeline construction and preserve the state monopoly on pipeline ownership.

Pipelines of power

In 2009, a revised Energy Strategy emphasised transit state dependence as a foreign energy policy problem (Ministry of Energy, 2009, p.35). Transit avoidance had priority (Ministry of Energy, 2009, p.48). In practice, Transneft's pursuit of transit avoidance had intensified ahead of the strategy's revision. Transneft's monopoly made customers look for alternatives. In Belarus and Ukraine, deprived of a part of Russia's oil export, Russian transit avoidance opened excess capacity in the downstream sectors. Their governments now periodically opened for oil from other suppliers like Venezuela (through swaps) and Azerbaijan. In the case of Belarus, the primary aim seemed to be to put pressure on Russia in the bilateral relationship, rather than pursuing any major change of primary oil supply.

Table 6.4 Transneft's charity donations and sponsorships, 2005–2017

Year	Charity donations	Sponsorships
2005	1600	nda
2006	5300	nda
2007	7200	nda
2008	1100*	nda
2009	nda	nda
2010	nda	nda
2011	8518	nda
2012	nda	nda
2013	nda	nda
2014	nda	nda
2015	8100	97.4
2016	14900	359
2017	4900	674

Million rubles
*first nine months of 2008
Author's compilation, based on Malkova (2009), Transneft (2011a), and Transneft's annual reports

As of 2005, Butinge was the largest foreign terminal for Russian crude export, but the volume had been reduced to around 5 million tpa (*Neft' i Kapital*, 2006a). However, Mažeikiu Nafta came up for sale again following the Yukos affair. The Lithuanian government, which held a 40.6 per cent stake in the refinery, used its right of first refusal to take control of Yukos's share, and offered 84.3 per cent up for re-privatisation (Rebrov, 2005). There were several offers, of which the best came from KazMunayGaz and the Polish company PKN Orlen, the former's slightly higher than the latter's (Rebrov, 2005; Shevel'kova, 2005; Rebrov, 2006; 2008). An offer from TNK-BP was lower. Lithuania's most important condition was a guarantee of oil deliveries to the refinery. KazMunayGaz promised to deliver 12 million tpa in the next ten years. As Kazakhstan's crude export reached a maximum on existing routes in autumn 2005, its problem was not supply, but transit capacity (*Neft' i Kapital*, 2006h). KazMunayGaz had a transit agreement with Transneft for the necessary volumes. Transneft, however, quickly and unilaterally abandoned the agreement, possibly on order from the government (US Office Almaty, 2006). Transneft now required KazMunayGaz to secure an amendment to the bilateral agreement between Russia and Kazakhstan which guaranteed transit of the increased volume through Russia (Rebrov, 2005; Shevel'kova, 2005; Tutushkin, 2005). KazMunayGaz had to retract its offer, and in consequence it remained dependent on Transneft's goodwill on this route.

Following KazMunayGaz's failure to go through with its offer, PKN Orlen acquired Mažeikiu Nafta in May 2006. Lukoil, Surgutneftegaz, Yukos (later Rosneft), Tatneft and TNK-BP continued to supply crude to the refinery and terminal. But in July 2006, one of the two pipes on the Baltic Druzhba branch broke down inside Russia, stopping the flow of oil to Butinge. The pipeline was not irreparable, but repair was too costly for Transneft. There was a possibility to redirect oil temporarily from BPS to Butinge, but Transneft ruled this option out (*Neft' i Kapital*, 2006g). Energy Minister Khristenko also ruled out repairs, advising Russian companies to use Primorsk and supply Butinge by ship (*Neft' i Kapital*, 2007e). This they did. There are indications that in the period around the Druzhba rupture, Sechin may have overruled Transneft and ordered TNK-BP and Lukoil not to supply Mažeikiu Nafta (Embassy Moscow, 2006). Rosneft cancelled supplies to Mažeikiu the month before the accident (Embassy Vilnius, 2006). Whatever the background, increasing reliance on BPS, instead of reconstructing the Baltic Druzhba branch, was a political decision (Kezik, 2007).

By 2006, oil transit relations with Belarus had become problematic. A full-blown crisis erupted when Gazprom in January 2007 increased the gas price to Belarus (Chapter 7). The settlement that followed introduced a Russian export duty on oil to Belarus. In response, Belarus introduced a transit duty, which Transneft refused to pay. Belarus then stopped around 79,000 tonnes of oil en route to Europe. Russia stopped all exports through Belarus in return (Khalip, 2007; Lavrov, 2007; Tomashevskaya et al., 2007). In the next settlement, Belarus cancelled the new transit duty and returned the oil, while Russia granted Belarus a discount on the export duty, which would decrease gradually until 2010, when the agreement expired (Anishyuk, 2010). Rents were again shared and transit resumed. But Russia's reputation as a reliable oil supplier to Europe had suffered.

A second BPS

The crisis accelerated progress on a new Transneft project, rumoured to have Sechin's support. A second pipeline to the Baltic Sea, BPS-2, linking Druzhba to Primorsk, would allow oil export to bypass Belarus altogether. The planned throughput was 50 million tpa (Savushkin, 2007), and the cost around 4 billion US$ (Socor, 2012). BPS-2 could reduce transit volumes also through Ukraine. Planning started in February 2007 (Gorelov and Tomashevskaya, 2007; Kulikov, 2007). Vainshtok indicated an 18-month construction period, declaring that Primorsk would be expanded if necessary. While Vainshtok preferred Primorsk, regional interests suggested Ust-Luga, to the south of St Petersburg (*Neft' i Kapital*, 2008a). For a while, the tide turned against BPS-2 (*Neft' i Kapital*, 2008a). There were doubts whether the pipeline could be filled. BPS-1, as the "old" BPS was now called, was utilised below capacity. In April 2008, the Energy and Industry Ministry said demand for BPS-2 was insufficient, and recommended the project be shelved (*Neft' i Kapital*, 2008a).

In May 2008, shortly after becoming prime minister, Putin declared that BPS-2 would be constructed, and terminate at Ust-Luga. The Transport Ministry, the Russian Railways and Gunvor, Timchenko's oil trading company, were reportedly in favour of Ust-Luga (*Neft' i Kapital*, 2008a; 2011d). Gunvor seems to have been close to establishing control over Ust-Luga's oil terminal at this point (*Neft' i Kapital*, 2009b). When the BPS-2 plan was finalised in November 2008, Ust-Luga was the endpoint, but overall volume projections were revised downwards, from 50 million tpa with an option of 75, to 30 million tpa with an option of 50 (*Neft' i Kapital*, 2011d). This was closer to actual demand forecasts at the time, but still appeared excessive.

There was a new oil transit crisis in Russian–Belarusian relations in January 2010. The two states again failed to reach a new agreement when the old one expired (Anishyuk, 2010). Russia may have pushed to get Russian oil companies to finally take over Belarus's refineries (Gabuev et al., 2010; Socor, 2010). The settlement in the end reduced Belarus's duty free oil import quota to 6.3 million tonnes for domestic consumption. Extra volumes would be subject to full export duties (Bilateral Protocol of the Government of the Russian Federation and the Government of the Republic of Belarus, 2010, quoted in Dyner, 2010; Yafimava, 2011, p.251 fn. 138). This was costly for Belarus, which now sought contracts with Venezuela (through swaps) and Azerbaijan (*Neft' i Kapital*, 2011c).

Putin was present at the opening of BPS-2 in March 2012 (*Neft' i Kapital*, 2011d). Due to the difficult seabed conditions, Ust-Luga would have to undergo a prolonged test regime of several months (*Neft' i Kapital*, 2012b). BPS-2 would therefore operate below maximum for an extended period, incurring losses for Transneft (*Neft' i Kapital*, 2012b). It was alleged that an inexperienced subcontractor, affiliated with Timchenko, had failed to address the fraught seabed conditions. The bulk of Ust-Luga's facilities was controlled by structures affiliated with Timchenko (*Neft' i Kapital*, 2012b). By now, there was considerable excess capacity in export pipelines, so overall volumes were unaffected.

In 2011, on the tenth anniversary of BPS-1's opening, Transneft's company magazine celebrated it as "the route of independence" (Marochkin, 2012, p.15). Special attention was given to the threat to Russia's economic independence of transit through Latvia and Lithuania. Their "monopoly position" had, against the background of their Nato accession, given these states an opportunity to blackmail Russia economically and politically. The article credited Putin for his role in moving the project forward (Marochkin, 2012, p.15).

As it appeared in March 2012, BPS-2 would take volumes from BPS-1, by creating excess capacity on export routes. Losses were likely. Primorsk and Ust-Luga competed for crude oil and diesel deliveries (*Neft' i Kapital*, 2012c). The rule of thumb for transit pipelines held true: alternative routes can be expensive (Stevens, 2009, p.20). However, most of this expense was financed by tariff surcharges and therefore covered by oil companies. Some of these resources may have been distributed within the ruling coalition as lucrative construction and service contracts. BPS-2 strengthened Russia's position in negotiations with Belarus and Ukraine. Belarus's opportunities to take a share of Russian oil rent through transit and re-export were curtailed. Transit volumes through Belarus and Ukraine decreased in 2011, but Druzhba did not become redundant (*Neft' i Kapital*, 2011d). Russian oil exporters still relied on it for export to Germany, Poland and Central Europe, where many refineries customarily worked on Urals (*Neft' i Kapital*, 2011d). In 2011, 77.5 million tonnes of crude oil were exported through the Druzhba system, including 2.2 million tonnes from Kazakhstan (*Neftegazovaya vertikal'*, 2012). But this was the peak. From 2012, the volumes exported through Druzhba were reduced.

Transit through Ukraine declined most. Russian crude transit decreased by about 25 per cent from 2006 to 2007 (Gorelov and Tomashevskaya, 2007), and by another 11.6 per cent in 2010–2011 (Socor, 2012). Transit relations had by then been disagreeable for over a decade, especially over the Odesa–Brody pipeline. The pipeline had opened in reverse in September 2004, ahead of the November elections (Ivzhenko, 2004; *Neft' i Kapital*, 2006d). The Ukrainian and Polish governments meanwhile worked to attract oil from Kazakhstan. Chevron was the most interested producer (Embassy Warsaw, 2005). While Kazakhstan looked for non-Russian transit routes to Europe, neither Kazakhstan nor Chevron wanted to antagonise Russia over Odesa–Brody, a route they had not asked for in the first place.

Ukraine explored the possibility of supplying Czech refineries through the Slovak part of Druzhba (Embassy Bratislava, 2006b; 2006c). In 2006–2007, Russia piled on the pressure to get Slovakia to agree to a Gazprom Neft takeover of Yukos's 49 per cent stake in the Slovak pipeline company Transpetrol (Embassy Bratislava, 2006a). Ukraine's Slovak route failed to materialise. But it remains questionable whether Ukraine's governments in this period could commit to a Polish extension, or any outlet option, while the flow direction in Odesa–Brody was caught up in a struggle among politicians and their business interests (cf. Embassy Warsaw, 2006; Balmaceda, 2008, pp.93–95). In 2009, Ukrtransnafta asked Transneft to allow a transit pause so that it could conduct a 48 hour trial flow in the original direction. Transneft refused. Tokarev called it a "risky venture" (Rebrov, 2009a). BPS-2 would in any event redirect oil flows away from Ukraine (Transneft, 2009a; Zuev, 2009). When the volume of oil transiting out of Russia decreased, Belarusian and Ukrainian refineries in 2011 contracted Azeri oil, and Odesa–Brody was put into operation in the original direction (*Neft' i Kapital*, 2011d; 2011c; 2012a).

Defending Transneft's share of Caspian transit

From 1996 to 2011, overall pipeline capacity for crude export from the Caspian region increased from 16 to 115 million tpa (Socor, 2009). With regard to export routes from Azerbaijan, Transneft and Russia were initially able to benefit from the increased demand for pipeline transport. Azerbaijan had planned to stop exports through Novorossiisk completely after BTC commenced operation in 2005. Baku–Novorossiisk was a reserve pipeline with a transit agreement for 5 million tpa (*Neft' i Kapital*, 2011a). But by 2011 it was operating at a loss to Transneft, and Azerbaijan proposed revising the volume downwards to 1.5 million tpa (*Neft' i Kapital*, 2011a).

In contrast, Russia retained around 80 per cent of Kazakhstan's oil exports in the 2000s in circumstances of high annual increases (Socor, 2009). This was to a considerable extent due to the Caspian pipeline. By 2006, Kazakhstan had increased its number of major export routes to four: BTC by way of a Caspian tanker service; the China pipeline under development in 2004–2009; CPC; and Atyrau–Samara (*Neft' i Kapital*, 2006b).

After BTC opened, Kazakhstan on several occasions seemed close to approving a trans-Caspian pipeline project, in effect a BTC feeder pipeline. There was however no final decision. Kazakh oil still reached BTC. In June 2006, a few months after BTC started to operate, Kazakhstan and Azerbaijan agreed to develop a tanker transport system with light Kazakh crude for BTC (Komsomol'skaya Pravda Kazakhstan, 2007). Parts of the planned system were operational by October 2008 (Guliyev and Arkhrarkhodjaeva, 2008, p.16), and a small but significant share of Kazakhstan's oil exports began to be shipped on the route. From 2010, the route took some oil from Turkmenistan (Rahimov, 2019). But the agreement had also included plans for a larger Kazakhstan–Caspian Oil Transport System in 2006, with a feeder pipeline in Kazakhstan and an expanded fleet (Butyrina, 2007). This did not materialise. In addition, KazTransOil acquired the Batumi oil terminal in Georgia in 2006–2008, while KazMunayGaz acquired the Romanian Rompetrol company in 2007–2008 (*Neft' i Kapital*, 2007b; Socor, 2007; 2008). The latter acquisition gave Kazakhstan access to considerable refinery capacity and an extensive distribution network around the Black Sea.

From the opening of the export leg of the Kazakhstan–China pipeline in December 2005, Russian companies found it a cost-efficient alternative to rail export to China. Rosneft tried to export 1.2 million tonnes oil to China in 2007 through Kazakhstan, and applied to Transneft for access to the adjoining Russian pipeline. Transneft declined, citing the lack of a regulatory framework (Derbilova, 2007; *Neft' i Kapital*, 2007f). Rail transit continued (*Neft' i Kapital*, 2006f). The Kazakhstan–China pipeline was completed to full length in 2009, with a nominal capacity of 10 million tpa (*Neft' i Kapital*, 2009a).

Expansion of the Caspian Pipeline was for a long time an unresolved issue (*Neft' i Kapital*, 2005b). In Kazakhstan, the lack of tangible progress on the CPC expansion most likely served to reinforce the government's determination to proceed with a pipeline to China, thereby reducing its oil transit dependence on Russia (Cutler, 2014, p.682). In Russia, there were frequent proposals, especially in 2005–2006, that Transneft manage the government's stake in the consortium. Transneft's management appeared reluctant, replying with statements like "[CPC] would be a burden", but always qualified by the standard assertion that any government decision on the issue would be carried out loyally (Derbilova and Bekker, 2006; Vin'kov and Rubanov, 2006). Eventually in 2006, the Russian government changed policy and made that decision. Following Russian pressure, in April 2006 the CPC General Director, Ian MacDonald of Chevron, was replaced by Vladimir Razdukhov, from Zarubezhneft (Gorshkova, 2007). And against Vainshtok's wish, the management rights to Russia's share were transferred to Transneft, effective from April 2007. Transneft was not obliged to return the favour by compensating the government, but it was free to decide how to manage the stake (Mazneva, 2007). The pressure on other consortium members to raise tariffs and restructure CPC debts became palpable (Derbilova and Borisov, 2006; Skornyakova and Skorlygina, 2006; *Neft' i Kapital*, 2007a). Russia used tax inspections and renewed tax claims to pile on the pressure further (*Neft' i Kapital*, 2006e; Gorshkova, 2007). An old Russian project intended to circumvent Bosporus and the Dardanelles (Karagiannis, 2002, p.133), a pipeline from Burgas on Bulgaria's Black Sea coast to Alexandroupolis in Greece, was also revived in 2006 (Reuters News, 1994; RFE/RL, 1997). While its main aim at this point was to boost exports from Novorossiisk and compete with BTC (*Neft' i Kapital*, 2007c), it was presented as a perfect onwards route for oil from an expanded Caspian pipeline (Kupchinsky, 2006; *Neft' i Kapital*, 2012a). By this time, the Caspian pipeline deadlock, and ensuing bottleneck, forced consortium members to ship surplus oil over the trans-Caspian route. In response to Russia's *fait accompli*, they threatened to increase trans-Caspian export.

At this point, Kazakhstan delayed the development of the trans-Caspian connection to BTC somewhat in a show of support for the CPC (Makarkin, 2007a; *Neft' i Kapital*, 2007a). In September 2007, Chevron and the other shareholders gave in to Russian demands, and agreed to CPC expansion in principle, on Russia's terms (Butrin and Rebrov, 2007). Tariffs were increased, interest payments reduced, and for the first time CPC ran a profit (Zotova, 2008). Russia suddenly achieved its primary objective with CPC, tax extraction. It had demonstrated the vulnerability of any trans-Caspian connection to BTC when faced with Russian pressure. When Oman left the consortium in November 2008, Russia acquired its 7 per cent stake, apparently just ahead of Kazakhstan (Zotova, 2008). The possibility came up quickly, and the 700 million US$ deal was financed from the pocket of Rosneftegaz, the holding company that controlled Rosneft, and the state's stakes in Gazprom and later Inter RAO, too (Yakoreva, 2016). Russia's share reached 31 per cent, managed by Transneft.

By late 2008, expansion had become a desirable prospect for Russia as well. Maximising Russia's share of oil export from Kazakhstan was a more urgent priority now that Kazakhstan had an outlet to China. The Russian government argued that the increased volume had to be sufficient to fill Burgas–Alexandroupolis (Gavshina, 2008; Mel'nikov, 2009). Kazakhstan again proceeded with the integrated tanker service on the trans-Caspian route (*Neft' i Kapital*, 2009c). Transneft then manoeuvred quickly in the consortium. It united forces with Chevron against BP, which held stakes in CPC through two JVs with Lukoil and KazMunayGaz. BP was not really interested in expanding CPC, as this would create competition for BTC (Gavshina, 2008). Following BP's divestment of its stakes in favour of its two partners in 2009, the CPC expansion finally moved forward (Mel'nikov, 2009; *Neft' i Kapital*, 2010b; CPC, 2019). The Burgas–Alexandroupolis project faltered in 2009, when the financial crisis hit Greece and Bulgaria (*Neft' i Kapital*, 2009c; 2010b; Daborowski, 2011; Eastweek, 2011; Gavshina, 2011). In October 2009 Russia joined an alternative project in Turkey, the Samsun–Ceyhan pipeline (*Neft' i Kapital*, 2012a), but this, too, failed to materialise. Nevertheless, the CPC expansion proceeded in two phases that were complete by October 2018.

CPC aside, Transneft remained unwilling to expand Kazakhstan's export capacity through its own system in Russia. In addition to denying KazMunayGaz additional throughput to Butinge, Transneft appeared to delay capacity increases in the Atyrau–Samara pipeline until BPS was fully developed (*Neft' i Kapital*, 2005e). The BPS-2 project propelled the expansion process for Atyrau–Samara forward. Following years of little or no progress, an agreement on a 25 million tpa expansion was finally reached in May 2008 (*Neft' i Kapital*, 2008a; IA FK-Novosti, 2009; Rebrov, 2009a). Atyrau–Samara would feed BPS-2 (*Neft' i Kapital*, 2008a; 2009c). However, on the supply side, Atyrau–Samara expansion now competed with the expansion plans for CPC as well as for expansion plans for the China pipeline. It lost out to the competition, and the expansion project was therefore shelved in 2009 (*Neft' i Kapital*, 2009c; 2011a; 2011d; 2012a). By putting a brake on Atyrau–Samara expansion, Transneft had jeopardised the possibilities of securing more of the increased oil flow from Kazakhstan for its own system. A few years later, the expanded CPC more than compensated the loss. However, Kazakhstan's development of oil export to China provided an illustration of how Russian intransigence pushed Kazakhstan in this direction.

Transneft and the reorganised ruling coalition: Staying the course

During the oil boom, the main bone of contention between Transneft and oil producers had been the speedy construction and specific trajectory of new export pipelines. Following the fall in global prices for oil, the main conflictual issue became Transneft's tariffs, a replay of the situation 15 years earlier. For the state, extracting dividends from this and other state companies again became more urgent. However, efforts to do so came up against the state's developmental goals, specifically Transneft's role in national development and in supporting political stability.

Following the completion of ESPO and BTS-2, Transneft's position in the industry was secure. The company continued to pursue investment programmes aimed at expansion, however, with few questioning their efficiency or overall effectiveness in the stagnating Russian economy. Transneft under Tokarev was seen as a successful company, in 2014 hailed by a major trade journal as the strong link of the oil industry (*Neftegazovaya vertikal'*, 2014b).

Transneft's position was not weakened by the international sanctions imposed on the energy sector in July to September 2014, following Russia's annexation of Crimea. Transneft was deprived of access to long-term European and US finance, however, it did not plan to alter its investment programme (*Neftegazovaya vertikal'*, 2014b, p.87). On the contrary, it began to pursue import substitution, planning to reduce its reliance on imported equipment from ten per cent to three (*Neftegazovaya vertikal'*, 2014b, p.87). But Russia's worsened financial position following the fall in oil prices and the sanctions did have an impact. In autumn 2014, Transneft traded in derivatives to hedge against currency and interest rate risks. The measure was unsuccessful, incurring a loss of 75.3 billion rubles, a sum that equalled its tax payments that year (Mel'nikov, 2015). The government was not pleased about this (Mel'nikov, 2015).

Nevertheless, Tokarev remained in place as head of Transneft for another five years in 2015 (Mel'nikov, 2015). He was loyal to Putin; this increased his lobbying powers. Towards the end of the period under study here, Tokarev was seen to be among the five most influential top managers in the energy industries. Another five to seven Transneft and Transnefteprodukt top managers were on the list of around 80 (Oilcapital.ru, 2012; 2016; APEK, 2017). Crucially, however, Transneft's lobbying power was surpassed by that of Rosneft and its head, Igor Sechin. This became apparent in a struggle over how to finance ESPO expansion.

Thanks to ESPO, 13 per cent of Russia's oil exports went to China in 2014 (Analiticheskii Tsentr, 2015, p.11). At that point, a new agreement between Rosneft and CNPC from 2013 had already come into effect, increasing the export volume from 15 to 30 million tpa, with options for more. This was in excess of ESPO's capacity of 20 million. In 2013, new contracts between Rosneft and Sinopec, and Gazprom Neft and PetroVietnam, added 16 million tpa to demand for pipeline transport (Solodovnikova, 2013). In light of this, the government required Transneft to increase ESPO's capacity to 80 million tpa not by 2030, as was the original idea, but by 2021 (Solodovnikova, 2013). The first ESPO project plan had included Chinese finance for Transneft as well as Rosneft. This time, however, no such support was forthcoming. Tokarev was reluctant to increase Transneft's debts, and preferred to let the oil producers, Rosneft in particular, bear the cost (Solodovnikova, 2013). Initially, Energy Minister Aleksandr Novak supported this view (Oilcapital.ru, 2013e). The stage was set for a lengthy struggle with Rosneft.

Rosneft was not going to pay for the ESPO expansion, and lobbied for a freeze in Transneft tariffs for 2014 (Oilcapital.ru, 2013d). Transit through Kazakhstan had become an option, and Rosneft did not rely only on Transneft's system to deliver the contracted volumes to China. The government, on its side, in September 2013 did decide to freeze Transneft's tariffs in 2014

(Oilcapital.ru, 2013d). In reply, Transneft increased the cost of a planned ESPO feeder pipeline, and suspended further development of another ESPO-related pipeline project relevant to Rosneft (Oilcapital.ru, 2013c; 2013b). Additionally, in November it asked for government permission to levy a surcharge on all companies to finance ESPO expansion (Solodovnikova, 2013). To increase the likelihood of government support for the proposal, Transneft planned to add an extra 10 US$/tonne to the surcharge. This would accrue to the state. But the proposal was rejected. The tariff freeze was retained through 2014 as planned. When the freeze ended, they were still indexed below the level Transneft had requested for 2015–2018 (Analiticheskii Tsentr, 2014b, p.29). In February 2014, the government decided that the company would not get access to any extraordinary funds or levies for the ESPO expansion (Ubushaeva and Ivankina, 2014). Rosneft's view had prevailed. In a meagre compensation, the government in September 2014 obliged Rosneft, Gazprom Neft and Gazprom to accept ship or pay agreements for two major ESPO feeder pipelines (Analiticheskii Tsentr, 2014a, p.29). Meanwhile, the tariff dispute continued, exacerbated by the low oil prices in 2016. By now, it involved also Gazprom Neft, Lukoil and Novatek (Kutuzova, 2017, p.71).

The issue of a quality bank scheme came up again in 2013 and 2017, this time raised by the Energy Ministry (Oilcapital.ru, 2013a; 2017). Transneft argued against this. In its view, exporting the high-sulphur, heavier oil from Bashkortostan, Tatarstan and Orenburg under a separate quality, Urals Heavy, would be the better solution to both the quality bank issue and the problem of maintaining a consistent quality for Urals (Kutuzova, 2017, p.72). This would again necessitate higher investment. Meanwhile, improving the quality in its existing system seemed to slip down on the list of priorities. In 2012 the Energy Ministry had relaxed chemical compounds regulation for Russian oil companies (Drankina, 2019). Oil producers and traders carried the responsibility for the quality of the crude that entered Transneft's pipelines. Overall export quality therefore depended on Transneft's capability to monitor quality and enforce standards. When in April 2019 scandal broke over massive contamination of the crude oil export flow to Europe, this capability appeared to be lower than most observers would have expected. The contamination was not discovered until the flow reached Mozyr refinery in Belarus, some 1,600 km west of its origins near Samara (Drankina, 2019). The damage to Russia's reputation as an oil supplier to Europe was substantial.

From 2012, the state took a more active stance towards extracting dividends from all the companies in the oil and gas industries, including Transneft. Government demands included dividends payment at the level of 25 per cent of profit across the board, and an increase to 35 per cent for the following year (Meshcherin, 2014, p.78). Another central demand was that companies calculate dividends from profits following international financial reporting standards (IFRS), generally a better guide to the actual financial position of large companies in Russia than Russian financial reporting standards (RSBU) (Meshcherin, 2014, p.78).[20] Transneft stood out in the oil and gas industries with a particularly impressive difference. Its profits by IFRS were more than ten times larger than profits per RSBU, due to its practice of accumulating profits in the subsidiaries (Meshcherin, 2014, p.75; Mordyushenko, 2016). Transneft, like Gazprom, did not heed the government's demand in 2013. It more than doubled its dividends payments from 2012 to 2013, as seen in Table 6.3. However, this was still less than the state would have received, had the dividends been calculated following IFRS.

In 2016, the government started to demand a dividends payment of 50 per cent of profits according to the reporting standard that would yield the higher sum, RSBU or IFRS (Mordyushenko, 2016). This was an unusually large share by international standards. Transneft responded by changing its policy to pay out 25 per cent of profits according to IFRS (Mordyushenko, 2016; Kozlov and Dzhumailo, 2017). Tokarev in 2017 declared that higher dividends payments were a possibility if the main shareholder decided to pay them (Mordyushenko, 2017), and the company management also stated that it would be possible to increase dividends payments after the end of ESPO construction (*Vedomosti*, 2017). In other words, before 2020–2021 the government would have to force Transneft to increase dividends payments.

While Transneft was loath to follow up on state demands for higher dividends, it did continue to supply quasi-fiscal services. Charity and CSR projects remained important. As seen in Table 6.4., in 2015–2017 Transneft contributed 27.9 billion rubles to charity. Relative to its turnover and profits, Transneft outspent Gazprom on charity. In 2015 its donations represented one per cent of its turnover, or 5.7 per cent of its profits. Gazprom's contributions was 17.6 billion rubles, about the double in absolute value, but this equalled only 0.3 per cent of that company's turnover or 2.2 per cent of its profits (Gazprom, 2016, p.60; RBK, 2018). The situation in 2016 was similar. While Transneft's donations equalled 1.8 per cent of turnover or 6.4 per cent of profits, Gazprom's 25.16 billion to charity was equal to 0.4 per cent of turnover, or 2.5 per cent of profits (Gazprom, 2016, p.60; RBK, 2018). Recipients of Transneft's charity were found across Russia, but concentrated in its main business regions, ranging from schools to cultural and sports centres, orphanages and religious establishments (Transneft, 2019).

Transneft continued its course amid criticism from the Audit Chamber on its lack of efficiency. An Audit Chamber control in 2015 found that Transneft only partly fulfilled its investment programmes. This was mainly due to a lack of interaction and contact with the Energy Ministry, but also with oil companies and refineries, resulting in insufficient project planning (Audit Chamber, 2015). The company was additionally found to purchase substantial parts of its pipelines without tender (Audit Chamber, 2015).

The tug-of-war over dividends continued in the government through 2018. Its problems in compelling Transneft and other state companies to pay out dividends were of a profound nature. There was a fundamental lack of coordination among government bodies, an issue raised by the Audit Chamber in

2017 in an audit of the 2018–2020 state budgets (Tkachev, 2017). The Finance Ministry, in charge of the budget process, and the Ministry for State Property (Rosimushchestvo), which oversaw the state companies, conducted their planning on the basis of different projections for dividends payments (Audit Chamber, 2017, pp.188–189). They did not share their principles for projections, nor the projections, with each other. On this background, Transneft's continued lack of compliance with the demand for 50 per cent of profits, based on IFRS, was unsurprising.

Maximum control of export accomplished

The relations between the state and Transneft in foreign energy relations became formally closer than before in September 2012 with the decree on protection of national interests in foreign economic relations (Decree No. 1285, 2012). The decree had immediate consequences for Gazprom's relations with its foreign customers. But it pertained to all the Russian companies the government had designated as strategic, including Transneft. From now on, Transneft would always have to obtain prior government approval for sharing any business information with a foreign organisation, and for all changes to contracts with foreign customers, including price changes. In the case of Transneft, this seemed to be more of a change to the formality of the institutional framework than to its content. However, it raised substantial hurdles to any development of greater independence from the state in the future.

In the final years analysed here, Transneft pursued international cooperation at a very modest level. For example, it joined a Czech initiative for a new international association of oil transporters (Transneft, 2018, p.47), and promoted a subsidiary in oil pipeline maintenance (Transneft-Diaskan, 2019). In addition, it carried out its tasks as Russia's manager of its CPC stake.

The annexation of Crimea and subsequent worsening relations with many European states had the effect of further strengthening the political priority on transit avoidance in the western direction. Transhipment through Primorsk and Ust-Luga increased by 11.1 and 16.1 per cent from 2014 to 2015 (Analiticheskii Tsentr, 2017a, p.10). From 2015 to 2016 the transit of Russian oil products in the non-Russian ports on the Baltic Sea was reduced from 9 to 5 million tpa, and this transit stream was expected to cease altogether in 2018 (Kutuzova, 2017, p.71). Ust-Luga now had an important resource export port (Analiticheskii Tsentr, 2017c, p.22). Altogether, in 2012–2018 Russia exported between 125 and 144 million tonnes of oil and oil products annually from its ports on the Baltic Sea, Primorsk, Ust-Luga, Vysotsk, St Petersburg and Kaliningrad (FGBU Administratsiya morskikh portov Baltiiskogo morya, 2019). In the same period, the share of oil products increased from a third to half of all liquid petroleum exports. Ust-Luga also increased its share of the export stream, taking around 40 per cent, a similar share to that of Primorsk (FGBU Administratsiya morskikh portov Baltiiskogo morya, 2019). This was now Russia's most important export route.

Transit through Druzhba did not cease, even as it was reduced. In 2012–2016, between 50 and 55 million tonnes crude oil transited through Druzhba annually (*Neftegazovaya vertikal'*, 2013; 2014a; 2015; 2016a; 2017b). Parts of the main branch into Belarus and the adjoining pipelines in Russia underwent considerable refurbishment in 2015, with more modernisation planned for the years ahead (Kutuzova, 2017, p.71). But when polluted oil was loaded into the system in April 2019, and discovered only on arrival at the Mozyr refinery in Belarus, this exposed Transneft's failure to control the quality of oil in the Druzhba system.

Around the Caspian Sea, there was little further development in non-Russian export routes after the completion of BTC from Azerbaijan, and Atasu–Alashankou/the Kazakhstan–China pipeline from Kazakhstan. Azerbaijan's main Azeri–Chirag–Guneshli field (ACG) had peaked in 2010, at a lower level than expected (Mishin, 2017, p.96). This came on top of the disappointment of Azerbaijan's other Caspian fields. As a consequence, the pipeline from Baku to Ceyhan in Turkey (BTC) was utilised not at its maximum capacity of 59.76 million tpa, but at the more modest level of 34 million tonnes a year (BP, 2019). In these circumstances, Azerbaijan's government made an effort to attract oil from Kazakhstan and other Central Asian states, like Turkmenistan. From 2010, some of Turkmenistan's oil went to Baku by tanker, and following the gas price dispute between Turkmenistan and Gazprom in 2016 (Chapter 7), the remainder was also transported to BTC on this route through 2018 (Rahimov, 2019). However, the efforts to increase transit from Kazakhstan on this route were unsuccessful. While the total volume of Kazakh oil export by tanker (mainly to Baku) in 2011 was 9.3 million tonnes, or 14.2 per cent of total export, this route's significance decreased thereafter (KazMunayGaz, 2012). In 2016, only 2.2 million tonnes, or 3.5 per cent of all Kazakhstan's oil exports, were shipped on Caspian tanker routes (*Neftegazovaya vertikal'*, 2017a, p.56). The route remained expensive due to many transhipment points. Expanding it with the planned feeder pipeline in Kazakhstan was risky and unnecessary, now that Kazakhstan had sufficient outlets to its main markets in Russia, China and Europe.

In the overall picture of Kazakhstan's export routes, export through Russia again began to increase. The CPC expansion was decisive. As it was completed, Kazakhstan by 2016 exported 65.7 per cent of its oil, or 40.8 million tonnes, through CPC, compared to 29.9 per cent in 2011 (KazMunayGaz, 2012, *Neftegazovaya vertikal'*, 2017a, p.56). Export on the Atyrau–Samara route remained important, staying stable around 14–15 million tpa, or 23.3 per cent of the total in 2016 (*Neftegazovaya vertikal'*, 2017a, p.56). Capacity on the Kazakhstan–China pipeline was expanded to 20 million tpa in 2013, and as a result, KazTransOil declared that the country had sufficient pipelines for existing and future production (Oilcapital.ru, 2014). With the pipeline to China, Kazakhstan had finally attained balance in its export routes. While Russia was the main export route, Kazakhstan no longer depended on Transneft only to reach its main markets.

The expansion of Kazakhstan's export routes had on the other hand resulted in overcapacity, particularly in the direction of China. This was due to a strategy of diversification from the Chinese market on the part of Kazakhstan, as well as national difficulties in replacing falling production at older fields (*Neftegazovaya vertikal'*, 2017a; Sharip, 2018). The route was therefore open to Russian oil export to China through Kazakhstan. Following Rosneft's new contracts for export to China, Russia and Kazakhstan in 2013 agreed on transit of six to ten million tpa Russian oil through Atasu–Alashankou from 2014 through 2019 (Oilcapital.ru, 2013f). Actual transit reached the 10 million tpa ceiling from 2017. Even so, Atasu–Alashankou was utilised significantly below its maximum capacity of 20 million tpa, with annual volumes fluctuating between 10 and 12.3 million tpa from 2014 (Kazakhstan–China Pipeline LLP, 2014, p.9; 2016, p.6; 2018, p.6).

Conclusions

Transneft appeared in the early post-Soviet period in many ways a Soviet holdover. It was a state-owned company with a monopoly transport service which it provided equally to all oil producers. But it offered little access for state organisations. In 1991–1997, central state organisations participated less and less in Transneft's development. Informal ties substituted for state access. Chernomyrdin's protection de facto minimised direct state involvement in Transneft's development. By 1996, the Fuel and Energy Ministry was well aware of Transneft's policy, and tried to access a greater share of Transneft's informal streams, remove Chernyaev, and make Transneft follow government instruction and become accessible to the state. With Chernomyrdin out of government, this was possible. The struggle for control over Transneft when Vainshtok replaced Savelev only 18 months later showed how much was at stake. Transneft's rent streams were an asset in the struggle for positions in Russian politics.

On a smaller scale, the privileged shares remained a constraint on Transneft's rent sharing with the government. The resolution of this conflict under Putin very likely involved a modification of rent management arrangements to give the ruling coalition a share of Transneft's dividends. Increasing state capacity at the expense of Transneft autonomy was a rather slow process. This may have been due to the perceived risks of upsetting the balance among key actors.

Informal rent sharing continued to matter in Transneft's relations with the state. By 2008, its monopoly and rent streams had political protection to an extent similar to that of Rosatom (Chapter 4), and possibly beyond Gazprom's (Chapter 7). Transneft's closeness to the regime affected power relations between the state and the company. What were most likely channels of informal rents to the ruling coalition associated with BPS-2 and ESPO promoted regime stability, but weakened state control. This also contributed to production and spending that was most likely excessive. It is reasonable to assume that many decisions that affected informal rent, such as choice of a particular business partner, were made based on considerations of business development. Taking on a particular partner who happened to be a friend of the president would simply be better for business, as "you can be sure there will be no problems with bureaucrats, as nobody in Russia will create trouble for a company whose co-owner is a close friend of the president" (Mokrousova and Reznik, 2013). On a smaller scale, Transneft's rents contributed to welfare and regional development. This was particularly visible from its extensive and expensive CSR programmes.

Savelev began to make Transneft more accessible to the state, a process that continued under Vainshtok. This went hand in hand with another policy promoted by Transneft, but strongly supported by the government, that of achieving control of oil export routes. The chapter shows how this policy first targeted Russian oil producers, which had to pay for the development of routes like BPS, and then turned into a policy of transit avoidance and control of transit routes to global markets. BPS first showed how Transneft could deliver infrastructural and economic development in a way that maximised state capacity and regime power over the economy. BPS delivered a new export route, but a commercially suboptimal one for oil companies. With transport routes a question of national policy, it was easier for the state to control Russian oil companies through Transneft. In the process, they lost control of route-related rent streams, which were now captured by Transneft. Now, concerns of regional development and the bypassing of Latvia and Lithuania overruled cost-efficiency concerns. The BPS tariff surcharge, levied from all oil producers in Russia, coerced oil companies into spending more of their income in Russia. They were now funding the development of regions and industrial sectors (concrete, steel, pipe, ports, etc.) as it suited the state, with the actual beneficiaries of these oil rents selected for their proximity to the regime. Pipeline construction became a source of infrastructural power to the state, but it also allowed the ruling coalition to dispense patronage and cultivate elite dependence on the company. Transneft's role as a source of authoritarian durability was then strengthened by the state's protection of Transneft's pipeline monopoly. This ensured that no oil company could grow beyond state control and challenge the ruling coalition's hold on power.

In light of this, it is ironic that, 12 years after the inauguration of BPS, Transneft's main challenger in its role as an instrument of state control over oil companies was a state-owned oil company, Rosneft. The tug of war between Transneft and Rosneft over the responsibility to finance ESPO expansion showed how increased state ownership in the oil industry did not deliver greater capacity to the state for making difficult policy decisions, or to turn the screws on oil companies in the manner of 1999–2001. Instead, the conflict turned into a stalemate of lobbying power. The personal relations between company heads and the regime deprived the government of policymaking power. When Rosneft prevailed, Transneft in turn failed to respond to state demands for higher dividends. In addition, it postponed major refurbishment, incurring further costs to other producers and the state. As illustrated by the criticism it attracted from the Audit Chamber, management practices did not become more efficient. The difficulties of resolving these conflicts, and the state's balancing among different industry interests, show how personal relations in the elite can result in a particular type of ad hoc balancing among different interests. In this political game, it is not possible to pursue long term solutions and institutional development.

Transneft was a domestic and foreign policy tool from the mid-1990s, but only in the 2000s under Vainshtok was its full potential realised. The state had better access to Transneft, and greater capacity to support development. Bypass pipeline projects were useful foreign policy tools. In relations with transit state governments, proposals for bypass pipelines could be used as sticks. Once in place, bypass pipelines maximised Russian control of export routes and simplified interaction with transit states.

But Transneft was more successful in promoting the avoidance of old transit routes to the west than in controlling the Caspian transit route. Russia's pursuit of maximum control of the Caspian transit route closed potential avenues for cooperation with oil producers in Kazakhstan and Azerbaijan. Transneft could have been a force of bilateral energy cooperation. Though never very likely, it was nevertheless an option in the 1990s. However, Russia's aim to achieve maximum control, interpreted rather narrowly by Transneft, made potential partners wary of its routes. Transneft was here a foreign policy tool that cultivated dependence on Russia to some extent, but also one that restricted Russia's ability to become a partner. Its heavy-handed pursuit of control and monopoly, instead of integration with the possibility of mutual advantage, made it less attractive to its post-Soviet neighbours. In this way, Transneft's role in Russian foreign policy contributed to centrifugal developments in the post-Soviet region.

Notes

1. Urals is the main crude oil blend in Russia, and a benchmark quality in global oil markets. It is a blend of heavy, sour oil from the Volga and Urals regions and light crudes from West Siberia.
2. This was the extent of the pipeline system after disintegration of oil products pipelines and non-Russian pipelines.
3. In a swap, oil delivered in one place is traded in for oil sold somewhere else, to minimise transport costs.
4. Supergiant fields have in excess of 1 billion barrels ultimately recoverable proven oil reserves or (for gas) oil equivalents.
5. This was the date confirmed by the Duma as per the ordinary election schedule (the previous presidential elections having been held in June 1996). When Yeltsin resigned on 31 December 1999, the election law required that elections be held within three months, and the election was pushed forward to 26 March.
6. Zarubezhneft, established in 1967, only had operations abroad. In 2000, its main activity was a joint venture in Vietnam.
7. The routes were Groznyi–Lysychansk and Samara–West.

8   In Russian: Vostochnaya Sibir–Tikhii Okean (VSTO).
9   In November 2017, Rosneft suggested the possibility of reopening the project and developing Indiga as terminal for oil and LNG from Timan-Pechora, but this was related to a business dispute with Lukoil and not pursued for long.
10 Pivdennyi terminal is Yuzhnyi terminal in Russian, meaning South terminal in English.
11 It was acquired by the Vitol Group in 2006.
12 The route was Vtorovo–Yaroslavl–Kirishi–Primorsk.
13 Crude oil quality is normally determined by sulphur content and gravity, and influences price considerably.
14 The 2228 km long pipeline goes from Atyrau by the Caspian Sea through Aktobe, Kenkiyak, Kumkol and Atasu to Alashankou on the Kazakhstan–China border. There it connects to the Alashankou–Dushanzi pipeline, completed in December 2005, which supplies a large refinery. The final leg on Kazakhstan's side, Atasu–Alashankou, serves China only.
15 FST existed from 2004 to 2015. It inherited the task of overseeing tariffs in the energy industries from the Federal Energy Commission (1992–2005). In 2015, the Federal Anti-Monopoly Service was placed in charge of these tasks.
16 In the first round of Western sanctions against Russian politicians and businessmen in March 2014, Timchenko was subjected to personal sanctions (asset freeze and denial of access to transactions) by the US, Canada and Australia. The US Treasury's grounds for designating Timchenko were that his "activities in the energy sector have been directly linked to Putin. Putin has investments in Gunvor and may have access to Gunvor funds" (US Department of the Treasury, 2014).
17 At average exchange rates for 2011. Annual average exchange rate for Euro for 2011 was 40.88 RUB/1 EUR (Statista, 2019). Annual average exchange rate for US$ for 2011 was 29.406 RUB/1 US$ (OzForex, 2019).
18 http://www.mbfk.ru/
19 In the event, the APEC summit fell short of expectations, and the local construction boom ahead of the summit was mired in corruption scandals (*Nezavisimaya gazeta*, 2012). The sea life centre opened in 2016 (Primorskii okeanarium, 2019).
20 In RSBU, there are strict rules as to how accounts must be presented, and what needs to be included or excluded, facilitating controls, taxation, and comparisons between companies. IFRS are principles-based and therefore give companies more flexibility in their reporting, but necessitate more information on a company's financial situation and accordingly hold greater information value for shareholders. Crucially, RSBU do not require integrated holdings to report consolidated financial reports, and large corporations may therefore report profits under RSBU only for the head company (cf. Wikipedia, 2019).

References

Aleksandrov, Yu. and Orlov, D. (2001) "Truboprovodnaya ekspansiya Rossii. Radikal'noe usilenie roli nashei strany na prostranstve SNG nachinaetsya so stroitel'stva magistral'nykh nefteprovodov [Russia's pipeline expansion. The radical strengthening of our country's role in the CIS begins with the construction of trunk oil pipelines]" *NG Politekonomiya*, 17 April, p.6

Aleksandrovich, S. (2001) "Moskva–Baku: soobshchenie vozobnovlyaetsya [Moscow–Baku: contact is renewed]" *Neft' i Kapital*, January

Analiticheskii Tsentr (2014a) *Stimulirovanie razvitiya vozobnovlyaemoi energetiki [Stimulating the development of renewable energy]*. Energeticheskii byulleten' 17, September. (Moscow: Analiticheskii Tsentr pri Pravitel'stve Rossiiskoi Federatsii/ Analytical Center for the Government of the Russian Federation)

Analiticheskii Tsentr (2014b) *Energeticheskaya bednost' i energeticheskaya obespechennost'* [*Energy poverty and energy prosperity*]. Energeticheskii byulleten' 10, February. (Moscow: Analiticheskii Tsentr pri Pravitel'stve Rossiiskoi Federatsii/ Analytical Center for the Government of the Russian Federation)

Analiticheskii Tsentr (2015) *Potentsial energeticheskogo sotrudnichestva stran BRIKS* [*The potential of energy cooperation among BRICS countries*]. Energeticheskii byulleten' 26, July. (Moscow: Analiticheskii Tsentr pri Pravitel'stve Rossiiskoi Federatsii/ Analytical Center for the Government of the Russian Federation)

Analiticheskii Tsentr (2017a) *V fokuse: Pribaltika – ozhivlenie posle Velikoi retsessii* [*In focus: The Baltic states – revival after the Great Recession*]. Byulleten' o tekushchikh tendentsiyakh mirovoi ekonomiki 20, May. (Moscow: Analiticheskii Tsentr pri Pravitel'stve Rossiiskoi Federatsii/Analytical Center for the Government of the Russian Federation)

Analiticheskii Tsentr (2017b) *Tekhnologicheskie prioritety v energetike* [*Technological priorities in electricity*]. Energeticheskii byulleten' 47, April. (Moscow: Analiticheskii Tsentr pri Pravitel'stve Rossiiskoi Federatsii/Analytical Center for the Government of the Russian Federation)

Analiticheskii Tsentr (2017c) *Novye prognozy mirovoi energetiki i mesto Rossii v nei* [*New prognoses for global energy and Russia's place in it*]. Energeticheskii byulleten' 54, November. (Moscow: Analiticheskii Tsentr pri Pravitel'stve Rossiiskoi Federatsii/Analytical Center for the Government of the Russian Federation)

Anishyuk, A. (2010) "Talks frozen in Belarus oil dispute" *Moscow Times*, 11 January, p.1

APEK (2017) "*Reiting vliyaniya krupnykh predprinimatelei i top-menedzherov toplivno-energeticheskogo kompleksa v iyune 2017 g.* [*Rating of the influence of major businessmen and top managers in the fuel and energy complex, June 2017*]" [online]. 29 June (Moscow: Agentstvo politicheskikh i ekonomicheskikh kommunikatsii). Available from: http://apecom.ru/projects/item.php?SECTION_ID=102&ELEMENT_ID=3803 [Accessed 18 March 2019]

Archi.ru (2019) "*Nauchno-issledovatel'skii kompleks 'Primorskii okeanarium' (g. Vladivostok, ostrov Russkii)* [*The science research complex 'Primore ocean centre' (Vladivostok, Russkii Island)*]" [online]. (Russia: Archi.ru). Available from: https://archi.ru/projects/russia/7750/nauchno-issledovatelskii-kompleks-primorskii-okeanarium-g-vladivostok-ostrov-russkii [Accessed 10 May 2019]

Audit Chamber (2009) "*Schetnaya palata proverila raskhodovanie sredstv na stroitel'stvo TS "VSTO"* [*The Audit Chamber has audited the expenditure of funds in the construction of the transport system ESPO*]" [online]. 2 February (Moscow: Schetnaya palata [Audit Chamber]). Available from: http://www.ach.gov.ru/press_center/news/318 [Accessed 1 April 2019]

Audit Chamber (2015) "*Investitsionnye programmy 'Transnefti' ne v polnoi mere sootvetstvuyut pokazatelyam strategicheskogo planirovaniya RF* [*Transneft's investment programmes do not completely comply with the Russian Federation's strategic planning indicators*]" [online]. 18 March (Moscow: Schetnaya palata [Audit Chamber]). Available from: http://www.ach.gov.ru/activities/control/21054/ [Accessed 1 May 2019]

Audit Chamber (2017) *Zaklyuchenie Schetnoi palaty Rossiiskoi Federatsii na proekt federal'nogo zakona "O federal'nom byudzhete na 2018 god i na planovyi period 2019 i 2020 godov"* [*The Audit Chamber's Conclusion on the federal law draft 'On the federal budget for 2018 and the planning period 2019 and 2020"*], (Moscow: Schetnaya Palata Rossiiskoi Federatsii)

Azarova, S. (1997) "'Baltiiskuyu truboprovodnuyu sistemu' reshili postroit' [Baltic Pipeline System decision made]" *Neft' i Kapital*, March

Babali, T. (2009) "Prospects of export routes for Kashagan oil", *Energy Policy*, 37: 1298–1308

Balmaceda, M.M. (2008) *Energy dependency, politics, and corruption in the Former Soviet Union. Russia's power, oligarchs' profits and Ukraine's missing energy policy, 1995–2006* (London/New York: Routledge)

Balmaceda, M.M. (2012) "Russia's central and eastern European energy transit corridor: Ukraine and Belarus" in Aalto, P. ed., *Russia's energy policies. National, interregional and global levels* (Cheltenham, UK/Northampton, USA: Edward Elgar), pp.136–155

Bazanova, E. and Petlevoi, V. (2019) "Dividendy ot sanktsii [Dividends from the sanctions]" *Vedomosti*, 18 April, p.10

Bekker, A. (1999a) "Sila i bessilie Putina [Putin's strength and impotence]" *Vedomosti*, 4 October

Bekker, A. (1999b) "Vainshtok stal tsarem truby [Vainshtok becomes tsar of the pipe]" *Vedomosti*, 17 September

Bekker, A. (2002) "Interv'yu: Viktor Khristenko, vitse-prem'er [Interview: Viktor Khristenko, vice premier]" *Vedomosti*, 25 March, p.A2

Bernstein, J. (2007) "Stanislav Belkovsky: Putin will leave power completely" *Eurasia Daily Monitor*, 19 November

Bernstein, J. (2008) "Belkovsky predicts Medvedev will tighten the screws" *Eurasia Daily Monitor*, 7 January

Bloomberg/*The Moscow Times* (2009) "Transneft in biggest bond issue" *Moscow Times*, 20 May

Bolukbasi, S. (1998) "The controversy over the Caspian Sea mineral resources: Conflicting perception, clashing interests", *Europe-Asia Studies*, 50 (3): 397–414

BP (2019) "Baku–Tbilisi–Ceyhan pipeline" [online]. (London: BP). Available from: https://www.bp.com/en_az/caspian/operationsprojects/pipelines/BTC.html [Accessed 2 May 2019]

Bradshaw, M. (2014) "The progress and potential of oil and gas exports from Pacific Russia" in Oxenstierna, S. and Tynkkynen, V.-P. eds, *Russian energy and security up to 2030* (London/New York: Routledge), pp.192–212

Bratersky, A. (2010) "Transneft accused of $4bln theft" *The Moscow Times*, 18 November, p.1

Butrin, D. (2008) "Pravila igry [The rules of the game]" *Kommersant*, 1 February, p.13

Butrin, D. (2010) "Goskompanii vnosyat v dokhodnuyu chast' byudzheta [The state companies will be transferred to the profitable part of the budget]" *Kommersant*, 26 July, p.2

Butrin, D. and Sapozhnikov, P. (2004) "Ukraine otkazali v legkoi nefti [Ukraine denied light oil]" *Kommersant*, 23 June, p.7

Butrin, D. and Rebrov, D. (2007) "Chevron vernula Rossii tarify KTK [Chevron returns CPC tariffs to Russia]" *Kommersant*, 20 September, p.14

Butyrina, E. (2007) "Berik Tolumbaev, AO 'KazTransOil': 'Glavnyi printsip nashei raboty – sozdanie sovremennoi integrirovannoi nefteprovodnoi sistemy Kazakhstana' [Berik Tolumbaev, KazTransOil: 'The main principle of our work is to create a modern and integrated oil pipeline network in Kazakhstan']" *Panorama*, 16 February

Buyantseva, L. (2000) "Baku zagruzit 'Transneft' [Baku loads Transneft]" *Vedomosti*, 19 September

Buyantseva, L. and Osetinskaya, E. (2000) "'Transneft' predlagaet skidku [Transneft offers a discount]" *Vedomosti*, 7 July

Chernitskii, O. (1999) "Mintop obvinyaet Dmitriya Savel'eva v rastrate [The Fuel Ministry is accusing Dmitrii Savelev of embezzlement]" *Vedomosti*, 12 November

Chernitskii, O. (2001a) "Vainshtok pozhalovalsya. V bor'be s KTK 'Transneft' rasschitivaet na pravitel'stvo [Vainshtok complains. In the campaign against CPC, Transneft counts on the government]" *Vremya novostei*, 6 June, p.4

Chernitskii, O. (2001b) "Igor' Yusufov: 'Sistema eksporta nefti budet spravedlivoi' [Igor Yusufov: 'The oil export system will be fair']" *Vremya novostei*, 14 September, p.1

CPC (2019) "Project chronology" [online]. n.d. (Moscow/Novorossiisk/Astana: Caspian Pipeline Consortium). Available from: http://www.cpc.ru/EN/about/Pages/chronology.aspx [Accessed 23 April 2019]

Cutler, R.M. (2014) "Chinese energy companies' relations with Russia and Kazakhstan", *Perspectives on Global Development and Technology*, 13 (5–6):673–698

Daborowski, T. (2011) "Bulgaria withdraws from the Trans-Balkan oil pipeline construction project" *CeWeekly*, 14 December

Davydova, M. (2000) "'Auktsionirovanie' neftyanogo eksporta. Pravitel'stvo izmenyaet poryadok vydachi kvot na vyvoz nefti [The auctioning of oil export. The government changes the order of oil export quota allocation]" *Segodnya*, 11 November, p.3

Davydova, M. (2001) "Neft' poidet s molotka [Oil will go under the hammer]" *Kommersant*, 29 May, p.8

Decree No. 327 (01/04/1995) *O pervoocherednykh merakh po sovershenstvovaniyu deyatel'nosti neftyanykh kompanii [On first measures to perfect the operations of oil companies]* (Moscow: President of the Russian Federation)

Decree No. 1285 (11/09/2012) *O merakh po zashchite interesov Rossiiskoi Federatsii pri osushchestvlenii rossiiskimi yuridicheskimi litsami vneshneekonomicheskoi deyatel'nosti [On measures to protect the interests of the Russian Federation when foreign economic activity is carried out by a Russian juridical person]* (Moscow: President of the Russian Federation)

Decree No. 1403 (17/11/1992) *Ob osobennostyakh privatizatsii i preobrazovaniya v aktsionernye obshchestva gosudarstvennykh predpriyatii, proizvodstvennykh i nauchno-proizvodstvennykh ob"edinenii neftyanoi, neftepererabatyvayushchei promyshlennosti i nefteproduktoobespecheniya [On the specificities of privatisation and conversion into shareholding companies of enterprises, production and scientific production associations in the oil and oil refinery industries and oil product distribution]* (Moscow: President of the Russian Federation)

Delovoi Peterburg (1999a) "Primorsk poluchil dostup k nefti [Primorsk receives access to oil]" *Delovoi Peterburg*, 24 March

Delovoi Peterburg (1999b) "Primakov b'et po interesam finnov [Primakov combats Finnish interest]" *Delovoi Peterburg*, 24 February

Derbilova, E. (2006) "Interv'yu: Semen Vainshtok, prezident 'Transnefti' [Interview: Semen Vainshtok, president of Transneft]" *Vedomosti*, 6 June

Derbilova, E. (2007) "'Rosneft' ne puskayut v Kitai [Rosneft is not let into China]" *Vedomosti*, 15 January

Derbilova, E. and Borisov, N. (2006) "Rossiya menyaet taktiku [Russia changes tactics]" *Vedomosti*, 13 January

Derbilova, E. and Bekker, A. (2006) "Vse sol'yut v trubu [Everyone will pour into the pipe]" *Vedomosti*, 4 May

Dmitriev, A. (2000) "Semen Vainshtok: Gosudarstvo dolzhno sebya zashchishchat' [Semyon Vainshtok: The state should defend itself]" *Komsomol'skaya Pravda*, 14 November, p.20

Dmitriev, A. (2002a) "Peremychka kak simvol kompromissa. Nefteprovod Baku-Novorossiisk i KTK budut soedineny blagodarya Vainshtoku i Alekperovu [A connection as a symbol of compromise. The Baku–Novorossiisk and CPC pipelines will be united thanks to Vainshtok and Alekperov]" *Nezavisimaya gazeta*, 29 January, p.11

Dmitriev, A. (2002b) "Snova Vainshtok. Godovoe sobranie aktsionerov 'Transnefti': s dividendami, no bez sensatsii [Vainshtok again. The annual shareholder meeting in Transneft: with dividends, but without sensations]" *Nezavisimaya gazeta*, 2 July, p.11

Dmitriev, A. (2003) "Sergei Grigor'ev: 'Vybor zavisit ot pravitel'stva, i tol'ko ot pravitel'stva'. Vitse-prezident kompanii 'Transneft' ubezhden o tom, chto chastnye nefteprovodnye proekty v Rossii ne slishkom perspektivny [Sergei Grigor'ev: 'The decision depends on the government, and only on the government'. Transneft's vice-president is convinced that there is little promise in private oil pipeline projects in Russia]" *Nezavisimaya gazeta*, 28 March, p.10

Dodsworth, J.R., Mathieu, P.H. and Shiells, C.H. (2002) *Cross-border issues in energy trade in the CIS countries.* IMF Policy Discussion Paper (Washington, DC: International Monetary Fund)

Dospekhov, A. (2008) "Rossiiskomu khokkeyu pokazali amerikanskie printsipy [American principles are held up to Russian hockey]" *Kommersant*, 12 March, p.24

Drankina, E. (2019) "Chastnyi punkt priema nefti [A private oil inflow spot]" *Meduza. io*, 7 May

Druzenko, E., Savushkin, S. and Chernov, M. (2002) "Politicheskie vektory novykh nefteprovodov [The political directions of new pipelines]" *Neft' i Kapital*, April

Dyner, A.M. (2010) "Is Russia getting closer to taking over Belarusian refineries?" *Eastweek*, 3 February

Eastweek (2011) "Russian Federation: Is the Burgas–Aleksandroupolis pipeline plan close to collapse?" *Eastweek*, 23 February

Embassy Astana (2008) Kazakhstan: Timur Kulibayev discusses oil transportation and Georgia Investments, 08ASTANA2081/Wikileaks #174382. Issue date 20 October 2008. *Cablegate* [online]. (Published by Wikileaks 1 September 2011). Available from: https://wikileaks.org/plusd/cables/08ASTANA2081_a.html [Accessed 1 April 2019]

Embassy Bratislava (2006a) Putin to Slovakia – Why would you want to own an empty pipeline?!, 06BRATISLAVA911/Wikileaks #85946. Issue date 16 November 2006. *Cablegate* [online]. (Published by Wikileaks 1 September 2011). Available from: https://wikileaks.org/plusd/cables/06BRATISLAVA911_a.html [Accessed 1 April 2019]

Embassy Bratislava (2006b) Russians waiting for clock to run out on Transpetrol, 06BRATISLAVA972/Wikileaks #89956. Issue date 18 December 2006. *Cablegate* [online]. (Published by Wikileaks 1 September 2011). Available from: https://wikileaks.org/plusd/cables/06BRATISLAVA972_a.html [Accessed 1 April 2019]

Embassy Bratislava (2006c) Slovakia pursues Transpetrol through murky legal waters, 06BRATISLAVA816/Wikileaks #80988. Issue date 6 October 2006. *Cablegate* [online]. (Published by Wikileaks 1 September 2011). Available from: https://wikileaks.org/plusd/cables/06BRATISLAVA816_a.html [Accessed 1 April 2019]

Embassy Moscow (2006) Russian oil to Lithuania – Mixing revenge and business, 06MOSCOW9482/Wikileaks #76658. Issue date 30 August 2006 [online]. (Published by Wikileaks 8 September 2011). Available from: https://wikileaks.org/plusd/cables/06MOSCOW9482_a.html [Accessed 13 February 2019]

Embassy Vilnius (2006) Two Russian oil suppliers cancel July crude shipments to Lithuanian refinery, 06VILNIUS618/Wikileaks #70128. Issue date 3 July 2006 [online]. (Published by Wikileaks 1 September 2011). Available from: https://wikileaks.org/plusd/cables/06VILNIUS618_a.html [Accessed 13 February 2019]

Embassy Warsaw (2005) Polish pipeline company finalizing a business plan for Odessa-Brody-Gdansk, still looking for Chevron support, 05WARSAW1282/Wikileaks #28330. Issue date 8 March 2005. *Cablegate* [online]. (Published by Wikileaks 1 September 2011). Available from: https://wikileaks.org/plusd/cables/05WARSAW1282_a.html [Accessed 1 April 2019]

Embassy Warsaw (2006) Poland's PKN Orlen discusses Mazeikiu Nafta, Kazakhstan, Azerbaijan, Odessa-Brody, 06WARSAW2008/Wikileaks #78600. Issue date 15 September 2006. *Cablegate* [online]. (Published by Wikileaks 1 September 2011). Available from: https://wikileaks.org/plusd/cables/06WARSAW2008_a.html [Accessed 1 April 2019]

Eremenko, A. (2011) "Energorynok: 20 let (ne) zavisimosti [The energy market: 20 years of (in) dependence]" *Zerkalo nedeli*, 26 August

FGBU Administratsiya morskikh portov Baltiiskogo morya (2019) "*Arkhiv dannykh po gruzooborotu [Data archive on turnover of goods]*" [online]. (St Petersburg: FGBU Administratsiya morskikh portov Baltiiskogo morya). Available from: https://www.pasp.ru/arhiv [Accessed 9 May 2019]

Fokina, E. (2006) "TEK. Bol'shaya proverka [The fuel and energy complex. A major examination]" *Profil'*, 15 May, pp.38–39

Fuller, L. (1995) "Azerbaijan: The 'Near Abroad'" *Transitions Online*, 28 April

Gabuev, A. et al. (2010) "Dmitrii Medvedev ogranichil Azerbaidzhan [Dmitrii Medvedev limits Azerbaijan]" *Kommersant*, 4 September, p.1

Gavrish, O. (2003) "TNK razvernula ukrainskuyu trubu [TNK unrolls a Ukrainian pipeline]" *Vedomosti*, 27 May

Gavshina, O. (2008) "BP vyzhivayut iz KTK [BP is being driven out of CPC]" *Gazeta*, 20 November, p.12

Gavshina, O. (2011) "Tanker vygodnee truby [A tanker is more profitable than a pipeline]" *Vedomosti*, 16 February, p.7

Gavshina, O. and Reznik, I. (2010) "Milliardy iz truby [Billions out of the pipe]" *Vedomosti*, 17 November, p.1

Gazprom (2016) *Vnutrennyaya sila. Finansovyi otchet PAO "Gazprom" za 2016 god [Internal strength. Financial statement for the public company Gazprom for 2016]* (Moscow: Gazprom)

Gordeev, I. (2007) "'Transneft' v bezopasnosti [Transneft is safe]" *Vremya novostei*, 16 October, p.8

Gorelov, N. and Tomashevskaya, O. (2007) "Podal'she ot Lukashenko [A little farther from Lukashenko]" *Vremya novostei*, 6 February, p.1

Gorshkova, A. (2007) "'Vainshtok umeet ubezhdat' ['Vainshtok knows how to convince']" *Vremya novostei*, 20 September, p.8

Government Resolution No. 512 (27/05/1998) *Voprosy aktsionernoi kompanii po transportu nefti "Transneft" [Questions concerning the shareholding oil transport company Transneft]* (Moscow: The Government of the Russian Federation)

Government Resolution No. 810 (14/08/1993) *Ob uchrezhdenii aktsionernoi kompanii po transportu nefti "Transneft" [On the foundation of the shareholding company in oil transport 'Transneft']* (Moscow: The Government of the Russian Federation)

Government Resolution No. 1325 (16/10/1997) *O proektirovanii, stroitel'stve i ekspluatatsii Baltiiskoi truboprovodnoi sistemy [On project development, construction

The oil industry: Transneft 245

and exploitation of the Baltic Pipeline System] (Moscow: The Government of the Russian Federation)

Government Resolution No. 1333 (17/10/1997) *O merakh po obospecheniyu gosudarstvennogo upravleniya zakreplennymi v federal'noi sobstvennosti aktsiyami aktsionernoi kompanii po transportu nefti "Transneft"* [*On measures to guarantee state management of the federal property of shares in the shareholding oil transport company Transneft*] (Moscow: The Government of the Russian Federation)

Guliyev, F. and Arkhrarkhodjaeva, N. (2008) *Transportation of Kazakhstani Oil via the Caspian Sea (TKOC). Arrangements, actors and interests.* RUSSCASP Working Paper. (Lysaker, Norway/Bremen, Germany: Fridtjof Nansen Institute)

Gustafson, T. (2012) *Wheel of Fortune. The battle for oil and power in Russia* (Cambridge, MA/London: The Belknap Press of Harvard University Press)

Harding, L. (2007) "Putin, the Kremlin power struggle and the $40bn fortune" *The Guardian*, 21 December, p.1

IA FK-Novosti (2009) "Transneft' rassmatrivaet vozmozhnost' perenapravleniya v Novorossiisk vsego neftyanogo tranzita Kazakhstana [Transneft is looking into the possibility of sending all Kazakhstan's oil transit through Novorossiisk]" *Kommersant*, 5 June

IEA (2002) *Russia energy survey 2002* (Paris: International Energy Agency)

IEA (2015) *Online Data Services*, Issue date [online]. (Published by International Energy Agency 2015). Available from: http://www.iea.org/statistics/ [Accessed 6 October 2015]

Ignatova, M. (2003) "Kachai nazad! 'Transneft'' uvelichit eksport za schet Ukrainy [Pump it back! Transneft expands export at the expense of Ukraine]" *Izvestiya*, 31 May, p.6

Inozemtsev, G. (1999) "Kogo ne ustraivaet 'baltiiskii proekt'? [Who isn't happy with the 'Baltic project'?]" *Rossiiskaya gazeta*, 4 August

Ivanov, N. (1997) "Transneft' sobiraet druzei [Transneft gathers its friends]" *Segodnya*, 5 December

Ivanova, S., Surzhenko, V. and Derbilova, E. (2008) "Beskontrol'nye milliardy [Uncontrolled billions]" *Vedomosti*, 24 March

Ivzhenko, T. (2004) "Kiev gotov reshit' vse problemy s Moskvoi do vyborov prezidenta. Ukraina namerena stat' osnovnym strategicheskim napravleniem tranzita rossiiskoi nefti [Kiev is ready to solve all problems with Moscow before the presidential elections. Ukraine wants to be the primary strategic route for Russian oil transit]" *Nezavisimaya gazeta*, 23 June, p.5

Kanevskaya, P. (2003) "Kon"yunktura ne dlya nas. Rossiiskie neftyanye kompanii ne uspeyut vospol'zovat'sya blagopriyatnoi situatsiei na mezhdunarodnykh rynkakh [Not our state of the market. Russian oil companies will not succeed in taking advantage of the favourable conditions in international markets]" *Nezavisimaya gazeta*, 13 January, p.4

Karagiannis, E. (2002) *Energy and security in the Caucasus* (London/New York: RoutledgeCurzon)

Kaz'min, D. (2012) "Ne ot chistoi pribyli [Not from clean profits]" *Vedomosti*, 10 August

Kazakhstan–China Pipeline LLP (2014) *Kazakhstan–China Pipeline LLP Financial statements for year ended 31 December 2014 with independent auditor's report* (Almaty: Kazakhstan–China Pipeline LLP)

Kazakhstan–China Pipeline LLP (2016) *Kazakhstan–China Pipeline LLP Financial statements for year ended 31 December 2016 with independent auditor's report* (Almaty: Kazakhstan–China Pipeline LLP)

Kazakhstan–China Pipeline LLP (2018) *Kazakhstan–China Pipeline LLP Financial statements for year ended 31 December 2018 with independent auditor's report* (Almaty: Kazakhstan–China Pipeline LLP)

KazMunayGaz (2012) "Transportirovka nefti [Oil transportation]" [online]. 13 April (Astana: KazMunayGaz). Available from: http://www.kmg.kz/manufacturing/oil/ [Accessed 30 April 2012]

Kezik, I. (2007) "'Druzhba' zakryta navek [Druzhba is forever closed]" *Gazeta*, 24 April, p.19

Khalip, I. (2007) "'Druzhba' so vsemi vytekayushchimi [Druzhba and all its meanderings]" *Novaya gazeta*, 11 January, p.9

Khikmatov, T. (2001) "Morskoi status. Rossiya ukreplyaet svoi pozitsii na Baltiiskom more [Naval position. Russia strengthens its positions on the Baltic Sea]" *Izvestiya*, 26 December, p.5

Kolesnikov, A. (2006) "Baikalspasaigrup [BaikalSaveGroup]" *Kommersant*, 27 April, p.1

Kommersant (2010) "'Rosneft' i 'Transneft'' protiv svoei privatizatsii [Rosneft and Transneft against their own privatisation]" *Kommersant*, 27 July

Kommersant-Vlast' (1999) "Nedelya 14.09.-20.09 1999" *Kommersant-Vlast'*, 21 September, p.20

Komsomol'skaya Pravda Kazakhstan (2007) "'AO KazTransOIL': Neft' idet zadannym marshrutom [JSC KazTransOil: Oil flows on the set route]" *Komsomol'skaya Pravda Kazakhstan*, 5 October

Korytina, E. (2010) "Uzakonennaya neft' [Legalised oil]" *RBC Daily*, 28 September

Kozlov, D. and Dzhumailo, A. (2017) "'Transneft' gotovyat k privatizatsii [Transneft is prepared for privatization]" *Kommersant*, 19 July, p.8

Kravchenko, E. (2003) "Ventspils prosit russkogo syr'ya. Latviiskii port mozhet ne vyderzhat' blokadu [Ventspils asks for Russian crude. The Latvian port may not endure the blockade]" *Izvestiya*, 14 March, p.6

Kulikov, S. (2007) "Berlin proverili na energozavisimost' [Berlin is checked for energy independence]" *Nezavisimaya gazeta*, 27 August, p.1

Kupchinsky, R. (2006) "Russia: Moscow extends its pipeline web" [online]. 23 June (Prague: Radio Free Europe/Radio Liberty). Available from: http://www.rferl.org/content/article/1069413.html [Accessed 1 April 2019]

Kutuzova, M. (2017) "Uspekhi i pechali Transnefti [Transneft's successes and sorrows]" *Neftegazovaya vertikal'*, Nos 1–2, pp.70–72

Lavrov, A. (2007) "'Druzhba' – za den'gi [Friendship at a price]" *Gazeta*, 9 January, p.1

Lee, R. (2013) "The Russian Far East: Opportunities and challenges for Russia's window on the Pacific", *Orbis*, 57 (2): 314–324

Makarkin, A. (2007a) "Eksportnye marshruty uglevodorodov [Hydrocarbon export routes]" *Neft' i Kapital*, June

Makarkin, A. (2007b) "Neftyanoi general [Oil general]" *Neft' i Kapital*, November

Malkova, I. (2009) "Komu pomogaet 'Transneft'' [Who does Transneft help]" *Vedomosti*, 7 May

Malkova, I. (2010) "Shareholder wins ruling against Transneft over charity funds" *The Moscow Times*, 7 May

Markus, U. (1995) "Belarus: Heading off an energy disaster" *Transition*, 14 April

Markus, U. (1996) "Energy: Ukraine and Belarus seek help abroad" *Transition*, 3 May

Marochkin, V. (2012) "Trassa nezavisimosti [The route of independence]" *Truboprovodnyi transport nefti*, 2012 (1–2), pp.14–25

Martynov, K. (2007) "Vozvrashchenie rezidenta [The return of the resident]" *Kommersant (Business Guide)*, 20 November
Martynov, K. (2008) "Pustaya truba [The empty pipeline]" *Kommersant (Business Guide)*, 24 March
Mazneva, E. (2007) "Upravlyat' konkurentom [To manage a competitor]" *Vedomosti*, 27 June
Mel'nikov, K. (2009) "KTK uzhe rasshiryaetsya [CPC is already being extended]" *Vremya novostei*, 17 December, p.8
Mel'nikov, K. (2015) "Glave 'Transnefti' dali eshche pyat' let [The head of Transneft is given another five years]" *Kommersant*, 27 April, p.7
Meshcherin, A. (2014) "Pir v preddverii chumy? [A feast on the eve of plague?]" *Neftegazovaya vertikal'*, Nos 13–14, pp.74–81
Ministry of Energy (2009) *Energeticheskaya strategiya Rossii na period do 2030 goda [Russia's energy strategy for the period to 2030]* (Moscow: Institute of Energy Strategy)
Ministry of Industry and Trade (2003) *Energeticheskaya strategiya Rossii na period do 2020 goda [Russia's Energy Strategy for the period to 2020]* (Moscow: Ministerstvo promyshlennosti i torgovli)
Mishin, V. (2000) "'Transneft' vryad li poluchit den'gi iz Baku [Transneft not likely to get any money from Baku]" *Vremya MN*, 7 July
Mishin, V. (2017) "Neft' Kazakhstana zhdut v Baku [Baku waits for Kazakhstan's oil]" *Neftegazovaya vertikal'*, Nos 1–2, pp.94–97
Mokrousova, I. and Reznik, I. (2013) "Chelovek s resursom [A resourceful person]" *Vedomosti*, 21 January, p.1
Mordyushenko, O. (2016) "Dividendy 'Transnefti' rassmotryat po sushechestvu [Transneft's dividends will be judged on substance]" *Kommersant*, 19 September, p.9
Mordyushenko, O. (2017) "Aktsii 'Transnefti' zhdut yuanei [Transneft's shares are waiting for yuans]" *Kommersant*, 4 August, p.9
Nazarbaev, N. (1997) "Pochemu Nazarbaev nedovolen Rossiei [Why Nazarbaev is unhappy with Russia]" *Novaya gazeta*, 26 May
Neft' i Kapital (1998) "Dmitrii Savel'ev: 'Seichas net smysla privatizirovat' Transneft'' [Dmitrii Savelev: 'There is no point now in privatising Transneft']" *Neft' i Kapital*, October
Neft' i Kapital (2002a) "Imangali Tasmagambetov: 'Kazakhstan stoit na pozitsiyakh postroeniya mnogovektornoi neftetransportnoi sistemy' [Imangali Tasmagambetov: 'Kazakhstan maintains its position of building a multivector oil transport system']" *Neft' i Kapital*, September
Neft' i Kapital (2002b) "Kachestvo opredelyaet napravlenie [The quality determines the direction]" *Neft' i Kapital*, September
Neft' i Kapital (2002c) "Torzhestvo zdravogo smysla [A triumph for common sense]" *Neft' i Kapital*, October
Neft' i Kapital (2002d) "Novaya severo-zapadnaya kontseptsiya [A new northwest concept]" *Neft' i Kapital*, September
Neft' i Kapital (2002e) "Tyazhelaya neft' mozhet pomoch' Ventspilsu [Heavy crude may help Ventspils]" *Neft' i Kapital*, January
Neft' i Kapital (2002f) "Truba chetyrekh [The pipeline of four]" *Neft' i Kapital*, December

Neft' i Kapital (2003a) "Yurii Medvedev: 'Polovina FGUP segodnya absolyutno ne nuzhny gosudarstvu' [Yurii Medvedev: 'Half the federal state unitary enterprises are today absolutely not needed by the state']" *Neft' i Kapital*, March

Neft' i Kapital (2003b) "Sergei Maslov: 'My rabotaem nad razvitiem sistemy magistral'nykh produktoprovodov' [Sergei Maslov: 'We're working on the development of a system of trunk oil product pipelines']" *Neft' i Kapital*, July–August

Neft' i Kapital (2003c) "Konkurent ne dremlet [The competitor is watching]" *Neft' i Kapital*, May

Neft' i Kapital (2003d) "Yanis Adamsons: 'Nam pryamo zayavili – problema v tom, chto v Ventspilse net rossiiskogo kapitala' [Janis Adamsons: 'We were told outright: the problem is that there is no Russian capital in Ventspils']" *Neft' i Kapital*, April

Neft' i Kapital (2003e) "Bol'shie nadezhdy [Great hopes]" *Neft' i Kapital*, June

Neft' i Kapital (2003f) "Gordiev uzel protivorechii [A Gordian knot of contradictions]" *Neft' i Kapital*, May

Neft' i Kapital (2003g) "Truba v Podnebesnuyu [A pipeline to the land under the heavens]" *Neft' i Kapital*, May

Neft' i Kapital (2004a) "Kaspiiskii truboprovodnyi konsortsium [The Caspian Pipeline Consortium]" *Neft' i Kapital*, October

Neft' i Kapital (2004b) "Baltiiskaya truboprovodnaya sistema [The Baltic Pipeline System]" *Neft' i Kapital*, October

Neft' i Kapital (2004c) "Transneft" *Neft' i Kapital*, October

Neft' i Kapital (2004d) "I vse-taki revers! [Reversed, after all]" *Neft' i Kapital*, September

Neft' i Kapital (2004e) "Ventspils" *Neft' i Kapital*, October

Neft' i Kapital (2004f) "Omishal' pobezhdaet Odessu [Omisalj is vanquishing Odesa]" *Neft' i Kapital*, March

Neft' i Kapital (2004g) "Poltora goda bez truby [One and a half year without a pipeline]" *Neft' i Kapital*, June

Neft' i Kapital (2004h) "Privilegirovannye aktsii Transnefti [Transneft's privileged shares]" *Neft' i Kapital*, October

Neft' i Kapital (2004i) "Sukhodol'naya–Rodionovskaya" *Neft' i Kapital*, October

Neft' i Kapital (2004j) "Mazheikyu nafta [Mazeikiu Nafta]" *Neft' i Kapital*, October

Neft' i Kapital (2004k) "Vagit Alekperov" *Neft' i Kapital*, October

Neft' i Kapital (2005a) "Semen Vainshtok: 'Transneft'' predlagaet sokratit' eksport nefti. Protsentov na 50–60' [Semyon Vainshtok: 'Transneft proposes to reduce oil export. By 50 to 60 per cent']" *Neft' i Kapital*, December

Neft' i Kapital (2005b) "Strana-khozyaika stavit usloviya [The host country sets conditions]" *Neft' i Kapital*, September

Neft' i Kapital (2005c) "Mechty sbyvayutsya [Dreams are coming true]" *Neft' i Kapital*, October

Neft' i Kapital (2005d) "Ventspils v ozhidanii peremen [Ventspils is waiting for change]" *Neft' i Kapital*, March

Neft' i Kapital (2005e) "Vse v Dzheikhan! [All to Ceyhan!]" *Neft' i Kapital*, December

Neft' i Kapital (2006a) "'Energeticheskii orel' priletel [The energy eagle has landed]" *Neft' i Kapital*, June

Neft' i Kapital (2006b) "Proyasnyayutsya perspektivy [The perspectives are becoming clear]" *Neft' i Kapital*, September

Neft' i Kapital (2006c) "Eto tol'ko nachalo [This is just the beginning]" *Neft' i Kapital*, October

Neft' i Kapital (2006d) "Kak obychno, 'v sleduyushchem godu' [As usual, 'next year']" *Neft' i Kapital*, October

Neft' i Kapital (2006e) "Svoya ruka – vladyka [One's own hand is sovereign]" *Neft' i Kapital*, December

Neft' i Kapital (2006f) "Trebuetsya neft' rossiiskogo proizvodstva [Wanted: Russian-produced oil]" *Neft' i Kapital*, January–February

Neft' i Kapital (2006g) "'Druzhba' otkhodit na zadnii plan [Druzhba is receding into the background]" *Neft' i Kapital*, September

Neft' i Kapital (2006h) "Kuryk ne nuzhen? [Is Kuryk superfluous?]" *Neft' i Kapital*, January–February

Neft' i Kapital (2007a) "Pora opredelyat'sya [It's time to make up one's mind]" *Neft' i Kapital*, September

Neft' i Kapital (2007b) "Dlya strakhovki [Just in case]" *Neft' i Kapital*, March

Neft' i Kapital (2007c) "Truba ne terpit pustoty [A pipe cannot be empty]" *Neft' i Kapital*, March

Neft' i Kapital (2007d) "Novoe litso 'Severa' [Sever's new face]" *Neft' i Kapital*, April

Neft' i Kapital (2007e) "Al'ternativno, no dorogo [Alternatively, but expensively]" *Neft' i Kapital*, June

Neft' i Kapital (2007f) "Semen Vainshtok: 'V blizhaishie neskol'ko let nashim prioritetom budet VSTO' [Semyon Vainshtok: 'In the next few years, ESPO will be our priority']" *Neft' i Kapital*, March

Neft' i Kapital (2008a) "BTS-2 [BPS-2]" *Neft' i Kapital*, August

Neft' i Kapital (2008b) "Semen Vainshtok [Semyon Vainshtok]" *Neft' i Kapital*, August

Neft' i Kapital (2008c) "Vse ne tak, rebyata… [This isn't all OK, guys…]" *Neft' i Kapital*, March

Neft' i Kapital (2009a) "Kitaiskii pauk [The Chinese spider]" *Neft' i Kapital*, November

Neft' i Kapital (2009b) "Kontekst. Gunvor konsolidiruet nefteperevalku v Ust'-Luge [Context. Gunvor is consolidating oil transhipment at Ust-Luga]" *Neft' i Kapital*, April

Neft' i Kapital (2009c) "Ty mne – ya tebe [You give me and I give you]" *Neft' i Kapital*, December

Neft' i Kapital (2010a) "Prizraki proshlogo 'Transnefti' [Ghosts from Transneft's past]" *Neft' i Kapital*, June

Neft' i Kapital (2010b) "Chistoe delo [A clear case]" *Neft' i Kapital*, September

Neft' i Kapital (2011a) "Slaboe zveno [The weak link]" *Neft' i Kapital*, October

Neft' i Kapital (2011b) "Ot kazhdogo – po sposobnostyam [From each on the basis of ability]" *Neft' i Kapital*, November

Neft' i Kapital (2011c) "Kaspiiskii priliv [A Caspian influx]" *Neft' i Kapital*, April

Neft' i Kapital (2011d) "Politicheskii marshrut [The political route]" *Neft' i Kapital*, August

Neft' i Kapital (2012a) "Ne ochen'-to i khotelos'! [Not that we wanted it in the first place!]" *Neft' i Kapital*, January–February

Neft' i Kapital (2012b) "Khoteli kak luchshe… [They wanted the best…]" *Neft' i Kapital*, April

Neft' i Kapital (2012c) "Smena orientatsii [A change of orientation]" *Neft' i Kapital*, January–February

Neftegazovaya vertikal' (2012) "Statistika [Statistics]" *Neftegazovaya vertikal'*, No. 3, p.87

Neftegazovaya vertikal' (2013) "Statistika [Statistics]" *Neftegazovaya vertikal'*, No. 3, p.115

Neftegazovaya vertikal' (2014a) "Statistika [Statistics]" *Neftegazovaya vertikal'*, No. 3, p.83

Neftegazovaya vertikal' (2014b) "Truboprovody. Sil'noe zveno [Pipelines. The strong link]" *Neftegazovaya vertikal'*, No. 23–24, pp.82–87

Neftegazovaya vertikal' (2015) "Statistika [Statistics]" *Neftegazovaya vertikal'*, No. 3, p.75

Neftegazovaya vertikal' (2016a) "Statistika [Statistics]" *Neftegazovaya vertikal'*, No. 3–4, p.123

Neftegazovaya vertikal' (2016b) "Mirnaya ekspansiya [Peaceful expansion]" *Neftegazovaya vertikal'*, No. 22, pp.32–39

Neftegazovaya vertikal' (2017a) "Ne tol'ko megaproekty [Not just mega-projects]" *Neftegazovaya vertikal'*, No. 9, pp.52–56

Neftegazovaya vertikal' (2017b) "Statistika [Statistics]" *Neftegazovaya vertikal'*, No. 3–4, p.127

Nezavisimaya gazeta (2012) "Sammit ATES ne opravdal ozhidanii [The APEC summit did not deliver on expectations]", *Nezavisimaya gazeta*, 29 December, p. 5

Nikolaev, N. (2003) "Truba u viska [A pipe at the temples]" *Rossiiskie vesti*, 29 January, p.7

Oilcapital.ru (2002) "Neftenalivnyi port Primorsk rabotaet na polnuyu moshchnost' [The oil port Primorsk is working to full capacity]" [online]. 11 July (Moscow: IG Industriya). Available from: https://oilcapital.ru/news/markets/11-07-2002/neftenalivnoy-port-primorsk-rabotaet-na-polnuyu-moschnost [Accessed 12 April 2019]

Oilcapital.ru (2009) "'Transneft' ne planiruet povyshat' tarif na prokachku nefti v blizhaishee vremya [Transneft does not plan to increase the tariff on oil transport in the near future]" [online]. 19 April (Moscow: IG Industriya). Available from: https://oilcapital.ru/news/markets/19-05-2009/transneft-ne-planiruet-povyshat-tarif-na-prokachku-nefti-v-blizhayshee-vremya [Accessed 1 April 2019]

Oilcapital.ru (2012) "Reiting vliyaniya krupnykh predprinimatelei i top-menedzherov toplivno-energeticheskogo kompleksa v dekabre 2012 g. [Rating of the influence of major businessmen and top managers in the fuel and energy complex, December 2012]" [online]. 6 December (Moscow: IG Industriya). Available from: https://oilcapital.ru/news/companies/06-12-2012/reyting-vliyaniya-krupnyh-predprinimateley-i-top-menedzherov-tek-v-dekabre-2012-g [Accessed 18 March 2019]

Oilcapital.ru (2013a) "Minenergo RF planiruet do kontsa goda podgotovit' model' 'banka kachestva' nefti [The Energy Ministry plans to prepare a model for a 'quality bank' by the end of the year]" [online]. 18 March (Moscow: IG Industriya). Available from: https://oilcapital.ru/news/markets/18-03-2013/minenergo-rf-planiruet-do-kontsa-goda-podgotovit-model-banka-kachestva-nefti [Accessed 9 May 2019]

Oilcapital.ru (2013b) "'Transneft' otkazalas' ot prorabotki proekta otvoda ot VSTO do Komsomol'skogo NPZ [Transneft refuses to develop the ESPO spur to Komsomol refinery]" [online]. 30 September (Moscow: IG Industriya). Available from: https://oilcapital.ru/news/transport/30-09-2013/transneft-otkazalas-ot-prorabotki-proekta-otvoda-ot-vsto-do-komsomolskogo-npz [Accessed 3 May 2019]

Oilcapital.ru (2013c) "'Transneft' povysila stoimost' nefteprovoda Kuyumba–Taishet do 120 mlrd rub [Transneft increases cost of Kuyumba–Taishet pipeline to 120 billion rubles]" [online]. 16 September (Moscow: IG Industriya). Available from: https://oilcapital.ru/news/transport/16-09-2013/transneft-povysila-stoimost-nefteprovoda-kuyumba-tayshet-do-120-mlrd-rub [Accessed 3 May 2019]

Oilcapital.ru (2013d) "Tarify 'Transnefti' v 2014 g. mogut byt' zamorozheny – gazeta [Transneft's tariffs for 2014 may be subject to freeze – newspaper]" [online]. 26 September (Moscow: IG Industriya). Available from: https://oilcapital.ru/news/ma

rkets/26-09-2013/tarify-transnefti-v-2014-g-mogut-byt-zamorozheny-gazeta [Accessed 3 May 2019]
Oilcapital.ru (2013e) "Rasshirit' VSTO dlya 'Rosnefti' mozhno za schet povysheniya tarifa dlya kompanii – Novak [Novak: ESPO may be expanded for Rosneft at company's expense]" [online]. 2 July (Moscow: IG Industriya). Available from: https://oilcapital.ru/news/transport/02-07-2013/rasshirit-vsto-dlya-rosnefti-mozhno-za-schet-povysheniya-tarifa-dlya-kompanii-novak [Accessed 3 May 2019]
Oilcapital.ru (2013f) "Kazakhstan utverdil tarif dlya tranzita nefti iz RF v Kitai [Kazakhstan confirms tariff for oil transit from Russia to China]" [online]. 27 December (Moscow: IG Industriya). Available from: https://oilcapital.ru/news/export/27-12-2013/kazakhstan-utverdil-tarif-dlya-tranzita-nefti-iz-rf-v-kitay [Accessed 3 May 2019]
Oilcapital.ru (2014) "Nefteprovody Kazakhstana obespechat transportirovku vsei dobyvaemoi v strane nefti – general'nyi direktor AO "KazTransOil" [KazTransOil General director: Kazakhstan's oil pipelines sufficient for transport of all oil produced in country]" [online]. 21 October (Moscow: IG Industriya). Available from: https://oilcapital.ru/news/transport/21-10-2014/nefteprovody-kazakhstana-obespechat-transportirovku-vsey-dobyvaemoy-v-strane-nefti-generalnyy-direktor-ao-kaztransoyl [Accessed 3 May 2019]
Oilcapital.ru (2016) "Reiting vliyaniya krupnykh predprinimatelei i top-menedzherov toplivno-energeticheskogo kompleksa v marte 2016 g. [Rating of the influence of major businessmen and top managers in the fuel and energy complex, March 2016]" [online]. 29 March (Moscow: IG Industriya). Available from: https://oilcapital.ru/news/companies/29-03-2016/reyting-vliyaniya-krupnyh-predprinimateley-i-top-menedzherov-toplivno-energeticheskogo-kompleksa-v-marte-2016-g [Accessed 20 February 2019]
Oilcapital.ru (2017) "'Transneft': ideyu banka kachestva nefti slozhno realizovat' [Transneft: The idea of a quality bank is difficult to implement]" [online]. 28 December 2017 (Moscow: IG Industriya). Available from: https://oilcapital.ru/news/markets/28-12-2017/transneft-ideyu-banka-kachestva-nefti-slozhno-realizovat [Accessed 25 April 2019]
Oliphant, R. (2010) "Putin orders openness at Transneft" *The Moscow Times*, 25 October, p.1
Osetinskaya, E. (1999) "Neftyaniki ne khotyat svyazyvat'sya s Chechnei [The oilmen do not want to associate with Chechnya]" *Segodnya*, 9 October
Osetinskaya, E. (2000a) "Tumannyi BTS [Foggy BPS]" *Vedomosti*, 11 February
Osetinskaya, E. (2000b) "Mintopenergo zhelaet znat' [The Fuel and Energy Ministry wants to know]" *Vedomosti*, 24 February
Osetinskaya, E. (2000c) "U Minenergo zabrali trubu [Pipelines taken away from the Energy Ministry]" *Vedomosti*, 9 November
Osetinskaya, E. (2000d) "Khristenko vzyalsya za trubu [Khristenko got busy with the pipelines]" *Vedomosti*, 24 November
Osetinskaya, E. (2001) "Eksport gotovyat k torgam [Export prepared for sale]" *Vedomosti*, 27 April
Osetinskaya, E. and Velikanov, S. (1999) "Truby goryat… [The pipes are burning…]" *Segodnya*, 17 September
OzForex (2019) "Yearly average rates" [online]. (Sydney: OzForex). Available from: https://www.ofx.com/en-au/forex-news/historical-exchange-rates/yearly-average-rates/ [Accessed 30 April 2019]

Paramonov, S. (2001) "Rynochnye obstoyatel'stva. Rossiya poluchila novoe 'okno v Evropu' [Market conditions. Russia received a new 'window to Europe']" *Rossiiskaya gazeta*, 17 August, p.26

Petrov, N. and Titkov, A. (1999) *Nachalo kampanii* [*The beginning of the campaign*] (Moscow: Gendalf)

Poluektov, N. (1999) "Vzyatie 'Transnefti' [The conquer of Transneft]" *Kommersant*, 22 September, p.3

Pravosudov, S. (2003) "Vagit Alekperov: 'Otkuda vy znaete, chto Kukuru ukrali beznakazanno?' [Vagit Alekperov: 'How do you know that Kukura was kidnapped with impunity?'" *Russkii Fokus*, 14 April

Prime-TASS (2006) "Pravitel'stvo RF utverdilo rekomendatsii federal'nym vedomstvam v otnoshenii pozitsii gosaktsionera po voprosam vyplaty dividendov i raspredeleniya pribyli [The Russian government has confirmed its recommendations to federal agencies on the state's position on dividends payouts and profit distribution]" *Prime-TASS*, 1 June

Primorskii okeanarium (2019) "Primorskii okeanarium – odin iz krupneishchikh nauchno-poznavatel'nykh kompleksov mira [The Primore ocean centre: One of the largest scientific educational complexes in the world]". Available from http://primocean.ru/primorskiy-okeanarium-odna-iz-samyh-cennyh-i-interesnyh-zhemchuzhin-kraya.html [Accessed 10 May 2019]

Protsenko, A. (1998) "Chetvertaya opora Rossii [Russia's fourth buttress]" *Trud*, 20 October

Pynnöniemi, K. (2008) *New road, new life, New Russia*. Ph.D. thesis, University of Tampere

Quiring, M. (2007) "Man sollte die aktive Rolle Putins nicht überschätzen [One shouldn't overestimate Putin's active role]" *Die Welt*, 12 November, p.5

Rahimov, R. (2019) "Turkmenistan redirects its oil export flows from Azerbaijan to Russia" *Eurasia Daily Monitor*, 25 February

RBK (2018) *RBK 500: Reiting rossiiskogo biznesa* [*RBK 500: The Russian Business Rating*] [online]. Moscow. Available from: https://www.rbc.ru/rbc500/ [Accessed 23 November 2018]

Rebrov, D. (2005) "Mazeikiu Nafta lishili kazakhskoi nefti [Mazeikiu Nafta is deprived of Kazakh oil]" *Vremya novostei*, 18 November, p.8

Rebrov, D. (2006) "Administrativnoe preimushchestvo [Administrative advantage]" *Vremya novostei*, 13 February

Rebrov, D. (2008) "Sergei Maslov ushel na birzhu [Sergei Maslov went to the exchange]" *Kommersant*, 3 October, p.17

Rebrov, D. (2009a) "'Stroit' mozhno chto ugodno, no tarif togda budet bezumnyi' ['You can build anything, but the tariff then becomes insane']" *Kommersant*, 3 December, p.14

Rebrov, D. (2009b) "Uspokoili spetskorrespondenta otdela biznesa Denisa Rebrova [The business section's special correspondent Denis Rebrov is reassured]" *Kommersant*, 10 February, p.9

Reuters News (1994) "Russia's Gazprom in oil pipeline deal with Greece" *Reuters*, 15 September

Reznik, I. (2000a) "'LUKoil' oboshel 'Transneft' [Lukoil gets round Transneft]" *Kommersant*, 8 September, p.4

Reznik, I. (2000b) "'My eshche ne znaem, kak delit' tarif' ['We still do not know how to divide the tariff]" *Kommersant*, 8 September, p.4

Reznik, I. (2001) "Interv'yu: Semen Vainshtok, prezident transportnoi kompanii 'Transneft' [Interview: Semyon Vainshtok, president of the transport company Transneft]" *Vedomosti*, 25 October

Reznik, I. (2002a) "Interv'yu: Semen Vainshtok, prezident 'Transnefti' [Interview: Semyon Vainshtok, Transneft's president]" *Vedomosti*, 14 October

Reznik, I. (2002b) "'Transneft'-kontroler [Transneft the controller]" *Vedomosti*, 3 June

Reznik, I. (2003) "Interv'yu: Semen Vainshtok, prezident kompanii 'Transneft' [Interview: Semen Vainshtok, president of Transneft]" *Vedomosti*, 26 November

Reznik, I. and Binchuk, P. (2000) "Putin podygral Alekperovu [Putin played up to Alekperov]" *Kommersant*, 11 February

RFE/RL (1997) "RFE/RL Newsline" *Radio Free Europe/Radio Liberty*, 14 November

RFE/RL (1999) "RFE/RL Newsline" *Radio Free Europe/Radio Liberty*, 27 September

Romanova, L. (1999) "Mintop obvinyaet eks-prezidenta 'Transnefti' [The Fuel Ministry is accusing the ex-president of Transneft]" *Nezavisimaya gazeta*, 2 November, p.1

Romanova, L. (2000) "Krizis ukrainskoi nezavisimosti [A crisis in Ukrainian independence]" *Nezavisimaya gazeta*, 25 January

Romanova, O., Volobuyev, I. and Useinov, A. (1997) "Rossiya otkazalas' ot transportirovki azerbaidzhanskoi nefti cherez Chechnyu [Russia refuses to transport Azerbaijani oil across Chechnya]" *Segodnya*, 5 February

Rosbalt (2007) "'Transneft' teryaet interes k nefteprovodu Khar'yaga-Indiga [Transneft loses interest in Khar'yaga–Indiga pipeline]" [online]. 6 January 2007 (Moscow/St Petersburg: Rosbalt). Available from: http://www.rosbalt.ru/main/2007/01/06/281207.html [Accessed 8 May 2019]

Rutland, P. (1999) "Oil, politics, and foreign policy" in Lane, D. ed., *The political economy of Russian oil* (Lanham, Maryland: Rowman & Littlefield), pp.163–188

Samoilova, T. (2000) "'Transneft' teryaet neft' [Transneft is losing oil]" *Vedomosti*, 31 August

Sapozhnikov, P. and Ovchinnikov, R. (2000) "Baltiiskaya truboprovodnaya sistema zakryta [The Baltic pipeline system is closed]" *Kommersant*, 6 September, p.4

Savushkin, S. (2003) "Igry patriotov [Patriots' games]" *Neft' i Kapital*, September

Savushkin, S. (2007) "Zadvizhka Moskvy [Moscow's catch]" *Neft' i Kapital*, January–February

Sborov, A. (2000) "Kalyuzhnyi poshel po delu 'LUKoila' v Baku [Kalyuzhnyi goes to Baku on the Lukoil case]" *Kommersant*, 14 July, p.3

Sharip, F. (2018) "Faced with Chinese expansion, Kazakhstan seeks alternative energy markets" *Eurasia Daily Monitor*, 30 April

Shevel'kova, O. (2005) "'Kazmunaigaz' ne puskayut v Litvu [KazMunaiGaz is not let into Lithuania]" *Gazeta*, 18 November, p.21

Shvedko, I. (2002) "Bor'ba za Slavneft' ne zakonchena [The fight for Slavneft is not over]", *Mirovaya energeticheskaya politika*, 1 (4): 69–71

Siddiky, C.I.A. (2012) *Cross-border pipeline arrangements. What would a single regulatory framework look like?* (Alphen aan den Rijn: Kluwer Law International)

Sim, L.-C. (2008) *The rise and fall of privatization in the Russian oil industry* (Basingstoke: Palgrave-Macmillan)

Skornyakova, A. and Skorlygina, N. (2006) "Rossiya nashla komu doverit' KTK [Russia found someone with whom to entrust CPC]" *Kommersant*, 13 January, p.5

Slyusarenko, S. (1999) "Primakov blagoslovil novye porty na Baltike [Primakov blesses new ports on the Baltic Sea]" *Kommersant*, 25 February, p.7

Smirnov, G. (1998) "'Svyashchennaya korova' 'Transnefti' [Transneft's sacred cow]" *Neft' i Kapital*, February

Socor, V. (2007) "Bridgehead in Europe: Kazakhstan acquires Romania's Rompetrol" *Eurasia Daily Monitor*, 7 September

Socor, V. (2008) "Oil-handling capacities growing and available on Georgia's Black Sea Coast" *Eurasia Daily Monitor*, 13 February

Socor, V. (2009) "Samsun–Ceyhan pipeline project designed to divert Kazakhstani oil" *Eurasia Daily Monitor*, 23 October

Socor, V. (2010) "Moscow tightens squeeze on Belarus oil industry" *Eurasia Daily Monitor*, 15 January

Socor, V. (2012) "Russia completing Baltic Pipeline system construction, reducing Druzhba pipeline flow" *Eurasia Daily Monitor*, 24 February

Sokolov, A. (1999) "S. i V. sideli na trube [S. and V. sat on a pipe]" *Nezavisimaya gazeta – Figury i litsa*, 8 October, p.4

Solodovnikova, A. (2013) "'Transneft' delit chuzhie sverkhpribyli [Transneft shares others' superprofits]" *Kommersant*, 25 November, p.1

Solov'ev, D. (2000) "Proshu slova. Truba nezavisimosti [In one's own words. The pipe of independence]" *Profil'*, 6 November, p.22

SPB *Vedomosti* (1999) "'I vse-taki v Porvoo!' ['And yet it will go to Porvoo!']" *SPB Vedomosti*, 23 February

Starinskaya, G. (2010) "Truba za schet neftyanikov [A pipeline at the oilmen's expense]" *RBC Daily*, 6 September

Statista (2019) "Euro (EUR) to Russian ruble (RUB) average annual exchange rate from 1999 to 2018" [online]. (Hamburg: Statista). Available from: https://www.statista.com/statistics/412824/euro-to-ruble-average-annual-exchange-rate/ [Accessed 30 April 2019]

Stevens, P. (2009) *Transit troubles. Pipelines as a source of conflict*. Chatham House Report (London: Chatham House)

Stolyarov, B. (2000) "Sensatsiya! Podvig Khristenko [Sensation! Khristenko's accomplishment]" *Novaya gazeta*, 20 November

Stratfor (2005) "Russia: Improving the oil infrastructure", Stratfor [online] (16 August). Available from http://www.stratfor.com/russia_improving_oil_infrastructure [Accessed 1 April 2019]

Strel'tsov, A. (1999) "Yuzhnyi marshrut neftyanoi reki [The oil river's southern course]" *Ekonomika i zhizn'*, 22 May

Surzhenko, V. (2007) "Den'gi v obmen na trubu [Money in return for a pipe]" *Vedomosti*, 20 September

Surzhenko, V. and Reznik, I. (2008) "'Vse ravno, skol'ko stoyat aktsii', – Nikolai Tokarev, prezident 'Transnefti' ['It does not matter how much the shares go for', says Nikolai Tokarev, Transneft's president]" *Vedomosti*, 18 February

Sysoev, G. and Gankin, L. (1998) "Rossiya ob"yavila Latvii neftyanoi boikot [Russia declares oil boycott on Latvia]" *Kommersant*, 9 April, p.3

Tkachev, I. (2017) "Schetnaya palata priznala nedostovernym plan Minfina po sboru dividendov [The Audit Chamber finds the Finance Ministry's plan for dividends extraction unreliable]" *RBC Daily*, 13 October

Tomashevskaya, O. et al. (2007) "Iz-za bat'ki – v peklo [To hell because of Batka]" *Vremya novostei*, 10 January, p.1

Tovkailo, M. and Biryukov, A. (2010) "Chastnaya ugroza [The private menace]" *Vedomosti*, 2 August

Transneft-Diaskan (2019) "AO 'Transneft-Diaskan' v 2018 godu vypolnilo diagnostiku bolee 4 tys. kilometrov truboprovodov za rubezhom [Transneft-Diaskan carried out diagnostics of more than 4000 km pipelines abroad]" [online]. (Moscow: Transneft-Diaskan). Available from: https://diascan.transneft.ru/press/news/?id=59611 [Accessed 6 May 2019]

Transneft (2006) *Godovoi otchet OAO "AK Transneft" za 2005 god* [*Annual report for Transneft for 2005*] (Moscow: Transneft)

Transneft (2007) *Godovoi otchet OAO "AK Transneft" za 2006 god* [*Annual Report for Transneft for 2006*] (Moscow: Transneft)

Transneft (2008) *Godovoi otchet za 2007 god* [*Annual Report for 2007*] (Moscow: Transneft)

Transneft (2009a) "Vo vtornik 26 maya prezident OAO 'AK Transneft' Nikolai Petrovich Tokarev vstretilsya s zhurnalistami [On Tuesday 26 May Transneft's president, Nikolai Petrovich Tokarev, met with journalists]" [online]. 26 May 2009 (Moscow: Transneft). Available from: http://www.transneft.ru/news/view/id/128/ [Accessed 1 April 2019]

Transneft (2009b) *Godovoi otchet za 2008 god* [*Annual report for 2008*] (Moscow: Transneft)

Transneft (2010) *Godovoi otchet za 2009 god* [*Annual report for 2009*] (Moscow: Transneft)

Transneft (2011a) *Informatsiya ob okazanii blagotvoritel'noi pomoshchi OAO "AK Transneft"'* v 2011 g. [Information about the rendering of charity aid by Transneft in 2011 (Moscow: Transneft). Available from: http://www.transneft.ru/files/2012-05/2Z56Q.x1sTBpubN.pdf [Accessed 1 April 2019]

Transneft (2011b) *OAO AK "Transneft". Godovoi otchet za 2010 god* [*JSC Transneft. Annual report for 2010*] (Moscow: Transneft)

Transneft (2014a) "Ustav [Statutes]" [online]. (Moscow: Transneft). Available from: http://transneft.ru/information/104/ [Accessed 1 April 2019]

Transneft (2014b) "Istoriya [History]" [online]. (Moscow: Transneft). Available from: http://transneft.ru/about/story/ [Accessed 1 April 2019]

Transneft (2018) *Godovoi otchet za 2017 god* [*Annual Report for 2017*] (Moscow: Transneft)

Transneft (2019) "Proekty 'Transnefti' v oblasti blagotvoritel'nosti [Transneft's projects in the charity sphere]" [online]. (Moscow: Transneft). Available from: https://www.transneft.ru/social_responsibility/charity/proekti/ [Accessed 10 May 2019]

Transnefteprodukt (2009) *Godovoi otchet za 2008 g.* [*Annual report for 2008*] (Moscow: Transnefteprodukt)

Tutushkin, A. (2005) "'Transneft' vmeshalas' v sdelku 'YuKOSa' [Transneft meddles in Yukos's deal]" *Vedomosti*, 18 November

Tutushkin, A. (2008) "V ocheredi k trube [In line for the pipe]" *Vedomosti*, 12 March

US Department of the Treasury (2014) "Treasury sanctions Russian officials, members of the Russian leadership's inner circle, and an entity for involvement in the situation in Ukraine" [online]. 20 March 2014 (Washington, DC: US Department of the Treasury). Available from: https://www.treasury.gov/press-center/press-releases/Pages/jl23331.aspx [Accessed 13 January 2017]

Ubushaeva, K. and Ivankina, E. (2014) "'Transneft' bez investtarifa [Transneft without an investment tariff]" *RBC Daily*, 12 February, p.5

US Office Almaty (2006) Kazakhstan: Kulibayev discusses energy with Ambassador, 06ALMATY1237/Wikileaks #59752. Issue date 7 April 2006. *Cablegate* [online].

(Published by Wikileaks 1 September 2011). Available from: https://wikileaks.org/plusd/cables/06ALMATY1237_a.html [Accessed 1 April 2019]

Useinov, A. and Klasson, M. (1999a) "'Transneft' stala zalozhnitsei Chechni [Transneft has become a hostage of Chechnya]" *Vremya MN*, 21 May

Useinov, A. and Klasson, M. (1999b) "Syurprizy dlya 'Transnefti' [Surprises for Transneft]" *Vremya MN*, 9 February

Useinov, A. and Tutushkin, A. (1999) "Nadoelo [Sick of it]" *Vremya MN*, 21 July

Vainshtok, S. (2000) "Transneft': 46,700 km of Oil Pipelines", *International Affairs (Moscow)* 46 (2): 44–47

Vasil'ev, A. and Suchkov, A. (1999) "Prirodnye resursy [Natural resources]" *AiF – Interfax*, 29 January

Vedomosti (1999) "Vainshtok stal tsarem truby [Vainshtok becomes pipeline tsar]" *Vedomosti*, 17 September

Vedomosti (2000) "Azerbaidzhanu ne khvatilo nefti [Azerbaijan does not have enough oil]" *Vedomosti*, 12 January

Vedomosti (2003) "'Transneft' khochet kupit' 50% Ventspils Nafta [Transneft wants to buy 50% of Ventspils Nafta]" *Vedomosti*, 11 April

Vedomosti (2017) "Vkrattse [In brief]" *Vedomosti*, 13 April, p.11

Verezemskii, S. (1998a) "'Transneft' stoit messy [Transneft is well worth a mass]" *Neft' i Kapital*, October

Verezemskii, S. (1998b) "Peremeny v Transnefti [Changes in Transneft]" *Neft' i Kapital*, August

Vin'kov, A. and Rubanov, I. (2006) "Osobo tsennaya gosudarstvennaya kompaniya [A particularly valuable state company]" *Ekspert*, 19 June, pp.82–88

Vin'kov, A. et al. (2004) "Tsena bezdeistviya [The cost of doing nothing]" *Ekspert*, 11 October, pp.38–43

Vinogradova, O. (2015) "Marshruty rossiiskoi nefti [The routes of Russian oil]" *Neftegazovaya vertikal'*, No. 7, pp.56–62

Vodyanova, M. (1999) "Zashchemlenie neftyanogo nerva [Pinching the oil nerve]" *Obshchaya gazeta*, 7 October

Vremya MN (1999) "Neft' propala [The oil disappeared]" *Vremya MN*, 30 November

Wikipedia (2019) "Russian Accounting Standards/Rossiiskie standarty bukhgal'terskogo ucheta" [online]. (San Francisco: Wikimedia Foundation). Available from: https://en.wikipedia.org/wiki/Russian_Accounting_Standards [Accessed 1 May 2019]

Yafimava, K. (2011) *The transit dimension of EU energy security* (Oxford: Oxford University Press for the Oxford Institute for Energy Studies)

Yakoreva, A. (2016) "Chernaya dyra s polovinoi trilliona. Skol'ko deneg skopil 'Rosneftegaz' [A black hole with half a billion. How much money Rosneftegaz accumulated]" *Republic (Slon)* 1 November

Zhiznin, S. (2010) "Nuzhna li Rossii 'Druzhba'? [Does Russia need Druzhba?]" *Nezavisimaya gazeta*, 9 February, p.11

Zhulebin, E. (1999) "Shchedraya ruka Viktora Kalyuzhnogo [Viktor Kalyuzhnyi's generous hand]" *Kommersant-Vlast'*, 14 September

Zimin, D. (2012) "How can foreign companies influence Russia's economic course? The cases of Finnish firms Fortum and Neste", *Post-Soviet Affairs*, 28 (2): 209–231

Zotova, E. (2008) "KTK pod kontrolem [CPC under control]" *Vedomosti*, 5 November

Zuev, A. (2009) "Eshche odin vykhod v Evropu [Yet another outlet to Europe]" *Truboprovodnyi transport nefti*, 2009 (5): 15–17.

7 The gas industry
Gazprom

Gazprom is the Russian company for gas production, gas pipeline transport, gas transmission and export. Two recurrent topics in the literature on this company are its position as a state within the Russian state (e.g. in Stern, 2005, p.172; Victor and Sayfer, 2012), and its role as a tool for the Russian state abroad (Hill, 2004; Finon and Locatelli, 2008; Sherr, 2013). In this chapter, it is argued that these two perspectives, which appear to contradict each other, represent the domestic and international sides of Gazprom's interaction with the state. In this respect, Gazprom is similar to the other cases studied here. The Soviet legacy of an integrated pipeline system, a natural monopoly, was the foundation for Gazprom's power, and a tool for the state. In this regard, Gazprom's relations with the state resemble those of both Transneft and RAO UES. But Gazprom's income from gas sales abroad made it, and continues to make it, more powerful and more important in the political economy. The volume of its rent streams matters. In the context of this book, Gazprom is both a typical case and an outlier due to its size and importance.

The Russian gas industry

Russia has the largest gas reserves in the world. Gazprom holds around 70 per cent of them, and produces 68 per cent of Russia's gas (Victor and Sayfer, 2012, p.655; Gazprom, 2019b). Gazprom Group is Russia's largest company, with a turnover of 6,546 billion rubles and 469,600 employees in 2017 (RBK, 2018). Gazprom began its life as something of an anomaly in the global hydrocarbon industry. It produced and marketed only gas, while other major, vertically integrated petroleum companies produce and market both oil and gas. This was a legacy of the planned Soviet economy, where the oil and gas industries were organised separately. In 2005, in an acquisition discussed in this chapter, it also acquired a large oil producing subsidiary, Gazprom Neft. Gazprom Neft is among Russia's top four oil producers. Another subsidiary, Gazprom Energoholding, generates around 15 per cent of all electricity in Russia, making Gazprom Group the largest electricity generating company. Gazprom Group now resembles its international peers more than it did in

1992 or 2005. But it remains very much a gas company, producing 12 per cent of global gas output (Gazprom, 2019b). Gazprom was for long the only significant Russian gas producer. Today, gas is also produced by two international consortia at Sakhalin, by Novatek[1] at Yamal, at few smaller independent companies, and by oil companies. A considerable part of the latter's gas production is associated gas.[2] In this chapter, unless Gazprom Group or non-gas based subsidiaries are referred to explicitly, the reference is to Gazprom's gas business.

With gas, consumption and production are closely connected (Ericson, 2012, pp.621–622). Gas demand is less elastic than oil demand, meaning that consumers in general are less responsive to price changes for gas than for example oil. Substituting oil for gas in primary energy supply can be complicated and costly. Arranging alternative gas supply is not always an economical, or even feasible option. Gas suppliers tend to have considerable market power over their customers. This is especially the case when a supplier controls both production and transmission. For this reason, policies to open up competitive gas markets will often prescribe ownership unbundling or limit the integration of gas production with transmission systems, in parallel to the measures advocated for electricity markets. This applies for example in the European Union's Third Energy Package.

Pipeline is the lowest-cost option for gas transport. The considerable cost of establishing such systems makes them a natural monopoly once in place. Once in operation, gas pipelines are cheap and efficient, and they link supplier and consumer in a close relationship. Stopping gas transmission bears the risk of damaging, even blowing up pipelines and other installations. Establishing such relationships requires a high level of trust.

The Russian pipeline system is massive, consisting of the United Gas Supply System (UGSS)[3], separate regional mains grids in parts of Russia, and local transmission lines. All told, this is a 172,100 km network (2019) that extends from some of the world's largest gas fields to end consumers in Russia and connects to grids in Europe and Asia. It is owned by Gazprom.

The break-up of the Soviet Union and Soviet legacies

Gazprom appeared in 1989 as a so-called concern in the Soviet gas industry. This implied some autonomy from the state (Kryukov and Moe, 1996, pp.7–9). Viktor Chernomyrdin, a former Gas Industry Minister (1985–1989), was the main force behind Gazprom, along with a close associate from the gas industry, Rem Vyakhirev (Bilanenko, 2013). Chernomyrdin aimed to channel income from gas exports into the investment-starved production and transport sectors (*Neft' i Kapital*, 2013c). In 1990–1991, he secured Gazprom's control over Soyuzgazeksport, the entity responsible for gas exports to Europe (Emel'yanov, 2003; *Neftegazovaya vertikal'*, 2003; Gustafson, 2012, p.70). Soyuzgazeksport's rent streams supported Gazprom's autonomy in the final months of the Soviet Union. The crisis in the wider economy created

Figure 7.1 Map of selected gas trunk pipelines in Russia and eastern Europe
The map is based on the author's compilation from a variety of sources.
(c) Anna Therese Klingstedt and Ingerid M. Opdahl, 2019

opportunities for insiders to consolidate and expand the gas industry under a single umbrella. Gazprom turned into an indispensable support for the Russian state and the ruling coalition.

During the first wave of privatisation in early 1992, First Deputy Prime Minister Egor Gaidar (Prime Minister from June) ordered an audit of Gazprom's foreign accounts (Bardin, 1992; Kirichenko and Solov'ev, 1992; Victor and Sayfer, 2012, p.662). This was an effort to gain access to Gazprom. Chernomyrdin, shortly afterwards appointed Fuel and Energy Minister, in practice reversed the effort by granting Gazprom control of foreign exports (Kirichenko and Solov'ev, 1992; Victor and Sayfer, 2012, p.662). That sealed the fate of this first attempt at reform. Gaidar most likely saw the exemption of Gazprom from structural reform as a necessary compromise to preserve stability (Gustafson, 2012, p.71). Gazprom's export monopoly was now connected to its role as a stabilising force in the economy. Gazprom was allowed to accumulate tax-exempt stabilisation funds under its autonomous control and accumulate export earnings in foreign currency accounts abroad (Victor and Sayfer, 2012, p.662), creating an informal channel for rent that could be directed towards the state's needs.

As a result, the Soviet legacy in the Russian gas industry was an integrated organisation that controlled the chain from production to consumer. Compared to other post-Soviet economic sectors, which were directly affected by the transformational recession, there was greater continuity in the gas industry.

Keeping afloat and muddling through

Vyakhirev succeeded Chernomyrdin, prime minister from late 1992, at Gazprom. During Vyakhirev's time as Gazprom's head (1992–2001), the gas monopoly was reinforced and extended into other areas, rather than encroached upon (Kryukov and Moe, 1996, p.3). Valuable staff had moved from the Soviet Ministry to Gazprom in 1989–1991. Gazprom assumed the strategic, regulatory and operational management of the gas industry from production to consumption. This was formalised in a November 1992 decree (Decree No. 1333, 1992); Gazprom was also entrusted with the management and development of the UGSS (Decree No. 538, 1992).

The decision to retain state ownership of Gazprom delayed reform of the company. Gaidar government reformers had intended to reform Gazprom at a later stage and open up for competition in the gas industry. This did not happen. Vyakhirev and the rest of Gazprom's management were a powerful brake on reform (*Neft' i Kapital*, 2004). They were hostile to any interference from market reformers, especially Anatolii Chubais, in 1992–1996 first deputy prime minister and until November 1994 responsible for state property (Rozhkova and Reznik, 2013). Gazprom was also stronger than the new Fuel and Energy Ministry, which found its ability to oversee the company restricted (Kryukov and Moe, 1996, pp.7, 16–17; Malkova and Igumenov, 2012; Victor and Sayfer, 2012, p.662). To Vyakhirev, late Soviet practices, including autarchy within Gazprom and autonomy from the state, suited Gazprom well also in the 1990s (Bilanenko, 2013). There was considerable support for his position in the population and among the political elite (Victor and Sayfer, 2012, pp.662–663). When so many other organisations were subjected to structural reform, many saw a priority in maintaining the status quo in one organisation that worked according to established principles.

Gas production continued with only a minor slump in demand in 1991–1992 (Stern, 1993, p.13). Gazprom's export earnings from its European customers provided the company with significant resources, especially compared to other parts of the Russian economy. Gazprom's rent streams stabilised society, the state, and supported the regime. In-house social services for 300,000-plus employees and their families contributed to social stability (Rozhkova and Reznik, 2013). More importantly, gas was delivered across Russia to factories, offices and private homes at still-subsidised prices, and in spite of chronic non-payments. Due to this, it is difficult to exaggerate the influence of Gazprom on the Russian state at the time. Gazprom was, in the words of Economy Minister Evgenii Yasin (1994–1997), "like a second Russian [state] budget when the first was exceptionally empty" (Rozhkova and Reznik, 2013). It included supporting President Yeltsin financially in the conflict with the Supreme Soviet in 1992–1993 and the 1996 election campaign (Popov, 2007). In this way, Gazprom enabled the ruling coalition to maintain its power advantage over potential rivals. This rent sharing protected Gazprom's monopoly in gas distribution, its extensive autonomy from the state, and discretion to regulate the gas sector. Any government contemplating reform of Gazprom would have to weigh the long-term benefits of profitability in Gazprom against the politically crucial considerations of maintaining stability and support for the ruling coalition (Ericson, 2012, p.634). Political survival in the shorter term was always a priority.

In return for acting as a stabilising mechanism, Gazprom enjoyed extensive autonomy. Vyakhirev set the terms of relations with the state as he saw fit, with the effect of gradually restricting state access to the company. In this way, Gazprom functioned as a classic state within the state. Partial privatisation was authorised by Decree no 1333, which was drafted by Chernomyrdin (Decree No. 1333, 1992). It also reorganised Gazprom, the state "concern", into a shareholding company. The decree enabled privatisation of up to 60 per cent of Gazprom's stock within three years, a period subsequently extended (Decree No. 1333, (1992) 1997). Two clauses further limited state participation in Gazprom's affairs. Clause 7 allowed Gazprom to retain at least 50 per cent of the dividends on state-held shares to finance maintenance works and other investment in the three years following the decree. Clause 8 entrusted the Board of Directors with the management of the state's shares on behalf of the state (Decree No. 1333, 1992). The government would appoint Board members, but the trustee mechanism restricted the state's access to Gazprom. Accordingly, the Board would have greater autonomy than indicated by the state's formal share. The clause had no time limit. Vyakhirev was shortly thereafter appointed Board Chairman. In effect, Vyakhirev managed the state's stake and controlled access to the company.

The state's share of Gazprom fluctuated between 35 and 40 per cent after partial privatisation (Gazprom, 2004a, p.16; Stern, 2005, p.170), as formalised by a 1998 decree (Decree No. 887, 1998). Taking advantage of new legislation on trustee management (Decree No. 2296, 1993), Vyakhirev in 1994 came to hold a 35 per cent share package in trustee management on behalf of the state, leaving only 5 per cent in actual state control (Nikolaev et al., 1994; Stern, 2005, p.172). The agreement was prolonged for three more years in 1996 (Decree No. 599, 1996), although conditions were revised somewhat in favour of the state in 1997 (Decree No. 478, 1997). Before this revision,

Vyakhirev had apparently had the option to buy out the state at a price of one ruble per share (Panyushkin and Zygar', 2007, pp.46–48). After revision, the management had a right to claim and acquire, at asking price, any stake put out for privatisation before 1 January 1999 (Decree No. 529, 1997). The right was never exercised (Popov, 2007). Other members of Chernomyrdin's government, and later governments, attempted – unsuccessfully – to abrogate the trustee arrangement (Kravets, 1998; Levin, 2000; Panyushkin and Zygar', 2007, pp.44–50). It remained in force to expiry (Popov, 2007).

Gazprom's management used privatisation of Gazprom's holdings to consolidate and increase insider ownership. A conglomerate of companies indirectly affiliated with Gazprom, or its management, began to appear. Vyakhirev was at the peak of this insider consolidation. The engineering and construction company Stroitransgaz, controlled by Vyakhirev's and Chernomyrdin's children, received around 80 per cent of Gazprom's construction contracts. Stroitransgaz held 4.83 per cent of the shares in Gazprom (Reznik, 2002b; 2009).

While Chernomyrdin remained Prime Minister (1992–1998), Vyakhirev had a powerful political patron. Yeltsin, on at least one occasion in 1997, vetoed changes to Vyakhirev's position (Rozhkova and Reznik, 2013). There was a limit to this support. Gazprom's 1996 tax arrears reached 70 trillion rubles (Rozhkova and Reznik, 2013). The government increased pressure on Gazprom in 1997 to pay taxes, and the imperative to collect some of it overruled informal constraints. Chernomyrdin now supported his ministers. Gazprom began to pay its taxes. Other businesses followed suit (Rozhkova and Reznik, 2013). But any government minister wanting to remove Vyakhirev, and embark on Gazprom reform, would still have to win over the Prime Minister, President, and Duma members (Bagrov, 2000).

A last, minor brake on reform was the lack of professional minority owners. From 1997 to 2005, there was a 9 per cent limit on foreign ownership. Initially a temporary provision intended to remain in force during partial privatisation, it proved difficult to abolish (Decree No. 529, 1997). Over time, it distorted Gazprom's share prices (Gustafson, 2012, pp.338–339). One consequence was low capitalisation, which, combined with management control, made Gazprom unattractive to active shareholders who potentially could have supported reform.

The 1997 decree on reform of the natural monopolies, which marked the beginning of electricity reform, included also Gazprom (Decree No. 426, 1997). First Deputy Prime Minister Nemtsov drafted the decree, but the Gazprom section was edited by Chernomyrdin (Berger and Proskurnina, 2008, pp.43–44). The resulting Gazprom reform plan was vague compared to the one covering electricity. With Vyakhirev in charge of Gazprom, the reform process did not start. The government ministers charged with decree implementation, not least Nemtsov himself, seem to have realised the difficulty of instigating major reforms without the Gazprom management on board (Ivanov, 1997). Without management cooperation, the state had no access to the organisation. Reform without access, if at all possible, might damage Gazprom, and the economy.

The trade collapse

From the moment Gazprom acquired control of Soyuzgazeksport, European markets became crucial to Gazprom and Russia. From its profitable gas sales to Europe, underpinned by long-term contracts with take-or-pay clauses,[4] Gazprom received a predictable income, and the state a revenue source. Europe was the only market where Gazprom made a profit, and this began to change only from 2004.

Gazprom's de facto monopoly in gas export to Europe rested on two provisions. After foreign trade restrictions were abolished in July 1994, Gazprom retained export control through an obligation to effectuate all gas export according to bilateral agreements between Russia and other states (Decree No. 2213, 1994). A lack of spare transit capacity in Ukraine completed Gazprom's control of the "single export channel" to Europe. Inside Russia, Gazprom's management of the gas grid placed it in control of other producers' transport options and customer relationships. With the new Gas Supply Law of 1999, Gazprom became the owner of UGSS (Yafimava, 2015, p.2). From 1997, it was obliged to give access to other producers (third-party access). However, it continued to exercise a high degree of control over the real access terms for third parties, restricting the possibilities for other producers (Henderson, 2015, p.356). Third-party access did not extend to export.

The important European market shaped Gazprom's priorities with regard to the post-Soviet states. It was paramount to maintain transit to Europe, with a high degree of control over export, and maximal control over transit routes. On its own, the post-Soviet region was Gazprom's smallest market by volume and income. Here, gas was still delivered as a subsidy, making gas markets in the Commonwealth of Independent States[5] (CIS) "[markets] in name only" (Mitrova, 2009, p.26). Due to its priority of transit to Europe, Gazprom accepted the transit terms of Ukraine, Belarus and Moldova (Stern, 2005, p.66; Mitrova, 2009, pp.26–28; Pirani, 2009b, p.8). In consequence, transit was often bartered for gas deliveries to the transit states (Mitrova, 2009, p.14). Cheap gas began to underpin Gazprom's relations with post-Soviet customers, and Russia's relations with its neighbours. In this way, a share of the gas rents from sales to European customers were distributed in the post-Soviet region. Gas relations were integral to foreign policy, and by maintaining the gas subsidy, Russia aimed to preserve regional stability (*Transitions*, 1995). In that context, subsidised prices and transit for barter were seen, by both sides, as Russian concessions that would ultimately infringe on the possibility of states like Belarus and Ukraine to achieve real economic and political independence of Russia (Markus, 1995; 1996). However, for Gazprom's post-Soviet customers it was impossible to pay the full cost of gas, and there was no feasible alternative supply.

In the early and mid-1990s, ten post-Soviet countries depended on imports for 80 per cent of their gas consumption or more (all data retrieved from IEA, 2015). Among these, five were 100 per cent dependent on imports:

Armenia, Estonia, Latvia, Lithuania and Moldova. Another four were close to 100 per cent dependent: Belarus, Georgia, Kyrgyzstan and Tajikistan, while Ukraine imported about 80 per cent. Only Kyrgyzstan, Tajikistan and Ukraine did not source all their imports from Gazprom. Azerbaijan, Kazakhstan, Turkmenistan and Uzbekistan had considerable gas production of their own, and relied less on imports. While Kazakhstan and Azerbaijan, and later also Uzbekistan, would develop their own gas production to further reduce their gas import, Turkmenistan's gas supply was covered by its own production from the beginning. The import-dependent states, on their side, were unable to pay the full, but still subsidised cost of Russian gas. Debts accumulated. Non-payment problems were gradually overcome after 2000, but the political and economic distortions of gas dependence continued to shape post-Soviet states' bilateral relations with Russia.

Gazprom's second priority was to retain its own transit monopoly for Central Asian gas from old and new sources. This included blocking or obstructing alternative transit projects for new gas from the Caspian Basin. Vyakhirev stated in 1997 that to purchase gas from Kazakhstan, and, by extension, give Kazakhstan access to the single export channel, would constitute "a crime against Russia" (Kravets, 1997).

When transit relations with Belarus and Ukraine became complicated and costly in the mid-1990s, this gave the impetus for Gazprom to develop a new policy, transit avoidance. To Gazprom it appeared attractive to establish alternative export routes, just as it was for Transneft. It meant investing in expensive excess pipeline capacity. But it mitigated transit risk and increased Russia's leverage over transit states, for gas as for oil. Gradually, this would become the backbone of Gazprom's strategy.

Transit avoidance towards Europe

Transit avoidance was a strategic choice. However, transit risk could be mitigated also in other ways, and these other policies were more prominent in the early 1990s. Beginning in 1994, Gazprom encouraged other companies to take over gas trade with post-Soviet countries. The Russian company Itera acquired a considerable share of Turkmen–Russian gas trade, and later supplied gas to several states (Stern, 2005, pp.22, 24–25; *Neft' i Kapital*, 2013d). Itera was originally a gas trader, and specialised in complicated gas barter. Only in 1998 did it begin to produce its own gas. Itera became an intermediary for Turkmenistan's substantial gas sales to Ukraine. Gazprom granted Itera preferential access to the grid for post-Soviet trade (Balmaceda, 2008, p.49). In this way, from 1994 to 2003, the post-Soviet region became an exception to Gazprom's export monopoly (Stern, 2005, pp.68–70).

This and similar arrangements relieved Gazprom of some of the difficulties associated with post-Soviet debt collection. These difficulties partly reflected state pressure. Recovering post-Soviet gas debts was difficult enough. The Russian government used subsidised gas and a tolerance for non-payment as rewards to states that maintained a pro-Russian foreign policy line (Bruce, 2007, p.44). In effect, closer relations with Russia maintained dependence on rent streams from cheap gas. Such tolerance, and rent sharing, was not extended to states that distanced themselves from Russia, beginning in November 1992 with the Baltic states (*Krasnaya Zvezda*, 1992). Debts from the Baltic states were recovered through equity acquisitions in national gas grids, first Estonia in 1994 (Gray, 1995, p.23). It took Gazprom much longer to succeed with this strategy for debt recovery in relation to transit states. Post-Soviet gas relations were therefore burdensome, even as they served the state. Itera, unlike Gazprom, was not expected to give price discounts according to the state of bilateral relations, and Itera's post-Soviet gas trade was profitable.

Relations with Ukraine were particularly difficult. Ukraine relied on gas for 40 to 50 per cent of its primary energy supply (IEA, 2015). In the 1990s, Ukraine transited up to 90 per cent of Russia's gas exports to Europe. Annual transit capacity was around 175 billion cubic metres (bcm). Ukraine also had underground storage capacity of 43 bcm (Pirani, 2009a, pp.109–113). This was essential to Gazprom, which invested little in storage facilities in Russia. Storage facilities smooth out seasonal variations and secure supply during interruptions. Transit and storage fees were low and paid in gas. Barter goods paid for the rest of Ukraine's gas imports (Balmaceda, 2008, pp.111–112; Pirani, 2009a, p.113). Along with some domestically produced gas, import from Russia enabled Ukraine to avoid significant cuts in its high and wasteful gas consumption. Gazprom refrained from cutting deliveries when Ukraine accumulated debts, and siphoned off gas not paid for (Yafimava, 2007, pp.72–73). Ukraine under Leonid Kuchma was too useful an ally for Moscow to "turn its perennial gas dispute with Kiev into a confrontation" (Pirani, 2009a, p.99). This also reflected Gazprom's reliance on Europe to make a profit, subsidise the home market, and thereby perform a quasi-fiscal service to the state.

In consequence, Ukraine often appeared to have a genuinely independent political position towards Russia (Yafimava, 2011, p.140). But Russian economic interests and the country's gas dependence defined much of Ukraine's domestic politics (Balmaceda, 2008, pp.23–32). For fear of Russian dominance, privatisation attempts would be blocked, and Ukraine's dependence on subsidised gas increased further (Balmaceda, 1998, pp.263–264). Gazprom was blocked from taking control of Ukrainian gas pipelines, despite the fact that Naftogaz Ukrainy, Gazprom's Ukrainian counterparty after 1998, could not afford necessary grid repairs. Gazprom would not upgrade pipelines outside its control (Yafimava, 2007, p.70). After Gazprom repeatedly failed to acquire the pipelines, both Gazprom and the Russian government made it a priority to scale down their reliance on transit through Ukraine (Balmaceda, 1998, p.269). This resulted in three large bypass projects, Yamal (through Belarus), Blue Stream (under the Black Sea), and Nord Stream (under the Baltic Sea) (Smith, 2012, p.122), although the latter lost momentum and was only revived in the 2000s.

Relations with Belarus were difficult, but less complicated than with Ukraine. On independence, Belarus inherited the modern pipeline system Northern Lights, established for deliveries to Belarus and transit to Poland and the Baltic states (Yafimava, 2009, p.139). Belarus relied on Russian gas for 50–60 per cent of its primary energy supply, and ran up debts to Gazprom and other suppliers (Yafimava, 2007, p.52). In order to regulate this debt, Belarus and Russia agreed to transfer Belarus's gas grid, Beltransgaz, to Gazprom, in 1993, on a 99-year lease (Markus, 1995). The deal was however criticised in Belarus's parliament and not ratified. When Gazprom in 1992 embarked on the Yamal project, this minimised transit reliance on the other pipelines in Belarus for the bulk of deliveries to Europe. Gazprom covered the four billion US$ cost and owned the Belarusian section. First deliveries were made in 1999 (Yafimava, 2009, pp.139–141).

Moldova was the third transit state, en route to Romania and the Balkans. Gas from Russia became more important in Moldova's primary energy supply, as it reduced its reliance on oil from around 40 per cent to around 20, and increased gas imports correspondingly, from 1992 to 2002 (IEA, 2015). Russia from the early 1990s used gas supplies and debts to pressure the Moldovan government in negotiations over the status of the secessionist region Transnistria (Bruce, 2007). The Transnistrian authorities also incurred debts to Gazprom.

Compared with other CIS member states, Moldova paid a high price: 80 US$ per thousand cubic metres (mcm) in 1995 (Stern, 2005, pp.101–102). This was offset by a high transit tariff, more than double Ukraine's and five times that of Belarus (Stern, 2005, pp.101–102; Yafimava, 2007, p.58; Bruce and Yafimava, 2009, p.177). By 1995, Moldova's debt to Gazprom stood at 300 million US$ (OMRI, 1995). Gazprom and Moldova then agreed on a debt-for-equity settlement, in which Gazprom took a share of Moldova's gas grid (Moldovagaz) in return for debt cancellation (OMRI, 1995).

Blue Stream was the second transit avoidance project in the 1990s, planned to supply up to 16 bcm annually to Turkey (Logvinenko, 2001). Turkey by 1997 received 6 bcm from Russia, transited through Ukraine, Moldova, Romania and Bulgaria. But Blue Stream was also essential in Gazprom's efforts to obstruct non-Russian transport projects from the Caspian basin. It would take a share of Azerbaijan's closest gas market. To Azerbaijan, the most attractive export route for new fields was the planned South Caucasus, or Baku–Tbilisi–Erzurum pipeline (BTE), parallel to the BTC oil pipeline. BTE could possibly attract also gas from Turkmenistan, and warrant a feeder pipeline across the Caspian Sea – a trans-Caspian connection (*Neft' i Kapital*, 2006b). Blue Stream offered Turkmenistan an outlet to Turkey through Russia. Blue Stream cost 3.2 billion US$ (*Neft' i Kapital*, 2005b). Gazprom in 1999 lobbied tax and customs breaks through the Duma to an estimated value of one billion US$ (*Neft' i Kapital*, 2003b). The Audit Chamber estimated in 2003 that the real value was higher, 130 billion rubles, or just over four billion US$ (Lyashenko, 2003). Its investigation concluded that Gazprom had exploited legal loopholes to a maximum (*Neft' i Kapital*, 2003b).

Control of Caspian transit

To develop its gas resources, Kazakhstan needed a route to Europe. With transit through Russia, Kazakhstan's gas would be competitively priced (Kravets, 1997). But this was not in Gazprom's interest, and Gazprom did not allow it. Kazakhstan's offers of stakes in its oil and gas fields did not change Gazprom's priorities.

Kazakhstan's gas industry was intertwined with Russia's. The giant Karachaganak gas and condensate field supplied pipeline gas to the equally giant Orenburg Gas Processing Plant in Russia. After the break-up of the Soviet Union, Karachaganak was owned by Kazakhstan and operated by Gazprom. To Gazprom, however, further development of Karachaganak was unwelcome competition to its Russian gas processing plant in Orenburg (Transitions, 1995; Brauer, 2002). It took little interest in Karachaganak, which sorely needed investment (*Neftegazovaya vertikal'*, 2011). Nevertheless, in the process of attracting an international consortium to Karachaganak's further development, Kazakhstan in 1995 offered Gazprom a 15 per cent stake (*Neftegazovaya vertikal'*, 2011). This was ceded to Lukoil in 1997 (Yenikeyeff, 2008). Lukoil took a more active role in the development of Karachaganak.

In the Soviet period, Turkmengazprom supplied gas to other union republics in return for hard currency, calculated on the basis of a stipulated export quota to Europe (Stern, 2005, p.72). After the break-up, Gazprom early on denied Turkmenistan access to the single export channel and to other post-Soviet markets. This also strengthened Russia's position towards a proposed pipeline from Turkmenistan through Iran to Turkey and possibly to Europe (Bolukbasi, 1998, pp.406–407).[6] Later on, Russia again opened for cross-border trade, but Gazprom demanded a high transit fee that made Turkmen gas uncompetitive (Savushkin, 2000). In 1996, Gazprom and Turkmenistan established Turkmenrosgaz, a JV between Gazprom (45%), Turkmenistan (51%) and Itera (4%). Turkmenrosgaz would handle Turkmenistan's gas trade, which was mainly with Ukraine, with a transit tariff discount (Smirnov, 1997; Bolukbasi, 1998). In 1997, Turkmenistan withdrew from Turkmenrosgaz due to non-payments by Ukraine, Armenia and Georgia, and disagreement with its partners (Smirnov, 1997; Savushkin, 2000). This in effect dissolved Turkmenrosgaz. For some time, Turkmenistan was forced to rely on intermediaries to export to Ukraine, and developed exports to Iran (*Neft' i Kapital*, 2008b; Lukin, 2011, p.87). Exports to Armenia and Georgia were cut off (Wyzan, 1999).

The integrated gas grid ended in Armenia, whose international isolation would have been alleviated by a gas connection to Iran. Both states lacked the funds (Verezemskii, 1997). On the other hand, there was a possibility that Armenia could become a route to the Turkish market for Gazprom. Only 25 per cent of Armenia's network capacity was utilised, and it offered underground storage facilities. Transit would require only minor additions and a new pipeline from Armenia to Turkey, as well as the involvement of a Russian company to minimise political risk (Verezemskii, 1997). In 1997, a debt-for-equity deal resulted in joint ownership of Armenia's gas pipelines between Gazprom (45 per cent), Itera (10 per cent) and the Armenian government (45 per cent) (*Neft' i Kapital*, 2005c; Stern, 2005, p.85). But the fraught relations between Armenia and Turkey stopped the transit project, and Gazprom decided to reach Turkey through Blue Stream (Verezemskii, 1997). Gazprom in 1999 offered to cover 60 per cent of the cost of a new pipeline from Iran (RFE/RL, 1999; *Vedomosti*, 1999). The project failed to materialise at that point.

The financial crisis

The dismissal of Chernomyrdin's government in March 1998 left Vyakhirev more exposed to demands from the state, especially for greater rent sharing. Improving state finances was an urgent task for Sergei Kirienko's new government. Gazprom's non-payment of tax was a recurrent source of tension. It was closely related to the issue of non-payment for gas, especially by government institutions, and Vyakhirev often made this point (Stern, 2005, p.56).

But the Kirienko government set itself greater tasks. There was a belief that it would be essential to curb Vyakhirev's power and enable a reform of Gazprom in the longer run (Levin, 2000), and it tried to put an end to the trustee agreement (Popov, 2007). The government demanded greater access to Gazprom's rent streams in the form of tax payments based on real numbers, no longer averaged out over the year (RFE/RL, 1998). Gazprom assets were sequestrated to retrieve taxes (RFE/RL, 1998; Popov, 2007). Gazprom in response mobilised the Duma, where it had widespread support and paid many deputies (Popov, 2007). The government was chastised. Wide-ranging reform was now off the table, still the resulting compromise increased tax extraction from Gazprom (Kravets, 1998; RFE/RL, 1998; Popov, 2007). As it turned out, this made a difference when the financial crisis hit a few weeks later. Gazprom contributed 25 per cent of all federal taxes in Russia in 1998 (Stern, 2005, p.56). It was now Russia's "largest foreign currency earning company", a position it held for several years (Stern, 2005, pp.128–129). The government struggled to maintain a power advantage among the elite, and Gazprom's sources of power could be mobilised against the government. It was therefore essential to have Gazprom's support.

By now, Vyakhirev's and Chernomyrdin's families were well represented in Gazprom subsidiaries (Butrin, 2001; Reznik, 2002a; Emel'yanov, 2003; Rozhkova and Reznik, 2013). Beginning in 1998, Gazprom also consolidated its ownership stakes in the media, notably including the nationwide broadcasters NTV (30 per cent) and ORT (3 per cent) and a long list of regional media. Gazprom's rent streams dominated the budget, promoted political interests in the Duma and the regions, and provided direct channels to voters through the media. Control of Gazprom gave access to a wide range of resources, and its infrastructure reached the majority of the population. It was a source of power.

New approaches to the post-Soviet region

Because Gazprom was being pressured to pay taxes in Russia, it pressured post-Soviet customers to repay debts (Balmaceda, 1998; Bruce, 2007). Gas supply cuts were used to recover debts from smaller states, like Moldova in 2000 and 2001 (RFE/RL, 2000; 2001a; 2001b). But the Russian government was against interrupting supplies to other CIS member states. Converting debts to equity stakes in gas-related infrastructure had already been practised in Estonia, Moldova and Armenia, and attempted in Belarus (Markus, 1995). This now became the preferred strategy for dealing with debts, and it gave Gazprom more leverage with host governments.

The Belarusian government was, however, adept at deflecting such pressure. Belarus remained reluctant to cede a stake in Beltransgaz to Russia, and it countered the pressure by buying more gas from Itera. In 1999–2004, Belarus consumed at least 16 bcm annually, a substantial part of which was sourced from Itera (Yafimava, 2007, p.58; 2009, pp.134–137). Itera accepted barter payment, which covered up to 80 per cent of supply (Yafimava, 2007, pp.52, 58). Belarus promised to implement the 1995 Customs Union Agreement to obtain reduced prices, but this was an empty promise. In the end, Belarus paid very little for Russian gas. Transit fees were low, too (Yafimava, 2007, p.58).

Regarding transit from the Caspian Basin, however, Gazprom was at the receiving end of others' efforts to avoid Russia. As the BTE project came closer to construction, the possibility of a trans-Caspian connection for gas from Turkmenistan remained on the table. To Gazprom, it was important to reduce the appeal of the Trans-Caspian pipeline project. Following the discovery of the giant Shah Deniz field in 1999, Azerbaijan demanded a 50 per cent share of BTE capacity for Azeri gas, to maximise its possibilities in the Turkish market (Savushkin, 2000). The Trans-Caspian pipeline project depended on sufficient capacity in BTE to be commercially viable, and Azerbaijan's demand deprived it of an outlet. Under orders from the new prime minister, Vladimir Putin, Gazprom bought a considerable volume of gas from Turkmenistan in 1999, and promised to reserve capacity for Turkmenistan in the Blue Stream pipeline (Savushkin, 2000; *Neft' i Kapital*, 2006b). Turkmenistan then withdrew the promised gas from the Trans-Caspian pipeline project (*Neft' i Kapital*, 2006b). At the same time, Gazprom had a domestic gas deficit, which it covered with Turkmen gas. This prevented Turkmen gas from reaching Blue Stream when it opened in 2002 (*Neft' i Kapital*, 2010c).

The new coalition: State access to Gazprom

Upon taking up the presidency, Putin refused to treat Gazprom with the now customary deference (Panyushkin and Zygar', 2007, pp.84–85; Makarkin, 2013). To Putin, the state's lack of access to Gazprom reduced overall state capacity. He clearly expected Gazprom to act as a tool of the state and the regime, particularly by providing media support for his own positions (Panyushkin and Zygar', 2007, pp.84–85). Putin also preferred to have loyal associates in central positions. Vyakhirev's position grew increasingly untenable. On expiration of his contract in May 2001, he was replaced by Aleksei Miller, who came from the position of deputy energy minister (Rozhkova and Reznik, 2013). Between 1991 and 1996, Miller had worked with Putin in St Petersburg, in the Committee for External Relations (Gustafson, 2012, p.241). His non-gas industry background, apart from the two years at the Baltic Pipeline System (Chapter 6) and the Energy Ministry, and his absolute loyalty to Putin were crucial to his appointment (Makarkin, 2013; Rozhkova and Reznik, 2013).

Miller was tasked with restoring state access to Gazprom, not with reform. The first aim was to re-establish majority control, 51 per cent, over Gazprom (*Neft' i Kapital*, 2013a). This was accomplished in early 2003, presumably by buying out the former management (Stern, J.P., 2005, p.171; *Neft' i Kapital*, 2013a). Vyakhirev and people close to him were also bought out from Gazprom-affiliated structures (Reznik, 2002b; 2009).

The second aim was to halt and reverse the erosion of Gazprom's control of Russian gas production and export. Independents, including Itera, had acquired minority stakes and lesser fields (Butrin, 2001; *Neft' i Kapital*, 2013d). After the management change, Itera's position in Russian gas production was reduced. It was also forced out of the post-Soviet gas trade. Itera's gas was partly sourced from Gazprom through barter payments of regional tax (*Neft' i Kapital*, 2013d). Itera had received credits from Gazprom on preferential terms (Popov, 2007). Gazprom's management under Vyakhirev was widely assumed to have benefited personally by letting Itera and affiliated structures take a share of gas sales (Butrin, 2001). However, later investigations by the Audit Chamber and PriceWaterhouseCoopers, Gazprom's auditors, into transactions and terms between Itera and Gazprom, and relations between Gazprom board members and Itera, found no evidence of wrongdoing (Jack, 2001a; 2001b; 2001c; cf. Stern, 2005, p.23 fn.49).

Miller's tasks were accomplished by 2003 (Popov, 2007; Makarkin, 2013). State capacity in the gas industry was restored. Barter and non-payment practices were reduced to below 5 per cent by 2004 (Gazprom, 2003, p.34; 2004a, p.73; 2005, p.44). There was now good reason to question whether Gazprom could keep up gas production sufficient to meet both export commitments and Russian domestic demand. The company's three main gas fields had peaked, and other major fields were close to peaking (Stern, 2005, ch.1; 2009). But exports now became even more significant to Gazprom and the state budget, as the oil price boom also affected gas prices in Europe. The inflow of rent increased.

The increasing deficit of domestic gas led the government to urge Gazprom to increase efficiency. But in contrast to the electricity industry, radical structural reform and ownership unbundling were considered, but not undertaken (Yafimava, 2015, p.3). Gazprom became a political tool of Putin's now much stronger state. Gazprom's minority stake in the television channel NTV was instrumental in 2000 in the government's attack on the powerful media owner Vladimir Gusinskii. Gazprom then acquired Gusinskii's large media holding (Victor and Sayfer, 2012, pp.684–685). NTV's broadcasts grew less critical towards the government.

A foreign energy strategy: Back in the CIS

The 2003 Energy Strategy envisaged substantial increases in gas export, with demand rising in Russia's traditional markets and in the Asia-Pacific region (Ministry of Industry and Trade, 2003, p.32). The post-Soviet share of Gazprom's gas sales was already growing. In 2003, Gazprom sold 9.1 per cent of its gas to customers in the post-Soviet region, a slight increase on the two previous years (author's calculations based on Gazprom, 2003, p.35; 2005, p.8). In the four years that followed, Gazprom's gas sale to the post-Soviet region would peak in absolute volumes, and grow to around a third of the size of its gas supply in Russia, or around 17.5 per cent of its total sales (author's calculations based on Gazprom, 2005, p.8; 2007, p.5; 2009, p.10).

From 2001, Gazprom began lobbying the government to adopt a different price calculation method and price level for CIS (and eventually also domestic) customers, with the aim of breaking even. During Putin's first term (2000–2004), the government refused even to consider this possibility (Pirani, 2009b, p.8). Cheap gas remained a bargaining chip in bilateral relations (Mitrova et al., 2009, pp.411–412). However, Gazprom was undercut on price by Itera, which in 2001 and 2002 came to cover a large share of CIS gas demand. In 2002, it supplied 47.6 bcm, slightly more than Gazprom's sale of 42.3 bcm (Gazprom, 2003; *Neft' i Kapital*, 2003a). Belarus and Ukraine were the main markets for both companies.

Yet signs of a new Gazprom approach were emerging. Gas relations with Ukraine became more regulated. An intergovernmental agreement replaced barter with partial cash payments in 2001, and a 2002 agreement opened for international consortium management of the Ukrainian pipeline network (Yafimava, 2007, p.75). The former was an important step towards a more business-like gas relationship with Ukraine. If implemented, the latter would bring relations with Ukraine much closer to Gazprom's ideal of control on transit routes.

Putin's initial approach to Belarus was different. He envisaged full political unification of Russia and Belarus, but Lukashenko rejected this (Yafimava, 2011, p.221). To Russia, economic relations then became more important (Yafimava, 2011, pp.222, 224). Gazprom was now allowed to pursue its commercial strategy of settling debts, avoiding barter, and establishing a commercially viable relationship. In 2002, Gazprom made continued gas supply to Belarus at Russian domestic prices contingent on its acquiring a stake in Beltransgaz (Yafimava, 2007, p.44). The two governments reached agreement on a Gazprom stake in Beltransgaz, in April 2002, but this was again not implemented (RFE/RL, 2004;

Yafimava and Stern, 2007). Gazprom then raised the gas price to Belarus by 50 per cent (Yafimava, 2007, p.52).

When the intergovernmental level failed to deliver better terms for Gazprom in Ukraine and Belarus, Gazprom had more to gain from controlling supply. In 2003, it forced Itera to give up CIS gas trade and exports by reducing its access to the Russian grid (*Neft' i Kapital*, 2003c; Stern, 2005, pp.24–25; Balmaceda, 2008, p.60). It then proceeded to assume control in the post-Soviet markets. Turkmen exports to Ukraine continued through opaque intermediaries (Pirani, 2009a, p.103), but elsewhere, Gazprom was again the main supplier, as seen in Table 7.1.

With government support for a more commercially based policy towards post-Soviet customers, Gazprom found it easier to progress on debt negotiations. Ukraine settled its debt incurred for 1997–2004 gas deliveries in August 2004 (Yafimava, 2007, p.74). The impending presidential elections in Ukraine made it easier to reach a deal. The settlement established principles for relations, giving Gazprom access to Ukraine's underground storage, and renewing the agreement on an international consortium for the Ukrainian pipeline network (Yafimava, 2007, p.75). The details were left until after elections.

Reaching a deal on Beltransgaz with Belarus was more difficult. Belarus again rejected Gazprom's price offer in 2003 (Mite, 2003). The Russian government then allowed Gazprom to increase prices further, insisting on actual payment (Mite, 2003; Yafimava, 2007, p.44). From that point, cheap gas deliveries to Belarus from Gazprom and Russia's side were contingent on, firstly, actual implementation of the Customs Union Agreement, and secondly, a finalised deal over Beltransgaz (Yafimava, 2007, p.90). But in practice, Belarus continued to drag its feet on both accounts.

Gazprom's approach to Central Asia also progressed in 2001–2002. Following 9/11 and the increasing competition over influence in Central Asia, Russia was more willing to engage. Gazprom also needed to import more gas. The aim remained to monopolise exports, but Gazprom would consider expanding import capacity, too. Central Asian gas was cheaper than Russian gas. When supplied to the Russian market, it freed up Russian gas for Europe. As long as Gazprom controlled transit, it could capture the price differential (Milov, 2011, p.92). Gazprom pushed Itera out of Central Asian gas trade (Flink, 2002). In the end, some of the Central Asian gas supplied Russia, but the bulk was sold to Europe (Stern, 2009, Table 2.1).

Gazprom's re-engagement with Central Asia came with an increased interest in the Central Asian upstream. Gazprom and KazMunayGaz together established KazRosGaz, which managed much of Gazprom's business in Kazakhstan. When Russia in 2001 began taxing Karachaganak gas en route to Orenburg, KazRosGaz stepped in as middleman to reduce the Russian tax burden (Tutushkin, 2001; Brauer, 2002). KazRosGaz also provided an outlet for Karachaganak's increasing production (Flink, 2002). The establishment of KazRosGaz delayed Kazakhstan's plans for a new gas processing plant in Kazakhstan (Tutushkin, 2001; Butrin, 2005).

Table 7.1 Gazprom's sales to post-Soviet states, 2002–2018

	2002	2003	2004	2005	2006	2007	2008	2009	2010	2011	2012	2013	2014	2015	2016	2017	2018
Armenia	—	0.3	1.3	1.7	1.7	1.9	2.1	1.7	1.4	1.6	1.7	1.7	1.8	1.8	1.8	1.8	1.8
Azerbaijan	—	—	0.8	3.8	4.0	—	—	—	—	—	—	—	—	0.1	—	0.4	1.0
Belarus	10.2	10.2	13.4	19.8	20.5	20.6	21.1	17.6	21.6	23.3	19.7	19.8	19.6	18.4	18.3	18.8	20.0
Estonia	0.6	0.9	0.9	1.3	0.7	0.9	0.6	0.8	0.4	0.7	0.6	0.7	0.4	0.5	0.4	0.5	0.4
Georgia	—	0.3	1.2	1.4	1.9	1.2	0.7	0.1	0.2	0.2	0.2	0.2	0.3	0.3	0.1	0.1	0.0
Kazakhstan	—	—	5.1	4	6.5	10	9.6	3.1	3.4	3.3	3.7	4.7	5.1	4.7	4.7	4.8	6.2
Kyrgyzstan	—	—	—	—	—	—	—	—	—	—	—	—	0.1	0.3	0.3	0.3	0.3
Latvia	1.1	1.2	1.5	1.4	1.4	1	0.7	1.1	0.7	1.2	1.1	1.1	1.0	1.3	1.3	1.8	1.3
Lithuania	2.4	2.9	2.9	2.8	2.8	3.4	2.8	2.5	2.8	3.2	3.1	2.7	2.5	2.2	0.9	1.4	1.4
Moldova	2.1	2.3	2.7	2.8	2.5	2.7	2.7	3	3.2	3.1	3.1	2.4	2.8	2.9	3.0	2.7	3.0
Ukraine	25.9	26	34.3	37.6	59	54.8	56.2	37.8	36.5	44.8	32.9	25.8	14.5	7.8	2.4	2.4	2.7
Uzbekistan	—	—	—	—	—	—	—	—	—	0.3	—	0.3	—	—	—	—	—
Total	42.3	44.1	65.7	76.6	101	96.5	96.5	67.7	70.2	81.7	66.1	59.4	48.1	40.3	33.2	35.0	38.1

Author's compilation based on Gazprom's annual reports

Billion cubic metres

Turkmenistan and Gazprom reached a first long-term gas trade agreement, valid for 25 years, in April 2003. The package deal between Russia and Turkmenistan cancelled dual citizenship arrangements at short notice, a decision that strengthened the Turkmen government's political control inside its own country (Dubnov, 2003; Panfilova, 2004). In return, Gazprom became the sole buyer of Turkmen gas through the Central Asia–Centre pipeline from 2007 (Butrin, 2003b). The deal deprived Ukraine of its separate contractual gas relations with Turkmenistan. Volumes were planned to increase with demand in Russia and Europe (*Neft' i Kapital*, 2003d; 2005a; 2008b). Gazprom accepted 50/50 cash/barter payment, but at advantageous terms that included a price discount (Butrin, 2003b; *Neft' i Kapital*, 2005a; 2008b).[7]

Commercial terms were also introduced for Georgia. Itera in 2002 planned a debt-for-equity swap with the gas distribution company Tbilgazi, Georgia's largest (Bakhtadze, 2002). When Gazprom replaced Itera, it concluded a 25-year strategic cooperation agreement with Georgia, just ahead of elections (Civil.ge, 2003b). The agreement stipulated that the gas grid would be renovated before Gazprom took over control. As argued by US representatives and the Georgian opposition, it could threaten Georgia's participation in the BTE pipeline (Civil.ge, 2003a; Gularidze, 2003a; 2003b)

The new stability: Gazprom the NOC

As discussed in Chapter 5, the Yukos affair affected the relations between the oil industry and the state. Indirectly it would also have effects on Gazprom's relations with the state. There was now a stronger emphasis on the primacy of the state and state ownership. Gazprom would be given priority in hydrocarbon development. After 2003, it acquired several stakes in the domestic oil and gas industry from less privileged owners. Room for competition in the oil and gas industries was limited; any wide-ranging structural reforms of the gas industry were shelved. Another effect was that Rosneft, in 2003 still a state-owned oil company of limited political influence, became a much stronger challenger to Gazprom.

In Putin's second term (2004–2008), energy policy was a means to increase state capacity. The government, and especially the president, aimed to make the state a driving force in societal development, political life, and increasingly, the economy. In the oil and gas sectors, the need for a stronger state was understood rather more narrowly to imply a stronger state in relation to private Russian companies and IOCs. A stronger state required strong NOCs, and Gazprom had a key role.

Gazprom would become even more important if it acquired Rosneft under a plan developed in autumn 2004. To proponents of NOCs, an integrated oil and gas entity based on Rosneft and Gazprom was a rational step. It would reduce competition between the two state-owned companies. A giant NOC would drive petroleum development. The playing field would tilt even further in favour of the state, and the benefits were seen to outweigh the drawbacks.

A merger would have an added bonus in enabling a relatively easy abolishment of the restrictions on foreign ownership of Gazprom, the "ring fence", which reduced its market value (Gustafson, 2012, pp.339–340). The Gazprom–Rosneft merger process stalled, most likely due to resistance from Sergei Bogdanchikov, head of Rosneft, and possibly Igor Sechin, who had just become head of Rosneft's Board of Directors (Gustafson, 2012, p.340). As the Yukos affair ran its course, in November 2004 a plan for integration of Yuganskneftegaz into Gazprom appeared in the Kremlin (Gustafson, 2012, p.343). Yuganskneftegaz was Yukos's main production unit. Gazprom managers less close to the Kremlin were less enthusiastic about preparing to take over an entire oil company (Gustafson, 2012, p.343).

When Gazprom later abstained from the Yuganskneftegaz auction, Yuganskneftegaz was acquired by the unknown Baikal Finance Group, which turned out to be a proxy for Rosneft. With Yuganskneftegaz added, Rosneft turned into a much larger entity, too large for Gazprom to acquire. The plan for a Gazprom–Rosneft merger was called off (Gustafson, 2012, p.350). There were now two NOCs of comparable significance to the state.

Nevertheless, Gazprom did enter the oil industry. After the Yukos affair, Roman Abramovich, the main owner of the large oil company Sibneft, was eager to leave the oil business. Sibneft and Yukos were in the latter stages of a merger as the Yukos affair unfolded. Abramovich had carefully reversed the process, but Sibneft at one point faced the same type of tax claims as Yukos (*Neft' i Kapital*, 2013e). When Abramovich decided to sell Sibneft and leave Russia, his loyalty to the state fetched him a good price. There may have been considerable offtakes for insiders, which may have enabled Abramovich to pay his dues (Embassy Moscow, 2007; *Neft' i Kapital*, 2013e). Gazprom acquired Sibneft, most likely because Rosneft could not shoulder the financial responsibility shortly after Yuganskneftegaz (*Neft' i Kapital*, 2013e). To Gazprom, the Sibneft acquisition offered few direct synergies. Importantly for the state, the share of oil production on its hands increased further. Sibneft became Gazprom Neft in 2006. After the dissolution of RAO UES in 2008, Gazprom also entered electricity production and became Russia's largest supplier.

Gazprom's restructuring programme enhanced the role played by formal institutions. The company was now well on a track to becoming a more efficient, more commercially oriented organisation, although its staff rosters remained inflated. While the state protected Gazprom's dominance and would not subject it to structural reform on the scale of RAO UES's, it was compelled to develop and restructure internally. Internal restructuring from 2005 enabled it to meet demands for efficiency from the state, and eventually to benefit from deregulated gas markets.

Domestic gas prices rose, through gradual, but incomplete deregulation. In 2004, Gazprom began to break even on some of its domestic gas sales (Gazprom, 2004b; Stern, 2005, p.173; Mitrova, 2009, p.23). The state was also more responsive to Gazprom's demands. In late 2006, the government supported a new policy, aimed at allowing Gazprom to reach equal profitability from domestic, CIS and European gas sales by 2011 (Stern, 2005, pp.173–182; Mitrova et al., 2009). In effect, the goal of equal profitability implied that Gazprom would increase prices also to CIS member states; the policy was already being introduced in relations with some customers. At home, Gazprom could, and did, participate in the partially deregulated wholesale market (*Neft' i Kapital*, 2013b). The regulated tariff reached break-even level in 2009 (Gazprom, 2013a). Its obligation to allow third-party access to UGSS was now increasingly enforced by the Federal Antimonopoly Service (Yafimava, 2015, pp.13–17). However, as discussed on p. 296, further deregulation stalled.

Gazprom remained important in the economy and to the state budget. In 2003, 20 per cent of all federal taxes came from Gazprom, which represented around 5 per cent of GDP (Stern, 2005, p.56). Gazprom's share of GDP increased to around 10 per cent in the period 2004–2008 (Gazprom, 2008, p.5). A new taxation system for the gas industry, introduced in 2004, reduced Gazprom's share of tax payments, and Rosneft became the largest tax payer (Stern, 2005, p.57). This was an implicit acknowledgement of the continued burden of informal taxation on Gazprom. However, the company remained an important tax payer, contributing between 7 and 10 per cent of all taxes in the years 2006–2011 (author's calculation based on Gazprom's annual reports and information on aggregate tax payments from Federal Tax Service, 2007; 2008; 2009; 2010; 2011; 2012).

Maximising market power, minimising transit risks

The 2009 Energy Strategy identified transit risk as the main obstacle to Russian access to the European market (Ministry of Energy, 2009, p.49). Consolidation of an integrated Eurasian gas pipeline system with Russia as the hub would minimise it (Ministry of Energy, 2009, p.54). Growing shale gas production and global liquefied natural gas (LNG) markets were in forecasts seen as having limited consequences for the Russian gas industry (Ministry of Energy, 2009, p.95). The new Strategy emphasised well-established aims, including Gazprom's equal profitability aim established in 2006.

But unlike the expectations presented in the 2009 Energy Strategy, the US shale gas revolution from 2007 and economic crisis in Europe from 2008 did reduce demand for Russian gas. Gazprom's future supply was now a less urgent problem than preserving its market shares. The dimensions of this change were only slowly grasped in Gazprom and the government. Gazprom's first reaction to the changing circumstances was not to offer European customers new negotiations on price, but abruptly to change its approach to gas producers in Central Asia and increase the pressure on its post-Soviet customers.

In late 2005, Gazprom announced a general gas price increase in the post-Soviet region from January 2006. This was the first real move towards achieving equal profitability from CIS gas trade and the European market, to be reached by 2011. This new pricing formula, which the company referred to as European netback prices,[8] linked prices for the post-Soviet region to those of European markets. Gazprom's equal profitability policy was in line with the higher priority accorded economic interests in foreign policy, following the "colour revolutions" in Georgia, Ukraine and Kyrgyzstan. There was an expectation in the energy industries that companies stood to benefit when economic interests now were more highly prioritised in foreign policy, and even a demand for tangible support from the state. For Gazprom, it now became possible to capitalise on the transit avoidance projects under development. They decreased the risks to transit of increased gas prices in the post-Soviet region. With more power over transit states, it was easier to acquire control of transit state pipelines. In annual price negotiations, post-Soviet governments were now willing to allow Gazprom to acquire stakes in gas pipelines, as long as it delayed a price rise by a year or two. Gazprom's position also strengthened as post-Soviet demand increased and peaked in 2006, as seen in Table 7.1. In 2011, 22.8 per cent of Gazprom's total gas sales income came from the post-Soviet region (author's calculations based on Gazprom, 2012b, pp.72, 74, 78). Gazprom's gain reflected its market power. The equal profitability policy was implemented over a short time period and with the balance of power heavily tilted in favour of Gazprom. As a result, Russia's foreign policy towards post-Soviet states moved further towards a coercive policy with more ultimatums than mutual gains.

Until 2006, Gazprom's control of the single export channel was a de facto monopoly. It served Gazprom well, especially in the European market, where a de jure monopoly would make Gazprom-owned marketing companies vulnerable to action under the Energy Charter Treaty. But in 2006, Russia introduced a de jure monopoly in a new gas export law (*Neft' i Kapital*, 2006c). According to the law, only Gazprom, now the owner of the gas grid, and its 100 per cent-held subsidiaries, could export pipeline and liquefied gas from Russia (Federal Law No. 117, 2006).[9] This removed the element of price competition in the post-Soviet region, however fictitious it had been (Yafimava, 2011, p.232).

Gazprom's reliance on transit through Ukraine decreased to 70–80 per cent of the total with Yamal (2001) and Blue Stream (2002) in operation (Yafimava, 2007, p.70; Mitrova et al., 2009, p.419). Gazprom assumed a prominent role in Ukraine's gas supply. Following Itera's exit, the intermediary company EuralTransGaz supplied Turkmen gas to Ukraine. In 2004 a new intermediary appeared, RosUkrEnergo. Gazprom owned 50 per cent and had a share in profits (Balmaceda, 2008, p.112; Pirani, 2009a, p.100). Yuliya Tymoshenko, Ukraine's Prime Minister from February 2005, tried to eliminate the persistently non-transparent intermediary companies from gas imports. She failed, but the two sides agreed on Gazprom Export as the sole supplier of Turkmen gas to Ukraine (Pirani, 2009a, p.100). Gazprom's leverage over Ukraine increased, with much better prospects of turning a profit from gas trade. Allowing this was a deliberate decision on Putin's side. After the Orange Revolution (2004), he made a point of ensuring that President Viktor Yushchenko had difficult relations with Russia.

In negotiations for 2006, Gazprom aimed to increase gas prices for Ukraine from 50 US$/mcm to at least 160 (Pirani, 2009a, p.100). Putin's participation in the negotiations, which included his public announcement of a 230 US$ price offer, escalated a nascent crisis (Grigor'eva, 2005; Panyushkin and Zygar', 2007, p.160). In the absence of a deal by 1 January, Gazprom reduced supplies to Ukraine and Europe for two days, until agreement was reached. The settlement appeared advantageous for Gazprom, with a price of 95 US$/mcm. RosUkrEnergo became party to the agreement, and had market access in Ukraine through a JV with Naftogaz (Pirani, 2009a, p.101; Yafimava, 2011, p.167). This organisation of gas supply was not transparent. Ukraine again accumulated gas debts, while Gazprom lost control of cash flows from gas sales. It was unclear where the bulk of gas debts accumulated, and it was difficult to establish their size (Yafimava, 2011, p.171).

When in early 2008 Tymoshenko returned as prime minister, she again attempted to introduce direct sales from Gazprom Export to Naftogaz (Pirani, 2009a, p.104). Gazprom's management were now in favour of direct sales too (Yafimava, 2011, p.172). A brief crisis in March was solved by replacing RosUkrEnergo with an intermediary owned jointly by Gazprom and Naftogaz. A share of the Ukrainian industrial market was also reserved for a Gazprom subsidiary. Ukraine now committed to discussing a higher price level based on the European price level in later negotiations (Pirani, 2009a, p.104). Bilateral gas relations moved closer to Gazprom's preferences. Further negotiations followed in October, and appeared to settle outstanding issues. In a crucial omission, RosUkrEnergo was not party to the new agreement. Gazprom controlled only half of RosUkrEnergo. The rest was owned by the Ukrainian businessman Dmytro Firtash, who did not approve of an agreement that removed his intermediary role (Yafimava, 2011, p.180).

Negotiations broke down in late 2008 with a new crisis emerging in January 2009. This crisis was unprecedented in the scale and duration of supply reductions to Europe. When Gazprom reduced the flow through Ukraine, Naftogaz in turn reversed Ukraine's pipeline network, supplying Ukraine from gas in underground storage. Gazprom's deliveries therefore stopped at Ukraine's eastern border (Yafimava, 2011, pp.186–187). While Russia and Ukraine negotiated over a new agreement, European customers questioned both Russia's and Gazprom's reliability as a supplier, and Ukraine's role as a transit state. Gazprom intensified its pursuit of transit routes that avoided Ukraine. It also reduced its reliance on Ukraine's overall infrastructure, for example, by ceasing to use Ukraine's underground storage and beginning to develop similar facilities further west in Europe (Yermakov, 2019, p.24).

Russia and Ukraine reached a settlement in late January. It was valid for ten years, had a high base price, starting at 360 US$/mcm, and included a take-or-pay clause that obliged Ukraine to take at least 80 per cent of 52 bcm annually (Yafimava, 2011, pp.191–192). The new transit agreement did not include a ship-or-pay clause that obliged Gazprom to ship the provisional annual volume, 110 bcm. Later in 2009, presidential candidate Viktor Yanukovych used the settlement to discredit Tymoshenko in the presidential election campaign. After his accession to the presidency in January 2010, Yanukovych initiated new negotiations with Gazprom. Little is known about these negotiations. An April comprehensive deal, the Kharkiv Accords (also discussed in Chapter 4), reduced the gas price somewhat (Pirani et al., 2010, pp.12–13; cf. Samokhvalov, 2015, p.1379). In return, Ukraine extended the lease for Russia's Black Sea Fleet, based in Sevastopol on Crimea, from 2017, when it was due to expire, to 2042 with an option for further extensions.

After the 2009 crisis, Ukraine consumed more coal and nuclear energy (Pirani, 2009a, p.93). When Ukraine opened its continental shelf for petroleum exploration in 2010, it was unwelcome competition for Gazprom. The most promising fields could potentially reduce Ukraine's dependence on Russian gas imports by 10 per cent. In 2012, Russia denied a drilling platform passage along the Russian coast to Crimea (Prostakov, 2012, p.30). Subsequently, Gazprom proposed to intensify development of an offshore structure under joint development by Gazprom and Naftogaz at the expense of other fields (Prostakov, 2012, p.31).

Russian–Belarusian gas relations came to a head in early 2004. Belarus rejected a price of 50 US$/mcm, and Gazprom cut supplies and let secondary traders supply Belarus (Yafimava, 2009, pp.154–156). After this arrangement expired, Belarus sifted gas from the supply to Europe (Yafimava, 2009, p.155). Belarus and Gazprom agreed on a 46.68 US$/mcm price in mid-2004 (Yafimava, 2007, p.97). Gazprom now delayed completion of Yamal to full capacity from 2005 to 2007 (Yafimava, 2009, p.141; 2011, p.220).

The crisis made plans for the pipeline across the Baltic Sea, Nord Stream, all the more attractive to Gazprom. Originally intended by Gazprom to bypass Ukraine, and underway before the crisis, Nord Stream also bypassed Belarus. In September 2005, Putin and German Chancellor Gerhard Schröder announced that Gazprom, E.ON and Wintershall would construct the Nord Stream pipeline (RFE/RL, 2005; Zimin, 2012, pp.222–224). When Schröder soon after lost parliamentary elections and resigned as chancellor, he became Gazprom's representative on the Nord Stream Board of Directors, and Chairman. Miller was not informed until just before the announcement (Panyushkin and Zygar', 2007, p.194). The decision appears to have been made by Putin. The consortium was led by Putin's acquaintance, the German banker Matthias Warnig (Crawford and White, 2005). Nord Stream's first branch opened in June 2011, the second in April 2012.

Nord Stream weakened Belarus's position towards Gazprom, particularly in regard to Beltransgaz negotiations. After international valuation in 2006, Gazprom offered to pay 2.5 billion US$ for 50 per cent of Beltransgaz (Yafimava and Stern, 2007; Yafimava, 2011, p.230). The transfer would take place in four stages from 2007 to 2010. These were the best terms Belarus could hope to achieve, and it was essential to finalise the deal before Nord Stream opened. Belarus now accepted a sliding scale towards paying the full European gas price by 2011 (Yafimava, 2011, p.231).

But in 2009, Belarus and Russia disagreed over these terms. Belarus experienced a severe economic crisis and ran up new gas debts. This escalated to a full-blown crisis in summer 2009, affecting bilateral trade in foodstuffs and oil transit. There was a new crisis in June 2010. But when Gazprom then reduced gas supplies to Belarus, Belarus turned the tables on Gazprom by demanding payment of its transit fee debts accumulated from late 2009 (Yafimava, 2010). Agreement was reached quickly. When Gazprom acquired the remainder of Beltransgaz for 2.5 billion US$ in November 2011, it was part of a package deal, advantageous for Belarus (Moshes, 2012). The deal included a gas price reduction from 280 to 156 US$/mcm from January 2012, debt restructuring for Belarus, and a ten billion US$ loan for a new nuclear power station in Belarus, discussed in Chapter 4 (Ioffe, 2011).

By 2003, Gazprom's relations with Moldova had deteriorated. Recovering gas debts from Transnistria was a particular problem. Gazprom failed in an effort to acquire the Moldova thermal power plant in return for Transnistria's debts, as discussed in Chapter 3. Reduced gas supply to Transnistria also failed to work (Bruce and Yafimava, 2009, pp.174–175). This was followed by a change of strategy. Pressure on the Transnistrian authorities in Tiraspol had not worked. Russia's relations with the Moldovan government in Chisinau had deteriorated after President Vladimir Voronin refused to sign a Russian plan (the "Kozak plan") to settle the secessionist conflict (Tomiuc, 2003; Tomiuc and Krushelnycky, 2003). In the following years, Gazprom gradually turned to pressure on the Moldovan government on Transnistria's debts. In 2005, Gazprom took over management of Tiraspol's stake in Moldovagaz (13.44%) through a debt repayment arrangement (Yafimava, 2011, pp.264, 266, 279). But more debts accumulated. Gazprom filed legal suits against Moldovagaz at the arbitration court in Moscow in an effort to make the Moldovan government responsible for Transnistria's debts. But debt collection was impossible as long as the government did not control Transnistria's territory. Transnistrian authorities used gas revenues to meet other obligations (Fedorova and Kulikov, 2007). Gazprom's management was unable, or unwilling, to reform its relations with Transnistria, but made little progress with its pressure on the Moldovan government.

From 2006, Gazprom wanted the price for Moldova to increase from 80 to 160 US$/mcm. Negotiations failed, and Moldova entered a severe energy crisis. New negotiations resulted in a temporary agreement of 110 US$/mcm. Gazprom offered to refrain from further increases in return for a greater share of Moldovagaz (RFE/RL, 2006; Sergeev and Grib, 2006). According to Gazprom, a similar arrangement could also cover Moldova's historical gas debt of 780 million US$. 560 million US$ were non-payments on Transnistria's part, and the Moldovan government refused to budge. No agreement was reached, and the gas price rose to 160 US$, and then, after further negotiations, to 170 US$/mcm for 2007 (*Neft' i Kapital*, 2011b). From 2008, the price would gradually increase towards the European level.

By September 2012, Transnistria's debts were around 3.5–4.1 billion US$ (Gamova, 2012; *Neft' i Kapital*, 2012a; Socor, 2012). Following the decree on protection of national interests in foreign economic relations, Gazprom was represented by the Russian government in this round of negotiations (Decree No. 1285, 2012). Chisinau offered Russia a comprehensive energy partnership within EU's Third Energy Package, to which Moldova had signed up in October 2011 and would implement in 2015 (Gamova, 2012; *Neft' i Kapital*, 2012a; Socor, 2012). Russia's position was that Moldova should refrain from implementing the Third Energy Package in return for a price discount, and assume responsibility for Moldovagaz's total debts (Infotag, 2012; *Neft' i Kapital*, 2012b). Russia aired the possibility of Moldova obtaining a price discount in return for joining the Customs Union with Russia, Belarus and Kazakhstan (Mordyushenko et al., 2012). Moldova then requested, and obtained, a four-year delay from the EU in implementation of the Third Energy Package to 2020. Russia granted a one-year contract prolongation with an element of price discount (Parfenova, 2012, Socor, 2012).

Maximising Russia's control of Caspian transit

Gazprom's efforts to limit the viability of non-Russian export routes for Caspian gas and promote Russian-controlled projects intensified in 2006–2007. Azerbaijan's Shah Deniz field was now close to production start. The opening of the BTE pipeline could make it easier for gas from Turkmenistan to reach markets. By minimising competition from Azerbaijani gas, Gazprom would also close possible export routes for Turkmenistan. In early 2006, Azerbaijan reinvigorated plans for a Trans-Caspian gas pipeline to feed BTE (*Neft' i Kapital*, 2006b; 2006d).

Azerbaijan already delivered gas to Georgia, after three explosions in January had cut its supplies (Civil.ge, 2006; Socor, 2006). When BTE opened in the autumn, Georgia's transit agreement included a transit fee levied in gas, with a right to take additional volumes at a discounted rate of 63 US$/mcm (*Neft' i Kapital*, 2006d). Georgia ceased buying Russian gas. The exception was South Ossetia, which in 2006–2008 was included in the Russian gas infrastructure development programme, at a loss to Gazprom (*Neft' i Kapital*, 2007).

Gazprom's increasing gas prices further accelerated Azerbaijan's gas development. After the opening of BTE, Azerbaijan pressured the AIOC consortium, in charge of the ACG field, to increase associated gas production at the expense of current and future oil production (*Neft' i Kapital*, 2006d). The date for full production at Shah Deniz was also carried forward. With Iranian gas supplying the domestic market, and fuel oil replacing gas in electricity production (Muradova and Abbasov, 2006), Azerbaijan became a net gas exporter in 2007 (Ismayilov, 2007; *Neft' i Kapital*, 2008a).

Gazprom's European customers now made progress on a new project, Nabucco, which would take gas from BTE at Erzurum in Turkey to Europe.[10] This would threaten Gazprom's market share in Europe. In response, Gazprom and ENI concluded in 2007 the South Stream pipeline project agreement, which would bring gas across the Black Sea from Anapa near Novorossiisk to Galata in Bulgaria and onwards to southeast Europe. Nabucco would thus become superfluous. South Stream was guaranteed supplies by Gazprom, while the Nabucco project did not include reserved gas supplies. South Stream was further strengthened as Gazprom embarked on construction of the domestic Bovanenkovo–Ukhta pipeline in November 2008 (*Neft' i Kapital*, 2009a). This was a feeder pipeline for both South and Nord Stream. When the Nabucco project progressed in spring 2009, Russia renewed and intensified contacts with Turkey over transit (*Neft' i Kapital*, 2009a). Gazprom also increased import from Azerbaijan (*Neft' i Kapital*, 2009a). This was expensive, as the Russian domestic market was saturated with gas (Afanasiev, 2009), but it limited the volume of gas available for Nabucco (Gabuev et al., 2010; *Neft' i Kapital*, 2010b). When the South Stream project progressed further in 2011–2012, this also increased Russia's possibility of pressuring Ukraine in negotiations over transit (Konończuk et al., 2012).

The policy of obstructing non-Russian export routes for Caspian gas was now coordinated at the top of the Russian state. In August 2009, President Dmitrii Medvedev held a conference with the foreign and defence ministers and the heads of Gazprom and Lukoil, to discuss the obstruction of pipelines that bypassed Russia in the Caspian region (Afanasiev, 2009; Gabuev and Granik, 2009).

Up to 2009, Gazprom had tried to capture as much of Central Asia's increasing production as possible for Russian-controlled routes. But Russian pipeline capacity from Central Asia expanded slowly, at a level just sufficient to make difficult the Central Asian states' pursuit of alternative routes to European markets (Yakuba, 2007). In this way, Central Asia's dependence on Russian routes continued, while Central Asian governments found it difficult to develop their export, and gas fields, optimally. To Gazprom, retaining as much of Kazakhstan's gas production as possible was crucial (*Neft' i Kapital*, 2006a). Without Kazakhstan on board, Uzbekistan and Turkmenistan would find it commercially unattractive to develop alternative routes.

In 2006, Kazakhstan planned to expand gas production from 26–27 bcm annually to around 53 bcm by 2010. Some 40 bcm would be exported (*Neft' i Kapital*, 2006a). Both its two main export routes, the Central Asia–Centre pipeline system and the Bukhara–Ural pipeline, went to Russia (Gazprom, 2012a). A lack of maintenance had reduced capacity from the designed 75 bcm annually to 60 bcm, and this limit was reached in 2006 (*Neft' i Kapital*, 2006a). Russia's gas imports from Central Asia increased from 2002–2003, and further increases were planned from 2006. At this point, the Central Asia–Centre pipeline was repaired (Gazprom, 2006; *Neft' i Kapital*, 2006a).

The gas industry: Gazprom 283

But capacity could be expanded to 100 bcm annually by adding a new leg along the Caspian shore: the Caspian Shore Project (*Neft' i Kapital*, 2006a). Turkmenistan had proposed this in 2003 (Butrin, 2003a). Gazprom had then given priority to the upgrade of the Central Asia–Centre pipeline system, even as actual repairs were only carried out in 2006 (Butrin, 2003a; Lukin, 2010). Three years later, Gazprom's transit monopoly was threatened by Nabucco, and by Turkmenistan's renewed interest in other routes. President Putin promoted the Caspian Shore project in May 2007, on a visit to Central Asia. The visit resulted in a joint declaration of intent by the presidents of Turkmenistan, Kazakhstan and Russia (*Neft' i Kapital*, 2006a; 2008b), followed by an inter-governmental agreement in December. Gazprom, KazMunayGaz and Turkmengaz finalised the project in 2008. It stalled in 2009, however, because Turkmenistan did not want to reserve gas for the pipeline (Blagov, 2007; Daly, 2008). Without this essential guarantee, Russia and Kazakhstan shelved the project (*Neft' i Kapital*, 2010b).

To the Central Asian states, access to China's gas market was now a realistic alternative (Ericson, 2012, p.642). In March 2006, KazMunayGaz and CNPC agreed on higher annual exports from Kazakhstan to China from 2012 through a new pipeline, Atyrau–Alashankou, which was parallel to the oil pipeline, discussed in Chapter 6 (*Neft' i Kapital*, 2006a). The pipeline would also receive gas from Uzbekistan and Turkmenistan.

Gazprom retained control of Karachaganak. Once more to pre-empt plans for a gas processing plant in Kazakhstan, Gazprom suggested in 2004 that Kazakhstan acquire a stake in the Orenburg Plant (*Neft' i Kapital*, 2006a). KazRosGaz came to supply Orenburg directly, and Kazakhstan would later have a stake in the plant (Butrin, 2005; Belyakov, 2006; Sokolov, 2007). To Gazprom, joint ownership would secure gas for Orenburg, which faced an impending shortage of gas (Verkhoturov, 2006). But when gas supply in Russia rose, the plan was shelved (*Neft' i Kapital*, 2006a; Gavshina, 2007; Zhelenin, 2007; Belyakov, 2008).

Kazakhstan, meanwhile, had tried to reach post-Soviet gas markets independently. Kazakh gas was already supplying Kyrgyzstan, and KazRosGaz supplied Azerbaijan and Georgia as a Gazprom agent (Vignanskii and Grivach, 2005). Georgia then tried to purchase cheaper Kazakh gas, not just Russian gas supplied by KazRosGaz. This transit was subject to Gazprom's approval (Grivach, 2005; Vignanskii and Grivach, 2005). Gazprom did not approve (Civil.ge, 2005). In 2006, KazTransGaz, a subsidiary of KazMunayGaz, acquired Tbilgazi (Prokhorov, 2006). As KazTransGaz supplied gas from KazRosGaz, it was believed that Kazakhstan could now sell gas to Georgia (IAA Trend, 2006). Also in May 2007, KazRosGaz obtained a marketing contract for Karachaganak gas (KazRosGaz, 2012). But KazRosGaz's marketing contracts for Georgia were later transferred to Gazprom Export (Grivach, 2010).

The Caspian strategy backfires

When the demand for gas in Europe began to decrease, Gazprom reduced imports from Central Asia. Overall gas imports from Central Asia decreased in 2009, 2010 and 2011. Kazakhstan, desperate for Gazprom to take the agreed volumes, managed to retain most of its share (*Neft' i Kapital*, 2011a). Gazprom's stake in KazRosGaz made imports from Kazakhstan more profitable to Gazprom than other imports from Central Asia (Lukin, 2012, p.18).

Gazprom had developed gas production in Uzbekistan from 2002.[11] It established a business partnership with the Switzerland-based company Zeromax at an early stage. Zeromax became a gas trade intermediary for 80 per cent of Uzbekistan's exports to Russia (*Neft' i Kapital*, 2011c). The company was widely assumed to be controlled by Gulnara Karimova, President Islam Karimov's daughter (Embassy Tashkent, 2008; 2010; *Neft' i Kapital*, 2011c).[12]

Gazprom expanded gas purchases from Uzbekistan from 7 bcm in 2004 to 14 bcm in 2008 (*Neft' i Kapital*, 2009b). In 2007, Uzbekistan's government asked for a new price formula based on European prices. The alternative was to sell gas to Europe on its own account. In the following negotiations, Gazprom agreed a price formula based on the European price from 2009. Gazprom now purchased around 85 per cent of Uzbekistan's gas exports (*Neft' i Kapital*, 2009b). When President Medvedev visited Uzbekistan, President Karimov declared that Uzbekistan sold gas "only to Russia" (*Neft' i Kapital*, 2009b). But when Gazprom curtailed gas imports in 2009–2011, Uzbekistan found it difficult to sustain exports. Unlike Turkmenistan, it had no take-or-pay clause, and unlike Kazakhstan, it offered no price discount (Lukin, 2012, p.19). In 2009 Tashkent offered 16 bcm and sold 12 to Russia (*Neft' i Kapital*, 2010a). In 2010–2011, Zeromax went bankrupt, and Uzbekistan's National Security Service took over control of its business activities. Gazprom limited operations in Uzbekistan (*Neft' i Kapital*, 2011c), while Uzbekistan increased exports to China (Lukin, 2012, p.19).

Between 2008 and 2011, Turkmenistan revised upwards its proven reserves from 2.6 trillion cubic metres in 2007, to 8.1 in 2008, 13.4 in 2010 and then 24.3 in 2011 (Chazan, 2008; Watkins, 2011; BP, 2012). This placed Turkmenistan fourth on the list of the world's gas reserves, behind only Russia, Iran and Qatar. In early 2005, Turkmenistan ceased gas deliveries to both Russia and Ukraine in order to obtain a better price and full cash payment (*Neft' i Kapital*, 2005a). In 2008, Gazprom paid 140 US$/mcm (*Neft' i Kapital*, 2008b). Gazprom then imported and re-exported 50 bcm annually, or two-thirds of Turkmenistan's production (Makarkin, 2009). But when European demand contracted, Gazprom was left with too much gas. For 2009, Gazprom and Turkmenistan had agreed on a price around 300–374 US$/mcm (Afanasiev, 2009; *Neft' i Kapital*, 2010c; Roberts, 2011, p.182). There was no market for gas at this price and volume (Afanasiev, 2009; Lukin, 2010, p.64). While defending the transit monopoly and its rents from the price differential, Gazprom had overcommitted. Gazprom renegotiated prices with Kazakhstan and Uzbekistan. Turkmenistan would not accept a lower price.

Early in 2009, Gazprom asked Turkmenistan either to reduce the agreed volume by 80 per cent, or the price by 40 per cent (Grib and Gavrish, 2009). Turkmenistan refused (Afanasiev, 2009; *Neft' i Kapital*, 2010c). Bilateral tension also increased over the terms of the Caspian Shore project, which Russia wanted to connect exclusively to Gazprom's system. Turkmenistan preferred to keep open a possibility of other connections (Voloshin, 2016). In April, the Central Asia–Centre-4 pipeline exploded, causing considerable damage to Turkmenistan's pipelines and gas fields. Export to Russia fell overnight by more than 90 per cent (*Neft' i Kapital*, 2010c; Roberts, 2011). Turkmenistan's government accused Gazprom both of reducing its offtake without notification and for causing the explosion. Gazprom officials blamed Turkmenistan for ignoring notifications and failing to reduce the volumes going into the pipeline accordingly (Embassy Ashgabat, 2009; Makarkin, 2009; Panfilova, 2009). Bilateral relations reached a nadir. They remained tense when trade resumed in January 2010, at a lower price and volume (Grivach, 2009; Lukin, 2010; *Neft' i Kapital*, 2010c). Turkmenistan now expanded exports to China and Iran (*Neft' i Kapital*, 2010c; Lukin, 2011, p.87). From 2011 onwards, almost all Turkmenistan's exports to China, 98–99 per cent, was gas (UN Comtrade database harmonised by Gaulier and Zignago, 2010, accessed through Simoes and Hidalgo, 2011).[13] This was a significant part of Turkmenistan's export.[14]

Armenia developed a pipeline to Iran beginning in 2004. Iran financed the project (*Neft' i Kapital*, 2005c), and import began in 2008. Armenia now had a surplus of gas for electricity production, and planned to invest in new generation for export to Iran. There were two alternatives. Armenia could raise funds on its own and construct the necessary domestic leg of the gas pipeline. It would be in control, but locked to the Iranian electricity market. Gazprom instead proposed that ArmRosGazprom develop the domestic pipeline, while Gazprom would invest in new electricity production at the Hrazdan thermal power plant (TPP) (Tatevosyan et al., 2006). The new unit would run on Iranian gas, and Inter RAO or Gazprom would own and manage the plant (*Neft' i Kapital*, 2005c). Inter RAO already managed the older parts of Hrazdan TPP.

Armenia chose to expand energy cooperation with Iran, which tried to secure a future option of exporting gas to Ukraine through Armenia and Georgia (Krashakov, 2006; Tatevosyan et al., 2006). Under the double pressure of Gazprom and the US, Armenia in March 2005 denied such transit (Embassy Yerevan, 2005). Gazprom also promised not to increase the gas price for two to three years (Danielyan, 2005a; 2005b). The diameter of the domestic Armenian gas pipeline was also reduced in response to Russian pressure (Danielyan, 2005c; Embassy Yerevan, 2005; Ter-Grigoryan, 2006).

In late 2005, Gazprom nevertheless included Armenia in the general price increase (Reznik and Egorova, 2006b). In negotiations, Armenia managed to postpone the increase from January to April 2006, followed by a price freeze until 2009. In return, Gazprom's share of ArmRosGazprom would increase to

75 per cent, and Gazprom would take over the new part of Hrazdan TPP (Reznik and Egorova, 2006b). Gazprom and ArmRosGazprom assumed the positions previously held by the Iranians, including control of the pipeline to Iran (Tatevosyan et al., 2006; Danielyan, 2007). The deal was rumoured, quite plausibly, to include arms transfers from Russia to Armenia (Tatevosyan and Reutov, 2006). Gazprom's share of ArmRosGazprom gradually increased in 2006–2012 (Gazprom, 2013b). With complete Russian dominance of Armenia's energy sector, Russia was in a position to control Iran's energy trade options through the country (Reznik and Egorova, 2006a; Ter-Grigoryan, 2006).

Gazprom and the reorganised ruling coalition

Also in the period 2012 to 2018, Gazprom's business and finances were profoundly influenced by its role in national development and in foreign policy. In return, it remained widely influential in Russian energy politics. Miller regularly polled first on ratings of influential business leaders in the energy industries, although he would on occasion come second, behind Sechin (Oilcapital.ru, 2012; 2016; APEK, 2017).

However, the government was firmly in the driver's seat on questions of gas market deregulation. Gas tariffs remained regulated, although the gradual increase continued. Political sensitivity was demonstrated when gas tariffs, like electricity tariffs, were subjected to a freeze ahead of the 2012 presidential election. Gas price deregulation seemed further off than ever, with global oil prices reaching 110 to 120 US$/barrel (Henderson et al., 2018, p.5). Deregulated prices were linked to the goal of equal profitability from domestic and European gas sales, implying that gas prices would be tied to the price of oil. The goal of equal profitability was now postponed to 2015–2018. It still remained an open question whether, and for how long, the government would allow continued subsidised prices in the Russian market. Subsidised prices meant continued high demand in the home market and Gazprom's continued reliance on high prices in global markets to increase profitability. On the other hand, if prices were allowed to increase in Russia, this could improve energy efficiency, release more gas for Europe, and in turn allow Gazprom to offer lower prices for European customers and secure a greater share of the market there. The equal profitability target was put on hold again during the crisis of 2015–2017 (Henderson et al., 2018; Yermakov, 2018, p.16). In the meantime, Gazprom continued to hold the export monopoly in return for fulfilling social obligations for the state (*Neftegazovaya vertikal'*, 2015). While other gas producers[15] could participate in a variety of wholesale markets and also compete on price, Gazprom was still obliged to offer gas throughout the country, at regulated tariffs (cf. Henderson, 2015; Yermakov, 2018, p.15). With the continued drive to develop infrastructure at home, the extent of this obligation widened.

Gazprom maintained a balanced financial position with a stable outlook. There were still reasons to worry, and a major reason for this remained the company's massive investment programme, infrastructure first and foremost. This again reflected the government's strategic priorities, both nationally and especially with regard to export. Infrastructure projects accounted for around 38 per cent of total investment spending in 2010–2017, or a bit more than the combined investments in gas, condensate and oil production (Kardaś, 2018, p.19).[16] This included the politically important gasification programme, which brought gas pipes to previously unconnected towns and villages in Russia, especially in East Siberia and the Russian Far East. However, while the gasification programme boosted domestic gas demand, it only accounted for a minor part of Gazprom's investment programme. The programme was partially financed by consumers through compulsory surcharges to gas tariffs. Therefore, gasification in Russia claimed on average 2.85 of Gazprom's investment spending in 2010–2017, or 7.5 per cent of infrastructure investments (author's calculation based on Kardaś, 2018; Gazprom, 2019a, p.19).[17] Gazprom also continued to develop underground storage both in Russia and abroad, allowing it to remain a flexible gas supplier (Gazprom, 2019d; Yermakov, 2019, p.18). A critical, unpublished report written by Sberbank analysts in 2018 raised the question of gains from the construction of new export pipelines, arguing that subcontractors in particular benefited from these megaprojects (Podobedova and Dzyadko, 2018).[18] It is difficult to assess the substance of such claims. This was not the first time the issue was brought up (Podobedova and Dzyadko, 2018). The continued priority on national and export pipelines amid an unresolved national gas market policy signified that Gazprom's role as a tool of the state mattered more than maximising its efficiency as a company. And Gazprom accomplished its politically important tasks. It retained and somewhat increased its European market share, as will be discussed on p.290. When Russia and China finally agreed on long-term gas trade in 2014, construction of the new Power of Siberia pipeline was added to the list of prioritised export projects. Also the mounting costs for the Power of Siberia indicated a preference for export route development over project efficiency.

Another reason to worry was partially related to the investment programme. Gazprom's debt burden increased threefold between 2012 and 2017, even as it remained well below a level where it would put the company's financial position at risk (Kardaś, 2018, pp.15–16). Around 75 per cent of the debts would mature in 2018–2023, indicating that the company's finances would be likely to come under some more strain (Kardaś, 2018, p.16). Profitability was another worry. From 2013, the falling oil and gas prices in global markets pressured its income downwards. Most worryingly, Gazprom seemed to develop in a suboptimal way, ineffective because of its size, monopoly position and state ownership. With its slow response to the gas market changes around 2007, it had also failed to develop LNG production when competitors, above all Novatek, grasped the opportunity. In 2017, only 1.93 per cent of Gazprom's gas sales volume were LNG (Gazprom, 2019c). Gazprom was perceived as having limited prospects of breaking into new markets (*Neftegazovaya vertikal'*, 2017a). Instead, it had pushed through massive pipeline projects, not all with the prospect of increasing its market share. The Power of Siberia pipeline seemed to run counter to the trend, as it accessed a new market. But even as the gas price in this contract is not known, the timeframe for recovering the investment is likely after 2030 (Gabuev, 2016, p.11). As stated in one trade journal in relation to the pipeline, "the economy of the specific investment project is by no means the primary issue for Gazprom" (Meshcherin, 2014b, p.42). When the contract was signed in May 2014, gaining a foothold in the Chinese market was more important.

Such priorities inevitably affected Gazprom's market capitalisation, which dropped from a historical high of 330 billion US$ in 2007 to a low of 53.5 billion US$ in 2017 (cf. *Neftegazovaya vertikal'*, 2017a, p.29; Barsukov 2018 cited in Kardaś, 2018, p.17).[19] The company's equity value in 2017 was only 16 per cent of its value ten years earlier. Some of the reduction undoubtedly reflected changes to the global markets for oil and gas, but the substantial change also reflected the fundamentals of its strategies and effectiveness. This was no reason to worry for the government, which held no plans to privatise Gazprom.

While Gazprom remained important to the state, its dividend payments became a source of contention (Sapozhkov, 2012). The trajectory was parallel to Transneft's relations with the state. The matter became urgent around 2012, when increased revenue from oil and gas production was needed to finance Putin's economic initiatives for his third term (2012–2018), known as the May Decrees (Meshcherin, 2014a, p.78). The government then introduced a new dividends policy for state-owned companies, as discussed in Chapter 6. Like Transneft, Gazprom did not comply with the demand to pay dividends to the state on the basis of its profits when calculated according to international financial reporting standards (IFRS), but instead continued to use Russian standards (RSBU). This deflated the level of dividends payment to all shareholders, including the state. The company had gradually raised its dividends payment level from 9.41 per cent of its profits based on IFRS in 2010, to 26.65 per cent in 2017 (Barsukov, 2018). The government's policy was that state-owned companies should pay half of their profits in dividends. In 2017, the Finance Ministry adjusted Gazprom's tax burden to compensate the shortfall in dividends (Barsukov, 2017). The low dividends payments in 2014 and 2015 coincided with a shortfall in tax payments. Gazprom had then paid only 7.3 and 6.7 per cent, respectively, of all Russia's taxes, this increased to above 8 per cent in 2016 and 2017 (author's calculation based on Gazprom's annual reports and information on aggregate tax payments from Federal Tax Service, 2015; 2016; 2017; 2018).[20] However, this was only partial compensation. It was indicative of a problem in the gas industry and outside, that of "manual control" or micro-management from the top, when frequent, targeted adjustments to taxation and regulation aimed at improving the situation in the short term, and often in other policy areas (Monaghan, 2012, p.14; *Neftegazovaya vertikal'*, 2015, p.54). This seriously affected the gas industry, and especially Gazprom as the most important, state-owned company in it (Henderson, 2015, pp.360–361). Making strategic priorities on the part of the company became more difficult.

Gazprom the tool of Russian foreign policy

The 2012 Decree on protection of national interests in foreign economic relations was especially important for Gazprom (Decree No. 1285, 2012). It came in force just as negotiations with Moldova came underway in September 2012. The timing indicated that it was intended to serve as a response to the deteriorating relationship between Gazprom and the EU. Less than two weeks before the decree was signed, the European Commission opened formal proceedings against Gazprom to investigate whether it breached EU antitrust rules in Central and Eastern European gas markets. If taken literally, the decree would deprive Gazprom and other strategic companies of much, if not all, of their autonomy when dealing with foreign entities. The decree made it mandatory for Gazprom and other companies to obtain government permission before responding to requests for information from foreign bodies, adjusting contractual arrangements with non-Russian customers, or alienating property abroad (Decree No. 1285, 2012). The decree stated further that government permission would be denied if "such actions would be conducive to incur damage to the economic interests of the Russian Federation" (Decree No. 1285, 2012). On the level of practicalities, the decree made Gazprom more dependent on the state when conducting its foreign operations. Moreover, the government now had greater formal powers to access Gazprom's internal business development. On the strategic level, Gazprom was obliged to pursue a business strategy that would not in any way affect Russia's economy negatively. In conceptual terms, the decree placed Gazprom's operations abroad firmly within the realm of Russian foreign policy. Any difference between Gazprom's foreign business relationships and Russian economic interests became arbitrary and temporary.

The international sanctions against Russian companies introduced in 2014 did not target Gazprom's gas business.[21] Gazprom Neft was affected by the restrictions imposed on the oil industry (Chapter 5). Due to the dependence on Russian gas across Europe, Gazprom was a less likely target for new sanctions. It did not face the same level of difficulty in obtaining credit after 2014 as did other Russian petroleum companies. However, there were other obstacles. Gazprom found it difficult to organise project financing for new pipeline projects like Nord Stream 2 and TurkStream. In the case of Nord Stream 2, which ran parallel to the existing Nord Stream pipeline, it had to rely on loans from its partners, a more costly alternative (Kardaś, 2018, p.15). The legal dispute with Naftogaz, discussed on pp.292–293, also reduced its financial flexibility (Kardaś, 2018, p.16).

The sanctions provided a renewed impetus to Russia's negotiations with China over gas export, which had lasted for about five years (Meshcherin, 2014b, p.37). Finally in May 2014, Russia and China agreed on long-term gas export through the new Power of Siberia pipeline. The pipeline was planned to run in parallel with the oil pipeline ESPO for most of its route. However, it was difficult to secure the financial basis for the new pipeline. Russia hoped for a 25 billion US$ loan from China to cover construction (Meshcherin, 2014b; Gabuev, 2016, p.11). In the event, it obtained a 2 billion Euro loan from the Bank of China (Analiticheskii Tsentr, 2016, p.28). With regard to deliveries to China, Gazprom faced competition on price from Turkmenistan (Gabuev, 2016, p.12).

Europe remained Gazprom's main market outside Russia, representing almost 42 per cent of its gas sales in 2017 (Gazprom, 2019c). Gazprom's share of the European gas market recovered to around 40 per cent in 2017, following a period of lower demand. In 2010–2012, it supplied around 25 per cent, and in 2013–2015, around 30 per cent (Vinogradova, 2017, p.44). Gazprom offered a competitive price, and a transfer for coal to gas in Europe increased demand, while the demand for LNG in Asia made this a less competitive option. In the period to 2030, these trends were likely to continue (Pirani, 2018b). However, the EU policy of energy security and alternative supply, introduced after the gas crisis in 2009 had been followed by the beginning of construction of alternative import routes. The Southern Gas Corridor, with the Trans-Adriatic (TAP) and Trans-Anatolian (TANAP) pipelines as the most important components, was underway from early 2018 (Gurbanov, 2018). There was considerable uncertainty as to the effect of these pipelines on demand for Russian gas from Gazprom.

Gazprom would likely face a stagnation in European demand. Its main advantage over competitors was that it offered abundant gas at a low price. However, this made it vulnerable to competition in a stagnating market: lower prices hit its profit margins, and led to a decline in its overall profitability (Kardaś, 2018, pp.9–10). In 2016, revenue from gas sales both in Europe and in the post-Soviet region decreased, even as the physical volume of gas sales to Europe increased (Vinogradova, 2017, p.49). To defend its position in the European market, Gazprom had had to reduce its price. While global prices for oil and gas were particularly low in 2016, Gazprom's declining profitability was a tendency over the entire period from 2012 (Kardaś, 2018). As for the post-Soviet region, the shortfall in revenue was caused by declining demand, as seen in Table 7.1.

In this situation, Gazprom's investment in new pipelines would be recovered only in the very long term. The construction of the seabed pipelines Nord Stream 2 and TurkStream required the construction of long feeder pipelines on shore in Russia. TurkStream also followed a different route across the Black Sea from the existing Blue Stream pipeline (Anapa to Kıyıköy on Turkey's Thracian coast), further increasing the cost. When added to the project cost for the seabed pipelines, total cost estimates for Nord Stream

2 and TurkStream reached 17 billion and 20 billion US$, respectively (Podobedova and Dzyadko, 2018). Gazprom bore sole responsibility for financing onshore infrastructure. When onshore infrastructure was included, Nord Stream 2 would begin to turn a profit after 21 years, and TurkStream after 40 (Podobedova and Dzyadko, 2018). While the former was not all that an unusual time period for recouping pipeline investment, the latter was an unusually lengthy wait.

Avoiding Ukraine

With regard to Ukraine, gas trade and pricing were important instruments used by Russia to entice Yanukovych and the Ukrainian government to refrain from further integration with the EU in 2013. By September 2013, Ukraine was well on the way to signing an Association Agreement and a Deep and Comprehensive Free Trade Agreement (DCFTA) with the EU. In November, Putin met Yanukovych in Sochi and offered a further discount on gas prices under the 2009 agreement as well as economic assistance from Russia to Ukraine (Bugriy, 2013). The aim was to convince Yanukovych to postpone integration with the EU and entice Ukraine to integrate with the Customs Union of Russia, Belarus and Kazakhstan. At the same time, Russia applied economic pressure on Ukraine by informally blocking Ukrainian exports to Russia of goods as diverse as confectioneries and freight cars, and threatened to apply sanctions should the Association Agreement be signed. These efforts were initially successful, as the Ukrainian government stopped preparations for the signing directly after Yanukovych's return to Kyiv. However, Yanukovych's about-turn was decisive in bringing about the Euromaidan protests in Ukraine. In February 2014, following the use of violence to disperse the persistent protests, Yanukovych's government collapsed, and he fled Ukraine.

Russia reacted to this by annexing Crimea, breaking international law. It seized the part of Ukraine's exclusive economic zone in the Black Sea adjacent to the peninsula. The Crimean de facto authorities took control of the Naftogaz subsidiary Chornomornaftogaz. Almost all Ukraine's significant new, conventional oil and gas resources at that point, 1971 bcm of gas and 435 million tonnes of oil, were located in the part of Ukraine's exclusive economic zone adjacent to Crimea (Vinogradova, 2014, pp.4–5). Altogether, Chornomornaftogaz had at least a dozen prospective fields under exploration and further development by early 2014 (Vinogradova, 2014, pp.4–5). The annexation thus closed Ukraine's possibilities for increasing oil and gas production in the future. The international sanctions that were introduced following the annexation targeted Chornomornaftogaz, thus in practice nullifying existing contracts for offshore development in this part of the Black Sea. By February 2014, one PSA was already signed and another was close to being signed. In October 2016, Naftogaz and its subsidiaries initiated arbitration proceedings with the International Court of Justice in The Hague to recover the damages, estimated at 2.6 billion US$ (Naftogaz Ukrainy, 2016). However, when the first part of the process ended with a ruling in favour of Naftogaz, Russia refused to recognize the decision (Krym.Realii, 2019).

The establishment of a new government in Ukraine also brought management changes in Naftogaz. A new management was in place already at the end of March (Naftogaz Ukrainy, 2015, p.7). Just like in the nuclear energy industry, Ukraine's efforts to diversify fuel supplies accelerated quickly under the new government. If anything, the turnaround was even swifter in gas than in nuclear energy. Naftogaz had purchased small volumes from Ukraine's western neighbours through a reversal of gas flows in 2012 and 2013. In 2014, a quarter of Ukraine's gas import and almost 12 per cent of its demand were covered by non-Russian imports (Vinogradova, 2015, p.28). The new Ukrainian government intensified the effort to reduce gas consumption, and new measures were taken to reduce overall energy consumption. Gas consumption in Ukraine had decreased from around 75–76 bcm annually in 2003–2005 to 57.6 in 2010 (Naftogaz Ukrainy, 2019). Now it was reduced further to 42.6 bcm in 2014 and 32.3 in 2018 (Naftogaz Ukrainy, 2019). Some of the reduction was due to the war in Donbas, while Ukraine's deep economic crisis also had an impact.

In spring 2014, relations escalated quickly also between Gazprom and Ukraine. In April, Gazprom cancelled both the price discount granted to Ukraine following Yanukovych's about-turn in late 2013, and the discount obtained under the Kharkiv Accords from 2010. Gas prices rose from 268.50 to 485.50 US$/bcm (Nikitin and Evdokimova, 2014; Varfolomeyev, 2014). Gazprom also demanded immediate repayment of Ukraine's 2.2 billion US$ debts for gas (Nikitin and Evdokimova, 2014). When Ukraine failed to comply, Gazprom in June suspended its gas sales to Ukraine. At this point, Gazprom launched legal proceedings against Naftogaz before the Arbitration Institute at the Stockholm Chamber of Commerce. When the parties returned to the negotiation table in September, the format was trilateral, with the EU acting as a mediator. This increased Russian pressure also on the EU (Łoskot-Strachota et al., 2014). However, a temporary settlement, the "winter agreement", was reached at the end of October (Kononczuk et al., 2014). In the final negotiation phase and subsequently when the agreement was prolonged, both Gazprom and the Russian government were more willing to discount the price than had often been the case before. The technicalities of the discount demonstrated the extent of the Russian government's support for Gazprom, as it in effect waived the export tariff on gas (RIA Novosti, 2015). Retaining a share of Ukraine's shrinking market and preserving some goodwill in Europe appeared to be important rationales for this policy. In November 2015, the agreement expired, and direct gas sales from Gazprom to Ukraine ceased altogether. From then on, Ukraine imported gas in reverse flow from Germany, Slovakia and Hungary. Ukraine also concluded agreements to establish gas interconnectors with Hungary, Poland and Romania (Vinogradova, 2015, p.29). Except in the case of gas obtained from Romania and partly Germany, gas that reached Ukraine from the west was sourced from Gazprom.

With support from the EU, Ukraine embarked on a long overdue gas sector reform in October 2015 (Kardaś and Iwański, 2018). This was part of a general policy to bring Ukraine's energy sector in line with EU and European Energy Community standards. Domestic politics complicated the process (Varfolomeyev, 2017). Another complication was the ongoing arbitration case in Stockholm, in what was claimed to be the largest arbitration case ever. The case was decided in December 2017 and February 2018 (Pirani, 2018a, pp.2–3). The tribunal's ruling was overall in favour of Naftogaz. Gazprom's reaction was unusual, as it refused to accept the decision, by partially appealing it, cancelling the planned resumption of gas export to Ukraine, and refusing to pay Naftogaz the outstanding compensation of around 2.56 billion US$ (Naftogaz Ukrainy, 2018). It was now very unlikely that Gazprom would sell gas directly to Ukraine again.

After the annexation of Crimea, Gazprom intensified its pursuit of transit routes that avoided Ukraine. Around 40 per cent of Russia's gas to European customers still transited Ukraine. However, in 2017 Gazprom and five other European companies, OMV, ENGIE, Shell, Uniper and Wintershall agreed on financing for a new pipeline under the Baltic Sea, called Nord Stream 2. In spite of considerable misgivings in EU member states and uncertainty on how changes to the EU gas directive would affect the pipeline, construction proceeded. Nord Stream 2 is likely to be operational in 2021–2022. In the south of Europe, the South Stream project was cancelled in December 2014. However, many of its advantages for Gazprom were preserved in TurkStream, announced by Putin simultaneously with the cancellation (Franza, 2015). TurkStream would still cross the Black Sea and serve the Turkish market, allowing Gazprom to compete in the Turkish market and against non-Russian routes from the Caspian Sea to Europe. Most importantly, TurkStream could take an increasing share of gas from transit through Ukraine and bring it to the EU's doorstep; crucially, it would not be subject to EU regulations on third-party access. TurkStream was unlikely to become fully operational until 2021–2022. Nevertheless, transit through Ukraine was likely to continue also after this point, even as the existing transit contracts were due to expire at the end of 2019.

Just as in the cases of Ukraine and Armenia (discussed on p.295), Russia tried to use gas to pressure Moldova to refrain from further integration with the EU. Ahead of Moldova's signing of an Association Agreement with the EU, and a DCFTA, in 2013, Gazprom brought the issue of debts for Transnistria's gas supply up again (Silady et al., 2013). Moldova's relations with Russia continued to worsen in the next few years, while Moldova's integration with the EU progressed. However, gas imports continued unperturbed. In 2015, Moldovans protested against electricity and gas tariff hikes, with some effect on tariffs (Calus, 2015). Indications were that the electricity tariffs did not reflect real production cost, as almost all Moldova's electricity supply came from the gas-fired Moldova TPP in Transnistria, which still did not pay for its gas (Popșoi, 2016). Meanwhile, Moldova and Romania had also constructed an interconnector (Iaşi–Ungheni), which enabled Moldova to import gas from Romania (Golub, 2012; Molnar, 2012). Romania's domestic gas production enabled it to provide small volumes of gas to Moldova (RFE/RL, 2015). While this improved Moldova's security of energy supply, it was not sufficient to replace Russian gas, nor was it intended to. In the event of a breakdown of transit relations between Ukraine and Russia, Moldova would be among the countries most affected.

The Caspian region: Foreign policy priorities

The problems with market access in Europe and gas transport and market access in Turkey led Gazprom to engage in downstream activities also in Central Asia, diversifying its operations in those states. On their side, states like Uzbekistan, Turkmenistan and Kazakhstan had accumulated several years' experience of relying on the Chinese market for their oil and gas exports, and on Chinese companies for investments in their oil and gas industries. While 15 years earlier, their governments saw Chinese companies as a welcome balance and complement to Russian companies, now, Russia served as a balance to China.

In Kazakhstan, gas export from Karachaganak to the Orenburg gas processing plant continued. In 2015, the KPO consortium and KazRosGaz agreed on a new contract for this export until 2038 (*Neftegazovaya vertikal'*, 2017b, p.56). One effect of the contract was that export to Orenburg became a priority also amid falling production. Therefore, lower production hit the local condensate processing factory instead of Orenburg (*Neftegazovaya vertikal'*, 2017b, p.56). While China was now a more important gas customer for Kazakhstan than before, Russia caught up with China as a trade partner from 2014 (Analiticheskii Tsentr, 2017, pp.10–11). Gas played a key role.

Russia was Uzbekistan's largest gas customer, followed by Kazakhstan and China. Beginning in 2016, Gazprom's relations with Uzbekistan intensified under President Islam Karimov's successor, Shavkat Mirziyoyev. The improvement was sealed in a deal under which Gazprom would export oil and invest in a new refinery in Uzbekistan, engage in other downstream activities, and buy 4 bcm of gas annually in 2018–2022 (*Neftegazovaya vertikal'*, 2017c).

Russia's gas relations with Turkmenistan remained tense. In 2016, Gazprom tried to renegotiate the price, leading to a new round of mutual accusations (Voloshin, 2016). The price, 240 USD/mcm left Gazprom in a squeeze, due to the pressure on prices in Europe. Relations, and gas trade, again broke down in January 2016, but picked up in 2018. One reason was that Turkmenistan faced difficulties in relations with Iran and Azerbaijan, both customers and potential transit countries for its gas and oil (Pannier, 2017; Rahimov, 2019). In that situation, it was left with only one gas customer, China, which was the destination for 83 per cent of its exports and close to 100 per cent of its gas (UN Comtrade database harmonised by Gaulier and Zignago, 2010, accessed through Simoes and Hidalgo, 2011).[22] The Turkmen economy was in dire straits. Importantly for Russia's position, in August 2018, the Caspian littoral states finally signed the Treaty on the legal status of the Caspian Sea. With a treaty in place, Russia was eager to prevent a situation in which the signing of the treaty would give a new impetus to the development of a trans-Caspian pipeline for oil or gas.

By September 2015, Gazprom's strategy of control of Caspian transit had become part of a comprehensive Russian effort to exert a maximum of influence over the development of north–south energy transit in the Caucasus. It had long been a goal to minimise Iran's reach in energy supply and transit in the region, especially in that country's best candidate for regional partner, Armenia. Following the annexation of Crimea, and especially, the beginning of Russia's military support for the Assad regime in Syria, Russia's policy turned more flexible. It became more important to engage with Iran in the development of energy relations in the Caucasus. After the 5+1 nuclear deal with Iran in summer 2015, it was possible to engage more comprehensively. Russia's aim to dominate the region's energy sector evolved into an effort to develop infrastructure and markets with a maximal Russian presence, with Iran on board. The policy complemented Russia's Syria policy well, turning the Russian energy component in the conflict into part of a more comprehensive regional effort. If successful, this would act as a counterweight to western influence, and possibly also China's efforts to attract states in the region to its Belt and Road Initiative.

This policy turn affected relations with Armenia and Georgia. In 2013, Russia had used Gazprom's dominance of Armenia's gas market to pressure Armenia on its conclusion of an Association Agreement and a DCFTA with the EU. In the run-up to Armenia's signing of the agreement, gas price increases and a weapons trade deal with Azerbaijan increased Russia's pressure on the Armenian government (Grigoryan, 2013). The pressure worked. Following a visit to Moscow, Armenia's President Serzh Sargsyan in September declared that Armenia would join the Customs Union with Russia, Belarus and Kazakhstan and subsequently, the Eurasian Economic Union. In the months that followed, details of the deal revealed that Gazprom had obtained a monopoly on gas deliveries to Armenia for 30 years, and the remaining 20 per cent share of ArmRosGazprom, against cancellation of a 300 US$ million gas debt, and promises of a freeze in gas prices for five years (Bedevian, 2013). The existence of the debt had thus far not been made public (Bedevian, 2013). Gazprom also acquired the pipeline that connected Armenia's gas grid to Iran (Abrahamyan, 2015). ArmRosGazprom, from 2014 Gazprom Armenia, retained full control of Armenia's gas market. However, in 2015, Russia widened its relations with Armenia in the energy sphere to a regional cooperation that included Georgia and Iran. This was followed by the development of four-party plans for electricity cooperation. But less happened in the gas industry. A lack of trust remained a serious obstacle to further development.

In Georgia, Gazprom's success in retaining a foothold began to deliver following the beginning of the four-party format. In September 2015, Gazprom and the Georgian government started consultations on payment for transit to Armenia, and on increased Russian gas supply to the Georgian market (Rukhadze, 2015). At that point, Gazprom supplied around 12 per cent of Georgia's gas, the rest coming from Azerbaijan (Rukhadze, 2015). Gazprom's goal was to cease paying the transit fee in gas, and begin paying it in cash. A monetised transit fee would buy Georgia a lesser supply of Russian gas than the commodity fee. In 2016, following popular protests, the Georgian government refused to consider such a deal. Instead, it increased purchases of gas from Azerbaijan (Vinogradova, 2017, p.48). However, a year later, the Georgian government agreed to transfer payment from gas to cash, to widespread public criticism (Civil.ge, 2017). The terms of the deal were not made public.

Conclusions

While other economic sectors disintegrated in the late 1980s and early 1990s, Gazprom emerged from the Soviet Union with control of the gas industry and access to external markets. This enabled Gazprom to provide indispensable capital needed for the stabilisation of the Russian state. Its informal rent streams, channelled through subsidies towards the population coupled with more selective rent sharing with the elite, gave the state infrastructural power and maintained regime stability. But this also sustained a status quo that inhibited institutional development and growth in state capacity. Gazprom's position as a linchpin of the state slowed the commercial development of the company.

Gazprom in the 1990s controlled sector policy and essentially regulated itself, as did Transneft, RAO UES and Minatom. This status quo was upheld by informal constraints, as were shared in the ruling coalition in return for protection of the monopoly. Rents from Gazprom sustained the ruling coalition and wider support in the Duma and the regions. These rent streams were considerable. State access to Gazprom through formal channels was restricted compared to other cases studied here. Trustee management and other institutions created barriers to the state's possibilities of overseeing Gazprom. As long as state capacity was low across all sectors, the difference was not so great between Gazprom and, for example, Minatom or RAO UES. But when the government in 1997–1998 attempted to gain access to all state-owned companies, there were more hurdles, secured in the formal institutional framework, to overcome to gain access to Gazprom. The balance of power had tilted away from the state towards Gazprom to a greater degree than in the other cases in this book.

State capacity increased under Putin's first presidential term. This was partly a result of improved access to Gazprom, with its rent streams, infrastructure, and media outlets. The return of state access to Gazprom was emblematic of this period when the state's ability to conduct economic policy increased substantially. For Gazprom, restored state control resulted in a more commercially oriented organisation, with consequences for the Russian and post-Soviet gas markets. Gazprom became a tool of the new regime. Gazprom had, of course, also been a tool of the regime in the 1990s, but that was negotiated access. Putin and the governments of the 2000s insisted on direct access to Gazprom. Gazprom was open to regime interference in the 2000s because it depended on the state and the ruling coalition. With greater specialisation among state organisations, it no longer regulated itself. In the 1990s, Rem Vyakhirev could pay Gazprom's taxes with considerable discretion. In the 2000s, Gazprom had to give real third-party access to UGSS and, informally, it could be instructed to acquire an entire oil company. In the 2010s, it had to deliver on infrastructure projects, while its gas tariffs remained regulated below the prices charged by other companies. Its central position in the Russian political economy meant that there were obvious limits to its possibilities for commercial development.

Gazprom was a tool of Russia's foreign policy in the post-Soviet region from its early days. There is an economic and political logic to this. Gas producers and consumers are always in long-term relationships, and gas pipelines lock the two sides together. Breaking out is costly. Pipelines are expensive, but bypass pipelines that offer excess capacity are even more expensive. Control of gas transit without an accepted dispute resolution mechanism makes a pipeline a political tool. In Russia, Gazprom held that tool. But, as Ericson puts it, mutual dependence can be used for cooperative development or geopolitical advantage (Ericson, 2012, p.617). Russia used its control of gas supply and gas transit for geopolitical advantage. Gazprom's control of post-Soviet states' access to subsidised gas in the 1990s was used to cultivate their dependence on Russian gas, and ipso facto enabled Russia to influence domestic economic and political development in these states. Gazprom's position meant that it could propose projects rivalling most alternatives, and thereby create uncertainty for lesser actors. This could be used coercively, as seen in Moldova and Armenia. The economic cost of post-Soviet gas dependence increased when Gazprom started to demand prices based on the price for gas in Europe.

Seen from Russia, Gazprom achieved foreign policy results in the post-Soviet region at a small cost in the 1990s. As long as there were no profits to reap, and transit was maintained, loss of revenue remained marginal. That the results were often symbolic, or that the other side delivered extremely slowly, did not automatically trigger a top-level Russian reaction. The use of gas as a geopolitical, not a cooperative, tool in the region ensured that at least Russia's short term aims could be reached.

In the 2000s, commercialisation of Gazprom's deliveries to the post-Soviet region strengthened company finances and increased revenue. It also transformed it into a more effective foreign policy tool. Bilateral conflict would now result in higher profits, while bilateral cooperation on Russia's terms could yield both profits and political returns in the form of leverage, often through equity. The mutual dependence between gas seller and buyer made it difficult for post-Soviet customers to protest against or exit the relationship. This delayed and lessened the negative political consequences for Russia when it used gas as a foreign policy "stick". However, when international gas markets changed in the mid-2000s and Gazprom continued to act in a ham-fisted way, this policy began to backfire. The repercussions had serious effects also on its relations with Europe, the most important market. The negative consequences seemed to accelerate from 2014, when Russian policy towards Ukraine further eroded trust in Gazprom. Subsequent increases in European demand for Russian gas showed that Gazprom would continue to play an important role. But its relations with post-Soviet customers and partners seemed less destined to improve without a change in Russian foreign policy. In that respect, Gazprom was set to remain an undisputed foreign policy tool also in years to come.

Notes

1 Until 2003, Novafininvest.
2 Associated gas is conventional gas that is produced during the extraction of crude oil. When the necessary infrastructure exists, selling it is an alternative to both flaring (burning to release the pressure) and reinjection into the field to maintain pressure and ultimately improve oil recovery rates.
3 In Russian *Edinaya sistema gazosnabzheniya*, ESG.
4 Under a take-or-pay clause (or take-or-pay contract), a buyer is obliged to take a certain volume of gas or pay a penalty for the shortfall. This provision reduces risk and can therefore also reduce the price, but it also represents a barrier to competition, particularly when combined with long-term contracts. Such clauses are especially common in gas trade, and uncommon outside the energy industries.
5 The Commonwealth of Independent States is comprised of all the post-Soviet states except Estonia, Latvia and Lithuania.
6 The project faltered due to US objections.
7 Turkmenistan exported around 40 bcm annually to Ukraine by 2007.
8 The term referred to a price level similar to that of Gazprom's European customers, minus transportation costs.
9 The exception was LNG exported to Asian markets.
10 The proposed route was from Ahiboz outside Ankara to Baumgarten in Austria, with a feeder pipeline from Erzurum to Ahiboz.
11 There were four main projects, Gissarneftegaz, Kokdumalak-Gaz, Shakhpakhty and Ustyurt, with total estimated gas reserves of around 320 bcm and oil reserves of around 20 million tonnes.
12 More evidence in support of this claim emerged during the Telia case (2013–2019), which exposed corrupt dealings between the Swedish telecommunications company TeliaSonera and several Uzbek companies, including Zeromax.
13 Data available from the Observatory of Economic Complexity (https://atlas.media.mit.edu/en/) (Simoes and Hidalgo, 2011). Values are calculated using current US dollars to exchange rates provided by the reporting nation.
14 Due to difficulties in obtaining statistics on the value of trade between Turkmenistan and Iran, it is difficult to estimate precisely the importance of China in Turkmenistan's overall trade.

15 The most significant other gas producers were Novatek, Lukoil, Rosneft and Surgutneftegaz.
16 Investment for Gazprom group as a whole, including Gazprom Neft and other subsidiaries.
17 Value of total spending on investment from (Kardaś, 2018), value of gasification programme spending from (Gazprom, 2019a). All numbers are ultimately derived from Gazprom.
18 Shortly afterwards, one of the authors behind the report left Sberbank CIB by mutual consent, as did his immediate superior.
19 Market capitalisation is the value of a company's outstanding shares (shares held by investors, not the company).
20 Calculated using Gazprom's consolidated tax payments, consisting of tax on profits and other taxes.
21 Aleksei Miller was in April 2018 added to the US list of persons subjected to personal sanctions in relation to the war in Ukraine.
22 While the reservation mentioned in fn.14 above obtains in general also after 2016, gas export to Iran stopped in January 2017. For this reason the numbers for 2017 are more accurate. Data available at The Observatory of Economic Complexity (https://atlas.media.mit.edu/en/) (Simoes and Hidalgo, 2011). Values are calculated using current US dollars to exchange rates provided by the reporting nation.

References

Abrahamyan, G. (2015) "Could Russia spoil Armenia's Iranian investment dreams?" *Eurasianet.org*, 17 July

Afanasiev, V. (2009) "Sector bridges great divide" *Upstream*, 20 August

Analiticheskii Tsentr (2016) *Trudnosti na puti vostochnogo gazovogo vektora* [*Difficulties on the road to an eastern gas vector*]. Energeticheskii byulleten'. (Moscow: Analiticheskii Tsentr pri Pravitel'stve Rossiiskoi Federatsii/Analytical Center for the Government of the Russian Federation)

Analiticheskii Tsentr (2017) *V fokuse: Kazakhstan – chetvert' veka reform* [*In focus: Kazakhstan – a quarter of a century of reform*]. Byulleten' o tekushchikh tendentsiyakh mirovoi ekonomiki. (Moscow: Analiticheskii Tsentr pri Pravitel'stve Rossiiskoi Federatsii/Analytical Center for the Government of the Russian Federation)

APEK (2017) "Reiting vliyaniya krupnykh predprinimatelei i top-menedzherov toplivno-energeticheskogo kompleksa v iyune 2017 g. [Rating of the influence of major businessmen and top managers in the fuel and energy complex, June 2017]" [online]. 29 June (Moscow: Agentstvo politicheskikh i ekonomicheskikh kommunikatsii). Available from: http://apecom.ru/projects/item.php?SECTION_ID=102&ELEMENT_ID=3803 [Accessed 18 March 2019]

Bagrov, A. (2000) "Kak delitsya Vyakhirev [How Vyakhirev will be divided]" *Kommersant*, 29 January, p.1

Bakhtadze, R. (2002) "Russian energy giant takes over Georgian gas distribution system" [online]. 16 August 2002 (Tbilisi: Civil.ge). Available from: http://www.civil.ge/eng/article.php?id=2490 [Accessed 15 May 2019]

Balmaceda, M.M. (1998) "Gas, oil, and the linkages between domestic and foreign policies: The case of Ukraine", *Europe-Asia Studies*, 50 (2): 257–286

Balmaceda, M.M. (2008) *Energy Dependency, Politics, and Corruption in the Former Soviet Union. Russia's Power, Oligarchs' Profits and Ukraine's Missing Energy Policy, 1995–2006* (London/New York: Routledge)

Bardin, V. (1992) "TsBR registriruet zarubezhnye scheta eksporterov nefti i gaza [The Central Bank registers oil and gas exporters' foreign accounts]" *Kommersant*, 25 May

Barsukov, Yu. (2017) "Nalog na dobychu dividendov [A tax on dividends extraction]" *Kommersant*, 13 June, p.1

Barsukov, Yu. (2018) "Dividendy poslednei nadezhdy [Dividends of the last resort]" *Kommersant*, 3 September, p.9

Bedevian, A. (2013) "New details of Russian–Armenian gas deal emerge" [online]. 17 December (Prague: Radio Free Europe/Radio Liberty). Available from: https://www.azatutyun.am/a/25204160.html [Accessed 20 May 2019]

Belyakov, E. (2006) "'Gazprom' pokoryaet Kazakhstan [Gazprom conquers Kazakhstan]" *Gazeta*, 26 October, p.13

Belyakov, E. (2008) "Energodiktat Moskvy i Astany stanovitsya yav'yu [The energy diktat of Moscow and Astana becomes reality]" *Gazeta*, 9 September, p.9

Berger, M. and Proskurnina, O. (2008) *Krest Chubaisa [Chubais's Cross]* (Moscow: KoLibri)

Bilanenko, P. (2013) "Eto byl stroitel' imperii [He was an empire builder]" *Kommersant*, 12 February, p.7

Blagov, S. (2007) "Russia struggles to finalize Caspian gas pipeline deal with Turkmenistan" *Eurasia Daily Monitor*, 1 November

Bolukbasi, S. (1998) "The controversy over the Caspian Sea mineral resources: Conflicting perception, clashing interests", *Europe-Asia Studies*, 50 (3): 397–414

BP (2012) *BP Statistical Review of World Energy June 2012*. London: BP. Available from: http://www.bp.com/statisticalreview [Accessed 14 June 2012]

Brauer, B. (2002) "Oil field hopes to become world power" *The New York Times*, 10 April, p.W001

Bruce, C. (2007) "Power resources. The political agenda in Russo-Moldovan gas relations", *Problems of Post-Communism*, 54 (3): 29–47

Bruce, C. and Yafimava, K. (2009) "Moldova's gas sector" in Pirani, S. ed., *Russian and CIS Gas Markets and their Impact on Europe* (Oxford: Oxford University Press for the Oxford Institute for Energy Studies) pp.170–202

Bugriy, M. (2013) "Kyiv testing 'pause' in EU integration" *Eurasia Daily Monitor*, 14 November

Butrin, D. (2001) "Nasledstvo Rema Vyakhireva [Rem Vyakhirev's heritage]" *Kommersant-Den'gi*, 6 June, p.12

Butrin, D. (2003a) "'Gazprom' sproektiruet gazoprovod iz Turkmenii, chtoby ego ne stroit' [Gazprom will plan a pipeline from Turkmenistan in order not to build it]" *Kommersant*, 25 July, p.6

Butrin, D. (2003b) "'Gazprom' stal importerom [Gazprom became an importer]" *Kommersant*, 11 April, p.13

Butrin, D. (2005) "Orenburgskii GPZ stanet napolovinu kazakhskim [Orenburg Gas Processing Plant becomes half-Kazakh]" *Kommersant*, 10 March, p.13

Calus, K. (2015) "A Moldovan Yerevan" *Transitions Online*, 22 July

Chazan, G. (2008) "Turkmenistan gas field is one of world's largest" *The Wall Street Journal*, 16 October 2008, p.A9

Civil.ge (2003a) "President makes new appointments as Energy Minister resigns" [online]. 13 August (Tbilisi: Civil.ge). Available from: https://civil.ge/archives/103878 [Accessed 15 May 2019]

Civil.ge (2003b) "GazProm, Georgia agree on strategic cooperation" [online]. 24 July (Tbilisi: Civil.ge). Available from: https://civil.ge/archives/103766 [Accessed 15 May 2019]

Civil.ge (2006) "Tbilisi receives Russian Gas via Azerbaijan" [online]. 23 January (Tbilisi: Civil.ge). Available from: https://civil.ge/archives/109637 [Accessed 15 May 2019]

Civil.ge (2017) "President, political parties, CSOs slam new transit deal with Gazprom" [online]. 17 January (Tbilisi: Civil.ge). Available from: https://civil.ge/archives/126087 [Accessed 21 May 2019]

Crawford, D. and White, G.L. (2005) "Dresdner official to get post with Baltic pipeline" *The Wall Street Journal*, 9 December

Daly, J.C.K. (2008) "Washington and Moscow vie for Turkmenistan's supplies" *Eurasia Daily Monitor*, 6 June

Danielyan, E. (2005a) "Putin visit highlights Russian interest in Armenia" *Eurasia Daily Monitor*, 29 March

Danielyan, E. (2005b) "Surge in Russian gas prices raises eyebrows in Armenia" *Eurasia Daily Monitor*, 7 December

Danielyan, E. (2005c) "Russian takeover of Armenian power grid prompts concern" *Eurasia Daily Monitor*, 21 July

Danielyan, E. (2007) "Soaring trade boosts Russian-Armenian economic ties" *Eurasia Daily Monitor*, 30 October

Decree No. 426 (28/04/1997) *Ob osnovnykh polozheniyakh strukturnoi reformy v sferakh estestvennykh monopolii* [*On the basic provisions for structural reform in the spheres of the natural monopolies*] (Moscow: President of the Russian Federation)

Decree No. 478 (12/05/1997) *O merakh po obospecheniyu gosudarstvennogo upravleniya zakreplennymi v federal'noi sobstvennosti aktsiyami Rossiiskogo aktsionernogo obschestva "Gazprom"* [*On measures to provide for state management of the shares of the Russian shareholding company "Gazprom" held in federal ownership*] (Moscow: President of the Russian Federation)

Decree No. 529 (28/05/1997) *O poryadke obrashcheniya aktsii Rossiiskogo aktsionernogo obshchestva "Gazprom" na period zakrepleniya v federal'noi sobstvennosti aktsii Rossiiskogo aktsionernogo obschestva "Gazprom"* [*On the order of circulation of the shares of the Russian shareholding company "Gazprom" in the period of federal ownership of the shares of the Russian shareholding company "Gazprom"*] (Moscow: President of the Russian Federation)

Decree No. 538 (01/06/1992) *Ob obespechenii deyatel'nosti Edinoi sistemy gazosnabzheniya strany* [*On securing the operation of the country's United system of gas supply*] (Moscow: President of the Russian Federation)

Decree No. 599 (22/04/1996) *O prodlenii sroka deistviya dogovora o doveritel'nom upravlenii zakreplennymi v federal'noi sobstvennosti aktsiyami mezhdu Pravitel'stvom Rossiiskoi Federatsii i Rossiiskim aktsionernom obshchestvom "Gazprom"* [*On prolongation of the agreement between the Government of the Russian Federation and the Russian shareholding company "Gazprom" on trustee management of shares held as federal property*] (Moscow: President of the Russian Federation)

Decree No. 887 (25/07/1998) *O realizatsii aktsii Rossiiskogo aktsionernogo obshchestva "Gazprom"* [*On realisation of the shares in the Russian shareholding company "Gazprom"*] (Moscow: The President of the Russian Federation)

Decree No. 1285 (11/09/2012) *O merakh po zashchite interesov Rossiiskoi Federatsii pri osushchestvlenii rossiiskimi yuridicheskimi litsami vneshneekonomicheskoi deyatel'nosti*

[*On measures to protect the interests of the Russian Federation when foreign economic activity is carried out by a Russian juridical person*] (Moscow: President of the Russian Federation)

Decree No. 1333 (05/11/1992) *O preobrazovanii gosudarstvennogo gazovogo kontserna "Gazprom" v rossiiskoe aktsionernoe obshchestvo "Gazprom"* [*On the reorganisation of the state gas concern "Gazprom" into the Russian shareholding company "Gazprom"*] (Moscow: President of the Russian Federation)

Decree No. 1333 (12/05/1997) *O preobrazovanii gosudarstvennogo gazovogo kontserna "Gazprom" v rossiiskoe aktsionernoe obshchestvo "Gazprom"* [*On the reorganisation of the state gas concern "Gazprom" into the Russian shareholding company "Gazprom"*] (Moscow: President of the Russian Federation)

Decree No. 2213 (26/12/1994) *Ob uporyadochenii eksporta prirodnogo gaza* [*On the effectuation of natural gas export*] (Moscow: The President of the Russian Federation)

Decree No. 2296 (24/12/1993) *O doveritel'noi sobstvennosti (traste)* [*On entrusted property (trust)*] (Moscow: The President of the Russian Federation)

Dubnov, V. (2003) "Rossiya – Turkmeniya. Istoriya darenogo konya, ili Gaz v obmen na ekstraditsiyu [Russia – Turkmenistan. The story of the gifted horse, or Gas in return for extradition]" *Novoe vremya*, 20 April, p.32

Embassy Ashgabat (2009) Turkmenistan: Gazprom and Turkmen government blame each other for April 9 pipeline explosion, 09ASHGABAT462/Wikileaks #201845. Issue date 10 April 2009. *Cablegate* [online]. (Published by Wikileaks 1 September 2011). Available from: https://wikileaks.org/plusd/cables/09ASHGABAT462_a.html [Accessed 15 May 2019]

Embassy Moscow (2007) Russian corporate statism: Watch this space, 07MOSCOW1442/Wikileaks #102758. Issue date 2 April 2007. *Cablegate* [online]. (Published by Wikileaks 8 September 2011). Available from: https://wikileaks.org/plusd/cables/07MOSCOW1442_a.html [Accessed 15 May 2019]

Embassy Tashkent (2008) Uzbekistan: Gulnora Karimova's Geneva UN appointment may reflect concerns about the future, 08TASHKENT1072/Wikileaks #170357. Issue date 18 September 2008. *Cablegate* [online]. (Published by Wikileaks 8 September 2011). Available from: https://wikileaks.org/plusd/cables/08TASHKENT1072_a.html [Accessed 15 May 2019]

Embassy Tashkent (2010) Uzbekistan: From A To Zeromax, 10TASHKENT27/Wikileaks #244365. Issue date 20 January 2010. *Cablegate* [online]. (Published by Wikileaks 8 September 2011). Available from: https://wikileaks.org/plusd/cables/10TASHKENT27_a.html [Accessed 15 May 2019]

Embassy Yerevan (2005) Armenia looking to Iran to reduce dependence on Russian energy resources, 05YEREVAN2005391_a. Issue date 4 March 2005. *Cablegate* [online]. (Published by Wikileaks 30 August 2011). Available from: https://wikileaks.org/plusd/cables/05YEREVAN391_a.html [Accessed 21 May 2019]

Emel'yanov, S. (2003) "Eksport rossiiskogo gaza: istoriya, sostoyanie, perspektivy [Export of Russian gas: history, position, perspectives]" *Neftegazovaya vertikal'*, No. 6

Ericson, R.E. (2012) "Eurasian natural gas: Significance and recent developments", *Eurasian Geography and Economics*, 53 (5): 615–648

Federal Law No. 117 (18/07/2006) *Ob eksporte gaza* [*On the export of gas*] (Moscow: The Federal Assembly)

Federal Tax Service (2007) Otchet po forme No.1-NM za 2006 g., svodnyi v tselom po Rossiiskoi Federatsii [Account for form No.1-NM for 2006, summarised for the

Russian Federation]. 1nm2006.xls. Moscow: Federal'naya nalogovaya sluzhba. Available from: https://www.nalog.ru/rn77/related_activities/statistics_and_analytics/forms/3832158/ [Accessed 13 June 2019]

Federal Tax Service (2008) Otchet po forme No.1-NM za 2007 g., svodnyi v tselom po Rossiiskoi Federatsii [Account for form No.1-NM for 2007, summarised for the Russian Federation]. 1nm2007.xls. Moscow: Federal'naya nalogovaya sluzhba. Available from: https://www.nalog.ru/rn77/related_activities/statistics_and_analytics/forms/3832160/ [Accessed 13 June 2019]

Federal Tax Service (2009) Otchet po forme No.1-NM za 2008 g., svodnyi v tselom po Rossiiskoi Federatsii [Account for form No.1-NM for 2008, summarised for the Russian Federation]. 1nm2008.xls. Moscow: Federal'naya nalogovaya sluzhba. Available from: https://www.nalog.ru/rn77/related_activities/statistics_and_analytics/forms/3832163/ [Accessed 13 June 2019]

Federal Tax Service (2010) Otchet po forme No.1-NM za 2009 g., svodnyi v tselom po Rossiiskoi Federatsii [Account for form No.1-NM for 2009, summarised for the Russian Federation]. 1nm2009.xls. Moscow: Federal'naya nalogovaya sluzhba. Available from: https://www.nalog.ru/rn77/related_activities/statistics_and_analytics/forms/3827841/ [Accessed 13 June 2019]

Federal Tax Service (2011) Otchet po forme No.1-NM za 2010 g., svodnyi v tselom po Rossiiskoi Federatsii [Account for form No.1-NM for 2010, summarised for the Russian Federation]. 1_nm_svod070411.xls. Moscow: Federal'naya nalogovaya sluzhba. Available from: https://www.nalog.ru/rn77/related_activities/statistics_and_analytics/forms/3827842/ [Accessed 13 June 2019]

Federal Tax Service (2012) Otchet po forme No.1-NM za 2011 g., svodnyi v tselom po Rossiiskoi Federatsii [Account for form No.1-NM for 2011, summarised for the Russian Federation]. svod030412.xls. Moscow: Federal'naya nalogovaya sluzhba. Available from: https://www.nalog.ru/rn77/related_activities/statistics_and_analytics/forms/3800184/ [Accessed 13 June 2019]

Federal Tax Service (2015) Otchet po forme No.1-NM za 2014 g., svodnyi v tselom po Rossiiskoi Federatsii [Account for form No.1-NM for 2014, summarised for the Russian Federation]. 1nm010115.xls. Moscow: Federal'naya nalogovaya sluzhba. Available from: https://www.nalog.ru/rn77/related_activities/statistics_and_analytics/forms/4621635/ [Accessed 13 June 2019]

Federal Tax Service (2016) Otchet po forme No.1-NM za 2015 g., svodnyi v tselom po Rossiiskoi Federatsii [Account for form No.1-NM for 2015, summarised for the Russian Federation]. 1nm010116.xls. Moscow: Federal'naya nalogovaya sluzhba. Available from: https://www.nalog.ru/rn77/related_activities/statistics_and_analytics/forms/5432274/ [Accessed 13 June 2019]

Federal Tax Service (2017) Otchet po forme No.1-NM za 2016 g., svodnyi v tselom po Rossiiskoi Federatsii [Account for form No.1-NM for 2016, summarised for the Russian Federation]. 1nm010117.xls. Moscow: Federal'naya nalogovaya sluzhba. Available from: https://www.nalog.ru/rn77/related_activities/statistics_and_analytics/forms/6040192/ [Accessed 13 June 2019]

Federal Tax Service (2018) Otchet po forme No.1-NM za 2017 g., svodnyi v tselom po Rossiiskoi Federatsii [Account for form No.1-NM for 2017, summarised for the Russian Federation]. 1nm010118.xls. Moscow: Federal'naya nalogovaya sluzhba. Available from: https://www.nalog.ru/rn77/related_activities/statistics_and_analytics/forms/6772396/ [Accessed 13 June 2019]

Fedorova, T. and Kulikov, S. (2007) "Pensii za Tiraspol' zaplatit 'Gazprom' [Gazprom will pay Tiraspol's pensions]" *Nezavisimaya gazeta*, 13 July, p.1

Finon, D. and Locatelli, C. (2008) "Russian and European gas interdependence: Could contractual trade channel geopolitics?", *Energy Policy*, 36 (1): 423–442

Flink, A. (2002) "Kazakhskii gaz pustyat v rossiiskuyu trubu [Kazakh gas allowed into Russian pipe]" *Kommersant*, 6 December, p.14

Franza, L. (2015) *From South Stream to Turk Stream*. CIEP Paper. 05 (Clingendael: Clingendael International Energy Programme)

Gabuev, A. (2016) *Friends with Benefits? Russian–Chinese Relations after the Ukraine Crisis* (Moscow: Carnegie Moscow Center)

Gabuev, A. and Granik, I. (2009) "Iran i Rossiya sovpali v Kaspiiskom more [Iran and Russia agree in the Caspian Sea]" *Kommersant*, 18 August, p.5

Gabuev, A. et al. (2010) "Dmitrii Medvedev ogranichil Azerbaidzhan [Dmitrii Medvedev limits Azerbaijan]" *Kommersant*, 4 September, p.1

Gamova, S. (2012) "Kreml' stryakhivaet pyl' s 'plana Kozaka' [Kremlin dusts off the Kozak plan]" *Nezavisimaya gazeta*, 12 September, p.1

Gaulier, G. and Zignago, S. (2010) *BACI: International Trade Database at the Product-level. The 1994–2007 Version*. CEPII Working Paper. (Paris: CEPII)

Gavshina, O. (2007) "Dorogie sosedi [Dear neighbours]" *Gazeta*, 11 May, p.13

Gazprom (2003) *Gazprom. Godovoi otchet 2002* [*Gazprom. Annual report 2002*] (Moscow: Gazprom)

Gazprom (2004a) *Gazprom. Godovoi otchet 2003* [*Gazprom. Annual report 2003*] (Moscow: Gazprom)

Gazprom (2004b) "Na puti k energeticheskoi kompanii – tezisi doklada Predsedatelya Pravleniya "OAO Gazprom" Alekseya Millera [On the way to an energy company – theses from a presentation by Gazprom's management chairman, Aleksei Miller]" [online]. 25 June (Moscow: Gazprom). Available from: http://www.gazprom.ru/press/news/2004/june/article54896/ [Accessed 15 May 2019]

Gazprom (2005) *Gazprom. Godovoi otchet 2004* [*Gazprom. Annual report 2004*] (Moscow: Gazprom)

Gazprom (2006) "Ob itogakh vizita delegatsii OAO 'Gazprom' v Uzbekistan [Results of Gazprom delegation's visit to Uzbkistan]" [online]. 17 May (Moscow: Gazprom). Available from: http://www.gazprom.ru/press/news/2006/may/article55734/ [Accessed 15 May 2019]

Gazprom (2007) *Gazprom. Godovoi otchet 2006* [*Gazprom. Annual report 2006*] (Moscow: Gazprom)

Gazprom (2008) *Gazprom v tsifrakh 2004–2008 gg. Spravochnik* [*Gazprom in numbers 2004–2008. A handbook*] (Moscow: Gazprom)

Gazprom (2009) *Gazprom. Godovoi otchet 2008* [*Gazprom. Annual report 2008*] (Moscow: Gazprom)

Gazprom (2012a) "Srednyaya Aziya – Tsentr [Central Asia–Centre]" [online]. n.d. (Moscow: Gazprom). Available from: http://www.gazprom.ru/about/production/projects/pipelines/central-asia/ [Accessed 4 July 2012]

Gazprom (2012b) *Rasshiryaya gorizonty. Godovoi otchet 2011* [*Broadening horizons. Annual report 2011*] (Moscow: Gazprom)

Gazprom (2013a) "Gazprom na rossiiskom rynke [Gazprom on the Russian market]" [online]. n.d. (Moscow: Gazprom). Available from: http://www.gazpromquestions.ru/russian-market/ [Accessed 19 June 2013]

Gazprom (2013b) "'Gazprom' planiruet uvelichit' dolyu v 'ArmRosgazprome' do 100% [Gazprom plans to increase share in ArmRosgazprom to 100%]" [online]. 17 June (Moscow: Gazprom). Available from: http://www.gazprom.ru/press/news/2013/june/article164593/ [Accessed 15 May 2019]

Gazprom (2019a) "Gazifikatsiya [Gasification]" [online]. (Moscow: Gazprom). Available from: http://www.gazprom.ru/about/production/gasification/ [Accessed 30 May 2019]

Gazprom (2019b) "Gas and oil production" [online]. (Moscow: Gazprom). Available from: http://www.gazprom.com/about/production/extraction/ [Accessed 1 June 2019]

Gazprom (2019c) "Marketing" [online]. (Moscow: Gazprom). Available from: http://www.gazprom.com/about/marketing/ [Accessed 1 June 2019]

Gazprom (2019d) "Podzemnoe khranenie gaza [Underground storage of gas]" [online]. (Moscow: Gazprom). Available from: http://www.gazprom.ru/about/production/underground-storage/ [Accessed 30 May 2019]

Golub, K. (2012) "Ot Ungen do Yass gazoprovodom podat' [Ungheni is just a gas pipeline from Iasi]" *Kommersant Moldova*, 14 March 2012

Gray, D. (1995) *Reforming the Energy Sector in Transition Economies*. World Bank Discussion Papers. 296 (Washington, DC: The World Bank)

Grib, N. and Gavrish, O. (2009) "Predlozhenie, ot kotorogo nel'zya ne uzhat'sya [An offer you cannot but shrink away from]" *Kommersant*, 2 June, p.1

Grigor'eva, E. (2005) "Putin – Yushchenko: Gazovyi torg neumesten [Putin–Yushchenko: Gas bargaining inappropriate]" *Izvestiya*, 9 December, p.1

Grigoryan, A. (2013) "Armenia chooses Customs Union over EU Association Agreement" *CACI Analyst*, 18 September

Grivach, A. (2005) "Sosedi. Syurpriz 'Gazpromu' [Neighbours. A surprise for Gazprom]" *Vremya novostei*, 4 October, p.8

Grivach, A. (2009) "Ob'yasnenie vzryva [An explanation for the explosion]" *Vremya novostei*, 2 June, p.8

Grivach, A. (2010) "Vostochnaya khitrost' [Eastern cunning]" *Vremya novostei*, 20 July, p.7

Gularidze, T. (2003a) "*Government Posed to Yield to the US Pressure on GazProm Deal*" [online]. 9 June (Tbilisi: Civil.ge). Available from: http://www.civil.ge/eng/article.php?id=4354 [Accessed 15 May 2019]

Gularidze, T. (2003b) "Georgia's pending GazProm deal stirs political controversy" [online]. 30 May (Tbilisi: Civil.ge). Available from: http://www.civil.ge/eng/article.php?id=4296 [Accessed 15 May 2019]

Gurbanov, I. (2018) "Southern gas corridor raises significant financing, but still faces provocations" *Eurasia Daily Monitor*, 3 April

Gustafson, T. (2012) *Wheel of Fortune. The Battle for Oil and Power in Russia* (Cambridge, MA/London: The Belknap Press of Harvard University Press)

Henderson, J. (2015) "Competition for customers in the evolving Russian gas market", *Europe-Asia Studies*, 67 (3): 345–369

Henderson, J. et al. (2018) "The SPIMEX gas exchange: Russian gas trading possibilities", *Oxford Energy Paper* [online] NG 126 Available from https://www.oxfordenergy.org/wpcms/wp-content/uploads/2018/01/The-SPIMEX-Gas-Exchange-Russian-Gas-Trading-Possibilities-NG-126.pdf [Accessed 1 June 2019]

Hill, F. (2004) *Energy Empire: Oil, Gas, and Russia's Revival* (London: The Foreign Policy Centre)

IAA Trend (2006) "Prirodnyi gaz v Gruziyu budet postavlyat' kompaniya 'KazRos-Gaz' [KazRosGaz will supply natural gas to Georgia]" *IAA Trend*, 22 May

IEA (2015) *Online Data Services*, Issue date [online]. (Published by International Energy Agency 2015). Available from: http://www.iea.org/statistics/ [Accessed 6 October 2015]

Infotag (2012) "'*Esli Moldova i Pridnestrov'e – obshchee gosudarstvo, to i gazovyi schet dolzhen byt' obshchim' – Dmitrii Rogozin* [*Dmitrii Rogozin: 'If Moldova and Transnistria are a common state, then the gas bill, too, should be common'*]" [online]. 19 November (Chisinau: Information Agency Infotag). Available from: http://www.infotag.md/news/598422/ [Accessed 15 May 2019]

Ioffe, G. (2011) "Washington struggles to formulate strategy on Belarus" *Eurasia Daily Monitor*, 12 December

Ismayilov, R. (2007) "Rich country, poor people" *Transitions Online*, 17 January

Ivanov, N. (1997) "Gazpromu mozhno tol'ko verit' [In Gazprom one can only believe]" *Segodnya*, 16 May

Jack, A. (2001a) "Link between Gazprom and Itera found", *Financial Times*, 14 March, p.33

Jack, A. (2001b) "Gazprom auditors to probe links with Itera", *Financial Times*, 15 March, p.29

Jack, A. (2001c), "Auditors find no evidence of deals that aided Itera", *Financial Times*, 6 July, p.22

Kardaś, S. (2018) *Neither Super-rich, nor Bankrupt. Gazprom's Financial Condition*. OSW Studies. 79 (Warsaw: OSW Centre for Eastern Studies/Osrodek Studiow Wschodnich)

Kardaś, S. and Iwański, T. (2018) "From vassalisation to emancipation. Ukrainian–Russian gas cooperation has been revised" *OSW Commentary*, 7 March

KazRosGaz (2012) *"KazRosGaz": soyuz Rossii i Kazakhstana* [*KazRosGaz: a union between Russia and Kazakhstan*]. Promotional material, KazRosGaz

Kirichenko, N. and Solov'ev, M. (1992) "Dom, kotoryi postroil Viktor [The house that Viktor built]" *Kommersant*, 21 December

Konończuk, W., Matuszak, S. and Paszyc, E. (2012) "Russian–Turkish agreement on the South Stream pipeline – an instrument of pressure on Ukraine" *OSW Analysis*, 4 January

Konończuk, W., Kardaś, S. and Łoskot-Strachota, A. (2014) "Success? The Russia/Ukraine/EU gas agreement" *OSW Analysis*, 5 November

Krashakov, A. (2006) "Erevan obmenyal trubu na gaz [Yerevan exchanged a pipeline for gas]" *Nezavisimaya gazeta*, 7 April, p.3

Krasnaya Zvezda (1992) "Pravitel'stvo Rossii izyskivaet sredstva dlya finansirovaniya rossiiskikh voisk v stranakh Baltii [The Russian government seeks out funds to finance the Russian forces in the Baltic states]" *Krasnaya Zvezda*, 12 November

Kravets, V. (1997) "Ni shagu nazad [Not a step back]" *Neft' i Kapital*, September

Kravets, V. (1998) "Do polnoi 'otklyuchki' [Up to full disconnection]" *Neft' i Kapital*, August

Krym.Realii (2019) "*Rossiya ne priznaet reshenie suda v Gaage po isku 'Naftogaza' ob aktivakh v Krymu* [*Russia does not acknowledge the Hague Court's decision on Naftogaz's suit for Crimea assets*]" [online]. 1 March (Prague: Radio Free Europe/Radio Liberty). Available from: https://ru.krymr.com/a/news-rossiya-ne-priznaet-reshenia-suda-v-gaage-po-aktivam-v-krymu/29798688.html [Accessed 24 May 2019]

Kryukov, V. and Moe, A. (1996) *The New Russian Corporatism? A Case Study of Gazprom*. The Post-Soviet Business Forum (London: The Royal Institute of International Affairs)

Levin, K. (2000) "Vyakhireva rezhut popolam [Vyakhirev will be cut in two]" *Kommersant-Den'gi*, 2 February, p.15

Logvinenko, E. (2001) "'Goluboi potok' s nebes – na zemlyu [Blue Stream: from the heavens down to earth]" *Neft' i Kapital*, April

Łoskot-Strachota, A., Konończuk, W. and Kardaś, S. (2014) "Gas negotiations Ukraine–Russia–EU: War of attrition" *OSW Analysis*, 8 October

Lukin, O. (2010) "Im ne zhit' drug bez druga? [Can they not live without each other?]" *Neftegazovaya vertikal'*, No. 6, pp.64–66

Lukin, O. (2011) "Podklyuchili Kaspii [The Caspian is connected]" *Neftegazovaya vertikal'*, No. 18, pp.84–87

Lukin, O. (2012) "Tsentral'naya Aziya: Usilenie gazovoi konkurentsii [Central Asia: The gas competition strengthens]" *Neftegazovaya vertikal'*, No. 9, pp.18–20

Lyashenko, G. (2003) "Byudzhetnye den'gi tekut potokom [Budget money runs in a stream]" *Kommersant*, 18 January, p.5

Makarkin, A. (2009) "Kaspiiskoe protivostoyanie [Caspian confrontation]" *Neft' i Kapital*, October

Makarkin, A. (2013) "Dva predsedatelya [Two chairmen]" *Neft' i Kapital*, January–February

Malkova, I. and Igumenov, V. (2012) "Poslednee interv'yu Rema Vyakhireva: 'Putin kogda uslyshal, chto ya ukhozhu, tak obradovalsya' [Rem Vyakhirev's final interview: 'When he heard that I was leaving, Putin was so happy']" *Forbes*, September

Markus, U. (1995) "Belarus: Heading off an energy disaster" *Transition*, 14 April

Markus, U. (1996) "Energy: Ukraine and Belarus seek help abroad" *Transition*, 3 May

Meshcherin, A. (2014a) "Pir v preddverii chumy? [A feast on the eve of plague?]" *Neftegazovaya vertikal'*, No. 13–14, pp.74–81

Meshcherin, A. (2014b) "Ne bylo by schast'ya… [There would be no happiness…]" *Neftegazovaya vertikal'*, No. 11, pp.36–45

Milov, V. (2011) "Ups and downs of the Russia–Turkmenistan relationship" in Dellecker, A. and Gomart, T. ed., *Russian Energy Security and Foreign Policy* (London/New York: Routledge) pp.89–106

Ministry of Energy (2009) *Energeticheskaya strategiya Rossii na period do 2030 goda [Russia's Energy Strategy for the period to 2030]* (Moscow: Institute of Energy Strategy)

Ministry of Industry and Trade (2003) *Energeticheskaya strategiya Rossii na period do 2020 goda [Russia's Energy Strategy for the period to 2020]* (Moscow: Ministerstvo promyshlennosti i torgovli)

Mite, V. (2003) "*Russia: Gazprom May Abandon Cooperation Deals with Belarus, Leaving Minsk in Economic Lurch*" [online]. 10 September (Prague: Radio Free Europe/Radio Liberty). Available from: http://www.rferl.org/content/article/1104305.html [Accessed 15 May 2019]

Mitrova, T. (2009) "Natural gas in transitions: systemic reform issues" in Pirani, S. ed., *Russian and CIS Gas Markets and their Impact on Europe* (Oxford: Oxford University Press) pp.13–53

Mitrova, T., Pirani, S. and Stern, J.P. (2009) "Russia, the CIS and Europe: Gas trade and transit" in Pirani, S. ed., *Russian and CIS Gas Markets and their Impact on Europe* (Oxford: Oxford University Press) pp.395–441

Molnar, S. (2012) "Romanian Government approves gas pipeline between Romania and Moldova" *Natural Gas Europe*, 6 June

Monaghan, A. (2012) "The vertikal: power and authority in Russia", *International Affairs*, 88 (1): 1–16

Mordyushenko, O., Rozhdestvenskaya, Ya. and Solov'ev, V. (2012) "Ukaz prezidenta Rossii nashel pervogo potrebitelya [The president of Russia's decree found its first user]" *Kommersant*, 13 September, p.6

Moshes, A. (2012) "Za retseptom dolgoletiya [For the recipe of a long life]" *Ezhednevnyi zhurnal*, 30 May

Muradova, M. and Abbasov, R. (2006) "Heat from the South" *Transitions Online*, 9 January

Naftogaz Ukrainy (2015) *Richnyi zvit 2014 [Annual report 2014]*. (Kyiv: Naftogaz Ukrainy)

Naftogaz Ukrainy (2016) "Naftogaz files arbitration against Russia to recover $2.6 billion for stolen Crimea assets" [online]. 19 October (Kyiv: Naftogaz Ukrainy). Available from: http://www.naftogaz.com/www/3/nakweben.nsf/0/DC8AA6A56E589FE3C2258 05100278490 [Accessed 24 May 2019]

Naftogaz Ukrainy (2018) "Win for Naftogaz in the gas transit arbitration with Gazprom. Gazprom to pay USD 2.56 billion to Naftogaz" [online]. 28 February (Kyiv: Naftogaz Ukrainy). Available from: http://www.naftogaz.com/www/3/nakweben.nsf/0/4927C1CECCAC4969C22582420076095F [Accessed 13 June 2019]

Naftogaz Ukrainy (2019) "Types of activities" [online]. (Kyiv: Naftogaz Ukrainy). Available from: http://www.naftogaz.com/www/3/nakweben.nsf/0/74B2346ABA0CB C69C22570D80031A365 [Accessed 24 May 2019]

Neft' i Kapital (2003a) "Gordiev uzel protivorechii [A Gordian knot of contradictions]" *Neft' i Kapital*, May

Neft' i Kapital (2003b) "Est' takoe slovo l'goty [There is a word called privilege]" *Neft' i Kapital*, March

Neft' i Kapital (2003c) "Lider menyaetsya [The leader is changing]" *Neft' i Kapital*, February

Neft' i Kapital (2003d) "Turkmenskie perspektivy 'Gazproma' [Gazprom's Turkmen perspectives]" *Neft' i Kapital*, May

Neft' i Kapital (2004) "Rem Vyakhirev" *Neft' i Kapital*, October

Neft' i Kapital (2005a) "Torg umesten [Bargaining is appropriate]" *Neft' i Kapital*, May

Neft' i Kapital (2005b) "Geopoliticheskoe ruslo 'Golubogo potoka' [Blue Stream's geopolitical turn]" *Neft' i Kapital*, December

Neft' i Kapital (2005c) "Iranskii gaz mozhet pomoch' Rossii [Iranian gas can help Russia]" *Neft' i Kapital*, May

Neft' i Kapital (2006a) "Proyasnyayutsya perspektivy [The perspectives are becoming clear]" *Neft' i Kapital*, September

Neft' i Kapital (2006b) "Bakinskii gazovyi uzel [The Baku gas junction]" *Neft' i Kapital*, May

Neft' i Kapital (2006c) "Nikto i ne somneval'sya [As nobody even doubted]" *Neft' i Kapital*, July

Neft' i Kapital (2006d) "Gazovyi debyut [A gas debut]" *Neft' i Kapital*, October

Neft' i Kapital (2007) "No transit!" *Neft' i Kapital*, May

Neft' i Kapital (2008a) "God gazovoi nezavisimosti [The year of gas independence]" *Neft' i Kapital*, November

Neft' i Kapital (2008b) "Turkmenskii gaz [Turkmen gas]" *Neft' i Kapital*, August
Neft' i Kapital (2009a) "Put' svoboden [The road is open]" *Neft' i Kapital*, November
Neft' i Kapital (2009b) "Bol'she, chem kazhetsya [More than meets the eye]" *Neft' i Kapital*, April
Neft' i Kapital (2010a) "Transaziatskii ekspress [Trans-Asian express]" *Neft' i Kapital*, October
Neft' i Kapital (2010b) "Shel'f za trubu [The shelf for a pipe]" *Neft' i Kapital*, October
Neft' i Kapital (2010c) "Igra na gazovoi trube [The gas pipeline game]" *Neft' i Kapital*, September
Neft' i Kapital (2011a) "Svoi chelovek v 'Gazprome' [A man at home in Gazprom]" *Neft' i Kapital*, July
Neft' i Kapital (2011b) "'Gazprom' i Moldova rassmotreli voprosy zaklyucheniya novogo kontrakta [Gazprom and Moldova consider questions related to the conclusion of a new contract]" [online]. 3 November (Moscow: IG Industriya). Available from: https://oilcapital.ru/news/export/03-11-2011/gazprom-i-moldova-rassmotreli-voprosy-zaklyucheniya-novogo-kontrakta [Accessed 15 May 2019]
Neft' i Kapital (2011c) "Polimery bez polumer [Polymers without half measures]" *Neft' i Kapital*, October
Neft' i Kapital (2012a) "Rossiya trebuet ot Moldavii otkazat'sya ot Tret'ego energopaketa EC vzamen na skidku na gaz [Russia demands that Moldova retracts from the EU's Third Energy Package in return for a gas discount]" [online]. 13 September (Moscow: IG Industriya). Available from: https://oilcapital.ru/news/export/13-09-2012/rossiya-trebuet-ot-moldavii-otkazatsya-ot-tretiego-energopaketa-es-vzamen-na-skidku-na-gaz [Accessed 15 May 2019]
Neft' i Kapital (2012b) "Moldaviya poprosit ES otlozhit' vnedrenie tret'ego energopaketa do 2020 g. [Moldova will ask the EU to delay implementation of the Third Energy Package to 2020]" [online]. 1 October (Moscow: IG Industriya). Available from: https://oilcapital.ru/news/export/01-10-2012/moldaviya-poprosit-es-otlozhit-vnedrenie-tretiego-energopaketa-do-2020-g [Accessed 15 May 2019]
Neft' i Kapital (2013a) "Po-prezhnemu nedootsenen [Undervalued as always]" *Neft' i Kapital*, January–February
Neft' i Kapital (2013b) "Gaz Rossii v Rossii [Russia's gas in Russia]" *Neft' i Kapital*, January–February
Neft' i Kapital (2013c) "Chto khorosho dlya Gazproma... [What is good for Gazprom...]" *Neft' i Kapital*, January–February
Neft' i Kapital (2013d) "Razvitie nezavisimykh [The development of the independents]" *Neft' i Kapital*, January–February
Neft' i Kapital (2013e) "Strukturnaya evolyutsiya neftegazovoi otrasli [The structural evolution of the oil and gas industry]" *Neft' i Kapital*, May
Neftegazovaya vertikal' (2003) "Vklad v delo razvitiya eksporta gaza [A contribution to the cause of gas export development]" *Neftegazovaya vertikal'*, No. 6
Neftegazovaya vertikal' (2011) "Karachaganak Petroleum Operating B.V." *Neftegazovaya vertikal'*, No. 18, pp.42–43
Neftegazovaya vertikal' (2015) "Gazovye golovolomki [Gas puzzles]" *Neftegazovaya vertikal'*, No. 3, pp.52–58
Neftegazovaya vertikal' (2017a) "Mikhail Krutikhin: Sozdanie VINK – men'shee iz zol [Mikhail Krutikhin: The creation of the vertically integrated oil companies was the lesser evil]" *Neftegazovaya vertikal'*, No. 21, pp.28–34

Neftegazovaya vertikal' (2017b) "Ne tol'ko megaproekty [Not just mega-projects]" *Neftegazovaya vertikal'*, No. 9, pp.52–56

Neftegazovaya vertikal' (2017c) "Uzbekskaya metamorfoza [Uzbek metamorphosis]" *Neftegazovaya vertikal'*, No. 18, pp.80–84

Nikitin, D. and Evdokimova, A. (2014) "Ukraina bez skidok [Ukraine without discounts]" *RBK Daily*, 4 April, p.4

Nikolaev, I., Privalov, A. and Kalinichenko, N. (1994) "Privatizatsiya Gazproma [The privatisation of Gazprom]" *Kommersant*, 8 February

Oilcapital.ru (2012) "Reiting vliyaniya krupnykh predprinimatelei i top-menedzherov toplivno-energeticheskogo kompleksa v dekabre 2012 g. [Rating of the influence of major businessmen and top managers in the fuel and energy complex, December 2012]" [online]. 6 December (Moscow: IG Industriya). Available from: https://oilcapital.ru/news/companies/06-12-2012/reyting-vliyaniya-krupnyh-predprinimateley-i-top-menedzherov-tek-v-dekabre-2012-g [Accessed 18 March 2019]

Oilcapital.ru (2016) "Reiting vliyaniya krupnykh predprinimatelei i top-menedzherov toplivno-energeticheskogo kompleksa v marte 2016 g. [Rating of the influence of major businessmen and top managers in the fuel and energy complex, March 2016]" [online]. 29 March (Moscow: IG Industriya). Available from: https://oilcapital.ru/news/companies/29-03-2016/reyting-vliyaniya-krupnyh-predprinimateley-i-top-menedzherov-toplivno-energeticheskogo-kompleksa-v-marte-2016-g [Accessed 20 February 2019]

OMRI (1995) "*OMRI Daily Digest*" [online]. 16 May (Prague: Open Media Research Institute). Available from: http://www.rferl.org/content/article/1140936.html [Accessed 15 May 2019]

Panfilova, V. (2004) "Molchanie patriotov. Shest'desyat tysyach rossii'skikh grazhdan v Turkmenii poboyalis' prinyat' uchastie v vyborakh prezidenta [The silence of the patriots. Sixty thousand Russian citizens in Turkmenistan were afraid to participate in the presidential elections]" *Nezavisimaya gazeta*, 19 March, p.5

Panfilova, V. (2009) "Dushanbe pred"yavit Moskve schet [Dushanbe gives Russia the bill]" *Nezavisimaya gazeta*, 20 February, p.1

Pannier, B. (2017) "Iran rejects Turkmen proposal for gas shipments to Turkey" [online]. Posted to the blog 'Qishloq Ovozi' on 30 October. Available from: https://www.rferl.org/a/iran-rejects-turkmenistan-proposal-gas-shipments-turkey/28824118.html [Accessed 22 May 2019]

Panyushkin, V. and Zygar', M. (2007) *Gazprom. Novoe russkoe oruzhie* [*Gazprom. The new Russian weapon*] (Moscow: Zakharov)

Parfenova, M. (2012) "Schetnaya palata nedovol'na 'Gazpromom' [The Audit Chamber is dissatisfied with Gazprom]" *Izvestiya*, 19 April, p.5

Pirani, S. (2009a) "Ukraine: A gas dependent state" in Pirani, S. ed., *Russian and CIS Gas Markets and their Impact on Europe* (Oxford: Oxford University Press for the Oxford Institute for Energy Studies) pp.93–132

Pirani, S. (2009b) "Introduction. Political and economic factors in the Russian and CIS gas trade" in Pirani, S. ed., *Russian and CIS Gas Markets and their Impact on Europe* (Oxford: Oxford University Press for the Oxford Institute for Energy Studies) pp.1–12

Pirani, S. (2018a) "After the Gazprom–Naftogaz arbitration: Commerce still entangled in politics", *Oxford Energy Insight* [online] (31). Available from https://www.oxfordenergy.org/wpcms/wp-content/uploads/2018/03/After-the-Gazprom-Naftogaz-arbitration-commerce-still-entangled-with-politics-Insight-31.pdf [Accessed 24 May 2019]

Pirani, S. (2018b) "Russian gas transit through Ukraine after 2019: the options", *Oxford Institute for Energy Studies* [online] Available from https://www.oxfordenergy.org/publications/russian-gas-transit-ukraine-2019-options/ [Accessed 23 May 2019]

Pirani, S., Stern, J.P. and Yafimava, K. (2010) *The April 2010 Russo-Ukrainian Gas Agreement and its Implications for Europe* (Oxford: The Oxford Institute for Energy Studies)

Podobedova, L. and Dzyadko, T. (2018) "Pribyl'nyi vsem podryad [Profitable for one after the other] (paper)/Pribyl' dlya podryadchikov: skol'ko aktsionery 'Gazproma' teryayut na stroikakh [Profits for subcontractors: how much Gazprom's shareholders lose on construction] (web)" *RBK Daily*, 21 May, pp.1, 10

Popov, I. (2007) "Staraya gvardiya [The old guard]" *Forbes*, April

Popşoi, M. (2016) "Are Moldovan consumers financing Transnistrian separatism?" *Eurasia Daily Monitor*, 21 April

Prokhorov, I. (2006) "A u nas – tbilisskii gaz! [But we have Tbilisi's gas]" *Kazakhstanskaya pravda*, 23 May 2006

Prostakov, G. (2012) "Chernomorskie kozyri Ukrainy [Ukraine's Black Sea trump cards]" *Neftegazovaya vertikal'*, No. 10, pp.30–32

Rahimov, R. (2019) "Turkmenistan redirects its oil export flows from Azerbaijan to Russia" *Eurasia Daily Monitor*, 25 February

RBK (2018) "RBK 500: Reiting rossiiskogo biznesa [RBK 500: The Russian Business Rating]" [online]. (Moscow: Available from: https://www.rbc.ru/rbc500/ [Accessed 23 November 2018]

Reznik, I. (2002a) "Vyakhirev ukhodit v otstavku [Vyakhirev resigns]" *Vedomosti*, 29 January

Reznik, I. (2002b) "Usmanov pomog Milleru [Usmanov helps Miller]" *Vedomosti*, 26 December

Reznik, I. (2009) "Chistil'shchik Ryazanov [Ryazanov the cleaner]" *Vedomosti*, 23 March

Reznik, I. and Egorova, T. (2006a) "'Gazprom' vmesto RAO EES [Gazprom instead of RAO UES]" *Vedomosti*, 10 April

Reznik, I. and Egorova, T. (2006b) "'Gazprom' propisalsya v Armenii [Gazprom settles in Armenia]" *Vedomosti*, 7 April

RFE/RL (1998) "RFE/RL Newsline" *Radio Free Europe/Radio Liberty*, 31 July

RFE/RL (1999) "RFE/RL Iran Report" *Radio Free Europe/Radio Liberty*, 22 November

RFE/RL (2000) "RFE/RL Newsline" *Radio Free Europe/Radio Liberty*, 2 March

RFE/RL (2001a) "RFE/RL Newsline" *Radio Free Europe/Radio Liberty*, 13 March

RFE/RL (2001b) "RFE/RL Newsline" *Radio Free Europe/Radio Liberty*, 16 March

RFE/RL (2004) "RFE/RL Newsline" *Radio Free Europe/Radio Liberty*, 28 June

RFE/RL (2005) "RFE/RL Newsline" *Radio Free Europe/Radio Liberty*, 9 September

RFE/RL (2006) "RFE/RL Newsline" *Radio Free Europe/Radio Liberty*, 30 January

RFE/RL (2015) "Romania starts shipping gas to Moldova" [online]. 4 March (Prague: Radio Free Europe/Radio Liberty). Available from: https://www.rferl.org/a/romania-moldova-gas/26882225.html [Accessed 25 May 2019]

RIA Novosti (2015) "Medvedev podpisal postanovlenie o predostavlenii Ukraine skidki na gaz [Medvedev signs resolution on extending a gas discount to Ukraine]" [online]. 1 April (Moscow: RIA Novosti). Available from: https://ria.ru/20150401/1055883614.html [Accessed 24 May 2019]

Roberts, J. (2011) "After the war" in Dellecker, A. and Gomart, T. ed., *Russian Energy Security and Foreign Policy* (London/New York: Routledge) pp.170–187

Rozhkova, M. and Reznik, I. (2013) "U nego bylo chut'e [He had a good nose]" *Vedomosti*, 12 February

Rukhadze, V. (2015) "Russia's Gazprom seems set to return to Georgia" *Eurasia Daily Monitor*, 21 October

Samokhvalov, V. (2015) "Ukraine between Russia and the European Union: Triangle revisited", *Europe-Asia Studies*, 67 (9): 1371–1393

Sapozhkov, O. (2012) "Gosudarstvo zabiraet chetvertinu [The state will take one quarter]" *Kommersant*, 17 November, p.1

Savushkin, S. (2000) "Turkmeniskii gaz snova v rossiiskoi trube [Turkmen gas again fills Russia's pipelines]" *Neft' i Kapital*, February

Sergeev, V. and Grib, N. (2006) "Moldaviya gotova otdat' chuzhoe [Moldova ready to give away what isn't theirs]" *Kommersant*, 18 January, p.7

Sherr, J. (2013) *Hard Diplomacy and Soft Coercion. Russia's Influence Abroad* (London: Chatham House)

Silady, A., Tesema, M. and Frye, B. (2013) "The Eastern Partnership Summit: A cheat sheet" *Transitions Online*, 22 November

Simoes, A.J.G. and Hidalgo, C.A. (2011) "The Economic Complexity Observatory: An analytical tool for understanding the dynamics of economic development" in Workshops at the Twenty-Fifth AAAI Conference on Artificial Intelligence

Smirnov, G. (1997) "Gazovyi bumerang vozvrashchaetsya [The gas boomerang returns]" *Neft' i Kapital*, July–August

Smith, H. (2012) "Russian foreign policy and energy: The case of the Nord Stream gas pipeline" in Aalto, P. ed., *Russia's Energy Policies. National, Interregional and Global Levels* (Cheltenham, UK/Northampton, USA: Edward Elgar) pp.117–135

Socor, V. (2006) "Russian energy supply cut off to Georgia: Another wake-up signal to the West" *Eurasia Daily Monitor*, 23 January

Socor, V. (2012) "Moldova's Filat discusses energy sector agreement with Russia's Putin and Medvedev" *Eurasia Daily Monitor*, 14 September

Sokolov, L. (2007) "'KazRosGaz' – pyat' let na gazovom rynke [KazRosGaz: five years in the gas market]" *Kazakhstanskaya pravda*, 21 March

Stern, J.P. (1993) *Oil and Gas in the Former Soviet Union*. Post-Soviet Business Forum (London: Royal Institute of International Affairs)

Stern, J.P. (2005) *The Future of Russian Gas and Gazprom* (Oxford: Oxford University Press/Oxford Institute for Energy Studies)

Stern, J.P. (2009) "The Russian gas balance to 2015: Difficult years ahead" in Pirani, S. ed., *Russian and CIS Gas Markets and their Impact on Europe* (Oxford: Oxford University Press for the Oxford Institute for Energy Studies) pp.54–92

Tatevosyan, A. and Reutov, A. (2006) "Armeniyu ubedili oruzhiem [Armenia was convinced by weapons]" *Kommersant*, 24 March, p.9

Tatevosyan, A., Reutov, A. and Grib, N. (2006) "Soglashenie. Armeniya perekhodit na 'Gazprom' [Agreement. Armenia transfers to Gazprom]" *Kommersant*, 7 April, p.1

Ter-Grigoryan, A. (2006) "V Armenii schitayut, chto otnosheniya s Rossiei napravleny na ukreplenie politiki Kocharyan [In Armenia, relations with Russia are seen as directed towards strengthening Kocharyan's policy]" [online]. 13 November (Moscow: Kavkaz-Uzel). Available from: http://www.kavkaz-uzel.ru/articles/103489/ [Accessed 15 May 2019]

Tomiuc, E. (2003) "Moldova: Caught between a hammer and a sickle as anti-Communist protests continue" [online]. 28 November (Prague: Radio Free Europe/Radio

Liberty). Available from: http://www.rferl.org/content/article/1105158.html [Accessed 15 May 2019]

Tomiuc, E. and Krushelnycky, A. (2003) "Moldova: Putin cancels trip to Chisinau as Moldovan, Transdniestrian leaders prepare to sign memorandum" [online]. 25 November (Prague: Radio Free Europe/Radio Liberty). Available from: http://www.rferl.org/content/article/1105122.html [Accessed 15 May 2019]

Transitions (1995) "Slow progress for CIS economics" *Transitions*, 25 February

Tutushkin, A. (2001) "Karachaganak spotknulsya o nalogi [Karachaganak gets stuck on taxes]" *Vedomosti*, 24 September

Varfolomeyev, O. (2014) "Ukraine readies to resume buying EU gas" *Eurasia Daily Monitor*, 14 March

Varfolomeyev, O. (2017) "Ukraine has gas for upcoming winter, but time for reform is running out" *Eurasia Daily Monitor*, 1 November

Vedomosti (1999) "Gazprom postroit gazoprovod iz Irana v Armeniyu [Gazprom will build a pipeline from Iran to Armenia]" *Vedomosti*, 16 November

Verezemskii, S. (1997) "Dobro pozhalovat' v 'kavkazskii gazovyi koridor' [Welcome to the 'Caucasian gas corridor']" *Neft' i Kapital*, October

Verkhoturov, D. (2006) "Karashagynak: vynuzhdennoe reshenie 'Gazproma' [Karashagynak: Gazprom's forced decision]" *APN Kazakhstan*, 5 October

Victor, N. and Sayfer, I. (2012) "Gazprom: The struggle for power" in Victor, D.G., Hults, D.R. and Thurber, M. ed., *Oil and governance. State-owned enterprises and the world energy supply* (Cambridge: Cambridge University Press) pp.655–700

Vignanskii, M. and Grivach, A. (2005) "Gaz s ubezhdeniyami [Gas with convictions]" *Vremya novostei*, 22 November, p.7

Vinogradova, O. (2014) "Neft' i gaz Kryma: Poteri i priobreteniya [Crimea's oil and gas: Losses and acquisitions]" *Neftegazovaya vertikal'*, No. 8, pp.4–7

Vinogradova, O. (2015) "Gazovyi revers Ukrainy [Ukraine's gas reverse]" *Neftegazovaya vertikal'*, No. 17–18, pp.26–30

Vinogradova, O. (2017) "Tsennik Gazproma ocharoval evropeitsev [Gazprom's price tag charmed the Europeans]" *Neftegazovaya vertikal'*, No. 1–2, pp.44–49

Voloshin, G. (2016) "Gas-rich Turkmenistan looks to export diversification" *Eurasia Daily Monitor*, 8 April

Watkins, E. (2011) "Turkmenistan claims supergiant gas find" *Oil & Gas Journal*, 13 October

Wyzan, M.L. (1999) "Mixing oil with politics" *Transition*, 15 March

Yafimava, K. (2007) *Post-Soviet Russian–Belarusian Relationships. The Role of Gas Transit Pipelines* (Stuttgart: ibidem-Verlag)

Yafimava, K. (2009) "Belarus: The domestic gas market and relations with Russia" in Pirani, S. ed., *Russian and CIS Gas Markets and their Impact on Europe* (Oxford: Oxford University Press for the Oxford Institute for Energy Studies) pp.133–169

Yafimava, K. (2010) "The June 2010 Russian–Belarusian gas transit dispute: A surprise that was to be expected", *Oxford Energy Paper* [online] NG 43 Available from http://www.oxfordenergy.org/2010/07/the-june-2010-russian-belarusian-gas-transit-dispute-a-surprise-that-was-to-be-expected/ [Accessed 15 May 2019]

Yafimava, K. (2011) *The Transit Dimension of EU Energy Security* (Oxford: Oxford University Press for the Oxford Institute for Energy Studies)

Yafimava, K. (2015) "Evolution of gas pipeline regulation in Russia: Third party access, capacity allocation and transportation tariffs", *Oxford Energy Paper* [online] NG 95 Available from https://www.oxfordenergy.org/publications/evolution-of-gas-pipeline-regulation-in-russia-third-party-access-capacity-allocation-and-transportation-tariffs/ [Accessed 15 May 2019]

Yafimava, K. and Stern, J.P. (2007) "The 2007 Russia–Belarus gas agreement", *Oxford Energy Comment* [online] Available from http://www.oxfordenergy.org/2007/01/the-2007-russia-belarus-gas-agreement/ [Accessed 15 May 2019]

Yakuba, A. (2007) "'Gazprom' produvaet truby [Gazprom blows the pipes]" *Russkii kur'er*, 14 May, p.9

Yenikeyeff, S.M. (2008) "Kazakhstan's gas: Export markets and export routes", *Oxford Energy Paper* [online] NG 25 Available from https://www.oxfordenergy.org/wpcms/wp-content/uploads/2010/11/NG25-KazakhstansgasExportMarketsandExportRoutes-ShamilYenikeyeff-2008.pdf [Accessed 18 May 2019]

Yermakov, V. (2018) "Shrinking surplus: The outlook for Russia's spare gas productive capacity", *Oxford Energy Insight* [online] (42). Available from https://www.oxfordenergy.org/wpcms/wp-content/uploads/2018/12/Shrinking-surplus-the-outlook-for-Russias-spare-gas-productive-capacity-Energy-Insight-42.pdf [Accessed 30 May 2019]

Yermakov, V. (2019) "It don't mean a thing, if it ain't got that swing: Why gas flexibility is high on the agenda for Russia and Europe", *Oxford Energy Insight* [online] (48). Available from https://www.oxfordenergy.org/wpcms/wp-content/uploads/2019/02/It-Dont-Mean-a-Thing-If-It-Aint-Got-That-Swing-Why-Gas-Flexibility-Is-High-on-the-Agenda-for-Russia-and-Europe-Energy-Insight-48.pdf [Accessed 30 May 2019]

Zhelenin, A. (2007) "Tsena gazovogo voprosa [The price of the gas question]" *Nezavisimaya gazeta*, 16 May, p.6

Zimin, D. (2012) "How can foreign companies influence Russia's economic course? The cases of Finnish firms Fortum and Neste", *Post-Soviet Affairs*, 28 (2): 209–231

8 Conclusion
Political economy and foreign policy

Over the quarter of a century studied here, the interaction between the state and energy companies played an essential role in the development of the Russian state. Due to Russia's resource richness, state relations with companies were to a significant extent relations with energy companies. And key actors shaped the central institutions that organised resource extraction, to their advantage. As shown in this book, actors perceive their advantage in many different ways. It can be profit-related, for private, state or developmental goals; derived from professional ethics and goals, or, when faced with disintegration in the state, in the preservation of a relative status quo in the short term. All the companies studied here appeared due to efforts to preserve intact some organisations, with some power over institutions and implementation. These strategies also shaped Russia's development.

The Russian energy companies having survived the Soviet collapse, started out with already existing ties to other post-Soviet states. Existing chains of supply and value, infrastructure for transport and technology united the Soviet successor states across the new borders and divisions. To Russia, the nave in the crashed Soviet wheel, these ties were the foundation of a foreign economic policy. From the beginning they were seen as a potential instrument for Russian influence over post-Soviet states, but the real economic and foreign policy priorities lay elsewhere, in integration into the global economy and particularly with the states and existing institutions of the West.

The lack of a foreign economic policy in the first part of the 1990s coexisted with a lack of state capacity to oversee the companies and participate in their development. In the ensuing policy vacuum, the priorities of flagships like Lukoil and Gazprom shaped policy on the ground. When overall policy changed, and greater importance was attached to the post-Soviet region, energy remained one of the few instruments that could be used to tie the other states closer to Russia. For some of the companies in this book, especially RAO UES/Inter RAO and the nuclear energy industry, this was an opportunity to recover lost ground, or expand their business. Nuclear energy in particular depended on state support to develop relations in the post-Soviet region. Also a company like Lukoil welcomed the increased level of support from the state for its foreign operations, while limiting the extent to which the state could influence its overall commercial development. Gazprom and Transneft's policies of transit avoidance and control fitted well into the new emphasis on regional integration with Russia as the dominant force. To a considerable extent, their transit avoidance plans and strategies of regional dominance shaped Russia's foreign policy in the 2000s. Russia's success in returning to the international stage as a regional great power would have been far more difficult to achieve without these companies. And Russia's strong position in turn helped them to success.

Mutual advantage

Mutual advantage characterised the state–business relationship over foreign policy and operations abroad in the 2000s. The companies found their place in the new foreign economic policy. Gazprom, Transneft, Inter RAO and Minatom/Rosatom acquired roles as tools, but their relationship with the state was more complex than the term alone suggests. Their monopoly or quasi-monopolistic positions in the Russian economy served as platforms ideal for the expansion of post-Soviet operations. Gazprom's dominance in domestic gas supply and its export monopoly were two sides of the same coin. Transneft's domestic pipeline projects went in tandem with priorities set for regional development and foreign policy. That Russia maintained and increased control over pipelines, or the electricity sector, was more than a business priority that arose out of considerations for enhancing a domestic monopoly. These were foreign policy priorities. The enthusiasm with which all the companies here, barring Lukoil, embraced these priorities, was connected to the business advantages they now possessed, simply by having the support of the Russian state. Lukoil, too, received some of this support in return for accepting the limits caused by state priorities at home and abroad. In the case of Minatom and the companies in the nuclear energy industries, state support for international expansion became a carrot in the reform process. Domestic institutional development and foreign economic policy went hand in hand.

Support from the state for individual investments, or projects, in turn shaped operations for all companies except Lukoil. Over time this shaped their overall business profile. This book includes major pipeline projects that would have been difficult to achieve without state support. It is unlikely that Gazprom's Blue Stream project, or Transneft's BPS and BPS-2, would have been accomplished without economic and political support from the state. Such projects had a decisive impact on company priorities and relations with customers, whether gas customers in Europe or Russian oil companies. Rosatom's international position and its technological strengths made it more difficult to check its sluggish performance. On a smaller scale, Inter RAO's investments in the post-Soviet region were often the result of a privileged position at home. By allowing it to maintain a de facto monopoly in export, the state in effect bolstered its position abroad. The investments were also sufficiently important to the state for it to shield the company from privatisation during reform.

When the drive for economic modernisation and restructuring stopped, giving way to greater concentration on state hands, state-owned companies assumed even more prominent roles in foreign policy. Some decisions concerning Gazprom's foreign operations were made by state actors, and Putin in particular. This was the case already by 2006 and the first crisis in gas relations with Ukraine. Inter RAO, too, openly acted in the interest of the Russian state. The fate of the company's foreign operations after the electricity reform of 2008 reflected its importance as a foreign policy tool. Rosatom's privileged position as a state corporation with a unique institutional framework allowed its foreign operations to expand. From 2004, the state had access to a cluster of companies in the energy industries that could be relied on to support and develop foreign policy initiatives towards prioritised states, including with investment. Lukoil would occasionally participate, like in the National Oil Consortium in Venezuela. All the other companies studied here were regulars in that regard.

The 2012 decree on protection of national interests in foreign economic relations formalised the close relationship and the function of many companies as foreign policy tools of the state (Decree No. 1285, 2012). It applied only to three of the five companies in this book. Lukoil was by then fully privatised, and not affected. Rosatom was an outlier in the opposite direction. After having been reformed, it was an autonomous state organisation. Any propositions it now received would come from the state's top decision-makers, and would be formally exempt from scrutiny. As its autonomy included also the privilege of maintaining autonomous relations with foreign bodies, any influence on foreign ties would have to be exercised informally at the top level.

Tools of national economic interest

Considering the importance, and finality, of the Decree on the protection on national economic interests in foreign economic relations, one could argue that carrying the analysis in this book beyond 2012 would have added little of substance. Rosatom, from 2007 a state corporation, was already a tool of the state. The decree turned three more of the companies analysed here into tools of the state. Considering the phrasing of the decree, managements had no choice but to act in the interest of the state. Moreover, the decree seemed to dispel any remaining doubt as to the answer to this book's main research question, how state–company relations at home mattered for Russian foreign policy. According to the decree, the companies are unambiguously subordinate to the state, also in their foreign operations. They are also compelled to ensure that their foreign operations are not harmful to Russian interests, ahead of any changes to those operations.

This book ends in 2018. Obviously, the author finds state–company relationships after 2012 less clear-cut than decreed. The analysis here shows how no relationship between the state and a major energy company in Russia can be changed only by decree. Informal institutions, personal relationships, and the resources available at times undermine the state's power, and the state's real possibilities of getting access to and shape business strategy in nominally state-controlled companies. There are no guarantees that the state's capacity for economic policymaking will not again be weakened by powerful company managers and their informal networks. Rosneft, Rosneftegaz and Igor Sechin provide us with a recent example of the mechanisms at work. Their appearance in four of the five case chapters in this book is not coincidental. The Russian state now is far more powerful, and advanced, compared to 1992 or 1998. However, its relations with some of the companies here, while more sophisticated and complex than 20 years ago, are still characterised by informal institutions that complement and undercut formal regulation. Relations of a state-within-the state-type are likely to develop, and be allowed to persist, as long as privilege and personal connections are pervasive and important enough to undermine the impersonal and predictable application of formal rules. Such relations may not always ease the use of companies as foreign policy tools. Quite the opposite, a company that acts as a state within the state can quickly become difficult to turn into a policy instrument.

For overall state–company relations, the annexation of Crimea in 2014, the war in Donbas and the introduction of international sanctions against Russian companies mattered more than any decree. It became more difficult to be a Russian company with a global presence. Contrary to what some observers expected when the first round of sanctions was introduced in March–April 2014, the main effect of sanctions was to tie the elite, including the economic elite, closer to the regime. In the months after the annexation of Crimea, declarations of loyalty proliferated among Russian businesspeople, including in the energy industries. This was no surprise, considering the haste with which the business elites distanced themselves from any politically resonant issue first in 2000 when Putin came to power, and then in 2003 with the beginning of the Yukos case. Continued weak property rights protection in Russia turned good relations with the state into a matter of business survival for the heads of large businesses. In 2014, the state was more powerful in relation to state-controlled companies than in 2003, reducing the scope for amassing power through informal channels and thus increasing company autonomy. It was still possible, as again Rosneftegaz's position shows. As always, there had to be some sanction from the top for it to work. For many others, the state's failure to uphold property rights as impersonal rights and not a privilege leads business owners to be loyal and defer to the political priorities of the regime. The extent to which the political priorities of the regime influence the commercial priorities of a company however varies with ownership. Private owners cannot set company priorities without taking state policy into account. In state-owned companies, state policies influence the fundamental commercial priorities even more.

The end of the post-Soviet period

The last few years also provide a study of how Russia's foreign economic policy in the post-Soviet region began to unravel. The push for regional integration under Russian leadership reached its limits with the strong pressure on Armenia, Moldova and above all, Ukraine, when these states prepared to sign association agreements with the EU in 2013. The reaction to the annexation of Crimea in Russia's closest partners, Kazakhstan and Belarus, was extremely cautious, also in regard to what was supposed to be their joint project, the Eurasian Economic Union (EEU). The reaction was a turning-point. In the post-Soviet period until 2014, Russia's regional leadership was a given, also when Russia was weak. Other post-Soviet states were in general weaker. This relative strength began to end in 2014. True, in absolute military terms Russia was stronger than at most points between 1992 and 2014. But in terms of converting strength to political influence, and of maximising economic influence, 2014 exposed profound vulnerabilities. Russia's interference and aggression in Ukraine closed that state to Russian influence and power for years to come. The consequences were much wider. The lack of Russian influence during Armenia's revolution in 2018; the measured steps to strengthen a non-Russian national identity in Belarus; Kazakhstan's overt building of a nation-state, and Russia's weakened power when faced with Chinese influence, all told of weakness, not strength. There were fewer conduits for influence. There were also fewer resources, as the Russian economy entered a protracted crisis, followed by stagnation. To project regional power after 2014, Russia had to be even more selective than before. Economic and political constraints reduced its available tools in the post-Soviet region, and their effect. Part of the picture was that it faced neighbours that harboured less trust and were less open towards Russia than before.

This outcome was not inevitable. The political and economic disintegration of the post-Soviet region in the 1990s was followed by a push towards selective reintegration. On the side of the other post-Soviet states, there was a demand for involvement by Russian companies. Investment in electricity and nuclear energy, technological know-how and experience in nuclear energy and oil and gas production were important reasons why some of the companies studied here were welcomed in many post-Soviet states in the early 2000s, and in the case of Lukoil, throughout the 1990s. Companies like Lukoil, Inter RAO and TVEL in the nuclear energy industry had a comparative advantage in the region. Increasing rents from higher oil prices contributed to a general economic upturn, making investments in neighbouring states profitable. This was also a desirable foreign economic policy development from the point of view of the Russian state. Better and more economic ties were instrumental in the drive in the 2000s to establish Russia as a great power with a post-Soviet base. But, like the liberal empire concept proposed by Anatolii Chubais, the policy was replete with contradictions. The aim to dominate and control economic development, so fundamental to the transit avoidance policies of Transneft and Gazprom, did not sit well with aims for more cooperative reintegration.

Russia's bilateral relations with its post-Soviet neighbours illustrate well how it takes two to tango. In each bilateral relationship characterised by dependence, there was a non-Russian side that also participated in managing that dependence. Post-Soviet governments faced difficult choices where considerations of political survival, domestic stability, national development, national security and the need, for all these reasons, to preserve a workable bilateral relationship with Russia were balanced against the political, human and economic costs of withdrawing from dependence on Russia. At best, pros and cons were considered consciously. Although this book has not analysed the non-Russian side of post-Soviet energy relations, it is safe to say that where some post-Soviet state leaders saw a narrow range of options for national development, others seized opportunities for economic gain.

As long as Russia's pursuit of regional economic dominance did not rule out mutual gains also for post-Soviet states, the energy companies could complement each other within foreign policy. Pipelines designed for transit avoidance and rising gas prices were tools of coercion, while electricity and nuclear industry development included more cooperative elements. An added bonus for Russia foreign policy was that cooperation, especially in the gas and nuclear energy industries, often furthered continued post-Soviet dependence on Russia. Upstream oil and gas projects stood out as especially important economic relations. Wherever Lukoil and Gazprom invested in production, they were in effect the most influential Russian companies. Because of this diversity, Russian foreign economic policy in the region, although in many respects dominated by energy ties, had at its disposal a good handful of tools. It was not all about gas and Gazprom.

After 2014, Russia had fewer resources. Some tools remained, however, even as the economic crisis dictated a partial retreat from an expansive regional economic policy. Hydrocarbon transit and sales and nuclear energy cooperation remain Russia's most important economic ties with other post-Soviet states. As Chapter 7 shows, gas and electricity relations could deliver on regional cooperation in the Caucasus, in a way that supported wider aims by including Iran. But in sum, Russia's inward-looking elite of the late 2010s found itself with a reduced economic footprint, and limited influence, in the post-Soviet region. This obtained even when the economic ties that remained supported Russia's global aims.

Resource abundance and development

This book takes as its starting point that energy resources make a difference in political development. The rents can be used to provide societal stability and regime support, as shown in the analysis. RAO UES, Transneft and Gazprom's rent streams made them reliable sources of patronage for the elite, and the population. In the 1990s, formalised and informal subsidies channelled through RAO UES and Gazprom stabilised society throughout most of Russia's regions. Select rent sharing with regional elites through the companies ensured support for the regime. At the very top, rent streams from Gazprom's European gas sales in particular were indispensable in securing cohesion in the ruling coalition, thereby directly underpinning regime stability. With a narrower impact in society, Lukoil's support for Yeltsin in 1996 broadened elite support for his ruling coalition. Transneft had a somewhat different relationship with the regime. It was instrumental for rent extraction from oil sales, and stabilised the oil industry with oil regions. But it was also an instrument of state control and coercion over oil companies. It had a narrower impact in wider society than Gazprom or RAO UES, but was still central to regime durability. The nuclear energy industry's contribution to stability was that it did not disintegrate, which would have deprived Russia of control over nuclear sector contacts in relation to other states. Its rent streams maintained the industry. As a consequence, the state was also relieved of a foreign policy challenge in nuclear proliferation.

Like the energy resources on their own, informality and a lack of transparency in the institutions that regulate them can also be sources of state strength. Close and less than transparent relations with companies give the regime access to foreign policy tools, and sources of infrastructural power at home, that also maintain stability and ultimately ensure political survival. Informality does not necessarily inhibit state strength in the short term. To the contrary, in this book state capacity develops as a result of the use of both informal and formal ties to direct the companies to support the state. But while successful in the short term, informality is a brake on overall economic and political development in the longer term.

Slowed development is observable at the industry level. The Russian energy industries developed considerably over the first 25 years after the Soviet break-up. State organisations and companies became more specialised, more clearly delineated and more stable. State–company interaction also set the parameters of companies' policy relevance to the state, according to their control of infrastructure, channels of rents or direct rent extraction, fuel production and markets. State–company interaction over institutional frameworks at home made the companies accessible, for purposes of foreign policy, to different degrees according to their ownership structure. Lukoil was privately owned and without infrastructural assets of major significance to the state, making it less integral to policy development and therefore accessible only through explicit arrangements. But informal institutions also persisted and placed constraints on the Russian government's room for manoeuvre. Regime balancing among different actors restricted the scope for government action. To survive, the regime needs to reward and bolster close supporters and subject every major decision to considerations of survival. Ultimately, this slows the development of industry policy, of economic policy, and of institutions in general. As a result, overall development in the state suffers.

After the initial attempts at reform in the early 1990s, institutional development in the energy industries slowed down, at the expense of keeping the regime in power. Pressure for company reform came from state actors, but this was staved off with reference to the companies' importance to regime and societal stability. The slowing down of reform in a period of crisis was clearly a consequence of resource abundance, or more precisely, abundant resources that the regime could employ relatively easily using informal means. These resources enabled the regime to prioritise stability. Reform pressures challenged the status quo, but were alleviated by resources accessed as informal rents. A favourable period for reform followed the 1998 financial crisis and Putin's new ruling coalition. Success with reform legislation and building wider elite support also increased state capacity. For the state-owned companies, increased state capacity meant that they now had to serve the state to a greater extent than private interests, at least private interests outside the regime. Sector autonomy in return for informal support and limited rent sharing with the regime was no longer an option. The state had to have access to the companies as well. Crucially, informal rent streams were now slowly but steadily redirected wholly towards the regime, resulting in greater regime stability. With stability improved and oil and gas rents boosting the economy, there was less need to continue with reform.

Towards the end of Putin's second period, state modernisation and reform stalled. Further electricity reform stalled after the dissolution of RAO UES, and crucial elements were reversed. Subsequent events deprived the government of control over Inter RAO's business plans and rent streams. Rosatom reform modernised the nuclear energy industry, but also institutionalised a lack of transparency in the state's top ties to the new corporation. A similar lack of transparency and personalised relations dominated the relations between the state and Transneft, and to a lesser extent, the state and Gazprom. The restoration of state capacity was not irreversible, and did not progress to a level where it would threaten regime stability. This was a brake on Russia's overall development, both economic and political.

The institutions discussed here are not unique to the resource industries. Informality and the persistence of privilege remain fundamental to relations between the Russian state and Russian companies. But in the hydrocarbon industries in particular they remain more entrenched. The vast resources generated by oil and gas extraction are shared across a substantial part of the Russian elites. However, as this book includes electricity and the nuclear energy industry, it shows that it is possible, and useful, to approach privilege, informality, and rent sharing in the Russian political economy as more general phenomena. The informal and formal rent sharing institutions of the hydrocarbon industries stand out because of the volume of the resource flows they organise and their ensuing political significance. Their existence, persistence and significance for elite makeup and change are less unique features. Rents and their sharing in an elite shape it by creating vested interests. Politicians may be tempted to use prolific rent streams to fix problems, both in domestic politics and in relation to bilateral relations with other states. Resource-rich industries are therefore particularly prone to generate many vested interests, and become significant political instruments. The general traits of how this works can be expected to pertain in other Russian industries as well. From the regime perspective, survival in the relative short term matters more than anything else. This has widespread implications for the Russian political economy.

Political economy and foreign policy

After 2014, Russia underwent crisis and protracted stagnation. The expectations for future economic growth are modest. There are reduced prospects that Russia will in the future use economic relations as a foreign policy tool on the scale and depth discussed in this book. But as the book shows, Russia's political economy still makes it possible to exert considerable economic influence towards several post-Soviet states. Energy resources remain a key part of the foreign policy toolbox. To a considerable extent, these tools are an extension of companies' roles in the domestic political economy.

Based on the findings in this book, one may point towards some more general insights on the connections between domestic political economy and foreign policy. Limited access orders can make use of more foreign policy tools, with fewer obstacles and less transparency, than open access orders. When the state only partially protects property rights, company owners may see it as expedient, or necessary, to accept some obligations on behalf of the state. Private companies open up for state influence, in order to survive, or to earn state support for some aspect of their operations. Similarly, when informal institutions dominate in state oversight of state companies, this can compromise more than real access and control. There are also fewer constraints on the instrumentalisation of company operations for state policy aims. In the case of Gazprom, Putin's direct interference gave that company's operations in post-Soviet states a special and prominent role in foreign policy. This came down to a lack of institutional boundaries, a lack of autonomy and overlapping responsibilities, between Gazprom and the Russian state. Such blurring of political and economic organisations at the peak of the state persists today, making it reasonable to expect the continued use of state-controlled companies as tools of foreign policy. Now, filling a particular role in the economy is the raison d'être for state companies generally, not just in limited access orders. But in limited access orders, state goals may override considerations of company development and efficiency, to the extent that efficiency and business strategy become less central to business operations. If the ultimate aim is to strengthen regime stability, regime survival, or international prestige, inefficiency can turn into an accepted, even expected feature of state companies in limited access orders. In that case, the companies are allowed to be efficient only when political survival does not dictate otherwise. However, the connections between domestic and foreign policy discussed have also been shaped by the Soviet past, which gave the companies discussed here a potential to become foreign policy tools in the first place. Integrated infrastructure and an addiction to cheap energy were inherited from the Soviet state. The legacy continued to shape the development of Russian foreign policy in the post-Soviet region for a quarter of a century after the Soviet Union broke apart.

Reference

Decree No. 1285 (11/09/2012) *O merakh po zashchite interesov Rossiiskoi Federatsii pri osushchestvlenii rossiiskimi yuridicheskimi litsami vneshneekonomicheskoi deyatel'nosti* [*On measures to protect the interests of the Russian Federation when foreign economic activity is carried out by a Russian juridical person*] (Moscow: President of the Russian Federation)

Index

Adamov, Evgenii 98–100
Aksenenko, Nikolai 204
Alekperov, Vagit 144–145, 149–150, 159–161, 172, 173
Armenia: and Eurasian integration 35, 295; "Electric Erevan" 36, 71; electricity relations with Russia 52, 56–57, **59**, 66, 71; gas relations with Russia; 267–268, **273**, 285–286, 295–296; nuclear energy relations with Russia 96, 103, 115, 121
ARMZ 90–91, 97, 111
Atomenergoprom 90, 105–106
Atomredmetzoloto see ARMZ
Atomstroieksport/ASE 90–91, 101, 114, 115, 121
Audit Chamber 106, 118, 212, 222, 233, 266
Azerbaijan: electricity relations with Russia 57; gas transit relations with Russia; 266, **269**, 281; Lukoil in 148, 152, 157, 174; oil transit relations with Russia 202, **210**, 217, 228, 235

Baltic Pipeline System (oil) 201, 204, 206, **208–209**, 214–215, 225
Baltic Pipeline System-2 (oil) *198*, 225–226, 230
Belarus: electricity relations with Russia 46, **47**, **48**, 52–53, 56; gas relations with Russia 263, 266, 269, 271–272, **273**, 279–280; integration with Russia 28, 34, 35–36, 202, 272; nuclear energy relations with Russia 115–116, 119; oil transit relations with Russia 170, 202, 215, 225, 226–227, 235
Blue Stream gas pipeline *259*, 266, 269
Brevnov, Boris 47

BTC oil pipeline 148, 157, 174, 202, 217, 228
BTE gas pipeline 158, *259*, 266, 269, 281

Caspian shore project (gas) 283
Chernomyrdin, Viktor 24, 145, 147, 199, 236, 258–259, 261–262
Chernyaev, Valerii 197, 199–200
China, Russia's relations with 64, 167–168, 172, **209**, 221–222, 231, 290; *see also* ESPO pipeline
Chubais, Anatolii 47, 50–51, 56, 98, 145, 260; and Yukos affair 60; "liberal empire" 51
ConocoPhillips 162, 163
corporate social responsibility (CSR) 12
CPC pipeline 148, *198*, 203, **210**, 218, 229; Transneft and 203, 218, 229–230
Customs Union between Russia and Belarus 202
Customs Union of Russia, Belarus and Kazakhstan 34–35, 281, 291

Druzhba pipeline 201, 213–214, 225, 227, 235; Transneft's plans for 207, **208**, 216
Duma 50, 100, 104–105, 155, 266, 268
Dvorkovich, Arkadii 69
Dyakov, Anatolii 43–44, 45, 47

Ekibastuz-2 TPP *see* Kazakhstan
Energoatom *see* Ukraine
Energy Charter Treaty 53, 157, 277
Energy Ministry (Fuel and Energy Ministry, Industry and Energy Ministry) 13; and electricity reform 61–63; and Gazprom 260; and nuclear energy industry 101; and oil industry 148, 176, 199, 204–205, 211, 232, 233

Energy Strategy (1995) 27, 29–30
Energy Strategy (2003) 29–30, 101–102, 106, 156, 212–213, 271
Energy Strategy (2009) 30, 107, 223, 276
ESPO oil pipeline *198*, 221–222, 231–232
Estonia 265, **273**
Eurasian Economic Space 34–36; *see also* Customs Union of Russia, Belarus and Kazakhstan; Eurasian Economic Union
Eurasian Economic Union 34–36, 295, 319

Federal Agency for Property Management *see* Rosimushchestvo
Federal Grid Company (FSK) 58
Federal Property Ministry 151
Fuel and Energy Ministry *see* Energy Ministry

Gaidar, Egor 145, 259–260
gas market, Russian 286–287
gas pipelines, Russia *see* UGSS
gasification programme 287
Gazprom: "single export channel" 258–260, 263–264, 267, 277; media ownership 268, 271; and European customers 33, 276, 278, 282; and Lukoil 155, 158, 163, 164–165, 167; and nuclear energy industry 99; and RAO UES/Inter RAO 45–46, 49, 51, 54; *see also* Gazprom Neft
Gazprom Neft 227, 257, 275
Georgia: electricity relations with Russia 46, **47**, **48**, 55–56, **59**, 66, 71; gas relations with Russia **273**, 274, 281, 283, 296
Glavtransneft 197
Group of Eight (G8) 36

Industry and Energy Ministry *see* Energy Ministry
Inter RAO relations with Rosatom 63, 69, 118
International Uranium Enrichment Centre (IUEC) 110
Itera 264–265, 269, 270, 272

Kalyuzhnyi, Viktor 150, 204
Kazakhstan: electricity relations with Russia 46, **47**, **48**, 49, 57, **59**, 66–67; gas transit relations with Russia 264, 267, **273**, 282–283, 294; integration with Russia and in Eurasia 34, 36;

Lukoil in 147, 152, 158, 167–168, 174; nuclear energy relations with Russia 97, 99–100, 102, 110–111, 119–120; oil transit relations with Russia 203, **210**, 217–218, 224, 227, 228–230, 235; *see also* Customs Union of Russia, Belarus and Kazakhstan
Kazatomprom *see* Kazakhstan
KazMunayGaz *see* Kazakhstan
Khristenko, Viktor 57, 211, 221, 225
Kirienko, Sergei 103–104, 107, 109, 117, 200, 268
Konovalov, Vitalii 93–94, 98–99
Kovalchuk, Boris 64
Kozyrev, Andrei 23–24
Kudrin, Aleksei 153–155
Kyrgyzstan 36, 67, 72, **273**

Latvia 201, 206, 214–215, 226, **273**
Likhachev, Aleksei 117
Lithuania 53, 70, 96, 115, 170, 206, 224, 226, **273**
Lukoil: and Gazprom 155, 158, 163, 164–165, 167; and Transneft 152, 155–156, 157, 203

Medvedev, Dmitrii 60, 105, 164
Megatons to Megawatts' programme 95, 98
Mikhailov, Viktor 95, 99
Miller, Aleksei 270, 286
Minatom: and Gazprom 99; *see also* Minsredmash; Rosatom
Ministry of Foreign Affairs 23, 95, 147–148
Minsredmash 92, 96, 107, 109
Moldova 53–55, **59**, 66, 70, 266, **273**, 280–281, 293–294

Nabucco gas pipeline project 33, 282
Naftogaz *see* Ukraine
Nemtsov, Boris 46, 98, 262
Nord Stream 1 and 2 gas pipelines 33, *259*, 279, 289, 290–291, 293
Nuclear fuel cycle 91–92

Odesa–Brody oil pipeline 207, 215–216, 227
oil quality 216, 221, 232

Power of Siberia gas pipeline *259*, 287, 288, 290
Presidential Administration 23, 50, 53, 67, 104, 171

Primakov, Evgenii 28, 148, 151, 204
Putin, Vladimir 29, 30, 31, 35, 68, 69, 151, 204, 269; and electricity industry 51, 56, 57, 61; and Gazprom 269–270, 278, 279; and Lukoil 151, 154, 161; and nuclear energy industry 101, 105, 109, 113; and oil industry 153–154, 159–160, 164; and Transneft 205, 221, 226

RAO UES relations with Gazprom 45–46, 49, 51
Rappoport, Andrei 52, 55, 58
Rosatom: relations with Inter RAO 63, 69, 118; *see also* state corporations
Rosenergoatom 50, 56, 58; *see also* Rosatom
Rosimushchestvo 69, 219; *see also* Federal Property Ministry
Rosneft: and Gazprom 274–275; and Lukoil 155, 160, 163, 164–165, 168, 172–173; and Transneft 215, 221, 225, 228, 231–232; *see also* Rosneftegaz
Rosneftegaz 68–69, 229
Rumyantsev, Aleksandr 100–101, 103
RusHydro 36, **59**, 62, 64

Savelev, Dmitrii 200, 203–204
Sechin, Igor 61, 63–64, 68, 164, 275
Shmatko, Sergei 63, 64, 109, 164
Sibneft *see* Gazprom Neft
Sobyanin, Sergei 104, 109
South Caucasus Pipeline *see* BTE gas pipeline
South Stream gas pipeline project 33, 282, 293
state corporations 105, 106
State Duma *see* Duma
Strategic Course (1995) 25, 27

Tajikistan 57, **59**, 67
technical oil 205
Tekhnabeksport 93–94, 107

Tenex *see* Tekhsnabeksport
Timchenko, Gennadii 222, 226
Tokarev, Nikolai 205, 221–222, 231
Transneft: and Lukoil 152, 155–156, 157, 203; *see also* CPC; Glavtransneft, Transnefteprodukt
Transnefteprodukt 197, 201, 207, 219
Turkmenistan 267, 269, 274, 283, 284–285, 294
TurkStream gas pipeline *259*, 290–291, 293
TVEL 93–94, 96, 97, 102, 107, 112, 114, 120–121

UGSS 258, 260, 263, 276
Ukraine: bilateral relations with Russia; 32–33, 35; electricity relations with Russia 47, **48**, 53, 66, 70; Euromaidan 35, 291; gas relations with Russia 265, 271, 272, **273**, 277–279, 289, 291–293; Kharkiv Accords 35, 113–114, 279, 292; Lukoil in 149, 153, 169, 175; nuclear energy relations with Russia 96–97, 100, 112–115, 120–121; oil transit relations with Russia 201, 207, **208**, 227
Uranium One 111, 118–119
Uzbekistan: gas relations with Russia **273**, 284, 294; Lukoil in 149, 152–153, 158, 168–169, 175; nuclear energy relations with Russia 112, 119

Vainshtok, Semyon 205, 211–213, 218, 221
Vyakhirev, Rem 260–262, 270

World Trade Organisation 34

Yeltsin, Boris 23–24, 34, 44, 47, 146, 261, 262
Yukos affair 159–160, 162, 176, 218–219, 275